Praise for Joe Stockdale

"Brave and experimental in his direction, Joe brought out a thread of my original talent, and under his guidance I came to life as an actress. In all my experience on Broadway and in Hollywood I was never as deeply touched or influenced as I was by him."

Frances Farmer
Film and Stage Actress

"I was finishing a high school drama workshop at Purdue when Joe Stockdale asked where I was going to college. Astonished that I had not applied anywhere, he called four top professional schools whose incoming classes had been filled. 'I'll get you into Purdue,' he said. Eight days later I was there. This was the first time that anyone had said, 'This is what you should do with your life.' I owe everything to him."

Peter Schneider
Film and Theatre Producer and Director
Former Disney President of Animation and Theatre
Tony Award Winner for *The Lion King*

"I wrote a letter to the *Berkshire Eagle* after seeing Joe Stockdale's production of *Guys and Dolls* at Williams College: 'Anyone in the mood for a big, fat, loud and lovely, red, white, black-and-blue, rip-snorting of a howling, infectious, hum-along-dinger musical joke book which is a joy to behold should hie himself up to Williamstown.'"

William Gibson
Playwright
Author of *The Miracle Worker* **and** *Two for the Seesaw*

"When I received an invitation to play Brecht's Mother Courage I recoiled at the multiple hazards. Under the best professional conditions the play is difficult . . . Luck, therefore, heralded my arrival at Purdue with a discovery doubly exciting in its totally unexpectedness . . . Dr. Joseph Stockdale, disguised as a professor, proved to be a talented and experienced young director."

Anne Revere
Film and Stage Actress
Oscar and Tony Winner

"My two most influential teachers were Joseph Stockdale, who taught me while I was studying for my master's degree at Purdue University, and Uta Hagen. Both know how to teach, know how to communicate, and are incredibly supportive of and nurturing to actors. They delight in imparting their knowledge and experience to young actors."

Stuart Howard
Legendary Broadway Casting Director
Broadway Salutes Award Winner

Stages

A Life in the Theatre

By

Joe Stockdale

Homo sum; hūmäni nihil a me aliĕnum puto
I am a man; and I consider nothing that concerns mankind a matter of indifference to me.

All I ask for is "your recognition of the me in you, and the enemy, time, in us all."
Chance Wayne in *Sweet Bird Of Youth* by Tennessee Williams

Hyphenates Books

Published by Hyphenates Books℠
A division of Hyphenates, Ltd.
P.O Box 3771
Danbury, Connecticut 06813
First Printing, August 2013
10 9 8 7 6 5 4 3 2 1

Copyright © 2013 Joe Stockdale.
All rights reserved

ISBN-10: 098388255X
ISBN: 978-0-9838825-5-8
Hyphenates Books is a service mark of Hyphenates, Ltd.
LIBRARY OF CONGRESS CATALOGING-IN-PUBLICATION DATA: 2013937887
Printed in the United States of America

Without limiting the rights under copyright reserved above, no part of this publication may be reproduced, stored in or introduced into a retrieval system, or transmitted, in any form, or by any means (electronic, mechanical, photocopying, recording, or otherwise), without the prior written permission of both the copyright owner and the above publisher of this book.

PUBLISHER'S NOTE

This publication contains opinions and ideas of its author and represents his personal observations. The author and publisher disclaim responsibility for any liability, loss, or risk incurred as a consequence of the use of the contents of this book.

The publisher does not have any control over and does not assume any responsibility for author or third-party Web sites or their content.

The scanning, uploading, and distribution of this book via the Internet or via any other means without the permission of the publisher is illegal and punishable by law. Please purchase only authorized electronic editions, and do not participate in or encourage electronic piracy of copyrighted materials. Your support of the author's rights is appreciated.

For all those with whom I ever shared the space of
a rehearsal hall, classroom, film shoot, or stage,
who gave me such a wonderful life.

Preface

STAGES IS A MEMOIR. MUCH of it is twice-told tales, some repeated over and over again throughout various stages of my life. My re-creation and reflection on the original event undoubtedly enhances it since my memory not only includes an interpretation of the original event, but also an interpretation of all the different times, places and given circumstances of the repetitions. This adds up to a unique point of view, one that hopefully adds some wisdom in what I think of as a reflection in real time, now, the present.

In every stage of my life starting when I was six or seven, books, radio, films, and theatre have played a major part. I've been an actor, director, designer, and writer, and taught theatre for 42 years. This results in enhancing the telling of my reflections.

Some memories have never before been told; in the very act of writing there has occasionally been a sudden triggering of an untold event that is still there in my memory bank: white-hot, fresh, and alive, as if it had just taken place. But is it "truth" or a figment of my imagination?

Nonfiction found out to be "lies" by fact checkers has taken a great deal of criticism recently, although without negative effect on sales. Charles Pellegrino's *The Last Train to Hiroshima,* James Frey's *A Million Little Pieces,* and Mike Daisey's critically acclaimed monologue, *The Agony and Ecstasy of Steve Jobs,* all received excellent reviews prior to post-publication disclosures.

When the authors admitted that they had fabricated some of the events in their works, they have argued that they did so to serve a greater narrative truth.

What constitutes "truth" has always been difficult to define, especially in the reporting of events in an autobiography. But what is truth? It can be viewed in a philosophical as well as a historically accurate sense, which accounts for those who read the Bible as fact and those who read it as metaphor.

Recently I watched two films—one a documentary, the other fictional—both titled *Gallipoli,* both on the same subject, the World War I battle between Australian, New Zealand, and British forces fighting Turkish forces to secure the Dardanelles. Both have the point of view that war is evil and dehumanizing.

A *New York Times* article on the documentary reported that the film drew upon the research of some sixteen historians in seventy European archives in order to approach the subject "from an objective vantage... never sacrificing historical fact for dramatic impact." At its end, the narrator cites the conclusive fact: 125,000 men were killed in these battles. After a viewing of one hour and 57 minutes, I received this final fact with a yawn, albeit a respectful one.

On the other hand, I stayed glued to the tube watching the fictional account played by Mark Lee and Mel Gibson as Aussies on the cusp of radiant manhood. The final shot of Lee's leopard-like sprint across no man's land, head thrown back and arms outstretched as he is about to breast the tape-line of the Turkish trenches and is hit by one of their bullets brought a gasp, and an *"No! Oh, God, no!"* right up from my gut. My emotional understanding of the absolute stupidity of war that cut short the maturation of this young man trumped the historic fact of 125,000 deaths.

In his *Poetics,* Aristotle writes, "The historian relates *what has happened,* the poet *what could happen.*" In his observations about the Greek drama Aristotle actually comes down on the side of the dramatists rather than Homer's narratives of the Trojan Wars—*The Iliad* and *The Odyssey*—because as he observes, dramatic storytelling "is something more philosophic and of more serious import than history; for poetry [theater] tends to deal with the general, while history is concerned with delimited particular facts."

Even in the legal profession, which prides itself on dealing objectively with facts, it is now well established that the results of eyewitness testimony gained through lineups for identity in court cases has resulted in electrocution of some of those so identified but later found innocent through DNA. It is now also accepted that no two persons even see and report the facts of an event in the same way.

In this memoir I have researched facts carefully and, I hope, accurately. In two cases I have put the absolute facts, the truth of the situation, as addenda because I believe they are essential in telling the truth of the story. The rest of the book is from my unique point of view, which certainly includes irony and exaggeration and is influenced by both the epic storytelling of Homer, as well as the principles of dramatic structure observed by Aristotle.

I hope that you will find what is written truthful, passionate and entertaining. If there is something depicted that tests your "willing suspension of disbelief," I hope you will smile and say to yourself, "Well, Joe has always been just a bit over the top."

Chapter 1

AUNT FLOSS, MY FATHER'S SISTER, became my surrogate mother when my Dad brought my sister Rachel and me to live with her. That I was not actually her birth child may have accounted for a different kind of bonding than is usual between mothers and offspring. My first memory of Aunt Floss and me—*us*—was (after I was delivered to her on a winter night) her rocking and holding me tucked up in a soft warm blanket as I watched flickering flames through the isinglass windows of a wood-burning stove.

The lack of an actual birth connection may have been the reason I was spared a Phillip Wylie kind of "mothering" that demands filial reciprocity. Finding myself at a no-strings- attached free-lunch counter of affection, I grew up doing pretty much what I felt like doing without an obligation that interfered with my sense of self, meaning I was probably just a selfish little pain-in-the-ass with an inordinate need for love, which aided me in developing an ability to absorb attention and affection, and to get my own way.

Dad was the third of five kids: Florence ("Aunt Floss"), Mary, Joseph, Rachel, and David. Their father Samuel (b. 1863), along with seven brothers and sisters, migrated to Michigan from Terrington, Norfolkshire County, England, in 1870. My only remembrance of my grandfather was of him being propped up by pillows arranged and plumped by his oldest child Aunt Floss (my grandmother Jenny and he were divorced) in a brass bed set up in the front parlor of his great white 12-room house built next to a magnificent horse-chestnut tree. Since he was sick and would soon die, the occasion was a farewell to his grandchildren. In an English accent and with little show of emotion he simply said: "Good-looking youngsters! Not one with a snotty nose."

⌘ ⌘ ⌘

Dad quit school in May of 1906 after completing fifth grade in the one-room township schoolhouse that accommodated grades one through eight. He would have been twelve at the time and Samuel needed his help on the farm. But Dad never much cared for farming. When I heard my aunts and uncle talking about him, it almost always concerned baseball. He joined a minor-league team and apparently showed enough promise to hope for recruitment by the major leagues. What interceded was the assassination of Archduke Ferdinand of Austria in June of 1914, an event that led to declarations of war, with Britain, France, and Russia, opposing Germany, Austria-Hungary, and Italy. Three years passed before the United States joined the Allies, declaring war on April 6, 1917.

Dad probably viewed the war as a potential for adventure, excitement, and change, and his joining the army can also be due to our family's fierce loyalty to England. He was 24 and his brother David 19 when they enlisted. Basic training was at Camp Custer near Battle Creek, Michigan, and from there they were sent to France.

As for our family's being pro-British, I can definitely attest. I was a sophomore in high school in 1940. The week following the bombing of Pearl Harbor, I was with Aunt Floss at a neighborhood grocery store. She had just leaned over to pick up a loaf of bread when the German grocer said, "Well, Floss, the goddamn English have gotten us into another war!" and without missing a beat the loaf flew through the air, hitting the grocer in the head, and we left the store, never to return.

On August 18, 1918, fortified with American troops, including the two Stockdale boys, the Allied offensive on the Western Front began. The German army was forced to retreat and less than three months later, on

November 11, the war ended on the eleventh hour of the eleventh day of the eleventh month. Dad's Great Adventure came to an end. He had been mustard gassed and was in and out of the V. A. hospital at Ft. Custer, as well as receiving special treatment for many years at Hines Hospital in Chicago. He received a small monthly V.A. pension until his death in January 1975.

He could not have been in great physical or psychological condition when, in 1923 at age 30, he married. On the marriage certificate our mother's birth date is listed as June 21, 1906 and her last name that of a previous husband. She was 17 and already had a daughter who was three years old. My sister Rachel was born in June 1924 and I was born 17 months later. According to the marriage certificate our parents lived in Otsego, a nearby mill town, where Dad worked. At some point they divorced and then remarried.

They eventually moved from Otsego to the great white 12-room house that my grandfather left Dad. That they quarreled was due to the fact that Dad was in bad health. I always thought that my own impatience and temper probably came from him, but on February 10, 2010, I got a call from a half-brother I had not realized existed, and in an eventual meeting he informed me that it was our mother who had the fierce temper. There were physical fights with his father, whom he described as a very easy-going man. I know that Dad did not suffer fools gladly but he was not short-fused.

Their marriage would not have been welcomed by Samuel. Our mother's family lived in a run-down house in the poor section of the county known as the "grub plains" with unproductive sandy soil. Samuel suspected my mother of wanting to marry my father knowing that he, as the oldest son, would inherit not only the large house, but also the lion's-share of the one hundred-acre property.

It may be difficult today for young people to understand the strong puritan ethic back then. At the time my mother would have been known as a woman who had been around the block a couple of times and as damaged goods. She lacked even a grade-school education and was known as being "fast." Nicknamed "Little Joanie Crawford" in reference to the sensational new star of *Our Dancing Daughters*, she was said to be a terrific dancer who resembled Crawford, especially the large expressive eyes.

If these reasons for not welcoming her into the family were not enough, her father's name was Solomon Christman indicating German origin, which would have been anathema to the Stockdales. When I was growing up, the worst admonishment I could receive was "You're acting like a Christman!"

⌘ ⌘ ⌘

I have a series of remembrances of this period: one was attending the one-room Clifford School when I was five and the other is of the great white-12 room house. I remember the house's interior: a large kitchen, a wood burning stove with a warming oven and a reservoir for heating and storing water, and not one but several pantries off the kitchen.

I have a very clear memory of visiting a neighbor lady who lived on the Kalamazoo River about two miles away and who showed us some jewelry. I took a great fancy to a blue-red stone, probably an amethyst set in a brooch. When we got back home and it was discovered that I had taken it, I was told to walk back to the woman's house, return it, say I was sorry and then walk back home by myself. I was always afraid of the dark and it had turned night when I completed this task and started back home through the long row of overhanging limbs that lined the roadway. I was absolutely terrified. I sobbed.

I remember a violent fight between my Dad and Mother and her hitting him with a poker from the fireplace as his hands clung onto the back porch. I remember a sandbar down by the creek and Rae and I playing with our half-sister and her attempting to put my "pee-pee" into her. There was nothing "traumatic" about the experience. I did not have any sexual feelings; she had simply put me on top of her and tried to insert my penis.

⌘ ⌘ ⌘

I hadn't been at Aunt Floss' place very long when it was decided that I needed to be circumcised. I assume it involved some matter of hygiene. Maybe Aunt Floss was shy about skinning my foreskin back in order to wash the penis' head; I just don't know. I don't even know if my Dad was circumcised because I never saw him naked. I doubt that he was, and that is why at birth I was not. I doubt that circumcision was done much in rural areas, especially during the Depression. I have spent very little time throughout my life thinking about this because of the painful memories it arouses in me.

I must have been at least six or seven; I remember being driven to the doctor's office in Allegan, the same doctor who later botched the job of removing my tonsils. I know exactly where it took place; I was taken upstairs into a small operating room. I remember the smell of ether absorbed in a gauze mask.

When I woke it was night and I was back at Aunt Floss's. Pillows had been stacked up on either side to prevent the blankets from touching my pelvic region. But I was thrashing about and after loosely reapplying the bandage that was soaked in blood, Aunt Floss sat on the side of the bed stroking my head with one hand and holding the blankets above my pelvis with the other.

Why had my father allowed it?

I have a strong feeling that the design of the human body, whether through creation or evolution, is best left to the creator and doctors shouldn't remove parts arbitrarily. I feel exactly the same way about "concept directors" who feel they can cut or rearrange a playwright's play. In both cases revision may be necessary, but not as a rule of thumb.

⌘ ⌘ ⌘

My father and mother's second divorce was messy. Initiated by Dad, there was enough evidence of bad behavior by my mother that she offered little if any resistance. There was a legal settlement. She got $500, which would have been a considerable sum in those days, and a signed agreement that he would have full custody without her having any visitation rights whatsoever to my sister and me.

This is why I had only three face-to-face spoken encounters with my mother during her lifetime. The first occurred when my sister Rae and I were attending the Baseline School. It was just before Christmas, perhaps the final day before vacation, and our mother arrived and asked to see us. She presented us both with rather large dolls, which were in long white boxes surrounded by white tissue paper. Aunt Floss was very upset and worried that my mother might abduct us (the Lindbergh kidnapping was on March 1, 1932).

Occasionally, I did see my mother from a distance because the small town in which we lived made sightings unavoidable. But the one I especially remember was when I was marching in the high-school band. I was bass drummer, and as we passed the only hotel in town, I saw her looking out from a second story white-curtained window. The place had a bad reputation. I was fearful that she might wave and the other kids would know of our connection.

The second face-to-face encounter was in my junior year in high school. I was at a party given for our Boy Scout troop. I made Life Scout and earned most, if not all, merit badges for Eagle. The boy at whose house the party was given and I were not good friends, not to imply enemies, but we just didn't go around with the same crowd. After scouting business had been taken care of, the kitchen door opened and my mother, in a serving maid's uniform, entered wheeling a rolling refreshment cart.

As my mother came toward me, handing out sandwiches and opening bottles of *Coca-Cola*, it seemed to me that the normal volume of rowdy voices lessened and all eyes were on me. I thought of leaving but the last thing in the world I wanted was any kind of a scene. When she greeted me by my first name, asking me how I'd been, I smiled, answering as if nothing untoward was taking place. I took my time listening and selecting the kind of sandwich she suggested. In short, I shut down so tight that *no one* would ever know what I felt. When she passed on to the next boy I took my time forcing down the food and drinking the Coke. After another boy left, I felt I could do the same without anyone suspecting I was running away. I left the party, hating the boy and his parents and suspecting them of instigating the encounter. But I felt that I had done a good job in hiding how badly I hurt inside.

The final encounter was during the summer of 1957 when I visited my dad's little cement-block house which he built some years after the big white 12-room uninsured house burned. My sister told me that our mother was dying of cancer. I called and said I would like to visit.

It was a hot day, about noon, and I felt some anxiety. I kissed her on the cheek because I thought I should. Neither of us knew what to say. She had heard that I had received my PhD a couple of years earlier and we talked about that and my teaching at Purdue. But there was simply no common ground of experience on which meaningful conversation or understanding could take place.

Although she had applied lipstick and some rouge and wore a flowered kimono, her obvious physical condition prevented us from saying things that might have been said, asking questions that might have been answered, voicing thoughts that might have been shared. The reality was that I simply did not know this woman; cheery, light-hearted repartee was not possible. The words *Mother, Son* were abstractions, and only the buzzing of a large green-backed fly was evident in the awkward, longer and longer silences that filled the room.

I attended her funeral, unnoticed.

⌘ ⌘ ⌘

The house where Aunt Floss and Uncle Sid lived on a one-acre plot of land was a mile or so from the village of Bloomingdale. Sister Rae was two grades ahead of me, and when I started at the Baseline School in second grade she was given the responsibility of seeing that I held her hand and walked on the side of the road. As soon as I heard the sound of an approaching automobile—there were not a lot of cars on the road in those days—I would let loose of her tightly held hand and run into the road, scaring the wits out of her. Why would I do such a mean thing since I always knew she loved me and tried to keep me safe?

⌘ ⌘ ⌘

Rae and I walked to school regardless of the weather conditions, including blizzards. The school bell rang at ten minutes to eight, so if we started out late and heard the bell, we would run. Being tardy was not accepted. There was a mid-morning recess for play out of doors in good weather, a lunch break when the kids ate what they brought in their lunch pails, or in our case, a brown paper sack, and in mid-afternoon there was another recess. School ended at four. The academic year lasted from the first of September till the end of May.

The one room had a row of pegs on which we hung our coats and a shelf above to stash our hats and lunches. Our yellow wooden desks took up the vast majority of the room. In front, stretching across the room was a recitation bench where students from each of the eight grades gathered to recite their lessons.

The teacher had to teach arithmetic, English, history/civics and geography/science all required by state law. Obviously such a schedule was impossible so the teacher figured out ways that included teaching certain subjects to more than one class at the same time, or teaching subjects only on alternate days or sometimes only once a week.

Most of these teachers were certified after one year of Normal School, a forerunner of teacher's college. Pay was about $50 per month, no peripheral benefits, and usually only one substitute teacher for an entire county; sick days were a rarity. The system was headed by a superintendent of schools whose office was in the town that was the county seat.

One advantage of the one-room setup was lower grades learned by overhearing the recitations of the older students. I can still remember and recite some of Leigh Hunt's poem:

> Abou Ben Adhem (May his tribe increase)
> Awoke one night from a deep dream of peace...

And this one:

> The wind was a torrent of darkness among the gusty trees,
> The moon was a ghostly galleon tossed upon cloudy seas.
> The road was a ribbon of moonlight looping the purple moor,
> And the highwayman came riding-riding-riding-
> The highwayman came riding, up to the old inn-door.

This poem by Alfred Noyes made a great impression on me, especially the cliff-hanging story and the rhythm of the words. You could have heard a pin drop when Miss Teusink finished reading and raised her eyes from the page. I was on the edge of my seat.

I learned other things from the back of the room. When a class was having problems with spelling the word "geography," Miss Teusink taught them to use the first letter from each of the words in the sentence "George Elder's own grandson rode a pig home yesterday." This was very helpful *then,* but throughout the rest of my life I have not been able to spell the word without reciting that sentence.

At home, Aunt Floss and Rae read aloud such books as *The Bobbsey Twins,* which bored the knickers off of me. I never found any event that captured my attention. Just listening to the twins blab on about everyday events in their upper-middle-class lives didn't correspond to anything in my life. And this was true of the conversations of the younger and older set of twins, their parents, and their stereotypical colored maid.

The book I never forgot was *Black Beauty.* I loved the story and the way it was told from the horse's point of view encompassing a lifetime of trials and tribulations, and Black Beauty's reflections on his fellow horses as well as mankind.

I felt anguish and fear when a fire ignited the hay in the loft and Black Beauty smelled smoke. From then on until the barn burst in flames I was holding my breath, and when some of the horses were burned to death, I cried my heart out.

I've always loved horses. We had a pony named Woody that my Dad bought for Rae when he got me a bicycle. Dad always had a dog and was in the habit of speaking for the horse and the dog, as well as himself. I grew up anthropomorphizing dogs and horses, fully believing they were endowed with the human attributes of thinking and understanding. I still believe this.

Check out Laurence Olivier's horse in the film *Henry V* when Olivier enters from the "a-little-touch-of-Harry-in-the-night" scene, where he psyches out the attitudes and feelings of his troops prior to the morning battle. It is here that he gives his stirring fifty line St. Crispin speech of which his horse understands every word. No, the English troops don't have a lot of men to fight the French but those who do, will, if they make it, someday remember this fight with great pride.

Obviously the horse is thinking, "Cut the blather, Harry, and bring 'em on!" That is why he will not—the motion picture people could not make him stand still—during this speech. They could whine all they wanted about the casting director pawning off an American horse schooled in Actors Studio's "method," but the horse would be true to his feelings and would not stand still.

⌘ ⌘ ⌘

I had terrible nightmares as a kid and was a bed wetter throughout all this early period and into the time I started high school. The nightmares and bed-wetting might have been caused by some of the books read to me, or the radio series I listened to, or seeing Lon Chaney in *The Hunchback of Notre Dame*, which was shown in the free-movie series in Bloomingdale's village park during the summers. Or they might have been a result of subconscious memories of a home life before my sister and I were brought to live with Aunt Floss, or what educators now call attention-deficit-hyperactivity disorder.

As I think back on this, I'm glad that I lived during a time when no big deal was made about my high energy level (which has lasted pretty much through my lifetime) or my bedwetting. Aunt Floss never scolded or belittled me. I can only imagine the work my bedwetting caused her. She would have to heat water on the top of the kitchen stove, lift it off the stove, pour it into a tub, scrub the heavy flannel sheets on the wash board, wring them out by hand, hang them up to dry, empty the tub, and do this almost every day. This could reasonably have tried the patience of a saint.

⌘ ⌘ ⌘

I was terrorized by snakes. My most vivid recollection was the time a thick blue racer slithered through the grass in the front yard and started crawling up a tree. I was so scared that Aunt Floss brought the double-barreled shotgun from the house and killed it. It's a wonder the tree survived. I also remember coming from the outdoor toilet at the Baseline School and stopping at the gnarled roots of a tree where a snake lay coiled. I was frozen in time, my skin gooseflesh, unable to call for help. Years later, son Joe and I were hiking on one of the trails near Murphy, North Carolina, a section of the country he loves, and I saw a snake coiled on the path ahead. The terror I felt was instinctive, a primeval warning from the muck and slime of eons past.

⌘ ⌘ ⌘

One summer, on a brightly moonlit night, I awoke from a sound sleep hearing a faint call, "Mrs. Ashbrook, Mrs. Ashbrook!" I woke Aunt Floss. She threw on a robe and we went downstairs. Across the front yard came our nearest neighbor, a frail, white-haired old lady, barefooted and in a white nightgown. Uncle Sid lit the kerosene lamp as Aunt Floss got her into the house and seated at the kitchen table, then hovered over her, finger-combing her hair which was in wild disarray and mumbling words of assurance to get her to quiet down and tell us what happened.

She'd been sound asleep and told of being unable to breathe and once fully awake realizing that someone was holding a pillow over her face trying to smother her. She struggled, overcame, and managed to get to our house.

Uncle Sid asked questions in an effort to find out suspects, to no avail, and finally Aunt Floss said she would drive our neighbor into Bloomingdale where her daughter lived. I tagged along because I was too scared and excited to stay home, and when we got to the daughter's place Aunt Floss was surprised to find her awake. The daughter said her mother was subject to flights of imagination. Aunt Floss was suspicious and said later that the daughter's reaction was not normal. It was only because she absolutely insisted, that the daughter called the sheriff—she had a phone, which was unusual at the time—and asked him to go to the family home and investigate. We drove home only to find that Uncle Sid was not there. It was only moments before he returned explaining that he had gone over to our neighbor's house to see if he could find out anything and had heard her two grandsons, who were bunking in the spring house, talking. These grandsons were the sons of the daughter we'd visited. Uncle Sid was not close enough to hear what they said, but their voices were loud and animated and he suspected that the one who had recently been released from the penitentiary in Jackson had schemed to murder his grandmother, pretend she had died in her sleep of natural causes, and take over the farm.

When Uncle Sid heard the sheriff's car coming, he flagged it down and told the sheriff about hearing the voices coming from the well house. However, when questioned by the sheriff, both boys acted as if they had been sound asleep and claimed that they had no idea what happened up at the main house. Both left soon after for jobs they hoped to get in another location; the daughter came to stay with her mother, and Aunt Floss never confided to our elderly neighbor about Uncle Sid's findings, or her own view that the reaction of the woman's daughter's had been unnatural. But our neighbor never seemed to suspect her daughter. What was left was unresolved: Was there collusion between the mother and her sons, or was the attempted murder a plot hatched only by the grandsons?

⌘ ⌘ ⌘

I remember magazines in connection with great-aunt Nell, my grandfather's sister, and one of the original eight children who came from England. Their mother, Mary Gagen, having had childbirth complications, was buried in the St. Clements Church in Terrington. The eldest, fourteen-year-old Elizabeth, had the responsibility of shepherding her siblings to the new country where their father had already gone to homestead. By this time he had laid claim to his 100 acres near Otsego where the family lived for three years when Charles, their father, died. Their Uncle Samuel and his wife Clarinda took responsibility for helping the family. When they were old enough, some were "indentured," meaning they were contracted as apprentices for some trade, including household servants, and were bound over to a master, usually for seven years.

Great-aunt Nell was indentured to a family, the son of whom was a University of Michigan Law School student. During a vacation, he brought home a fellow classmate named John Dwan who in 1889 married great-aunt Nell. The wedding took place in St. Ignace, Michigan, and the couple settled in Two Harbors, Minnesota, on the shore of Lake Superior.

John Dwan was one of the five founders of a mining and manufacturing company. At last report (in 2008) the 3M Company had an operating income of $5,218 billion, a net income of $3,406 billion, total assets of $25,547 billion, and employed over 85,000 workers.

During the Great Depression, great-aunt Nell would come for family reunions held fittingly enough on the farm homesteaded by her father, and eventually owned by her youngest brother John Charles. A view at the back part of the farm, which bordered the Kalamazoo River, offered a panoramic view. There were two great trees atop this hill and it was in their shade that tables and chairs were set up and an all-day family reunion was held.

Great-aunt Nell was very generous and gave even the youngest of us a $20 bill, which was considerable in the mid-1930s since the *average* national income was about $1,200 per year. Uncle Syd was gone by that time and twenty bucks could buy necessary groceries for our patched-together little family for a month.

At that time University of Minnesota students at the extension center in Duluth would sell magazine subscriptions to help pay their tuition. Those who stopped by the Dwan home in Two Harbors, which was 25 miles north of the campus, almost always hit the jackpot because to help them, great-aunt Nell subscribed to magazines for family members, including her niece, Aunt Floss.

So on our shabby house on the one-acre "farm," I thumbed weekly through *The New Yorker* (loved the cover and the cartoons!) and the monthly magazine *Town and Country,* whose targeted audience was old-money New York families, Boston Brahmins, and social-register types and included social events such as coming-outs (in the old-fashioned sense of the word) and debutante and cotillion balls. We also received *Country Life* which featured golf, horseracing and manorial estate sales throughout the nation, and its cover was often graced by a picture of England's Queen Mother. All three of these magazines used the thick shiny slick paper which, unlike the Sears, Roebuck Catalogue, was unusable in our outdoor privy.

⌘ ⌘ ⌘

As for how we scraped together a little money during the height of the Depression: I was a hot-shot picker of strawberries. The work began at a very cool 6:00 A.M. with me crawling between rows when the dew was still on the vine, and when the day warmed up with the rising sun. I loved to work. As soon as I picked 16 quarts (one crate) I had earned 25¢, and in addition I ate as many berries as I liked. I also picked string beans, but stood tall picking blackberries, or red and black raspberries, and then later in the season I was back on my hands and knees gathering cucumbers. We often ate—boiled with a little bacon—dandelion greens dug up in the yard, along with the very expensive delicacy (if bought on the open market), morel mushrooms which we gathered from around dead tree stumps during spring in a nearby forest. And occasionally, Dad would bring over a rabbit or squirrel he had shot.

There was a bi-monthly sale of "day-old" baked goods hawked from the back of a truck for twenty-five cents a bushel basket. The contents were mostly various kinds of breads, but sometimes, very rarely it is true, but sometimes, "lady fingers" filled with a frosting. And of course Aunt Floss raised a few chickens, so there were eggs and an occasional chicken to eat which was boiled in order to make dumplings or home-made noodles in the broth. In summer we went to a swamp. It took a lot of dead frogs to feed three of us, but when we got that many, their legs were really good eating.

For a time, we owned a cow and had a vegetable garden of potatoes, corn, peas, cabbage, carrots, lettuce, radishes, turnips and parsnips. There were also occasional handouts of a side of beef or a smoked ham from good-hearted neighboring farmers aware of our circumstances. Our grandmother, Jenny, worked seven days a week for room and board at a nearby farm, and once in a while slipped us some of the largess from the farmer's pantry, justified by the fact that she received no cash wages, not even in threshing season when she had to prepare huge midday meals for the workers.

What did we do for entertainment? I became a whiz at "cat's cradle," a two-person hand game played with a long piece of white store string, ends tied to form a circle which I would shape into a cat's cradle which would be re-formed by another person (Rae or Aunt Floss or whoever I could get). Various configurations were made by pulling different strings with the thumb and index finger until coming back full circle to the cat's cradle.

We also had a table-sized, curved-top RCA radio which provided a wealth of entertainment sponsored by various food, drug, or soap companies. Comedy programs: Jack Benny, Eddie Cantor, Burns and Allen, Edgar Bergen and Charlie McCarthy, regular drama programs such as *The Lone Ranger, Jungle Jim, Sherlock Holmes, The Green Hornet, Calling All Cars,* and best of all, as far as I was concerned, *The Lux Radio Theatre,* in the latter half of the decade, with Cecil B. DeMille as host. This show offered classic and contemporary dramas and adaptations of stories, all presented with major Broadway and Hollywood stars.

There were also musical shows headed by Bing Crosby and Guy Lombardo, as well as Rudy Vallee's *The Fleischman's Yeast Hour.* Yeast was used not only to make bread dough rise but also to cure pimples and, eaten raw, to build muscle so you wouldn't look like a 98-pound weakling on the beach.

I loved popular music and sang not only for Aunt Floss and Rae, but any audience I could get. I quickly learned lyrics, and even today when I hear a song from that decade I can usually sing right along:

'Twas on the Isle of Capri that I found her
Beneath the shade of an old walnut tree...

In addition to radio entertainment, we listened to the news and I remember listening to FDR's first inaugural address. I would have been eight years old; old enough to recognize the president's unique voice and realize the special relevance of what he had to say to people in our circumstances. FDR said, "This great Nation will endure as it has endured, will revive and will prosper. So, first of all, let me assert my firm belief that the only thing we have to fear is fear itself, nameless, unreasoning, unjustified terror which paralyzes needed efforts to convert retreat into advance."

Although Aunt Floss made no sound when he said this, I knew she was crying. And someplace deep inside me "convert retreat into advance" echoed many years later during a summer theatre season when all the apprentices wore tee-shirts stenciled with "negation is debilitating," words I had used constantly. I had told them, "If the director says we need a pink elephant in this scene don't waste your energy and my time being negative. Call the hardware store to see if they have plenty of pink spray paint and then look up the phone number for the nearest zoo!"

By March of 1933, we were at a point when we could no longer survive on the kindness of neighbors and something had to be done. In his speech the President specifically mentioned that farmers could no longer find markets for their produce. I remember a couple of months later a local farmer came along on a horse-pulled wagon hauling crates of eggs into town and pulled the horses up under the shade of a tree to answer Aunt Floss' question (she was forever trying to hatch up some way to make a buck) about the egg market.

"Flossie," he said, "truth to tell, eggs ain't worth the wear and tear on a hen's hind-end."

It was around this time that Dad was in bad health and out of work. What Aunt Floss did—go on relief—was to her the most humbling and humiliating experience she ever went through, but she did it because she had us two kids to take care of. She applied for a small amount of money per month plus some basic food supplies from the government through the Federal Emergency Relief Act passed just two months after the President's address. This Act was "the opening shot" fired by "The New Deal" against poverty.

Thanks to welfare, when going to bed hungry was no longer an absolute certainty, the bicycle Dad gave me, which did not have balloon tires and was built for a full grown man, became very important in my life. In my beginning attempts—with many spills—to ride it, I laid stones strategically at intervals along the road for mounting purposes so I would not have to wheel it home to get back on. As for getting on and off in the front yard, there was a snowball bush that had a substantial forked limb, and I could ride the front wheel into the fork so the bicycle would remain upright as I carefully dismounted.

I found great freedom riding up and down the road, being by myself, and not having anyone hold my hand or being watched over. That was the only bike I ever owned and I had it all the way through high school when my buddy Lloyd and I would ride to Blue Clay Ridge or take a twenty-five mile trip to camp overnight on the shores of Like Michigan.

Chapter 2

WE MOVED TO THE COUNTY seat, Allegan, during the summer of 1936 and I entered the fifth grade at Dawson Elementary School in September. Oil had been discovered near Allegan by a wild-cat driller and suddenly there was an actual oil well pumping out real oil on a farm close to Dad's. He got an option on a section of land and was hoping for the rigs to come, drill, a geyser blowing black gold, and cause happy days to be here again. That didn't happen, but it was some of the option money, plus money Aunt Floss got from the Bloomingdale property, that paid for our house on "The Flats."

The move would be good for Aunt Floss because she would have a chance of finding a job she could walk to; the school system would be better for us kids; and Allegan would be less than five miles from the cement-block house Dad had built near where the uninsured great white 12-room house had burned to the ground.

On the fiftieth reunion of my graduating class of 1943, a female classmate, whose family's wealth and social standing was built on money made from state highway contracts—a girl I liked who had no intention of putting me down, not having seen me in fifty years—identified me musing, "Joe... Joe... let me think... oh, yes! I remember. You were the boy who lived down on The Flats!"

"The Flats" was a small section of town down by the river comprised of a half dozen run-down houses with outdoor privies. And this *did* make a difference. But I was lucky; I became the best friend of a kid named Lloyd, a genuine genius with an off-the-chart IQ who happened to be the son of the superintendent of schools.

Lloyd, born on the eighth and I on the sixth of December of the same year, became inseparable. We differed in two instances: first, his family was Presbyterian and mine was Methodist; and second—thanks to a young blond English teacher, a kind of sultry Lauren Bacall-type who taught me—I became a very good dancer, and attended all the free weekend dances in the high-school gym so I could cozy up cheek-to-cheek with pretty girls

I don't believe Lloyd ever learned to dance.

⌘ ⌘ ⌘

The Dawson School where I started the 5th grade was some distance from the junior high school where Rae went. This meant that I was now totally on my own.

At the beginning, of course, I knew no one and most of the other kids had known one another from the first grade. I was cautious and shy, conditions that affected me for much of my life but which gradually left me. My memory bank has chosen not to retain much of the two years I spent at Dawson. I was basically illiterate, and when a book was passed around the room for a demonstration of each student's reading ability, I would be in agony waiting my turn, since I knew any attempt I made would fail. Most of the other kids' reading ability was acceptable and some read very well, but I had never read anything myself because Aunt Floss and Rae had always read to me. When the teacher instructed me on how to sound out a word's syllables, I felt such pressure I could not think. And when the other kids laughed, I was humiliated.

This memory stayed with me all my life. Even when I could read to myself, the thought of reading unfamiliar material before others could bring about sweat-producing panic. During my lifetime I devised all sorts of stratagems to avoid such situations. But there are some situations, such as auditions, when a director will want an actor to read a scene other than the one he has prepared. Such situations are unavoidable, and that is one reason, even though I absolutely loved acting, that I eventually gave up on being an actor.

I had no problem memorizing the multiplication tables, addition, subtraction, division, and multiplying, but understanding how to apply what I had memorized was difficult. And my self-confidence was not increased when at recess the boys played baseball and the team captains always chose me last. I was worthless at batting, catching, and pitching. Dad never understood that I needed training in these skills and I was too shy, or maybe too stubborn, to ask for help. Physically, I was underweight, pale, and frail, and had not yet become friends with any of my classmates.

I do remember life in the new house on The Flats. Aunt Floss got a job helping the cook and the dishwasher at a restaurant-bar (mostly bar) called The Stable, which was on a scuzzy street with a history of liquor and beer-joints. It was closed down by the Eighteenth Amendment, but when that was repealed in 1933, it was happy-days-are-here-again.

Aunt Floss also rented out a couple of bedrooms to oil riggers, who, because of their occupation, found it difficult to find living accommodations. Our property was big enough so the oilmen could park their rig, and our nearest neighbors were understanding enough never to complain. There was an older man and a young guy named Rex who worked for him. They spent most of their time at the drilling sites, so we hardly ever saw them. They left early and came home late after they had gone to a local eatery. If I remember correctly, Aunt Floss charged $5 per week per room (without a bathroom) which brought in a handy $40 a month; that, plus salary from her job, was enough to take us off welfare and provide for basic needs.

During that first year at Dawson, I started going to the Regent Theatre for the kids' Saturday matinees. I'd already been exposed to drama by listening to radio shows, and seeing half a dozen free films during the summers in the park in Bloomingdale. Then, too, living through the first decade of my life, given my family situation and the economy, afforded me a kind of heightened sensitivity, so I was instantly hooked on stories told on the big screen. I also liked the serials, a single episode (one usually of fifteen) ending in a cliff-hanger in which the hero is in some kind of life or death situation such as being tied to a tree while an evil "redskin" on the verge of snagging another scalp for his trophy belt raises his tomahawk. I was anxious each week to hustle back to the theatre to see how the hero would resolve the situation.

The admission price was 10¢ for kids under twelve. My sister, Rae, had already reached that age and Aunt Floss had advised her to simply scrunch down and plunk down her dime. But eventually the manager questioned her. She told the truth and had to pay a quarter. Aunt Floss intervened, telling the manager that I would not be able to go to the films unless my sister was with me. She suggested that Rae be allowed to continue to pay a dime until I'd reached the age of twelve when we would both pay a quarter. Aunt Floss assured the manager that this arrangement would be strictly between them and that no one else would know.

The arrangement worked out well and I was some months past the age of twelve before I had to start paying the regular price. But long before that, Rae's enthusiasm for films had waned. At the time I thought she just wasn't interested, but perhaps she was embarrassed at not paying her rightful entrance fee. Then again, maybe she was just weary of looking after me.

I enjoyed the feature film, usually a western, along with the action and suspense of the serials' episodes. I loved the cinematography of both, and adored the hero's horse. I quickly figured out that I could also attend Sunday matinees, and argued that since there was no school on Saturday, I could attend the seven o'clock show on Friday.

I can't remember Aunt Floss ever saying I could not see a film. The same would be true of books when I finally started to read. As a high school freshman I attempted to check out *The Grapes of Wrath,* and was told by the librarian that I was too young to read it. Aunt Floss returned with me to the library and informed the sweet elderly lady that I was not to be denied checking out any book. When we left, I had the Steinbeck in hand, eager to find out for myself if what other kids said was true, that in it a young mother lets a man suckle at her breast to save him from starving.

Watching films became the major focus of my existence, and by the time I entered high school, I was a veteran moviegoer. I lived vicariously through all the stories, empathizing with the good guys, knew the names of the actors, loved the Movietone News, the Travelogues, the Disney animated cartoons, and the previews of coming attractions. Often on Friday nights or at Sunday matinees, there would be an adult double-feature, so I got two for the price of my dime.

By the time I finished high school I was a Bette Davis fan, having seen her in such films as *Dark Victory, The Old Maid,* and *Now Voyager.* She was not a conventional beauty and I can't remember her in plunging necklines. (If that was a guy's major attraction why didn't he just take up dairy farming?) And even though the plots of her films edged perilously close to "over the top," she always played the larger-than-life characters with such truthfulness and passion that I couldn't help but be awed.

I loved her performance in *Jezebel*. In the last scene, with torches and big guns blasting in the harbor to rid the air of yellow fever which had ravaged the town, she sits atop a load of yellow fever victims, including Henry Fonda, being pulled by a team of wonderful horses, headed off to the quarantine island where, against all odds, she is determined to nurse the man she loves back to health. I loved that film!

I'll never forget Henry Fonda's last speech in *The Grapes of Wrath* when he is running from the law and his mother, played by Jane Darwell, expresses the fear that she may never see him again. He assures her, "I'll be all aroun' in the dark. Wherever there's a fight so hungry people can eat, I'll be there. Wherever there's a cop beatin' up a guy..." is where she can *always* see him... some of Steinbeck's best writing, so moving it brings tears to my eyes.

And it wasn't only Judy Garland's truthfulness and simplicity in *For Me and My Gal*. It was her one-of-a-kind singing of a great score—popular songs from the 1910s—that was so memorable. And my favorite Laurel and Hardy scene is in *Swiss Miss,* when they attempt to move a baby grand piano across a swinging bridge in the Alps with intervention by an ape. I laughed at that one until my stomach ached.

For dramatic scenes, I think of *Waterloo Bridge*. Vivian Leigh is waiting for her lover's mother (played by Lucille Watson) to arrive for lunch. She sees, through a water glass on the table, her lover's name in a newspaper's missing-in-action column. Distraught, she misses a rehearsal, is kicked out of the ballet, and eventually she becomes a prostitute. And then one day she sees her lover, played by Robert Taylor, returning from the war .

I have a thousand such memories from the movies.

⌘ ⌘ ⌘

Allegan was blessed with one striking visual element, the Allegan County Courthouse, a magnificent red-brick Romanesque structure built in 1889 that occupied the elevated center of an entire block, with great shade trees and sloping green lawns leading to the streets that constituted downtown. Across the street on its west side was the county jail and the Methodist Church. Southwest was a charming tile-roofed library built with a 1913 grant of $10,000 from Mr. Andrew Carnegie. Next door was the Griswold Auditorium, a splendid municipal building housing a theatre in which the Community Players, under the direction of Abbie Smith, produced plays.

The ceilings of both the first and second floors of the courthouse were eighteen feet high topped by a sloping attic roof with three dormer windows. The building was crowned by a square tower housing the gigantic bells which resonantly intoned the quarter, half, and hours of day and night, and the steeple rose from it.

In the southeast corner of the green sloping lawn was a pedestal on which a statue of a veteran of the Civil War in full uniform held a historically correct sword, which somehow had been broken off so that only the hilt remained in his hand. What this looked like, viewed in profile and at a certain angle and time of day, was never acknowledged, and face was saved when dignitaries from the town's historical society had the full sword replaced.

There was something both unifying and magnificent about our courthouse that tied the whole town together, both by sight and sound. Holding the entire county's civic offices and records, it also boasted an architecturally beautiful and sizable courtroom on the north side of the second floor with an impressive bench for the judge, polished wooden balustrades stretching across the front, and a small statue of Themis holding the scales of justice in one hand and a sword in the other.

⌘ ⌘ ⌘

Sometime during those two years at Dawson Elementary, and two at the junior high school, I took up roller skating. Since there was only a narrow sidewalk leading up from The Flats, this activity was carried on around the courthouse and downtown. The four wheelers I bought were fairly expensive but I pestered Aunt Floss until I got them.

Skinny as a rail, and close to six feet tall, in spring, summer and fall of my junior high school years, I would routinely skate after school let out at four o'clock, then about an hour later go to the grocery store where we "traded." I'd buy a Powers Bar, the largest of the nickel candy bars. I had Aunt Floss' permission to tell the clerk to "put it on our bill." I've always had a sweet tooth and the candy bar helped sustain my energy for another hour and a half before I went home for supper.

I was still in junior high school when Aunt Floss came home from work one night after a fight with the cook, in which she'd dumped all the potatoes she had just peeled onto the kitchen floor before storming out. It was raining, and she was soaking wet and totally disheartened. In the days that followed, she made up her mind to do something else. That something turned into action when she decided to take refresher courses at Western Michigan Teacher's College (now Western Michigan University) in Kalamazoo to earn a renewal of her teaching certificate. By the time I entered high school we had moved from The Flats to a house on Arbor Street, which boasted an indoor bathroom—but not a water heater. Instead we used an electrical coil device that was plugged into a socket and dropped into the water. I was warned that if I ever stuck my hand in to test how hot the water was, I could be electrocuted .

The little white house was only two blocks west of the high school, reached by a path through neighbors' backyards. Aunt Floss signed a contract to teach at the Pickle Street School. And our grandmother Jenny came to live with us.

⌘ ⌘ ⌘

In September of 1939, I entered Allegan High School. I was twelve with pubic, armpit, leg and arm hair, and raging hormones. The English teacher who taught me to dance also introduced me to two great short stories, "To Build A Fire" by Jack London, and "The Yellow Wallpaper" by Charlotte Perkins Gilman. She read parts of Don Marquis' poetic *Archy and Mehitabel* to me after school and urged me to read the rest at home. Archy is a cockroach who hangs out in and around the desk of Don Marquis at his newspaper office in New York. Archy is able to leave notes to Don by jumping from one key of his typewriter to another but can't, of course, make capital letters since it is impossible for him to work the shift and home key at the same time.

Mehitabel is a fascinatingly immoral female cat claiming to be descended from Cleopatra, and nothing I can remember so caught my fancy as this premise. The conversations between these two, along with Mehitabel's tomcat friend, an actor, were very humorous. The tomcat's theatrical remembrances included the playwright Bill Shakespeare, whom he claimed had gotten sucked into show biz by Producer Burbage for financial reasons when all he really ever wanted was to become "an honest sonneteer." These characters captured my interest and commanded my attention.

I also had the impression—wrong or right, probably wrong—that the English teacher not only liked me but was attracted to me. Nothing ever actually happened along those lines, but this was my first time for fantasizing such a relationship. This ability to fantasize would stay with me throughout my life.

Puberty is an extraordinary time in one's life and I was unusually fortunate in not having biological parents, or Aunt Floss, or minions in the church to tell me that if I masturbated I'd go crazy, grow hair in the palms of my hand, or go to hell or purgatory. Like Topsy in *Uncle Tom's Cabin*, "I just growed," receiving nature's reward of wet dreams and eventually the knowledge that the creator designed my fist not only to be able to wrap itself around a tree limb but around anything vertical like the joystick on small aircraft.

Ironically it was my Sunday school buddies who instructed me in self-pleasure. One, Bill, got me to tag along with him on a hike during which we watched an older Sunday school friend jerk off. Bill and I later enjoyed a vacation together and shared a bed. The first night of the trip his hand strayed over and into the fly of my pajamas. The next night there was reciprocity. There was never any mutual affection in this act; it was only a pleasant relief for two horny adolescents. And after the vacation was over, "Bill" went his way—which was sports—and I went mine .

A young adult substitute Sunday school teacher clued us in on the sexy sections of the Bible such as "The Song of Solomon" and sometimes drove a bunch of us on swimming trips. On the way to the lake he would tell us dirty jokes about Mae West or the Fuller Brush man, and a couple of times he even shared with us one of his pornographic comic books.

The first time I actually ejaculated was when I was working as a soda jerk. With no customers at the fountain, I went to the bathroom and was amazed to see sperm shoot out. I cleaned up the mess, washed my hands carefully, and went back to the bar to jerk sodas, dip ice-cream cones, blend malted milks, cut bananas for splits, and make sundaes and/or the then-popular tin roofs: two dips of vanilla ice cream with chocolate syrup covered with peanuts.

There was nothing I remember that was traumatic about my pubescent sexuality, and I suspect that it probably was no different than any other adolescent's. It was just something natural, necessary and most of all, pleasant, since it was soon clear to me that neither tennis nor bike riding nor cold showers could stun my surging horniness into submission.

Not having access to a family car like most of the other guys was a problem. But I was a good dancer, including cheek-to-cheek, and once in a blue moon there would be a hay ride in the summer, or a sleigh ride in the winter and I would hook up and neck with a girl. I was a passionate kisser but too shy and inexperienced to go all the way.

⌘ ⌘ ⌘

During my freshman year, I experienced a major frustration. Every boy was required to take a course called "Manual Training," that had traditionally been known as "Shop." And I was surprised just now to check the dictionary and find: "Manual Training: A course of training to develop manual dexterity in practical arts as woodworking or handcrafts."

The first requirement was to saw a two-inch piece of yellow pine and then use a plane to smooth the ends. For most of the guys, handling carpentry tools was nothing new, having helped their fathers with all sorts of household or farm jobs including building construction. The only carpenter's tool we had was a small hammer used to drive nails into the wall in order to hang a picture, and Aunt Floss usually did that. So it took me some time to get a perfect two-incher sawed to the satisfaction of the teacher, but I never could plane the ends. My fellow students kept telling me to plane with the grain. But the grain at the end was rough and ran in different directions.

After the teacher used a T square to sight both sides of the 2" x 4" block and found it evenly sawed, my confidence was restored. I clamped the block into the vise, gently lowered the plane on it, and passed the blade evenly along the end. Success was near, but at the last minute I *always* hacked off a goodly chunk of that damn 2" x 4" piece of yellow pine and, like Sisyphus, was doomed to start all over again.

The rest of the class already had passed this requirement and moved on to other projects. Some were even on their third or fourth—*manually* building all sorts of wondrous inventive items such as a double deck electrically driven lazy-Susan condiment/spice holder for their mothers to proudly display on their kitchen counter—while I still plugged away at smoothing out the grained end of the block. Now the joke of the class, I was destined throughout both semesters to provide entertainment for the others guys.

With six weeks to go in the second semester I composed a note to the teacher—with a sub-text intimating suicide if the idea were not approved—in which I admitted defeat, begged clemency, and stressed that the quality of mercy was not strained because it blessed him who gave as well as him who received. "Could I please have your permission to enter the end-of-year competition with prizes awarded the three most inventive projects?"

He reluctantly agreed when I suggested that the project would at least manually train me to cope with a coping saw, used for sawing curves.

What I did was construct a likeness of Popeye from a four-foot piece of three-quarter plywood—anything to get away from yellow pine! Between Popeye's spread feet, I installed a traditional magazine rack; to the top of Popeye's held-out fist I attached a Maxwell House coffee can lid to be used as an ashtray. The piece was intended for the Man of the House as he sits in his easy chair after a hard day's work, scratching his belly, smoking his pipe, and reading the sports section of the newspaper.

Upon sight, the contest judges went into gales of thigh-slapping laughter and awarded me third place in the contest. My teacher, capitulating to popular opinion, grudgingly passed me with a D-.

⌘ ⌘ ⌘

I can't remember touching any carpentry tools for the next two years, but in my senior year Lloyd got an appropriation of $35 from the administration to build a set of flats that would be used as scenery for plays we put on for assembly. With aid from a book on how to construct scenery, he ordered the yellow pine, the muslin, and sizing glue, and we went to work. I successively helped him assemble the frames for the muslin covering for a dozen flats which were 12' x 5'9" (including those constructed for plug-ins: a fireplace, windows, and French and regular door frames). The odd measurements the book told us were because the flats would be able to fit into railroad boxcars when the show was touring. Since we had no intention of taking our shows on the road, these specifications made no sense, but I was delighted to find out about this theatrical tradition. In addition, we constructed half a dozen one-inch wide by twelve-foot tall "jogs" which were designed to aid in supporting the larger pieces of scenery that were lashed together by lines, and supported by adjustable stage braces attached to the back of the flat and secured to the stage floor.

After we assembled the frames we were about to cut the muslin, but I could not understand why the instructions were to glue it to the flat's front rather than wrap it around the edge of the yellow pine and glue it in back.

Lloyd was eventually persuaded to do just that—and remember he was a genius—and so we "sized" (painted) the muslin with a mixture of glue and water to tighten it up.

The next day, after the size dried, we could not wait to inspect our handiwork: standing and lashing two flats and jogs together, we quickly saw what was wrong. The yellow pine—wouldn't you know?—had warped so badly that the flats and jogs did not fit together. Only with effort could we lash and stand them up as a stage set. We did find ways—drapes and moldings—to conceal the cracks through which could be seen the backstage. I assume that the school eventually tossed them as unusable. But given the opportunity, and failing, I learned a lot about stagecraft.

⌘ ⌘ ⌘

In my senior year I became a debater, mainly because Lloyd talked me into it. Every year there was a national debate topic, and I assume that to give some status to this ancient and most honorable tradition, the debate officials found it necessary to defer to the teacher in charge as the coach of the team, and indulge in the scheduling of home and away debates. It sometimes happened that a debate was scheduled at the same time as the baseball game and we were allowed to ride on the school bus—Jim-crowed to the backseats—and while 99.9 percent of everyone in the visiting high school were at the baseball game, we debated the local team in the high school auditorium in front of a couple of adjudicators plus our respective "coaches." Why an extracurricular activity that employed reasoned arguments wasn't as popular as kicking, shooting or batting a ball escaped me then, and escapes me now.

There was a dress code honoring the seriousness of the occasion and we were suited and wore neckties—the first suit and tie I owned. What was most important in winning points was presenting *logical reasoning and supportable conclusions*. Lloyd did an enormous amount of research in newspapers, magazines, books, and shared all this with me on file cards that included the sources of quotations and statistics. Lloyd, with his brainpower, and me with my passionate conviction, turned out to be a winning team.

⌘ ⌘ ⌘

The bandmaster was Herman Priebe, a very quiet little man who was born near Berlin, Germany, and was in charge of instrumental music, the orchestra, and the band. I was asked to join the band when I was in the eighth grade, probably because I was the only one big enough to carry the drum in the marching band. The only thing I ever remember Mr. Priebe telling me was that I had a good sense of rhythm and that without a conductor, as in an orchestra, it was the bass drummer, not the drum major, who set the rhythm for the band's marching. So I got my uniform and did all the drumming for the next five years for shows at halftime for football, basketball, and sometimes on special occasions for events in town such as the Memorial Day Parade.

I had wanted to play snare drums, and every once in a while at band practice the snare drummer let me use hers. I did learn to play the smaller drum, but buying one to practice on, and practicing at home, was out of the question. Having now lived through the experience of raising my own drummer son, it probably was a good thing that Aunt Floss or Dad didn't have the money to buy a snare drum for me.

⌘ ⌘ ⌘

Typing was an elective, and there were very few boys in Miss Dunkley's class. I actually don't know why I wanted to take typing but I liked hands-on learning better than learning out of a book. I have used my typing skills almost every day throughout my life. I started with an old Underwood I bought for five bucks after World War II and used for almost 40 years. In 1985 a friend urged me to get my first electric typewriter, which had an eraser tape, a storage box with a large saving capacity, plus the ability to cut and paste as well as copy on 3x2 floppies.

In 1997, after my retirement, son David urged me to buy a computer. I spent the first six months cursing my HP tower, monitor, printer and scanner, occasionally threatening to throw them out a window of our 21st story apartment. But I grew used to computing and now cannot compose with a pen or pencil; it's just too slow. And when I hurry, my handwriting is illegible. I now do even the first draft on my computer because it allows me to record my thoughts almost as quickly as they occur and this has affected my writing style, perhaps adversely.

⌘ ⌘ ⌘

I loved the initial training in tennis which started with how to hold the racket, and how to swing with a follow-through motion with the strings slightly tilted upward so the ball would clear the net. I loved a fast serve: standing relaxed, tossing the ball up with my left hand, swinging the racket up, over and with a powerful downward motion, slamming the ball just
inside the serving box and acing my opponent.

I took to tennis like a duck to water and played not only after school, which was the time set aside for the practice of all sports, but whenever anyone was available. I quickly learned how to score games, matches, and sets. And most important, I was good at it. I loved playing net in doubles and sending the ball over so easy that my opponent couldn't get to it before the second bounce; loved to hit the ball just barely inside the far or side line when my opponent thinks it is going out of bounds; loved to hit it so hard that it made my opponent run backward, face in the sun, unable to return it. I loved the away games, especially the ones held in Kalamazoo when our team would meet some of the best players in southwest Michigan and we would rack up wins; loved the feel of my body and mind in hard-won sweaty competition; and most of all, loved to get an accepting slap on the back by the man in charge and know I was good and belonged to the competitive male species.

⌘ ⌘ ⌘

Masque and Sandal was the fancy name for the Drama Club. I was a member all four years of high school and served as vice president my junior year, and president my senior year. We presented three one-act plays for assembly. I remember that "The Last Curtain" was about backstage activities of the cast of *Our American Cousin* the night Lincoln was shot. I recall doing research on this play, finding out about the assassination, Lincoln, Ford's Theatre, John Wilkes Booth and his brother Edwin, the famous actor, and even read some of *Our American Cousin.*

You'd think since this experience was my introduction to theatre that every detail would stand out in my mind. But I can't remember what "One Room Apartment" was about because nature in its infinite mercy erased it from my mind. In addition, I know I got the leading role in the junior class play, *The Phantom Tiger,* and a character role in the senior class play *Ever Since Eve,* but I remember nothing of either of them other than memorizing the lines and showing off. I'm also listed in the yearbook as being in the freshman play but I haven't a clue as to what it could have been.

I did write a short skit (and typed it myself) called "Good-bye Grandma," a thinly disguised episode based on the real-life death of my grandmother, Jenny, which was presented at the all-school assembly. I'm more than chagrined to recollect that it was a comedy with a kind of Joe Orton point of view that the old girl was gone. When I reflect back on this I'm surprised that anyone at home or school allowed it. But the truth was that while she was dying she lived with us and was very cranky, and anti-young people, including me.

In addition to being in plays, club members of Masque and Sandal went to productions offered by the Kalamazoo Civic Players, under the direction of Sidney Spayde, and one of the best community theatres in the country. I especially remember *The Women* and *Angel Street,* and also saw the road show *The Black Hills Passion Play.* Lloyd and I went to see *The Show-Off* with Joe E. Brown at the Cass Theatre in Detroit.

It was thrilling to see the great Ethel Barrymore in *The Corn Is Green,* and the New York company's production of *Watch on the Rhine* with Paul Lukas, Mady Christians, and Lucille Watson. And there was *Spring Again* with C. Aubrey Smith and Grace George. All those shows played one-night stands at Kalamazoo's 2,500-seat State Theatre.

Our annual yearbook, *The Echo,* listed accomplishments beside each senior's picture. It recorded my nickname, "Barrymore," and on the "consensus of opinion" page I was voted "Most Talented Boy." I had tied with

Tucker Nash for best dancer, but that honor was given to him since I had already received one award and he had enlisted in the Marines.

I served in some capacity on the yearly Carnival my freshman, sophomore and junior years; I was club editor for *The Echo;* and in physical fitness for Uncle Sam during my senior year, I came in second to Leroy Gibson on the cross country run and received special praise from teacher Bob Peckham, who wrote on my report card that he had been surprised and pleased with my running ability and wished that I had been more active in track and other sports. I took part in paper drives, served on the Youth Council which sponsored the Friday-night dances, and however slim the chance that the Japanese or Germans were plotting an aerial attack on Allegan High School, I took my duty as air raid warden seriously.

⌘ ⌘ ⌘

My first regular paying job during these years was at a radio shop that, in addition to Philco Radios, also had a soda fountain that sold not only the usual cones and sit-down ice-cream dishes, but an occasional sandwich, too. I began this job the second week of June 1939, just after finishing eighth grade. Hours were from 10:00 A.M. to closing, which was usually about 10:00 P.M., after which I not only cleaned up the soda fountain area, I mopped the tile floor of the whole shop while the owners played Pinochle in a back booth. I usually rode my bicycle to and from work unless the weather was bad, at which time I walked, or the owners, Mr. and Mrs. Franz, dropped me off on their way home.

The next summer I had the same job. When two of us were offered a trip to San Francisco to see the World's Fair by our Sunday School teacher, my sister replaced me for a month, and the money she earned went to help pay for the trip. We picked up my friend's aunt who lived in Chicago and the four of us were off on a great adventure. Highlights? Mount Rushmore in the Dakotas; the Continental Divide in Colorado and seeing snow in July; swimming in the Great Salt Lake in Utah; Old Faithful in Yellowstone National Park; and the Pacific Ocean glistening on our right as we drove through Washington and Oregon on Highway 101 to San Francisco and the World's Fair—where we sneaked in to see Sally Rand and her famous fan. Then on to Los Angeles to see Hollywood Boulevard and Grauman's Chinese Theatre, and to San Diego, and over the border to Tijuana, Mexico to see "the longest bar in the world." We crossed the desert, and in Arizona visited the Petrified Forest, went north to the Grand Canyon, and back to Allegan, and my soda jerking job until school began.

The next summer, 1941, Aunt Floss, Rae and I all got jobs in the famed resort town, Saugatuck, about 25 miles west of Allegan. Aunt Floss and Rae worked as chamber maids in a resort home-hotel, and I got a job as dishwasher-busboy (mostly dish and pan washer) at Mrs. Stilson's Green Candle Tea Room for twelve big ones a week plus lunch and dinner. I shared a room with a guy who was the busboy and occasionally helped me with the pots and pans. We each paid $2.50 a week for the room. I liked the responsibility of the work and keeping ahead of the waitresses' need for clean glasses and silverware.

Prior to going to Saugatuck, I had insisted on seeing a Sunday matinee of *A Woman's Face* with Joan Crawford, and was also finishing reading *The Grapes Of Wrath,* which Aunt Floss had convinced the librarian I was old enough to read. She and Rae had to report for their jobs two days before I did, so Dad drove them down to Saugatuck while I stayed home alone. I finished *Grapes of Wrath* on the trip and sent it back with Dad to return to the library.

There is no doubt on which side of the political fence I stood after reading the Steinbeck book, probably the greatest epic story ever told by an American author. I was for the underdog: I was for the one black kid who was in our class. He lived up near the old brickyard just above the Flats and I occasionally ran into him on my way to school.

In the third week in June, Mrs. Stilson closed early and came into the kitchen and plugged in a portable radio. We all gathered round and listened to the broadcast of the fight at the Polo Grounds in New York City between "the Brown Bomber," Joe Louis, the heavyweight champion, and Billy Conn, the light-heavyweight champion contending for Louis's title. Everybody except me wanted Louis knocked out by the white guy. I kept my mouth shut.

I was the only one in the kitchen who was happy when, with only seconds to go in the thirteenth round, Louis knocked out Conn. Everyone in town wanted Conn to win in a rematch. But this was the summer of 1941, On December 7th the Japanese attacked Pearl Harbor and Joe Louis went to war.

I'm not sure why I was so affected by the racial prejudice that night. It was pretty common knowledge—all you had to do was drive along the highway or the shore road and see the "Gentiles only" signs—to know there was anti-Semitism, as well as disrespect for Negros in this area of the state. I *did* know and respect my dad's politics. He was responsible for fighting and winning pensions for widows whose husbands had died in World War I. He did not like Republican Congressman Clare E. Hoffman who became famous for his fight against government public health, specifically FDR's anti-polio immunization program, claiming it was backed by Russian-born doctors. Dad's thinking was that Hoffman's view was motivated by his hatred for the president who, a victim himself of polio, had a special interest in this program.

Hoffman was also anti-Semitic and a supporter of The America First Committee and Father Coughlin of Detroit, whose weekly radio program was estimated to reach nearly 40 million listeners, or one-third of the nation, and generated 80,000 letters a week. He not only worked against the president but shared some of the same views as Hitler and Mussolini. He was re-elected for thirteen succeeding terms, serving as representative of Michigan's fourth congressional district from 1935 through 1963.

Toward the end of the season at Mrs. Stilson's, Olive, a very pretty waitress, another waitress, the busboy, and I rented a couple of canoes after work and paddled down the Kalamazoo River into Lake Michigan. It was a beautiful moon-lit August night. Olive was in my canoe and I felt very grown up. We built a fire on the beach and roasted marshmallows and sat watching the stars. I knew she chose me as her date because she was engaged to a guy in the service. I suspect that she also knew that I was too grassy green to come on to her. But still, except for the marshmallows, this was an almost grown up experience.

My third job was at Johnson's Dairy on the highway. Once again, my bike was my transportation. I was a soda jerk and ice cream and milk seller, but this time I made 18¢ an hour plus all the ice cream I could eat. I worked there on weekends until June when I got a really terrific job at the Kroger Store. The only test I had to pass for manager Bud Warden was to demonstrate that I could lift a hundred pounds. For 25¢ an hour, I sure as hell could, but as I bent over and reached for a sack of sugar, he stopped me. "You'll wreck your back that way," he warned. Squatting on his hams, he said, "Let your thighs and legs take the weight." Bud was a young guy and advice from him was like advice from an older brother. It felt good.

Customers, usually with a list, would tell me what they needed, and I would fetch it from the shelves that I stacked, always rotating the cans or boxes so the new was behind the old. I wrote down the cost of each item, and when the order was completed, added it up twice, let the customer check my addition if they wished (mostly they didn't), then rang it up and deposited their money in the cash register. I always thanked them for coming in when giving them their change and said that I hoped to see them next week.

After a while I had certain customers who always wanted me to wait on them. Because of the war, many items such as butter and sugar, were rationed and I had to account for those sold with coupons. Some items such as canned salmon, which was scarce, were stashed under the counter and sold only to our most loyal customers, surreptitiously of course.

Bud taught me to work the meat counter so I could take over when the butcher went to lunch. After I had that job under my belt, he made me produce manager. I came in early, before we opened, and retrieved the produce which was stored in a walk-in refrigerator overnight. I cut off outer leaves of cabbages and lettuces if they needed trimming and arranged the various vegetables and fruits attractively. When they became messed up as the day went by, I saw to it that they were rearranged.

I worked six days a week until school started and then Saturdays only. Bud raised my pay to 30¢ an hour and eventually to 35¢. By that time I was making the same as a man with a family and saving my money for one thing. Against all odds, I was determined to go to drama school.

Chapter 3

THE SIXTY-EIGHTH ANNUAL COMMENCEMENT OF Allegan High School was held at the football field on Wednesday, June 10, 1943. I was the last of five speakers, my topic, "America, Our Future," and my speech ended with "We entered to learn and go forth now to serve." These speeches were followed by the presentation of the class, the conferring of diplomas, benediction and recessional.

I worked at Kroger's right up to the end of June, and on Friday, July 2nd, left Allegan at 6:00 A.M. on the bus to Kalamazoo. There I caught the train to Detroit, and on to New York City, riding overnight and arriving on a Saturday. I walked from Grand Central Station over to Broadway and then up to the YMCA at 5 West 63rd Street, just off Central Park West where, on the advice of the school, I had pre-arranged for a room. I checked in, got some much needed sleep and the next day—The Fourth of July—had a very inexpensive but hearty breakfast at the Y's cafeteria. I walked south along Central Park to Columbus Circle, then east on the Park side of 59th Street and then south on 5th Avenue to Rockefeller Center. The Feagin School of Dramatic Art was on the sixth floor of the International Building, Rockefeller Center, guarded by the statue of Atlas.

How had I come to know about this school? Miss Towne, our drama club's advisor, had introduced me to a monthly magazine called *Theatre Arts*. Its major focus was Broadway, the "legitimate" theatre as Broadway fare was then called. But it also covered national as well as one-night-stand road companies. I read it cover to cover each month, including ads for professional drama schools. And now I stood in front of one not knowing anything about Atlas's shrug.

With my directions squared away, I went over to Broadway and explored the side streets between 43rd and 56th Streets where most of the shows that I had read about in *Theatre Arts* played. I was surprised to find many of them closed for the summer. In those days air conditioning was problematic. The theatres still open advertised either "air cooled" (which could have meant an electric fan blowing over a keg of ice) or "air-conditioning" which could have meant anything, although the Plymouth Theatre, where *Skin of Our Teeth* played and which I saw, boasted "air conditioned to 68 degrees."

That first afternoon I checked out cast pictures that were displayed and the price of tickets. There were some variations, but the cost to see Helen Hays in *Harriet* was what most shows were asking which was from $1.10 (balcony) to $2.75 (mezzanine and orchestra), although you could get into *Junior Miss* and *Angel Street* for 55¢ to $2.20. I spent that afternoon getting used to the fact that *I* was walking on Broadway, the most famous theatre street in the world.

I wasn't scared being so far from everything I knew, but for the first time in my life I was lonely, even though the streets swarmed with people. Back home, I knew everybody and everybody knew me. But here, in Times Square on the 4th of July, there were more people than the population of Allegan—all seemingly going someplace, having friends—and I knew absolutely no one. Aunt Floss did get a phone in our house after she started teaching, but the only time I remember long-distance calls was when someone in the family had died. Just to call for a reassuring voice was unheard of.

I was excited and thrilled seeing the theatre marquees and advertisements, and looked forward to the next day when I would start school. But as I headed back up to Columbus Circle in late afternoon I knew I did not want to sit in my room alone. Instead, I sat on a bench on Central Park West people-watching and feeling like I was going to cry. But seventeen-year-old guys as tall as I was did not cry even when, for the first time in their life, they experienced this unfamiliar emotion—loneliness.

Toward dusk I went back to the Y, had an inexpensive supper in the cafeteria, and moseyed around the lobby where I looked at newspapers and magazines until I began to wonder if the desk clerk thought I didn't have any place to go. I went up to my room and wrote a letter to Aunt Floss extolling the city. Then, being conscious to lock my door, I went down the hall with the towel the Y provided, went to the toilet, then to the adjoining shower room, showered, dried, put on my shorts, and, key in hand, went back to my room, closed and locked the door, put on my PJs, looked out the window that overlooked the courtyard of the Y and saw lights in other windows and an occasional moving figure. I turned off the overhead light and lay down on the bed, the lights from the courtyard shining through, casting a reflection of the window frame on the dark brown linoleum-covered floor.

⌘ ⌘ ⌘

If you look up the Feagin School on the Internet you will not find any substantive facts, or history of the school. There are, however, seemingly endless entries about alumna Angela Lansbury, probably one of the most-written-about actresses to ever tread the boards of Broadway or be seen on the silver screen. The full-time faculty members at Feagin were Helen Claire, Grace Mills, and John Kirkpatrick.

Helen Claire was in her forties when I attended the school. She eventually ended her 21year-career in the theatre with 17 Broadway credits. Her first three big hits were followed by seven years of shows that lasted from two to 32 performances before she played the lead in *Kiss the Boys Good-bye*, which ran for 286 performances, followed by five that lasted from 12 to 36 performances. She played a total of 1,085 performances on Broadway and worked with two stars, Texas Guinan and Lillian Gish. Neither she nor any of the plays or musicals would be remembered in the history of the American Theatre.

Grace Mills was 60 years old. Her Broadway career totaled 21 years in 17 shows including five hits for 812 performances, 12 others for 278 performances (average run 23 performances), making a grand total of 1,090 performances. She worked with six stars: Ruth Gordon, Alla Nazimova, Clifton

Webb, Judith Anderson, John Gielgud and Florence Reed, and in five plays that are still remembered.

John A. Kirkpatrick's list of credits and shows went back to 1919. He was an actor, then a stage manager, then a director and finally a playwright. In 1921 he stage-managed *Nice People,* starring legendary actresses Katharine Cornell and Tallulah Bankhead. Just above his cast listing in the 39 *East* program is listed actor Henry Hull, who would later create the role of Jeter Lester in *Tobacco Road,* which famously ran 3,182 performances as a *success de scandale.*

These three teachers were the real thing. The two actresses had been around the Broadway block more than a couple of times and were obviously now "between engagements," and Mr. Kirkpatrick is credited with a number of one-acts published by Samuel French, which made him enough money to survive since one-acts were produced by high schools and little theatres all over the country.

⌘ ⌘ ⌘

At Feagin, lessons in stage deportment (how to conduct oneself in a given manner) taught us: how to walk, how to sit and how to rise from a chair (step off from the most forward foot: "unnecessary action not wanted"); girls were taught how to cross their legs (avoid pressing the calf of one leg against the other, press *the side* of one leg against the other to make both look thin); how to open and close a door; how to fall (three sequential movements: to the knees, then sideways to the hip, followed by torso to the floor); how to laugh (start with ha, ha, and repeat, increasing the rate until laughing); to cross downstage of a fellow actor when the focus of the scene is on you and up stage when it isn't; always to turn to the audience since your face is more revealing than your backsides; how to slap and get slapped; how to take snuff, and all such deportment issues of period style.

Scene study stressed analysis of the structural elements of the scene as an adjunct of acting. In that class I played the wonderful role of Stanhope in the climactic scene in *Journey's End.* We also had lessons in makeup and had to go to Gray's Drug Store at 43rd Street and Broadway and get a makeup kit. The clerk advised me to use 7A Stein's stick greasepaint as a base because of my dark complexion; buy liner brushes to apply brown, black and white grease paint for highlights and shadowing; rouge for cheeks and lips; powder to set the base once it is applied, and a small brush to dust off the excess. The *de rigueur* [for good luck] rabbit's foot was included in every kit although we were cautioned never to utter "Good luck" prior to going on since it was bad luck. What we said was "break a leg," or, if German, "neck and leg break."

Perhaps the major training I needed was in voice and speech. In voice class, the emphasis was on diaphragmatic breathing ("up from the stomach"). I remember being laid out on the floor and given sounds or words or sentences to say while Miss Claire's hand was placed on my lower abdomen about an inch above my dingus so she could feel if I was breathing from the diaphragm. All this did was tense me up—who needs an in-class erection?—and so, rather than relaxing me for proper breathing, it did just the opposite.

And how could my voice be coming from down there when my vocal chords were in my throat and my breath came from my lungs? So it all got kind of confusing. The bottom line was that I became aware that there was something wrong with my voice, but couldn't find a way to fix it. At that age almost everyone is interested in a quick fix, when in reality voice work—read Chuck Jones's book, *Make Your Voice Heard*—takes a lifetime of exercise.

Voice production—don't confuse this with singing lessons—has rightly become more and more important in the training of actors. But when I went to Feagin, it was taught simply for projection. Today the technology of sound—amplification—has been given emphasis in some university curriculums because there are few, if any, Broadway shows, straight or musical, that aren't miked. In 1943 there was no such thing; it was the actor's voice you heard, even up in the back row of the top balcony, and if you couldn't be heard up there, chances were you weren't working.

Then there was my speech; I got cast as Bobby—the closest role to a prototype of the playwright, in Noel Coward's *I'll Leave it to You*. What I most remember was that during the first rehearsal, the director, Miss Claire, constantly stopped me and corrected my pronunciation and accent, which no one had ever criticized when I was in shows in high school or on the debate team.

"Just, not jist," "*mothah, fathah,* not moth*ur* and fath*ur,*" "kaant rather than caan't." She imitated the nasality of the worst sort on the "caa," plus my habit of skipping the ending *g* in words due to my lazy, nay "slovenly," modifiers, saying "goin," "doin," "mowin," "chewin," god help me! etc., etc., etc., *ad infinitum.* What I remember her saying to me after that painfully long first rehearsal was that if I repeated any of those mispronunciations the next day she would have to recast. If I'd had any street smarts, I would have known she was bluffing, because I don't remember there being any more than four guys in the class, and the other three looked more like character juveniles.

But I was taking no chances. The next rehearsal was total hell, not only for me but probably for everyone in the room. I'd come to a line like "I just can't do that, mother." And forcing myself to say the words correctly, there would be these long pauses between "I" and "just" as my tongue, teeth, lips and jaw eschewed 17 years of mispronunciation and my brain was *telling* me, 'say the bloody word correctly or else!' Thus, with the sword of Damocles hanging over my head, I corrected my slovenly enunciation and pronunciation and, in addition, I subtly tried to draw some much needed sympathy from the others, especially the beautiful Rosemary Culligan whose face had appeared on the cover of a magazine, which I bought for her to sign. But she took my agony in stride, while the girl playing Sylvia—who had a head of hair that had been marcelled so often with a hot curling iron that the ends of each split follicle stuck out like a singed overgrowth—comforted me during breaks.

In addition to classes and rehearsals, I quickly learned from the other kids that one could go to the Astor Hotel in Times Square and for ten cents buy a copy of "Cue," which came out once a week as a mimeographed fold-over listing all the open calls for Broadway and road shows. I pored over this little rag and decided to audition for a projected road company of *The Front Page* because it had so many roles for men. It was being cast by producer Chamberlain Brown. This being my first audition, I had taken a picture from my senior class play and left it with his assistant with my address at the Y and the phone number for messages.

When I got a message from the front desk that Mr. Brown had called asking me to come to his office it was seven o'clock; he wanted me there at eight. Excited? You better believe it! I fantasized on my walk down about becoming a Broadway star. There was an elevator which took me to an upper floor of the building where I found Mr. Brown's name etched in the glass. I knocked. I obeyed the "come in" and after closing the door, explained who I was.

Mr. Brown, seated behind his desk, looked me over, got up and came around to me and held out his hand. I held out mine to shake and found his face very close to mine and his other hand fumbling the zipper of my fly. I backed away fast. He followed. I moved behind his desk to get a fix on the door. He followed and when he got to the back of the desk, I ran to the door and fled down the stairs.

I was scared, my heart pounding as I hurried along the crowded street, wondering why this had happened. Why, why, why my mind was asking. Was there something wrong with me? I had never heard the word homosexuality. That spring I had read a popular novel *Kings Row* that was made into a movie, and remembered the vague feeling I had, but did not understand about the relationship between the two boys. After a very bad night, I went to school early and asked to talk to Miss Claire. Both she and Miss Mills were in the office and seeing that I was upset sat me down and I blurted out what had happened. Was it something about me?

Both women were wonderful. Miss Mills took my hand and held it as Miss Claire told me that there were many older men in the theatre, just as there were conductors of orchestras (she had been in musicals as well as plays), who were attracted to young men who had to "cater" to them as a condition for being hired. Both told me that Mr. Brown was notorious for this and that I was not to blame for what happened. Miss Claire said I was a good-looking young man and that my looks were an asset as far as acting was concerned, but that I should know the facts because this same thing would probably happen again. I had done the right thing to tell them what happened.

Miss Mills had some additional advice, which has stayed with me throughout my career: "As bad an experience as this was for you, remember that all experience can be beneficial *if you make it so,* because you can use it in acting." Although the situation that brought on the emotions in a play might be different, what I felt could be exactly the same, and I could use my memory of this emotion to turn something bad into something of benefit: a useful recapitulation of Stanislavski's principle of "emotion memory."

It was past time for classes to start; both women hugged me, and we went into the rehearsal hall with me feeling much better. But I didn't, couldn't, get the experience out of my mind.

Sometime later—after I had learned to take a short cut through Central Park back to the 63rd Street Y—I was returning after a day of classes and rehearsals when I saw three guys in uniform coming in my direction. One started singing to the tune of three blind mice, "One 4-F, One 4-F, see how he runs, see how he runs ..." and I knew they thought I had not joined the service because there was something physically wrong with me. Although I was certain I would be in the service as soon as I was 18—that is what my commencement speech "go forth to serve" was all about—I'd been thinking about staying in New York through December and going to the American Academy Of Dramatic Arts for their fall term. But now I didn't want to stay. Now all I wanted was to join up.

⌘ ⌘ ⌘

I don't actually remember the occasion, but there was some kind of party at the school, probably at the end of the term. And I bought a bowtie to wear. Frank Sinatra was my favorite singer and I wanted to look like him. I tried and tried to get the tie right (if they had clip-ons in those days, I didn't know about them) and then I *had* to get underway or be late.

There was this woman who ran the elevator—those were the days when elevators had an attendant and you just called out the floor you wanted and they took you there. She had been nice to me and if I had a friend at the Y, it was certainly her. As soon I got on and the door was closed she told me my tie was not tied correctly, stopped the elevator between floors and instructed me how. When I botched it she tied it herself in a perfect Frank Sinatra imitation, restarted the elevator and took me to the lobby. With my black wavy hair and my big nose, I felt a little like Sinatra. I have never forgotten this kindness from the elevator lady at the Y.

⌘ ⌘ ⌘

I came back to Michigan wearing my bow tie and thinking of myself differently. I had been to New York City! I had one date after arriving home with the girl I most liked in high school and Aunt Floss loaned me her car. I got as far as parking and "necking," but the truth was she was in love with a guy who was a couple of classes ahead of me and was in the army.

I met with Abbie Smith, the theatre director with whom I wanted to do *Ghosts,* to tell her about the Feagin School and that I had decided to join the Navy. Abbie, a very accomplished actress, told me to see Sidney Spayde, the director of the Kalamazoo Civic Players, and try out for *Claudia,* in which she would be playing Mrs. Brown.

Mr. Spayde saw me (I'm certain Abbie had called him in advance) and cast me as Fritz, an elder German servant who was in a few scenes. Today, such casting would be unthinkable, except in high school productions. But no one had TV sets in those days and audience expectations were different. Sidney Spayde enjoyed casting young actors to play character roles of any age. He understood that audiences took delight in seeing a young person convey age in a way that made them believe a mirror was being held up to nature. This was accomplished by good acting, not by bending over and talking in a wavering voice, but understanding that older people might be bent, but they attempted to stand tall and walk steadily. Secondly, and equally important, Spayde believed in the art and craftsmanship of makeup and delighted in plays with historical characters where the actors had to resemble their real-life prototypes.

I got a job as a busboy—which included a room—at the Burdick Hotel cafeteria for breakfast and lunch, with evenings free. Rehearsals were a wonderful experience and I watched all the scenes I was not in. For my scenes, I delighted in the demands of a different body and an accent. But although I loved being in the show, I was still determined to enlist in the Navy. During a break between work and rehearsals I went to the recruiting office in Kalamazoo with a permission letter signed by Aunt Floss.

I took the physical on a day I was not on-call at the theatre. A car took three of us to Detroit for the day-long series of tests and examinations: standing in line naked for hours with the other guys, giving urine samples (a couple of guys were unable to pee and others shared theirs), and when all the physical stuff was done being ushered individually into the psychiatrist's office.

We all knew we were to be asked why we wanted to join the Navy and the talk would be pretty much patriotic, so after asking me if I had a girlfriend and then asking why I wanted to join the Navy, the doctor probably expected a variation on the patriotic theme. I hesitated but said what was the truth, "I want to make a man of myself." I've never forgotten the way he responded or what he said. He was an older gentleman, probably my dad's age, and he looked at me for a moment, then smiled and said, "You look to me like you're pretty much of a man already, son."

That was something really good. I was pleased that I passed all my tests and was given a specific induction date after *Claudia* closed. Later in the week, after lunch hour at the Burdick. I hitch-hiked to Allegan to tell Aunt Floss. I prolonged my stay and she told about her own plans to get a job at the Willow Run defense plant. She gave me her car to get back to rehearsal on time and said that after it was over I could drive it back to Allegan, stay overnight, and go back to Kalamazoo on the 6 :00A.M. bus the next morning in time for work.

On the drive to Kalamazoo, I had a flat tire. I wasn't experienced in changing a flat, but I did know how, though it took time and I knew I was going to be late for rehearsal. When I walked in, Mr. Spayde was furious. He explained how much time for rehearsal had been lost because of my lateness. He stated the time—perhaps 20 minutes—and multiplied it by the cast and crew members who were there waiting. Then he told me the time taken for rehearsals for productions in New York and compared it to the lesser time taken for a community theatre production, and that being on time meant being ten minutes early.

Only after he was finished did I explain. He listened steely-faced. Through clenched teeth, he said, "If you are ever in a similar situation and there is even a remote possibility of having a flat tire on the vehicle you're driving, start an hour early so you are not late for rehearsal." And he meant exactly that! In my telling I had attempted to gain the advantage via empathic sympathy and patriotism but that didn't work. Screw my enlistment in the armed forces of World War II where I might be killed in action. Screw any filial obligation I might have for the woman who raised me. To heck with my father who had gone to war once again for his country. No sentiment offered or understanding given. There were no possible excuses EVER for being late to rehearsal. Just, goddamn it! BE ON TIME, which meant ten minutes early. Period!

Throughout the 138 productions I was to direct in my life, this was my own feeling exactly!

⌘ ⌘ ⌘

There were only a few of us being driven from Kalamazoo to the bus in Detroit. When the bus came back through Kalamazoo, I wondered why didn't it just stop and pick us up there? When I voiced this to the guy who had the window seat, his response—uttered in a barely understandable accent—was something to the effect that "There's the right way and the wrong way and the Navy way. So keep your yacker shut!" I caught enough of "Ours is not to question why, ours…"

When I joined him in the punch line, "… is but to do or die?" he was not amused.

Most of these guys knew each other. They were from Hamtramck, a town almost completely surrounded by Detroit. Their families had been there to wave them off: their dads, mothers, and younger brothers. They were first generation American sons whose parents had emigrated from Poland and come to Hamtramck to work for the Dodge Motor Company. All were devoted Catholics, loved baseball, and not one of them had pronunciations that honored the *ly* or *ing* of the English language. I knew instinctively that if I spoke as I was taught at Feagin, I would not survive boot camp. And yes, since what I told the psychiatrist was true, it would be best if I talked as little as possible. I did not acquire a single friend, a special buddy I could talk with.

Basic training taught me things I never knew. I learned ship language: the floor was the "deck," steps were "ladders," a mop was a "swab," we were "swabbies," the bathroom was "the head," undershorts and shirts were "skivvies," my bed was "the sack," sleep was to "sack-out," food was "chow," to eat was to "chow-down," coffee was "cup o' joe," and cold cuts of meat were "horse cock." Then there were the nautical terms such as "aft," "starboard" (right side), "port" (left side), and so forth. We learned to correctly pack our canvas sea bag and our smaller ditty bag, how to make our sack with squared corners, how to scrub the deck, how to swab out the head. Then there was the marching and the commands—dress left, right face, forward "harch," and "at ease."

We learned the history of our dress uniforms. The 13 buttons that constituted the fly of our trousers stood for the original 13 states. My "mates" called them "13 chances to change her mind." There were swimming classes where we learned life-saving techniques while the teacher vividly captured our attention with tales of sinking ships and sharks. There were the usual calisthenics (I was never able to bend and touch the floor because my femur—the bone from the knee to the hip—is out of proportion with the rest of my body. (Wouldn't you just know I'd be given a *long femur?* Thanks for nothin'!) Try to explain that to the "chief" petty officer! I could do all the other exercises and was very good at push-ups, since I was now down to 120 pounds distributed over my six-foot-plus frame.

We also had hand-to-hand combat during which we were not supposed to hurt one another, so it usually turned into wrestling and being pinned. I had never had a fight or wrestled or even roughhoused in my life. The boys from Hamtramck had a fetish for delivering a hard punch to the muscle in the upper arm that hurt like hell, although they seemed to think of it as some kind of bonding love tap. But I didn't have a lot of muscle and what my upper arms developed was an interesting black-and-blue-turning-yellow coloring.

We did a regular four hour "watch" although it was questionable if any Germans or Japanese were lurking outside the gates of the Great Lakes Naval Station. And we had to learn how to fire a rifle ["This is my rifle, this is my gun, this is for fighting, this one's for fun"] and were scored on our accuracy. Surprise of surprises I got the highest rating possible—I can't remember if it was called "sharpshooter," "marksman," or "Annie-Oakley"—but I got the highest mark for both stationary and moving target, and my dad had never even taken me duck hunting. In fact, only once in my lifetime had I ever fired a shotgun. I guess I just had a good eye.

I survived those two months as company drummer (I volunteered) and doing everything else with sleep deprivation like I had never known. Before graduating exercise in the drill hall in December, we were assigned our next duty. Most of the guys went to the Naval Base at San Diego, which meant they would be assigned to a transport ship that would take the Marines to the South Pacific to retake Japanese-held islands. I was assigned for further training to the Hospital Corps School at Great Lakes.

As corpsmen we not only served the Navy but were the official medical unit for the Marines. When we finished those two intensive months we were prepared to assume a position comparable to that of a trained nurse. This might be in a base hospital or a hospital ship, or we might be assigned as the only person who could take care of a medical situation from a hot appendix aboard a submarine to the Fleet Marines in battle on a South Pacific island. We were taught how to apply a tourniquet to stop bleeding, give morphine, sprinkle sulfa (sulfanilamide) powder to allay infection, and dress wounds.

When units of sailors or Marines were transferred from one place to another, all were checked for "crabs" (body lice) and venereal disease. We were known respectfully, even affectionately, as "Doc," but unofficially—albeit with the same affection—as "shanker [canker] mechanics," a cancroid being a lesion resembling a cancer on the penis caused by a sexually transmitted bacterial infection contracted during unprotected sex. We were also called "pecker checkers" because of the ritual dropping of skivvies to "milk it down" to check for a yellow discharge that meant "clap" [gonorrhea], then "skin it back" for the uncut or just a look to check for *lymphogranuloma venereum* (yes, we had to learn the Latin) which was revealed by genital lesions and warts, again from unprotected sex. Finally it was "Turn around. Bend over. Spread the cheeks," looking for crabs.

The first time I ever actually had to do this was in Norfolk when a company of Fleet Marines boarded our ship. I saw this long lineup in the aft cafeteria and spoke to the old salt who was our chief petty officer. "That's a lot of guys for short arm inspection," I said with a hint of complaint in my voice. "You'll get used to it," he answered. "In my time I've checked enough of 'em to spike a railroad track from here to Frisco." And we were in Norfolk!

Of course our main duty was to attend the sick either in out-patient treatment or in the sick bay aboard ship. Our routine was to take TPRs (temperature, pulse and respiration) four times a day at 0800 hours, 1200 hours, 1600 hours and 2000 hours. The telling and writing of time was another thing we had to get used to, because there was no A.M. and P.M. in the U.S. military, which used (and still uses) the 24-hour clock.

We also studied *Materia Medica* in Corps School. All ships had some variation of a pharmacy aboard and a variety of pills and liquids that were shipped in or concocted aboard via a mortar and pestle to grind down one substance into—whatever was needed. The PAC was our standard pill taken every four hours (Q4H) for everything from the common cold to double pneumonia. I had just turned 18 when I took the pledge on graduating from Corps School:

> I solemnly pledge myself before God and these witnesses to practice faithfully all of my duties as a member of the Hospital Corps. I hold the care of the sick and injured to be a privilege and a sacred trust and will assist the Medical Officer with loyalty and honesty. I will not knowingly permit harm to come to any patient. I will not partake of, nor administer, any unauthorized medication. I will hold all personal matters pertaining to the private lives of patients in strict confidence. I dedicate my heart, mind and strength to the work before me. I shall do all within my power to show in myself an example of all that is honorable and good throughout my naval career.

I loved Hospital Corps School, but on graduation most of our group—maybe two hundred or so—were sent to San Diego. I was among 20 who were assigned to the Brooklyn Naval Hospital. On hearing this, I was of two minds. I still wanted to see action, but on the other hand I would be in NYC where I could see Broadway shows. Secondly, Brooklyn Naval Hospital was the major hospital for Marines who had contracted malaria while on duty in the South Pacific. At least I would get to serve in that way. But still as twenty of us departed from the Chicago train station, I felt some disappointment.

Maybe what I actually felt was what I woke up with in my berth in the middle of the night. I had a raging fever along with chills. I was sweating and my throat was burning. I roused the guy in the lower bunk and he got the chief, who took my temperature which was 103.7^0 and immediately put me in isolation in a berth away from the others, and gave me two PACs.

Next day when the train pulled into Grand Central Station, there was an ambulance waiting. I was taken to it on a stretcher and driven to the Pearl and Sand Street Naval Hospital where I stayed on a sick ward for two weeks with pharyngitis, acute (we always used the adjective after the noun) which is similar to strep throat.

While a patient, I witnessed the Golden Gloves on TV. They took place at Madison Square Garden and were transmitted electronically over to the hospital. All I really know about this is that it may have been one of the earliest broadcasts in the history of TV. I was treated well in the hospital. But, as in boot camp, I made no special friends and no one came to see me. When discharged, I was looking forward to duty on the malaria wards but they did not need any more corpsmen. But they did need….

How in hell was I going to write to that girl from high school whose picture I had cut out of our yearbook and placed in my wallet and tell her I was working on the maternity ward at Brooklyn Naval Hospital? I could hardly believe it; *no one* would believe the Navy ran a maternity ward! But they did. It was for the officers' wives. This was going to be my war experience? Three times a day going to the main mess hall where they had, ready and waiting, a chow wagon that I would wheel over to the maternity ward and, after the patients had finished eating, wheel it back to the kitchen in the main mess hall?

The maternity ward kitchen was staffed by civilians, mostly Italian women from Brooklyn. I've always looked like someone from the Mediterranean areas because of my dark complexion, so the women took me as one of their own, including inviting me to their homes for the weddings of their elder daughters and to meet their younger daughters. Some guys might have relished duty that allowed so much liberty. but I was too embarrassed to even let anyone at home know what I was doing. Every other day for two months I went to the office of the commanding officer and put in for a transfer to the Fleet Marines.

My routine was as soon as I finished hauling chow, which was at 1900 hours, I would go on liberty, walking the Brooklyn Bridge over to Manhattan and then uptown. I went to Feagin to see if any of my classmates were around. None were, but I did discover that Miss Mills was in a play at the Belasco, called *Decision*.

The American Theatre Wing's Stage Door Canteen was where I went to get a sandwich and hopefully a dance, but jitterbugging seemed to be the main dance. I was looking for a little cheek-to-cheek action. As a part of the Theatre Wing's service they also gave out free theatre tickets. On one occasion I got tickets to two shows on the same weekend, one for a Saturday evening performance of *Othello* with Paul Robeson, Uta Hagen, and Jose Ferrer, the other for a matinee of *Decision*.

I shall never forget Robeson, who would certainly be in my top 50 list of great actors. I idolized him. I was at the Belasco the next day to see Grace Mills in *Decision*. I went to the stage door and left a note with the stage manager saying that I would like to see her after the performance. When it was almost curtain time there was a rustling in the back of the theatre. Heads turned. There was a murmur that turned into something much louder. And who do you think it was? Paul Robeson! *Othello* did not play Sunday matinees.

After the show, as I walked up the alley anticipating seeing Miss Mills, a hand was placed on my shoulder. It belonged to the six-foot, six-inch, Paul Robeson. He called me "Sailor," asked my name, and he said he was pleased to meet me. I told him I had seen him the night before and how great a performance I thought it was. He deflected talk of *Othello* and wondered how I liked *Decision*. I told him I liked it and was going back to see Grace Mills. He opened the stage door for me and insisted that I precede him. I was first up to the stage manager who told me the room number on the third tier and that Miss Mills was expecting me.

It was great to be greeted by her. She wanted to know what I was doing. I told her I was waiting to be assigned, probably to the Fleet Marines, and would go to the Pacific. A call from the stage manager interrupted our talk and she went out on the balcony. I followed. Below, the stage manager individually introduced Paul Robeson to each of the actors in the company. When he got to Miss Mills, she turned to me and said, "I'd like to introduce my friend and former student, Joseph Stockdale." And Mr. Robeson replied, "Thank you, but Joe are I are old friends. We met as we walked up the alley together." That drew a chuckle from the assembled actors.

Can you imagine how proud I felt?

⌘ ⌘ ⌘

It was sometime in late March when my Dad was honorably discharged from the Army in Texarkana, Texas after basic training after it was discovered that he had lowered his age to enlist. He decided to come to New York to visit me before going home, and I got two tickets for us to see a matinee of *Over 21* by and with Ruth Gordon. What I most remember is my dad, still in uniform, and the women who came up to him commenting on and even touching his ribbons He explained that they were from World War I. For the first time, I saw him from an outsider's point of view. Even with graying hair, he was a good-looking man and, of course, fit as could be having just gone through basic training. Women were naturally attracted to him.

We had dinner together after the show and I walked him back to his hotel where we shook hands and said good-bye. He was only there for the one night. I told him that I was waiting to be shipped out but never mentioned the maternity ward. I had the feeling he was pleased to see me in uniform, albeit that of the Navy rather than the Army. But in truth, our talk was filled with silences, since we did not really know what to say to one another.

⌘ ⌘ ⌘

It was sometime in April that I got my wish and was transferred. The women on the maternity ward wished me well and I was off to Norfolk's Naval Operating Base (receiving) where I would be waiting to be assigned. I was totally out of touch with Aunt Floss, who was at Willow Run. I sent a card prior to leaving Brooklyn to say that I was being transferred and that I would let her know just as soon as I knew where. I waited there for weeks, hoping each day I'd get assigned. We had liberty every night, but the base was a long streetcar ride from the heart and bowels of wartime Norfolk. There were some movies shown on the base, but otherwise it was just waiting. I didn't make any friends. No one did because there was no reason to since we never knew if and when we would ever see each other again.

The only thing I remember specifically about those weeks is that I went to the burlesque theatre on Granby Street, which I enjoyed, and for the first time in my life got drunk. On the streetcar back to the base I rang the bell to get off at the next stop, where I puked out my guts. There was a chapel nearby and I went in. It was 2300 hours and I had to be back by midnight but I walked to the front—there was no one there—saw this beautiful statue of Jesus, knelt down and prayed.

I went to the Methodist Episcopal Church in Allegan while I was growing up, and had Epworth League medals (one for each year of perfect Sunday school attendance) halfway down my chest. Just as there are no atheists in foxholes, there were none at NOB waiting to be shipped out. I felt like I was going crazy waiting, waiting alone, and I prayed hard to get my orders that would allow me to see some action.

When my assignment finally came through, I was ecstatic. The *USS Wyoming*! I was going to be on *a battleship*. It seemed as though my prayers were answered. I would see some real action, and believed that this was, after all, the best of all possible worlds.

Much, much, later, of course, I learned the facts. The *Wyoming* (BB-323) was one of the oldest ships in the fleet. She was launched on the 25th of May, 1911, and could accommodate 60 officers and 1,000 men. She had a history of being in and out of Brooklyn Navy Yard for repairs, overhaul, and alterations an inordinate number of times. Between fixes she took

Annapolis midshipmen ["middies"] on high-end cruises, and was the flagship for various Admirals.

In World War I, she joined the British Navy for maneuvers and tactical exercises and was inspected by King George V. Although she dodged a couple of "torpedo wakes," she was never involved in anything so John Wayne as actual combat. After World War I, she cruised the East Coast, became part of the Pacific fleet, and in 1931 put into the Philadelphia Navy Yard where she was demilitarized and converted into a gunnery training ship.

The point is that during her first 30-plus years, there was never a hint of conflict; rather, her mission seemed to serve as poster-ship fodder for the Navy's recruiting efforts, gathering photo-op sessions, picturing gobs in various ports of the world with hot-looking babes hovering in the background near the slogan "Join the Navy and see the world."

During WWII, she served for over two and a half years in the lower reaches of Chesapeake Bay in countless gunnery training drills for thousands of Fleet Marine Corps gunners, and was referred to as "The Chesapeake Raider." In brief, the entire history of the *U.S.S Wyoming* gave new meaning to the word *dreadnought*.

⌘ ⌘ ⌘

Highlights of those two years?

One weekend when I had treatment-room duty and all three doctors were ashore, a guy came in with a severe pain on the right side of his lower abdomen. I had learned in Corps School that if you suspected a hot appendix the best way to tell was to press down (with your four fingers clamped together) two-thirds of the way from the crest of the ilium in a direct line toward the navel and then release quickly. If the patient experienced severe pain, chances were he needed an appendectomy.

Fairly well convinced that this guy should be transferred to Portsmouth Naval Hospital, I called the captain who was ashore, but his yeoman, on my recommendation, ordered a special liberty launch to get the patient to the hospital. They reported that his appendix was indeed hot and if I had not done what I did, it would have ruptured.

⌘ ⌘ ⌘

One day while I was making the rounds with one of the doctors, a patient claimed he was seasick. The doctor ordered that the patient be moved to a "fracture sack," a bunk with a very thin mattress, take castor oil Q4H, and be placed on a liquid diet. I asked the doctor why, and he said the guy was faking sea sickness to try and get discharged. I told him I didn't know how he could be certain of that. He said it was obvious. I asked him how. He said he just knew. I said how? "Experience," he said. I thought for a moment and then said, "No, I will not do it." He looked at me, and I knew that he was not so much angry as he didn't know how to deal with what was clearly insubordination. But I also knew he knew that I would not carry out his orders. He finally drew a deep breath and said, "Okay, cancel. Just continue what you've been doing."

⌘ ⌘ ⌘

Six of us took liberty with the expressed intention of visiting a whorehouse in Norfolk. We registered at the hotel where the women worked and made the arrangements, paying in advance. I was edgy and volunteered to be first, but got more and more embarrassed because I couldn't get it up. She grew impatient and asked me if this was my first time. I said yes. She said I probably needed special attention and she didn't have time for that. I said that was okay, told her she could keep the money, and asked her not to tell the other guys.

When one by one the other guys came back, none of them talked about their experience with her. She was older and not at all attractive, at least not to me, and the approach—her just getting naked and lying on her back in the bed waiting for me to undress—was not conducive to any feeling of sexual desire on my part; in fact, it was a turnoff.

Afterwards, as I lay in bed, not being able to sleep, I tried to figure it out. I had to feel something, either because she was pretty, or because she was nice, or was attracted to me. I just could not be aroused when this woman spread her legs and expected me to hop on. And I never could, not that I ever tried at a whorehouse again. I had to feel something that started with sight; I just couldn't do it without the stimulation of—what? Love.

One of our doctors aboard ship knew I liked to read. He was from Asheville, North Carolina, and one day said that I should go to the ship's library where I would find a book written by an author from his hometown named Thomas Wolfe. The book was *Look Homeward, Angel.* I started reading and could not put it down. I took it topside, read it on the forecastle with the sea all around me. To this day there are passages that I can recite by heart. "We can believe in the nothingness of life, we can believe in the nothingness of death, but who can believe in the nothingness of Ben. Like Apollo, he came, a God with broken feet..." and I could go on and on. I fell in love with Thomas Wolfe's writing. I'd loved books before but nothing had ever so affected me as this one. I was Eugene Gant, "young and drunk and twenty-one and knowing I could never die."

⌘ ⌘ ⌘

It was in the treatment room that this same doctor dealt with my chronic stuffed-up nasal passages. He wrapped cotton around a steel prong, dipped it into liquid medicine and gently put it up my nose. As he pulled out the prong, he left the saturated cotton and I was high as a kite! I loved the euphoria, and for months aboard, I was free to medicate myself with this seven percent solution of cocaine in sterile H2O. After I was discharged I had a nose operation to alleviate the problems of my deviated nasal septum and never thought of the cocaine high again . . . until a later incident in my life.

⌘ ⌘ ⌘

I saw a production of Ibsen's *Ghosts* one weekend in Norfolk with two great actors, Alla Nazimova and Francis Lederer. It blew me away. This is the story of a young man, a congenital syphilitic, who is going mad. I coveted the role and wanted to play it with Abbie Smith as Mrs. Alving. Aboard the *Wyoming* we had some crew who were receiving injections of Salvarsan to kill the spirochetes that caused syphilis. The problem was that this compound contained arsenic and only a small amount could be administered for the body to withstand it. The average time was 18 months, and a "cure" could not be assured. I often assisted one of the doctors in these treatments and was in charge of sterilizing the equipment.

The week after I saw *Ghosts* a new medicine arrived. Made from the mold that produced penicillin, taken by injection it would, within one week, cure syphilis. The doctors explained that this was one of the great landmarks in medical history, and the coincidence of seeing the production of Ibsen's *Ghosts* and getting the first batch of this medicine aboard was memorable.

⌘ ⌘ ⌘

I absolutely loved the two years of my life aboard. I was tight with the guys I served with, had fun, learned a lot since I not only did duty in the medical office, but also served regular watches in sick bay, occasionally in the operating room, the autoclave room where we sterilized instruments, and I also stood regular duty in the outpatient treatment room. I felt respected not only by the guys in my division, but also by the men of other divisions and the Fleet Marines we trained.

⌘ ⌘ ⌘

The *Wyoming* was tied up to the dock when I boarded her in April 1944. The Normandy invasion— D day—was on June 6, 1944 so I missed that action. But it was still possible, I told myself, to see action in the South Pacific. Then, almost a year of gunnery training later, on May 7, 1945, Germany surrendered and some weeks after that on June 30, 1945 the *USS Wyoming* cautiously ventured out of Hampton Roads into the ocean.

I remember that day very well. Sailing out of the 12-mile limit into international waters meant we would receive overseas severance pay when we were discharged. We could buy duty- free watches at the ship's store. Although I was a bit seasick, I was still elated until one of the signalmen in the Morse code room finally caught on to the fact that SOS meant danger, and relayed the message to the captain that the tail end of a hurricane was coming up from the Keys.

All hands were ordered topside and instructed to gather on the starboard side, then on command run to the port side, then back to the starboard side, etc. etc. The point was to try to get her rocking and rolling so the captain could ascertain how much list she could take before rolling over. The problem was that even if all the hatches were battened down tight, there was not a watertight compartment on her; even the portholes leaked. The captain cautiously took thirty knots to turn her North.

It was a glorious sunny mid-morning when we sailed into New York Harbor. I was topside to see the New York skyline, the Statue of Liberty and the Brooklyn Bridge. As I watched I heard the noise of welcoming ships in the harbor, and in the distance saw a tugboat making its way toward us. As it neared I saw a WAC band on its bow and debutantes swaddled in red, white and blue bunting waving tiny American flags. Across the side of the tug was this big sign, "Welcome Home Boys."

I just went below.

We went into dry dock at Pearl and Sand Street until July 13th. We had liberty every night and I saw such shows as *Dark of the Moon* with Richard Hart, *Anna Lucasta,* and the musicals *On the Town* and *Carousel.*

And unforgettably, I saw *The Glass Menagerie* on a freebie from the Stage Door Canteen. Nothing I had seen up to this point could compare with the acting and writing of *Menagerie*. I had seen Ethel Barrymore, Katharine Cornell and Helen Hayes, but knew nothing about Laurette Taylor. Every moment of her performance was spontaneous; she was never thinking ahead, she was always in the scene, living it, moment by moment. Her acting was as different as the acting of Marlon Brando was to people a few years later except for one aspect: every syllable of her mumble was articulated so it could be understood up in the balcony where I sat.

The Glass Menagerie is my most memorable evening in the theatre.

⌘ ⌘ ⌘

On the 13th of July the *U.S.S. Wyoming* left Brooklyn Navy Yard to once again venture out into the ocean where she headed for the North Atlantic, Casco Bay, and Portland, Maine. Our mission was to develop the Mark 8 director (directors were the rotating compartments on the top of a ship, which controlled firepower) by way of firing not at enemy aircraft, but rather at radio-controlled drones towing sleeve targets. This was about the extent of my wish to experience the clamor of fife and drums. All this was calculated to aid our guys in the Pacific who were dealing with the Japanese *Kamikaze*. We were hard at it in late July when Hiroshima and Nagasaki were bombed, and we sailed back into Casco Bay the afternoon of August 14th when Japan surrendered, ending World War II.

Chapter 4

ONE OF THE FIRST THINGS I did at home after I was discharged was to go see Abbie Smith and tell her that I was thinking about applying to The American Academy of Dramatic Arts in New York. She was not against the idea but asked me if had thought about going to Western Michigan and getting a teaching certificate in case I needed something to fall back on. She also mentioned that there was a show already in rehearsal at the Civic that had still not cast a nice character role, and that I should see Gerhardt Lindemulder, the Civics' new director. I got the part and it was great to be back in rehearsal and meeting cast and crew. Betty Ebert was the Civics' intern that year and I got to know her and her husband of only a few months, Jack P. Ragotzy, who would play an important part in my life.

There was a woman connected with the show who offered me a lift home after an early rehearsal, but instead of dropping me off at the apartment Aunt Floss had rented for us in Kalamazoo, she invited me up to her apartment. We listened to Noel Coward's "Mad about the Boy," and another with lyrics, "It seems like happiness is just a thing called Joe. He's got a smile that makes the lilacs want to grow… Does he love me good, that's all I need to know…" and drank a couple of beers. Hugs and kissing resulted and it all happened naturally.

I liked her a lot. She loved undressing me and getting me in the sack, and since this was my first time, she gently guided me, and reached down and put me in. After I came and was up again, we changed positions. I watched her face and as she rode me listened to her special sounds. I couldn't get enough of her.

We saw movies together sitting in the back of the balcony of the State Theatre where no one else sat, she with her hand high on my thigh and then into my fly, and oh did I love it! She was in her late twenties and I was twenty and a half, and as I look back on my life, I thank my lucky stars for this wonderful woman who so wanted me, and who I so wanted and needed. We had sex every evening after rehearsals and performances of the play.

It was during this time that I enrolled, at least for the summer, at Western Michigan on the GI Bill of Rights. But during the short time between the end of the show and the start of school—and despite how much enjoyment there was being with this woman—I decided to make a trip to New York to see shows, and then go up to East Long Meadow, Massachusetts, to visit a shipmate buddy, John Stacy Beebe.

The train trip was memorable because this was a time when the nation was converting from war to peacetime. There were labor disputes which had been absent during the war because it wasn't patriotic to strike while others were putting themselves in harm's way.

A national railway strike was called, and President Truman threatened to have the armed forces take over the railroads. When I left on my overnight train ride, I knew there might be problems. Our train stopped just short of reaching New York. It stopped in the middle of nowhere. I made a friend on the hike to the nearest town; he called his dad; and I rode into the city with them, checking in at the 63rd Street Y.

The shows I saw were the Kazan-directed agitprop *Deep Are the Roots* (which I loved), *O Mistress Mine* with Alfred Lunt and Lynn Fontanne, *Pygmalion* with Gertrude Lawrence and Raymond Massey, *Show Boat, State of the Union, Dream Girl* with Betty Fields, and the innovative musical by Rodgers and Hammerstein, *Oklahoma*, based on Lynn Riggs' *Green Grow the Lilacs*. The most interesting innovation I saw was when the Lunts dovetailed the dialogue (one line of dialogue was not completed when the other actor started), a technique that Robert Altman later used in films.

The trip up to East Long Meadow was fun, not only to renew an acquaintanceship with my *Wyoming* buddy, but to find out that this was the home of Paul Robeson where he was a football player in high school. I also met my buddy's girlfriend who took an intense interest in me and me in her.

⌘ ⌘ ⌘

When I returned home I got a call from Jack Ragotzy, who wanted me to come to a meeting to launch a summer theatre. Jack had gotten out of the Air Force in December 1945 and was immediately cast in a Kalamazoo Civic Players production where he had met intern Betty Ebert. A whirlwind courtship followed and marriage. She wanted to go away to summer stock but Jack, who had enrolled for the spring semester in Kalamazoo College, wanted to go to summer school in order to keep his subsistence checks coming, and to more quickly complete his degree.

Betty, having queried various eastern summer stock companies, found that even with a BA degree in English Literature from UCLA and a year's internship with the prestigious Kalamazoo Civic, she would be expected to pay over a hundred bucks for the season, plus her room and board, to be an apprentice and do coolie-labor with no promise of even a walk-on. So Jack suggested they start their own summer theatre.

The meeting was at their apartment at 527 S. Park Street where a dozen young hopefuls, including me, would soon be incorporated into a legal partnership agreement known as The Village Players, our own summer stock theatre in the rented Richland Community Hall. All were picked because of their expertise in specific areas, and if you want to know who they were read my 50-year history of The Barn Theatre, *The Man in The Spangled Pants*, which you can find on Amazon.com.

It would be storybook perfect to be able to report that at that meeting, where I first laid eyes on Robin Fastenrath, that it was love at first sight. That didn't happen because I was far too absorbed in trying to give a decent reading for the leading role of Jack Chesney in Brandon Thomas's

Charley's Aunt. Never feeling the necessity of dressing up or making up, Robin, with her long auburn hair, perfect oval face, beautiful brown eyes set against unblemished skin and a dimple in her cheeks, plus a suggestion of one in her chin, was easily the most beautiful woman in the company. Hell, why qualify it? Better to say, with no exaggeration, she was the most beautiful woman I had ever seen.

We were naturally drawn to one another and our relationship grew quickly once we became involved in everything from building scenery to acting. Since I did not have a car and neither did she, we would find ourselves after rehearsals or performances huddled together in the back of a pickup truck, wind in our hair, headed the ten miles back to Kalamazoo with me whispering Omar Khayyam's "…A loaf of bread, a jug of wine—and thou beside me in the wilderness."

After we were dropped off, I would walk her home and eventually was allowed in to her parents' living room for "necking" and eventually foreplay on the sofa, after which I hurried home to get some sleep before attending Professor Frank Householder's 7:40 A.M. English class, followed by Albert Becker's Rhetoric class, then a full day's work at the theatre and, at the same time, reading textbooks, writing assigned papers, and having time with the woman I got to calling "my lost lane-end into heaven," from Thomas Wolfe's *Look Homeward, Angel* which I could recite by heart, and did.

⌘ ⌘ ⌘

That first season we offered four performances, Wednesday through Saturday evenings every other week, of five plays. In *Charley's Aunt,* I was thrilled to get the longest role in the show until I eventually found out that the role Jack cast himself in was the show stopper and got all the laughs. During the rest of that season I played a minor role in *The Bishop Misbehaves;* the hero in *Pure as the Driven Snow or A Working Girl's Secret;* a featured role as Homer, the bashful bachelor in Paul Osborn's *Morning's At Seven* opposite Robin as Myrtle Brown, a shy old maid. In *Goodbye, Again* I played a bit part and Robin played the leading female role.

The Village Players started with $350 capital ($25 from each of the fourteen legal partners). Ticket prices were 75¢ for Wednesdays and Thursdays and 90¢ for Fridays and Saturdays, and this was subject to a twenty percent federal entertainment tax. With the hall comfortably seating about 175, we ended the season with a total attendance of 2,359 paying customers (lowest night 56 and highest 222), and at season's end each partner received back his $25 plus $8.40 profit.

⌘ ⌘ ⌘

I entered Western Michigan as a Speech major with minors in English and History, and completed my 120 credits required for the BA degree in December 1948. I was on the GI Bill of Rights which paid for tuition and books—$35 for tuition and fees, with textbooks averaging about $12 per semester. My monthly subsistence allowance was $65. When I was married on July 4, 1947 it was raised by $25 so I got a check for $90 per month. In 1948 it was raised to $105, and after the birth of our first child in August of 1949 it went up to $120.

Aunt Floss had put a down payment on a run-down house with an upstairs rental at 824 Academy, which was just below Kalamazoo College and only a short walk up Oakland Drive to Western. That's where I lived for the first year going to school. I was able to live on my allowance and still contribute some for my room and board.

As I reflect on these years, fragments of remembrances come back.

Lucille Nobbs (so perfectly named), my professor for American Prose, looked very much like the actress Josephine Hull, whom I saw in the Broadway production of *Harvey*. Not only did she look like Hull, but there was a similar askew manner—with one eye that darted in an opposite direction on occasion and a wisp of unruly hair that she swept away from her face with the back of her hand. She stood barely five feet so her ample bosom was disproportionate to the rest of her body, so much so that as she made her way from the door to the lectern it seemed as though she might fall flat on her face, but she always managed to grasp the podium in time.

None of the veterans in the class will ever forget her Benjamin Franklin assignment. She said that all non-veterans would be responsible for reading Franklin's "The Virtues." Then growing confidential, she told the veterans they might profit more by substituting Franklin's little essay, "Advice To A Young Man..." She leaned dangerously forward and gave a wink—a rapid *tic douloureux* fraught with innuendo and elliptic subtext.

Of course we all rushed to the library to find a copy. It turned out that the full title of this "essay" (actually a letter to a friend) was "Advice on Choosing a Mistress," the gist of which was that he (Ben) "knew of no medicine to diminish the violent natural inclinations" his friend had written him about, but he strongly advised marriage. If, however, the friend did not take this counsel, then he would advise "that in all your amours you should prefer older women to young ones" and he went on to suggest reasons why. Since aging appears first in the highest parts of the body, "the lower parts continuing to last as plump as ever so that covering all above with a basket, and regarding only what is below the girdle, it is impossible to know an old woman from a young one. And as in the dark all cats are gray, the pleasure of corporal enjoyment with an older woman is at least equal, and frequently superior, every knack being by practice capable of improvement. And they are always so grateful!" Just by the way she taught, you knew that Miss Nobbs was in love with literature, and rather than some stuffy puritan listing of virtues, how much more relevant—not to mention useful—advice it was at our age to encounter Ben in this context. Of course we had all heard this advice in one form or another (he gave it in 1745) during our time in service when an older guy would council us: "If she's older just hang a flag over her head and fuck for old glory."

⌘ ⌘ ⌘

The formidable Laura V. Shaw not only headed the theatre, she chaired the Speech Department, which included Argumentation and Debate headed by Anna Lindblom, and Speech Correction headed by the legendary Charles Van Riper. Miss Shaw was my most influential teacher not only in studies for the BA but throughout degrees to follow, plus 42 years of teaching and directing. She had a BS from Ohio Wesleyan University in 1914, an MA in speech from the University of Michigan in 1917, summers at the Bread Loaf School of English, and in 1931/32 she studied in New York with Maria Ouspenskaya and Tamara Daykarhanova at the American Laboratory Theatre, both of whom were members of the Moscow Art Theatre and had acted in plays directed by Stanislavski.

An absolute disciplinarian in both the classroom and rehearsals, she knew her Stanislavski backward and forward, and as was usual for me I gained more in a practical situation than in theoretical classroom discussions. Miss Shaw's rehearsals were from 7:00 to 10:00 P.M., and for a major production—actually, everything she deigned to work on became major—there were three weeks to a month's preparation in readings and discussions of the play before we attempted to put the show on its feet.

I remember one such reading when, after two and a half hours, my body shifted slightly from forward leaning to rest against the chair's back. Miss Shaw stopped the discussion in midsentence and wanted to know if I was bored. She was absolutely relentless in her view that the body must be relaxed *but* in an attentive position for full concentration in order to discover and understand that which would undergird the play's mounting.

She believed, as I came to believe under her tutelage, that the essential creators in theatre production were the playwright and the actors. But both create *within the parameters of the order and symmetry* of a prime creator. In short, they imitated the order of nature: the world, the universe, and man. Directors and designers are interpretative artists who serve the same higher order. In such a system the tipping point in which destructive ego can run rampant is eliminated because the work of each is eventually judged by its faithfulness to nature. Hamlet's advice to the players says it all: "Suit the action to the word, the word to the action, with this special observance, that you o'erstep not the modesty of nature. For anything so overdone is from the purpose of playing, whose end, both at the first and now, was and is to hold as 'twere *the mirror up to Nature*—to show Virtue her own feature, scorn her own image, and the very age and body of the time his form and pressure."

What Laura Shaw had us searching for was the *theme* of the work. The *subject*, expressed in a word or two, is what the play *is about;* theme, on the other hand, is the author's *point of view* on the subject. In O'Neill's *The Iceman Cometh* the subject is "illusions"; the theme is that "the lie of the pipe dream is what gives life to the whole misbegotten mad lot of us."

My initial experience of working with Miss Shaw in a production was during my first year at Western. I suggested that she consider *Deep Are The Roots,* which I had just seen in New York, for the midwinter production; I did this because I passionately agreed with the point of view of the author on the matter of racial prejudice.

I remember with great pleasure the intensity of a month's reading and discussion followed by that first rehearsal when we got the play "on its feet." Miss Shaw did not "block" the scenes; our movements were dictated by our characters' actions to fulfill the specific objectives, which illustrated the play's theme which Stanislavski calls the "super-objective." I was cast in the major role of Howard Merrick, a young lawyer from the North who is in love with the eldest daughter of the Governor of the Southern State (Alabama) where the story takes place.

When it came time to make my entrance I was primed. Already having learned my lines plus having acted a good character role at the Civic Theatre and roles in our summer theatre, I came on like gangbusters and was about to say my first line when I heard Miss Shaw from the auditorium.

"Excuse me. What are you doing?"

The questioned stunned me. Wasn't it obvious? "I'm making my entrance," I said defensively.

She gave a slight laugh. "Yes, I couldn't help but notice."

I understood immediately. "Let me try again," I said, going offstage. While the scene prior to my entrance was being repeated, I was concentrating—Concentration was one of Boleslavsky chapters in *Acting: The First Six Lessons*—on getting into character by saying to myself, "You are Howard Merrick. You are a lawyer from Albany, New York; you are thirty years old…," when I heard Miss Shaw call, "Now what are you doing?"

I came on stage. "Sorry to miss my cue," I said. "I was getting into character."

"Meaning?"

"I was reminding myself of who I am. I'm Howard Merrick...."

She was amused. "This morning," she said, "prior to class you came to see me in the office?"

"Yes?"

"Prior to your... entrance, were you standing in the hallway saying to yourself, 'My name is Joe Stockdale, I am twenty years old, and I was born in Allegan, Michigan'?"

"Well, of course not," I answered.

"What were you thinking about?"

"What I wanted to talk to you about."

"Your objective, yes. Concentrate on your character's scene objective within the author's given circumstance and you will have your character."

I entered to talk to my girlfriend about my objective, but this time my actions—how I talked to her and what I said—revealed my character.

⌘ ⌘ ⌘

In the spring, I suggested that the directing students direct each of the major scenes between two characters in Irwin Shaw's antiwar play *Bury the Dead*. Bits and pieces that glued these seven scenes together were also assigned, and eventually the whole play was put together and given public presentation under the supervision of Miss Shaw. I played the Captain and Robin played one of the whores.

Miss Shaw was always right. Always. But in discussion of the play she made the only mistake I ever heard her make. She used the word *whore*, pronouncing it with the *w*. I informed her how the word should be pronounced and she accepted the correction and somewhat humorously admitted to her sheltered upbringing (her father was an ordained minister of the Methodist faith).

⌘ ⌘ ⌘

The following year Miss Shaw chose André Obey's *Noah,* translated from the French by Arthur J. Wilmurt, which tells the story of the biblical character embarking on the ark with his wife, three sons, three neighbor girls and the animals. It ends when the water recedes and the ark lands on Mount Ararat.

I was cast as the title character and did a good job with makeup, which included a long beard. In addition to the month of discussion and readings, we rehearsed for another six weeks. At one rehearsal I became so rattled and enraged by Miss Shaw's eternal striving for perfection that I left the stage with a roar, continued out the back door of the theatre, and ran wildly around the building three times in a snowstorm's drifts up to my ass before I had cooled off and was once again ready to "get it right." But by the time the production opened, I felt we had gotten it right. I was proud of the production and my performance. It was one of the few roles in my life that I felt that way about.

I had written a play that included a thinly disguised Laura Shaw character. Unfortunately I gave it to someone at the Civic Theatre to read, who did so and then immediately turned it over to Miss Shaw. She was more than a little upset. I told her the character was not based on her but on the rigidly inflexible ballet mistress in the film *Waterloo Bridge.* Miss Shaw knew I was improvising this fib. What I had done tore apart the fragile bond of codependency of teacher and student. For the first time ever, the midwinter production was cancelled, and since I had no more classes from her before I graduated, that was essentially the end of our relationship.

Several years later Robin and I were driving along a road near Saugatuck, Michigan, and in the car ahead I saw the short stiff-necked, severely combed-back gray head of hair of the driver. I knew at a glance that it was Miss Shaw, and riding with her was a new young teacher, Clara Bush. On impulse, I passed, honking, waved my hand and pulled off to the side of the road. She stopped behind me. I got out and ran back, hoping against hope that she would realize how glad I was to see her. She attempted a kind of cordial civility but it didn't play, or maybe it didn't match my own hopeful expectation of reconciliation.

Many years later, I had occasion to return to Michigan. I called ahead and asked if I could see her. She agreed. It was wintertime. I went to her house. I apologized for causing a break in our relationship and told her she was the best and most influential teacher I ever had. Any success I had in teaching and directing I owed to her, and I said that many times I told my students of her influence.

She was old, and hard-of-hearing. She accepted my apology but the acceptance was guarded and cold, and I know the hurt I had caused her was still inside. I guess I had thought and hoped that time had mitigated her hard feelings. I should have known that once convinced of something, nothing could penetrate her certainty. The portrait I drew of her in my play was still present, and maybe she knew that it was an honest picture. For that I was terribly sorry.

⌘ ⌘ ⌘

Professor Russell Seibert was my history professor. I was strictly a C student throughout. I thought highly of his lectures, knowing he was a class act and the real thing as a scholar, but I couldn't find a connection in history that would sustain an abiding interest and appreciation of the subject—that is, until he lectured on Karl Marx and Friedrich Engels. These lectures just happened to coincide at a time in my relationship with Robin when I was doing everything I could to make an impression.

I can still see her sitting in the Union building, serenely beautiful, smoking a cigarette, playing bridge, discussing politics with a circle of friends that included an older guy named Trevor, a young intellectual named Jeannie, another friend named Marge (and occasionally her boyfriend, Gordon), and Ella, a real bohemian.

A peroxide blond sylph, wearing clown white make up, red lipstick and black eye liner, Ella was famous, or I should say infamous, for claiming not only to have bedded most of the male professors whose courses she had taken at Western, but after reading *Sanctuary* of having hitch-hiked to Oxford, Mississippi to try to do the same with William Faulkner.

Robin often says that I was not political in those days, but I was born a member of the proletariat. All of her coterie, as well as fellow debaters, were political radicals. She had walked in a picket line in support of Kalamazoo's Shakespeare Fishing Tackle Company strikers. To feel a part of this group, I not only read *The Communist Manifesto* by Marx and Engels, which was one hundred years old in 1948, but I one-upped the rest of the coterie and read Engel's edited fourth volume of *Das Kapital*, which dealt with "The Theories of Surplus Value."

It was on this issue that I outdid some of her radical clique, and for the first time gained her attention and admiration as a thinker. She was vitally interested in politics during the heady period right after World War II: The United Nations, Labor disputes, the Nuremberg trials, peace treaties, the Marshall Plan, and the partition of Palestine.

⌘ ⌘ ⌘

I was not at all pleased with the Education Department. I simply did not fit into a four-year time frame because of my speeded up schedule to qualify me for a Michigan Secondary Teaching Certificate. I was in the gymnasium where we signed up for classes and asked the little man seated behind the desk for cards for two courses. He brought out a card for Human Growth and Development and signed me up.

"I also will be taking Introduction to Directed Teaching," I told him.

"You can't take that."

"Why not?"

"Because," he smiled, "Human Growth and Development is a 200 level course and a prerequisite to the 300 level course, Introduction to Directed Teaching."

I explained that in order not to stay another semester I would have to double up on these two courses. "I can't help that," he said. "You will have to take Introduction to Directed Teaching in the second semester.

"No," I said with some heat, "I will be taking these two courses together this semester."

"No, you will not!"

"I wish to speak to the head of the department."

"*I'm* the head of the department," he answered, and without missing a beat I said, "Then I will speak to the dean."

Dean Lofton Burge seemed friendly enough, but I entered with a head of steam. I told him that I needed to take both courses in the same semester and explained that I would be kept from graduating for another semester if I could not. I was an adult male, served in the U.S. Navy for three years, was married, on the G.I. Bill of Rights, knew exactly what I was doing, and would take full responsibility for my work and the grade I received in both classes.

And then I kind of lost my head and added, "As I understand it, you could take the content of all the requirements deemed necessary for certification as a secondary teacher in the State of Michigan and wrap them up in a six-week workshop and that would be more time than needed."

He didn't smile, he laughed—a big laugh and genuine. He was an old guy. When he finished laughing he said, "I like your style, young man. Permission granted." And he wrote out the note for me to take back to the head of the department waiving the requirement that made one course prerequisite to the other. I finished both courses without any effort, receiving a B grade in both.

In addition to Miss Shaw and Dr. Seibert I was influence by a fairly new member of the Education Department, Dr. Violet Beirge, who did her graduate work at the University of Chicago where President Robert Maynard Hutchins became president at age thirty and famously eliminated the school's football program in the Big Ten. When one of their coaches, in exasperation, asked what he did when he felt like exercising, Hutchins is reported to have said, "I lie down until the feeling has passed."

Dr. Beirge was influenced by President Hutchins' ideas. She not only taught the Socratic Method but her course was based on great books. Hutchins once said that he advocated the Great Books idea simply because it was "teacher proof." Beirge's class had nothing to do with lesson plans or six-week units on subject matters that focused on why a child could not read in the dark.

Nor did she lack for a kind of dramatic flair. Her first day in class she arrived just in the nick of time, making her way hesitantly to the desk. She reached into her clutch bag, took out two small pills, slowly put them on her tongue, and washed them down with water (at least I assumed it was water) she had poured into a paper cup. Then, taking a moment to recover she said slowly and in a clear, if somewhat sepulchral voice, "The Impact of the Automobile on American Society (long pause). The Impact of the Automobile on American Society (another long pause). The impact of the Automobile that turned out to be a whorehouse on wheels."

She was interested in teaching us to think, and the subject matter was anything that dealt with great ideas, properly communicated and reasoned. The whole course was like that, without dictating what was right or wrong and using Aristotelian and Thomistic Methods.

⌘ ⌘ ⌘

In adhering to a through-line of random thoughts on my undergraduate education, I have skipped over much of my personal relationship with Robin. Now let me fill in. After our getting acquainted in summer stock, there came a time just after when there was a serious rift. I had fallen in love for the *first* time in my life. Then, during the weeks that followed, between our last show, the striking and storage of the sets, as well as figuring out what courses I should take for the fall semester and a tentative schedule of what would constitute my entire BA degree, I became inattentive and uncommunicative.

She began to wonder if ours was just a summer romance and whether it was over. She was much more experienced, and more intelligent and mature than I; of that, I had no doubt. She had boyfriends in high school, and after graduating from Central High she'd received a rare, full-tuition scholarship from Kalamazoo College, one of the best of the small colleges in the country. She did very well there in everything except her second semester of biology, when she refused to dissect a frog.

Only a fool would expect this bright and beautiful woman to lack opportunities for male companionship while she waited around for me. I, of course, found out about it and confronted her. We were lovers. I had thought that meant we were exclusive. I was devastated—jealous really—by her going out with another man, and even more so by her trying to fib her way out of it.

During the week that followed our breakup, I saw my high-school girlfriend once, but it was obvious that she was involved with another guy and no substitute for the relationship I had with Robin. I was lovesick, so depressed and low of spirits that I could not eat, couldn't sleep; all I could do was think of her. It was during this time that I again thought of her in the terms of "my lost lane-end into heaven," and I still believe this was an apt description of her, not only then but throughout all the stages of my life.

After thinking over the situation from her point of view, I came to the conclusion that I had no right without talking to her about it to expect that our relationship was exclusive. I had to see her at once. She worked part time at Lerner's Dress Shop, but I could not go in. I walked past it several times, fearing a possible rejection. But when I took courage, opened the shop's door, and saw her in the distance among the dress racks talking to a customer, I knew that if this did not work out I just wanted to die.

When she finally saw me, her dimpled smile told me it was okay. I moved toward her bloodied and humbled. All I said was, "I need to see you." And the way she smiled told me that nothing had changed; she loved me as much as I loved her. She asked if I could meet her after work. The hours of waiting seemed like days and I was there at five. When we were out on the street, she said she wanted to take me to dinner at the Chinese restaurant. There she told me that when she saw me come in the store, her stomach did flip-flops and that she had never been happier in her life.

It would be almost a year before we married. All those months, the fall leaves, the winter when she wore a cloth coat and I walked her home at night, lingering in the park and holding my body against her to keep us both warm; and then *she* asked *me* to marry *her*. She would graduate, I said, and— But no, she said, she would *not* graduate. Why? Because she hadn't taken a single physical education course and 12 credit hours were required for graduation. But, she assured me, she didn't care about the degree. It wasn't important. Yes, it was, I insisted. No, she smiled. She didn't care about it.

She had that something about her—was it obstinacy? Yes, it was but hidden by that angelic smile. I would not be conned. In acting class I had studied beats in Petruchio's big speech in *The Taming of the Shrew* about taming Katharina. True, my assuming a character to claim her was not fair, but to this day I think my move was a wise one. Robin certainly was not a shrew, but she did need a little taming. So I told her that if she didn't have her degree by June, I wouldn't marry her.

"But how?" she asked, all innocence. "How would it be possible?"

"Just take four classes of PE in the spring semester," I said, cold as ice and without an ounce of sympathy .

She was strong-willed, but like Katharina, as Shakespeare wrote her (rather than as so many modem day revivals play the ending), she complied as Shakespeare intended.

She dutifully signed up for Swimming, Tennis, Folk Dancing and Badminton in the spring semester. In addition she took Dr. Seibert's history class that I was in. She would come in breathless from swimming, looking frazzled, her long auburn hair hanging limp and wet, and sit next to me breathing heavily like a beautiful retriever, and I could hardly control myself from capitulating and telling her she didn't need to graduate. But I stayed the course, and as I've already mentioned I think it was a damn good thing. Someone's got to wear the pants in the family, I thought, before I realized how inappropriate that was.

⌘ ⌘ ⌘

Although we knew after our reconciliation that we were exclusive, she was the one who took the necessary steps for our life together. She induced her mother to give her one of her diamond rings and had it reset in a new band, which she gave me with the requirement that I get down on my knees and ask her to marry me. She voluntarily said that when we got married, she would take the vow to "love, honor and obey." She also said that I did not need to, and would never have to wear a wedding ring, which I never did.

I think she knew what a needy guy I was. I think she knew and loved me for it. Hell, Robin was a woman's righter before Simone de Beauvoir wrote

The Second Sex. I think she pretty much knew herself: beautiful but vain, subject to flattery, without a lot of drive or energy, little sense of rhythm, or, in fact direction, or sense of order, and occasionally enjoyed being a provocateur. She could not dance, and had not an iota of good taste in clothing, nor did she care about it. I always went with her to shop and helped her select her dresses.

She was challenged by my drive, my energy, my rhythm, my talent and my looks, especially my height which was 6'3", almost a head taller than she was. She was aware of my major drawbacks and faults: a man without a cent, but certainly not without a dream, jealous by nature, lacking patience, excessively romantic, and unable to spell *cat*. I think like most women, she made her choice of mate by an instinctive gene-pool guess about the father of her children. I would probably be the one who would be there for the long haul. If I strayed, which I did on occasion, it would not destroy what the two of us had together since her self-confidence precluded jealously.

She made all the arrangements for our wedding at St. Luke's Episcopal Church in Kalamazoo. I rented a room with a shared bath down the hall at 525 South Westnedge Avenue, the only place I could find given the time I had for apartment hunting, and the fact that apartments were scarce in this post-war year.

The second summer season of the Village Players opened with only seven of the original partners asked back. Robin and I both played small roles in *Kiss and Tell*, and then I played a huge role, the villain, and she a character part, in *Dirty Work at the Crossroads, or Tempted, Tried and True*. This was, in fact, the show we were playing on Saturday July 4th, 1947, when we were married at 11:00 A.M. There was a reception, and that evening I donned my top hat, spats just above my black shoes, and sweated through my long black cape worn over a black wool suit.

We spent our honeymoon night in our room and how perfect to be with this beautiful girl all night for the first time. The next morning Robin's picture was in the *Kalamazoo Gazette* along with an article about the marriage and a honeymoon trip to Chicago. (Robin's mother had given them the story.) So on impulse I said, what the hell? Let's catch the train and see a matinee. We did exactly that, seeing *Call Me Mister*. Years later we found out

Wayne Lamb had been in that cast. We got back at midnight, and the next morning I was off to my 7:40 A.M. class, and she was off to the dress shop. The busy routine of our lives continued.

For the rest of the summer-stock season I played a character role in *Laburnum Grove,* the Syrian Peddler in *Green Grow the Lilacs,* and an absolutely dumbbell Hollywood cowboy star in Bella and Sam Spewack's *Boy Meets Girl* in which Robin played the leading role of Susie, her first, under her new last name.

Total attendance nearly doubled that of the first year: 4,035. The lowest night's attendance was 99 and the highest 307, which filled the theatre's auditorium to the breaking point. Ticket prices were upped to 90 cents for Wednesdays and Thursdays and $1 for Fridays and Saturdays. Total income, including program advertising, was $4,497.60. Cost of the five shows was $2,370.23. After paying back the partners their $25, the net profit was $1,752.37, less salaries of $450 to Ragotzy, $300 to Betty Ebert, $300 to technical director Art Crain and $150 to me as secretary/assistant. The total profit of $552.37, minus $1.87 to cover writing the final checks, split among 15 partners, was $36.70, or $3.05 per week.

With summer stock over, I could spend the necessary time to find an affordable apartment which I finally did, a wonderful apartment at 515 S. Rose Street at a cost of $50 a month and with a terrific landlady. It was on the ground floor and had a large living room that faced the street, a good-sized bedroom, a bathroom with tub and shower, and a small furnished eat-in kitchen in which I hoped I could teach Robin to boil water.

Just outside our bedroom window with a broken shade was a doghouse, home to a huge brooding and introspective (hairy but friendly) Russian wolfhound we named Dobrolyubov who turned out to be a serial voyeur, standing on the top of his house to look in the bedroom window and watch our lovemaking.

We lived here for 15 months, from September 1947 through December 1948, when I completed requirements for the BA degree and teaching certificate. Robin worked at Lerner's until she found a better paying job as a saleswoman and occasional model at The Gown Shop— "smart apparel for Women and Misses"—of which Helen E. Boylan was the proprietress in a beautiful old house at 507 W. South Street. I found work on weekends, and sometimes extra hours on weekdays, at a small Kroger store working behind the meat counter. Robin's parents, Olga and Frank Fastenrath, and her brother, Jimmy, moved in the spring from the rental house on East Walnut Street to the new house they had been building for the past two years at 2255 March Street. We spent a few afternoons visiting and arguing politics, especially about African-Americans in society.

Aunt Floss had sold the place on Academy Street, giving us basic furniture when we moved into our apartment. She was married for a fourth time to a Theodore Boven about three weeks after we were, on August 1, 1947. We visited her several times. The house was small and cramped. She was cheerful about the situation, but in late fall got a nursing job in a home for the old and indigent where she got room and board plus a salary.

We decided to go to New York and see shows during Christmas vacation and began saving our money by cutting down on food. We got a ride with fellow student Dick Kishpaw, and made hotel reservations at the Piccadilly Hotel in the theatre district. *A Streetcar Named Desire* had just opened with spectacular notices and we got to see it because Alma Johansson, an intern at the Civic, had married cast member Rudy Bond who played Steve Hubbell, and he got us standing room. Afterwards, he showed us around the set and backstage area. By the time we finished, all the cast members were gone, but we looked into the open doors of the dressing rooms and on the shelf of each—except for Miss Tandy's—was a copy of Stanislavski's *An Actor Prepares*.

Robin and I went to the White Rose Bar on 7th Ave. where there was a free lunch counter. We ordered beers and ate, and argued about the show until three o'clock in the morning. We both loved the hell out of *Streetcar,* but I had reservations about Brando's interpretation since it tipped the balance of the show toward Stanley, making it seem about a woman who almost breaks up the marriage of this nice young couple.

That is not, I told Robin, what Tennessee Williams had in mind. She, of course, hot for Brando, argued that Blanche got exactly what she had coming to her. I said that structurally the protagonist was Blanche, and although I too thought Brando a mesmerizing, handsome male with a powerful sexual presence who moved with the grace of a panther, I still thought he skewed the author's intent. We argued back and forth for years about this.

Other shows we saw were *Allegro* with John Battles, whom I would meet years later; *Annie Get Your Gun* with Ethel Merman; *Born Yesterday* with Judy Holliday, Paul Douglas, and Gary Merrill; *Brigadoon; Finian's Rainbow* with Ella Logan and David Wayne; *Medea* with Judith Anderson, Dennis King, Florence Reed, and my teacher from Feagin, Grace Mills, whom we saw backstage after the performance; *Harvey* with Frank Fay; and *The Heiress* with Wendy Hiller and Basil Rathbone. But what I remember as well as all those shows was that after a bout of lovemaking one morning with her in the dominant position, Robin told me it was the first time she'd achieved orgasm.

That spring she auditioned for and got the role of Jean Maitland, the bad girl in *Stage Door*. Going along for the ride, I played a walk-on in this Civic Theatre production. The apartment on South Rose was where I read such books as *The Naked and the Dead* and *The Young Lions*. And Robin read to me *Ethan Frome*, the dramatization by Owen and Donald Davis of Edith Wharton's novel, and *Liliom* by Ferenc Molnár on which the musical *Carousel* is based. At the end—when Julie says to her daughter, "It is possible, dear that someone may beat you and beat you and beat you and not hurt you at all," referring, of course, to her husband and the girl's father, Billy—we both burst into tears.

In the summer of 1948 we opened the Saugatuck Summer Theatre playing two terrific roles, Mr. and Mrs. Manningham in *Angel Street*, the Patrick Hamilton melodrama. I still have a letter from a fan who said they had seen Charles Boyer and Ingrid Bergman in the film and thought we were better! After the final dress rehearsal a local woman brought in supper for the cast and crew, but wanted me excluded because, as Mr. Manningham, I was so mean to my wife.

We returned to the Village Players almost immediately for roles in *Love Rides the Rails or Will the Mail Train Run Tonight*, in which I played the hero, and Robin played Fifi, the maid, and then *Petticoat Fever* in which Robin played the lead. I had a nose operation to help correct the deviated nasal septum (and hopefully make my voice less nasal), and just four days before *Petticoat Fever* opened, Jack asked me to replace an actor in the role of Sir

James Fenton. I was a fast study, but blood was still coming from my nose. For the first couple of days of rehearsal I used a handkerchief a great deal and Jack insisted I keep it in as business, even when it was no longer necessary because it was so effective for this wonderfully vague and delightfully obtuse Englishman.

I had taken only one full summer school session, and we decided not to become partners in The Village Players because we had accepted my sister Rae and her husband Bill's invitation to go with them for a month's vacation to California. We had a wonderful time, with me scaring Robin by hanging my legs over a cliff, which overlooked the Grand Canyon a mile below. And then two days before we got home I ran out of money and my ever-generous, big-hearted sister, who always saw me as her special concern, paid for our lodgings and meals and urged us to eat more.

That fall I did my last courses at Western, including the previously mentioned, Human Growth and Development, and Introduction to Directed Teaching, which consisted of practice teaching at Western's experimental high school. I had read in *The New York Times* about the University of North Carolina at Chapel Hill and decided that we would go there for my master's degree. The next day I sent a telegram to Samuel Selden who headed the theatre, followed by copies of transcripts of credits from both my high school and Western. On December 11, 1948, Sam Selden sent me a letter of acceptance with the proviso that I would not be officially accepted into the program until after I had taken the Graduate Records Examination sometime in the spring.

It was also about this time that we decided we wanted a kid. Up to this point I was opposed to the idea and to tell the truth, I have no idea why I changed my mind. But I did. Robin stopped using the diaphragm, which was great since there was something just a little off-putting about getting the urge and then having her run to the bathroom to insert it. When, after that first month without it, she had her period, she broke into tears, certain that there was something wrong with her. I was a rock at that point and told her not to worry. Sure enough, after yet another period had come and gone, in late November one didn't. She went to the doctor and he confirmed that she was pregnant.

⌘ ⌘ ⌘

Just before Christmas, Aunt Floss was admitted to the Allegan Hospital. I remember our landlady coming to knock on the door to tell me I had an emergency call. The diagnosis was carcinoma of the liver, a malignant cancer. The doctor's prediction was that she would not last six months. Heavy of heart, I hitched over to Allegan to see her. She was in a wing of the hospital which was actually one large room with a half dozen patients. She had been in pain for some time before she finally allowed herself to be admitted. She was under no illusions, and confided to me that she did not want to go on much longer. She was receiving pain killers every four hours around the clock but was saving some of them for a time when the pain was not bearable.

I told her of our decision to go to Chapel Hill and that we were going to have a baby. She was pleased, but I know also saddened by the fact that she would not be there to witness the end of either of these events. I kissed her good-bye. It's hard to know what I felt. When I got down to the first floor I went to the men's room and cried.

Her impending death was not soul-destroying, and thinking back on it I believe that this was because she never asked for, or demanded, or wanted me to feel that kind of filial connection. I never told her how much I loved her or thanked her for all she had done for me. I didn't need to. She knew. And she made me know she knew. What I had experienced was a pretty wonderful time growing up. She had a great sense of humor. We had laughed a lot and sometimes cried a lot and I was not alone now. I had Robin, and we were going to have a kid.

It was a cold day. I was wearing my Navy Pea jacket. I walked the few blocks from the hospital to where I could hitch a ride. We would be leaving soon for Chapel Hill. Aunt Floss was a very special woman; she didn't want me devastated by her death, and I would not be.

Chapter 5

WE TOOK THE TRAIN FROM Kalamazoo in late January. With Robin pregnant I was more focused than at any other time in my life. We had a layover of five hours in Cincinnati, and the train to Durham was slow and overnight. Robin snoozed and snuggled up beside me, but I stayed awake anticipating what was in store. We took the bus to Chapel Hill and found a basement apartment for rent at 107½, Rosemary Street that first afternoon. Although we weren't thrilled with it—especially the cost per month and the dampness—we were pretty exhausted from the trip and desperate to settle in. It was when Robin was fixing sandwiches for supper that I heard the scream.

There were *flying* cockroaches! She was hysterical, and I knew that we could never live in this place. I'd already paid the first month's rent of $70 and after getting her calmed down, I went to the landlord to whom I had already explained our circumstances—on the GI Bill of Rights with not much money—when I signed the lease. I told him Robin was pregnant, and we would need our rent money back just as soon as I could find another place.

We found an apartment out on the Durham Road at 51 Davie Circle. It was upstairs, partly furnished and was only $50 a month, and dry. I went through every drawer and cupboard in the kitchen—no cockroaches. It would be farther to walk to the campus but I was used to walking. The

Rosemary Street landlord was not too happy refunding our rent but I told him I would go to the University Housing Office if he refused.

The Davie Circle house was large and held four apartments. Ours was upstairs on the left with a wide entrance hall. We had two rooms One was the kitchen, dining and living room area; the other at the front of the house was our bedroom. The bathroom was at the end of the hall. Directly below us was a larger apartment with an extra wing at the back where Edward and Margaret Woodhouse lived. Edward was a beloved Political Science professor at UNC who'd married Chase Going, a congresswoman from Connecticut. When they divorced he married Margaret Kinsman, a graduate student in one of his classes.

Opposite them lived Hans Freistadt, a graduate student in physics who wrote for the *Daily Worker*. An avowed Communist Party member, his writing was said to have "tarnished the reputation of the Atomic Energy Commission." He headed the student Communist Party at UNC and at several other southern schools. I don't believe we saw him more than three or four times during our eleven month stay. The apartment over his was never rented, giving us a private bathroom. Although not as nice as our apartment in Kalamazoo, and missing our voyeur canine friend Dobrolyubov, this was still a place in which we were happy.

The first thing Robin did after we moved was to walk into the middle of town where she had seen a bakery with a sign, "Help wanted" and get a job. She stayed with it until late May when her pregnancy was obvious.

As soon as I saw Samuel Selden, any anxiety I had was allayed. He was a short man, slightly plump with receding reddish hair, wore very thick (Mr. Magoo) glasses behind which his eyes seemed to squint, and he always had a smile. I believe the very first thing I said to him was, "How long is it going to take me to get out of here with a degree?" I explained our financial situation and that my wife was pregnant. He understood and sympathized, and I felt immediately that he was in my corner.

Since the new quarter did not start until mid-March, he told me I could work in the shop under Professors Harry Davis and Lynn Gault and prove to them that I knew my way around a scene shop, building sets and hanging lights. He said that Lou White, the department secretary, would schedule me to take the Graduate Record Examination for which I would have to pay $15.

It was soon after this interview that I got a letter from Nyburg's funeral home in Allegan. It included a paid receipt for Aunt Floss' urn, the cost of which was $12.50. I had not paid for the urn, but the receipt was clearly marked that the payment was by Joseph G. Stockdale, Jr. It struck me that Dad had paid for it and put the receipt in my name. I was moved by this.

Harry and Lynn liked my shop work and waived the required courses in stagecraft, but it would be a few weeks later—when a major production was mounted—that I would have an opportunity to test out of the required lighting course by demonstrating my skill and knowledge. I was wearing shorts—spring had sprung as glorious as I had ever seen it as I walked through the gravel paths of the arboretum to get to classes. The night after a main stage rehearsal of a show about to open, I found myself straddling an A-frame ladder to support myself while bolting a light instrument—a leko—onto an overhead pipe, when I felt a hand moving up inside the leg of my shorts. I got myself un-straddled as quick as I could and finished hanging the lights. The faculty member whose hand I felt was a hell of a talented man. He waived my lighting course requirements; I never mentioned this incident, and neither did he.

Frederick Koch was responsible for the Theatre Department at UNC. He had joined the English Department faculty in 1919. In 1925 he turned the oldest building on campus into the Playmakers Theatre, and a decade later his one-man theatre division in the English Department morphed into a Department of Dramatic Art, its two major graduates being Thomas Wolfe and Pulitzer Prize winning playwright Paul Green.

For my first quarter I signed up for 15 credits: History of the Theatre, Playwriting and Advanced Play Direction. Kai Heiberg-Jurgensen was my professor in Theatre History. The brain damaging textbook *A History of the Theatre* by Freedley and Reeves was a 784-page listing of facts; every word had the effect of one of those self-administered morphine drips given terminal patients in hospices. Since the GI Bill was paying for all textbooks authorized by the department, I bought *The Theatre: Three Thousand Years of Drama, Acting and Stagecraft,* a 558-page tome by Sheldon Cheney that was so un-interesting I often wondered if the pulp for the paper it was printed on had been laced with some kind of morphine that paralyzed the eyeball's macular. Why else did my brain turn blue moldy every time I opened its cover?

The book I found most useful for fact checking (although it got some things badly screwed up) was the 866-page *The Theatre Handbook and Digest of Plays,* edited by Bernard Sobel. It was laid out in alphabetical order by name, giving dates and plot summaries. It cost only $4 plus 12¢ tax. Two books I loved were *A Handbook of Classical Mythology* by faculty members George Howe and G.A. Harrer, which cost $1.85 plus 6¢ tax, and my favorite: *The Poetics of Aristotle,* translated by Preston H. Epps, which cost 75¢ plus 3¢ tax. I have had these last three books with me for over sixty years and frequently consult them, although my copy of *Poetics* now has to be handled with great care since some pages are literally disintegrating, having probably been made from the pulp of yellow pine.

Kai Jurgensen was a short, odd-looking man—one eye seeming not to work with the other—but a swell guy, about thirty years old, and very understanding. Although I did not do well in Theatre History—undoubtedly the result of sleeping sickness—Kai gave me a P (only H for honors, P for pass and N/C for no credit grades were given) and we became good friends. Kai was a womanizer par excellence, and used his photographic skills to good advantage in his pursuit of attractive young women. Sometime after I had left UNC he married Jo Reynolds of the Tobacco family, who certainly was young and attractive.

In my playwriting class, the one-act I wrote and read to the class on May 19, 1949, was titled "Dad Voten." Dad's sons are to be honored at the annual father/son athletic awards banquet, the speaker to be Jud Helmer, a rich businessman who was a classmate of their father and famous major league baseball player. When the sons realize that Dad expects to be at the banquet, the oldest son tells him he is not welcome. He is nothing but the town drunk, and both sons are ashamed of him. At the banquet, Jud presents the boys their awards, but says that the only reason he was there was to see their father and recount some of his former glories. Others at the banquet are soon swept up with the speaker's remembrances, and Helmer cuts short his speech, saying he came to visit "Dad" and is going to do just that. At home, Dad's wife, Abbie, has been trying to buck him up with remembrances of his glory days but he is heartsick and broken and has gotten drunk. When the youngest son, who has come ahead of the crowd, bursts in telling what is happening, Abbie realizes that such a meeting cannot take place. Pouring a glass of wood alcohol that Dad uses for his arthritis she recalls one of his most famous games, as-drink-in hand-she leads him into the bedroom. The youngest son has rejoined his brother and the two try to head off the crowd that is shouting for Dad to appear. Abbie comes out on the porch. Dad died of a heart attack. She thanks them for remembering. As Jud and the others express their sorrow and condolence to the now bereaved sons, telling them of their father's greatness, the editor of the local paper talks of a special edition, the mayor of a "day of remembrance." Abbie asks the boys to give her a moment alone with her husband before they come in. Inside, she goes to the door of the bedroom. As the town clock begins to strike eleven, she turns and listens as do the boys as the lights slowly fade to out on sound of the last bell.

⌘ ⌘ ⌘

The first draft of this one-act play included the actual names of the prototypes that lived near us when we moved to Arbor Street in Allegan. I got a lot of compliments from fellow students after the reading. Sam Selden told me how much he liked the play and suggested that I expand it into full-length which could be my thesis play and would receive a full production. You must know how all this made me feel. But there was no time for basking in reflected glory because I had been cast in Ann Martin's (a beauty, with terrific talent) one-act play *The Vanishing American* for which I stripped down to war paint, feathered headgear, a jockstrap covered barely by a ripped loincloth, and played an American Indian. This casting would prove to be important to me for future summer work.

⌘ ⌘ ⌘

I enrolled for both six-week summer sessions taking Greek Drama, Playwriting, and Special Readings, and those sessions were some of the best educational experiences I ever had. But the one I worked hardest in was Greek Drama taught by Professor Epps. On the first day of class he handed out a single sheet of paper on which were 39 specific questions on the *Poetics*. We had to know—memorize verbatim—the definition of tragedy, the constituent parts, and the definition of the tragic character—and it had to be *exact* on our final exam.

Although a real scholar, Professor Epps was not a hard-ass, and the first paper I did for him was a comparison of Sophocles' and Seneca's handling of the title character Medea with Maxwell Anderson's leading character, Oparre, in *The Wingless Victory*. I worked my butt off on this paper and felt it was excellent, but Professor Epps returned it marked "unacceptable (see me)." After class he told me that none of my references could count. I pointed out that they were all authors of the textbooks we were using in the Drama Department. He replied, simply, "They are not accepted scholars," and urged me to use the books on the reading list he had passed out at the beginning of the term in rewriting the paper.

I ran to the library and started reading. I was now pouring over S.H. Butcher's *Aristotle's Theory of Poetry and Fine Arts;* Gilbert Murray's *Euripides and His Age;* and Ingram Bywater's *Aristotle on the Art of Poetry,* along with other yellowed-with-age tomes. When the rewritten paper was turned in, Epps gave me an H and I was proud as hell and you know what? The paper *was* much better than that first one I had written.

Another of my one-act plays, "Turkey's in the Thirties" set in a farm kitchen during the Depression, was chosen for production. I also wrote two other one-acts. "Reflected Glory" dealt with a couple of old-time actors and their son whom they have dominated all his life, and who brings home a young woman and tells them he is going to marry her.

The back story of the other one—titled "Anna Lindquest"—was based on my great-uncle Joe, who with his brother Samuel had emigrated to America just prior to my great-grandfather. There is a grave stone in the Trowbridge cemetery where so many of the Stockdales were buried that faces north and south, rather than east and west—indicating that it's a memorial marker and that Joseph is not buried there. Aunt Floss explained, with some embellishment, that after Colonel George Armstrong Custer discovered gold in the Dakotas in 1874, great-uncle Joe had sallied forth to make his fortune in the gold rush and never returned.

In 1948, when Robin and I had traveled with Rae and Bill to California, we insisted on stopping in Deadwood City to check out great-uncle Joe's famous grave. I had come to think of him as an eccentric family hero, fixing him in my imagination as a gun-slinging Indian fighter who was killed in a barroom brawl after taking a bullet for his buddy Wild Bill Hickok, or had passed happily after a prolonged fornication with Calamity Jane resulting in an erection that lasted more than four hours.

In Deadwood City's Mount Moriah Cemetery we immediately found the graves of both Wild Bill and Calamity, so where was great-uncle Joe's? The sexton was in a rinky-dink office in an alley in the center of town where we were allowed to check the actual record books dealing with burials. We eventually found Joseph Stockdale but he wasn't chumming around in heaven with Wild Bill or Calamity. He had been buried in an unmarked grave in a Potters' Field for paupers; the cause of death was inflammation of the bowels.

My one-act play was about a truth-telling Swedish grandmother helping her widowed daughter raise two grandsons. In hard times, to cheer the boys up, she told them stories of their great-uncle Joe who was killed fighting Indians in the North Dakota gold rush. The boys, now teen agers, are on a trip to California and have written that they decided to veer off course and visit their great-uncle's grave in Deadwood City. When the grandmother hears this she breaks down and tells her daughter that the stories she told were fabrications. He had actually died an ignominious death, and now the grandkids would not only be disillusioned but would take her for a prevaricator. The postman arrives with a postcard for her. Anna is in agony, fearing the reprimand of her grandsons. Her daughter reads the card which says they visited the grave and yes, she was right. "Great-uncle Joe is buried right next to Wild Bill Hickok and Calamity Jane." Anna is moved and after a moment she turns to her daughter and says: "We raised a couple of good boys, yes, real good boys." Curtain.

⌘ ⌘ ⌘

That summer I was also stage manager for Kai's production of *The Merchant of Venice* in the Forest Theatre. The night before it opened I had to leave early before notes were given, and an assistant took my place. On opening night just before Ann Martin reached her cue for "The quality of mercy" speech, there was sudden quiet and I saw her moving slowly down left. I waited and waited for what seemed like hours and finally whispered "The quality of Mercy..." She turned, and if looks could kill....

What had happened was that on final dress rehearsal Kai changed the blocking, and my assistant never told me. Still, how could I have ever imagined that she would go dry on one of the most famous speeches in all of Shakespeare? I took a lot of razzing for this, and only recently in a talk with Bill Hardy in Chapel Hill did he tell me he related that story to almost every stage management class he taught.

⌘ ⌘ ⌘

On the home front it was drawing near to the birth of our first child. There was no hospital in Chapel Hill, and Margaret Woodhouse had been driving Robin over to Duke Hospital in Durham for the necessary checkups. Close to the time of delivery we found out that we would need $100 as a deposit before she could be admitted. We didn't have it. I'm positive that we could have borrowed from Edward and Margaret, but I was too proud to ask. I went to the financial office at the university and asked for a loan. I do not remember the actual details but this turned out to be a humiliating experience. The man who interviewed me treated me like he probably treated all poor people, and it brought me up short. I guess this was the first time I ever desperately needed money and had to get it from a source other than family. With the baby coming I realized that I had to get a job by the end of the fall quarter.

Robin and I talked over names for the baby and decided that if it was a boy he would be named after me. If it was a girl, I suggested the name Laurel, after the mountain laurel in western North Carolina. The due date came and passed and we were on tenterhooks waiting. Then on the morning of August 12th Robin told me that she thought her water broke and the baby was about to be born. I remember sucking in a breath and tears springing to my eyes.

Margaret kept her cool as she drove us to Durham, but she had to go back to Chapel Hill and told me she would call to find out how things were going. In Robin's room all I could think of was what she was going to have to go through. Instead of being some kind of tower of strength, when the pains became more intense so that she yelled, I could not stand it and just broke down. After the third contraction she said, "Look, Joe, I am going to have to go through this alone, you can't do it for me. I love you, so please, for my sake, just leave." I went to the men's room and was racked with sobs.

Margaret came over again in the early evening and was told that it would be okay to take me out to get something to eat because Robin was not yet ready to deliver. At midnight, Margaret drove back to Chapel Hill and I sat in the waiting room with other expectant fathers, none, in my view, who seemed to understand what their wives were going through.

Margaret returned at noon the next day. Robin was going through one of the longest labors the nurses could remember, so again Margaret took me out to get something to eat. When we got back I was told that I was the father of a seven-pound baby girl. I went to the room and saw Laurel (from here on, Lory) and Robin, too filled with emotion to talk. I held the baby and kissed her and then kissed Robin. When I was able, I asked her if there was anything I could do. "I'm hungry," she said. "How about running out and getting me a chicken sandwich and ask them to put a little mustard on the side."

That certainly wasn't like the dialogue in any movie I'd ever seen. When I returned she wolfed down that sandwich like she was starved, and after a few minutes fell fast asleep and snored. Joan Crawford or Bette Davis *never* snored after giving birth in the movies!

Why the delivery had taken such a long time was later explained. Robin had not been able to take the pain and asked the doctor to give her something to put her under. She had received the medicine via a spinal, which slowed the process considerably and was found later to be counterproductive to birthing.

Margaret picked up Robin and the baby the very next day and brought them home where Lory's first bed was the lower drawer in the bedroom bureau. Almost from the first she was a remarkably docile baby. Robin's milk came in and her breasts were about twice their normal size. I got the feeling that she kind of enjoyed this. She had already decided that she would breast feed. It was an amazing and wonderful sight, and I turned out to be Dobrolyubov watching through the window.

There were some new expenses: inexpensive disposable diapers in those days were not an option. Robin would flush the cloth ones out in the toilet, wash them in the bathtub, and dry them out on the clothesline on the upstairs back porch. Within a couple of weeks, friends loaned us a small electric washing machine (was it Mo and Doodle Huntley?) and that made the diaper chore a lot less work, and cleaner. I did the grocery shopping as well as my class work, and our lives were very full.

I signed up for 15 credits for my fall quarter. Renaissance and Baroque in the Comparative Literature Departure under Dr. Frederick was a real ball-breaker. He had a list of 50 books we were responsible for "knowing" in order to pass the final exam. One was Cervantes' *Don Quixote* which I "knew" by reading the summary in Master-Plots but didn't actually get around to reading until I retired 43 years later. I loved it! My other two courses were Literary Criticism which I liked. But the third course, Seminar in Modem Drama, was something special, focusing on all the published plays of Eugene O'Neill (five volumes costing $12). Sam Selden supervised the course and his assistants were Kai Jurgensen, Paul Green, Walter Prichard Eaton, and Archibald Henderson.

You already know something of Kai and Pulitzer-Prize winning dramatist Paul Green; Sam Selden was a Yale graduate who had taken George Pierce Baker's courses in playwriting as had O'Neill. After graduating he worked as an actor, stage manager, and technical director with the Provincetown Playhouse which did a lot of O'Neill's early works. Until Professor Koch retired, Sam had been his assistant. In later years he wrote a number of successful textbooks including *Modern Theatre Practices* with contributions by

Hubert Heffner and Hunton D. Sellman, plus *The Stage In Action*. Arguably his most successful book was *Stage Scenery and Lighting* on which Professor Sellman collaborated.

Walter Prichard Eaton, in his 70th year, was a graduate of Harvard and in 1933 had become associate professor of Playwriting at Yale. Prior to this he was drama critic for the *New York Herald Tribune*, *The New York Sun* and *American* magazine. He authored many books on drama including *The American Stage of Today* (1909), *At the New Theatre and Others* (1910), *Plays and Players* (1916), *The Actor's Heritage* (1924), and *The Theatre Guild: the First Ten Years* (1929).

Archibald Henderson was sixty-two in 1949 and interested in any number of subjects, first and foremost of which were mathematics and its allied sciences, physics and astronomy. He was also deeply interested in literature, drama, history and philosophy. Fascinated by Einstein's theory of relativity, in 1923-24 he spent a sabbatical studying at Cambridge and at the University of Berlin where he came to know Einstein personally. What drama connection qualified him as one of the adjunct teachers in the O'Neill Seminar was that after seeing an amateur production of Shaw's *You Never Can Tell* in 1903, he began to study and write about GBS, and in 1905 Shaw made him his "authorized biographer."

I think we can agree that no course in drama was ever taught in the same room by so much brainpower and experience. We read all the plays of O'Neill and listened to fascinating stories and had stimulating discussions. I shall never forget it.

⌘ ⌘ ⌘

The fall quarter had barely started when I got a letter from my sister Rae asking me—no, it was much more than asking—to please come to Detroit for a couple of days. She wanted to see me and would pay for the round-trip air ticket. This could not have been more than six weeks after Lory was born and I did not like the idea of leaving her and Robin even for a few days or missing classes. But something told me I probably should take the time; Margaret and Edward would look after Robin.

Bill picked me up at the airport and told me on the drive home that their baby—born a week after our Lory—was not doing well, nor was Rae, who was extremely depressed. Baby Eric was thin and emaciated and looked nothing like our Lory. Rather than breast-feeding him, Rae had put him on the bottle from the get-go, and she was nervous and not sleeping well.

I've always been able in other people's toughest times to stay cool and play the fool, get people laughing *if* I thought that was the best way to go. Although I didn't know much about bottle-fed babies, I just took the little fellow up (by that time I knew how to hold a baby!) and put the nipple in his mouth. He tried to suck for only a couple of minutes and then gave up. There were no bubbles coming from the bottle. I handed him off to Bill and took the bottle, put the nipple in my mouth, and sucked. I couldn't get anything out of it either. I asked Rae for a needle and plunged it into the nipple, rotating it around. We re-sterilized the cap and nipple, put it back on the bottle, and once again I took up baby Eric and put the nipple in his mouth. *Voila!* Bubbles appeared and he sucked like a little pig. I had them get some Gerber's strained plums, dipped my well-scrubbed finger into it, put it in his mouth and moved it around his gums, which he seemed to like. The bottom line was that in only two or three days he was more active and had taken on weight. Years later, after my sister's death, Bill told me that he was sure I had saved Eric's life with that visit.

I had an extraordinarily wonderful experience on that trip. At the Cass Theatre, Arthur Miller's *Death of a Salesman* was playing and Bill drove me down to catch a matinee. Thomas Mitchell, who had replaced Lee J. Cobb at one point in the New York production, starred as Willie in this national company. I no longer remember the rest of the cast, but the play was one of the best I would see in a lifetime.

⌘ ⌘ ⌘

That fall I went to the library, got a book listing all the colleges and universities in the United States, and wrote down the names and addresses of 100 schools that had courses in theatre. Margaret had loaned me her portable Underwood and I wrote a brief letter to heads of departments explaining that I was finishing my course work in December, would be available for teaching the second semester, and to please let me know if they had a vacancy so I could send a resume. There were no duplicating machines in 1949, and the carbon-paper industry, like the oil cartel today, was fighting tooth and nail to keep it that way. Each letter and envelope had to be typed individually. It was almost impossible to erase mistakes, especially on the carbon copies, so it was important to take time and avoid errors. But taking the time, going to school, plus revising the one-act "Dad Voten" into a full length entitled *October In The Spring*, along with everything else, left very little sleep.

⌘ ⌘ ⌘

Later that fall, Margaret and Edward moved to the country. Never very good at organization, they called me at the last moment and asked for help. The van was coming and they had only started packing. Of course! I would do anything for them considering what Margaret had done when Lory was born. I was a good organizer and had already moved a few times, so I went down to their place and did a whirlwind job. I even helped load the van. Margaret invited us to their new home for a Thanksgiving dinner of roast beef and Yorkshire pudding and all that goes with it; it was a rare and wonderful holiday for us. Margaret and Edward, with their incredible age difference, was a dear and wonderfully happy married couple.

⌘ ⌘ ⌘

One last word about Chapel Hill. It is said that when the North Carolina State Legislature was discussing the possibilities of creating a state zoo, Senator Jessie Helm's advice was: "Why spend the money? If you want a zoo, all you have to do is put a fence around Chapel Hill." Well, what can one say about Jessie, the quintessential icon of southern conservatism?

To me Chapel Hill was the most beautiful and exciting place I'd ever lived, a place where I felt at home, worked hard, and was very happy. The beauty of the campus and the village itself conjures up the names of students and townspeople who preceded me, or were there at the same time, or who came after. In addition to the extraordinary faculty I think of writers: Thomas Wolfe, Paul Green, Howard Richardson, James Street, Josefina Niggli, John Ehle, and Betty Smith, author of *A Tree Grows in Brooklyn*. Actors: Douglas Watson, John Forsythe, Louise Fletcher, Andy Griffith, George Grizzard, Eugenia Rawls, Kay Kyser, Randolph Scott, James Pritchett, Shepperd Strudwick, and Bill Trotman. Fellow students: Don Treat, (a lookalike for a young Sterling Hayden), the incredibly talented Tommy Razutto, Ann Martin, Frank Groseclose, and so many more. Townspeople: Jofine Sharkey; Louise LaMonte (who claimed kinship to Tallulah Bankhead); and then there was a kick-in-the-head thrill of passing *Life*-cover football hero Charley "Choo-Choo" Justice moseying to class after seeing him play so brilliantly in the Duke/UNC game, which we won.

Oh yes, the gravel walks, the magnolia trees, the arboretum, the roses, the old Playmaker's Theatre, and the glorious weather. But especially the people. Chapel Hill was wonderful.

⌘ ⌘ ⌘

I had surprising responses from my query letters. Not that there were a lot of jobs open starting second semester. In fact, there were fewer teaching jobs available at that particular point then there had been in many years. Still, about seventy-five percent of the heads of departments wrote notes of encouragement. There were three openings. After sending them my resume, my transcript of credits from Western Michigan, and my incomplete transcript from UNC plus letters of recommendation from Sam Selden and Zack York at Western, I got job offers from all three: Asheville Biltmore College, the University of Missouri, and Purdue.

Asheville Biltmore was tempting because of its beautiful campus, and that great city, Thomas Wolfe's birthplace, and where Scott Fitzgerald had visited his wife Zelda who was incarcerated in a mental institution where she burned to death. What was *not* tempting was the semester teaching load: being responsible for two or three classes of a basic speech course plus acting, directing, journalism, and if I wished, playwriting. Faculty responsibilities included advisor to the Drama Club, for which I would direct, design and technical direct a couple of productions a year, and advisor to the student newspaper. The salary offered was $2,200 a year.

I thought of writing and saying I would take the job but only if, in addition to my other duties, I was allowed to coach the foot, basket, and baseball teams. But I had a feeling that irony was not going to play there, so I restrained myself.

At the University of Missouri, in addition to teaching three sections of the basic speech course, I would be allowed to teach one course in theatre, either acting or directing, plus design, and would technical direct two productions a year. The pay would be $2,800 per year.

The offer from Purdue included teaching four sections a semester of the basic speech course to engineering and agricultural students, and being technical director for two shows a year. The pay would be $3,100 a year. Sam Selden had been to an Educational Theatre convention in Chicago where Ross Smith, who headed the Purdue theatre, interviewed him about me. After Sam's recommendation Ross decided I was the one he wanted and asked the head of the Speech Department, Alan H. Monroe, to send me an offer.

Robin said the choice was up to me. I, of course, wanted the University of Missouri job because I would get to teach a theatre course. But I also knew that we needed the extra $300 per year. I made my decision and wrote Professor Monroe my acceptance. At the end of the quarter, we knew that I would start teaching on February 2nd. In the meantime, with me being so busy on the production, we decided that Robin should visit her family and that I would pick her up when I went to West Lafayette.

October In The Spring was a major hit. I remember that in the darkened auditorium there was a moment of total silence after the curtain closed, and the applause was so heartfelt that I was near tears. In the discussion that followed, Walter Prichard Eaton opened by saying, "Thank God! To see a play by an author who isn't afraid of emotion." And he called the play first-rate. There were many great comments that night and I was high as a kite, and even higher the next day when I read Vestal Taylor's review in the *Daily Tar Heel*.

The Carolina Playmakers have taken a long stride forward with their production of Joseph Stockdale's original, "October In The Spring." Stockdale's work is a refreshing change from the usual run of student originals when all plots are similar. "October In The Spring," while telling the interesting story of a retired baseball player struggling against social condemnation... weaves a moral lesson that is gripping and always timely.... For once the audience was living with author and characters in a real sense and sharing each breath of their lines. Tears were seen when the final curtain fell. This is sufficient evidence that we need more work of the same caliber and that this particular work deserves more recognition.

On Feb. 11, Mr. Taylor wrote a follow-up article for *The Daily Tar Heel:*

For those of you who missed Joe Stockdale's experimental play, we can only say that you missed the finest production in this category since the end of the war. With just a little polish, this could very easily merit billing as a major production in community theatres.... This, in short, was a work that any neophyte playwright might well be proud of.

But by that time I was far from Chapel Hill and going through what I felt was one of the worst times of my life.

Chapter 6

I FLEW FROM DURHAM TO DETROIT where I stayed overnight with my sister and Bill. Rae loaned me her car to drive to West Lafayette where I met Dave, the moving man from Allegan, who brought our meager possessions to the barracks apartment we were assigned. The next morning while I was painting the bedroom, Ross Smith, who headed the theatre, came over and introduced himself, giving me a warm welcome. By late afternoon I was ready to head out to pick up Robin and the baby, thinking how great it was going to be to see them again.

When I arrived at eight, Olga, Robin's mother, said that she was at a reception of some sort up at Kalamazoo College and that I should pick her up there. I cuddled Lory a bit and gave her a "raspberry," which sent her off into gales of giggles. I warmed a bottle, fed her, tucked her in and was about to take off when Olga said there was something I should know. I had known from the get-go that she didn't think I was the right husband for her daughter.

Sometime during her visit, Robin had met an old boyfriend. The night before I arrived, he had taken her to dinner and she had not gotten home until 3:00 A.M. Even as I write this, that moment is difficult to relive. I couldn't wrap my brain around it. The implication was so clear that my mind reeled. I was an instant basket case. I didn't want to reveal myself to my mother-in-law and knew that I had to get the story straight from Robin.

All those jealous feelings I had three years before when we were still a year from marriage welled up in me. She had dated an old boyfriend. But why had she stayed out half the night? What about our baby? My world had just been blown apart. There was no ground under my feet.

As soon as I entered the reception room, Robin knew just by looking at me that something had happened. She was spectacularly beautiful but I couldn't put my arms around her. She asked me what was wrong. I said we had to leave. In the car I told her what her mother had said. She was the startled deer caught in the headlights, stopped cold and not knowing which direction to turn. I demanded the truth. She knew from the way I acted that she was on thin ice. She admitted that she had gone to dinner with the guy, and then cautiously tried to make light of it. But I was taking no hostages—the truth, the whole truth and nothing but the truth—everything that happened after dinner until 3:00 A.M.

The truth eventually came because it could be no other way. The one thing she insisted on was that she had not had sexual intercourse with him. Yes, she had been drinking. Yes, they had parked. Yes, he had kissed her. At one point she said she had scratched his back to keep him from going further. But that only told me that he either had his shirt off, or her hands were up under it.

The thought of this made me go completely berserk. I wanted to kill him. I demanded she tell me where he lived. I did not have a gun, but I would use the tire iron from the car's trunk and smash the life out of him. I was just one raw piece of meat with all my nerve endings exposed. I kept after her for a couple of hours until she had absolutely no defense and swore to me that she had not gone all the way. But that depended on the definition of "all the way" and I knew I would never know.

It was getting late and we had to get back to her mother's place to feed the baby. After that I lay beside her rigid with anger and fear. She tried to get me to hold her but I could not or would not. My mind was searching for some way to get through this. Were we going to get a divorce? What would happen to our baby? What about my job a Purdue? My play? What about the fact that not once through this horrible night had I even thought of hitting her, not once, although I would have killed the guy. Why she would do such a thing was the one thought that kept running through my mind. Was he a better fuck?

Throughout that long sleepless night I lay wide awake as she managed to get some sleep. At about seven I told her we had to get underway. I wanted to avoid her mother. Even as I was being torn apart, the one thought that came through, over and over again, was that I desperately wanted her. Above all, *I* needed *her*. She was "my lost lane-end into heaven." If I lost her what would become of me?

If the circumstances at this stage of my life had been different, I don't think I would have had the same thoughts and feelings. Maybe if I had had more experience with girls I would not have been so destroyed. I felt like I was in a vise and there was no way to turn, no way out. How could trust ever be restored? How could I understand that there might be a difference between just a roll in the hay and love? How was I going to survive? But I stopped the self-inflicted ripping apart of my mind. I *would* have to survive. In two days I had to walk into a classroom for my first day of teaching.

I had a meeting scheduled for late that afternoon with Professor Lee Winch, who was to explain the schedule and syllabus of Speech #114 to those of us who were new to the faculty. When we reached West Lafayette, I stopped at a grocery store and told Robin to get what she thought we needed while I waited in the car with the baby. At the apartment she said some nice things about it, although I knew it was not nearly as nice as our apartments in Kalamazoo or Davie Circle.

We sat at the card table and ate. I had to read the first chapter of the textbook I would be teaching from. I needed to know how to pronounce a word. She told me. I left her for the meeting without saying good-bye, because I didn't know if I was coming back. But I did know. What I didn't know was how I was going to manage to do so. I would have to take one step, and then another, to get through time, then try to get through more time, get through the everyday things that had to be gotten through and try to do well in my work.

Within a few days I could not stand not to touch her, to hold her. I had the shakes—I wanted her so much that emotions melted my mind and she responded with tenderness and love. Yes, we made love, and yes, I felt needed, and yes, my lost "lane-end into heaven"—Robin—was there again.

⌘ ⌘ ⌘

Sixty-five years later, I reflect on this event. First and foremost, I wish my mother in-law had minded her own business and never told me. Ignorance of the fact that my wife had accepted a date with another man and was out half the night would probably not have had any effect on our future lives. Perhaps what motivated Olga's telling was good intentions, you know, the things *the road to hell* is paved with? My ignorance of Robin's actions, in fact, could have saved both of us—but me especially—a lot of doubt, a lot of misery.

When I think of this event—and I do not think of it very often—I cannot help but remember Ibsen's play *The Wild Duck* about a perfectly happy family, a husband, his wife, and their daughter. A neighbor informs the husband that his wife was formerly the mistress of another man which raises paternity questions. The truth-monger then tries to persuade the daughter to restore the tranquility and happiness of the family and prove her love for her father through a sacrificial act of redemption by killing a wild duck she has kept as a pet. The distraught daughter kills herself instead, leaving the relationship between the husband and wife shattered and their lives in shambles.

I believe Ibsen was right about societal "truths," imposed in order to control what cannot be controlled—our humanity, including our frailty. I would eventually understand this by my own conduct when I, too, would stray from what society professed were social norms by doing the very thing that had so shattered me. The big difference? No one told on me.

⌘ ⌘ ⌘

One of the first things I had to do that afternoon when I met Professor Lee Winch was to sign a loyalty oath. I knew it was part and parcel of the "Red Scare" that permeated the United States since I was discharged from the Navy. Both Robin and I had voted for Henry Wallace, Secretary of

Agriculture under FDR, who ran for president on the Progressive Party ticket in the 1948 campaign and who was often called a socialist or a communist. And although I resented my having to sign, I sucked up my reservations and did so.

⌘ ⌘ ⌘

Much of the basic body of knowledge I learned as a high school debater—and what Robin knew even better from her three years on the college debating team—was included in Alan H. Monroe's textbook *Principles and Types of Speech*. Speech #114 was a core requirement in the Schools of Agriculture, Business, Engineering, and Science. Speech #116 was the same core course that served the departments in the School of Humanities, Social Science, and Education, as well as the School of Home Economics, and therefore there were women in these classes. There were some 60 sections each semester of approximately 25 students in these two speech courses. All classes were scheduled three times a week for 50 minutes; semesters were 18 weeks.

I thrived on it. I had a job and was making $3,100 a year!

⌘ ⌘ ⌘

The Speech Department, which had been separated from the English Department for only a few years, was divided into three parts: Classical Rhetoric included debate and graduate work leading to the PhD, and the same for Speech Correction; Theatre and Interpretative Reading piggybacked an occasional advanced degree by stressing scholarship rather than anything as ephemeral as creativity. Ross Smith was administrative head of theatre, Sam Marks headed the technical area, Earl Harlan and Erling Kildahl were directors, and Owen Stallard, Allan Fletcher and I were technical directors.

The term "technical director" meant being responsible for the design of sets, lighting, and costumes for two of the five productions per year. Since there was only History of the Theatre, which Ross taught, plus a couple of stagecraft courses that Sam offered, the rest of the theatre faculty taught either Speech #114 or #116, and Professor Harlan taught Oral Interpretation.

Over fifty percent of the men who were taking Speech #114 were veterans on the GI Bill of Rights. I remember being astonished my first day in class. I had just turned 24 and half the students were older than I was; one, in fact, had just finished his last four-year hitch in the Marines and had retired after 20 years in service. I cannot remember how far into the course we were when one day this guy raised his hand and said, "Joe, this is bullshit!"

What was I going to do—defend the teaching of the text, or go against it?

It took me only a moment before I answered this guy. "I agree with you," I said. "However, all of these motive appeals we are studying are used—and have been—since Quintilian's *Institutes of Oratory* over two thousand years ago. Recognizing and understanding how they work does not necessarily mean you have to approve of their use. You might use your knowledge about them to inform your family and friends how they are being manipulated. That's one reason for their inclusion. Another is that, as we all know, knowledge of them will be tested on the departmental IBM scored tests on which fifty percent of your final grade will depend. So for both intellectual and practical reasons, this 'bullshit' may be necessary."

The guy who made the observation was not being over-familiar when he addressed me by my first name. During my initial lecture I'd asked permission to call the students by their first names because I felt it was more conducive to a give-and-take communication, the result of which would more likely produce a thinking person. When the students agreed, I told them that the same would apply to me, and my first name was Joe.

It took this student a moment of reflection before, shaking his head; he said, "Yeah, I see your point." And I was eternally grateful for his challenge. Right then and there I learned *never to demand* that I was right and that the student was wrong on subject matter simply because of my position as their teacher.

⌘ ⌘ ⌘

My first show as technical director was *Shadow and Substance* by Irish playwright Paul Vincent Carroll, which had only one interior set. I knew I was inadequate to do a really professional job as a set designer. I just did my best and depended on my knowledge of the play. Thank god for well-constructed standard flats and jogs—including French doors and window frames—which had already been built under Sam Marks' watchful eye (he had an undergraduate engineering degree from Purdue) and were recycled from one show to another. All I had to do was figure out what the author had envisioned, arrive at a serviceable floor plan, a basic color approved by Earl Harlan, the director, and fit all this together in some aesthetic arrangement.

We had a slew of Playshoppers who vied for the honor of heading the various crews and areas of duties, and lots of students to serve on these crews—which I had the good sense, as new man on the block, to let the crew heads choose. There were some amazingly talented kids in the area of backstage technology as I should have expected at an engineering school.

Why was the organization called Playshop? This was theatre from the point of view of an engineering campus. If something needs assembling, or something goes wrong with your car or any kind of mechanical thing, what do you do? Why, of course, you take it into the "shop" where they'll fix it. It was natural that these kids figured the play script was taken into Fowler Hall and assembled into a serviceable production. Anything I could dream up got done in a professional, albeit, engineering manner. The kids saved my ass on all five productions that I— using the word loosely—"designed." The only thing I insisted on was final say on such matters as budget, historic style, taste, color, and what costume I thought was right or wrong for a specific character. I also required the student designers to make colored renderings or 3-D models for the director's approval.

These talented kids taught me a lot. I would not take anything for the experience of working with them, not only on *Shadow and Substance,* but also *Macbeth, The Playboy of the Western World, Tartuffe, Hedda Gabler* and co-designing with Allen Fletcher, *Oedipus Rex.*

⌘ ⌘ ⌘

This stage of my life cannot be complete without special mention of Allen Fletcher. He had also been hired as a "technical director" and although he was more knowledgeable in such matters as historic style than I was, he was no more capable of the basic technical skills. Having gotten his master's degree from Stanford, Purdue was his first job and he was hired only one semester before I was. Allen did not care for teaching four sections of speech #114 per semester. He was much more interested in directing the technical work, so he was not a happy camper, and would soon leave for graduate work at Yale. Two years later he joined the Carnegie Tech theatre faculty and went on to become a nationally known director in the burgeoning professional regional theatre movement.

Allen and I shared a sense of humor, as well as an interest in the same kind of shows, and in seeing professional productions. Although smarter, he was less outgoing. His father was a career military man and Allen had been raised on various military bases. He was a good-looking guy, about my height, and under that rather dark sense of humor there was something just a little sad.

We shared the "foggy notion" that Charles Staff, the drama critic for the *Indianapolis News*, once wrote about Purdue as "a boiler factory hard by a cow pasture." True, its architecture was pretty much brick factory with the possible exception of University Hall, its oldest building, in front of which was the grave of John Purdue enhanced by a small bargain-basement fountain. Fowler Hall was opposite, across the Oval, a good chunk of land forming the main entrance into the campus.

Allen's desk was in the same large room, at the back of Fowler Hall, as were Owen Stallard's and mine. There was an unscreened window about eight feet tall and five feet wide facing University Hall across the Oval. The ledge of this window was a good eight feet from the ground. One miserable, dark, last-of-winter day we were all correcting students' outlines for their next speech when Allen said, "Suicide is the only answer." He rose from his desk, raised the window and hoisted himself up on the ledge.

Owen was a thirty-second-degree Mason (with the ring to prove it), who taught sections of Speech #114 his entire life, lived and breathed the course's "motivated sequence," and viewed both Fletcher and me through a jaundiced eye. Looking up from dutifully correcting papers, he was obviously alarmed.

"Wait a second," I said, "I'll go with you." On the ledge, I took Allen's hand, and dramatically turning toward University Hall we closed our eyes and leapt. Racing across the mall we war-whooped like Indians on the warpath and stomped on John Purdue's grave, eventually returning to mount the dozen or so steps to the back door of Fowler Hall.

These were the same steps that the following fall Allen and I would be coming down when Ross Smith, a classical opera enthusiast and duck hunter, scarf around his neck flying in the wind, blew on his new duck-calling horn. "Look, look," he shouted to us, pointing up as the flock hung a U. "They are returning." Having reached the bottom step at that moment, Allen warmly pressed Ross's arm, looked deeply into his eyes, and said, "That must make you very proud." And we continued on our way across the campus to the Quonset huts to teach yet another section of Speech #114.

Within weeks of arriving, Robin and I had Allen over for dinner served on our card table. This was just the beginning of his visits. Actually, I don't remember—in fact I don't believe I ever knew—where he lived during the year and a half we knew him, probably in a furnished room on the East side since apartments near campus were scarce and expensive. But he visited us a lot, bringing over a six-pack or a bottle of wine and sharing what we had for dinner. He was very fond of Robin and baby Lory.

In the spring, Playshop produced Sophocles' *Oedipus Rex* directed by Erling Kildahl, with Allen as technical director and yours truly as his assistant. The title role was played by the talented Vladimir "Wally" von Cott, an Arnold Schwarzenegger look-alike wrestler, who won honors for Purdue in Big Ten competitions and eventually went to Hollywood where it is rumored he auditioned by ripping off his shirt and doing a speech from *Oedipus Rex*.

The annual spring Harlequin show—a dual effort by the Purdue Glee Club under the legendary musical director Al Stuart, and Ross Smith of Playshop—was *The Vagabond King* on which both Allen and I worked. I vividly remember Allen's solving the problem of the very slow exit of a chorus of thousands by telling the first ones to exit and then *run* to the pin rail rather than stopping in the wings and clogging the exit for the hordes of Glee-clubbers and Play- shoppers who followed.

⌘ ⌘ ⌘

In the summer of 1950, Robin, Lory and I returned to Chapel Hill, and I signed up for six credits of independent study and six more for Theatre Workshop in order to complete my required credits for the master of arts. Our return to Chapel Hill was eventful. During our semester away there had been a lot of promoting of *October In The Spring* on the part of the department. True, much of the interest came from people like the woman who operated a touring theatre who said she "needed a drama to produce between two comedies." And if they liked my show they would produce it, "without paying royalties, of course." The business office politely explained that I would not be interested.

But John Parker of that office had connections with Warner Watson, head of the new play division at the American National Theatre and Academy (ANTA) in New York, and he also knew John Byram of Paramount Pictures who read the play and was interested in me. And there was interest from a couple of literary agencies.

Lou White had suggested we sublease Bill and Martha Nell Hardy's apartment, which was practically on campus. But as soon as we opened the door a swarm of fleas—you could actually see them fly through the air—attacked Robin's silk stocking legs. The Hardys' dog had obviously left a few in the apartment and they had multiplied and grown very hungry in the week the apartment had been closed. It needed an exterminator to do what exterminators do. I can't remember where we stayed—it most likely was with Margaret and Edward Woodhouse.

The Playmakers had scheduled a main-stage production of *Born Yesterday*, and remembering what a great job Robin had done in the role of Suzie in *Boy Meets Girl* in summer stock, I thought she should audition. This suggestion was not totally altruistic. Since my oral examination was over, and

October had made a pretty big splash on campus and the faculty committee was high on the play, I did not have a hell of a lot to do. I could baby-sit and read at home for my independent study project.

She read for director Bill MacIIwinen and within a minute had the part. There were four weeks of rehearsals. The guy who played Brock was a jock type. The actor who played Paul, the reporter with whom Billy has love scenes, was a good-looking nice guy. And then there was Kai Jurgensen, who was doing publicity and wanted a shot of her looking startled and holding only a towel over her nude body—a scene not in the play. That picture did sell quite a few tickets.

There was no doubt that I sometimes got nervous as a cat on a hot tin roof when she did not arrive back at the apartment in about fifteen minutes after they were scheduled to break. But I also knew that rehearsals were sometimes delayed and that I must not show the anxiety I felt, or question her with any kind of attitude if we were going to survive as a couple.

I had come to accept that this would be the pattern of our lives. My lifework was to be in the theatre. Rehearsals in the collegiate theatre were usually in the evening, and I would be meeting a lot of people. She couldn't just sit home and raise the baby. She would get all sorts of opportunities to be in plays, which would undoubtedly mean other opportunities as well. This would be our lives, and it seemed to me that if it was going to happen, it would have to be with trust and without imposed restraints from either partner, a tall if not impossible order for me. This was a very difficult time for me, but I made it.

As it happened, Robin was an absolute sensation in the role and the campus and I were agog with her portrayal of Billy Dawn. And her last line, "Do me a favor, will you Harry? Drop dead!" was greeted with a laugh that rocked the campus. Wink Locklair of the *News and Observer, Raleigh, N.C* wrote: [7/14/1950] "As Billy Dawn, Robin Stockdale gives one of the best performances seen here in a long while."

⌘ ⌘ ⌘

It was a Sunday afternoon that a call came from Harry Davis, who was director of Kermit Hunter's outdoor drama *Unto These Hills.* The show opened on July 1st and had been running for two weeks. A member of Ross Durfee's family had called to tell him his father had died and his mother had had a heart attack. Ross, who played Junaluska, the leading role, told Harry he would play his last performance that evening and would not return after the funeral. Harry asked me to take the role. I would be given room and board and $50 a week, my contract running for the rest of the season ending on Labor Day.

I asked him if I could read the script and get back to him. He said no, he knew I could play the part from seeing my performance in Ann Martin's one-act *The Vanishing American* which his wife, Suzie, had directed. If I could not accept he would have to start calling other actors. I said okay, I would do it. But Robin and Lory had to follow within the week. He said that would be impossible, that the company could not accommodate wives and children. I played hardball. Well then, I told him, although I would have loved to do it, I would respectfully have to decline. But thanks for thinking of me.

Harry went silent for more than a moment before he said he would see what he could do. The script was in Sam's office. He would alert Lou White to go to the office and give me a script and I could start going over it while he called whomever he had to call to make possible arrangements.

I rushed to Sam's office. I couldn't have been there more than an hour when Harry called. He had a room in the Indian Teachers' Faculty Club right in the same area as the cafeteria and the girls' and boys' dorms where most of the company was lodged. The room was on the second floor and had access to a large screened porch. There were only two members of the Indian School's faculty who lived in the house during the summer and they had agreed. "Thanks," I said. "I'll learn as much as I can tonight and be on my way tomorrow morning."

I went home and told Robin of our plans. She would follow just as soon as she could close up the apartment. The rest of the day she helped me with pronunciations of the difficult Indian names and other unfamiliar words as I studied my scenes. I then started memorizing and going over scenes, with her cueing me. We did this till past midnight when I was exhausted.

She said I should probably get some sleep; we would get up and continue until I had to leave.

The script was written in a kind of poetic style and had to be memorized verbatim. There was little room for substituting another word in the speeches, let alone improvisation which I had become good at in summer stock. Learning the lines was tough sledding.

The next day I kissed Robin and Lory good-bye and was on my way, a couple of peanut butter sandwiches packed in a brown paper sack. I caught the bus to Durham where I had an hour to wait, boarded, and doggedly set out getting the cues and lines in my head.

The following morning stage manager Ed Loessin met me at the bus station and the first thing he did was ask if I'd had any breakfast. When I said no, he took me to a little place in the village for eggs, bacon, toast and coffee before he drove me to the Indian School, where in addition to dormitories and a cafeteria, I saw the Faculty Club where Robin, Lory and I would be housed. In the meantime, I was assigned a room in the girls' dorm where other cast members lived. We then went to the Mountainside Theatre which seated 3,000, including temporary seating in the rain shelter, which was often used for overflow crowds during this first season. Backstage, Harry and Susie Davis welcomed me along with Ed's assistant stage manager and two costume crew members. No cast members were present; Monday was their day off and they would not have to report back until 7:30 P.M. on Tuesday.

The outdoor stage consisted of a huge main acting area and two side stages where various small scenes took place: Stage Right for exterior scenes and Stage Left had a platform that rolled out to be redressed for various interior scenes. At the back of the main stage area was a twelve-foot-high stockade wall constructed of split trees. Further up, behind the dressing rooms and costume shop, the trees of the forest could be lit at night for a breathtaking view of the mountains. There was a ready-room for quick costume changes on either side of the stage. Directly in front of the stage was a small rectangular building recessed under the mountainside amphitheater in which the narrator, Mr. Henry Joyner, along with the lighting console, the lighting designer and his assistant, plus the music/sound director, were stationed.

We rehearsed each scene twice and then went through the entire play. After this we focused on costume and makeup changes. Costumer Suzie Davis was there to make suggestions to her assistants assigned to me. In the fast changes, I was simply to hold my arms out while they stripped and redressed me, and occasionally white shoe polish was added to my hair to show the progression of age. We then did a run-through of the entire show in full voice with Ed in the auditorium checking my vocal projection. By that time it was late afternoon, and although we were in the mountains, there was still sweat-inducing heat in the sun and I was pretty well brain dead.

I've never been in any play that I didn't have stage fright prior to my first entrance. Never! But as soon as I heard the cue and concentrated on my scene objective—what was my character there *to do*—I was released from stage fright and could listen and respond in character. The spontaneity of my listening and responding that night was in no way faked since I was seeing and hearing the other characters for the first time .

I did know some of the cast, but the majority of them were strangers, so this was as close to moment-to-moment reality as one could get. Added to this, I knew that I had to try to project my voice to the back row, which meant I had to play my lines as much as humanly possible, "out and up," or "front," yet at the same time seem to be talking to the character(s) I addressed. This was something that could only have been accomplished while rehearsing with the full company, so I had to improvise as we went along.

Just before Junaluska's death of old age (If one actually goes through the script and figures out the time that passes, I think it is something like 123 years!), he moves toward the audience like the blinded Oedipus with the line, "twilight makes mist through the beech trees…" I was struck with such feelings that it was all I could do not to be overcome by pity for the character and at the same time be aware that these feelings must not swamp my vocal projection; as the lights slowly dimmed my body slumped in death.

After the curtain call, I staggered offstage, with back slaps and congratulations by Ed, the other actors, and many of the Cherokee Indians when Harry Davis arrived to give me my first and only note: "Tomorrow night you gotta be louder."

Harry was Harry. Never prone to say more than was necessary, but physically and psychologically I was at the absolute end of my rope and I never forgot this "note." All I did was say, "I'll try harder tomorrow." Instead of going back to the dressing room, I went into the bushes and just let go, crying as hard as I ever had, not for Harry's insensitivity, but because I was totally exhausted.

⌘ ⌘ ⌘

Robin and our "plum-Dum," as I had nicknamed the baby for her fondness for strained Gerber's plums, came up to Cherokee and we lived in our very pleasant room with its wonderful screened-in second-story porch where we often made love.

The only negative event of the summer was that after I had played for about a week, I picked up a program and realized that my name was not in it. I went immediately to Ed who, in the rush of getting me blocked, rehearsed and through opening night and beyond, had not thought to check this matter.

What he found out was that the business office had ordered enough programs at the beginning of the season to last for three weeks and had decided to use them. Ed told the business manager that when cast members changed it was standard practice to slip-sheet the program or make an announcement over the loudspeaker. The general manager argued that that would have a negative effect on the audience since they might feel an understudy was on. I told Ed I'd go to the office with him and we could talk to the general manager.

The meeting was not pleasant. He couldn't understand what the "fuss" was all about, and it got to the point where I told him that if they were going to use the programs they either had to be slip-sheeted with my picture and bio, or there had to be an announcement. I would not continue appearing under the name of Ross Durfee. A hard-ass business type, the manager tried to win until I was too pissed to argue and simply said, "Okay, if one of these solutions is not done before tonight's performance, I will not be appearing," and walked out. That night an announcement was made, and the next night they had slip-sheeted the programs with my bio and picture, and within a week they had new programs.

The only other negative remembrance was that I was stunned when I discovered that the theatre had a Jim Crow section for Negroes. This was both unacceptable and patently ridiculous. The play about the history of the Cherokee was nothing if not about racial prejudice. Bernie Barrow and his wife Jane were as surprised as I was, and with their support and the backing of others, there was a company protest.

What we found out was that the vast majority of the Indians wanted the Jim Crow section. There was a pecking order among the disenfranchised. The Indians, who were sometimes mistaken as Negroes, instead of empathizing with and relating to that, were insulted.

⌘ ⌘ ⌘

It was a wonderful summer. My $50 a week was equal to what I would have received under an Equity contract in summer stock; plus board and room not only for me but for Robin and the baby. We played only six performances a week through Labor Day. There were various arts and crafts activities such as pottery making, which Robin took up while I became proficient in the art of weaving. Tourists timorously peeked into the loom room and cautiously entered to ask questions. My skin was very dark from the summer sun and in Pigeon English and pantomime they would ask "Are you a real Indian?" I would turn with a fearful facial expression and growl, "ja <u>na</u> ha!" If I ever knew what that meant in Cherokee, I've forgotten, but the tourists would wither in fright and slink off, much to the delight of the actual Cherokee Indians.

On August 13th, we had a birthday party for Lory. Kai Jurgensen and Jo Reynolds had married in February and they and Nat and Lou White came up to Cherokee for the party. Lory was dressed in a white dress, and one of my favorite memories of her is me lying on my back on the lawn, her on my chest, and me suddenly lifting her in the air which brought on shrieks and giggles and then lowering her. After she was comfortable, we did it again, much to her delight.

⌘ ⌘ ⌘

Back at Purdue in September, I again taught four sections of Speech #114. I found a vacancy at the caretaker's house for the Potter Apartments on State Street. There were two apartments in this house, one rented by Judge Lightcap and his wife, Edna, with whom we shared a porch from which both apartments were entered via large eat-in kitchens. I mention this because if things were not going well in her kitchen, Edna would often say, "Oh, shit!" and if the weather was warm and both kitchen doors were open, we could easily hear her. In fact, Lory's first words were in imitation of Edna during a meal preparation gone wrong.

We were glad to be out of our barracks apartment. We were now closer to the campus and to the village that constituted the business section of West Lafayette, where the mom-and-pop grocery store run by Russ Printy allowed us a monthly charge account.

At the theatre, with Ross' permission, I branched out from my technical work and directed some one-acts. Among them were an original, *Values* by Rosemary Peachen; *The Lady Will Jump* by Brad Arrington, a fellow student at Chapel Hill; and a longer piece, Terrence Rattigan's *The Browning Version*. I also wrote a one-act, *Evolutionary Synthesis,* which was directed by Erling [hereafter "Gene"] Kildahl, and a "meller-drama" (parody of the old-fashioned melodramas) that was included in *The Harlequin Minstrels* for the annual "gala week" show that took place in the Hall of Music.

In the past they had done standard kitsch pieces such as 1920s operettas, but this year decided to do an old-time minstrel show (white performers made up in blackface, which clues you in to the prevailing racial sensitivity). The one-act parody I wrote as a part of the show ended with the iconic scene in which the hero has been tied to the railroad track. The desperate heroine, now ready to sacrifice her modesty to save the man she loves, is about to remove her red petticoat to flag down the train while the villain hisses and twists his mustache in sadistic delight.

Technical director Sam Marks ratcheted up the sound of the train to an ear-splitting volume as this miniature train rolls onstage under its own power, Sam himself straddling the engine. This bit brought down the capacity house filled with happy Gala-weekers in Purdue's 6,006-seat Hall of Music.

⌘ ⌘ ⌘

Robin was cast as Irene Livingston in Moss Hart's *Light Up the Sky*, directed by Ross, for the Lafayette Little Theatre. The role was a thinly designed portrait of actress Gertrude Lawrence whom Mr. Hart had found problematic when he directed her in the musical *Lady in the Dark*. The role would have been perfect for the throaty voiced Tallulah Bankhead in full-throttled camp mode, but Robin was definitely not that type, neither vocally nor personally. Although all the best of the Lafayette Community Theatre talent pool were in this production, it was perhaps her least favorite role.

What good that came out of her participation were lifetime friendships with cast members Page Karling, Dorothy Harlan, Stuart Main, and Tex Burdick. Socially, we became the exciting, new couple on the block and stayed that way for the majority of our twenty-five and one-half year Purdue career. We also used lines from that show in everyday conversation for years. "The play's an *allegory*? Great! I'll tell our Texas investors, they'll think it's an oil well."

When Ross directed *Born Yesterday*, casting Pam Printy as Billy, and knowing of Robin's success in Chapel Hill, he asked her to work with Pam. Robin did it to great effect, including the voice and accent. Ross encouraged Pam to cut her waist-long hair and dye it blond to the horror of her mother, but it was an absolute life-changing event toward freedom and independence for Pam. And of course, she became one of our dearest friends and continued to be until her death a few months prior to this publication.

⌘ ⌘ ⌘

We made a down payment on a record player at Loeb's Department Store, paying the balance in monthly installments. I had just returned from a trip to New York to keep up with the theatre scene and brought back records of Edith Piaf *("La Vie En Rose"),* Josh White ("One Meat Ball"), and an album with all the songs from the musical *South Pacific* starring Ezio Pinza and Mary Martin.

Allen and I spent hours together both socially and in rehearsals, and conferences on the two shows he directed and on which I served as technical director. I used stenciled wallpaper for the room in which *Hedda Gabler* took place. After the flats were lashed together, the moldings attached, and the set was upright and dressed, Allen said, "The wallpaper pattern is too prominent. It takes focus and has to be toned down."

After rehearsal the paint crew and I dismantled the set, laid the flats on the stage floor, and barely dipping a paintbrush into a darker colored paint, spackled fine bits of paint onto the flat. The spackling had to be consistent over all the walls, no mean trick. We then reassembled the flats and reattached the moldings, which took the entire night. When Allen saw it the next day he was pleased. As inexperienced and incompetent as I was as a "technical director," it never occurred to me to say no to a director who felt some doable change was necessary regardless of the amount of time it took. This remained my view after I became a full-time director.

On *Tartuffe,* for which Allen used the English actor Miles Malleson's version, the set was basically wing-and-drop with a raked floor, both painted in perspective. I decided to paint on the second wing Stage Left—which was, of course, just a flat—a three-dimensional niche in which I would paint the sculptured bust of a female nude in perspective.

The truth was I could not paint a still life of a bowl of cherries in perspective let alone a nude, but I spent most of the night doing my best. Fortunately the student crew head who was an excellent painter saw it before Allen did. "Sorry, Joe but the breasts—just too pornographic."

"Could you fix it?" I pleaded.

"Sure," she said, painting over what I had done. In no time she had a three dimensional niche, which you would swear was really receded into a wall, containing a statue of a perfect look-alike bust of Aphrodite with capable three-dimensional tits. Allen was delighted and devised a wonderful bit of business: on Tartuffe's first entrance, seeing the bust, he whipped off a neck scarf and sanctimoniously pinned it over Aphrodite's breasts, demonstrating his piousness. We both gave the paint crew head full credit for one of the biggest laughs in the show.

⌘ ⌘ ⌘

In addition to the teaching and the theatrical activity, my writing became increasingly important. Thelma Anton, my undergraduate journalism teacher at Western, introduced me via letter to a young relative who was interested in the theatre, and it was he who suggested I send *October In The Spring* to Tom Hill, director of Originals Only, an Off-Broadway producing group. Almost immediately Tom wrote back and said he wanted to produce it.

On May 23, 1951, I received confirmation that for the next academic year at Purdue I would receive $3,550, a raise of $45 a month. Robin and I were ecstatic. Things were looking up! In addition, just before we left for Cherokee that summer, I received a letter from Bertha Klausner, International Literary Agency, 130 East 40th Street, New York, 16, N.Y. saying that Tom Hill had told her he was producing *October In The Spring* and was very excited by it. "If you are not committed to any agent," she wrote, "I would like very much to represent you and get as many Broadway producers as possible to see your play when it is performed."

Chapter 7

WE RETURNED TO CHEROKEE FOR the full summer of 1951, including two weeks rehearsal prior to the show's opening in mid-June. I had to have summer employment since Purdue paid ten monthly checks and we had no other income for July and August. This time I played "the flaming Tecumseh" in full body paint with zigzag stripes across my stomach, chest and face along with loincloth, and a wooly cape that was attached around my neck but hung over my back (presumably this was for warmth?). Since this was the second scene in the show, I could shower and then change into a couple of feathers, or whatever, to play an Indian or a settler in one of the crowd scenes. In addition, I played the leading role of Junaluska every Sunday evening.

This second season, Harry told us to contact Peter Strader, who played Reverend Schermerhorn, and see if Robin and Lory could share his and his wife Helen's apartment in the village, while I had a room in the girls' dorm along with meals in the cafeteria as a part of my salary. This arrangement, although not perfect, worked out well because of the Straders' hospitality and Robin's adaptability, and proved to be a good summer in the mountains away from West Lafayette. Helen would babysit Lory so that Robin could join me at the canteen after the show and we could spend some time alone in my room before she went back to the Straders'. And vitally important, it gave me a room where I could write all day and sometimes most of the night, working on a novel.

On June 12th I received a one-year contract from Bertha Klausner with a clause that stipulated she receive "25 percent from the first one thousand dollars and 10 percent thereafter, in the U.S." of all money from the sale of my writing. The twenty-five percent was necessary, she wrote, "when there is no fee for reading and criticism services." She also said she sent the one copy she had of my *October In The Spring* to Joe E. Brown in Hollywood "because he was interested in baseball and perhaps might see a part for himself as 'Dad'." Since I had seen his films—all farce comedies—plus him onstage in the farce *The Show Off*, this submission did not inspire confidence that she knew much about casting, so of course I was not surprised when she sent me his rejection letter.

How did getting a literary agent make me feel? For most of my life I have thought of myself as a director, and although that is what I did, the letters I received from Bertha Klausner clearly show that what I was most passionate about was my writing. In all aspects, the theatre—acting, directing and designing—is an ephemeral art but the written word is forever.

She did inform me that the critic for *Women's Wear Daily* wrote that my show "was excellent." This drew big yuks from me down in Cherokee until a New Yorker in the cast explained that *Women's Wear Daily* was published by the National Garment Association and buyers from all over the country read what it had to say about New York theatre's offerings. Its critic, Kelcey Allen, was a member of the Drama Critics Circle, who voted each year for Broadway's best play award. *Then* I was interested in reading Allen's review, but neither Tom Hill nor Bertha ever sent it.

She did send an ad from *The Villager* (a forerunner of *The Village Voice*) about the play premiering on "actors night" July 23rd, plus their review which called the play "warmly sentimental ... a plain, honest story, without fancy trimmings... with a compact book [and] down to earth dialogue." The critic said that I "appeared to have great potential," and praised Netha A. Stanton who played Abbie "with grace and understanding," Otto Lohmann, currently a guest on "The Danny Thomas Show," as Dad, and Carolyn Brenner "who captured the audience's fancy with her delightful vivacity as the barmaid, instilling into that role a sparkling Carmen-like quality." Would that be like in Bizet or Miranda? I wondered. In either case it didn't sound like anything I had written.

On August 7th, Bertha sent me a response from John Byram of Paramount Pictures who informed her that he had "...originally read this script after its presentation at UNC" and said that he'd had another look at it and thought "the dialogue reaches a professional level and that the characterizations, particularly the older people, are convincingly managed, but the play strikes me as a bit confused...."

⌘ ⌘ ⌘

That summer at Cherokee was not all writing. I found out that a run of approximately 70 performances could get pretty boring in this kind of presentational show in which there was not much chance of any empathic feedback from the audience, or of conquering the almost hopeless task—for me, at least—of vocally projecting to 3,500 tourists in the Mountainside Theatre. I suppose this was one reason we did some pretty unprofessional things. We were at an age when we justified bad behavior by "the devil made me do it." The following antic was a product of my less than perfect nature and not to be emulated.

If you are acquainted with Cherokee's surrounding area, you can't avoid the signs that advertise "See Rock City" which tops Lookout Mountain near Chattanooga and from which "you can see seven states." One night, as a crowd-scene-Indian in loincloth and beaded headband, I "oohed" and "aa-hed" as directed in shock and awe when Hernando De Soto's soldiers appeared. But instead of reaching out tentatively to touch the armor plate of the soldiers, I moved my loincloth aside to reveal a sign I had painted high up on my inner thigh: "See Rock City."

As De Soto's solders marched off, doubled up with laughter, the audience must have thought they were drunk. Harry came backstage like J. Edgar Hoover on a bloodhound determined to find out what happened, but none of the Spanish solders ratted me out.

⌘ ⌘ ⌘

Featured dancer that second season doing "The Great Eagle Dance" was David Vaughan who became a lifelong friend. A Brit, David came to this country in 1950 at the behest of Lincoln Kirsten, co-director with George Balanchine of NY's City Ballet, "having danced, sung, acted and choreographed in London and Paris." He was a friend of dancer Ruth Sobotka, who appeared in many of Balanchine's ballets, and was, at that time, film director Stanley Kubrick's wife.

She served as art director on Kubrick's and Jim Thompson's film *The Killing* starring Sterling Hayden. This was/is a must-see suspense flick about a racetrack robbery. One day when Kubrick was still working on the screenplay, David read a letter from Ruth and went into gales of laughter. She had written that when the first version of the screenplay was submitted for registration by the Screen Writers Guild, it had not been approved because of the title, *The Big Snatch*.

⌘ ⌘ ⌘

Another cast member was Hal Hackett who played Major Davis. Hal was one of the few actors who did not have a Chapel Hill connection. After being in WWII, he did a three-year stint in Hollywood. His first film in 1946 was *The Secret Heart,* followed by *Love Laughs at Andy Hardy, Undercover Maisie, Living* in *a Big Way, Dark Delusion, Campus Honeymoon, Summer Holiday,* and *Tucson*. Disillusioned because most of the roles in these films were bit parts, he went to New York and landed a job in the Broadway cabaret *Lend An Ear.* Then in the spring of 1951, he auditioned for the role of Major Davis and came to Cherokee to enjoy the mountains, seek new adventures, and be away from the heat of a New York summer.

Hal drove one of those two-door convertibles with a wood paneling interior that obviously cost a lot of money. I remember him taking Lory and me for a ride one day. We had a six-pack in the car. I finished one and tossed it, only to look back to see a state police car.

When the lights started flashing and the siren wailed, Hal immediately pulled over. I was petrified while the cop took down the license plate number. When he started toward us, I called to him to please come to my side of the car since I was the one who tossed out the beer can. Admitting that I knew it was against the law to drink on the reservation, I told him I was a cast member in *Unto These Hills*.

He said he had seen and liked the show. Lory, who I was holding on my lap, stood up and reached out to touch his badge. I gently pulled her hand back but he said it was okay. Yes, I was her father. Yes, she was just two years old. And yes, living on the Cherokee Reservation was a bit of a problem since one was not even allowed a beer. He ended up returning Lory's smile, and when she held out her arms to him—although he did not pick her up, he did put both hands around her waist. She'd totally charmed him.

This incident ended with me getting a warning to *never* toss a beer can out on the highway, not only on an Indian reservation but *any* highway, and although he knew and ignored the fact that there was drinking on the reservation, to keep in mind that it was against the law. And have a good day.

During all of this Hal never uttered a word. It was his cool unflappable demeanor—beyond worry of anything that would happen, an acceptance without judgment as if he had pre-mellowed-out all eventualities, but at the same time felt for what I was going through—that left an indelible impression. His attitude was not quite sardonic, but beyond caring in the face of what for me was sweaty-armpit inducing.

Hal had a terrific wry sense of humor and we became friends. I was fascinated with his war experience and tried to get him to talk about it, and although there was an undeniable subtext, he never told me anything specific of his experiences during the Battle of the Bulge or in Hollywood. He was good-looking with curly dirty-blond hair and had an extraordinarily rich baritone voice.

As Tecumseh in full body makeup, I was usually ready before the show started and would sit on one of the built-in benches backed by a railing for the runway that went from the dressing rooms down to the stage. Since Hal's entrance was a couple of scenes later we would sit and talk. There were times when he suddenly stopped and looked at me and slid his tongue in a circular motion around his lips. When I finished my scene and was in the shower, he sometimes showed up to take a leak and before leaving, would stop and look at me. Embarrassed, I would turn my back to him. Now, of course, it is impossible to see these actions as I saw them then, as just odd, something that was crazy and wild, but nothing more. That is the quality I believe I captured in using him as the prototype in my short novel *The Adventures of Allen Hack*.

⌘ ⌘ ⌘

When we returned to West Lafayette, I found a small but newly built white house at 101 East Wood Street, the last house before the River Road. It was owned by a professor in the English Department. The rent was $50 a month. Because Robin had spotted a couple of rats in our place next to the Potter Apartments, she wanted to move, and this would be the nicest house we had lived in.

⌘ ⌘ ⌘

Except for seeing Robeson in the New York production of *Othello*, stage managing *The Merchant of Venice* in Chapel Hill's Forest Theatre, and furthering my ignorance by talking my way out of having to take the required Shakespeare class as an undergraduate, I was inexperienced even in the reading of his plays. But now, back at Purdue, I had to read and become acquainted with one because I was technical director of *Macbeth*, which Ross Smith would direct. My solution to the problem of multi-scenes was to do it in three basic areas as in a musical: "in-one" being downstage, "in-two" being mid-stage, and "in-three" being upstage, with travelers to separate the three areas when necessary, and to use side stage areas as in the architecture of The Globe Theatre's "Inner above and inner below" during Shakespeare's time.

The gals doing costumes, headed by Rosemary Peachen, had me make the chain mail. I had never knitted in my life but as I remember I found out how to make chain-mail tunics in a costume book by the legendary Fairfax

Proudfit Walkup. I used half-inch rounded doweling sticks and knitted, and got anyone who happened to be sitting idly in the greenroom to knit the tunics. They were composed of a single piece which was tapered (you had to drop stitches at the middle and make a hole in the center for the actor's head). Separate knitted units were then attached to each of the side for the arms. (I left this fancy stuff for the gals to figure out). They also, thank god, advised me that I had to allow for about thirty-three percent shrinkage because of the large cotton string I was using. After the arm sections were attached I dyed the tunics grey, brushing each lightly with silver paint while they were still damp.

If I do say so myself, under lights they looked terrific!

Sam Marks gladly took over the John Wayne task of creating the broadswords which required metallurgic/welding skills. They were so heavy that the guys playing Macbeth and Macduff had to get into training as weightlifters to swing them—but what the hell? As I reminded them, there were no pussies in the Scottish army at that time.

I had taken a trip to NYC the year before when I had bought the recording of *South Pacific* and other great albums. Robin had stayed home with six-month-old Lory. This year, I wanted to go again, but I also thought that Robin should go. But if we went together who would take care of Lory? It wasn't fair for me to be the only one who kept up with the New York theatre scene. Robin loved seeing shows, too. The only solution I could think of, since we both agreed that her mother would not want to baby-sit, was for her to go for a week during the Thanksgiving vacation, and I would go after Christmas.

There is no point in detailing the activities centered around a year-and-a-half infant cutting her teeth except to say I longed for her nappy time, which usually lasted no more than an hour and then, at the end of the day, putting her to bed for a solid eight or nine hour sleep, interrupted by one middle-of-the-night feeding during which I hummed to induce heavy eyelids and drowsiness. I loved our baby but in truth, I found her—as well as all babies—heavy duty until she was old enough to reason.

She loved time in the bath splashing and kicking in the warm water with me kneeling attentively at the side of the tub fearing that she might decide to flop over and drown. She loved time in her playpen, discovering new delight in the various objects we had bought for her amusement. And, as previously mentioned, she could now say words so I had to guard against my use of "bad" ones such as Edna Lightcap used. I mean, what would Robin think if she came home and baby Lory called out, "More fucking plums"?

So much for good intentions. Robin took care of and nurtured our children during their baby and growing-up years. She watched football, baseball, and basketball with them and taught them all they knew (which was considerable) about sports, which I'm certain she had learned dating jocks in high school and college before I showed up with my interest in theatre. After they reached puberty and beyond, I took over and continued the takeover throughout their adolescence and young adulthood and . . . oh, hell, let's be honest: being the one to remember birthdays and taking some kind of never-ending care of them, from getting Joe out of jail to shopping with Larkin for both her Junior and Senior Class prom dresses—apparently it was considered absolutely necessary *not* to appear in the same dress twice.

In my mid-eighties, I did the ordering of the DVDs of Larkin's second marriage. This is the kind of care that, for the most part, I have done with only occasional grousing. Robin took the long haul that lasted perhaps thirty of the best years of her life, and I've taken over the adult caring that has lasted fifty years and continues.

I was pleased that I had not gone crazy while she was away for a week. And I encouraged her to do more acting, which she did, being cast in the title role of another Lafayette Little Theatre production, this time opposite a handsome guy who worked for the Purdue Radio Station WBAA and who played her lover in Zola's *Therese Raquin*. This gave her time away and I could baby-sit during evening hours when blissfully the kids slept, or when they were older and I could let them watch television beyond their normal bedtime. But more important I was also testing myself to see if I could control my jealousy and strengthen my ability to trust.

Why we decided to have another kid I'm not sure, but we did. Perhaps because that's what was expected of young couples during the Eisenhower years when some of our well-to-do friends got a colored TV set that cost twelve hundred bucks to watch Lucille Ball in *I Love Lucy*, Jackie Gleason and Art Carney in *The Honeymooners,* or *The Arthur Godfrey Talent Show.* And also because young couples then knew that babies should have baby brothers or sisters and.... well, maybe also that sex without using the diaphragm was freer and more spontaneous.

When I went to New York City after Christmas, I saw: *Caesar and Cleopatra* with Vivian Leigh and Laurence Olivier; *Call Me Madam* with Ethel Merman; *Don Juan in Hell; Gigi* with Audrey Hepburn (now getting star billing in the ads and the top price $3.80); *Guys and Dolls; I Am a Camera* with Julie Harris; *Point of No Return* with Henry Fonda; *Saint Joan* with Uta Hagen; *South Pacific; The Constant Wife* with Katharine Cornell; *The Fourposter; The King and I;* and *The Moon is Blue* with Barbara Ben Geddes, Donald Cook and Barry Nelson.

Thirteen shows in 10 days? You better believe it! This became my usual schedule when I went to New York. Besides the nominal Wednesday and Saturday matinees there were often special Thursday, Friday and Sunday matinees. David Vaughan was looking after a friend's apartment and I was allowed to stay there. I got to meet his friend Ruth Sobotka and have late suppers with them at the Carnegie Grill where a lot of hungry dancers went for wonderful German food, like beef stroganoff with dumplings and red cabbage, at inexpensive prices.

⌘ ⌘ ⌘

How was my writing going? From May 24, 1951, to October 1, 1953, some 80 letters, clippings, rejection slips, and readers' reports came from Bertha Klausner. My reworking of *October In The Spring* into a novel called *The Dark Limbo* reveals the influence of William Styron, whose *Lie Down* in *Darkness* had just been published. I loved the story, his stream-of-consciousness style, and his characters, especially the one who commits suicide at novel's end.

Bertha submitted this novel—a "partial"—to Little Brown, Rinehart, Bobs Merrill, Prentice Hall, A.S. Barnes, and Harpers. My short stories were submitted to *Colliers, Esquire, Good Housekeeping, Cosmopolitan, McLean's, Blue Book, Argosy, Lion Books, Western, Harpers, Atlantic Monthly,* and *The Saturday*

Evening Post, and in all cases there were encouraging remarks about my writing, but no takers.

⌘ ⌘ ⌘

During the second semester I was in rehearsals until mid-February, directing my first full-length play. Since Allen Fletcher had departed, and Ross was aware that being a "technical director" was not my forte, rather than firing me he allowed me to direct. I had chosen *The Glass Menagerie.* I was in love with the play, having seen it with the original cast.

We spent the first part of rehearsal in discussions and readings, but not taking nearly as much time as did Laura Shaw. I felt I could tell when the actors had the structural components of the play in mind as well as the connecting back story, and it was time for them to be on their feet. Blocking rehearsals dealt with when and where the actors should move; when they should move dealt with their relationship to the furniture and stage properties, their relationship to one another, and their relationship to the scenes' subtexts. All this was, of course, to form an aesthetically pleasing stage picture that aided in conveying the play's meaning, just as a painter does in a painting, or a film director does in each frame of a film. In addition, I used George Bernard Shaw's ideas from his letter to an Irish director, which was originally published under the title *The Art of Rehearsal.*

After going through the blocking once or twice I often asked the actors to put down their scripts and improvise, then go back to the lines as written. I sometimes took an actor aside and if they answered "yes" to another character, I would tell them to say "no" and allow them to improvise a scene as a result of this change. All of this was to train them to be "in the moment," to listen and respond to what had famously been called "the illusion of the first time." I told actors never to memorize lines aloud, and often in early readings I had cast members exchange roles so that the focus would be on clarity of meaning, and melody patterns could not be set.

This process of improvisations produced one of the most astonishingly first-rate moment- to-moment pieces of business I have ever seen. It was during a final dress rehearsal: Linden Chiles, as The Gentleman Caller, revealed to Amanda and Laura that he is engaged to be married and is off to pick up his girlfriend. When leaving the apartment and going down the alley, he characteristically puts his right hand into the pocket of his jacket and touches the little glass unicorn Laura had given him. Removing it, he stops for moment, then tosses it into the empty garbage can.

The sound of its shattering tore me apart and was one I never forgot—a totally unintentional act of cruelty akin to what he had just done to Amanda by telling her he had a girlfriend—as well as a metaphor for our thoughts on the play's theme, which was printed in the program—"the lives of most people are insulated by a corresponding monotony in their own souls, alas for the poet, the dreamer, who is cast into the world, without this indispensable insulation."

In May, when Playshop Awards were given out at a banquet, *The Glass Menagerie* was judged as Best Production, Pamela Printy Best Actress, Adrian Robinson Best Actor, and Katie Neff as Best Supporting Actress. All members of the cast went on into various aspects of theatre and television and all have been lifetime friends. The two whom I have seen and communicated with the most were Pamela and Linden Chiles. The one with the longest sustained professional resume (which you can access on the Internet) is Linden Chiles, whom I felt deserved but did not get the award for Best Supporting Actor.

⌘ ⌘ ⌘

I also found myself, for the first, if not the last time, not to be on the same page with the "designer" of *Menagerie*. I naturally suggested we talk over the design but he did not wish to do that; he wanted to create it the way he saw it. "Okay, but have the floor plan and rendering done early in case there are changes to be made," I said.

He did not have them done early and there were changes to be made. Tennessee wrote, "The scene is memory and therefore nonrealistic. Memory takes a lot of poetic license. It omits some details; others are exaggerated, according to the emotional value of the articles it touches, for memory is seated predominately in the heart. The interior then, is rather dim and poetic". When I saw the rendering I was appalled. There was nothing about it that was poetic. It was ugly. The alleys had solid realistic walls, constructed with bricks (obviously fresh from the brick factory); the fire escape was real. But what struck me as absolutely not to be believed was that there was a kitchen added next to the dining room, thereby throwing it partially out of the sight-line triangle that is formed when lines from the extreme DL and DR proscenium meet upstage center. Now that this upstage-center area was expanded to include a realistic kitchen with tile floors and running water from the faucet over the sink, the characters at both ends of the table would be out of sight for those in the farthest right or left seats in the auditorium.

I didn't give even a nod to the idea that this was acceptable. No, I told him everything had to be changed and said that there was to be no further discussion. He went to Sam Marks, who headed the technical direction/design area. Sam went to Ross Smith, in defense of the "designer." Ross saw the rendering and floor plan, called me in, heard my demands for change and agreed.

No love was lost between Ross Smith and Sam Marks, but in this instance the argument was ended. I had final say and the technical director had to yield to my point of view in all artistic matters of *Menagerie's* production. This chain of command set a precedent—at least for the moment.

While we're on problems in production, let me segue into my reflections about the rehearsal hall. I start with a premise that as far as creative activity is concerned, the rehearsal hall is the *most needed large space in any theatre complex*. Now think back. Have you ever found a theatre building where this is the case?

The Glass Menagerie played in Old Fowler Hall, and rehearsals were held in various spaces: the costume room if it wasn't busy, sometimes the greenroom, occasionally the stage and very often classrooms in other buildings. Seldom *if ever* was the floor plan taped on the floor so we could be sure of the exact amount of space we were working in while blocking.

⌘ ⌘ ⌘

In the summer of 1952, I played the ninth president of the United States, William Henry Harrison, in *Unto These Hills,* and found out that Stanislavski's homily about there being no small parts, only small actors, was wrong. Harry Davis was not exactly helpful as a director.

Larry Randolph, who was in the show in various roles for some 18 summers, remembered when he played President Harrison. From the middle of the amphitheater Harry called, "Larry, what the hell are you doing?" After a moment Larry called back, "Well, I thought I was acting." "Well, stop it!" Harry growled.

⌘ ⌘ ⌘

Robin was pregnant and the baby was due in early August. I had to make money for the two months we were without income, and her staying in West Lafayette was not an option. She and Lory again lived with the Straders, who found a nice three-bedroom house along the Oconaluftee River about a quarter of a mile away, and only half that distance by using the swinging bridge over the river. Since she did not fancy the swinging bridge, the place was not convenient for her to walk to our after-show canteen performances as had been the case when she stayed in the Village. On the other hand, I could make enough money for us to live on, see both Lory and Robin during the day, and occasionally go swimming. In short, it was a two-month summer-in-the-mountains vacation for them, and three months for me.

Again I was assigned a room at the girls' dorm along with a writing desk to work on, and meals at the cafeteria. I was very much interested in my short novel *The Story of Allen Hack* which was eventually turned into a short story titled "Sailor From Nowhere." I had also started writing a play called *Interim* about the modern day Cherokee. Thanks to the beautiful setting and the ever so hospitable and interesting Straders, the situation, although not perfect, was very good indeed.

Robin and Lory flew back to West Lafayette the last week in July but the baby was not born until the eighteenth of August. The Harlans, Earl and Dorothy, met them at the airport, saw to their needs, and when the time came, took Robin to St. Elizabeth's Hospital while Lory went home with them. The birth was another very long process, only this time, life threatening, since the umbilical cord somehow wrapped around the baby's neck which could have resulted in strangulation.

I was swimming in the Oconaluftee River with Moe and Doodle Huntley when a messenger came from the business office telling of the birth of Joseph Gagen Stockdale, III whom we would call "Thirdy" during his baby years. I was overjoyed, but when I called Robin and she told of the complications, I knew she needed me and I desperately wanted to go home. Dorothy would stay with her until my sister came, but I asked Harry whether I could leave a week early. He agreed since there would be time to work in an understudy.

When I got home and met "Thirdy" (noting that he had all his toes and fingers and accruements), Robin and Lory and the new baby brother and I were a happy family. Thirdy was beautiful as was Lory, who had reached her third birthday a week before his birth. I was so glad to be home.

Chapter 8

DURING THIRDY'S FIRST YEAR, WHILE he was still nursing and didn't cost much to feed, the average wage in the United States was $3,515 a year. Bread averaged 16¢ a loaf, a dozen eggs was 24¢, milk was 25¢ a quart, gas was 20¢ a gallon—but since the average price of a Ford was $1,955, we walked. I was earning just *over* the average wage, $3,550 a year, plus what I brought in during summer employment at Cherokee. But it was obvious that we needed more money. At one point I remember Robin had to turn in milk bottles and get the 15¢ refund so we could buy a pack of cigarettes.

Dad would come to visit, during which time he would, in his generous and quiet fashion, drive Robin to the mom-and-pop grocery store run by Russ Printy and pay whatever amount we had not been able to pay of the previous month's bill. I finally went to talk to my boss, Ross Smith, who by now felt like the older brother I never had, and ask him about a pay raise.

Ross received his BA from the University of Iowa where he helped pay his way by being janitor of the theatre complex. He also served a stint in New York City working at a settlement house on the Lower East Side—whether for Emma Goldman or not, he never mentioned—and then went to the University of Minnesota for his master's degree. He was hired as an instructor in Purdue's Speech Department in 1942. Within a year however, with the draft board breathing down his neck, he enlisted and went to officer's candidate school in San Diego before boarding a destroyer and sailing to those islands in the South Pacific that had to be taken.

When he was discharged in 1946, he went back to Purdue where he soon realized he wasn't making enough money and would have to get a PhD if he was going to make the university his career. He went to the University of Utah to study under Dr. Lowell Lees, who had been his major professor at Minnesota, and received the degree in 1948, returning to Purdue to head the theatre and to run the Convocations and Lectures program.

Based on his own experience, Ross advised that if I was going to make teaching a career, rather than being an actor or a writer, and make enough to get a car, a house, support a family and eventually see the kids through college, I would have to get a PhD. Since my focus had obviously been on playwriting at Chapel Hill—and during my time at Purdue I had demonstrated that my talent and interest was in directing—his advice was that I should take a part-time sabbatical and get the degree.

Purdue, in order to attract and keep highly qualified young faculty members, often took a vested interest in their obtaining an advanced degree by offering them such a sabbatical. Since sabbatical was usually awarded only after six years of service (with the proviso that the recipient return to the university for at least one year) and awardees received half pay, this would mean quarter-time in my case since I would by that time have been there two and one half years.

What they offered averaged $88.75 a month for 10 months, but I would receive an allowance of $135 per month under the GI Bill, plus all tuition and books. Figuring that we might be able to squeeze by on $223.75 a month for 10 months, Ross pointed out that at least I would have a start on my PhD and could finish it up during future summer sessions.

I went for the idea hook, line and sinker. But not with the idea of "just getting started" on the degree and then spending future summer sessions working to finish it. No way! If I was going to do it, I'd damn well do it in the time I had left on the GI Bill of Rights.

⌘ ⌘ ⌘

I wanted to be a playwright *and* a novelist *and* short-story writer and thought that I could accomplish this within the security of the university where I would be allowed to teach advanced courses, including playwriting and directing. There was only one problem. Most of what was offered for the PhD was exclusively "academic," and that was counterproductive to what I valued most in myself—my creativity. I could not and would not do work that narrowed my view from one hundred and eighty degrees down to one, such as a dissertation on Geoffrey Chaucer's use of the strophe and antistrophe in *Anelida and Arcite*. I wanted to be allowed to do a creative dissertation that would include plays or film scripts that used my imagination and sense of humanity.

The only two universities I found that offered creative PhD dissertations in Theatre were the University of Iowa, where Tennessee Williams had taken graduate work, and the University of Denver. The University of Iowa had an excellent reputation for its writers' workshop, but the theatre was headed by Edward Charles Mabie. There were a lot of crazy stories going round about his loose cannon behavior. I wrote Campton Bell, who had just taken over as director of theatre at the University of Denver. Since I had an excellent recommendation from Sam Selden as to my talent, and my play *October In The Spring* had not only been produced by the Carolina Playmakers but also Off-Broadway, Bell wrote that I could submit two plays and one film script with this proviso: one of the plays had to be historical in both time and place that would force the use of footnotes and a bibliography—in short all the paraphernalia that the graduate faculty understood and insisted on; and one of the plays had to receive production, preferably by a professional company with Actors Equity Association director and actors.

He went along with a pre-registration agreement that my MA degree, which constituted 60 graduate credits, be accepted *in total* and that I would take another 60 graduate credits at the U. of Denver. In addition, rent for a two-bedroom furnished apartment in the veteran's housing in U. of Denver's Pioneer Village bordering the campus would be $50 per month. When all this was agreed to, I wrote a letter to Dean Ayers and requested a quarter-time sabbatical in which Purdue would pay one quarter of my annual salary. In return, I would get the degree, which would qualify me to become a member of the Purdue graduate-school faculty, and offer not only playwriting but other graduate-level courses. And, of course, I would return for another year after the degree was awarded.

I received a handwritten note from Dean Ayers: "I found your proposal most interesting and hope you pursue these plans rigorously. The program seems very ambitious to me and you may find it requires some limitation of scope later." What he meant was the problem I would face after paying the rent and living on $178 a month, or $5.96 per day, for everything for a family of four. When I thought of what Robin faced, making do on this amount, ripped me apart.

If only I could get published...

⌘ ⌘ ⌘

Bertha Klausner had three and sometimes four readers giving their opinions with suggestions of markets for submission. The following are reports on *The Story Allen Hack*.

> In this short novel I felt the author deliberately dragged in as much nauseous slime as possible simply for shock effect. He is often self-consciously poetic and calculatedly obscene. The book is full of cheap dramatic tricks... A great part of it is chaotic, stagey, superficial—surface drama, with no depths.... However, in spite of the foregoing, I am convinced that he has an authentic, if undisciplined, talent.

A second reader wrote:

> Allen Hack, who is in the navy, wanders into a group of army men on the warfront in Europe in WWII. He just happened to be the kind of guy who likes to do unusual things. His philosophy is terrific. You just can't help loving the guy. A crazy, wacky, wonderful story written with sharp insight and depicting war exactly as it is... All I can say is—this is, in my considered opinion a great piece of writing.

John Bender, Associate Editor, at *Argosy*, in a letter dated 9/8/1952, rejected the novella, saying, "despite its many instances of good writing and its accurate scenes of men at war, [it] remained too narrow and limited a piece of work for our novelette length."

⌘ ⌘ ⌘

As technical director in the fall for Gene Kildahl's production of *The Playboy of The Western World,* I could not find this production of Synge's "masterpiece" either relevant or special. Helmed by Yeats and Lady Gregory, history has it rated as one of The Abbey Theatre's best and most controversial productions. The story is of Christie Mahon, who strikes his father in anger and believes he has killed the old man. He runs off to County Mayo to tell a friend and is sheltered by the friend's beautiful daughter, Pegeen. The story of what he has done leaks out and he becomes a hero, not only to the community but also to Pegeen, who falls in love with him. When his father arrives—he was not killed after all—Christie wins even more respect from the locals when he makes another attempt on the old man's life.

Synge, of course, is making fun of the Irish adoration of myth and fantasy, meaning that the play is supposed to be satiric. But I never felt that patricide as a means of illustrating the Irish whim (gullibility), worked; and particularly I did not feel that any of the author's intent was realized in the acting and direction. The result, played as a kind of straight romantic comedy, was simply unbelievable.

⌘ ⌘ ⌘

Needing a little extra money at Christmastime and beyond, and desperate for what only publication could give me—a sense of success—I wrote Mr. Bender and asked him if he really meant what he said in his letter about *The Story Allen Hack,* why didn't he tell me what changes to make to get the story published?

⌘ ⌘ ⌘

That Christmas, Robin stayed home with Lory and Thirdy and I made my annual trip to New York to see shows. During my ten days, I saw Bette Davis in *Two's Company* with young leading man Peter Kelly, formerly Pete Smith from the Purdue Glee Club; Shirley Booth in Arthur Laurent's *The Time of the Cuckoo;* Maurice Evans in *Dial M for Murder;* the incredible dancer/singer/actor Harold Lang in one of the great musicals, *Pal Joey;* Margaret Sullivan in *The Deep Blue Sea,* which would be her last show; the University of Denver student Mary Chase's *Mrs. McThing* starring Helen Hayes; the splashy swimming-pool musical *Wish You Were Here;* Patricia Neal with Kim Hunter in Lillian Hellman's *The Children's Hour;* and a spectacular, albeit a terribly misguided opera updating the Civil War, *My Darling Aida,* with music by Giuseppe Verdi! I also saw young Robert Preston in James Thurber's *The Male Animal;* Tom Ewell in *The Seven Year Itch;* Katharine Hepburn in Shaw's *The Millionairess;* and finally at Circle in the Square, in the Village, Tennessee Williams' *Summer and Smoke* with Geraldine Page. Along with so many truthfully acted private moments, the show did not end until well after midnight. I also saw the film *Come Back, Little Sheba,* which had just opened.

With tickets costing an average of $3 to $3.50, the 13 shows I saw came to under $50 and I made do by cadging a place to sleep via the kindness of various friends, eating *very little,* occasionally being taken to dinner by people like Lou and Nat White who had moved from Chapel Hill to the city, and catching a ride in, and back, with a Purdue student who lived in New York.

I had fun on these junkets. I was in love with the theatre and the movies. But now in addition to loving them, I also considered viewing shows as absolutely necessary if I were going to teach and work in theatre and understand professional standards. Love is never totally altruistic, and I had a keen eye and a good memory for stage business which I used a lot of in the shows I directed. And no one, I mean no one, could have visited New York and seen all these shows for less money.

In February (1953) I directed my second major production at Purdue, William Inge's Tony Award play, *Come Back, Little Sheba* with Katy Neff and Linden Chiles as Lola and Doc. Although not Inge's most popular play, the relationship between Lola and her husband Doc interestingly reveals a profound codependency of two tragic lives, both repressed sexually by the couple's puritanical parents.

The final scene is very moving, very Freudian, and profoundly dark, especially when one thinks of Inge's eventual suicide. I was having a difficult time in casting the ingénue role, Maria, a pretty college student who roomed at Doc and Lola's, and also a young actor for the role of Turk, her Adonis-like boyfriend who poses in brief attire for her art-class drawing. With this problem uppermost in my mind, I happened to be taking the Lafayette bus back to Purdue when I became aware of a young couple, she, blond and pretty and he tall, dark, and handsome.

The bus was approaching the stop where I would get off and run across campus to teach, so I quickly introduced myself and asked them if they had ever been in a play. They had not. I wrote down my name and the location of my office and told them to come to audition that evening. They did, were cast, and both were excellent in their roles. On final dress rehearsal, Tom Tsatsos, who played Turk, had kept on his white socks in "The Discus Thrower" posing scene. Although costumed in the briefest of briefs, he still insisted on wearing his socks. In giving notes I mentioned that since it was winter and Fowler Hall was drafty, it would be okay to continue wearing his gym socks, but of course, he could not do so in performance.

A nice cooperative young man up to this point, he suddenly balked. He would not reveal his feet. Why? He just couldn't appear without his socks on. I would have been surprised if he objected to appearing nude, but I knew from this sudden refusal that he actually would not go on stage unsocked. So, without making anything of it, I simply said, "Okay." And that is the way the scene played throughout all performances.

As I write this, I have a vision of this guy—neither of the two kids from the bus ever did another show at Purdue—reading this, and now 59 years later, the phobia, or whatever it was, of revealing his feet having left him, he picks up this memoir, reads about himself, and calls and tells me what so embarrassed him. Was there a sixth toe? Acne skin from athlete's foot? Had he been molested by a foot fetishist as a baby? What? Not knowing could drive a person crazy .

The other interesting remembrance was that in the climactic scene when Doc goes after Lola with a hatchet, Linden Chiles, who was especially vulnerable and open to truth in acting, almost slipped over the edge.

⌘ ⌘ ⌘

Amazingly, on February 25, 1953 John Bender, editor of *Argosy*, sent a two-page letter giving me comments and suggestions and telling me to make it a short story and "stick to a singular point of view." For some reason I hadn't thought of telling a story in only the first person (heard, saw, touched, smelled, tasted or thought) or third person (he or she heard, saw, touched, smelled, tasted, or thought) or an omniscient point of view (where the author has access to what every character hears, sees, touches, smells, tastes or thinks). I chose to use the third person point of view and this created the most difficult technical problem I had, since Allen Hack (whom the story is about) is seen through another character's eyes.

With help from Robin, I spent a lot of time revamping and shortening the novella to the 20 double spaced pages John Bender suggested. On April 23, 1953, he again wrote a two-page letter giving me further suggestions.

⌘ ⌘ ⌘

One night, sometime after the production of *Come Back Little Sheba*, Linden Chiles knocked on our door at 3 AM. "Tell him this is no time to visit," Robin said. But he was in some kind of emotional state, and I sat him down at our kitchen table and listened. He made very little sense and at one time in his ramblings, he said he was going to kill himself. I laid a kitchen knife on the table in front of him and he broke down completely. Before he left, he had pulled himself together. On reflection, and after our lifetime friendship, I think what I did was right, but I also realize that it was probably very dangerous.

At the Awards banquet in the spring, the Best Actor award did not go to Linden. Best Actress was awarded to Katy Neff, and Best Supporting Actress to Flurry La Sage who played the neighbor lady, Mrs. Coffman.

⌘ ⌘ ⌘

It was in early May of 1953, after the decision had been finalized to start my PhD at the University of Denver, that I received another letter from John Bender saying, "At long last I can report to you that you have been successful in cutting your novella, *The Story of Allen Hack,* down to a short story entitled "Anchors Ashore" which we feel we want to use. The general consensus of opinion here bears out my original contention that it is a very nice piece of work; and we are prepared to offer you $400 for it, subject (as most editorial offers are) to these conditions:...."

He then explained that there were some spelling errors to be corrected, some sentence strengthening needed, and that the death of one of the characters was "too grim," and he would edit the scene and allow the character to live. "I've been pretty close to this story, as you are well aware, and I propose to do nothing violent to your text, but I should like to have your okay on editing it." On the next line, he added, "Good enough?"

You better believe it!

Bertha, who up to this point had no knowledge of my correspondence with him, took $100 as her commission and sent me a check for the rest.

⌘ ⌘ ⌘

I knew we would need transportation to Denver. That spring I bought a 1935 Cadillac for $50—not because it was the perfect car for us to travel in but just because it was so beautiful with its slightly altered imitation of the Winged Victory of Samothrace stretching out at the front of the elongated hood, under which was presumably an engine that I knew nothing about. But the interior was plushy upholstered and roomy with pull-down shades over the windows, plus a specially installed footrest that could elevate one's feet after a shopping spree on Fifth Avenue or Rodeo Drive. And with gas at 20¢ a gallon, why not some New York/Hollywood elegance now that I had an extra $300 check coming in from my writing?

⌘ ⌘ ⌘

The Cadillac actually got us to Denver. Before we even arrived, I had mapped out *exactly* what I had to do, and read up in their current catalogue about the number of credits received for each course and the various academic timetables, such as prelims, comprehensives, and final oral examinations by my graduate committee. In short, all requirements that *were legally binding*.

All my life people have commented about my energy level, medics thinking I was probably hyperthyroid with high blood pressure. But a hyperthyroid diagnosis was never established, and all my life my blood pressure has pretty much been 120/60. I was, however John Wayne on steroids when it came to being a PhD candidate.

When John Bender found out that Bertha Klausner had taken twenty-five percent of his payment for the story, he suggested his agent friend Rogers Terrill, whom I queried in late July from Denver. In early August, Rogers answered that on the basis of my Off-Broadway production, my short-story sale to *Argosy,* and John Bender's recommendation, he would "like to see samples of work." At the bottom of the letter was a P.S., "This agency makes no charges other than the usual ten percent commission on manuscript sales."

He wrote again a couple of weeks later after reading two of my short stories, "Turkey Run" and "The Congresswoman and the Bosun's Mate." He said that the stories were not saleable, qualifying this by adding that the former—which dealt with soldiers in the Korean war and using the major plot element I cannibalized from my one-act play "Turkeys in the Thirties"—was a "good try" and that it had a "nice simplicity," but added that my "handling of character and situation is not quite sure enough to successfully put over your ending," which was having the main character killed trying to hook a turkey for his buddies for Thanksgiving. He suggested I not spend more time on the story at present.

"Congresswoman," he said was a "fresh and amusing situation... a perfect vehicle for the sort of light romance which is so well received by many of our national magazines." But he believed "much of the trouble you've had stems from bad—or at least inadequate—plotting." His suggested change was that I have "a Congresswoman, who during her college days has campaigned with her father. He dies in office suddenly and a Governor makes a smart political move by appointing her to fill the rest of his term." So why didn't I do this? Aside from my work on the PhD, I thought that a romantic relationship between an older woman and a younger man of totally different backgrounds and experiences was much more unpredictable and interesting. What I did not know was that this was a taboo in the slicks in pre-Helen Gurley Brown days. But Roger's point was absolutely right: If I wanted to be a professional writer by starting in the popular magazines, I had to learn—clearly impossible at the time—what was acceptable to their readers.

By September 11th, Rogers had read my novella *The Story of Allen Hack* and said he wanted to read my play *October In The Spring*. He said he accepted me as a client based on my submissions and observed: "I am inclined to think that you do better with more serious subjects."

In late September, he wrote, "You have a fine situation in your 'The Lie,' and I feel that with not too much fixing we should have a saleable story here." He went on to suggest a plot change. In November, he still had not been able to get a copy of my play *October In The Spring* from Bertha, but spent most of this letter on *The Story of Allen Hack* novella.

> You've done some strong writing here, but you're beginning to lose some of the direct drive and clarity which characterized the action in Europe. I've the feeling you're becoming too subjective, and in spots the reader begins to lose himself in Hack's own confusion. It's becoming more a story of mood than movement, and this tends to emphasize the organizational weakness which is more noticeable in your other novel, *The Dark Limbo*. This mood writing may explain the trouble you've had in plotting. By submerging yourself so completely within a character, you lose control of your story. You do the mood writing extremely well, but I am not sure that the average reader, anxious to get on with the story, will be too tolerant of these continued submersions...

He was right, of course. I was truly enamored of the prose-poetry of my favorite author, Thomas Wolfe, and had adapted his short story, *Only the Dead Know Brooklyn*, as a one-act play for one of my classes with Campton. I was also immersed in writing a potboiler since one of the plays for my dissertation had to be of a "historical" nature so that I could demonstrate my knowledge of traditional scholarly research, along with their hundreds-of-years-old reference notations such as *op. cit., loc. sit.,* and *ibid.*

What I wrote to fulfill this academic criteria was suggested by a course I took in Elizabethan and Jacobean Drama, which included the force-fed *Endymion: the Man in the Moon* by John Lyly. My reflection is that in a class discussion, Professor Bob Mead justified the assigned reading of this visual-Sominex, because John Lyly's euphuism had influenced Shakespeare. I, in turn, perversely emulated such overuse of language in a well-made sex farce with stereotype characters satirizing the dishonesty of what has been termed "the cult of flattery" that existed in the Court of Queen Elizabeth I. This would be in total contrast in both style and genre to my other works. And it sure as hell could use footnotes!

In late December, Rogers wrote: "Your novel *The Dark Limbo* has come so close with so many publishers that it would seem time we got down to cases with one of them. Dodd, Mead seems like a good bet, partly because they are so interested in young novelists, but especially so because Ray Bond told me just last week that you are easily the most brilliant young author whose work he has seen in a long time."

In early January, he wrote:

Am much impressed by your play *Interim.* It won and held my interest to the point where I resented interruptions and did not want to lay it aside until I had finished it. I don't feel that I am a good judge of the present play market, but I should certainly like to offer this, and I appreciate your willingness to discuss markets. I have no sound basis for determining in advance how such a play will be received. It is real, it is well done, and it is moving. If it can break through the present day indifference to our neglected Indian problem, it could be successful.

Do you, the reader, have any idea what such words of encouragement could mean to a guy like me at age 27?

About both novels, *The Dark Limbo* and *The Story of Allen Hack,* Rogers wrote, "I little doubt that you will someday become a very successful novelist, but... the chief fault is... you are so anxious to portray the basic tragedy of life... I know you want to portray life as you see it (a rather grim picture, I'm afraid) but you must sell to get started in this writing game. Later on, if you're big enough and successful enough, you can probably write whatever you damn well please."

In early March he wrote, "Thought I'd check with Janet Cohn of Brandt and Brandt, one of the top theatrical agencies in New York, on your play *Interim*. She said it was exceptionally well done but that she couldn't herself guess if anybody on Broadway would go for such a subject." On St. Patrick's Day he wrote: "The news on *Interim* is disappointing… Friedman is very enthusiastic about your handling of the play, but feels almost certain that the Indian subject is too remote to win Broadway backing. As you probably know, Mr. Friedman's reputation as a play broker is pretty close to tops, and I think he knows the current market very well. I think his willingness to handle the play, is in itself, a fortunate circumstance." On April 28th' he said, "Friedman promised to get in touch with you and said he thought your idea of a summer production was excellent and might prove helpful to them in promoting the play here in New York."

Getting a production came about because I had sent a copy of *Interim* to Jack Ragotzy of The Barn Theatre, who by now was making quite a reputation in the summer-theatre circuit. His lineup included ten shows, 13 Actors Equity Association [hereafter AEA] members and 11 apprentices. Jack had responded immediately that he liked the play, that he already had scheduled one premiere, but liked my play so much he would schedule another. I, of course, was not only seeking recognition in the professional theatre, but also to impress Campton Bell by gaining an AEA production, which he wanted as a requirement for my dissertation. And then, at the perfect time, the following was printed on May 12, 1954, in the Bible of show-biz, the national entertainment weekly *Variety*, headlined in their characteristic jazzy show-biz style: "Ragotzy's 'Time' Try, Kalamazoo," followed by… "Production rights to the tentatively-titled *The Time Between*, a new play by Joseph G. Stockdale, Jr., have been acquired by Jack P. Ragotzy, who operates The Barn Theatre, Augusta, Mich. Ragotzy plans to tryout the work at his strawhatter July 27-31, with a Broadway production contemplated for next fall if the Barn engagement is promising."

My short story "Sailor from Nowhere" had come out in the March issue of *Argosy*, and the screenplay of this was to be a third of my dissertation.

Now a production of my play in the up-and-coming Barn Theatre season, plus an interest by Harold Friedman of Brandt and Brandt in NYC, went a long way to help Campton support my candidacy for a creative dissertation. Jack wanted an option of six months on the play, which I decided I would give him, because it would not only help to shore up my reputation at the University of Denver, but because there was a real chance Ragotzy might get some Broadway interest.

By mid-March, the deal was settled with Jack, and in early May, I wrote Rogers to tell him of my decision. In late June, he wrote back: "I'm sorry to report that Scribner's has turned down *Dark Limbo,* but the refusal letter from Burroughs Mitchell, which I am attaching, is by far the most encouraging we've had." Mitchell wrote: "As I told you the other day at lunch, Joseph Stockdale's novel, *Dark Limbo,* doesn't seem to us to come close enough to success. In a number of places it has very real force—both emotional and satirical.... I do want to say, though, that the author of this novel seemed to us a serious writer of genuine ability. We would very much like to see the next piece of work he does."

On July first, I was scheduled to take the oral examination over my dissertation. Four final copies had to be in to the committee three weeks in advance. My Aunt Mary, who had been secretary for Mr. Gray of the Ambassador Bridge in Detroit for some 40 years, was now retired in Florida. I asked her to type the final copy of the dissertation, which she did, including all the footnotes, end notes and bibliography in a professional manner which, if I had attempted the job myself, would have taken several frustrating weeks.

On June 28th, I was so sick with a high fever, swollen lymph glands, and a sore throat that I had to go to the University Health Center where the doctor diagnosed infectious mononucleosis, the worst case he had ever seen. He ordered enforced bed rest in the Center to prevent serious complications to the liver and spleen. I broke down, telling him I could not do that because I had my final oral examination in two days. He was understanding and kind, although he warned me of the risk I was taking. He gave me medications for pain, told me to rest as much as I could, and to gargle with salt water.

I took my orals as scheduled and failed to answer one question about Moliere. But Campton laughed this off, informing the committee that I knew the answer full well, but was just a little nervous. I passed.

The next day we bundled the kids in the '35 Cadillac along with the few possessions we had and left Denver for the trip home. Since the distance from Denver to Allegan, Michigan was over 1,100 miles and we did not have money for a motel, we had to make it in one haul. To avoid Chicago, I chose highway 70 across Kansas, through St. Louis and up to Lafayette, so that if anything happened to the car, I would at least be in known territory. The midday temperature was terrifyingly hot and I didn't dare take the car much over 50 miles per hour. We left at the dot of 6:00 A.M., which would mean that with luck I might make it to Dad's place the next morning about seven or eight.

When we stopped to get something to eat, I thought it had started to rain. But the waiter told us that the restaurant had a tin roof and when a cloud passed between it and the sun it caused expansion and contraction which sounded like rain. Because of the mononucleosis I was probably at my lowest ebb physically. Robin kept us all drinking water she had brought along in jars. The misery was countered somewhat by the fact that I could not help but feel elated that I had passed my exams; we had accomplished what we had set out to accomplish.

Three A.M. was the worst time on the trip for me. Robin and the kids had been sleeping as we passed Lafayette and got on that two-lane highway, 421 north. I was at a point when my eyes would close and then snap open; I was panicked because I was afraid I'd drive off the road. Exhausted beyond measure, I forced myself to stay awake by putting my head out the window to get the night breeze, slapping my face hard. I've driven before while exhausted, but this was the worst experience I'd ever had.

By six, I was on I-94 in Michigan that would take us to Dad's. We had enough gas to make it but not enough money to get breakfast, so we arrived at his place about eight, more tired than I had ever been in my life. As he got breakfast for Robin and the kids, I went to sleep on the cot on the screened porch and was out until mid-afternoon.

⌘ ⌘ ⌘

During the last portion of that horrifying drive I spent time thinking over our experiences in Denver. Some are worth telling:

The day we arrived at our new address we looked around the living room-kitchen combination, and the two bedrooms, and decided not to do any painting, put up any pretty curtains, or make any improvements. We wanted where we were living to remind us daily that we had a job to do that would take over a year, and that our entire focus had to be on that job.

I remember coming home one day and Robin telling me that Thirdy had fast-crawled out the front door, down the two wooden steps, and had climbed up the "A" frame on one side of the swing set and hung by his hands on the crossbar. He still wasn't walking but he was a whiz-bang climber and crawler.

I've always thought that if I were tied up and placed on a floor, not able to move, if I only knew that at a specific time in the future I would be released, I could stand almost anything. The trick was to firmly believe that there would be an end to what we were going through, which sometimes was plain misery.

This was okay for me because that was the way I was and still am. But Robin had to feel the same about our circumstances, and that is not the way she was or still is. At *first* I worried about this, but through it all, she helped me do the things I had to do, took care of the kids and handled the money—what little there was. We bought only a desk and a washing machine, both at the Salvation Army, but the beds, bureaus, sofa, chairs and kitchen table in the apartment were furnished by University Housing. Occasionally the couple next door went out and asked Robin to baby-sit, which she did for a little extra money. Dorothea Smith would occasionally write, and in her letter enclose a $5 bill—$10 at Christmas—which was appreciated more than she would ever know.

At one point we all came down with some kind of stomach flu with high temperatures and vomiting that was so disabling that Robin and I could hardly drag ourselves from the bed to care for Lory and Thirdy. But we made it through and I was back at school in three days.

⌘ ⌘ ⌘

The play by Robert Ardrey, *Thunder Rock,* in which I played the leading role of Charleston, was not a rewarding experience. In it, however, were two guys in the theatre department playing bit parts—about the smallest I've ever seen in any play—whose job it was to carry on my luggage at the play's beginning. They were Michael O'Sullivan, who later joined William Ball's APA Company, and Norman Kean. Michael won the Tony Award for best supporting actor for his portrayal of *Tartuffe* in the Lincoln Center's 1965 production. His life ended in 1971 when he was found dead in his San Francisco apartment, sleeping pills at his side. As for Norman, I'll have much to say later so consider yourself Scheherazaded.

Another remembrance: Sometime in January, Campton called me into his office. He had that sardonic grin on his face when he asked, "How do you strip?" quickly continuing in case I might miss the intended irony. Director George Somes, married to the legendary Helen Bonfils who had inherited *The Denver Post,* called that morning. When my face lit up, Campton looked at me, shook his head and with some weariness said, "You're thinking writing or acting, right?" I confessed that I was. "No," he said gently. "He's 'staging' James Bridie's play, *Tobias and the Angel* at the Denver Civic Theatre and he's interested strictly in eye candy with a good physique to play a walk-on... and welcome to the real world."

The worst period of apprehension I had in Denver was when I had to take my foreign-language examination, which I had scheduled during the winter quarter with a prior written agreement that it would be in Spanish. The Foreign Language Department told us in advance the books from which the selections would be taken to translate. In my case it would be excerpts from two different plays. My thinking was that they probably would not take scenes randomly, but rather would choose from beginnings of one of the acts, probably the first. I found copies of the plays in Spanish in the library, checked out a Spanish dictionary, and Robin, who is very good at languages, helped me with translating the three or four pages from the beginning of *each act* of both plays.

Knowing enough cognates to recognize the various selections, I went to the examination and, thank God, they had indeed taken their selections from the first act of the plays in each book. A couple of days later, Campton told me that I had passed. That was the day that I felt the most relief during the entire time I was there.

This may be rationalization but I don't believe I cheated. The Foreign Language Department at the University of Denver was progressive enough to have as their criteria for passing the student's ability *with a dictionary*, to be able to make a reasonable translation of a foreign language, and to understand some basics such as adjectives coming after the noun. They did not expect the student to be fluent in the language.

The national touring company production of *Picnic* played Denver's Elitch Gardens. I told myself that because I had missed the New York Theatre season that year I had a right to see this 1953 Pulitzer Prize winner. It was directed by Joshua Logan with a brilliant cast, and seeing it was like manna to one starving in the wilderness.

On my prelims, which I took after my first quarter, I misspelled Inigo Jones' name, writing "Indigo" and Campton wrote in the margin: "write correct spelling 100 times." The next morning, I got up very early and went to the bus stop where he got off in front of the Theatre Arts building. With a couple of pieces of chalk and taking my time, I wrote the number and the name on the curbstone; then, following the sidewalk that led to his office building, up the steps, into the hallway right up to his office where I wrote: "100. I N I G O."

He was totally delighted and never forgot it.

I remember only once blowing up. I was in Campton's office talking and something I took as criticism set me off. I yelled, "What the hell more do you expect of me? I'm working my ass off about 18 hours a day, from 6:00 A.M. to midnight and doing the best I can!" He looked at me and smiled, and without an ounce of pity said with what was profound tough-love torn from his guts after years of pain, which he kept to himself without complaining, letting me know I was capable of doing the same: "So what are you doing after midnight?"

One last story about him. In early 1953, Ethel Merman married Robert Six, president of Continental Airlines, and moved to Denver where they resided in the exclusive Cherry Hills Country Club section. Ethel, a native New Yorker, decided to ingratiate herself to this wild-west community by giving a free concert at Red Rocks Amphitheatre, located some miles west of Denver.

On the day of her freefer I happened to pass Campton's office in the late afternoon and on impulse peeked in and asked if he was going to see her show. "Why bother to go clear out there," he said casually, making a mark on a paper he was correcting. "We'll be able to hear her from here."

Chapter 9

IT TOOK A WEEK TO recover but only a day to confess that I was flat broke. Dad knew how difficult it was for me to ask for money. Our worlds were so far apart; he did not understand, and I could not explain, why I needed the degree. He was proud in his own quiet way of the fact that I was now Dr. Joseph Stockdale. For me it seemed just another hurdle jumped in the long-distance race I was running.

Rehearsals for my show would start on Tuesday the 19th of July, while the two-hander, *The Fourposter*, was given a two-week run, leaving us with a blessed 16 days of rehearsal right up to the 8:30 P.M. curtain on Tuesday the 3rd of August. In the meantime, the only sensible thing to do—or more accurately, the only thing possible—was to hang out at Dad's little cement-block house and what was left of the farm, including the creek, the pond, the woods, a vegetable garden, and berry bushes.

The house was cramped quarters but there was not a rainy day and the outside was glorious. When rehearsals started I would be over at the theatre most of the time anyway. In the meanwhile there were relatives—Uncle Dave and Aunt Nellie's kids, cousins Bob, Jean, and Lois, close by—and I am certain that Dad felt genuine enjoyment having Robin and his two grandkids there. He would let Lory pet Jumbo, put the saddle on him, and lead her around the yard, and Thirdy bonded with Dad's dog "Jackie," and fast-crawled around the house and yard with him. Robin always liked

Dad, and he liked her. When the kids were napping she liked to sit out on the screened-in porch and read while I lay on the cot and listened to the sounds of the water splashing over the dam that Dad had built to back up the creek and form a pond for fishing and swimming.

We visited in Kalamazoo with Frank and Olga, Robin's mother and father, and her brother Jim, who was out of the Marines and going to Western Michigan. We drove or walked over to Pike Lake which was less than a mile away, and sometimes we would drive the twenty miles over to the Allegan County Park on Lake Michigan. But mostly we just vegged-out, which Robin, always so confident and relaxed in her own beautiful skin, was so good at, and in those days was so difficult for me. We also drove over to The Barn Theatre to catch Betty Ebert and John Newton in *The Fourposter* while Dad gladly baby-sat.

After Jack got his MA at UCLA, he and Betty moved to New York, and since he had time remaining on the GI Bill, he decided to get his PhD at NYU. He had completed his prelims and all of his course work and was working on his dissertation—forty pages having already been approved by his major professor—when one evening, tired after the summer season and pissed off about something that had to do with referencing, he said to Betty, "For two cents I'd quit the whole damn thing." Betty went to her purse, came back and laid two pennies on the typing table. That was all he needed. He never completed the degree. And yes, we had taken different directions, he heading a first-class 1954 professional summer theatre hoping to get a show on Broadway, and me to Academe hoping to find enough free time to write a best-selling novel.

1954 was a landmark season for The Barn. During the winter, Jack had had a few acting gigs on TV which he found unrewarding and spent much of his time designing a new wing to be built on The Barn, which he fondly named "The Growth." It was an 18 x 30 foot space which would alleviate the necessity of rehearsals being conducted in The Barn's auditorium where we had to fold up chairs after the evening performance to ready the space for the next day's rehearsals, and then set them up again for the 8:30 P.M. curtain. He was now able to put in permanent raised seating in the auditorium; and the box office could rack up and sell tickets for specific seats, rather than having a general admission policy.

Jack knew that the new addition would make The Barn much more valuable, and he and Betty decided to settle in for the long haul. They purchased The Barn and a little over six acres for $16,500. With their talent and work ethic they—and their apprentices—made it possible to pay the debt in six years. The Barn became one of the best known summer-stock companies, not only in Michigan, but throughout the country.

That season there were two new leading men. John Newton was one hell of a good actor and a knockout at comedy timing. His looks were such that he could stretch from a Tom Ewell-type character role of almost any age to leading men roles. The other new guy was the handsome and talented James T. Pritchett, who had graduated from the University of North Carolina at Chapel Hill with a pre-law degree to satisfy his parents and then became an actor. The Barn season opened with a two-week run of *Mr. Roberts,* with Jim playing the title role. It became a smash hit, setting box-office records.

There were 20 characters in my play and Jack would be using all the AEA members, as well as over half of the acting apprentices. Betty played the leading role of Ann, the assimilated Indian girl who had gone off the reservation, gotten a university degree, a job with the United Nations, and a boyfriend, Mike. She was in love for the first time. But before their romance had gone beyond a goodnight kiss at the door of her apartment, she wanted to have her guy see where she came from—her roots—the Qualla Indian Reservation in Cherokee, North Carolina, where he would meet her sister Agnes, brother Lee, and her alcoholic father, "the Chief."

I had recommended Norman Kean from Denver as an apprentice. Jack was impressed with Norm's talent, intelligence and amenable personality, and cast him in good roles in the first two shows. These roles were followed by routine crew assignments on the next two productions. Now, cast in the important supportive role of Ann's younger brother Lee, Norm was chafing at the bit and ready to get his teeth into this stand-out role in my play.

The ad in the Sunday *Gazette* of the other new play which preceded mine had stressed the pre-Broadway production aspect of the premiere, and the critics had responded accordingly: "While it has some interesting moments it doesn't seem worth the effort," followed by "It is a good play, though it is not yet ready for Broadway," and "At this point it appears to be a questionable bet for B'way."

Jack had come to the conclusion that the emphasis in that ad had the effect of putting the critics in an awkward position of predicting a Broadway success, so he was not going down that path again. Instead, he took another route, starting with re-naming my play *Desire Is A Season*.

I was not happy about the title change, but I knew he could design the ad so that the word desire was in a large shimmering font to suggest sex. Just in case there was any question he put "ADULT ENTERTAINMENT ONLY." And below that added: "A lusty new play about the passionate daughter of a Cherokee tribe whose love would not be suppressed!" He then added a third line: "Sensational new play by Michigan's brightest young author!" These three lines and all the newspaper articles not only furthered the sex angle, they appealed for support of a hometown boy with lust in his heart.

Rehearsals were exciting and Jack worked well with the company. He was always specific about rewrites. In addition, I could rewrite a page and hand it to Jim Pritchett who would read—or most of the time, just glance at it. The scene would be rerun with the new material and Jim would be word perfect. I've never known anyone before or since with that kind of photographic memory.

Opening night, Ross and Dorothea Smith drove over from Michiana Shores on Lake Michigan, where Ross was running a summer theatre, and, of course, Robin was there with me. I was excited and happily frightened and pleased when, in Jack's curtain speech, he introduced me to the audience. The show went very well and it got incredible applause and several curtain calls. I was moved by the production and by the actors' performances, and anxious to read the reviews the next day. Mayer of *The Kalamazoo Gazette* wrote:

> Stockdale's frequently moving, tragic story of a Cherokee Indian family in North Carolina is more than a big play. It sprawls, moving in 'giant steps' from skillfully done propaganda about the very real problems of the Indians' racial twilight to the sheer theatrics of an onstage suicide and an over-wrought seduction scene. It's strong stuff ably

written but done with more courage than discretion. His play has a large dose of interesting sociology and too much "kick 'em in the gut" melodrama. That's a large order to force feed any audience. Eugene O'Neill tried it over and over again—and failed as many times as he succeeded. When the show's at its best it recalls some of Tennessee Williams' tinted realism. But the play ran aground on the shoals of Mickey Spillane, and beached on *Tobacco Road*.

Dolliver of *The Enquirer* praised the actors and setting and noted:

Old –timers who turned the police on *Sappho* because her lover carried her upstairs to her bedroom, or were shocked by *Tobacco Road*, would probably pass out completely upon contact with *Desire Is A Season*. In many years of play going, this writer can recall no scene as sexy as the mutual seduction of hero and heroine in Act II and no scene more morbid than the suicide in the same act. It is doubtful that even blasé Broadway would accept either for public presentation...

Norman Kean, a less known member of the company, steals the show as the brother who doesn't intend to be downtrodden because of his race. He looks like an Indian, acts like an Indian, and displays a fine conception of the role.... The first night audience was large and seemed to accept sexiness and stark realism as if accustomed to it. Applause was generous and there were several curtain calls.

I felt sick at heart as I read these. The sections of the reviews dealing with the play did not seem real, especially after the reception the audience had given it. I was too thin-skinned to remind myself that critics such as Alexander Woollcott and Dorothy Parker often tossed the reader a comic zinger with such cracks as, "she runs the gamut of emotion from a to b" more to make their reviews interesting reading than for any real critical value.

Not wanting to see anyone, I walked up to the woods just to keep in motion and try not to think. But moving could not shut down my feeling of sickening personal failure. The misery just kept coming. I had totally believed in my play. I had lived through every emotion of those characters. I was them, feeling all they felt! The hurt was beyond despair or anger, beyond crying which would have released the ache I felt in my guts. I must have walked or just stood still—I know I never sat down—trying to shake off what I felt, but there was no escaping this sense of failure.

When I finally looked at my watch I saw it was just a little less than an hour before curtain. I went to The Growth through the back steps so I could avoid seeing anyone. I did not turn on the lights. I just sat on a bench hunched over and waiting, not being able to find a way out of my feelings. Then vaguely I began to hear the distant sound of the box office phone, technicians and actors coming back for half-hour call. Outside it was approaching dusk and when I looked out there seemed to be a steady stream of cars, their headlights moving on the road and turning into the parking lot.

Hallelujah! That night, and for the rest of the run, we had huge crowds and SRO on the weekend. When I told Jack how I had felt after reading the reviews he sat me down. "How many playwrights get compared to Eugene O'Neill and Tennessee Williams?"

"Yeah, but what about comparisons to Erskine Caldwell or Mickey Spillane?" I asked.

"We did *Tobacco Road* and *A Streetcar Named Desire* three years ago in the same season and both drew SRO crowds. And Dolliver's review was pure box office gold."

Jack told me the story about producing and directing his thesis play *Country Mile* (written for his MA at UCLA) as The Barn's last show of the 1949 season. Dolliver had written that it was as "sordid as *A Streetcar Named Desire*" and described the story as "coarse, with dialogue that reeked with profanity and suggestive words." Jack said he too had been down in the dumps until the show drew more audiences than any other show of the season. Dolliver had thrown in the caveat—something to the effect that "people who were not too upset by foul language and coarse behavior in a play might find *Country Mile* interesting dramatic fodder." And Jack said he finally figured it out. "The old fart was savvy enough to etch his review with enough frowning old-maid head-shaking/tongue clicking disparagement to appease the paper's editor and bible belt readers, but at the same time lace it with the titillating promise of abundant risqué sexual behavior that promised them a throbbing blue-veiner." Jack said he laughed his ass off when the reviewer wrote that audiences who saw *Sappho* would "pass out completely" when they saw *Desire Is A Season*. And then he looked at me, shook his head and said, "Doesn't that tell you anything, *Dr*. Stockdale?"

When Jack Bell's review came out in *Variety* a few days later I was elated: "There is a promise of commercial possibilities in this new play. An unusual theme and background, with which the author is obviously familiar, heighten audience interest...." He, too, mentioned apprentice Norman Kean, calling his performance "outstanding."

While reflecting on this episode in my life, I started wondering about some of the people who were in my show. There isn't much else in life—outside of sex—that I can think of, that is as intimate as doing a show together. It is where actors and director use their emotions and brains to put flesh on the bones of an author's creations. Via Google I checked IMDb (Movie and TV), IBDB (Broadway), and the Lortel Off-Broadway Database on the Internet on the cast of *Desire Is A Season*, and discovered there was no information on eight of the actors in the cast. But a dozen of them are listed and had various kinds of careers in some aspect of show business, and four of them had very successful careers.

William Bramley created the role of Officer Krupke in *West Side Story* on Broadway, playing the show's entire run, and then did the role in the film. He has a total of six pages of credits from TV series and 12 movies.

Jim Pritchett played Dr. Matt Powers in TV's *The Doctors* for 21 years and received a coveted Daytime Emmy Award as Outstanding Actor. On Broadway he was Jerry Ryan in *Two For The Seesaw* after Henry Fonda left the cast, and was also in *Sail Away* with Elaine Stritch

John Newton had the longest and most varied career. In addition to 52 productions at The Barn Theatre, he was in enough TV and films to be vested in SAG (Screen Actors Guild) as a pensioner. John was also in a dozen Broadway shows including 600 performances in *The Best Little Whorehouse in Texas,* as well as Mitch in *A Streetcar Named Desire* with Lois Nettleton. He also did Off-Broadway, notably as The Grave Digger in the Roundabout's 1992 production of *Hamlet,* and Off-Off B'way in any number of shows at the York Theatre He played in more Regional AEA Theatres than any actor I know in both musicals (including Emile de Becque in *South Pacific* and

Frederick in *A Little Night Music*) plus leading and character roles in some 300 straight plays and many commercials and voice-overs.

The fourth person who had a long professional career in the Theatre was the kid who played Lee in my play—the one who I recommended as an apprentice from the University of Denver, Norman Kean.

In the climactic scene of *Desire Is A Season,* Virgil Downs, a lonely and sexually repressed white teacher from the Indian School, commits suicide. Lee, Ann's brother—a Korean War vet who has been making up a course with kindly Virgil Downs, intends to apply for admission to the University on the GI Bill, but is wrongly accused of the teacher's death. He has known the prejudices and abusive treatment of young Indians by the white law enforcement officers all his life, and is now on the run from a posse of newly sworn-in deputies with hounds. He has avoided them by swimming the Oconaluftee River to get back to the trading post where he intends to take refuge in the crawl space until he can safely leave the area and hide in the hills.

With two of the posse outside, Ann's boyfriend, Mike, confronts Lee, making him realize that he will put them all in jeopardy if he is discovered inside "The Post," and Lee decides to make a run for it. He has just gone through a side window and headed for the river to make his escape when his father, the Chief, sodden with drink, sees him and calls out, alerting the deputies.

> Slim whirls and races outside. Lee slips behind a rock. Slim raises his gun. Agnes grabs the gun. They struggle. Ann screams. "Lee! Come back. He's going to shoot." Slim throws Agnes to the ground as Walt, the other deputy, runs up the path to join him. Ann screams again. "Lee. Stop. Don't run or he'll kill you." Lee comes back into sight. He stands in full view. The deputies raise their guns. Ann turns back to the guards, pleading. "Don't shoot! Please don't. He's not running." Suddenly Lee starts to climb up the rocks where he disappears for a moment, then reappears moving to the edge of the rock, his back to them.
>
> Suddenly both deputies have no intention of firing. They lower their shotgun to watch in fascinated horror as Lee leaps.
>
> The sky has now turned from early morning pink to red.
>
> They wait.

"Son of a bitch! Did you see that?"

"Jesus! He stood up there and... from that rock... "

Agnes, Lee's younger sister, wraps her arms around her chest tight as though protecting herself. Ann moves to put her arms around her. Mike stands speechless on the porch. After a long pause Ann turns to him. "Did you see it? (etched in her memory forever.) "He was tall on the rock. His shirt was off. He held out his arms. He dove... beautifully... onto the rocks below.

Jack Ragotzy was not exactly a "method" director—who can be in summer stock?—but when Jack blocked the play's climax, Norman did have a question about his actions: when *exactly* does Lee decide to kill himself? At first Jack wondered if it made any difference when there was so much action on stage. But Norman said he thought a moment of decision was necessary so that, in reflection, the audience would remember it, connect the dots, and it would be clear that his suicide was intended—that his hitting the rocks was not an accident.

⌘ ⌘ ⌘

Three years after that Barn season, Norman Kean was stage-managing the premier of Tennessee Williams' *Orpheus Descending* for its original Broadway run. A year later he stage-managed *The Waltz of the Toreadors*. His third Broadway credit was as assistant stage manager for *A Touch Of The Poet*, and ten days after that opened he married Gwyda DonHowe, whom he met in summer stock in Nantucket. Two years later Norman became general manager of the Association for Producing Artists (APA), a position he held from 1960 to 1970.

During these years, he was connected with a great number of shows in either a managerial or entrepreneurial capacity in various venues. In mid-October 1970, he became the long lease holding tenant of the 499-seat Edison Theatre, converted from the ballroom of the hotel of the same name. There he produced the legendary revival of *Oh! Calcutta!*, a series of sex sketches by Kenneth Tynan, Samuel Beckett, Sam Shepard, John Lennon, David Newman, Leonard Mielfi, Jules Feiffer and others, which ran from late September 1976 through early August 1989, playing 5,959 performances.

In 1978, Norman was 44 years old. His wife, Gwyda, was a year older. They had been married 20 years, had a four-year-old son, an eight-room apartment on the fashionable Upper West Side's Riverside Drive and a summer home in Montauk. In the decade 1978-1988 he spent most of his time managing *Oh! Calcutta!* During this time, his wife's career, which was mostly due to Norman's influence in the theatre, ended and her career in TV had slowed down. It would end with a role in *Another World* in 1981-82.

And now I must go from personal knowledge to an article written by Jeremy Gerard and published in *The New York Times* on February 9, 1988. Apparently no one suspected any trouble existed between Norman and his wife. All the personal information related in the article was based on a first-hand report from a private investigator.

Gwyda was having an affair.

Norman attempted to salvage the marriage by staying away from *Oh! Calcutta!* and became a stay-at-home husband, cooking and giving parties to raise money for good causes. But he also hired a private investigator. When the investigator reported that Gwyda had again visited her lover, his view was that not only was Norman depressed because of her unfaithfulness, she had been a heavy drinker for twenty-five years. He also said he "knew Norman was in love with his wife and could not live without her."

Norman decided on a divorce, the papers to be delivered on Thursday the 14th of January. On Monday, after their son David, 14, had left for school, Norman went to the bedroom and killed Gwyda, stabbing her to death. The maid came at 9 o'clock but didn't enter the bedroom because she knew that Gwyda was accustomed to sleeping late. That afternoon, Norman paid the maid in cash, and gave her three letters, and a tape recording to leave in David's room. Then he went to the roof of the fifteen story building and dove to the flagstone courtyard below.

Chapter 10

WE RECEIVED OUR LAST SUBSISTENCE check on the GI Bill the day before my show closed at The Barn. I was on the road on Monday at 7:00 A.M. headed to West Lafayette in the Cadillac, Robin and the kids staying behind until I found a rental. I got to West Lafayette by noon, went to the office of the *Lafayette Journal and Courier,* and found out from the gal who worked the ads that there was a new one just placed for a house on the West Side a quarter of a block from the little white house we had rented on Wood Street.

I went there immediately. This two-story older house at 129 South Ellsworth Street on the River Road, just off State Street, was next to the Henry Poor lumber company. Floors were hardwood, the interior had been kept up, and after our time in the barracks of Pioneer Village the space was mansion-like: a small covered porch entrance led into the living room with a smaller room in front which could serve as an office. There was a big kitchen with refrigerator, stove and a table and chairs. The upstairs had a full bath with an old-fashioned tub, a master bedroom and two smaller ones—one considerably smaller which would be great for Thirdy's crib, and a room of her own for five year old (no longer "plum-Dum" but "Lory") who would be entering kindergarten.

The rent was $65 per month, walking distance to Purdue, the grade school, and the Printy grocery store where we could get a charge account.

The owner of the lumber company interviewed me, made a call to the Speech Department to confirm that I was on the payroll and was married with two kids, and found me acceptable. I paid the first month's rent (thank god he didn't ask for an additional month in advance) and called a student who owned a pickup truck and had helped me get through my technical direction days. He drove to where we had stored our pathetic furniture, including Aunt Floss' sofa-bed which weighed about twelve tons. We moved it in along with our bed, plus smaller items we had stored. This guy brought his toolbox along, knowing me well enough to know I wouldn't have tools.

We finished work by 7:00 P.M. I grabbed a hamburger at the Triple X and headed back to Michigan, got there by midnight, and we left the next morning. Dad gave me a couple of hundred bucks to get settled and worried as usual—god bless him!—about us getting through till our first paycheck at the end of September.

In the middle of all my work at the University of Denver, I had taken time to write Alan Monroe, giving him a progress report, and raising three points. Would I be promoted to assistant professor? He replied: "Promotions for this year were processed in December and therefore I should not expect to be on the list for the coming year." About an increase in salary: "I have recommended an increase in salary for you beginning this fall. I will not know the exact amount which is finally approved by the university budget committee." And his answer to my third question about teaching playwriting: he "had no idea yet" what courses I would be teaching. That remained to be worked out with Professor Smith "in terms of prospective enrollment..."

He added, "I presume you have heard from Ross that plans are progressing for the new theatre, but we shall have to operate rather primitively since Fowler Hall will come down before the new theatre is completed."

On August 12th, I wrote the official letter to President Hovde informing him that I had fulfilled all requirements for the PhD. I also thanked Purdue, Ross, Monroe, Dean Ayers, and the Board of Trustees for granting me this opportunity, adding that I sincerely hoped that I would be better able to serve Purdue through playwriting instruction as well as my work with experimental theatre and original scripts.

⌘ ⌘ ⌘

I had a letter from Rogers dated July 6th and forwarded saying, "I'm very pleased with the final version of *Allen Hack* and am sending it as is to my friend Burroughs Mitchell at Scribner's. I want particularly to congratulate you on your ending, and in general on your amazing ability to turn out good copy so fantastically fast."

On August 28th he wrote: "I am very sorry to have to forward you the enclosed note from Burroughs Mitchell, for as you see, a decision at Scribner's has gone against *Allen Hack*... He has the feeling that you haven't found yourself, but he seems as sure as I am, that you have the makings of a successful novelist."

Toward mid-September we ran out of money and I sold the Cadillac for $65. Vapor lock aside, she had served us well and I hated getting rid of her. We had to park her on the street and she had sprung a leak, so I had to remember to put a tarp over the roof when it rained to avoid the upholstery in the backseat from being ruined. We were close enough to my office, Lory's kindergarten, and the Printy grocery store to walk, and we didn't feel the need for a car over and above eating. And I just could not ask Dad to kick in any more money.

When the fall semester started in September, I was disappointed that I was once again teaching four sections of Speech. Unhappy about coming back without being advanced from instructor to assistant professor, I was pleased that Ross said I would be teaching a playwriting class during the second semester if he could get it through the curriculum committee. As for my salary, it was raised only $500, to $4,000 per year.

I had scouted around the campus and found what was called the Tower Room—a third floor in the Memorial Union—with a small stage and a seating area that could hold about 75 folding chairs. I wanted to do some experimental productions, and the Tower Room was the perfect venue. When Ross returned from Michiana Summer Theatre he made the necessary arrangements, and since the room was seldom, if ever, used, he got it for us for the entire year. We would be able to put up freestanding light-trees to hold the lekos and fresnels for stage lighting, and we would limit the technical aspects to a minimum, using only hand and set props plus costumes and music. I absolutely loved this room.

Our first production played two different nights and consisted of three short plays each night: *Cracked Record Blues,* which had been adapted by one of the students at Chapel Hill into a play based on a poem by Kenneth Fearing; my adaptation of Dorothy Parker's *Here We Are* about a newlywed couple on a train headed to their honeymoon hotel attempting to hide their anxiety about the consummation of their marriage; and *House Party* about a New York chorus girl invited by a freshman pledge to a Princeton fraternity party who totally blindsides her well-to-do very upper-class date by proving to him that he can't be absolutely certain that the four faces of the bell tower clock are in sync. Juanita Carpenter, Purdue marching band's first Golden Girl, was perfect for the chorus girl.

Our second series consisted of *I've Got an Anchor on my Chest* from a *New Yorker* short story by R.H. Newman, which took place in a chow wagon in the 1930s. A hungry Dust-Bowler hitching his way from Oklahoma to California has several tattoos he is willing to display for a sandwich. The anchor on his chest is a come-on to reveal an in-the-buff tattoo of Mae West on his thigh, which he can make dance with muscle movements, but is booted out of the eatery when he attempts to do so. *Only The Dead Know Brooklyn* was based on a story by Thomas Wolfe that I had adapted, plus an original, *Late Summer '44,* which I had written for a tutorial taught by Campton Bell. These short plays, together, made quite a splash with very simple staging and gave the kids who acted and worked crew an interesting, fun-filled extracurricular activity. I absolutely loved the work.

Money was not plentiful enough this Christmas for me to get into New York and see the best of Broadway. Instead we had a family Christmas at home with a tree and presents. I worked on a theatre novel, and also *A Streetcar Named Desire,* which would go into rehearsal as soon as the second semester started; the play would open in late February.

On January 20th Rogers wrote: "Janet Cohn called yesterday to tell me that Friedman agrees with her that *The Time Between* [title changed because I did not care for Jack's rename, *Desire Is A Season*] is much improved by your cutting and revision. They still feel that they would like to try first for an Off-Broadway production, but both are now enthused about your play and I feel sure will push it in every way they can. If this is satisfactory with you, I'll give them the green light and you will no doubt hear directly from Cohn or Friedman."

February 18, 1955, a letter from Janet Cohn via Rogers: "I am sending you the original copy of Stockdale's play; also the bill for typing the new copies. As you suggested, it can be paid in installments. Among other things, I wrote a note to Arrow, Inc. and they have asked me to let them see a copy of the script. I think they might be interested in investing in it."

From her lips to God's ear! But it was not to be. Her reason for sending the play to them resulted in probably the worst gut-grinding experience I had in my early writing career. Even now, as I start to go over this, my heart sinks.

⌘ ⌘ ⌘

The production I directed of *A Streetcar Named Desire* was presented for three nights in the Purdue Hall of Music on February 24, 25, and 26, 1955. I had a first-rate cast with Karlene Counsman playing Blanche DuBois, Andy Rasbury as Stanley Kowalski, Donald Bain as Harold Mitchell ("Mitch"), and Carolyn White, Stella. The set and lights were designed by Sam Marks—and eventually a picture of the set, which I sent to Sam Selden, was published in the textbook *Stage Scenery and Lighting* (1959) authored by Sam Selden and Hunton Sellman. On the copy below the picture it did not mention me, but did say it was designed by Sam Marks, and the recognition of this creative credit was used as support when Sam made full professor.

On the front cover of the two-fold black-and-white program of *A Streetcar Named Desire* are printed the four lines from Hart Crane's "The Broken Tower" which Williams used as an epigraph:

> And so it was I entered the broken world
> To trace the visionary company of love, its voice
> An instant in the wind (I know not whither hurled)
> But not for long to hold each desperate choice.

In the program note, I wrote: "Without doubt, Tennessee Williams is one of the most important playwrights of contemporary theatre and *A Streetcar Named Desire* is one of the theatre classics. It is for this reason that Playshop, in line with its policy of presenting the classics from all periods, is proud to offer one of the first University productions in the United States of this play."

I cannot find any reviews of the production but it was a knockout, with big houses and outstanding acting. I recall it as one of the best productions I've ever directed; same for *The Glass Menagerie.* My love for both of these plays was the beginning of a lifelong reading of all of Tennessee Williams' work and everything about him in (and out) of print.

The relationship between Sam and me went very well at first. He submitted for approval his rendering and floor plan of *Streetcar* which included, by mutual agreement, a backing of flats which would vaguely look like New Orleans and serve as a sounding board to help the actors' voice to project in the Hall of Music.

For the first technical rehearsal, however, the setting was backed by black velour drapes which did not add any sense of a New Orleans background, and sucked up and absorbed the sound of the human voice. Since Sam and I had gotten along so well up to this point, I never thought he would take offense if I said I hoped the flats would be in place for the next rehearsal. He responded with some annoyance that there would be no flats because he had decided to use velour drops. I said this was not acceptable since backing flats had been agreed upon. He said this was not going to happen and that was that. I went immediately to Ross, who agreed with me and said he would see Sam the next day. Sam essentially told Ross that he would not accommodate me, so Ross went to Alan Monroe. But Sam, who was the good soldier as far as Monroe was concerned, had already been to Monroe, who told Ross that Sam was right. The show would go on regardless of a previous agreement between director and designer. There was nothing to do but accept what was clearly unacceptable, and this gave me an uneasy feeling about the future.

⌘ ⌘ ⌘

In a contract dated March 21, 1955, from the Cherokee Historical Association, Inc., I was offered the job of company manager for the coming season with a rent-free two bedroom apartment in the boys' dorm for our family, and Robin and I would be house parents. I would teach a speech lab three times a week at the Mountainside Theatre to company members and would play William Henry Harrison. Rehearsals ran from June 6th to 24th at $45 a week and thereafter $70 a week for 11 weeks through September 5th. This work would provide me with a total of $860 for the summer. I signed immediately and we looked forward to our summer in the Great Smoky Mountains.

My sister Rae, hearing of this and having been told that we'd sold the Cadillac, gave us the Hudson in which we had traveled west with them in 1948. I offered to pay for it, but she insisted on giving it to us. She and Bill were getting a new one and would not get much for the trade-in anyway. Of course, this was her way of making us feel that we were not getting a handout.

⌘ ⌘ ⌘

Then the devastating news came. In mid-April Rogers wrote:

> I am sorry to report that I have had rather frightening word from Janet Cohn. It seems you have made the almost incredible mistake of using real people in *The Time Between*, without bothering to camouflage them at all. As a result, you have made several important people very unhappy and have exposed yourself to criticism which is obviously based more on emotional involvement than objective opinion.
>
> The attached photostatic copies of the letters Miss Cohn sent me are self-explanatory. She has not lost interest in your play but would like an explanation from you. And of course it will be necessary to change names and perhaps make other changes before your play could conceivably be produced by anyone.

The copies to which he referred were from Paschal Sherman of the National Congress of American Indians and sent to Mrs. Ruth M. Bronson, Vice President, Arrow, Inc. in which he wrote:

> Dear Mrs. Bronson: In my opinion the playlet is a libel against Chief Saunooke and others in the cast of characters, whose true identity have been ill concealed and is actionable at law since, as pointed out by Arrow's correspondent, it was tried out very successfully last summer in the west.... As a general rule, agents, publishers and producers not

only will have nothing to do with a play that attempts to use real people as characters but will see to it that the author never again will impose on them and their craft.

Two days *after* Mr. Sherman's letter was written, Mrs. Ruth M. Bronson, wrote a two-page letter to Janet Cohn, which included the following comments:

> The author has shown a singular lack of imagination, even in the naming of his characters. He has used actual names of living individuals and/or identified them in such a way that it seems to me there can be no mistaking about whom he is writing... While we have not consulted legal counsel on this, it is my opinion that this play is libelous... I am convinced Chief Saunooke would have a good libel case against the author and against your firm for distributing the play.... I should think Mr. Stockdale's portrayal of him could be seriously damaging to his business and to his prospects of continuing as a publicly elected official. The author shows the same type of lack of imagination in giving names to his characters who are government officials, and the same type of false reporting. The Government official in the play is called "Mr. Jennet," The actual superintendent in charge at Cherokee Agency for many years was... Likewise, the teacher in the play who killed himself is called Virgil Downs, while at Cherokee for many years, there was a government employee by the name of... who befriended Indians and counted many of them as his personal friends. I was shocked at the misrepresentation of these men by the author, for I do not think I am far-fetched in thinking these were the men whom the author took as models for his characters in these two respective parts.

What was my reaction? My guts were grinding and I was traumatized because I understood completely, agreed with them on the single charge that could lead to a libel suit against me and possibly affect my advanced degree, my job at Purdue, my future as a writer, and our limited financial resources as a family if it resulted in my contract being withdrawn for summer. I had absolutely no defense and could only think of the old adage, "Life is tough but it is a hell of a lot tougher if you're stupid"—and that is exactly how I felt, totally stupid.

However, I could not understand how anyone could read *The Time Between* and feel that I was maligning the Indians. I was nothing if not sympathetic to all underdogs. But why hadn't I learned from experience not to use identifiable names and characteristics for my characters? After all, I had been through this before with Laura Shaw, the teacher I most admired, who confronted me about using her as a prototype in a play. And in two other cases I used real names for characters in one-acts. I mean, how more stupid could I get?

On reflection I think I can—without rationalization—understand why this happened. First and foremost I did, and still believe, that Thomas Wolfe was right when he wrote something to the effect that a man must use the materials and experiences of his own life if he is to write anything of substantial value. I don't see how it can be otherwise. In addition, the "folk play" emphasis by the Carolina Playmakers inadvertently promoted this. Look what happened after Thomas Wolfe's novel *Look Homeward, Angel* was published. The citizens of Asheville rose up in anger, recognizing themselves as well as all the members of the extended Wolfe family.

Did Thomas Wolfe learn from this experience that he had to disguise his prototypes? No way! After his last novel, *You Can't Go Home Again,* his mistress, Aline Bernstein, was reported to have said that she loved the novel but was it necessary to use her real phone number?

When I was writing, I sometimes used actual names, not wanting to stop the creative flow by taking time to think of fictitious ones. Then as the play went through revisions the names I had used *became* the characters so that I forgot all about the need to change them. This is not a defense for what happened, but however stupid, I hope aids understanding. My absolute terror of a libel suit pretty much stopped me working on the theatre novel or anything else, and my greatest fear was that Harry Davis might hear about all this and revoke my contract. What would we do for money?

And now that I reflect on all of this there is yet another more oblique factor. I had so enjoyed directing *The Glass Menagerie,* the six one-acts and *A Streetcar Named Desire* that subconsciously comparing the rewards I felt as a director with the disappointments and rejections from publishers, I may have been like Pavlov's dog—subject to salivating at the thought of another play to direct in contrast to getting stomach cramps at the thought of all that it takes to be a writer

On April 19th Rogers wrote:

> I have read carefully your long letter to Janet Cohn and forwarded her the original copy. It seems to me that you have successfully defended yourself on all major points

except the obvious and incontrovertible fact that you elected to use names so similar to living people in positions which invited identification with your fiction characters. I think that your Dad Voten character in *October In The Spring* pretty clearly establishes the fact that you used him as a similar character of Chief.... without reference to any living person. What worries me is that two such identical characters in two separate plays also establish a kind of self-plagiarism... I have told Miss Cohn not to spread your letter around but have passed along your permission to use whatever quotes seem reasonably necessary in her efforts to placate Mrs. Bronson.

In May I had a reading performance of a full-length play, *Spring Was Late,* in the Tower Room of the Union. This work was by a student in my first playwriting class, Alice Dowling, a mature woman with a son at Harvard. I found it blissfully diverting from my immediate problems to put all my energies into this activity. This reading started the tradition at Purdue that I had experienced at Chapel Hill: audience participation with views and suggestions after the reading, which was very successful. At least with this I had demonstrated that I could attract enough students to justify the course, and it would become permanent as a once-a-year offering by the Department of Speech.

On May 20th I received the following letter from Janet Cohn. "I was awfully sorry that Arrow, Inc. was so unfriendly toward *The Time Between*. This is going to make the chances of a sale extremely improbable, as I think any announcement of the sale of the play might bring unfavorable pressure from them, and while I am entirely sympathetic to the point of view expressed in your letter, I think that I cannot be very encouraging about the future of a professional production. They returned the play to us with their letter and as far as I know, no scripts were made. Sincerely yours.

⌘ ⌘ ⌘

Robin, Lory, Thirdy and I were at Cherokee for the summer and our situation turned out fine with Harry apparently not knowing anything about *The Time Between* brouhaha. This time after opening night Harry did not come back to give me his notes about my projection. I figured he'd either given up on my ability to project, or maybe he finally realized that he had been losing his hearing for years.

Added to all my writing problems, I had learned in May that in spite of the fact that Ross had supported my advancement to assistant professor for the fall semester, Alan Monroe had not made an effort to do so. Why? Was there some relationship to this and my disagreement with Sam over the *Streetcar* set? I concluded that regardless of the support I was receiving off and on campus, especially from Dean Ayers, Monroe was not going to be supportive of me except on his terms, which basically meant that he would not allow me to go up for promotion until after I had served five years as instructor. He would then want another five years to pass before he put me up for associate professor, which would guarantee tenure.

Ross had told me the best way to get ahead in academia was to get a firm offer from another school and force Purdue to meet what the other school offered. So I started to read the job openings and send out query letters along with a brief résumé. I received several job offers, but it was one in California that seemed most promising. It was at the University of California, Santa Barbara College, and I would be hired as an assistant professor, would be technical director/designer, but would also direct a show a year.

I called Ross at Michiana Sumner Theatre and told him that I wanted a promotion to assistant professor at Purdue, and would accept the other offer if didn't receive it. Ross did not want me to leave and said he would call Monroe. I told him that Theodore Hatlen, who headed the department in Santa Barbara, wanted a firm answer from me as soon as possible and I didn't feel that I could take more than a few days to make a decision.

On the 2nd of August, just two days later, came a two word telegram from Alan H. Monroe: "Release Confirmed." I was thrown a bit off balance by the implication, speed and brevity of this communication, but on the other hand wasn't upset. California was, after all, where almost everyone in academia wanted to get a job, and Santa Barbara was touted as one of the most beautiful and perfect places to settle and raise a family.

⌘ ⌘ ⌘

On August 15, 1955, I heard from Rogers. "I hope the summer has gone well for you and that you have been able, perhaps through Mrs. Bronson's daughter, to straighten out your difficulties with her organization."

I was so traumatized by the threats of legal action that my recollection of the meeting with Mrs. Bronson and her daughter—which took place in Cherokee—is clouded. I presented my case sincerely, was apologetic and explained the changes I would make, and stressed that my sympathy was all for the Indians. I believe I made a good impression on the daughter.

In any case, neither mother nor daughter acted in such a manner as to make me feel defensive. In fact, my remembrance was that they treated it rather lightly, seeming to want the issue to go away so there would be no problem. In light of the congeniality of the meeting, I believe that the daughter must have convinced her mother not to make any trouble. Since the two had come to our apartment in the men's dorm, they also met Robin and the kids, and the meeting was so absent of conflict—more like a nice visit from friends—that I was thrown totally off balance. How could the threat in those two letters, triggering visions of me being clamped into leg irons in a chain gang with Paul Muni, suddenly be spoken of as a minor frivolity in a *tête-à-tête* over pink lemonade? I was still troubled, although Robin tended to pooh-pooh my worries and sided with Rogers that indeed it was all a "tempest in a teapot."

Was Higgins right? It's disconcerting why a woman can't think like a man!

After the closing performance of *Unto These Hills*, we got an early start and were back in West Lafayette prior to midnight on the 7th of September with tons of work to do the next day getting ready to leave for California. Our lumber company landlords let us leave what furniture we had accumulated—I hated leaving the desk that I got at the Salvation Army—and did not charge us for the partial month of September. There was a big sentimental farewell party given me in a nearby field where the students knew they could drink without being entrapped by the campus police, and the next morning we left for the new adventure—California, here we come!

Chapter 11

IT WAS NOT A LEISURELY trip since the first day of classes was less than a week away, but we spent four nights in motel rooms and had just enough money to eat before getting settled. We took Route 66 across the desert into California in darkness, and then up the coast road to Santa Barbara. I called Ted Hatlen as soon as we arrived. His wife, Edna, who was in real estate, or had friends who were, was prepared for us.

The first place she showed us overlooked the Pacific and was as beautiful a house as I had ever seen. It was listed for $200,000. We went through the entire house and grounds and I fell in love with it, but after fantasizing about living there the rest of our lives, listening to the Pacific Ocean and bathing in the sun each day, I had to tell Edna that we would need an inexpensive rental. She explained that the down payment was only $10,000 for a veteran who could qualify for a GI thirty-year loan, and that our monthly payments would actually be pretty low. But no, no, no, that house was not for us.

Edna—probably thinking back to the time she and Ted left Indiana for their dream job in Santa Barbara—had been looking around and was prepared for all eventualities. The next house was a Spanish-style bungalow in midtown. To get there you crossed the Pacific Coast Railroad tracks on which fast trains headed two hours south to L.A., and headed up the Mesa, from where one could look out over the Pacific Ocean in all its blue wonder and see the Channel Islands. Looking east, one saw the foothills and the umber-colored magnificence of the Santa Ynez Mountains.

Halfway to the top of the Mesa, at 1230 West Valerio Street, sat a white stucco bungalow with a dull red tile roof. There was a nice cement driveway and well-manicured front lawn which had a built-in underground sprinkling system. In the quarter-acre backyard were fruit-bearing orange and lemon trees, and a small building that at one time served as a chicken coop that I saw as a place where I could write. Inside the house were two bedrooms, one bath, a living room with fireplace and a furnished kitchen, plus a live-in back porch. There was a bed in the master bedroom and a few pieces of furniture—two of which we still have.

Edna was very persuasive about buying rather than renting since a starter-house like this went for $25,000 and could be gotten for $1,000 down. With a twenty-year GI loan, the monthly payments would be less than any rental we could find. The only problem was we didn't have the down payment. I called Dad and explained the situation: I needed to borrow $1,000. He had objected to our move, but he said he would go to the bank and see if he could mortgage a part of what was left of the original 100-acre farm. He wired the money that afternoon, we stayed overnight in an inexpensive motel, and the next night we slept in our new home.

Santa Barbara was indeed all that it was advertised to be. Driving south on Highway 101 you could see the panoramic curve of the blue Pacific and Santa Barbara Bay with yellow sand and stately palm trees with high up foliage; and in the sky, always and forever, comforting great white fleecy clouds.

The University of Southern California, Santa Barbara College was a dozen miles to the north on Highway 1 and was being built on a former Marine base that carried the distinction of being the only piece of USA that was shelled in World War II when a Japanese submarine lobbed in a few before scooting away. I'm certain there must have been at least one new college building but in truth I can't remember it. What I remember were the Marines barracks in which a junior theatre student, David Hale Hand, jerry-rigged a small theatre of sorts for the shows, and classes were held in adjoining barracks.

I thought of the times Allen Fletcher and I criticized Purdue University's brick-factory exteriors but believe me, I now looked at this Santa Barbara campus with its awful impermanence, and it made the Purdue's campus look like Oxford. Further, no organ in my body was ready for this year-round perfect weather. Now however, having gone through many winters of my discontent with the wind-chill below zero, I look back on such minor inconveniences as the campus's impermanence and Santa Barbara's weather quite differently.

⌘ ⌘ ⌘

Robin, now four months pregnant, struck up a good relationship with a neighbor lady. I had to use the Hudson auto Rae and Bill had given us to get back and forth to school so Robin had to plan grocery-shopping trips carefully when I was home. Lory was in first grade and we did not have a television set, but Robin's temperament and genius for adjusting to whatever—how else could she have managed all these years with me?—allowed her to take care of the kids, the checkbook, the cooking and washing (we bought a used washing machine) and, of course, to come up with plenty of reading material.

At school, I taught a couple of courses in Speech plus a beginning course in Stagecraft. My first assignment in the theatre was to design the set, costumes, and lights for an original play written by Ted Hatlen. A lot of this, of course, was extracurricular evening work when I could get crews to work on the various assignments. The experience I had in high school, summer stock, college, plus what the Purdue kids taught me, was excellent, but I had never before had the chutzpa to stand before tuition-paying students and pretend I knew a thing about teaching set construction, lighting and costume design. These kids were presumably going to teach Speech or English in California high schools and be responsible for the junior and senior class plays.

Fortunately, while at Cherokee the lighting designer, Jessie Jacobs, had a copy of the 1948 edition of Milton Smith's—he headed Theatre at Columbia University—textbook on play production, which had a big section on design and technical matters. Since Jessie knew I was going to be teaching this material for the first time he gave me the book. It was an absolute godsend! Brander Matthews, who wrote the introduction to that first edition, put it exactly right when he said the book's content was "intended to guide the faltering footsteps of the novice and supplied practical directions for 'putting on a show.'" Unlike Purdue where there was a great deal of know-how and interest in the area of technical theatre, only one student at Santa Barbara matched it.

David Hale Hand kept in touch long after he graduated, but then we lost touch. Recently I gave David one of those "are you sitting down?-voice from the past" calls and he filled me in about his highly successful career, sounding as full of energy as he did 55 years ago. The kids in my classes were terrific. They gave me a gold Oscar mounted on a wooden base on which was inscribed "Outstanding Service/ Theatre/ U.C.S.B.C 55-56 /Joe Stockdale." If I can turn my neck enough, I can see it at the top of a bookcase as I write this.

⌘ ⌘ ⌘

I was glad to get a letter from Rogers dated the 29th of September saying:

I have talked with Janet Cohn and she has promised to write tactfully to Mrs. Bronson -- though she is by now annoyed by the lady's meddling and particularly so by her presuming to suggest the deletion of that perfectly inoffensive sex scene. What's more important, perhaps, she still thinks very highly of your play and has promised to get back to work on it. She says not to worry about changing the names now. They can be switched at any time-when and if she succeeds in finding a producer. I suggested she re-approach the one she said was interested last spring.

⌘ ⌘ ⌘

An event I vividly remembered in those early months in Santa Barbara was when our Provost, Clark G. Kuebler, went to New York. On Sunday, November 7th, *The New York Times* printed a brief story headlined: EDUCATOR

Arrested on Morals Charge, which told of Dr. Kuebler being arraigned on a charge of felonious assault by Detective Eugene Kelly of the vice squad.

Kuebler was quoted as saying that his arrest was "a gross mistake." Magistrate Hilda G. Schwartz set his bond at $25 and a hearing on Thursday. Detective Kelly said that Kuebler had stopped him on the street, asked for the time, invited him to the Biltmore Bar for a few drinks and then up to his room, "where he made an immoral proposal." When Dr. Kuebler attempted to run from the room, the detective stopped him; Kuebler struck Kelly, causing the detective to handcuff him to a chair.

The story printed on the front page of *The Chicago Daily Tribune* was accompanied by a picture of Kuebler and under banner headlines—Prof. Insists He's Innocent in Sex Case—said that when Kelly approached him on the street, Kuebler introduced himself as "Karl Kress, a shoe-manufacturer representative" and added that "Kelly, married and the father of two children, is a veteran officer of five years in the Marine Corps and has been a policeman for three years and a pre-law student at New York University," while Kuebler was "a bachelor who lives with his mother... and served as a layman in various parochial, diocesan, and national capacities for the Episcopal Church."

These stories hit Santa Barbara and the University like a ton of bricks and little else was talked about while Kuebler awaited trial. On November 11th *The New York Times* printed: Educator Upheld in Morals Case. The article noted that "several hundred spectators" were present, and after the trial Dr. Kuebler said, "he would have to discuss with his attorneys whether or not to bring charges of extortion against Detective Kelly."

The next day, *The New York Times* printed a brief article to the effect that allegations against detective Eugene R. Kelly of the Commissioner's morals squad were under investigation, and that Kuebler had been cleared of "disorderly conduct and felonious assault." When asked if charges had been made against the detective, Commissioner Kennedy's spokesman said, "The allegations are under investigation."

Finally, on December 18th, *The New York Times*—under a headline Kuebler Leaves Post—and the sub-heading "Character Assassination Forced Move," wrote that Dr. Kuebler "angrily denounced" the "character assassination" that forced his decision. The fact that the case drew national attention to Kuebler's prominence in the field of education and that "no mention of the case was made when the Board of Regents accepted his resignation..." noting that the publicity given to "the false accusations had done me irreparable damage" but he was determined that "his personal tragedy not stand in the way of the university's future" and thus was "formalizing and making irrevocable his resignation."

⌘ ⌘ ⌘

Now, skipping 57 years ahead, I have been saddened by the news of the death of playwright Romulus Linney. Rom shared an apartment on the Upper West Side with my friend Ed Loessin, and I sometimes crashed on their sofa when I was in New York. Although I can't claim him as a close friend, he certainly remained alive in my memory.

With my background of using real people for characters, I was struck while reading Rom's *The Love Suicide at Schofield Barracks* when I came across a character with the name Edward E. Roundhouse. I instantly recognized his back story as that of Clark G. Kuebler. When I contacted Rom he was surprised that I knew about Kuebler and said that no one else had ever brought this connection to his attention. Yes, the prototype of Roundhouse was Kuebler, and Rom told me the circumstances of their meeting.

Rom, an Army draftee and private, was stationed at Schofield barracks in Hawaii.

He met Kuebler bending an elbow in a bar and was dazzled by the man's knowledge, especially of Greek drama. Their evening ended with Kuebler inviting him to lunch the next day. They became friends and Romulus accepted more invitations to lunch, and more talk including words one might hear while hanging out under a tree near Areopagus in Greece during The Golden Age.

In *Schofield Barracks,* the character Roundhouse is a witness at an informal inquiry about the double suicide of General Michael and his wife, Sheila, at the Officer's Club. When the officer in charge inquires about his background, some of Roundhouse's reply includes the following:

I was president of two American universities. After a very distinguished education in classical studies I graced several advanced faculties, and in due process... turned my hand to university administration. In 1945, I became president of Triton College in Ohio and in 1951, president of the University of the Southwest.... In those lost days of my academic glory, I traveled, often... then time up, I returned home, to give my incoming freshman class my most stirring speech on the advantages of being an American, of the endless possibilities therein appertaining, of their duty to the very best in themselves, and after that, promptly took myself to New York, and in a perfectly respectable hotel bar, I met a young man who thought me equally charming, we adjourned to my room, where he turned out, of course, to be cruising for the Vice Squad. He arrested me, that little Benedict Arnold, whose legs, by the way, I can still remember, o perversity of memory. Those were the days of terror, you recall, when you were probably not merely a homosexual, debauching poor innocent policemen, but also most likely a Communist, since both vices were obviously intimately connected. When I got out of jail, what the Hearst papers in Chicago didn't do to me, the faculty and board of trustees at Southwestern University did.

Making this connection was closure to the story of what ever happened to Provost Clark

G. Kuebler, of Santa Barbara College. His brief unrecognized reappearance on Broadway as a prototype took place on February 2, 1972, when Rom's *The Love Suicide at Schofield Barracks* previewed for seven performances, opened, played for five more and closed after some very bad reviews. And as far as I know, only I connected the dots.

⌘ ⌘ ⌘

December 5th, Rogers wrote: "It was good to get your fine long letter and to learn that you will at least have a draft of the new novel ready by the first of the year. Why not let me read it at that time and judge whether or not it shows enough promise to show to Burroughs Mitchell? Mitch is one of my oldest friends in publishing and if the novel is sufficiently impressive I would not hesitate to let him look at it even though it might still need more work."

I asked Ted Hatlen that if it was within the divisional secretary's duty to type a professor's scholarly articles, why wouldn't it be okay to have her type my novel? Ted agreed, with the caveat that she should do so only if she had free time. She wasn't thrilled about it, but agreed to give it what time she could. This never worked out because I don't think she wanted to do it, so I ended up typing the 350-plus page novel myself in the little chicken coop behind our bungalow on Valerio Street.

On December 28th, I delivered a paper in Los Angeles at the American Educational Theatre Association convention. My subject was the huge influx of veterans guaranteed an education by the GI Bill of Rights, who were granted advanced degrees in acting, directing, design (sets, lighting and costumes) and playwriting. I urged my listeners to rabble rouse for equal recognition of creative work for their dissertation/theses up through the PhD. Such work must be recognized by administrators as on a par with the *op. cit., loc. sit. ibid.* scholarly research required for those in the humanities for tenure-track appointments, promotions, and increases of salary.

Ross and Dorothea came to Los Angeles for the convention and to visit us in Santa Barbara. Ross asked me whether I would come back to Purdue if I received an assistant professorship and more money than I was making at Santa Barbara. "Yes," I replied. We had a great reunion and when they left I knew that when I went back to Purdue I would not only have the promotion and raise, it would not be long before Theatre would split from the Speech Department. By April 1958 The Loeb Playhouse would be completed and I would be the artistic director of the Experimental Theatre.

⌘ ⌘ ⌘

On January 27, 1956 Rogers had finished reading my new theatre novel, *The Spirit and the Fire,* and wrote:

> I believe you have the making of a fine novel… it so successfully presents the comprehensive and exciting story of a Broadway play in the making that I decided Burroughs Mitchell should see it now, with the understanding that you felt it might need some further work. I had lunch with him yesterday and since he was anxious to read it, I gave it to him… Whatever happened to it—and I believe it will make a successful book—it shows throughout a maturity of thought and perceptive adult tolerance which was completely lacking in *Dark Limbo* and, to an almost equal extent, in *Allen Hack.*

After reading *The Spirit and the Fire*, I believe that you could now rewrite both of those novels and so improve them that both would sell—though I am not suggesting that you tackle any such project at this time. Later, when you've authored a successful novel or two, such rewrites might prove both profitable and satisfying.

One more thing—I think your novel deserves a stronger, more basic title than *The Spirit and the Fire*. Perhaps something as simple as *Broadway Play* or *The Playmakers*—or perhaps even *Opening Night*.

⌘ ⌘ ⌘

How did I feel after receiving this letter while I was already up-in-the-air-crazed waiting for the new baby to be born? I was ecstatic! I was against the title change because I thought the titles Rogers suggested were trite and uninteresting, whereas my title, rather than limiting the subject—theatre—expanded it and made it more universal. For me, spirit and fire were a metaphor for what got actors through opening night, just as it got soldiers over the top and on to the next trench.

Rogers had established a good relationship with Mitchell and they were not shy about adding their points of view about what constituted good writing based upon their knowledge of the market. After receiving Rogers' letter my hopes were high about this novel's success. And no amount of money could equal the thrill of publication.

About this time I was *desperate* to feel some kind of acceptance that went beyond what Robin already gave me. Like most writers, I wanted encouragement, plus, of course, feedback on spelling and grammar errors, clichés, and technical matters. But more important I wanted discussion on the substantive issues of story and characters.

In West Lafayette, there were three women whose opinions I most respected: Alice Dowling who had taken my playwriting class; Dorothy Harlan, a first-rate actress and the wife of a colleague; and Page Karling, who taught English part-time at Purdue. I decided to send a copy of the novel for them to share. Alice wrote a two-pager, some of which is below:

I just finished reading and I want to write while it is still hot. First of all -- it is GOOD. Good style, wonderful pace, and you are really saying something. When it is *you* talking it is really moving. The theatre atmosphere is grand -- authentic -- the reader believes in it. The plotting is good -- it all falls into line. At first I was put off when you inserted the play. It changes the pace so completely. But after I got used to it I liked it. I think, on the whole, it adds depth... Can't tell you how another reader would react.... The characters of the players have variety and you have carried through their stories.

About sex -- there is a lot and it is the hard-hitting kind, but it is my belief that it along with cigarettes and liquor fits into this world of tension... therefore, I felt no striving toward sensationalism on your part -- it all seemed to come naturally...

Well, Joe, what can I say? It is the most interesting novel I have read in years. It is so much better than *The Man in the Gray Flannel Suit* that if you do not make a million I shall scream. I think you are on your way and I am proud of you. I am positive of publication.

Later, Alice called me and said Dorothy Harlan brought the book over and she was almost in tears – said it was hard to be objective – wondering if it could possibly be as good as she thought it was. Page also raved, said it puts her work in the dark; she considered it really professional. So relax. Your worries are over.

Page Karling wrote seven and a half pages with hardly any margins, which obviously has to be cut. But I include all her points of view, since she figures importantly in my story—as well as my family's story—as a lifelong friend who took a genuine interest in my work and in me.

Joe - I read it in one sitting - five hours - and I have a lot to say.... First, let me disqualify myself as an objective critic. It was utterly impossible to forget that you wrote it - you're on every page - and my opinions cannot be impersonal. What judgment I pass on Nick, I pass on you. You must understand that. If an author is his own worst critic, then an author's friends are the second worse. You say you don't bother about minutiae. I did, because except for a mighty few sweeping generalities, the only things that bother me are details, things that a good eraser can correct.

Can I just throw this at you as it occurs to me?

The technique is pretty damn near flawless. You handle these people going on and off the scene as if you'd been writing slick professional stuff all your life. I'm constitutionally against the overworked flashback but I accept yours, because it isn't done so briefly, exactly to the point in each case and not belabored. The dialogue rings as true as a tuning fork.

... Let's take the play first... I think it is entirely unnecessary. Note that last word. Unnecessary. It adds nothing to your story... OK?

I think your pin-point vignettes of background, appearance and characters, are excellent. I like the way you simply present each character with a complete caption as to who he is, why, what he's doing, what he looks like and so forth. Wonderful....

Is Abbie put in for a change of pace? For honest sentimentality as it realistically exists in the theatre? Because that's what she does — Introduces the only note of tearful pathos... If you must cut, take out the doctor's office scene. I knew she had cancer the minute she doubled up with pain....

I like the title, but doesn't your quotation put the emphasis on acting? You're talking about the whole intimate psychology of creating theatre - writing, producing, acting, standing-by, - you're not limited to acting... let the title stand on its own feet as relevant to the entire story.

I like it, Joe. I like it very much. I think it's fantastically good by the standards and comparison with amateur drivel. I think it's solid and skillful and taut and says something beyond the mere plot and I could pick up any ten books off the West Side Library shelf and find it better than eight of them.... I do not think it's the great American you-know-what. But then, neither do you, I am sure.

I think her critique reveals one hell of a lot of the love and care that she always felt for me. She ends by saying that "any second-rate proofreader could correct it up to publication shape in a couple of days. If Terrill doesn't sell this one for you, I'm going to stop trying to write and go back to making doll clothes."

⌘ ⌘ ⌘

Our baby was born on February 13th while I was off teaching. The neighbor lady drove Robin to the hospital. Although late in arriving, he weighed 10 pounds. We decided that since we already had a Joe we might name this one after my dad's brother. I called Michigan and asked cousin Bob Stockdale's wife, Gail, if they intended to have any more kids. If not, was it okay for us to name our new addition to the family David? She said that was fine. We gave him the middle name of James in honor of Robin's brother.

It's always hectic when a new baby is brought home from the hospital. Lory and Joey seemed to like him okay and I hung around the house for a couple of weeks except for classes. David was as remarkable and loveable as the other two, but I was determined that this would be our last. I was 31 years old, which meant that he would start college about 1975, when I was 50 and thinking of retirement. It's amazing how we think of our future when we're young.

In a letter dated February 28, 1956 Alan H. Monroe wrote: "In a conference yesterday, Dean Ayers authorized me to reappoint you as assistant professor of Speech beginning September at a salary of $5,500, for the 1956/7 academic year."

Rogers forwarded a letter from Burroughs Mitchell written in March.

Dear Rogers: Joseph Stockdale's new novel, *The Spirit and the Fire*, seems to me to show a considerable advance in craftsmanship over his earlier work. He knows the theatre and all his detail about the making of a play reads most interestingly. But... the book needs revision. For one thing, it needs to be cut.... As to the play itself, I'm troubled by the way he renders it in full. I don't think most readers will stay with that rendering.... What troubles me most of all about it is that while all the characters are competently handled and several of them - the blond in particular - are quite good, no one in this book seems to me fully to take hold of the reader. With none of them does the reader become deeply involved. One does not care as much about the people as about the production and I think that's a lack in the book. But I don't know just what is to be done about it.

Of course it was the play that was the protagonist of this story, and each character's

objective was to make it succeed against all the obstacles. That's why in the birth of a play it takes spirit and fire to do so. This was what I liked and thought unique, rather than the usual single point of view (I or He) novel that the vast majority of readers were used to.

Being susceptible to opinions of others, I was pretty much depressed about Burroughs Mitchell's point of view and tried to avoid thoughts about it. Thanks to my lucky stars, it was during this time that I directed the department's major production, presented in the famed old Santa Barbara landmark, the Lobero Theatre.

The Rainmaker was a hot title. In our production a very talented Miriam "Mimsy" Birch played Lizzie. She later became "Miss Santa Barbara" and had a long career, starting with her wearing a fish tail as a mermaid for Bill Burrud Productions, and eventually directing and writing for *National Geographic* TV productions. This should have been predictable since not only was she a knockout, she also had a D-cup sized brain.

I remember the technical rehearsals in the dark and dank of the old Lobero Theatre, with David Hale Hand in charge of the set and lighting—away from thoughts about my novel—as among my happiest times in beautiful Santa Barbara. In addition, I enjoyed getting to know Win Park, who directed a production of *Medea* for which I was technical director, and Lory played her first role as one of the children. Win was later hired at Purdue but lasted only a year because of personal problems caused by an impending divorce.

I also vividly remember a first-rate production by the Santa Barbara Repertory theatre company who did Ibsen's *A Doll's House*. It blew me away with its interpretation—which I later used in my own production of that play—emphasizing not solely Nora's liberation as a woman but her husband's tragedy as a man conditioned by social norms of the time, unable to escape this conditioning.

⌘ ⌘ ⌘

On March 12, 1956, Rogers wrote:

I returned *The Spirit and the Fire* to you on Friday, first class mail, so you may have it by the time you receive this note. I'm glad you've been working on the revision and shall be able to return it sometime soon. If I think it sufficiently improved I'll either give it to Mitch for another reading or offer it to some other publisher, but if, as you suggest, I think it needs further fixing, I shall return it to you again for additional work.

As for titles, I don't feel that *The Fourth Wall* would mean enough to the average layman though it has possibilities. *Back Stage* and *Curtain Time*, and the others of that kind seem trite. *Hour of Eternity* has weight and authority and teaser value. Though it doesn't very clearly indicate theatre, it might be the best bet.

⌘ ⌘ ⌘

Sometime that spring Dorothy, the department secretary, did not show up for work and we learned that she had been committed to Camarillo State Mental Hospital in Ventura County. It was some distance, but I drove down to visit her and was struck immediately by the view as I turned off the coast highway and drove east. The first things I remember on that drive were the telephone poles! Crucifixes holding sloping-in-the-middle lines as far as the eye could see. These poles reminded me of the poster and ads for *A Streetcar Named Desire*. In the upper left corner the same telephone poles; crucifixes diminishing in perspective to out-of-sight endlessness in the dead hills.

I imagined what it was like for Blanche Du Bois to experience approaching such a hospital and the horrors that happened inside, and yet be led off to one after her climactic struggle against the nurse and doctor. Much of my feeling stemmed back to seeing *The Snake Pit*, Camarillo State Hospital being one of the sites where the film was shot. At that time, the hospital was close to being overcrowded with 7,000 patients. It was a snake pit, with doctors giving lobotomies, and hydro-therapy in ice-packed bathtubs, and I could only imagine the types of people who worked there.

Nothing I saw as I approached the sprawl of buildings appeased my apprehension. At the end of a hall I looked into a ward through a wire cage to where Dorothy lay. I tried to stay objective, but when Dorothy was led toward me and we went to one of the rooms to "talk" with a nurse in attendance, my feelings only grew. During our brown-bag lunches at school I never observed any mental instability. And if there was, could I ask questions about why she had been confined? No. All I could do was talk about nothing, nothing important, nothing I really wanted to say; just nothing. I could lie and say she looked good and that I was sure she would be well enough to go home soon.

I did take her hand and said that we missed her at school, and that all the kids had asked about her and the faculty would be glad to have her back. And then there came a time I simply could not think of anything else to say. Emotion welled up in me. Saying that it was close to the time traffic would be heavy north to Santa Barbara, and holding back from taking her into my arms and hugging her, I left.

I never saw Dorothy again and don't know what happened to her—whether she was ever released or not.

⌘ ⌘ ⌘

On April 12th Rogers wrote:

For the most part, I think you have done an excellent job of tightening and shaping your manuscript. The removal of the verbatim play scenes has, of course, helped a great deal, but the improvement goes far beyond that basic need, and your novel is much more cohesive and for the most part much more real and moving.

Unfortunately, I don't think that Walter Hackett's death scene is or can be quite as moving without the detailed play background, but I don't know what can be done about that.... I must confess that I am also a little worried by the sense of inevitable tragedy which hangs over so many of your characters in their last scenes. This concern has nothing whatsoever to do with the soundness of your work as a novel, but comes from a bitter knowledge gained through actual experience that the average publisher, unless he is convinced beyond reasonable doubt that he is about to publish a totally noteworthy work, is more inclined to favor the up-beat ending.

On May Day he wrote again:

As we both half-expected from Mitch's original reaction, Scribner's has refused *Hour of Eternity*. He said in effect that the book had been greatly improved by cutting the long play sequence, but he feels that the characterizations of too many of the story's people lacked real depth and were in some instances more inclined toward types than real people. He adds that though the center of the story is the production, rather than any one character, he feels there should be deeper interest developed in the people who make the production.

⌘ ⌘ ⌘

Before we left Santa Barbara I got a big send-off from the kids; it was "roses, roses, all the way and tears and cheers and good-bye Mr. Chips."

The trip back was not boring because even though this was the fourth time I had taken Route #66 since 1939, this "Mother Road"—as Steinbeck named it in *The Grapes Of Wrath*—was constantly changing. It took Robin and me five days to drive with the three kids to Dad's place where I paid him back the money we had borrowed to buy and sell the house.

Robin and the kids stayed with Dad and I went to West Lafayette to find a rental. Very little was available on the West Side, but we did not want to live in Lafayette proper. We wanted the kids to have access to the West Side schools. I looked at what we could afford and got an older house at 414 North Salisbury that had three bedrooms upstairs used for student rentals with a private back entrance, while downstairs we had a three-bedroom apartment. The location was great: about three or four blocks to State Street and the Triple X, I could walk to school, it was close to the kids' school, and the student rentals would pay much of our rent.

The downside was that the place looked like a slum. There was very little backyard, we had on-street parking, and worse, there was no space for me to use for writing. Fowler Hall had been torn down; Ross's convocations office was in the lobby of the Music Hall, and no space was available for theatre faculty there or in the building where the Speech Department was located. Regardless, we were glad to be home.

On June 21st, Rogers wrote that he had not had a report from Western Printing because there was a writer's conference in Santa Fe that half their staff attended and would not be back for a week.

> In the meantime, I am glad you feel how you do about a quick sale on *Hour of Eternity*. It is still at Doubleday, but if they refuse it I am strongly tempted to try for a quickie at Gold Medal, where I just placed another book which had been refused by many of the hard-cover people. I took Bob Amussen at his word and sent *The Dark Limbo* to McGraw-Hill, where it is still unreported... I hope you have a pleasant, productive summer.

⌘ ⌘ ⌘

In mid-summer Harry Davis called to tell me that he had to let the actor who was playing Andrew Jackson go because of a serious problem and asked me if I could come. This was a Monday afternoon; I would be playing the role the next night. Of course, I already knew the lines from playing in that scene as an Indian, so all it would take would be a refresher look/see at the script on the way down.

Getting settled in our rental had taken some extra money, and I desperately needed a place where I could write. Harry offered me $75 a week, plus board and room and transportation. We decided I should take the job. As it turned out the best I could do was to get to Asheville at 6:00 P.M. the next afternoon. Kai Jurgensen met me and drove me directly to the theatre where the show was just starting. I made up, was fitted into the Andrew Jackson costume by Suzie Davis, practiced the fight with the actor playing the Indian who tries to kill me at Horseshoe Bend, and before I knew it, my cue came, and I was on.

When the show ended cast members came to congratulate me. Harry arrived to give me two notes: "Joe, tomorrow night you gotta be louder" and "You know that line where Jackson says, 'I got a dang nail in my boot?' We cut the word 'dang' because members of the Andrew Jackson Society of Tennessee said it sounded like "damn" and claimed Jackson never swore."

Andrew Jackson never swore! Gimme a break!

⌘ ⌘ ⌘

On August 23 Rogers wrote me c/o *Unto These Hills*:

It has never been my intent to limit you to the so-called popular themes, but I feel very strongly that you would have been selling long before now if you could have sincerely interested yourself in something a little less spectacularly off-beat than the several things you have so far shown me. I've shown you enough publishers' reaction to *Hour of Eternity* to indicate pretty clearly, I think, that it was basically your decision to make the play itself your protagonist rather than to build your novel around a central character that has made this one more difficult to place than such a novel should be. Now that I have put this on paper, I wish you would at least give it some further thought and write me again before going further on this new project.

⌘ ⌘ ⌘

This was to be my last year at Cherokee. Robin, the kids and I had enjoyed the summers we spent there with a wonderful group of theatre folks. Louise Fletcher, who was a student at U of NC at Chapel Hill, was in the cast, and many nights after we finished the show we would have a sloppy-Joe at the canteen, then go up to the day room in the girls' dorm and play bridge, Louise and me against the Gordon brothers. Sometimes we played so late that the brothers would drive us to Bryson City for an early morning breakfast.

In 1975 Louise received an Academy Award for her role as Nurse Ratched in Ken Kesey's *One Flew Over The Cuckoo's Nest*. As I watched the Awards I was aware that both her parents were deaf-mutes and had raised Louise and her siblings to communicate in sign language, and knew exactly what was happening when she "signed" a special message for them in her acceptance speech. She was a wonderfully talented and pleasant gal without any affectation, and tolerated my bidding with an abundance of patience.

The highlight of all the mistakes made in my five summers with *Unto These Hills* happened that summer. When the old Shakespearian actor Mr. Henry Joyner, who had never made a single mistake in all the years he narrated the show, introduced the author, Kermit Hunter, in the beautiful well-modulated voice he made the perfect spoonerism: "Please welcome the author, Mr. Hermit Cunter."

On the bridge backstage waiting to go on, we all fell to the floor shrieking and rolling about in hysterics.

Chapter 12

I ENJOYED THE BEGINNINGS OF CLASSES at Purdue, the faculty meetings and going to football practice with Ross. There is something special about fall and the death of the green leaves and grass, and the vital energy and hopeful promise associated with the first semester of an academic year on a college campus. Nothing could daunt my spirit about this return to Purdue, not even the endless waiting and the emotional ups and downs—the yo-yo existence—of a positive message from Rogers followed by yet another rejection.

Enclosed in a letter sent by Rogers was one from Jean Crawford, Associate Editor at Rinehart dated September 20, 1956:

I'm sorry to be returning the *Hour of Eternity* to you. We have had a number of readings on it and certainly found it to be a readable book, if not a completely satisfactory one. The idea of putting on the play is an interesting one for this *Grand Hotel* type of book. Its drawbacks, we feel, are a flatness of style and the total lack of humor. This didn't worry me personally as I regard actors as a fairly humorless lot, but some other readers were quite upset by it. I hope you will place Mr. Stockdale's book but if you do not, we shall be interested to see his next manuscript.

Rogers' letter that enclosed the above was dated October 4th:

I talked with Jack Goodman, of Simon and Schuster today and he tells me that they are very anxious to expand their fiction list, so I told him I would send him *Hour of Eternity* on the promise that he would give us a report in two weeks or less. Despite our several turn downs, I still feel that this is potentially a good novel and I am still hopeful of finding a publisher who will share my enthusiasm for it.

⌘ ⌘ ⌘

My writing was on hold because of full attention to my fall production of two one-acts: T. S. Eliot's, *Sweeney Agonistes* (1932) and Edna St. Vincent Millay's *Aria da Capo* (1920). Getting to know an author when directing his/her play became a lifetime habit. Once introduced through the play, they become a special kind of friend, and during the years that followed I would accumulate various bits and pieces of information as one does with any friend. The following was gathered during and after my production of "Aria."

I knew Millay's most famous, "My candle burns at both ends, it will not last the night, but oh, my foes, and oh, my friends it gives a lovely light!" but didn't know that she had said it. I was fascinated to find that she was an early feminist. In high school and college, and later in life, she had sexual affairs with women; her husband (she married Eugen Boissevain at age 31) did all the household duties and supported them. They had an "open marriage" in which he too had affairs and she, believing in equal opportunity in her choice of sex partners, had an affair with George Hill Dillon, a dozen years her junior and Pulitzer winner in 1932 and editor of *Poetry* magazine from 1937 to 1949.

At various times in my life, after I heard the news of a tsunami, war, earthquake, plague, tornado, hurricane—whatever—I'd read that verse in Millay's "Epitaph for the Race of Man" which I had slapped into my "favorites" file whenever I needed a quick fix in my waning belief in man's survival. The poem tells of a primitive man who experiences an earthquake and with "dread and dismay" sees his bamboo home sucked into the vortex. That afternoon the sun calmly sets...

> *Days pass; the ashes cool; he builds again*
> *His paper house upon oblivion's brim*
> *And plants the purple iris in its roof*

Aria da Capo's setting consisted of props: a banquet table covered with a long cloth and two tall-backed chairs; foodstuff for the table along with a single rose. At rise, two stock characters from the *Commedia dell arte*—Pierrot and Columbine—are dining and when she disclaims herself as an actress he reminds her, "You are blond, are you not? You have no education. Can't act? You underrate yourself!"

If anyone in the theatre needs a play with five characters, good but not complicated lighting, costumes that will take talent and skill to design and construct plus a little money spent at your local fabric store and collecting stage props, you would enjoy working on this play. It should definitely be done on its one hundredth birthday. I can assure you that its point of view on human nature will be just as timely in 2020.

Eliot's *Sweeney Agonistes*, a short 20-pager, was the most daunting and challenging I had encountered as a director. It was actually a fragment, or an unfinished play, and Eliot's first attempt at dramatic writing. When you boil down the plot of "Sweeney" what have you got?

It's a short piece, perfect to play last on this double bill, but how in hell will I direct it if I don't know what it means? Eliot gives its genre as "an Aristophanic melodrama." Does Eliot know what he is talking about?

"Sweeney" is in verse with everyday language, including slang, and an early twentieth century jazz rhythm. None of the endless research helped me so I chose to do it with a chorus line facing front and sometimes dancing to the rhythms, and delivering the lines directly to the audience. That may or may not have been "right" but it did hold the audience for the 20 or so minutes after *Aria Da Capo*. And in truth, none of Eliot's major plays are remembered and only one had a substantial run—the original run of *The Cocktail Party*—and that was mainly because of its cast and staging. What T.S. is known for is the musical *Cats*, based on his *Old Possum's Book of Practical Cats*, which ran 7,485 performances on Broadway and made him rich. Go figure!

⌘ ⌘ ⌘

Rogers wrote on December 11, 1956:

"This will show you that at least I am still trying. *Hour of Eternity* has been at Random House for almost a month now and I am once more mildly hopeful. I am also hoping that the Christmas recess will give you time to finish the synopsis of your new book and send it in to me."

This was the longest lag between letters in our relationship and indicates exactly what was happening. My focus, of necessity—how often could I beat myself up for failure?—was switching from writing to directing. This time it was the December production in the Purdue Hall of Music, which followed without interruption my direction of the two short plays.

The Desperate Hours, a novel by Joseph Hayes (who was born in Indianapolis and a graduate of Indiana University), started out as a thrilling page-turner about a brutal killer, Glenn Griffin, his brother, and a third inmate who escaped from the federal prison at Terre Haute, Indiana, and, at random, selected and held hostage, a family in an upscale Indianapolis suburb.

After publication, the novel was quickly adapted for the stage by Hayes and won a Tony Award as best play of the year. Its cast included Karl Malden as the father and a young Paul Newman as the sociopath killer convict. Even before the Broadway run of 212 performances ended, the film was being edited by director William Wyler with an aging Humphrey Bogart as the killer, and Fredrick March as the Father. It won a 1956 Edgar given by the Mystery Writers of America for distinguished work in their genre.

If name value and close proximity to where a film's story takes place gets attention, doesn't it seem obvious why I would want Purdue to be one of the first universities to produce this play? Although I didn't know it when they took my Introduction to Theatre class that fall, two footballers, Doug Streff and Gene Salaskie (who would be co-captains of Purdue's Big Ten team a year later), along with Don Rosenberg (whom I knew before my year in Santa Barbara) would be damn near perfect for the convicts, Streff especially because he was lithe and had a kind of nervous intensity. We also had an older man, Al Culver, who would be fine for the father, and Schorling Schneider, a kid from Indianapolis' Ben Davis High School, was right out of central casting for the role of Ralphie.

Yet this was the worst production I ever directed. Why? Very simple, and it didn't take any reflection to come to this conclusion. In fact, I called the cast together just prior to curtain on the final performance and told them where I had gone wrong and urged them, if possible, to try to kill any emotional recall stuff I had imposed and to pick up their cues and play the show loud and fast.

My mistake was falling in love with the idea of giving dimensionality to the killers and trying to eke out understanding and sympathy for them. It didn't occur to me that no one gave a rat's ass about how or why they got to be killers—they just were. End of story. *The Desperate Hours* was a cliff-hanging melodrama asking only one question: will the family get through this nightmare alive?

So how did I go about royally screwing it up? We didn't just sit around intellectualizing about the killer's back story and what kind of hell prison must have been for the poor guys. Oh, no! I got on the horn and called the warden of the federal prison at Terre Haute and got an appointment for us to visit the very prison they escaped from. What did the prisoners have to eat? How much sunlight and exercise did they get? Were they allowed conjugal visitations from wives and sweethearts? How about an interview with someone on death row just before they go to the electric chair?

The warden must have thought I was a nut case, but since I was a university professor he figured there was no point in the prison getting a bad rap by disallowing higher education to take place, and so pretty much give us full access. In addition I probed the actors to find the author's "objective correlative" (to toss off a little T.S. Eliot) in order to evoke sympathy and if they found none, they could search, and hopefully find, something in their emotional memory. If that was lacking, I urged them to invent imagined childhood horrors: being spanked by their teachers, going to bed without supper, or being pulled from their mother's breast before they had quite finished supper! Above all, no one was to bother with such tawdry commercialism as feeling they had to pick up their cues if they felt more like picking their nose. In short this must have been the only production in history that dealt with hostage-taking murdering convicts that so induced sleep that it was an effort to listen to the next line.

In addition, I disliked Sam Marks' set which turned out to be a heavy-handed two-story well-constructed box that stood alone in the center of the Music Hall stage and seemed to cry out for something resembling the exterior of the neighborhood such as other houses, trees and shrubs. To me, the setting was more an object, an engineering feat of construction. However, I did not insist that Sam change it.

⌘ ⌘ ⌘

Robin and I and the kids had a great Christmas with the student roomers on vacation and the house to ourselves. She baked a huge turkey refraining—bless her—from any symbolic comparisons to my recent production. Dad came for a couple of days, Page Karling invited us to a terrific after-Christmas party at which time, still believing *Hour of Eternity* would be published, she suggested that I apply for a Purdue Research Foundation grant to work on it, or, start a new novel. And a few days later as a climax to 1957, we went to Ross and Dorothea's New Year's Eve party in which Ross always got the family shotgun (remember he was a duck hunter), went out on the front porch, and fired it into the stroke-of-midnight sky.

⌘ ⌘ ⌘

In a letter dated January 16th, Rogers sent his view on the synopsis of a new novel I had been working on which included some of the story of the secretary at Santa Barbara who was committed to Camarillo State Mental Hospital and would eventually morph into a play called *The End of the War.*

I am very disappointed to learn that your new novel will be so largely concerned with human maladjustment, frustration and bitter tragedy. I have, of course, sensed your predilection for this type of thing and there is always the chance that you will be able to develop the solid characterization, emotional insight and honestly motivated dramatic impact which alone can overcome the natural publisher's resistance to such a theme. Judging from the synopsis and from your previous work, I can honestly say that I am not at all optimistic of your success in this venture...

I had taken Page Karling's advice and sent in a proposal to the Purdue Research Foundation asking for a summer grant to research a new novel. On February 5th, I received a letter from Director Ralph A. Morgen saying that my request was among those which the Council found that it could not recommend.

I had to think of some way to get myself fully employed on a 12-month rather than 10-month basis.

⌘ ⌘ ⌘

As soon as the second semester started I held auditions and cast Jean-Paul Sartre's *No Exit* for a late February showing in the Tower Room. I loved the play, which had been done on Broadway a decade earlier lasting for only 31 performances (the Main Stem was never very receptive to French intellectualism!) It was basically an agitprop piece for existentialism, the characters residing in what they eventually found out was Hell. And after an hour or so of talk and little action, they came to the conclusion that "Hell is other people."

This doomed-to-be-disconnected roundelay of the three characters illustrated the essence of the post-WWII fashionable philosophy—that the human condition boils down to the unfortunate fact that existence *precedes—in* fact, *trumps*—essence. In short, *you* know who you are but who you are never jibes with the default summing-you-up by others, which, like it or not, becomes your essence. Was this an "objective corollary" for my life? I saw myself as a novelist, but I had no novels published so, was my hell not to be recognized by others for what I was?

A young woman who was not enrolled in school but whose husband, Eddie Black, was an engineering student, auditioned. Obviously she was talented and very pretty, but there were only two women in the show, and Karen was not at all right for Inez, the lesbian, and looked too young for Estelle, the nymphomaniac.

When I posted the cast outside of Ross' Music Hall office, Karen Black was there waiting. Seeing that she was not cast, she broke down and ran into the ladies' room. I felt badly but there was nothing I could do. Ross' secretary later told me Karen had spent much of the day crying in the john. I think this was one of the few times I ever saw an actor openly reveal genuine and deep disappointment about not being cast in a role—and such openness was truly sad.

That spring Karen got her break. Ross directed *Ten Nights In a Barroom* and cast her as little "Mary Morgan, the drunkard's daughter" who dies and is seen ascending to heaven. Most theatergoers today think of such flying scenes as originating in *Peter Pan*, or if they're young and rich, *Spiderman*. Sam Marks, the show's designer, was wildly happy at the prospect of lifting Little Mary from her death bed and flying her straight up into the flies of the Hall of Music.

The author of the play, Timothy Shay Arthur, was a prolific writer with over 200 publications to his credit. His greatest success, *Ten Nights in a Barroom and What I Saw There* published in 1854, was quickly turned into a play, and proved to be a major success for well over half a century.

Ross decided that he would play the play straight, meaning he would not satirize it or make fun of the Delsartian method of acting. He feared that his choice was problematic, because the acting might look hammy, and the play itself seemed hopelessly outdated. Not to worry! The Purdue faculty/student/town audience, quite used to weekend cocktail parties, got the joke with no need to gild the lily, and showed their pleasure with gales of laughter and applause at sermonizing lines such as "Lips that touch Liquor shall never touch mine!" In short, they joined in the spirit of the play and hooted when Little Mary, accompanied by heavenly music from the Purdue Glee Club, was hoisted into the flies.

When the show was taken on the road, I drove five members of the cast—including Karen—to Kokomo. Used to the hilarious reception it received from the Purdue crowd, the actors were stunned to hear no laughter and indeed, audible weeping at the death of Little Mary. Driving back, their consternation soon turned to light heartedness, and by the time we reached Lafayette they were a merry band of giddy troupers.

In dropping off the students at their place of residence the last one just happened to be Karen Black. Still in high spirits about the performance, she told me that Eddie was out of town and asked me if I would like to come in.

It was possibly just an offhand remark, but I didn't think so. She was lovely, we were both in high spirits and I was attracted. I had felt sadness by her reaction at not being cast in *No Exit*. I had experienced young women students coming on to me occasionally—at Santa Barbara, Mimsy Birch and I had carried on an innocent flirtation—but I hadn't given it much thought. In this instance I did. I was married and deeply in love with a beautiful and intelligent woman. We had three kids. I was sexually satisfied and very happy. But life happens! That moment happened. She was quite close and I wanted to kiss her but I did not. And I couldn't help but think as I drove home what it might have been like. So like Jimmy Carter, I only lusted in my heart – this time.

⌘ ⌘ ⌘

February 14, 1957 Rogers wrote:
 I admire your courage in coming back so quickly with another outline and I am again impressed by the terrific energy with which you tackle these things... I think your selection of a contest-winner's wife is an excellent idea and certainly there should be a good novel in such a woman. I'm afraid, however, that Kay Maning as an interest-worthy person falls a little short of this mark, and I don't think that her husband makes much better material for use in such a conventional plot as you have deliberately chosen. Both may be typical of their times, but I'm afraid you have made them, perhaps deliberately, so immature as to be almost totally lacking in interest, except in one of those clinical type studies which lay bare to the morbidly curious reader all of those innermost secrets and intimate personal foibles.

Of course I couldn't say this at the time but on reflection I asked: then how why was Oprah's TV show such a success? The rest of his very long letter detailed in no uncertain terms that he was totally against this story and that the people were "almost incredibly immature" and "so completely blind as to be inordinately stupid." Both were "completely selfish" and the wife sought the "pleasure and thrill of an affair, without the costs." He concluded: "I'm sorry to be so negative, but there isn't much else I can say."

Of course, I was pretty well knocked out by this letter. In late February, using my original title *The Spirit and the Fire,* I decided to send that novel to

Bobbs-Merrill Company located in Indianapolis. I knew full well that this was circumventing Rogers but decided to do so anyway. They had published William Styron's first novel *Lie Down In Darkness* in 1951, and when I had submitted *The Dark Limbo* they'd kept it for a long time before rejecting it.

On March 1st, I received a notice of receipt of the manuscript from Anne McDowell of Bobbs-Merrill saying: "Thank you for your manuscript... and we shall be glad to give it our most careful consideration and will let you knows our decision as soon as possible."

I'm not certain if there was any communication between publishing houses and agents but on March 27th, Rogers wrote:

> I feel very badly that I have not been able to be of more help to you during these past several years, and I certainly would not blame you if you had decided by now that some other agent might do a better job. I've enjoyed working with you and I am not in any sense hinting that I'd like to terminate the relationship. It had been so long, however, since I sent you that last harshly critical letter that I have become concerned.... In any event, I'd appreciate knowing your plans.

About the same time as I got this letter I got my teaching contract for 1957/8: My tenure-track assistant professorship salary would be $6,000 for 10 months.

On April 9th, Rogers wrote:

> Buz Wyeth, of Harper's, has just given us a quick reading of *Hour of Eternity*, and although he thinks the manuscript would need a terrific amount of work to make it publishable, the idea interests him and he would like to meet you when in town. I have set up a tentative luncheon date for the three of us on Friday the 19th. I am looking forward to meeting you after all these years.

The very next day, April 10th, he wrote again: "Buz Wyeth has taken the time to put his reactions to your *Hour of Eternity* on paper with the idea that having them and thinking them over you will be in a better position to discuss the manuscript with him at lunch on the 19th."

Wyeth's comments were:

> ... the whole thing lacks restraint, subtlety, discipline, not in plotting and length, but in selection, in motivation and action, in too many characters, in too many distractions.... It is still a good idea for a novel, but to make this version of it into something

publishable will take a great deal of work... The novel needs a hero, a central focus, predominantly sympathetic and likeable, or an engaging rascal (the character Roger for one, Mickhouskie for the other).

⌘ ⌘ ⌘

It was good to meet Rogers face to face at a little French restaurant and I found Buz Wyeth energetic, intelligent and very much set in his decision that my story should emulate the form of Scott Fitzgerald's *The Last Tycoon*. Had I read it? No, I told him, I was familiar only with *Tender is the Night, This Side of Paradise* and, of course, *The Great Gatsby*.

I was not very forthcoming at this luncheon. In the first place I did not really know what to order at a classy French restaurant and wasn't very hungry because I was nervous. I basically I kept my mouth shut and was a good listener, agreeing with almost anything either Rogers or Buz said.

I hadn't been to NYC to check out the Broadway theatre for some time and decided that this was the perfect opportunity to do so. I thought to myself that I would probably see an increase in the price of theatre tickets but that didn't happen. I saw Rosalind Russell in *Auntie Mame* (with Peggy Cass as Agnes Gooch, and Polly Rowles as Vera Charles) which opened at the end of October. The top price for an evening performance in the orchestra section was $6.90 but you could get tickets for $4.05 ($3.45 and $2.90 seats were "completely sold out"). At Wednesday or Saturday matinees, an orchestra seat cost $4.60 but the least expensive seats in the balcony were $2.

I saw Frederick March, Florence Eldridge, Bradford Dillman, and Jason Robards, Jr. in O'Neill's *Long Day's Journey Into Night*, which had opened five months earlier and is one of the four great American plays of the 20th century and provided one of my greatest evenings in the Theatre. Because of its length it had a 7:30 curtain and played only six performances a week. The cost ranged from $6.90 to $2.90. Tickets to *My Fair Lady*, which had opened in March the previous year but still had Rex Harrison and Julie Andrews as Higgins and Eliza, ranged from $8.05 to $2.30.

I also saw the musical *Damn Yankees;* Tennessee Williams' *Orpheus Descending; Separate Tables; The Tunnel of Love;* Shaw's *Major Barbara* about to close after a six-month run (but still with Charles Laughton as Undershaft, Glynis Johns as Barbara, and supported by the likes of Burgess Meredith, Cornelia Otis Skinner, and Eli Wallach, among others); and a final show about to close, Jean Anouilh's *The Waltz of the Toreadors*.

Nine Broadway shows for which I had great seats—ordered in advance via US mail with a return-self-addressed-envelope with a 3¢ stamp, spending less than $50. I stayed the week at the Claridge Hotel for something like $35, which was opposite the Astor Hotel on Broadway and 44th Street. Theatre buffs eat your hearts out! And to think that *New Yorker* critic John Lahr (arguably the best theatre critic still standing) paid $250 for *Spiderman* without a single name in the cast—at least a name any legitimate theatre person would recognize.

When I returned home after this wonderful trip and studied Fitzgerald's *Tycoon, I* found that if I told the story from Mickhouskie's point of view (as a "more amusing, delightful, ingenious, raffish, and rascally character" than I had written) and used a combination of the "I" *and/or* "He" *plus* third-person-omniscient as Fitzgerald actually did, rather than a singular point of view, I would have to toss the work I had done and start afresh on a story about the production of a Broadway play where the conflict was between either the author, the director, or a big-time producer. I knew this was a possibility, but I also knew it was a total overhaul that would take me a couple of years—the same time as it took me to write it in the first place.

I *did*—I swear I did—try to write an outline plus sample scenes but I just could not get it right. For me, the story was still about getting a play on the boards from the point of view of those most concerned. I don't believe I was being stubborn. Going to lunch with Buz and Rogers was a great experience and I certainly appreciated the time, money and energy spent on me for the trip. But every time I rolled a blank sheet into the Underwood I just sat there and felt the same way I felt when I went to the whorehouse in Norfolk. I just couldn't get it up.

On June 6th, Rogers wrote:

> I am much happier with your new outline, and I think your opening characters are fine. They have gone down to Buz Wyeth today and I'll let you know as soon as I have any word from him. Will you send me additional copy as you do it? I'd like to have more on

hand in the event that Buz feels he needs more to get you a contract. I am hoping that this is it, Joe, and that *Hour of Eternity,* once sold, proves to be the first of many.

> Rogers forwarded Buz's comments on June 17th:
>
> I am sorry to say that Joe Stockdale's seventy-five page revision of *Hour of Eternity* is not what I hoped. In general, the total impression is too pat; too slick seemingly too quickly envisioned and put down on paper. In particular, Mickhouskie is too crude and unattractive to appeal, and there is too much of Joe Malbee, whose thoughts and problems I found dull... The idea remains a good one, but I think the treatment requires more thought and much more subtlety and restraint in execution. If you want Joe to take his time and take another crack at it with these comments in mind I would be glad to look at it again.

I worked hard; it is hard work to write when your heart is not in it. That summer of 1957 was a difficult time for me. I was without a paying summer job but Robin had saved for just such an eventuality; we were getting along on as little as possible to make the money stretch until that first paycheck at the end of September.

Robin drove the kids up to Michigan for a vacation with Dad and to go to the beach, and I stayed home writing and minding the house where we had three guys rooming upstairs for both summer sessions, thank god! I wrote with discouragement and knew it was no good. Finally, I had to do something else or go nuts. I decided to direct a play and got some of the kids I knew to be in it.

S.M. Behrman's *No Time For Comedy,* a high comedy—my first in that genre and also the first and only show I ever directed in the round—was done in one of the barracks Purdue erected during World War II and used by the theatre throughout the rest of the century. Originally staged on Broadway in 1939, it begged the question: with the world facing another world war, wasn't *this exactly the right time* for comedy? Contemporary, smart, literate, well written, well structured, and sophisticated, I enjoyed being in the company of Behrman's characters, their speech, milieu, dress and manners; all upper-class theatre people. And oh what a joy it was to get away from what I was breaking my brain doing—trying to write something in which I was no longer interested.

I had first-rate actors in the cast: John von Szeliski, Karlene Counsman—who had been so incredible as Blanche in *Streetcar* and who was now and forever after Mrs. John von Szeliski; and a newcomer, a brunette beauty named Jo Hulley who was married to a guy in the Air Force who was on active duty. There were a total of seven cast members and I found blocking in the round with audiences on all sides and entrances and exits through the aisles very difficult. I kept asking the actors for too much movement in order for the audience to see their faces. Finally I knew that the blocking was arbitrary and awkward and I cut back, discovering that less was more and hoping that if the scene was fairly long with the actors' backs to half the audience that they would remember how the actors looked.

We used the light trees and instruments and a portable light board which had been stored while the Loeb Playhouse was being erected, and I got someone to help me with hand and set props. The space was not air-conditioned, it was mid-summer and our program was a single-page mimeographed sheet. But I loved the work and I pretty much decided that this was what I wanted to do rather than being a writer. In addition, thoughts of a regular summer theatre started to germinate in my head along with my being hired on a twelve-month salary schedule.

⌘ ⌘ ⌘

The opening show of the 1957/8 season in the Hall of Music was John Patrick's *Teahouse of the August Moon,* which had premiered on Broadway in mid-November 1953 and played 1,027 performances. The film, released in December 1956 less than a year prior to our production, starred Marlon Brando (miscast) as Sakini, Glenn Ford as Captain Fisby and Paul Ford recreating his role as Wainright; so the show had terrific name value when the curtain went up on our production with a young, very talented grad student named Jack Booch in the role of Sakini.

Sam Marks designed the setting and lighting and the major stage properties and costumes, all of which were good. I found an assistant and advisor, a Japanese student Tom T. Miyazaki (Mechanical Engineering 1959) who also played a small role. Tom later worked for Rexnord International,

Inc., in Kamakura, Japan and in a letter to Arthur Hanson, then president of Purdue, wrote that "playing a minor role in *The Teahouse of the August Moon*... was one of the highlights of my student life at Purdue."

⌘ ⌘ ⌘

It was a very long time before I heard from Rogers again, but on December 23rd he wrote in answer to a request I had made: "Here's the letter for the Purdue Research Foundation people.

I hope it's about what you wanted—and I hope you get the grant."

During the several years I have known Joe Stockdale he has demonstrated both unusual talents as a creative writer and a rare determination to persevere under very difficult conditions.

Despite heavy teaching loads at the several colleges where he has served and the necessity of taking summer jobs, he has somehow managed to earn his doctorate and write two new novels, a couple of plays and do extensive revision on some earlier work. Although neither novel has found acceptance, both have received considerable praise from publishers, and Harpers asked for revision of *Hour Of Eternity.* Had Dr. Stockdale been less pressured by his many responsibilities I believe he could have done this rewrite successfully and would by now be an established Harpers novelist.

I have known few authors so worthy of a grant in aid and none so immediately in need of financial help—for I feel that just one summer free of other responsibilities may well mean the difference between failure and the successful launching of a distinguished writing career.

On December 27th, I presented a paper, "The College Adviser," delivered at the Central States Speech Association in Chicago about a Summer Theatre Project I had been thinking of. This paper outlined the beginning of what would eventually be the Purdue Summer Theatre. It was to incorporate the talents of students and townspeople, plus apprentices selected from junior and senior high schools throughout the country.

⌘ ⌘ ⌘

The Loeb Playhouse, Main Stage and Experimental Theatre opened in April 1958 with Ross directing and Sam designing a production of Shaw's *Caesar and Cleopatra* and me directing *Northern Lights,* a play written in my Playwriting class by graduate student Douglas Denbow. I knew I would be directing a student-written production and slaughtered a couple of goats left over from *Teahouse* in homage to Dionysus, praying he would deliver a gifted young Jewish Irish playwright raised in the South named Arthur Tennessee O'Neill.

But that didn't happen. So I selected the best of what we had—even though I had serious reservations—and focused on making a statement about the function of the Experimental Theatre. I did this by attempting to give the new play a staging that I felt reflected its essential style—which was *not* the realism of real things happening to real people.

On reflection, I suppose I was doing what "concept" directors do, pay little heed to the author's intent but rather use the script as a mounting block for their own creativity. In short, I was trying to make of Doug's play something better than it was. Of course the result felt alien to him rather than something birthed from his own brain and guts.

Just before we opened, Doug came to me and threatened to withdraw the script. Since I had not anticipated any such problem, and the cast was working hard and was excited about *the way* the production was shaping up, I was blindsided by this threat. To have a graduate student withdraw the script and not to open as we had advertised (copy for a commemorating program for the Loeb's opening was already at the printers) took me back to the fear inducing tension I had experienced when Mrs. Bronson threatened possible legal action regarding *The Time Between.*

I continued to rehearse, but Doug did not withdraw his verbal threat, and I was unsure of what legal action he might take. I *did* understand his complaints and had some sympathy for them, but I also felt strongly that to open with a flawed script, would at least establish the fact that this facility was to be a place where dramatic experimentation—even if flawed—could take place. This was necessary since the theatre faculty had decided that each graduate student would be required to direct and design a full-length play, and I was artistic director of the Experimental Theatre.

To cut short what was a nerve-racking and gut-wrenching experience, Ross settled the problem in a talk with Doug, which I did not attend. Ross's solution was simple: Doug was a grad student on a tuition-free scholarship plus monthly stipend working for a master's degree. If he chose to withdraw the show, Ross, with the support of the theatre faculty, would ask him to leave the program, explaining that his decision could, of course, be challenged by a review from the School's academic disciplinary committee, but gently reminding Doug that he needed the degree to insure continued advancement as a high school teacher.

And so the problem was settled by fiat, one of those ugly realistic quid pro quo face-saving arrangements, which I have always hated to be a part of. But in this instance I was.

Actually, the production did make a bit of a splash as an avant-garde presentation, thus supporting, furthering and justifying the intended image we had for this beautiful little theatre. But I count this experience as one of the worst of my life, and cannot recall even the story *Northern Lights* was telling.

Years later, during one of the reunions of alumni, Doug Denbow showed up and wanted to talk to me, essentially apologizing for his actions during this period. I listened and was polite, but this kind of trauma lives forever inside, or at least it did in my guts and nerves. I wish I had been a little more unbending and gracious when after so many years he attempted to right what for him was a situation that he wished had not occurred, and for that I'm sorry.

⌘ ⌘ ⌘

On April 29, 1958, I received a letter from Albert J. Berdis, president of Wieland Steel, from his 460 Park Avenue, New York address. His son Bert, Jr. had asked me to write his father who was disappointed about him devoting so much time to extracurricular activities and not buckling down to his engineering studies. In fact, Bert was hoping to switch to a theatre major. He had been first-rate playing Sgt. Gregovich in *Teahouse*, and was in

Northern Lights as well as other plays that season. I had my eye on him for a role in my first show in the Loeb, and I was eager to help. I wrote the letter.

Bert's father replied, "We feel that an engineering curriculum will provide him with the essential foundation to go on to any graduate work or other fields of endeavor he may choose. This we feel is important if he is to earn a living and if he is to learn how to live." Bert did eventually switch his major to theatre and I found him intelligent and talented, and an exceptionally fine comic actor.

Eventually I lost track of Bert and did not hear from him until sometime after the turn of the century, when he came to Purdue for one of those alumni banquets. Last I knew his company, Dick and Bert, was on N. La Brea in Hollywood but that phone number is no longer in service.

⌘ ⌘ ⌘

June 9, 1958 Rogers wrote: "Thanks for the beautifully done programs. I can imagine what a bang you get from working in two such beautiful theatres and I have an idea you especially enjoy your work in the Experimental Theatre of which you are director. I forwarded this other copy to John Ehle and you have probably heard from him before this."

June 10th, the extremely talented John Ehle (whom I had met in a playwriting class in Chapel Hill) of 14 Washington Place, New York wrote:

> Dear Joe: I was just looking through this beautiful booklet Rog and Lyn sent down, and which you were kind enough to send to me; and I was thinking about UNC and how the Drama Department needs something better than they have. Better and in one place. It's certainly a beautiful plant at Purdue, and it's good to know that you're a part of their work and are doing so well. Rog tells me you're writing a book. I would send you my best luck and sympathy, but I'm working on one too and anybody working on a book doesn't have either luck or sympathy to spare. Best wishes. Sincerely, John Ehle

⌘ ⌘ ⌘

And, oh yes, of course, how could I have forgotten to mention? On May 15th we received a check from Ralph A. Morgen, Director of the Purdue

Research Foundation, for $1,100, representing payment of an XL Grant for the summer. I was now ensconced in my air-conditioned office in The Loeb Playhouse and had started to work on a play based on my novel *The End of the War.*

So Hail Purdue! Eternal thanks and god bless the Research Foundation!

Chapter 13

AT THE END OF THE spring semester I held auditions and cast *Mister Roberts* before anyone went home for summer vacation. I got Ross's approval to cast early and picked out my four leads, plus the fourteen supporting roles, along with another dozen guys for ensemble and shore patrol. I handed out 18 scripts and asked the actors to familiarize themselves with the show, although I was adamant that they not consciously memorize and *never* say the lines aloud to avoid setting melody patterns. I asked these 18 to come back to school four days early so that we could schedule full days, 9-12 and 1-5, standard professional rehearsals before classes started. We would then work in the dozen ensemble members after school commenced, those rehearsals from seven to ten. All this was necessary, I felt, because the opening date set—October 10th—for the fall did not allow sufficient rehearsal time to mount a first rate production.

Jim Stephens played Lieutenant (JG) Roberts and was absolutely outstanding, as was the rest of the cast. All great guys, perfect in every role, however few lines they had, but who were *there* acting and interacting in almost every scene in the play. The show is a perfect one in which to develop an esprit, hard work and a hell of a lot of laughter during energized rehearsals, plus a few beers after. The payoff of this bonding was that staggering moment when the crew hears that Roberts, who finally got his request for transfer to action, was killed in combat.

On opening night—the second show to play The Loeb—we knew we had a smash hit. The cast and crew and I cried for joy, just as if we were members of the Purdue football team when they stopped Notre Dame's 40 consecutive wins.

For that one female role, I cast Nancy (later changed to "Nanci") Hall, a vivacious blonde with a great sense of humor. She was wonderful in the role of Lieutenant Ann Girard, one of the nurses stationed on a nearby island. If memory serves it was Insignia, played by Bert Berdis, who discovered via his binoculars that these nurses usually took their outdoor showers at the same time, and had shared the information with most of the crew.

When one of the nurses invited to come aboard arrives, it is Insignia who famously identifies her, during a moment of silence as the one with the "Strawberry on her ass." This is one of the great laughs you will find in show biz, first on the line itself, and then as the nurse who has heard turns her head on the "take."

After the final curtain on *Mister Roberts* I was casting *Death Of A Salesman* for a December opening. Nanci was not the slender Mildred Dunnock-type, but she was determined to be in the show. She figured that I would cast her as "The Woman in Boston," but I asked her to read Linda in the "Attention must be paid" scene with the boys played by David Blakeslee (Biff) and Dick Guhse (Happy). The reading made the hairs on my arm stand up. I knew she would be absolutely first-rate and truthful to the role.

During rehearsals she worked like hell and had only one problem, the Requiem scene. Miller is absolutely clear in his stage directions at the end of the long final speech as she is kneeling at Willy's grave: "(A sob rises in her throat) We're free and clear. (Sobbing more fully, released) We're free. We're free... We're Free..."

She was such a truthful actress that it was difficult for Nanci to hold in the emotion until that exact moment and still have the breath to project the words during the early and midsection of this speech. Holding it in, trying not to cry, always makes not crying more difficult. If you're a singer, which Nanci was, you understand the problem of "breaking" at a specific time, and prior to that time getting the notes out clearly and without strain requires technique that must avoid real feelings. Nanci wanted it both ways.

She wanted to not be crying when she said, "Forgive me dear, I can't cry," but she also wanted the emotion to build organically and truthfully rather than relying solely on technique, and at the same time be able to project the words, and then break at the point Miller (and I) wanted her to. She was not successful until opening night when she got it and as the lights began to fade one could hear audible weeping throughout the theatre.

Salesman was a great production! I shall never forget it.

⌘ ⌘ ⌘

Having mentioned earlier what I considered the four great plays of the of the twentieth century let me now be specific as to their authors: Tennessee Williams gets my vote for *Streetcar* as number one, Miller is second for *Salesman*, O'Neill is third for *Long Day's Journey*, and Albee is fourth for *Virginia Woolf*. Even so, I believe that the greatest of all their collective plays is *Death Of A Salesman*. This is true because it deals not only with personal problems, including sex (as in Williams) or family (as in O'Neill) but also politics. In the overwhelming tragedy of our beloved country and where we went wrong, *Salesman* is absolutely on target. Although theoretically, by leaving us with that enormous feeling of grief it is not a perfect tragedy, since pity is not nullified through terror to purge us of these emotions. I've directed the play three times and this first student production was the most special, partially because I was younger and this was my first time. Like a first great love affair, it was remembered.

⌘ ⌘ ⌘

February 16, 1959, Rogers wrote:

Once more I am concerned by your choice of subject matter in *The End Of The War*. Though there is plenty of precedent, of course, for novels based on insanity, your method of developing your theme in this novel puts the reader so completely out of sympathy with Frances Hays so early in your story that I am very much afraid the average reader will lack sufficient interest to read on.

On April 17th, Rogers finally heard from Mitch.

We have to decline Joseph Stockdale's *The End of the War* and I am of course sorry for that. I am afraid that I won't be able to give him the sort of specific analysis he has asked for.

On April 21st, he wrote:

It has now been a long while since we started working together and I am finally forced to the reluctant conclusion that I have been of almost no help to you—though you must admit that I have tried to the best of my ability. I am, therefore, somewhat sorrowfully, returning your novel under separate cover and I sincerely hope that you prove both Mitch and me wrong by promptly placing it with a good publisher.

Again, Joe, I am sorry that I haven't been able to help you more and I am sure you know how strongly I'll be rooting for your future work in the writing field.

⌘ ⌘ ⌘

It was during this academic year that my relations with a student went beyond minor flirtation into kissing—which I always enjoyed—after some of us had met for a beer. Shortly after that she invited me to come to her home. Of course, when I went I wasn't anticipating much more than a little necking, but we listened to records and talked and I had couple of beers and then the kissing started. I got aroused and she simply led me to a space in back and we took off our clothes and got into bed. I enjoyed it a lot and I knew she did, too.

Robin and I were fine. We were now raising three kids. Life in general was good as was our sex life. I did try to observe the rules of the game by having excuses for my lateness in getting home. Once I even said that I'd fallen asleep in my office. But I don't believe Robin ever suspected, or if she did, she was wise enough to not show it. I did not have any great problem with the fact that the girl was a student and I a professor, as I would probably have today. It would not have happened if she had not been willing, or truthfully, even a little more than willing.

One time when we were in bed there was a knock at her door that would not go away so she told me to just lie still, got up, threw on a kimono, and closed the curtains that separated the bed from the living room area. What

I overheard was a conversation from her explaining to a professor from another department that she had just gone to bed. It took a little time to get rid of him. My car was parked outside and since I knew him I was a worried he might recognize it. Actually, I think he did because many years later after I retired and was visiting Purdue, he brought her name into the conversation and asked if I ever heard from her.

This was not, however, just a one-night stand roll in the hay. The affair lasted several months. And yes, I had enormous feelings for her and knew that she did for me. There came a time however, when it had to be over. She came to my office which was isolated and off the beaten path. I told her—not I'm sure in a very clear way, but by circumventing the physicality—that the thing we had was over. Had I been in love? Yes, I think so. But it was different from the love I had at home, probably because there is always that sense of excitement when something is new and different, especially if it feels prohibited.

⌘ ⌘ ⌘

During this stage of my life— particularly the academic year 1954/5— two really big events, equally important, happened. I was notified that I would be promoted to associate professor starting in September of the following year with an increase in salary to $7,000 for ten months of teaching. And, we bought a house.

Purdue had been reluctant to accept tenure, which they considered unionization. Making the rank of Associate is a major step for anyone in higher education because this is when tenure is awarded. And Purdue was one of the last universities to concede. They did so only because they had to in order to be included in the American Association of University Professors.

Practically speaking, tenure meant that I would be free to speak my mind on all academic subjects in my field of expertise, and could feel free to disagree with politicians, colleagues, or administrators without fear of being fired.

The second great event: The house we bought which, when you made a left turn off the River Road on to Robinson Street, was halfway up the hill, number 435, second house on the left; the one that in the spring of the year always had the redbuds and the white dogwood in blossom near a large front window, as well as a crab apple tree just to the left of the porch. It was the Stockdale Family home for the next 16 years, as well as for hundreds of kids plus professional actors who were in shows at Purdue.

There was a very large walnut tree close to the street that eventually had to be cut. There was also a large hickory nut next to the driveway that had to go, and an old two story barn behind the house which I eventually tore down. The lot was three quarter acres with a large backyard, two thirds of which had grown to weeds and which I eventually cut back to the fence that separated us from Charley Dietrich, a West Lafayette policeman.

To the left side of that fence, a path led down to a wide alleyway that sloped upward to Littleton Street. Charley's house was on the right and the Tinsleys, he the Episcopal priest in the Lafayette church—Ben and Evelyn—on the left. In the junction where our path met the alleyway, the road went straight to where the Costs lived—Donna and Jim—he a metallurgic engineering professor and their four kids, Holly, Heidi, Amy and Jamie. Yet another road turned right and led to the Engels—Gerald and Marilyn—and their two boys. Moshe and Hodya, who would often come over on Saturdays and ask either Joe or David to return with them to perform some small task that their religion did not allow them to do. Gerald was the Rabbi of the local synagogue and they were Orthodox Jews.

So how could we buy a house, you may well ask? We were at Page and Jack Karling's at a party one night, it was late and Page and I were slow dancing in the kitchen and she asked in her best Tidewater, Virginia accent, "Joe honey, why don't you buy a house, now that you have your associate professorship and tenure?"

"Very simple," I answered as I dipped her. "We don't have any money for a down payment."

After I righted her there was that momentary pause as her mind took in the fact that it was possible that I didn't actually have any money for a down payment and she said, "Oh. Well, is that all?'

"Well, yes."

"Well, I'll loan you the down payment if that's all that's keeping you from buying."

Page took three percent interest and after the loan was paid back, she gave the accumulated interest to David, who was her godson.

⌘ ⌘ ⌘

I contacted Hal Hackett at some point in the spring of 1959. It seemed odd to contact *him* since in my imagination I'd been with Allen Hack as the character I created in my novel and short story for years. I had sent Hal the *Argosy* story, "Sailor from Nowhere" and let him know that it had been listed by Martha Foley in her *Best American Short Stories* for 1954 as a "Distinctive short story in American Fiction." He responded by calling me at home. He loved the story, elated and flattered that he was the prototype for the main character.

Later on that spring, I read about the new musical with Ethel Merman called *Gypsy* which was opening on Broadway. In mid-May I decided to get into the City and catch up on shows, and in a letter mentioned this to Hal. He called and said I must stay with him. He had an apartment in midtown. I said yes because it would save money, and because I wanted to update our friendship. When I asked him what he had been doing he was characteristically vague and finally told me he had played in the Broadway musical *Kismet* in 1953/4.

What I actually knew of him was reflected in the pages of the story I wrote, in which the character is basically an enigma. When he suddenly turns up at the Battle of the Bulge, who is he? A sailor that far inland and how did he get here? I think I did this to fill in the blank about Hal's war experience, which he was never specific about and that had piqued my curiosity and drove the story. I liked the guy I created because I liked the real guy's silent support when I tossed that beer can out of his car and it landed in front of a State Trooper's car. It was going to be good to find out who the real Hal Hackett was.

In the bio section of the program for the Paper Mill Playhouse production of *Brigadoon*, Hal's is the longest I have ever seen in a theatre program and reads (in part) as follows:

Hal Hackett (Jeffrey Moss), who can currently be heard in the role of Bob Lyle on CBS Radio's long running "Ma Perkins" serial, was born in the town of Sleepy Eye, Minnesota, and when he was a year old his family moved to Madison, S.D. After high school Hal went to South Dakota Teacher's College for a time, and then moved to Southern California, enrolling in UCLA as a pre-medical student, working at the same time as head of industrial compensation for the midnight shift of an aircraft plant. In his third college year he joined the Army and was assigned to the Division Surgeon's office and was sent overseas where he was severely wounded, during the first month, in France. Shipped back to the States, he was hospitalized in Gardner General in Chicago until the broken neck and back mended. After his discharge he was given a boost up by Sophie Tucker, was signed for the Radio Broadcast of Chicago Theatre of the Air, and several film companies became interested in the good-looking sergeant.... [a listing of his movies included previously]. On the Broadway stage he was a principal in *Kismet*.... had the juvenile lead in *Bonanza Bound*, was a principal in the popular review *Lend an Ear*... In radio he has been both actor and singer on all major networks; and, in television [8 major listings] and Industrials and the International Automobile Show.

I arrived in NYC in late May and went to Hal's apartment. My flight got in early evening and I bussed in, which took over an hour, arriving at 9:30. He greeted me warmly and we settled down in his small living room with beers—a couple of which were about all I could drink without getting a little high—and talked, he characteristically asking the questions. It must have been toward eleven o'clock when I yawned. He saw I was tired and said it was time for me to hit the sack.

When I went to shower, I realized that the bathroom was the only other room in the apartment except for an open kitchen. When I came out, the sofa I had been sitting on was turned into a bed. I was used to sleeping naked and did not own pajamas, but while he was in the bathroom, I hopped into bed in my T shirt and shorts.

It had been eight years since I sat on that bench at Cherokee in my loincloth and body makeup as Tecumseh, and Hal would stop in mid-sentence, look at me, and slide his tongue in a circular motion around his lips. When he came from the bathroom in his PJs—I never saw him undressed—I feigned sleep. He turned off the lights and lay down, and it wasn't long before his hand was right there, and it wasn't long after that I was ready to be gentled.

The sex was fellatio, which I had experienced only a couple of times with the girl who first took me to bed after I got out of the Navy, offering it as a most agreeable substitute when she had her period. All the unstated parameters for the act were set that first time. I did not kiss guys; anal sex was out and so there was no reciprocity on my part.

What follows is reflection and I wish I had known all of this when I was young and it mattered: In Richard Greenberg's Tony Award play *Take me Out*—based on a real event—a baseball player comes out. What starts to erode the unity of the team is not that the guy is gay, but the fear of what others might think if they associate with him. They stop looking at each other in the shower and stop slapping one another on the butt after a spectacular play. In short, what causes the problem is their deep-rooted fear of being thought gay.

We should all examine our sacred shibboleths. We are all sexual mammals. Period. We are designed for that incredible gift of orgasm. Yes, the design of male and female facilitates the survival of the species but I don't for a moment believe the design was exclusively for that purpose. It also gives pleasure, in fact the most sought after of all pleasures.

I'm not one hundred percent sure of this but aren't we damn near the only animal—other than penguins—that constantly disappoint ourselves because we have set up a standard of monogamy and exclusive heterosexuality? How did that start? We know from all sorts of historical records—the Greek especially—and on down through the ages that both expectations are pretty much impossible. About the only effect monogamy has had is an over fifty percent divorce rate; and insisting on exclusive heterosexuality mostly with the guy on top (those missionaries really screwed up!) as the only way we can have our orgasm is just malarkey.

A year or so ago, I read Blake Bailey's biography, *Cheever: A Life* and was saddened by the absolute torture that was so much a part of the end of his life because of his sexual affair with a young ex-marine. Since the book was

784 pages I'm not going to re-read or try to find the quotes, but I remember Bailey quoting Cheever as saying he could not think of any action more decent or satisfying than being "gentled" by sex with his ex-marine buddy.

Sex with Hal was not mutual, but it worked for him as well as me and I never bothered to categorize myself as either "heterosexual" "closeted bisexual" or "homosexual" or "sexual narcissistic" or "sexual omnivore." Screw it! It was, for that week in my life, exactly how Cheever described it, "being gentled," which was highly enjoyable, and in truth I don't for a moment regret or feel guilty about it.

Some time ago I was watching a DVD of George Eliot's novel *Daniel Deronda*. All that is necessary is to say that the title of the book is the name of the protagonist and his thru-line objective is to discover his "birthright"—i.e. who he is. When he finally meets his birth mother expecting her to be "a mother," she says something to him that I think is very important. She says: *"I had a right to be free. I had a right to live the life that was in me. We all have that right."*

If you want to understand more, I advise that you start by reading Kinsey's first two books on sexual behavior in the human male (1948) and female (1950). In the former the finding was that "nearly forty-six percent of the male subjects had "reacted" sexually to persons of both sexes in the course of their adult lives, and thirty-seven percent had at least one homosexual experience"—and this was 65 years ago! Or if you want the short course rent the DVD *Kinsey* starring Liam Neeson, Laura Linney and Chris O'Donnell. Or you might want to know what anthropologist Margaret Meade writes about sex in her book on the Samoan Islands.

⌘ ⌘ ⌘

On that trip to New York I saw *A Raisin In the Sun* which was one of the most exciting evenings I ever had in the theatre. The standing ovation this performance received was totally spontaneous and universal—I mean every member of the audience stood and clapped and yelled at the same time. Of course, I remember the terrific performances by Sidney Poitier, Ruby Dee, Diana Sands and the rest of the cast, but when I went backstage it was to ask the stage manager if I could see Claudia McNeil. The answer was yes, although I had to wait while she got dressed and out of makeup.

When I walked into her dressing room I was shocked to see a well-dressed and well made up—she even wore false eyelashes—young woman (she was actually 42) who played the mother of Poitier and grandmother of Diana Sands and did so convincingly. When I remarked on this and told her that up to that evening the greatest performance I had ever seen in the theatre was Laurette Taylor in *The Glass Menagerie,* and that I thought she equaled it, she burst into tears, threw her arms around me, and gave me a big hug. She, too, had seen *Menagerie* and said that my comment was the nicest compliment she'd ever received. We talked for 20 minutes and when I was ready to leave she asked for my address. The week I got home I received a wonderful long letter from her which I treasured.

I saw Archibald MacLeish's Pulitzer Prize play *JB* directed by Elia Kazan, which I found interesting (the most ambivalent backstage word in show biz), but overrated—as the Pulitzer committee is wont to do—although I knew that Kazan directed it because it was poetic and he needed to direct that kind of play for himself. I also saw his *Sweet Bird of Youth* with Paul Newman and Geraldine Page which I loved, especially Tennessee's last line delivered by Newman directly to the audience: "I don't ask for your pity, but just for your understanding—not even that—no. Just for your recognition of me in you, and the enemy, time, in us all."

Of Cyril Ritchard and Cornelia Otis Skinner in Samuel Taylor's *The Pleasure of His Company* I have no memory other than that it was a high comedy. And I saw the great *West Side Story* in its last six weeks, still with Larry Kert after 685 performances under his belt and the last man standing through the total run. I loved it as I did Meredith Wilson's hit *The Music Man* with Robert Preston. To round out my play-going, Hal and I saw a couple of shows together.

He was busy doing singing rehearsals for the Paper Mill production of *Bells are Ringing,* which would open in early June. I had no idea then that a Paper Mill production was considered a big deal so I took his word for it as "Just a summer stock production." The two shows we saw together were *Gypsy* and *Our Town.*

I remember the boxed announcement for the opening of *Gypsy* in the *New York Times* on Thursday the 21st, and on Friday morning we read Brooks Atkinson's review calling it "the most satisfying musical of the season" and Ethel Merman's "Rose's Turn a "song and dance of defiance," her performance "cocky and aggressive, but also sociable and good hearted," and ... "not for the first time in her fabulous career, her personal magnetism electrifies the whole theatre. For she is a performer of incomparable power."

Since I already had my ticket ordered through the mail, Hal got one at the box office. It was a Saturday matinee and at intermission we met for a cigarette. He said that he saw in the program that a friend of his, Chotzi Foley, was playing the role of Electra, one of the three strippers, and we should go backstage. At the final curtain the house went crazy and there were a lot of curtain calls. Even more could have been taken except that there was another performance that evening.

When the stage manager let Chotzi know that Hal Hackett was there with a friend, we were invited to her dressing room. In addition to Chotzi, there was Faith Dane who played Mazeppa; Maria Karnilova, who played Tessie Tura; and a little blonde girl, Merle Letowt, who played Thelma, one of the Hollywood Blondes who later took over the role of June. The talk was more colorful than any I ever heard during my time in the Navy. I remember telling Robin I was shocked that they put that little blonde girl in the same dressing room with the strippers where she obviously had picked up their really "racy" language.

Let's skip ahead four years for closure to this story. In July 1963, I was at The Barn Theatre seeing Jack Ragotzy's production of *The Unsinkable Molly Brown* in a final dress rehearsal. The gal playing the title role dried up on a line and out of her pretty little mouth came language I had not heard since that backstage visit with the strippers. Guess who? None other than Merle Louise Letowt, now just Merle Louise because her show business friends had taken to calling her "Lay Twat."

What a hell of a great performer/actress for both musicals and straight plays she is. Merle and I became fast friends—in the best sense of that word—and remain so to this day.

The second show Hal and I saw together the next day was *Our Town* directed by Jose Quintero. I had gone to church with Hal that morning—a really beautiful church on either Fifth or Park Avenue, after which we went down to the Village, had some lunch, then to Circle in the Square. In the performance when Emily is allowed to return to earth, Hal became very emotional and reached over and took my hand. I was a little embarrassed, but I figured what the hell? I had no idea why he was so affected by the scene (of course it *is* affecting) but there was something more Hal saw in it. Had he himself been close to death when whatever it was happened to him in France during the war? Or was this hand holding strictly related to me?

When I got home from my New York trip, Hal started calling. Of course, Robin knew that I had stayed with him and was always pleasant on the phone, as she still is even when we all get those political calls during elections—but the frequency of his calls became worrisome and got to be a little much. I never thought of another guy being "in love" with me as he professed and so I tried to end conversations as quickly as I could. He was persistent. Sometimes his calls would be late at night when he was a little drunk. I finally told him he had to stop calling. I did not reciprocate his feelings; I was in love with my wife and we had three great kids and he should not call again. He started crying. I said good-bye and hung up.

I hated doing that but that's the way it was. I liked Hal and I am not proud to say that I never saw or communicated with him again. I never found out about the war wounds he had received in France, or attempted to keep up with his career. In 1967 he died at the age of 43 in New York City, but I only found that out when I started researching this book and the source didn't give any cause of death.

⌘ ⌘ ⌘

On June 24, 1959 I received a rejection on a short story I had submitted to *Argosy* from Bruce Cassiday, Managing Editor. "Many thanks for letting us read 'That's What Sergeants Are For.' Although very well written and certainly a fine story, it still isn't quite suited to *Argosy* at the present time, therefore, we are obliged to turn it down. We appreciate your having thought of us all the same. Cordially,"

On July 15, 1959 Rogers wrote: "I called Bruce Cassiday this week and he tells me, I am sorry to say, that his letter to you on "That's What Sergeants Are For" is the usual style he uses when rejecting stories which just don't hit his magazine's requirements, but which are written by men whose ability he respects.... If you want to try it around yourself I suggest the other men's magazines and I certainly hope you prove my judgment wrong."

This was a nice way to tell me that editors' rejections don't always mean what they say, and asking whether I no longer wanted him to represent me.

⌘ ⌘ ⌘

September 29, 1959 *The Purdue Exponent* published a long Letter to the Editor I wrote concerning the fact that prior to participating in extra-curricular activities, a student had to be approved by the Dean of Men or Women. Approval was granted only if they had a 4.0 academic index (out of a possible 6.0 at that time), and it applied to the debate teams, glee club and university choir, program directors or technical directors at WBAA, the Purdue radio station, and to cast and crew members in Playshop.

The faculty had also passed a ruling that students needed a 4.0 index to graduate. Discovering that a number of students who had gone to school for four years and were about to graduate did not qualify, they changed it back to 3.5. In actuality they sometime lowered it to 3.0 to avoid trouble with irate tax-paying parents. I saw no point for this policy of *loco parentis*. Kids had to grow up, and making mistakes is a part of the process. What was the point of this knuckle-slapping rule? "You've been a bad boy, so next semester you may not participate in activities?" They could do shows with the local Civic Theatre over which the University had no jurisdiction. In fact, some students working on shows got better grades, because with rehearsals they learned to manage their time and were stimulated by being with friends and doing something they loved. In short, both class work and activities were important in the education of the student.

Albert P. Stewart, who headed the Purdue Musical Organization, wrote: "Dear Joe Stockdale: Thank God for men with both brains and 'guts.' You really hit the nail squarely on the head in the morning *Exponent*. This note is to say three things: (1) Thanks. (2) Congratulations. (3) Count on me if I can be of any help or support. Cordially, Al Stewart."

Only a few days later, Jan Barrett, the theatre secretary, handed me a letter with the return address of the Governor. The first thing I thought of was that I was in BIG trouble for criticizing education at Purdue. Despite now having tenure and free to voice my opinions, the suspense was a real pants-wetter. I went immediately to my office and tore open the envelope:

Dear Mr. Stockdale

Your letter to the editor in the Purdue Exponent of Tuesday, September 29, was forwarded to me by my good friend, Al Stewart, since he felt the content would be of interest to me. I read the letter with a great deal of interest and want you to know that I agree wholeheartedly with every word. You have shown a great deal of insight, as well as common sense, with regard to this area of higher education. I am in wholehearted agreement with you that academic excellence is not based on a one-sided man trained in a vacuum for a specific purpose. We need more young men of your kind of thinking and I do hope that, as you prepare for the responsibilities of the years ahead, you will consider the interesting area of governmental affairs. Sincerely yours, Harold W. Handley, Governor.

Letters to the editor followed on one side or the other and I enjoyed the fact that this issue was being discussed by the students and faculty. There is no question that it helped in the lessening of control by the Deans in dictating to the students whether or not they could participate in extracurricular activities. Al Stewart, who had received a copy of the Governor's letter to me, sent it on to President Hovde who, of course, had great influence on such policy matters. This did not make a whole bunch of friends for me at the Dean's office.

At the end of October I had cast my December production, *The Diary of Anne Frank*. There was only one problem: the subject of *Diary* came with a flood of emotional conditioning. We assumed that the immense tragedy of the Holocaust, dealing as it did with the extermination of six million human beings, would be written as a drama with in-depth characters. I cast Nanci Hall as Mrs. Van Daan. She was determined to do a great job and tried to give dimension to the character, the same mistake I made in the direction of *The Desperate Hours*. She couldn't understand why a back story and private moments were counterproductive when in fact every character in the play was one-dimensional and the play was basically a melodrama.

Our production was well received, but throughout rehearsals the actors really wanted more in-depth characterizations to work with, Nanci most of all. All I could say when she begged for ideas to improve her performances was that I didn't have any. The character of Mrs. Van Daan was played by Shelley Winters in the film, who did a first-rate job within the parameters of the stereotype. That's the only thing one could do. And I should have scheduled a shorter rehearsal period, just enough time for the cast members to get their blocking, learn their lines, have a few run-throughs, go into tech rehearsals, and open before they had time to realize that there wasn't a lot to think about character-wise. The play's initial success, both on Broadway and in films, was very much based on what viewers brought to the material, rather than what the material brought to them, a kind of shared sense of sympathy, guilt, and interest in keeping the subject matter alive, more a duty homage that worked against any objective thoughts in terms of dramatic story telling.

⌘ ⌘ ⌘

Purdue's Hall of Music technical staff (former motion picture projectionists) were members of The International Alliance of Theatrical Stage Employees (IATSE) and now had their eye on the new venue. The gift by the Loeb family specifically stipulated that the theatre was for exclusive use by Playshop. However, lectures, small music groups or plays—such as *The Four Poster* brought to the campus by Convocations and Lectures, might better be served playing the 1,200-seat Loeb rather than the 6,006 seat Hall of Music. If so, it would require a union crew for load in, performance, and strike.

Although the union never bothered with Eliza Fowler Hall (a real firetrap) where Playshop had produced plays since 1928, it now saw some possible expansion of its jurisdiction by making The Loeb a union house.

To this end it convinced the administrative head of the Hall of Music to send over its fire inspector. Up to this point Sam Marks had always trained his students as a part of their technical education to fireproof flammable aspects of scenery and stage properties. But since it was a first-of-its-kind event, when the Hall of Music's fire inspector showed up late on the afternoon of our opening of *Anne Frank,* our stage manager and technical staff accommodated him.

Finding nothing untoward on the flammable aspects of the set or stage props, he checked the hand props and noticed that the cage in which the cat was kept by the Frank family had a bed of straw, which he sprayed with a flame retardant liquid. When the cat was put into the cage just before the curtain went up, it took a few minutes to attempt to find a dry spot. Unable to do so, it became agitated and gently mewed for some attention. Not getting it he became pissed off and mewed loudly. Of course, the entire show rests upon the secrecy of the Franks hiding in the attic. If there were any Nazis roaming around the streets or in the offices below, as the situation implied in order to set up the suspense factor, the Franks certainly would have been discovered.

At first there were a few audible titters from the audience. The girl who played Anne was too inexperienced to try to comfort the cat; Bob Cowan, who played Mr. Frank, attempted to quiet him and at the same time keep up the pace of the dialogue, but nothing short of taking him out of the cage—and risk his escape, possibly through the audience—would work. And so we had a situation where everyone in the audience was actually amused, but most of them were polite enough not to laugh, while on stage actors attempted to make the audience believe real things were happening to real people.

Sympathy for the actors turned *The Diary of Anne Frank* into *The Emperor's New Clothes:* actors and audience vainly attempting to ignore what was patently evident to anyone who was not stone-deaf. It wasn't until intermission that Elaine Goldman, our stage manager, discovered the wet straw and replaced it with a non-fireproofed pillow that was comfortable for our pussycat, who quietly snoozed throughout the rest of the show.

⌘ ⌘ ⌘

In the program for this production is the first official notice of the gathering and compiling of two programs from all past Playshop productions, which I had volunteered to do in order to keep the history of the organization alive. One set of programs was to be filed in the Playshop office, the other framed and hung along the hallways and walls of the trap room. For years, during Gala Week especially, one could find alumni showing their children and then their grandchildren their name and picture on the programs and telling stories about their experiences with Playshop.

Thanks to Richard Cordell, Al Fulton and others in the English Department, I had collected two programs from all but 27 productions since 1928, and listed the titles of those we still needed in the *Anne Frank* program. This succeeded in closing the gap a bit. The public display lasted until I left Purdue in 1975 and then disappeared under an administration that seemed intent on destroying past history, and fostering the notion that nothing went on before its reign.

⌘ ⌘ ⌘

In the new year of 1960, after all the parties and Ross getting out his rifle from under his and Dorothea's bed and firing it into the sky from his front porch on New Year's Eve, I was heavily involved in directing *The Glass Menagerie* for the Lafayette Civic Theatre, for which I received a small stipend. The show opened in early February. I had a solid cast, all perfect for their roles with Lily Fisher as Laura, David Blakeslee as Tom, Michael O'Brian as the Gentleman Caller and a first-rate actress, Martha Nell Hardy, as Amanda.

And oh, how good it was to direct a play for the second time with enough depth to provide creativity and emotional stimulation throughout rehearsals and performances, when the audiences teach the actors about what works and what doesn't. This was Martha Nell's first show in Lafayette. Bill Hardy, her husband, had joined the faculty after I alerted him to an opening. Years later, at the 50th year anniversary of *Unto These Hills*, Martha Nell told me at the party she and Bill hosted that I was the best director she had ever worked with. She was certainly one of the really first rate actresses I was fortunate enough to direct.

⌘ ⌘ ⌘

Sometime during the spring I got a call from Jack Ragotzy. He had just received an offer from the director of The Bucks County Playhouse to direct *Happy Hunting*, which would open toward the end of August. He said he would like me to come to The Barn Theatre as his assistant that summer. I told him of our opening of the Purdue Summer Season. He said that if I could make it by Sunday the 17th of July that would be fine. I would direct *Look Homeward Angel*, and he would sign me to an Equity contract.

Chapter 14

ON JUNE 7TH, ROGERS TERRILL wrote of a short novel I had written called *Everything's Coming Up Roses*: "Although you have characteristically set yourself a very difficult writing chore you have, it seems to me, in this one succeeded in creating a very real set of characters and built slowly but surely to your wonderful suspenseful and dramatic climax...Your story is handicapped by the all too familiar situation of a professor becoming enamored of one of his students..."

I had already started rehearsals for the summer theatre when Rogers again wrote:

> I decided to call Ray Bond, of Dodd, Mead, and discuss our problems with him, including the shortness of the novel and the obvious similarities to other properties he has used. He responded with a cordial invitation to enter your novel in their yearly contest for mysteries written by college professors, and I have already sent it down to him with the understanding that you will be glad to fatten it if he likes the novel in other respects.
>
> Since your letter which arrived this morning makes such good sense, I am going to send it along to Ray so that he can attach it to your manuscript and I'll let you know as soon as I have any further word from him.

⌘ ⌘ ⌘

The Purdue Summer Theatre opened with *Tunnel of Love* by Peter DeVries and Joseph Fields on June 15, 1960 and played through the 26th. Directing would constitute my sole job. I would be using local actors plus students, doing entertaining shows with small casts that we would not do for our main-stage season. *Tunnel* was entirely unmemorable a half hour after leaving the theatre, let alone half a century later, but Bill Hardy liked the play and wanted to be the husband, Augie, to Helen Mahon's Isolde. Since I was anxious to have a good actor, which Bill was, plus an audience pleaser, it proved to be an excellent choice.

The Experimental Theatre's permanent seating was 187, but extra identical folding seats had been made that could be set up quickly in the back of the theatre as favors to special customers, and we sometimes played to 200. Since the weekends quickly sold out and ticket buyers had to be turned away at the box office, this set a precedent for our audience members: get your tickets early.

Our next production—June 29th through July 6th—was Noel Coward's *Private Lives,* in which Martha Nell Hardy played Amanda, I played Elyot, Robin was Sibyl, Tony Buckley was Victor and his wife, Mary Foley, was the French maid. Stage manager for this first season was Elaine Goldman, and since I was also in the show, she became a trusted co-director.

The subject of this play is normality and Coward's point of view is expressed in Amanda's line: "I think very few people are completely normal really, deep down in their private lives. It all depends on a combination of circumstances. If all the various cosmic thingagimmys fuse at the same moment, and the right spark is struck, there's no knowing what one mightn't do."

Elyot has some beautiful lovemaking lines: "You're looking very lovely you know, in this dammed moonlight. Your skin is clear and cool, and your eyes are shining, and you're growing lovelier and lovelier every second as I look at you. You don't hold any mystery for me, darling, do you mind? There isn't a particle of you that I don't know, remember, and want." The degree of reality, which is almost always present in the theatre, got a bit fuzzed. Martha and I became fond of one another although it never got to the point of an affair.

The third production was F. Hugh Herbert's *The Moon Is Blue*—July 13th through 24th which had premiered on Broadway in 1951 and lasted for 924 performances. It had been turned into a very successful film which was released in 1953, providing just enough lapsed time so that audiences remembered that the play was slightly risqué, something about a young actress determined not to give up her virginity before marriage. The house was full for every performance.

Gene Kildahl played the middle-aged roué, David Slater. Thanks to the play's reputation and Gene's popularity with the Lafayette Little Theatre crowd, plus his impeccable timing on comedy lines, the play helped cement the relationship between town and gown theatre devotees.

Private Lives' technical crew transported the set, props and costumes up to Michiana Shores after opening night of *Moon* and had it set up by late morning when Robin and I arrived, followed by Martha Nell and Tony and Mary Buckley. The technical run-thru went well with the Michiana crew and we opened that night and played the following three, going swimming in Lake Michigan every night after performance. It was actually a kind of vacation while Elaine oversaw *The Moon Is Blue* back at Purdue.

⌘ ⌘ ⌘

After Saturday night's performance of *Private Lives* with an especially good crowd, Robin, Tony and Mary rode back to West Lafayette with Martha. I then took off for Dad's place which was about a two-hour drive, stayed the night, got up early the next morning and drove to The Barn Theatre.

I signed my Equity contract and was pretty excited about going pro. The job paid $50 a week—same as actors' minimum—and after working during the afternoon with the lighting people, I managed to catch the final "early bird" 7:30 performance of *Can-Can* and was stunned to see the name of Susan Willis (who had played Sally Cato in the *Auntie Mame* national company that played Purdue) now in the sexy role of Claudine. I thought she was terrific! After the performance I went backstage where I saw stage manager Andy Rasbury, who played Stanley in *Streetcar* at Purdue,

Flo Dire who was also from Purdue, and Jim Pritchett, whose wife Cindy, a Kalamazoo girl, had seen the show, and re-introduced myself to Susan. She remembered our meeting at Purdue, seemed glad to see me, and knew I would be directing *Look Homeward, Angel* in which she was scheduled to play Mrs. Gant.

I helped out with the *Can-Can* strike and the load-in for *Kiss Me Kate* for a while only; the change-overs from one show to another required overnight work in which all the apprentices were involved. When I cut out about eleven, I was hungry and went to Ford's where some of the Equity cast members, including Susan, were hanging out. I sat alone and she soon came over to join me. We had a couple of beers, and since I had a meeting with Andy the next morning I said I had to split. Susan asked if she could ride with me. The hotel was no more than a couple of blocks. Her room adjoined mine. I said goodnight, grabbed a quick shower down the hall and crawled into bed.

When I had checked in that afternoon, I saw that there was a door between the rooms, and assumed it could be used as a double. I was about to fall asleep when that door opened. There was Susan in a robe. I sat up in bed and pulled up the sheet since I slept naked. She smiled, dropped her robe, threw back the sheet and got in.

She stayed with me all night.

I don't know how long it was—certainly months later—when I wrote a short story called "The Man Downstairs." I always liked it, but it was rejected by everyone to whom Rogers submitted it. I liked it so much that I rewrote it over and over again throughout the years. It was a fictitious account of our meeting that night, but I know there's a truth in the fiction. It reminds me of the 1950 Humphrey Bogart flick *In a Lonely Place* where he plays a writer named Dixon Steele who has a line of dialogue but can't find where to put it in a piece of writing he's working on. I knew exactly where to put it: as an epigraph for my short story:

> Millie and the Man Downstairs
> "I was born when she kissed me
> I died when she left me.
> I lived a few weeks while she loved me."

In A Lonely Place

It was almost midnight. I couldn't sleep, so I went to Harry's to drink. That's where she found me, sitting at the bar. She was short; about five foot six, with long black raven's hair that hung down to her ass and shimmered in the light. Her face was sharp; prominent cheeks and a chiseled jaw bone; with keen black eyes in milk-white, blue-veined skin. A slash of red outlined her smallish mouth. Just looking gave me a throbbing hard-on.

Getting up from the table where she sat partying with her theatre friends, she came and introduced herself, bought me a beer and aware of the tension in my groin took me back to her room like a stray dog she found, needful of tender loving care, where we fucked and sucked away the dark night until dark turned day.

In the story, Joe stays in Millie's apartment on Charles Street in NYC in a sexual relationship that feels slightly uncomfortable/unfamiliar, since he is not used to dealing with such a woman, but which he desperately wants/needs. Millie gets a replacement job as second lead in a retro-Shakespeare, girl-disguised-as-a-boy, fairly funny long-running Off-Broadway musical, while he spends time writing about the city and their relationship.

It was a quarter past five, end of November, time between day and night in the city. Sidewalks were crowded with hurrying people and I remembered how lonely the city was until I found Millie, or, she found me.

No one could say we were a galaxy streaming outward into curving, infinite space. No, no galaxy, we, but only small unstable particles of electrons twitching and inching our way through the crowds, with no thought of how fragile the fabric of time and space could be; how easily it could be torn.

A man moves into the downstairs apartment and puts up a sign in the window written in colored crayons: "Professional Listener, Guaranteed Never to Reveal Anything Spoken."

It was after midnight; we were naked, sweaty and spent; me soft, but still inside her sweetness, on my back, hands under my head, wet armpits open for air, looking up at those gorgeous tits and the long black hair matted against her face and the shaft of ivory that was her neck.

"Joe," she said, "did you have an illustrated Bible when you were a kid?"

"I guess."

"We did too. A big book with pictures. When I was little I looked at it all the time. This guy moving in downstairs looks like that."

"Like what?"

"Like those colored pictures of Jesus."

Susan had come to the Barn that season for specific roles. Her first was a two-week run in *Two For The Seesaw* opposite Jim Pritchett in which she had gotten rave reviews: "Miss Willis is devastating as Gittel Mosca. She captures the hearts of the first-nighters." And then right into *Can-Can* which broke all The Barn's records for a two-week run. Since she was then scheduled to play Hattie in *Kiss Me, Kate,* Jack had given her the week of *Teahouse* off, but she asked him if she could play the Old Woman who enters on top of a carriage dressed in rags with betel nut-stained teeth. Susan gave that bit everything she had. She was, in fact, a real Carnegie Tech-trained actress. When she spoke there was that homage to speech teacher Edith Skinner—something of a mid-Atlantic high-toned, intellectual thing that made an unusual, but intriguing sound, combined with her throaty voice.

I enjoyed my work as Jack's assistant on both *Kiss Me Kate* and *Call Me Madam.* It was like old times when we first started out together. Both shows ran for two weeks. Jack split after opening night of *Madam* for his job at Bucks County Playhouse and I directed *Look Homeward, Angel.* Rather than starting with describing the set and going right into blocking the action, I addressed the cast by simply quoting by heart Thomas Wolfe:

"... a stone, a leaf an unfound door. ... Naked and alone we came into exile. In her dark womb we did not know our mother's face; Which of us has known his brother? Which of us has looked into his father's heart? Which of us has not remained forever prison pent? Which of us is not forever a stranger and alone? O waste of loss... lost, among bright stars... lost! Remembering speechlessly we seek the great forgotten language, the lost lane end into heaven, a stone, a leaf an unfound door...."

Then after a pause, I said, "Underneath the relationships, and the things in life we laugh at in this play that are so wonderful—those words I just spoke are... *are the essence* of Thomas Wolfe."

I still think that was exactly the right thing to have done: Poetry *was* Wolfe's essence, and in fact mine at this stage of my life. I then went about describing the set, telling them that I had visited Wolfe's mother's Old

Kentucky Home boarding home—"The Dixieland Boarding House" in the play—run by her in Asheville NC, but fictionalized as Altamont, Catawba, and I had read his four major novels.

Then I started blocking each French scene, asking the actors if the movements felt comfortable, and if they were not, addressing their comments and/or suggestions and then re-running it again without interruption to set the blocking in their muscle memory, all of course connected beat by beat with the thru-line objective of the characters that supported the author's super-objective.

This was not what the cast expected, or were used to, especially in summer stock, and several spoke to me with enthusiasm about the approach after the rehearsal. There is no doubt I was well prepared, having done much of my work on this script before my first rehearsal for the Purdue Summer Theatre. Organized I was and am.

I did this not only because I was in love with the writing of Thomas Wolfe, but desperately wanted Jack's acceptance. Throughout rehearsals the only resistance I felt was from Betty, who was cast as Madam Elizabeth. What she would have preferred was a basic blocking and line memorization approach without any talk about the world of Wolfe, her character's objective, or how it fitted into the play's structure and theme. On the other hand, I felt I had absolute support from all the other actors and the production staff.

At the Sunday run-thru, Jack, having gotten back in the early morning from his drive from Bucks County, was present. He had not had much sleep and didn't seem himself. Before we started he said he wanted to say a few words. Those words were to the effect that "This show is not about loneliness, it is a comedy of family life and I want it played for comedy." Each word he uttered felt like a whiplash, but I did not reply. I knew that he was shooting himself in the foot because I felt confident of the company's support.

After we started, Jack stopped the run-through a few times to give comments on line reading, which the actors accepted. But the stops were basically addressing minutiae, and eventually he settled down and listened, and let the show run. But when it came to the scene with Madam Elizabeth he stopped the show and had words with Betty, made her redo a part of her scene, got angry and yelled at her, and took her into their apartment just off the rehearsal room from which we heard a slap and shouting.

During the act break his attitude had changed and he made an effort to be solicitous and supportive, which told me he knew his mercurial temperament had come into play and he wished to make amends. It's hard to ascribe motive, but I think Betty was worried that Jack's control and interest in The Barn might lessen as he did more directing in other venues. She felt *he* should be at The Barn keeping a firm hand, not leaving that job to anyone else.

A scene I shall never forget near the end of *Look Homeward* was when Eugene, knowing that his brother Ben is going to die, is sitting on the porch staring straight ahead, as his brother Luke, sister Helen, and mother talk. Luke, remembering the good times, tells them of "...the early morning when Ben and Gene and I used to take the paper route together, remember, Gene? Old Ben used to make up stories for us about all the sleeping people in all the sleeping houses! He always used to throw the papers as lightly as he could because he hated to wake them. Remember, Gene?"

"And that book of baseball stories Ben used to read to us by the hour, what was it, Gene?" Helen asks.

"*You Know Me Al* by Ring Lardner," Gene answers. And just as he started to say the author's name he broke into tears. The truth of Dale Helward's emotions was undeniable and at the end, after Ben's death, Eugene sinking to his knees, saying: "Whoever You are, be good to Ben tonight. Whoever You are, be good to Ben tonight... Whoever You are... be good to Ben tonight... be good to Ben tonight...." was unforgettable, and I knew I had to work with Helward again.

After the "early bird" final performance of *Call Me Madam* that evening, I helped the crew strike and load in the *Angel* set, working most of the night. I got some sleep the next day and then the dress rehearsal started at seven o'clock. It went extremely well, with Jack stopping it only for changes in lighting intensity. That night Susan and I were together again, and we both knew this was our final night. We slept late the next morning, had some breakfast at Ford's and then went to The Barn for the afternoon dress, which was splendid. I knew that it was my show and that Jack was pleased with it.

Curtain was at 8:30. The Michiana Summer Theatre had ended its season a couple of weeks earlier, and Ross and Dorothea drove up from West Lafayette with Robin. I was nervous as hell but there was not a hitch in the performance. Timing was right on the button and the cast received wonderful applause on the curtain call. Robin, as well as Ross and Dorothea, loved the show, but the Smiths had a four-hour drive back home and had to leave. The plan was that Robin and I would go over to Dad's after the opening night party and drive home the next day.

The most difficult part of the evening was when I took Robin backstage to introduce her to cast members, and Susan came from her dressing room. Everyone staying at the Augusta Hotel had to know what was going on—that first night was in my room, but after that I spent my nights in her room—and Dale Helward's room was just across the hall.

I was introducing Susan to Robin—both women were gracious, Robin was always gracious—when Jack appeared and told me he had something important to do the next day and needed me to take the rehearsal for *Dark at the Top Of the Stairs* at 10:00 A.M.

I had not read or seen the play. I wanted to play ball with him because of possible future work, and let's face it, I was addicted to the theatre; it was what I loved. But I knew that to block that first act, I'd not be able to walk into rehearsal until I had time to read the play and break it down into French scenes and beats. But I was feeling guilty. I told Jack I had planned on going home, but Robin offered that she could ride back to West Lafayette with Ross and Dorothea, if I needed to stay. Ross wanted to get underway; there was a blissfully short time to say good-bye and I told Robin I'd be home in a couple of weeks.

I got the script from Jack, and when Susan and I drove back to the hotel, I said I was going to have to get the first act under my belt before I went to sleep. Uppermost in my mind was my wife, the most beautiful woman in the theatre with whom I had three great kids, who was totally supportive and trusting of letting me do what I wanted/needed to do, and me in a whirligig of emotions, feeling awkward with another woman with whom I had made love for five weeks.

Susan understood my unexpressed feelings, knowing I could not talk about them, hadn't faced and figured anything out yet, and needed to be in my own room. I worked till a little after 3:00. I made it through the first act okay and went to sleep in my own bed.

Using the same technique I always used by blocking a French scene, then going over it to set the action before moving on, the theatre provided me with such intense focus as to blot out everything else in my life. After rehearsal the next day, Jack came with the reviews for *Angel*.

Bockstanz of *The Gazette* wrote that the production was:

> ... one of the finest Broadway dramatic productions in recent years, thrilled and pleased a sellout audience of first nighters... and earned loud and continued applause for Jack Ragotzy's summer theatre company at numerous times during the presentation and following the final curtain.
>
> For Joe Stockdale, a member of the original Village Players from which The Barn was born, the comedy drama turned into a homecoming triumph. Stockdale, now an associate professor of Drama at Purdue University, served as director and guided the cast into a nearly perfect production.... Making the role of Eugene Gant come to life is Dale Helward, a young actor in the first summer at The Barn. His is, without doubt, the finest dramatic role seen this season at Ragotzy's Theatre.

Humphrey of *The Enquirer* added, "Helward left no doubt that he is a true Broadway star of the future." Susan, too, got a very good review from the *Gazette* in a role that is most difficult because Eliza is not the one to whom the author gives sympathy. Of her work Bockstanz said, "A powerful performance is contributed by Susan Willis, as Mrs. Eliza Gant, who masters the role of a grasping dominating mother and wife. Her performances earned for her, in turn, contempt, pity and at times, love by the audience, but most of all praise for a splendid job."

Of course I was euphoric and I know Jack was thrilled for me. I read and studied the rest of *Dark At The Top* twice, and since Susan was performing in *Angel* that night, I paper-blocked the second act for Thursday's rehearsal. After the performance, we went to Ford's to celebrate, had a couple of drinks and went back to her room and did what we had been doing since that first night.

On Friday I blocked and rehearsed act three, and on Saturday, with only three hours of rehearsal because of the two performances that day, we ran the entire show off-book with prompts for lines still to be learned, knowing that the next day Jack would be there to check on the run-through. Susan perfectly played the challenging role of Aunt Lotty. I waited with some apprehension to see what Jack would say at the Sunday run-thru.

When we drove to the theatre at 9:30, Susan had something she had to do before rehearsal, so I let her off at the backstage door of The Barn and went to park. But before I had gotten out of the car, Betty was headed toward me. She handed me a check, saying that I would not be needed any more and that Jack would take over the rehearsal. I was stunned. I asked her if there was anything else he wanted me to do. She said no, and that I could go home. At that point my short fuse ignited and I looked at the check and, controlling my anger, told her that Equity rules require a two-week written notice of dismissal, or, two-weeks payment. I would, of course call Equity the next day and see if this was correct, but I was sure it was and handed back the check.

There was that anticipated standoff moment between us. Betty, more than a little frugal, had instigated the nail-straightening-for-reuse detail that first season in Richland, but she knew the rules as well as I did and knew that the last thing Jack wanted would be problems with Actors Equity. Thin-lipped, she told me to wait, she would be right back. I waited. She returned with a check for the proper amount signed by Jack, or, one she'd signed for him. Equally thin-lipped, I thanked her and drove off.

Between The Barn and the hotel there was a field where wild flowers grew, and Susan had regularly had me stop so she could pick bouquets for her room. I got out, picked flowers I knew she liked, drove back to the hotel, got the vase she used, filled it with water, placed it on her bedside table, went to my room, got my gear together, wrote a note telling her that I had been fired and that I knew she would be wonderful in *Dark*, signed it "always, Joe," went back to her room, and put it on the nightstand by the flowers. I gave one last look around and left, torn apart by feelings I could not fuse, knowing I would have a four-hour drive to get back home to a loving wife and three loving kids, who would all be glad to see me again. All I could wonder was: was I worth it?

⌘ ⌘ ⌘

It was sometime later that I found out from Dale Helward, who played Sammy Goldenbaum, that Susan gave Jack two weeks' notice but said she would prefer to leave after *Dark* closed—which she did—and that he thought it was just as well that I was not there when Jack made script changes. In *Dark,* the character of Sammy, a Jewish military school cadet whose mother, an actress, had cared so little for him that he had not developed the necessary protective insulation for "the thousand natural shocks that flesh is heir to," commits suicide. Jack cut the suicide. Actually, I should have anticipated this since on the cover of the program for *Look Homeward, Angel,* in the lower right quarter which promoted the next attraction, under *Dark At The Top Of the Stairs* was written, "William Inge's newest and finest comedy!"

During our short rehearsal period we all came to the conclusion that what Inge meant by "dark" in his title was a metaphor for the fear most of us as little kids experience when we're told to go to bed; the light from downstairs always faded as we climbed the stairs and soon we faced that moment of darkness at the top, where we feared the bogeyman might get us. In short, the tragedy of Sammy's suicide most dramatically and clearly illustrated the necessity of living our lives in loving support of one another so we can twitch and inch our way through that dark space, not knowing how fragile the fabric of time and space is, or how easily it can be torn.

On June 10, 1973, playwright William Inge committed suicide at the age of sixty.

⌘ ⌘ ⌘

The new school year had started off well. In late October I cast one of my favorite plays, Tennessee William's *Cat on a Hot Tin Roof Tin Roof,* which would play The Loeb in December. The casting was difficult. I had a Big Daddy in graduate student Floyd Herzog, but in Playshop's stable of actors there was not a "Brick" or "Maggie." I finally cast two young people, George Dandrow and Virginia Carnes, both physically perfect for their roles but who had very little, if any, theatre experience. We all did our best, but I never felt I achieved a really first-rate production. A good part of the fault was mine, not the fledgling actors who beat their brains out to do a good job. I just could not see Maggie, the Cat, as a really likeable leading character. Years later I figured how that play should be directed, but by that time my directing career was over.

⌘ ⌘ ⌘

Sometime at the beginning of 1961, after Ross had fired his gun from the front porch on New Year's Eve, I saw an ad in the *Educational Theatre Journal* for a one-year replacement for Professor Giles Playfair, who headed The Adams Memorial Theatre at Williams College. James Phinney Baxter III was the president of Williams but in his retirement year. I decided to apply. When I first talked to Ross about this he was more than a little nonplussed. I suggested that IF I got the job, he could use the money from my faculty line and hire a nationally known playwright to teach my playwriting class for one semester, and then perhaps get a nationally known designer for the second. He began to see this as an excellent idea.

I was surprised when I got a letter from President Baxter asking me to come to Williamstown for an interview. I did just that, flying to New York in the early morning at the beginning of February and taking the train to Albany where a student driver picked me up for the two-plus hour drive to Williamstown. Giles, who was right out of central casting as the quintessential Brit/Britannia-rules-the-waves type, took me to lunch at the charming Williamstown Inn before going back to The Adams Memorial Theatre where I met Ruth Sanford. At first glance she was a frail senior citizen, a quiet and unassuming secretary whom I would find a dynamo of energy and the spirit of The Adams Memorial Theatre, as well as Williamstown; housemother to the theatre students during the academic semesters and in the summer, friend of the professional actors and apprentices who swamped Williamstown to be in first-rate productions by the best playwrights, both international and native, produced and/or directed by artistic director Nikos Psacharopoulos.

I loved The Adams Memorial Theatre, which seated close to 500. I met Jack Watson, the technical director, who took me all over the building and showed me the small theatre below which would be fine for student-directed productions. I ended my interviews with a revealing hour with James Phinney Baxter, the president of this absolutely first-class all-male college where only later I learned that about eighty percent of the students were from prep-schools such as Lawrenceville, Exeter, or Groton.

It was a couple of weeks later that President Baxter called and told me that they wanted me. I was elated. When I told Ross I got the job he was supportive. The position was a prestigious one, and he had already started thinking about whom he could hire from the professional theatre to replace me. All the paperwork for the Williams job was soon completed and I went to work on planning the second Purdue Summer Theatre Season.

⌘ ⌘ ⌘

I read in *Variety* that *Gypsy* closed its NYC run and Merman was taking the show on a national tour. I suspect that the show actually could have run on in Gotham, but Merman was of the tradition of those big stars like Ethel Barrymore and Katharine Cornell who believed it was important not to ignore her loyal road audience. If they couldn't see her on Broadway she would go out to see them. In the cast, playing the small role of Miss Cratchitt, was Susan Willis.

We had not talked after I had left The Barn. Seeing her name, I wanted to see her again, wondering if she might be a little PO'ed with me for not getting in touch with her. I didn't want our relationship to end that way. I contacted her at the Croydon Hotel in Chicago. She sounded surprised but also happy and said that she understood my not getting in touch. She suggested that I come up and see the show.

I told Robin I needed a little beach time. If memory serves, this is the first time I deliberately lied to her and didn't feel comfortable doing it, fearing complications when I took off. Arriving late afternoon I went to the hotel where the desk clerk had a note for me. Susan wrote that I could get her key and go up to the room, and if I liked, I could go to *Gypsy* that night—she had informed the box office—and she would be back as soon as possible. Or, if I wanted to, she was doing the role of Aunt Lily in the musical *Take Me Along* at one of the professional tent musicals in-the-round and I could come there. Curtain was at 8:30 and there would be a ticket for me at the box office; she'd explain everything later. Having already parked in the "long-term" section of the hotel's garage, I took the bus, arrived in the nick of time and was just being seated when the announcement came over the loudspeaker about the role being taken that evening by.... and the lights dimmed.

Take Me Along is a musical based on Eugene O'Neill's *Ah Wilderness* and was produced on Broadway by David Merrick, who also produced *Gypsy*. From what Susan told me later, the actress playing Aunt Lily had gotten ill just after the Tuesday performance and the management had called David Merrick to see if there was a possible replacement since there was no understudy to go on for the Wednesday evening performance. Susan had been hired late in the *Take Me Along* run as an assistant stage manager, and to understudy a couple of roles including Aunt Lily.

I found her absolutely wonderful with her impeccable speech distancing her from Uncle Sid's drinking, yet regardless of their differences, with a smashing need-to-be-loved vulnerability of a woman dangerously close to the cusp of becoming an "old maid." After curtain calls, I went backstage and very shortly—since they said they would need her the next night—we were being driven back to the Croydon.

We got pretty much locked together as we drove, and I don't remember even getting anything to eat before we went up to her room where we spent a lot of the night doing what we had done at the Augusta Hotel. I have no idea where the energy came from after the day we had both just experienced, but energy we had in abundance; again, without an Edith Skinner accent or vocabulary, she was vocal as hell.

We got up very late the next day and she made breakfast in the room using an immersion rod in a bottle of water to make soft-boiled eggs. Later that afternoon we went to one of those great downtown Chicago restaurants and then back to the Music Tent. I loved seeing the show again since it had that special energy because of someone new in a role. But this would be her last performance; the actress who'd gotten ill, would be back the next day. Afterwards, I went back to her dressing room and a lot of the cast came in and thanked her for saving them a couple of performances and saying how great she had been. She introduced me to them, which made me a little uneasy.

Our next day was like our first day, breakfast and coffee in her room, back in bed, a late dinner at the same great restaurant, and then to the theatre where *Gypsy* played. The performance was very special because the next day, Saturday, the entire company was to board the train which would get them to Seattle, Washington, sometime early Monday where they would perform the show that night.

There was a big party after the show. Miss Merman was with a guy she'd met in Chicago, and everyone in the company knew that she was sorry to be leaving him. Susan introduced me to her as "Professor Joe Stockdale from Purdue," with no airs, just being what she was, energetic and friendly, showbiz meeting academia. She was much shorter than I had imagined. She scanned my 6'3" frame, shook my hand with a strong grip and in her distinctive Bronx voice said, "Glad to meetcha, professor."

Flash cameras went off and I got more than a little worried fearing I might turn up the next day in one of the Chicago newspapers. I whispered to Susan to just call me Joe. But she liked the professor tag and so why not? There was a lot of hard partying going on and an open bar. We stayed late and had a hell of a good time.

This was our final night. Susan, who was also an assistant stage manager, had to be up early to see that every person in the company was packed, checked out, and in the lobby to be picked up to get to the train station by 1:00 P.M. All this was right up my alley (remember my moving Margaret and Professor Woodhouse to new digs in Chapel Hill?). I'm nothing if not organized. I was a big help getting everyone to the lobby—especially the musicians who were still a little drunk from the night before—and there were mothers of some of the young cast members, and the lamb that appears on stage, and if I remember correctly a monkey! Transportation came and we headed out, Susan and I following in the last taxi.

The company occupied three or four Pullman cars—one being special for Merman—and by this time they had kind of adopted me as Susan's guy. The train whistle blew, we kissed good-bye, and as she boarded someone yelled, "Hey, don't leave her," and others joined in. "Come on." "We got room." "Take the trip with us." "Come on!"

It actually flashed through my mind that I could leave my car where it was parked, go with them, and fly back. I looked at Susan. She had not yet gone to her seat. I knew she wanted me. I smiled, and folded my arms as the train started to move. I stood there alone until the caboose was out of the station.

It was a time in my life when I desperately wanted to do something and didn't. Of course I didn't. I had a beautiful and loving wife and three kids in a wonderful house/home in West Lafayette, Indiana, and I was a tenured associate professor at a major university where my 12 month salary line for 1961-1962 would be $8,500. I had lots of friends among the students and the faculty at Purdue, and I had rehearsals coming up for the summer theatre. I was one lucky guy having met Ethel Merman and knowing Susan, and I'd wanted like hell to take the trip.

But I loved all those things I had in West Lafayette, *too!*

⌘ ⌘ ⌘

We opened our second summer season with *The Marriage-Go-Round* by Leslie Stevens. Stevens said that the play was inspired by Isadora Duncan, who, when she met George Bernard Shaw, suggested they have a baby together because "with my body and your brains, it would be near perfect." Shaw answered, "Yes, but what if it had my body and your brains?"

The story concerns a couple of academics. Gene Kildahl played the professor of Cultural Anthropology, and Martha Nell Hardy played his wife, a professor and Dean of Women at the same school, both with a serial-killing list of academic acronyms after their names. With an academic setting and these characters, *plus sex,* it didn't take a rocket scientist to figure it would prove to be great box office. Maida Rusk Withers, the sole dance professor at Purdue, tucked away in the woman's physical education department under healthy exercise rather than art, played the Swedish sexpot and was perfect for the role.

In our second production, *The Dark at the Top of The Stairs,* Robin played Cora Flood, with Arlen Withers as her husband Rubin, and Mary Helen Kahn, who was the drama teacher at West Side High School, as Lottie. She brought one of her students to audition for the role of Sammy Goldenbaum, but he looked far too young and emaciated for the role, so he was used as a "rehearsal assistant." This was "H. Thomas Moore" *aka* Tom Moore, the original *Grease* director who morphed into the director of a dozen or more Broadway shows, including the 1983 Pulitzer Prize winning drama *'night, Mother.*

Only in the past decade has Moore begun to look a bit older, but there is a huge difference: the toothpick arms and 97-pound-weakling look had developed into rock star status on the high-wire-trapeze-strength-and-health-circuit. He recently sent bare-chested pictures from Rio de Janeiro, posing in front of The Christ the Redeemer statue atop Mt. Corcovado.

Who could have known?

Dark was also the production in which I told the designer I had to have a period chaise longue. He said that probably would not happen. I said it would and to find one. On the first tech rehearsal when it did not appear, he said that it was impossible to find. To prove how wrong he was, I assigned the task to the two leading ladies, Robin Stockdale and Mary Helen Kahn, and said if they did not find one by the next day we would not open.

They came up with the idea that in the movies, psychiatrists often interviewed patients resting on chaise longue, so they called the psychiatric hospital on the River Road. No, they did not have *one,* they had a *roomful* of them. The two leading ladies selected a horsehair chaise perfect for the early twenties in rural Oklahoma, the play's setting, and it was there the next day for the final run-through, serving as a cautionary tale to *never* say finding a stage prop is impossible; "negation is debilitating!"

The two-hander *Two For the Seesaw* proved to be good choice for actors Bill Hardy and Millie Loeb. I really liked the play and empathized with Jerry, a kind of square Nebraskan lawyer who is in a sexual relationship with Gittel Mosca, a Greenwich Village dancer—definitely *not* the ballet type.

Our final show of that season was Brandon Thomas' *Charley's Aunt*. This was the first time I directed the play and I felt it was a shoo-in, easy farce comedy that would be perfect for a laugh-filled evening as the last show of the season. It is, in fact, an immensely difficult play to make work because the task for the actors at the beginning is not to try to make the audience laugh, but to layer in the exposition so as to make believable the actions that follow.

It is only after Lord Fancourt Babberly, a friend of the two undergraduate Oxford students Jack and Charley, enters to show them his costume for an Oxford Dramatic Society production in which he plays an elderly female, that news comes that the aunt has been delayed in chaperoning the two girls. In desperation, the decision is made that Fancourt must substitute for the real Aunt.

The farce actions that supply the laughs work *only* if the actors keep the audience in a state of belief in the situation. As Samuel Coleridge advises, this can only work if the audience is guided into a *willing* suspension of their disbelief and become participants, and this only happens if they believe that real things are happening to real people. With Roger Hill playing the leading role I think we accomplished a good production that achieved this end, however hoary this old chestnut was.

⌘ ⌘ ⌘

William Saroyan decided to accept Ross's offer as a visiting artist at Purdue; in fact he was happy to do so since he was in deep doo-doo with the IRS for unpaid back taxes. He was to occupy my office, and during the summer I took to writing notes to him on my page-a-day calendar. My first one was toward the end of September when I copied his beautiful and most famous: "In the time of your life, live so that in that wondrous time you do not add misery or suffering to the world, but smile to the infinite delight and wonder of it." Then I added, "Anyone who would write this has got to be bonkers!." As I suspected, he enjoyed this Scheherazade of dark-humored notes and eventually sent me a note of thanks saying they lightened his days at Purdue where he wrote and directed *High Time Along The Wabash.*

⌘ ⌘ ⌘

I had decided against attempting to ascertain the talent pool at Williams College and Bennington, or locally, for the season of shows I chose. If one loves the show they can instill that love by securing *a truthful representation.* This has always been my working method, whether with Academy or Tony Award-winning actors, or simply with students who had never been on stage. The season I chose was: *Death of a Salesman, Tartuffe, Oedipus Rex, Guys and Dolls,* and *Romeo and Juliet—Tartuffe* to be directed by my assistant, Phil Meeder, the others, by me.

During the summer I wrote Lee Strasburg explaining that I would be visiting professor at Williams and would like to be an observer of his work at The Actors Studio. I received a reply saying that I would be welcome; that meetings were Tuesdays and Fridays from 11:00 to 2:00; that I would not be allowed to comment on the scenes; and that the door to the studio would be locked promptly at eleven. I looked forward to these observations with great anticipation, and I also looked forward to seeing all the best of Broadway, which was only a four-hour bus trip to the Port Authority at 42nd Street and Eighth Avenue.

Chapter 15

WE WERE FORTUNATE TO RENT 435 Robinson Street to responsible students for enough to pay the mortgage payments. The trip east was made in our new Volkswagen, Robin in the passenger's seat or sometimes Joe III there, and Robin, Lory, and David in the back. It was good to have money and a good car so we did not have to rush the trip. We took Highway 421 north to the Indiana Toll Road, then 80/90 east: Toledo, Cleveland, Buffalo, Albany and Highway 7 north to Williamstown. The scenery in that northwest corner of Massachusetts was spectacular, especially on 3400 foot Mt. Graylock showing the beginning of fall. Finally we arrived at beautiful Williamstown.

The college assigned us the house right next to the theatre that had a couple of classrooms downstairs, but up the back stairway were two apartments, which combined into our living space with two bathrooms and 3 bedrooms. Laurel was eleven (sixth grade), Joe eight (third grade), and David five (kindergarten) and it had been arranged that Robin would teach at the private school, Pine Cobble, in exchange for free tuition for the kids.

A major issue was that the theatre was a four-person department: Ruth Stanford, secretary and box office; Jack Watson, technical director and lighting designer; Phil Meeder, who taught a basic theatre course and directed one show; and me as producer/director. In our talks, Jack recommended that we job-in designer Robert T. Williams, who turned out to be one of the best designers I have ever worked with. As for costume construction, Purdue grad Rita Bottomley was now living in New York City, and was happy to work with us. I jobbed-in Wayne Lamb as choreographer for *Oedipus, Guys and Dolls,* and the single dance number for *Romeo and Juliet,* and Monte Aubrey, pianist and musical director at The Barn, who could always find a bass player and drummer, to form a trio that sounded like a full pit orchestra. Trust me, these job-ins were not only talented and professional, but much, *much* less expensive than hiring an academic.

⌘ ⌘ ⌘

Williamstown was the quintessential small-college town, and the village was charming. One of the first things we did was drive to Pittsfield and buy Lory clothing since she was at an age where these things were important. While Robin was getting us settled, and she and the kids started school, I met the faculty plus the new president, John "Jack" Sawyer, a class act who was incredibly supportive.

The day soon came when the freshmen arrived on campus. Tradition had it that they were all taken for a hike up and over the mountain, and since I was, in my own way, a freshman, albeit faculty, I asked to go along. At some point a dirty blond, shaggy-haired kid who gave the impression that he did not have a lot of money—no socks, wrecked sneakers, ripped jeans, and skuzzy T-shirt—got to walking alongside me. He said he was interested in theatre and had graduated from Exeter (for all I knew at the time this could have been a Catholic orphan's home) and had written a play. I asked him if I could read it and he said he would get it for me just as soon as we got back to campus, which he did in ten minutes. I read it that same evening and talked to him the next day. He was obviously unprepared for so fast a response, and although there were problems with the play, it did show talent. During our talk I decided he would be right for "Happy," the younger brother, in *Salesman.*

On the first rehearsal two cast members were late. I explained that this was unacceptable and must not happen again. If they would rather meet from 7:15 to 10:15, or 7:30 to 10:30 rather than 7:00 to 10:00 that would be fine with me, but once set and agreed upon, there was no lateness—in fact "consider being on time five minutes early!" This came as a surprise to the upper classmen who said that Professor Playfair hardy ever started rehearsals on time, and they were simply unused to such a requirement. But they now knew that if even one person was five minutes late, an hour of accumulated time was wasted for the company, let alone pissing me off.

I went to the theatre in the afternoon of the day we were to open to ask Ruth what kind of a house we were going to have, and was surprised to hear that she expected an attendance of about 180. The theatre had 479 seats. Ruth explained that the talk around town was that the play was much too difficult for college kids and was sure to be a tedious evening. However, the show went extremely well with Wood Lockhart, Phil McKnight, Peter Simon and Deb Hays from Bennington in the leading roles (Robin played the woman from Boston). At the end the response was pretty overwhelming for that small an audience. There was a first-night party at our place, and Robin and I didn't get to bed until 2:00 A.M. I slept in and didn't appear in the office till late the next morning. When I came in Ruth was on the phone taking ticket orders, and Jack Watson and a student assistant were working the two windows in the box office and had been all morning. The word of mouth around town, Ruth said, was very good.

By late-afternoon, the epitome of politeness on the phone, Ruth explained that there were no more seats for the Saturday performance. "No," I heard her sigh, "I'm afraid that includes all the extra seats we will have to put up in the back, Professor...." She was talking to a certain look-down-his-nose member of the English Department who had voiced the opinion that the show was "too difficult" for amateurs. I couldn't help but notice under the layer of tact in her voice a note of satisfaction. "I'm so sorry you'll miss it, Professor... It's a splendid production. Please try to call a little ahead of time on our next one."

Ruth told me that the cleaning person had mentioned that the dressing rooms had been left in a terrible mess. I found this to be true and talked to the cast that night prior to curtain: It was not the janitor's job to clean up cold cream-saturated Kleenex they had thrown on the floor rather than in the wastebasket; it was also not the janitor's job to hang up their clothing and other personal items of apparel dropped on the floor, or slung over the backs of the chairs. It was their responsibility to leave the rooms in order and their assigned makeup spaces clean and free of half-filled coffee containers with floating cigarette butts. "I realize that many of you have maids to pick up after you at home, but you are no longer at home and should know that I do not tolerate your leaving the dressing rooms looking like the wreck of the Hesperus. I hope my message is coming through to you loud and clear!"

I heard a muffled response and added pleasantly, "Pass this info on to any of your buddies who are in shows for the rest of the season. And by the way, we lack about a dozen seats of selling out tonight, and tomorrow night is already sold-out, including the extra seats Jack will put up in back. You'll be playing to about five hundred."

Whoops of joy were sounded.

I liked almost all these kids, and there is nothing better than success for unification. A handful of the guys, including those who held office in Cap and Bells, seemed to suffer from a kind of casting-pearls-before-swine syndrome and felt utter failure if a show turned out to be a hit. It seemed to me that this kind of look-down-your-nose negative response had come to be the glue that held this little band of brothers together.

A centerpiece of the brothers was a constant critic who was vice president of Cap and Bells. But I vaguely remember (I was slightly drunk) that at the final party just before I left Williamstown, he did have a few good words for me. This was because I allowed him to direct a play in the experimental theatre. He was very intelligent and the play seemed to hold a special interest for him.

A friend of his, Bill Prosser, was also imbued with the same kind of negativity. He questioned whether or not *Salesman* was "a true tragedy." My response was decidedly un-Williams: "Who gives a rat's ass? And spare me your intellectualizing!" He played Bernard in the production and seemed flummoxed by his conflicting feelings: glad of the show's success but if it sold out how could it possibly be any good?

Later, pleading on behalf of officers of Cap and Bells, he asked me to cancel *Guys and Dolls,* which "was far too commercial," and substitute

Voltaire's *Candide*. I said no. I was running the theatre because I had more experience than he did, or the coterie in Cap and Bells, and cast him as Nicely-Nicely Johnson. He stopped the show every performance with "Sit Down You're Rockin' the Boat." The "kid," Bill Prosser, was to become a lifelong friend. He came to Purdue to take his master's degree with me, and sadly I spoke at his funeral about a decade ago. Much more on Bill later.

When *Salesman* closed I had time to get into the city to The Actors Studio and don't believe I missed a session for about six weeks before I was in rehearsals for *Oedipus Rex*. Even then I sometimes cut out on Friday and scheduled work on the choral odes with choreographer Wayne Lamb. I never saw Brando, Dean, Cliff, or Monroe, all of whom were touted as members of the Studio. I eventually found out that they took private classes with Mr. Strasberg. However, I most often saw actors like Madeleine Sherwood, Shelley Winters, Geraldine Page, and Rita Gam.

I did see Paul Newman as Petruchio give the "This is a way to kill a wife with kindness" speech from *The Taming of the Shrew*. There was nothing spectacular about it, and when he finished he turned a chair around, straddled it, sank down, elbows on the back of the chair and head in his hands. Strasberg asked his usual question, "What were you specifically trying to accomplish in this scene?" Newman heaved a sigh, smiled, and said, "Just... to get through." It was a wonderful spontaneous truthful moment, but Strasberg was not amused. Newman added, "I was scared to death."

Another scene I remember was one in which (I am almost positive) Rita Gam removed most of her clothing, leaving only a bra and a thong. Her answer to Strasberg's question about what she was trying to accomplish was that she had begun to think that the only reason she got roles was that people wanted to see her body. She had to free herself from self-consciousness and strengthen her concentration on a scene's objective. I thought she did a hell of a great job, but her improved concentration did not lessen the attractiveness of her body one bit!

My experience at the Studio also got me thinking of what is the difference between learning acting from an acting teacher, or from a director? The obvious answer is that the director is preparing the actor for a scheduled performance while the acting teacher is not. Acting teachers concentrate on helping actors find a way to achieve their best work. Probably the best advice is the oldest—*Est modus in rebus*—"There is a middle course in all things." At the Studio, I came to some temporary and long-term conclusions. Actors can be wonderful, but very few of them, if any, can do it all. Paul Newman was not Brian Bedford and Brian Bedford was not Paul Newman. Each of us fulfills a specific job—that is, what we are good at—and it is foolish to beat one's self up for failing to be able to be all things to all people.

⌘ ⌘ ⌘

The first show I saw in New York was *A Far Country*. I went to see Kim Stanley who had created the role of Elizabeth von Ritter and would be a nominee for best actress for it in the 1962 Tony Awards. But the house lights were about to go down when an announcement came that Miss Stanley's standby, Joan Potter, would be appearing in the role at that performance. Lights gave enough time for a few angry patrons to scurry up the aisle to get to the box office before the curtain rose.

The play is problematic in as much as it centers on what is arguably Sigmund Freud's most famous case: a woman who is not "crazy" but communicative and is even a bit flirtatious, despite having lost the use of her legs and anticipating life in a wheelchair. Steven Hill gave a very fine performance as Freud, as did Lili Darvas (a wonderful character actress, wife of Ferenc Molnár) as Amalie Freud, along with Salome Jens and Patrick O'Neal. But the center of focus was Joan Potter playing Elizabeth. I shall always remember it, although I did not remember her name.

Of course, I glutted myself seeing shows, since I now had the money and access to NYC, and viewing the professional theatre would be a major part of my education as a director. I saw the only preview of Robert Bolt's *A Man For All Seasons* with George Rose as The Common Man and Paul Scofield as Sir Thomas More. Afterwards, I went to a Thanksgiving party at Jim and Cindy Prichett's and I told everyone at the party what a brilliant play it was and they had to see it. Some doubted my enthusiasm but it was confirmed the next day by the reviews.

It was during the Christmas break that I saw Tennessee William's *The Night Of The Iguana* just after it opened with Patrick O'Neal, Margaret Leighton, Bette Davis and Alan Webb. I count it as one of my great nights in the Theatre. Davis, of course, had the star power box office draw, but during the star curtain call Alan Webb was first, second was Davis who quickly yielded to Patrick O'Neal, and then Margaret Leighton. This was Davis' choice and I respected it because Maxine Faulk is *not* the starring role; the stars are the actors playing Shannon and Hannah Jelkes.

I saw Harold Pinter's *The Caretaker* which I absolutely loved, especially for the pauses in which much of the story is told, and also because of the incredible way the actors dared to play these pauses. I also loved Terrence Rattigan's *Ross* [the assumed name of T. E. Lawrence when he was hiding while being disciplined for alleged misconduct by the Royal Air Force]. Knowledge of this play helped my understanding of David Lean's great film *Lawrence of Arabia*. I saw the Off-Broadway production of Brendan Behan's *The Hostage*. Less memorable, but still important were *Purlie Victorious* with Ossie Davis and Ruby Dee; *How to Succeed in Business Without Really Trying* with Robert Morse; and *Milk and Honey,* a musical celebrating the new state of Israel, featuring Molly Picon, an icon of the old Jewish Theatre in NYC; Alfred Drake in *Kean; Daughters of Silence* with Emlyn Williams; *Subways are for Sleeping* with Sydney Chaplin and Carol Lawrence; and *Take Her, She's Mine* with Elizabeth Ashley and Art Carney. At that time, NO ONE did it better than Broadway. Seeing these shows was the best thing I could do to learn.

On December 28, 1961 I chaired a panel at the Speech Association of America meeting in New York City. The subject was "The New Script" and panel members included New York Agent Annie Laurie Williams, Director Allen Fletcher, Playwright Joe Caldwell and drama Professor Webster Smalley of the University of Illinois. I actually didn't have a lot of use for these meeting, but I was aware it was prestigious to chair them.

⌘ ⌘ ⌘

I had scheduled *Oedipus Rex* for a three-night run, but during the semester Bill Prosser told me he desperately wanted to be in *Endgame,* and one of the Cap and Bell boys wanted to direct. I suggested that we do the two in repertory, which appeased the Cap and Bells contingency who were all for the avant-garde. I figured these two shows side-by-side would give the Williamstown students, and the town a chance to compare classic tragedy with its existential modern view.

For *Oedipus,* I cast a young man whom I thought enormously talented but who had a severe stuttering problem. In everyday conversation Claude M. Duvall could scarcely get through a single sentence without blocking. I knew from Charles Van Riper's class in Speech Correction at Western Michigan that it was possible for an actor playing a character to do so without stuttering. The other aspect that I don't think anyone ever knew was that Robin, very early in life, also stammered and feared that if Claude had a block she would too. But I said to hell with the forecasting of what might happen! I believed they would make it and they did, beautifully; Claude and Robin never blocked on a single line.

Critic for *the North Adams Transcript* (remember that all these critics reviewed the productions of the highly acclaimed Williamstown Summer Theatre) J. Gordon Bullett wrote of *Endgame:*

> While the play is of limited appeal it is the type of theatrical work that can best be presented by an experimental group and best kept out of the professional theatre.... The author is like a man let loose with a new toy, in this case a dictionary, and he pours words over one in a title wave that sometimes has meaning and sometimes not. One of the author's better lines is 'this is deadly.'

Of *Oedipus Rex* Bullett wrote:

> ...one of the greatest tragedies of all time, was given a presentation last night... that was worthy in every respect of the greatness of this work and of the many luminaries of the stage that have appeared in it. Such productions... restore one's confidence, if this confidence has at times slipped, in the worthiness of college dramatics. The play has been directed by Joseph G. Stockdale, Jr. acting director of The Adams Memorial Theatre in the absence of director Giles Playfair who is on leave. Mr. Stockdale has directed with simple and loving care as well as with complete understanding, and an audience that filled

the theatre showed its appreciation through a concentration that passed from one to another in an electrifying, though absolutely quiet awareness, of the story being unfolded.

⌘ ⌘ ⌘

It was about this time that we were eating dinner at home one night—we usually sat down to dinner together—and six-year-old David said, "Please pass the fucking butter." Robin and I were, of course, aghast. He had obviously picked up that word someplace and did not know what he was saying. Robin kept her cool but said: "We do not use such language at the table." When David politely said something to the effect that the table was the only place he'd be asking "for fucking butter," I tried to keep a straight face but it was difficult. Thin-lipped now, Robin said she would talk to him after dinner and immediately launched into the subject we had been talking about—something like the Etna Bay encounter by the Dutch and Indonesian navies. We tried for years to talk about *important* subjects at the dinner table.

True to her word she took David aside after dinner. When he argued his case for free speech she said, "No, you are not free to use such language;" and when he wanted to know why, unlike me who would have said, "Because I said so!" she eventually said: "If you want to use such words, I give you permission to do so, but on one condition. You may whisper them to me but say them to no one else." He agreed cheerfully—David was nothing if not cheerful about almost everything—and that ended the discussion.

She pillow-talked to me that night about the agreement they had reached but she wondered where he had heard such language. I said that he had perhaps picked it up from Ash Crosby, who during afternoon rehearsals of *Oedipus* had taken to carrying David on his shoulder to the snack bar and treating him to an ice-cream cone. I figured the issue was settled.

The very next day as Robin was driving the kids to Pine Cobble, David leaned forward and whispered in her ear. "Fuck. Shit." Robin kept her cool and let this incident pass, but it kept recurring. In truth her nerves were frayed since he had also taken to eating the white paste they used in art class and she was trying to break him of that. One morning when he whispered the forbidden words she suddenly slammed on the brakes, turned to him and yelled, "You are NEVER to say those words again! You understand?"

"Okay, mom," he said pleasantly and thus the dirty words issue was settled—at home at least. Now the only thing we had to worry about was what he might say when Ash carried him to the snack bar and he ordered ice cream.

These little problems in raising the kids was why, in mid-November, when Robin missed her period and we found out she was pregnant, I was more than a little flummoxed. I will not say that I was angry, but this had not been thought out in advance, nor my agreement sought. She was in charge of the birth control issues and we already had three kids. I hinted that if she wanted an abortion...but she got miffed at such a suggestion. So that was that. She seemed happy and looked forward to having another baby to hold in her arms and nurse, but still.... As I think back, I believe that during Robin's pregnancies she was always happiest.

It had been six years since David was born. Maybe the diaphragm didn't work or she failed to put it in. Maybe she had not put it in on purpose, or maybe I got a little drunk and didn't pull out fast enough. Who knows? Although neither of us was especially religious I think she thought of being pregnant as a gift from heaven. At any rate, there it was and I adjusted quickly, looking forward for the baby to be born in mid-July.

⌘ ⌘ ⌘

Word had gotten to Giles Playfair in England about the good feeling within the community about the theatre's successes. He called President Sawyer to tell him that his legal work was going to keep him in England for another year. Jack told me that if I would stay on he would give me a generous increase in salary. I explained that I had tenure at Purdue, and although I would enjoy staying it would depend totally on Purdue granting me another leave of absence. Jack said he had a sense that Giles did not really want to return and that he would then hire me; tenure would be included along with my associate professorship.

I absolutely loved the place and was flattered by Jack's offer. But there was no guarantee that Giles would not return, so I suggested that Jack write Monroe and ask him if my leave of absence could be extended for another year. In his letter to President Sawyer, Alan Monroe said, "I can appreciate the problem with which you are faced... and have discussed this matter with our Theatre Director and with the Dean.... It would be extremely difficult for us to get along without Dr. Stockdale for another year. I am writing him and hope that you will be able to find some other way of handling your problem."

In Monroe's letter to me he answered questions I had asked:

> The Dean has assured me that your job as Summer Theatre Director will continue. In addition, he indicated that an increase from your presently budgeted salary of $8,500 could be made at $750. Making a total of $9,250 for the academic year. This is in addition to your summer salary, of course. Although the budget instructions have not yet been issued the Dean was sure that this could be done, and so am I. You should remember that TIAA and Social Security benefits should be added to your academic year salary since these are now paid for by the university, making your total take-home pay considerably more than it appears to be. Putting all of these things together, I have the feeling that your financial situation, to say nothing of your friendships here at Purdue, should be such that you would want to come back with us. I know that Ross wants you here and so do I.

Always nice to be wanted, but what a lot of effort it is to force the issue of raises and promotions! Why should that be necessary?

⌘ ⌘ ⌘

It was during Thanksgiving vacation when I stayed with Ed Loessin and Romulus Linney that Ed mentioned the national company of *Gypsy* had closed in St. Louis. I found Susan's phone number and called. She answered. I was headed to The Actors Studio and she asked if I could come to her place afterwards. Yes, I could. She lived on Charles Street in the Village.

From then on her apartment—on the second floor, a roomy studio—was where I stayed when I was in town to see shows, or to go to The Studio. I remember our renewed relationship first of all for the sex, and then the talk. This soon became a habit and I had my own set of keys.

We saw a lot of the Off-Broadway shows together at such theatres as the Cherry Lane, the Theatre de Lys, and Circle in the Square, and others within walking distance. I introduced her to James Earl Jones, whom I had first met when Pamela Printy was in summer stock with him in Manistee, Michigan. We saw him in *Moon of the Rainbow Shawl*, and we spent a couple of great evenings with Ed Loessin and Rosemary Murphy, who was going with Ed at the time. During post-Christmas vacation Susan invited me to The Plaza for Carnegie Tech's annual Christmas Party, which Bess Kimberly and Edith Skinner hosted for their alumni, grandly ladling out punch from a large cut glass bowl. It was an outrageously classy affair and I met a lot of people there who had known Susan at Carnegie Tech.

Susan introduced me to a community, not of stars, but of theatre workers who lived in The Village and were her friends of fascinating people such as John Battles and his partner (who had us to dinner and who I remembered from his Broadway role in *Allegro*); Sudie Bond, Vince Romeo and Jackie Brooks. I have always felt something special for talented theatre people who had to keep hope alive under circumstances that are almost hopeless. In those days there were about 35,000 members of AEA who lived in, or within commuting distance, of New York City.

Like Susan, they keep auditioning and being rejected, not for lack of talent, but because of a reliance on typecasting that is reinforced by authorial descriptions such as in O'Neill's *Long Day's Journey Into Night*. With the size of the talent pool of AEA members it was possible to audition maybe 50 actors who met the physical requirements for O'Neill's Edmund, and find a dozen who you felt had the talent to play the role.

⌘ ⌘ ⌘

Naked and spent, Susan and I were lying in bed talking about my need for security late one evening. The conversation was low-keyed and dreamy, face to face, so I could look and admire her. Robin had never been the subject of our conversations, but I said something about not only did we have three kids, but there was another one on the way.

What followed was a volatility that was instantaneous and with the force of a short-fused Roman candle. She was physically pummeling me and pushing me out of bed, screaming at me to get out. I could not understand it; we had just made love. She knew I was married. She had met my wife. What did she think, that I was not sexually active at home? She was out-of-control angry, screaming that I was a bastard and demanding that I leave. I attempted to calm her but she would have none of it.

I dressed and packed my things. She wanted the set of keys. I put them down on the stand next to the bed. I tried to tell her I was sorry. It seemed only to make her angrier. Outside in the hall, the door slammed behind me. I stood there trying to understand. I felt sad as hell. It was the end of our affair for certain and I knew it.

It was something like 1:00 A.M. I went down the flight of stairs and walked to the public phone booth on the corner. Ed answered on the seventh ring, said yes, I could stay there. I hailed a cab and wondered what could have made her turn so quickly to what felt like absolute hatred. She'd started our affair.

Maybe she felt sorry for Robin and wondered what she would have done if she were in her place and found out that I was sleeping with someone else. I never figured it out. I tried to call her a couple of times the next day and left messages with her answering service, but she did not respond. Several years later she came to a reading of my play *Taking Tennessee To Hart* at the York Theatre, but when we spoke, she acted as if there had never been anything between us—all that passion she had expended and now... nothing. I could have been a stranger she met for the first time and that was it.

She died a couple of years ago. A friend sent me the news. Susan kept working right up to the end. I saw her in an HBO special, playing the music teacher Irene Tewilliger for Jim Carey in *The Majestic*. I thought she was absolutely right for the part. She also had a small, but memorable scene as Mrs. Prior in Clint Eastwood's *Mystic River*. Stuart Howard used her in a Noel Coward show he directed in New Jersey. "Hope," indeed, for the vast majority of actors "perches in the soul and sings the tune without the words and never stops at all."

⌘ ⌘ ⌘

I suppose I should bring closure to this by some thoughts on monogamy. It may be possible, but I think it is very rare. So what is to be done? I don't know. Does anyone? Life happens! What I said when I was married was: "I, Joseph, take you Robin, to be my wife, to have and to hold from this day forward, for better or for worse, for richer, for poorer, in sickness and in health, to love and to cherish, from this day forward until death do us part." And I have been true to the vow. We have been married for more than 65 years.

Are women sexually wired the same as men? The problem is that after marriage, if women feel free to have sex with other men, men feel cheated, and isn't male jealousy hot-wired because of the paternity issue? How come over fifty percent of marriages end in divorce? Why are there so many households where there is no biological father present? Would it be better if when straying happens, the partner is not told? Isn't it better for each of us to try and understand that we are human and take that for exactly what it's worth?

What actually constitutes a marriage where the partners stay married for sixty-five years as Robin and I have? I think that we learned what "love" means and that there are different kinds of love for different stages of life. For the most part it isn't just going nuts like we did in the first years. Maybe the God of evolution has helped create the invention of cyberspace so both sexes can have virtual sex without actually meeting the other person in the flesh.

Why the craziness over Monica's blue dress? If she didn't have the money to send it to the cleaners, why not just go to the store and get a can of Spot-Off? Think of the billions that would have saved our nation! "We expect a higher standard from the President of the United States!" I say, why? To be honest, I'd much rather have a president who is sexually active than one who isn't. Why do so many people go ballistic because a couple of guys, or girls, fall in love and want to get married? I have a former student friend from Purdue who has been a lesbian forever, and who wanted to get married to a woman she had been living with for 30 years but couldn't under

New York State law. The law eventually changed and they were married. Good for New York State. Why would ANY human being be against that union? Why in hell do we all play these morality games that bring so much unhappiness?

⌘ ⌘ ⌘

Directing *Guys and Dolls* was one of the happiest experiences of my life. Robert T. Williams' designs for sets and costumes were incredible, Wayne Lamb did a great job as choreographer (the guys and dolls of Williamstown loved working with him), and musical director Monte Aubrey and his musicians could not have been better.

Headlines in the *Albany Times-Union* in a review by critic Michael Pilley read: "They're Going Wild in Williamstown."

"So rapturous was its reception... and so heavy has been the demand for tickets that an extra matinee will be presented tomorrow. And if you want to reserve one of the few seats remaining for the matinee your telephone call needs to be good and early today. It is a pleasure to report that this reception—one of the warmest seen in this area in many a production—is fully deserved. Joseph G. Stockdale has put together a humdinger of a show—a racing, entirely refreshing version of the story of the weird guys and dolls of Broadway immortalized by Damon Runyon.... You simply can't apply the word amateur to a show like this. It zips and zings with a professional pace. And never have there been such jokingly joyous performers."

There was a belated article in *The Williamstown Record* with terrific pictures of the show and a long write-up: "A total attendance of 3,039 for six performances (including a special matinee) of *Guys and Dolls,* is one indication of how successful the musical fable was received last month...." The story went on to quote Dr. C. Frederick Randolph, Jr. who wrote, "Not since the days when Mark and Albert Hopkins succeeded in launching religious revivals in the month of March has such good use been put to this dreary time of year in Williamstown."

"Why all the shouting? Staging the musical required 75 people—50 of them on stage—and it was whipped together in five weeks, with only seven full rehearsals. Most oft-heard comment in the AMT lobby was, 'I saw it in New York (or London) and this is every bit as good.'... Although Director Stockdale emphatically praised the students as the key factor in the success, they tossed the bouquet back to him. Personal touches by the director—such as a hand-written note to each member of the production on opening night—help place credit where it belongs. His attention to detail is evident by a personal check to make sure a local school principal would not object to one of his teachers appearing in the stripper scene.

As we went to press, one of the cast was scheduled for a Broadway try-out. All in all, the show captivated everyone, with not a single negative vote."

William Gibson, author of *Two For The Seesaw* and *The Miracle Worker*, saw the show opening night with friends, including Director Arthur Penn, and sent a letter-to-the-editor the next day to *The Berkshire Eagle*:

Since the Eagle did not review the Williams College production of *Guys and Dolls*, may I suggest to your readers that anyone in the mood for a big, fat, loud and lovely, red, white, black-and-blue rip-snorter of a howling, infectious, hum-along-dinger musical joke-book which is a joy to beholders, should hie himself to Williamstown this Thursday, Friday, or Saturday evening.

The week after the show closed Louis Rudnick asked Nikos Psacharopoulos, "Why don't you do a show like *Guys and Dolls* for the summer theatre audience?" and I got a letter from Jack Sawyer enclosing a check for $300 saying, "I know that you go to the New York Theatre and I know that it takes money, so this is for you to finish off your year at Williams going to the theatre. Thanks for the great job with *Guys and Dolls*. We all loved it."

⌘ ⌘ ⌘

I took Jack Sawyer at his word and kept going into New York for sessions at the Studio and to see shows. Among others, I saw *A Passage to India*, *The Aspern Paper*, *No Strings*, *I Can Get it For You Wholesale* with Barbra Streisand, *A Thousand Clowns* with Jason Robards, Jr., all new that season, and catching up from past seasons *The Sound of Music*, *Camelot* with Richard Burton and Julie Andrews, and *Carnival* with Jerry Orbach.

Off-Broadway and special events on Broadway included The Martha Graham Company; Arthur Kopit's *Oh Dad, Poor Dad, Mama's Hung you in the Closet and I'm Feeling so Sad* (a house seat since Flo Dire was working the box office); and at the old Yiddish Folksbiene Playhouse on the lower East Side, Ellis Rabb's productions of *The School for Scandal* and *The Seagull*.

I saw all of these shows and more on the $300 check that Jack Sawyer gave me.

⌘ ⌘ ⌘

I started rehearsals for *Romeo and Juliet,* which would be my swan song at the college. I again had Robert T. Williams to design the set and costumes, and it was he who suggested the approach the show took. I instantly agreed and added to his concept: What kind of place was Verona in 1594-1595? There were goatherds, prostitutes, and the contents of slop pots were thrown out the windows to quiet rival rowdy gangs. Romeo was horny and in love with Rosaline prior to going to the Capulet's masque ball and seeing Juliet—which gave him an instant boner.

One night at rehearsals, after the second balcony scene a cast member said, "Why in hell don't they just run away together?" It was a question shared by the entire cast. "Okay," I said, "every one of you write a scene as if you were Shakespeare explaining just why they can't elope, and we'll put in the best one. But you must swear to keep this quiet so absolutely no one knows about it." The one that I thought best was by Peter N. Simon, whom I had cast as Romeo.

Romeo:
Farewell, farewell one kiss and I'll descend.
Juliet:
O, leave me not alone. Take me with thee
Fear not my father's anger and pursuit.
We hide in tiny hollows in the ground
Where swelling rage can never find it out.
I'll with thee to Mantua.
Romeo:
It cannot be.
Thy vengeful kin desire more thy death than

> Thou be wedded to one of Montague.
> On being discovered, thy life would
> Not be spared, and in that death would I
> Die twice. Await with joy my quick return.
>
> (exits)
>
> **Juliet:**
>
> Art thou gone...?

There was a lot of controversy about this production, but we had great houses and a lot of excitement, even though criticism was leveled by various Shakespeare scholars. We even had one critic from Boston see the show. But you know something? Out of all those scholars *not a single one* detected those added lines. Peter Simon and I have since laughed and conjectured on the possibility that someone will find a copy of our script in an attic and get a PhD for their discovery of lost lines that Shakespeare wrote.

⌘ ⌘ ⌘

When Lawrence Olivier and Vivian Leigh did their production of *Romeo and Juliet,* Olivier got the idea that in the tomb scene, when Romeo bids Juliet's body farewell, Romeo crosses downstage to take the Apothecary's poison. Just after, as he feels it coursing through his veins, he turns upstage for a final look. At that moment Juliet begins to waken from the Friar's potion and moves her arms. She is not dead! Romeo staggers upstage toward her but is felled by the poison.

Has this business ever been copied? You better believe it! For all I know, it may not have been original with Olivier. I do know I copied it in that 1962 Williams College production, and it caused a matinee audience from Miss Hall's girl's school to gasp and weep.

⌘ ⌘ ⌘

Indeed, it had been a record year at the Adams Memorial Theatre. Bill Prosser wrote the history of that year in the student newspaper, giving events, dates, number of performances, and attendance, all of which Jack

Watson and I (as head of AMT) booked. Among them, on May 2nd, was Dame Judith Anderson in her one-woman show of scenes from *Macbeth* and *Medea*, which drew a full house.

The Dame traveled to these one-night gigs in a Winnebago in which she lived and slept. After the show, I escorted her to the Williamstown Inn where many of the theatre guys were waiting to meet her. She ordered a double Beefeater gin "with a splash" and asked to see the menu. The embarrassed waiter said the kitchen closed at nine. It was now almost eleven and he apologized.

This closed kitchen did not placate The Dame. She was hungry! One of the Williams boys hovering around the table sucking up insights into the legitimate *"theatah"* offered to drive her to North Adams for a sandwich. After a fraught pause with subtext, she countered with the suggestion that he "run on over" and bring her back *two* ham-and-cheeses-on-rye with a couple of dills on the side. While we waited, she slugged down a few more double Beefeaters "with a splash," presumably of quinine water, although since it was now past closing time I would not have blamed the waiter if… but let that thought pass.

When the sandwiches finally arrived, she ate half of one, wrapped the other half and second one in one of the Inn's linen napkins, tucked it in her clutch bag, and grandly left the Inn to go to her Winnebago. One of the people who traveled with her confided in me as she was making her exit that she would be having the other sandwich and a half the next day for breakfast and lunch. She did this at every one of these one-night stands. "She is, you know," he whispered, "the biggest tightwad in show biz."

As for her performance, I felt it was about the most professional technical acting I had ever seen. I loved her acting in *Medea* when I saw it on Broadway, but that was in 1948. This was 1962, and she was now on the road on cruise-control with a vocal-only rendition.

⌘ ⌘ ⌘

President Sawyer was at the final performance of *Romeo and Juliet*. At the final curtain call he brought me to the stage on behalf of the faculty, students and townspeople. He thanked me for the season, saying some very kind words about my contribution to the college, and presented me with a token of the college's esteem, a Williams College football sweater (the only other person who was *ever* awarded one, who did not actually play football for Williams, had been James Phinney Baxter), along with an accessory. When I later opened the box, it turned out to be the team's sacred purple-cow jockstrap.

After a wild party in a house on lower Spring Street and a few hours' sleep, Jack Watson drove me to Albany to fly to Chicago. Robin and the kids would stay on in Williamstown and finish the school year at Pine Cobble, after which Jack would drive them to Albany to fly home. Jack would then return to Williamstown, pick up Bill Prosser and our excess baggage and drive to West Lafayette where Bill would be an apprentice in our summer theatre, and Jack would design scenery and lighting.

1961-2 at Williams College had been a never-to-be-forgotten one hell of a great year!

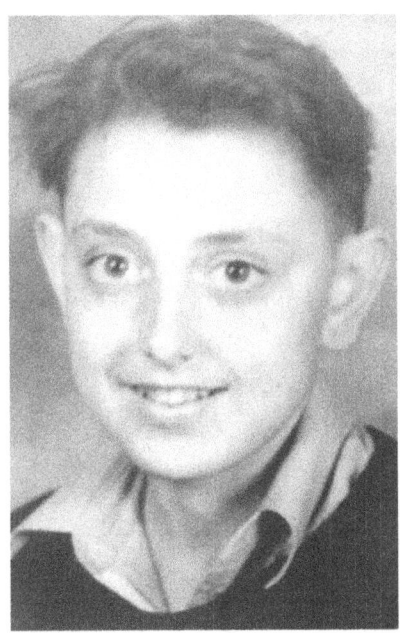

5th grader, Joe the Kid

Aunt Floss

Band of Brothers: Pharmacist Mates on the U.S.S. Wyoming.
(Joe, fourth from left, second row.)

Joe PhM2

Robin, the girl from Kalamazoo with engagement ring.

July 4, 1947. Married.

Robin and Joe in *Boy Meets Girl*.

The kids from Santa Barbara. "Mimsy" Birch on the right turning to face Joe.

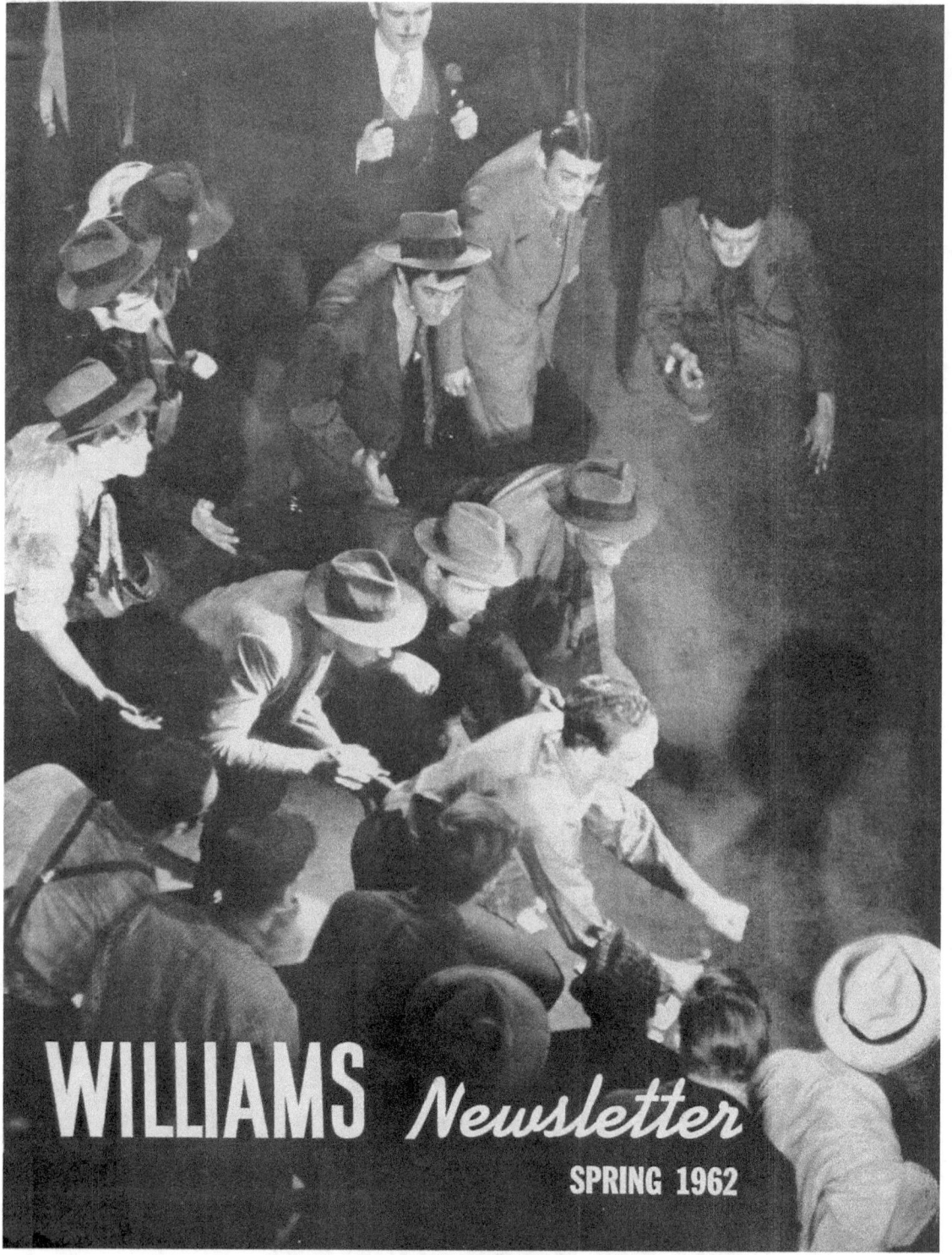
Guys and Dolls, Williams College.

Guys and Dolls

Anne Revere in *Mother Courage and Her Children*.

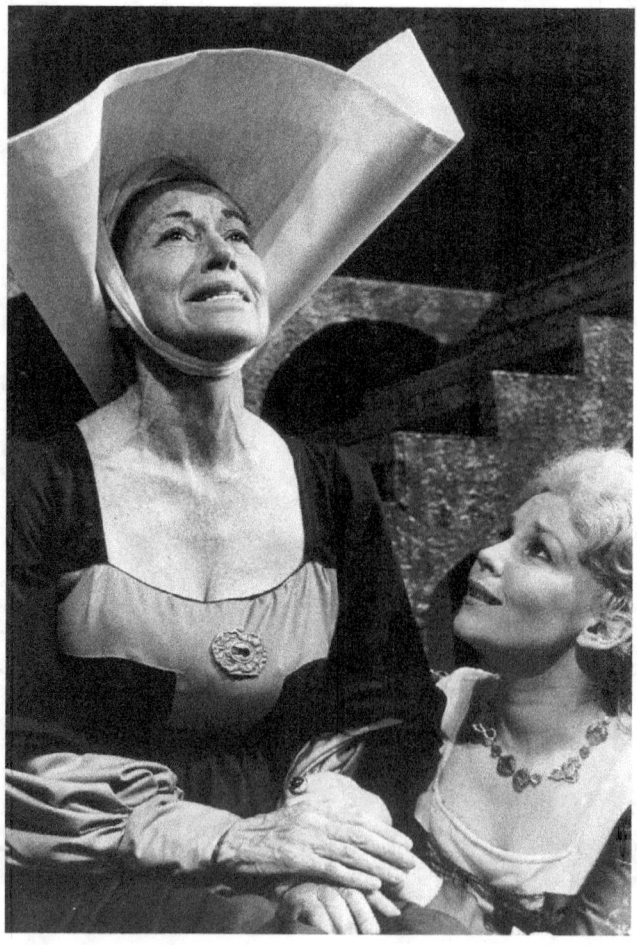

Anne Revere and Merle Louise as the Nurse and Juliet.

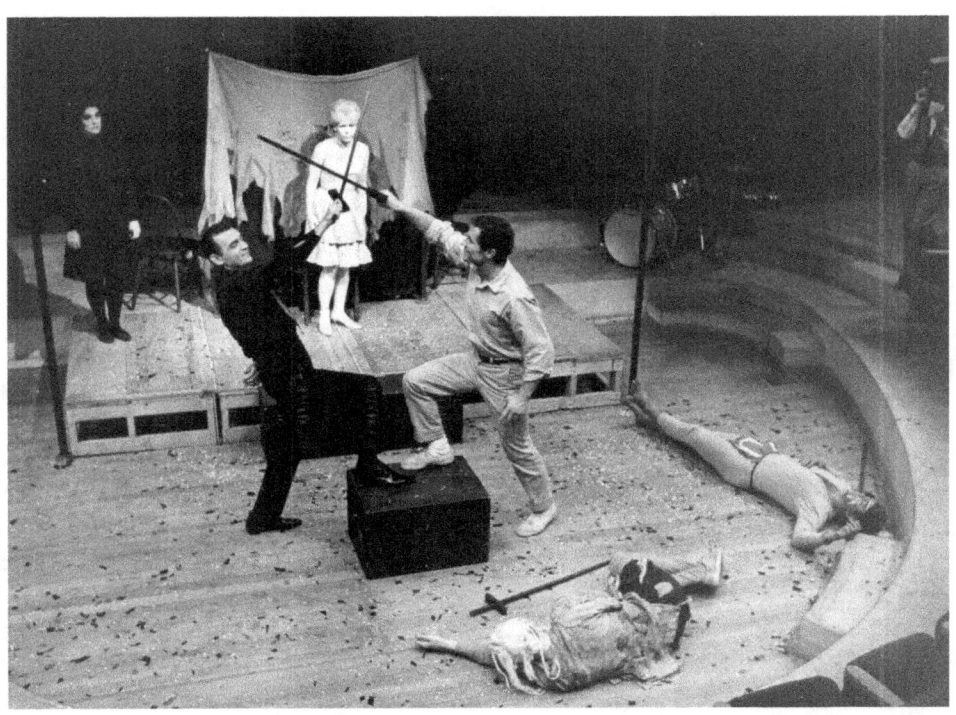

The Fastasticks, a great small musical, performed at Purdue as are all the following plays unless otherwise specified.

Ladies of the Evening with Macheath played by Dale Helward in *The Threepenny Opera*.

Pygmalion, from left, Dale Helward, Richard Newdick, Merle Louise, and Marilynne Black.

Larry Kirk (white shirt) in *West Side Story* with Joe (left) as Shrank.

(L. to r) Miriam Birch as Eve, Carole Lockwood as Susan, Royce Lenelle as Jane, and Stuart Howard as Littlechap and in *Stop the World, I Want to Get Off*.

435 Robinson Street, West Lafayette, Indiana.

Above Erling Kildahl and Frances Farmer in *The Visit*.

Dale Helward and Frances Farmer in *Look Homeward Angel*.

Joe and Purdue President Frederick L. Hovde at *The Visit* reception for Frances Farmer.

Robin Stockdale and Mark Lenard in *The Night of the Iguana*.

Ardele, an interesting French play without much name value, featured Stuart Howard, Dale Helward, and Janet Hayes.

Tartuffe

Oh What a Lovely War, Karen Woodward sings recruiting song for WWI "I'll make a man of you."

Uncle Vanya, Will Gregory as Astrov and Catherine Damon as Yelena.

James Earl Jones and Ed Setrakian in *Of Mice and Men*.

A Funny Thing Happened on the Way to the Forum, Reid Shelton as Miles Gloriosus with Lycus's girls.

Forum's curtain call.

Incident at Vichy

Bus Stop

Born Yesterday

You Never Can Tell

The Little Foxes with Robert Donley, Connie Heaver, and David C. Jones.

God's Peculiar Care with Preston Maybank and Tracy Kolis, performed at SUNY Purchase.

Robin and Joe at Lake Michigan.

Chapter 16

I LANDED IN CHICAGO AND HAD to catch the train down to Purdue in time for the Awards Banquet. The train got in late, and I had to get into my thrift-shop *Private Lives* white-tux-jacket outfit. During the last couple of months in Williamstown I had not shaved and when I walked into the banquet hall of the Memorial Union Alan H. Monroe called out as if in pain, "Oh, no! He's grown a beard!" But his dismay was drowned out by welcoming applause.

It was good to be home.

During my year at Williams, I had been so busy that I hadn't noticed that major changes were going on in the educational theatre. In the May 1962 issue of the *Educational Theatre Journal,* the lead article was an address given by W. McNeil Lowry, director of the Ford Foundation's Program in Humanities and the Arts, titled, "The University and The Creative Arts."

Even though I had a lot of work getting ready for the summer theatre, I started reading this article and could not put it down. At 8,042 words, it was overlong, digressive, qualified, and circumlocutory. But to me, being at a school noted for science and engineering, in a situation where the theatre had emerged from an English department and was now about to split from a Speech department, Lowry's words packed a wallop. What grabbed me was his discussion of the theatre training in a university setting. Purdue's

Dean of the Humanities, Social Science and Education was soon to create a Department of Creative Arts as part of that School.

Lowry observed the emergence in America of the vague idea that the a-r-t-s were somehow good for people. There was an increase in audiences—which he credited to a larger proportion of the population being university trained—along with a greater share of both private and corporate funding.

But funds were given largely, he observed, for the building of theatre (Harold Clurman called it the decade of the "Edifice Complex") which Lowry noted housed work "with amateur directors and amateur acting ensembles, and if criticized at all, criticized by amateurs" with little or no understanding that "it is the highly talented and professionally trained artist on whom all depend."

Lowry's conclusions were:

> The university has largely taken over the functions of professional training in the arts but in the main has sacrificed professional standards in doing so.... The trend is irreversible. The future of professional training in the arts depends, first, upon a radical shift in the university atmosphere surrounding students considered potential artists, and, second upon the provision of postgraduate opportunities for professional apprenticeship removed from an academic environment....

It was the next section that skyrocketed me into the final focus of my lifework.

> The Spartan effect one detects in professional environments has much to do with the drive or fanaticism or whatever of the person who has made his choice, and will eschew anything else—money, the elite identification of a university degree, even health—to develop the talent he hopes he has. It comes also from the pride of doing for oneself, of making ends meet, of giving society what it will pay for even if what it pays is inadequate to sustain a normal life, of working in the midst of a fraternity that will show the same fanaticisms and abnegations. It comes from the endless time, time, time spent on doing one thing, only one thing, and then starting all over again. It comes, finally, from the acceptance of such distortion as a way of life, a way of life, you will note, that is in some ways completely antithetical to the ideal objectives of a liberal and humane education.

I can remember no other time in my life when I was so intellectually and emotionally stimulated by an article. I found myself in those words; they were my energy, my rhythm, and what was true to my nature. Whatever happened, this was how I was going to live my life. What appealed was the impossible dream, the idealism. And perhaps because of my frustration at being a failed writer, I knew that intense focus on theatre was the answer of what I wanted most and it was—especially at Purdue—up to me whether or not I achieved it. I trusted both my talent and drive to do so.

Lowry waived the question whether the Deans wanted that sort of atmosphere on their campuses, and whether they could have it if they wanted it.

But if the university is going to allow the student's distorted concentration on hard-nosed doing and redoing, it cannot also require of him all the courses in humanities, the social sciences, and the natural sciences that are even minimally thought to constitute a liberal education. Nor can the professors and students be selected for a professional curriculum and atmosphere according to the patterns now employed in universities.

Roughly eighty per cent of the university students now concentrating in one of the creative arts have chosen to major in art education; they are insuring their ability to have a second vocation if the first fails. For four fifths of the students, then, no special atmosphere, no distorted concentration need be attempted. By all means excuse them from none of the normal requirements of a liberal education. *Their hunger for the arts* is *not fanatical enough.*

To face the necessary distortion of the primary objectives of a university, to reflect that distortion in a highly concentrated curriculum, to open that curriculum only to the students with the most fanatical drives, to give to the artist-professor *responsibility for testing both the drives and the talents*—these motives and procedures may go part way toward producing a professional atmosphere. [italics mine throughout.]

And this is *exactly* what I would be doing for the rest of my theatre career, and thank my lucky stars that I had married exactly the right mate to be able to do this.

⌘ ⌘ ⌘

The summer of 1962 was the first in which we advertised for apprentices. Out of some 30 applications, I selected ten. In addition, we had three grad and three undergraduate students working on the shows. Our first was *The Fourposter,* a two-hander by Jan De Hartog, which premiered on Broadway in October 1961 with Hume Cronyn and Jessica Tandy. It is the life story of Michael and Agnes, starting on their wedding night in 1890 in their bedroom, where a four poster is the major set prop, and continues for the next thirty-five years—through major events in the life of a marriage.

With such identifiable material, plus good actors—our Agnes was Helen McMahon and Michael was William ("Bill") M. Hardy—we played from June 19th to July 1st. Both were excellent in their roles, although Michael was a perfect match for the fine comic talents of Bill Hardy, whereas comedy was not McMahon's forte, or at least she approached it differently.

Concurrently with all our productions I scheduled two shows for children which would play every weekend. These shows were cast and crewed with members of the apprentice company. Both were musical plays: *Tom Sawyer* by Austin O'Toole and *Circus Is A Happy Thing* by Joe Gage [*aka* me] with music and lyrics by Jack Foley Horkheimer. I directed both productions; scenery and lighting were designed by Jack Watson. Both played on the forestage and in the pit area of the Experimental Theatre, which reduced seating capacity to 132 and sold out every performance.

In brief: four performances per week totaling 40 performances for an audience of 132 equaled 5,280 at 50¢ per, which gave us an income of $2,640 for the production costs. And at every performance we had wiggle-room for some harried mother who would appear with two extra neighbor kids for whom we set up a few more seats in back. Bless the house manager and ushers for facilitating, managing, and being aware of customer relations and goodwill in the community without sticking to "rules" and going totally nuts.

Our second major production playing July 4th through 15th was *Angel Street* with Martha Nell Hardy as Mrs. Manningham, and me as Mr. Manningham. Now you may wonder why Robin was not Mrs. Manningham since we had played it as the first show of the Saugatuck Summer Theatre in 1948. If so, you have not remembered that our fourth baby was due on the 15th of July.

⌘ ⌘ ⌘

It was just a little before this date that I got a call from producer Paul Day at the Bar Harbor, Maine summer theatre. He explained that I had been recommended by the Williamstown Theatre people and wanted me to come at once to direct the rest of the season. I told him this was impossible. Could I be there by the first day of August for rehearsal for the last three shows? Of course I wanted to do this, and after talking it over with Robin—both of us reasoning that she would have the baby almost two weeks before I had to leave—I called Paul back and said I would take the job.

As for births we had been there, done that and had three kids to show for it, so on July 15 we did not go ballistic when it did not happen. I, of course, had Tennessee Williams' *Suddenly Last Summer* to think about, it playing from July 18-29. I believe that *Suddenly* is Tennessee's best Aristotelian (time-place-and-action) structured play and is written to be played with no intermissions. Its subject matter is the predatory basis of nature which is typically portrayed by the praying mantis or the Venus flytrap, the insectivorous plant in the garden where the play takes place.

In fact everything, in this jungle garden setting—from the vegetation, to the birds that fly overhead, the Spanish moss, and the people—exemplifies evolution's predatory nature. As Tennessee describes it, "The set may be as unrealistic as the decor of a dramatic ballet." Backed by a part of a New Orleans mansion built in the Victorian Gothic style... in front of which is...

> A fantastic garden which is more like a tropical jungle, or forest, in the pre-historic age of giant fern forests when living creatures had flippers turning to limbs and scales to skin. The colors of this jungle garden are violent, especially as it is steaming with heat after rain. There are massive tree flowers that suggest organs of body, torn out, still glistening with un-dried blood; there are harsh cries and sibilant hissings and thrashing sounds in the garden as if it were inhabited by beasts, serpents and birds, all of savage nature....

In the *Lafayette Journal & Courier* (7/19/62) critic B.B. wrote: "You won't get much better drama anywhere this side of Broadway, and there have been some things in that area which were not as awesomely moving as this production."

During the playing of *Suddenly,* and as I directed *Teahouse of the August Moon,* I became more and more concerned that our baby had not arrived. Robin suggested we go for rides over bumpy roads in hopes it would bring on the birth, but that didn't work. It was when we were both at wits end on July 31st that I decided to call Paul Day and tell him that I had to break my AEA contract, which would cause them problems. Robin's water broke and I drove her to the hospital. After Dr. Peyton got there, I called Dick Newdick, the stage manager, and explained that he should proceed with the final dress rehearsal of *Teahouse* without me as I didn't know what was going to happen; I might or might not be there for the opening the next night.

Jack Horkheimer was standing by to drive me to Chicago's O'Hare field. The baby was born about 8:15 P.M. I was gowned and masked and went in to see Robin, who was very together at that point and was holding the baby. I asked her if I should cancel the trip. She said absolutely not, that she would be fine, and that I should go and not worry about anything. I kissed her good-bye and then I kissed John Williams Stockdale (his middle name was for the College). Jack drove fast, as the flight was scheduled about midnight.

I freaked out when we were halfway there and became so emotional that I cried. I had a terrible feeling that I was doing the wrong thing. Jack pulled off to the side of the road and told me to make up my mind. He'd have to drive like hell to get me there, and we had no time to waste. I told him to drive on.

In New York I had to change for my flight to Boston, and then another change to fly to Bar Harbor. It was 6:00 A.M. when we approached that small airport, in fog so thick I could not see the ground. I thought of Robin and John, and thought of death as the plane descended. Suddenly I saw earth so close that I thought we were going to crash. The pilot aborted the landing and the plane lifted sharply upward. We circled through the fog as thick as the proverbial pea soup, and the pilot made his decision to try again. He had to abort that landing, too, veering upward so sharply that the lower back section of the plane touched the runway.

When the plane was again horizontal and at altitude, the pilot announced that we would have to go on to Portland. Nelson Rockefeller had landed at Bar Harbor just an hour previously, but that was it. The airport was closed. We flew to Portland over a hundred miles away, and after safely landing there, I took a bus back to Bar Harbor.

I was an hour late for the first rehearsal of *Private Lives*. When I was met by the producer, Paul Day, he told me the problems he had had with the company's leading actress, Olive Deering, and how the director who preceded me had literally been carried out onto a plane with bleeding ulcers the morning after the opening of Saroyan's *The Cave Dwellers*. I had been without sleep for 30 hours—experiencing some of the worst stress I would ever know—not to mention that I was so hungry I could eat the back end out of a skunk—but since this was Wednesday, on a one-a-week summer-stock schedule, I had to block the first act.

I spent no more than a few minutes explaining my absence and mentioning the birth of my son. I don't think it was more than a half-hour while working on a new French scene that Olive took an unusual pause in the middle of a beat. I said, "No, Olive, there is no pause there. Wait until you end the beat on line…" She seemed astounded and looked out at me with those beautiful green eyes and said, "But I need a private moment at this point and…" "No," I interrupted her, saying very firmly on which line the beat started, the beat's objective, and where it ended. There was no question that she was about to challenge me, but I looked at the intensity in her eyes with the same (if not a bit more) intensity in my own, and after only a moment her expression changed. She hunched her shoulders and said, "All right then, you're the boss."

And you can be sure I saw to it that she was on time and ready for her entrance on the date the show opened. To do so I had to win her full confidence, which I did. I dined with her that evening before curtain time for *Cave Dwellers* at the local eatery, Joe Testa's restaurant, which had its own herb garden in a small attached greenhouse. I think she was intrigued by my eating—I was famished—and also because I was someone without any New York theatre credits.

She was dallying with her food when I finished a second cup of coffee and said I'd walk her back to the theatre for half-hour call. Sounding very cavalier she said there was no hurry. I asked for the check, telling her what her share of the bill was. I could tell by the way she dug into her purse that she hadn't expected to pay. I settled up, tipped the waiter, and we headed out.

Paul was stunned when he saw us come in and told me the curtain had not gone up on time since she had been there because she deliberately delayed it, sometimes as much as 15 minutes or more. But the curtain went up on time (five minutes after advertised time) that night and each successive night of *The Cave Dwellers,* a play I found pretentious. I went backstage to tell her she was wonderful, which wasn't just bullshit because she *was* a very talented actress, and to ask her if she wanted to go for a quick drink. She did.

I had a gin and tonic but she drank tea. After about half an hour, talking mainly about *Private Lives,* I suggested we run the lines of those scenes we blocked in the first act and she agreed. So we went back to her room at the hotel. I believe she assumed I was going to make advances but instead I started immediately on her first scene.

Yes, I knew all the lines because I had done the show three times. In fact, I had brought one costume that Martha Nell wore in the Purdue production, knowing that whoever played the role would love it. And the next day after rehearsal I gave it to the costumer, who thought it perfect and Olive absolutely adored it, thank god! It fit her with very few alterations.

I did not dine with Olive opening night. I needed a nap before coming to the theatre for the performance. She went to Testa's as usual and it seemed that I had just put my head on the pillow, although I had actually slept an hour, when Paul called: Olive had gone crazy at the restaurant and he asked me to get down there. I literally ran the five blocks.

Olive's voice, passionately alive with sibilant threats and plans of revenge, sounded much like Judith Anderson as Medea in 1948 having just heard that Jason was about to ditch her and marry "Little Creusa." And the language was a little bluer than the strippers I had heard backstage at *Gypsy.* I pushed my way through the fleeing customers and sank to one knee, taking her hands, and telling her to breathe deeply. When she was calmed, she said she had taken a *Private Lives* program and stuck it in her bag. When she finally looked at it after dinner she saw that *once again* it did not have her name over the play's title and she was certain Paul had done this deliberately.

I immediately sided with her and she began to relax. I told her we were going to the theatre and that before the curtain went up, we would have it out with Paul. I said I thought the best thing was to let me do the talking so she could not be accused of egotism, and I would tell him that the William Morris Agency had said that this was a breach of contract and that she would be within her rights to refuse to perform. But, I added quickly, since she was a consummate professional, I knew she would never refuse to perform out of loyalty to her fellow cast members and her audience. The person who should be taken down was Paul, and I would see to it.

He was in the lobby waiting. I took a position just in front of Olive and winked at him so he understood that I was staging a scene, although, in truth, my feelings were genuine to the degree that what he had done for spite was pretty stupid. He immediately picked up a program and said that this was the first he knew about her name not being printed over the play's title.

I told him we would accept his word. However, it had happened. As producer he was still responsible, and Olive had every right to call her agent.

He apologized immediately and his words reflected sincerity because, in fact, this was an unfortunate oversight. He offered to make an announcement and would try to get new programs made for the rest of the run. I said I didn't think that would be necessary, that Olive was above such pettiness, but he must know that violation of contracts with William Morris could result in repercussions both for him and the theatre.

Olive then spoke, saying that no announcement or second printing of the program was necessary, that she accepted his apology, and that she now had to get ready for the performance. Paul took her hand and thanked her.

That night Olive was ready when the stage manager called "ten," "five" and "places please" and the curtain rose on time. She was word-perfect and did not work in any extraneous pauses. She played the play as Noel Coward wrote it and as it was directed. In truth she was a Tallulah-Bankhead-at-her-best *perfect* Amanda, and I was very proud to have worked with her and grateful for this experience because it gave me insight into actors known as "difficult."

After *Private Lives* opened I had dinner with Olive each evening and walked her to the theatre to see that she got there and that the curtain rose on time. She was fine throughout the rest of the week without a new part to work on and no rehearsals. During the days I rehearsed *The Moon is Blue*, which would be followed by *Gaslight* (original name of *Angel Street*) in which I again played Manningham, the leading role.

⌘ ⌘ ⌘

Perhaps the most important national event that happened after I arrived in Bar Harbor was on August 5th. I was having breakfast prior to going to rehearsals when I heard two tight assed up-east accents. "Well, she certainly got hers, didn't she?"

"Ayuh, and rightly so," answered the other woman through a down-turned mouth.

"What happened?" I asked.

"Marilyn Monroe killed herself," was the woman's gleaming-eyed answer.

"Ayuh," the second one added self-righteously, "she finally got her just deserts. Ayuh, Marilyn Monroe's dead!"

I was devastated. Marilyn was 36 years old and I was one year older. Her death made me as sad as I had been in a long time.

⌘ ⌘ ⌘

It was great to see the family again. The first thing I heard from Robin was the story of the bat. She had been in the hospital two nights while Doe Harlan stayed with the kids before Earl Harlan—who would be one of baby John's godfathers, the other, Wayne Lamb—brought them home. After she nursed him and he was settled in his basinet, which was placed in a crib in the small front room with the big window—a room not connected with the two living rooms and accessible only by the upstairs hallway—a bat flew in and Robin became hysterical.

Scared for the new baby, Lory grabbed him and sent Joe III running down the alleyway to ask our neighbor, West Lafayette policeman Charley Dietrich, for help. He came at once, captured and killed the bat, and then closed the flue in the fireplace. Rather than regaling me, this story made me realize that as a husband and parent, going to Bar Harbor had probably not been a good choice. But—the paradox—as for what I liked to do, it was.

⌘ ⌘ ⌘

As previously arranged I would direct Chekhov's *The Sea Gull*, which was to open the second week in March (1963). A pesky schedule conflict had reared its ugly head and Ross wondered if I would also direct *Our Town*, scheduled for October.

To tell the truth, my first thought was, "No, I would not like to direct that hoary old chestnut." I had read the play in college, seen community theatre productions, and during my second year at Purdue had been called by the frantic director of the Lafayette Civic Theatre telling me that the actor playing Professor Willard had taken ill and could I go on that night and for the rest of the run? Of course I said "yes," not realizing that the old professor was a stereotypical academic geologist/meteorologist/anthropologist/statistician whose monologue concerned these subjects and all their unpronounceable words that had to be memorized, along with the hour it would take me to do the complex age makeup including the obvious gray beard.

So NO, I did not want to even hear the name of *Our Town*, let alone direct it, but I was far too busy at the time to answer with anything but yes. Once I started working on the play, I realized how wrong my first reaction had been. I came to realize that it is the ordinariness of Wilder's characters, the episodic structure of *Our Town's* lifelike, strung-together events, its lack of scenery and big dramatic scenes, its antithesis to the razzmatazz of Broadway that unifies the play's universal subject, revealing the simplicity and beauty of its theme.

After dying, when Emily is allowed a momentary return to earth and for the first time *sees* the beauty in random, everyday events, she breaks down sobbing.

"I didn't realize." She says, "So all that was going on and we never noticed. Take me back-up the hill-to my grave. But first: What! One more look. (pause) Good-by. Good-by, world. Good-by Grover's Corners… Mama and Papa. Good-by to clocks ticking … and Mama's sunflowers. And food and coffee. And new-ironed dresses and hot baths…and sleeping and waking up. [now with full realization] Oh, earth, you're too wonderful for anybody to realize you." She looks toward the stage manager and asks abruptly, through her tears: "Do any human beings ever realize life while they live it?—every, every minute?

"No," the Stage Manager answers and then adds, "The saints and poets, maybe—they do some."

I had a really splendid cast of actors, some 45 in number, and the night the show opened I came down to the trap room to make my traditional fast rounds of the dressing rooms and to call "Break a Leg!" I found both cast and crew assembled. On behalf of all of them, E. Allyn Thompson presented me with one of those Gorham Giftware gold plates, inscribed:

> Ayuh. Right Smart Director
> OUR TOWN 1962
> Joe Stockdale, Jr.

This was not a razzmatazz event on the Great White Way, like a chorus member getting the Gypsy Robe on opening night of a new musical, but one so simple and truly felt I have never forgotten it.

I also loved Anton Chekhov and had read his major short stories and plays. Up to this point however, I had not dared to direct one because of the complicated mixture of the comic and tragic genres and their obscure (to me at that time) universal subject and point of view. Now faced with the fact that I was to direct *The Sea Gull* in a March production, the show was constantly on my mind.

One afternoon in the late fall of 1962, while watching a film on a TV program from Indianapolis station WFBM called *Frances Farmer Presents,* an idea struck me. Clurman's *The Fervent Years,* a history of the Group

Theatre (1931-1940), chronicles the most important attempt in the history of the American Theatre to form a permanent repertory company. Frances Farmer, having reached stardom in Hollywood, had been a part of the Group during its final years.

Watching her in the brief sections in which she appeared between advertising and segments of the film she was airing, I felt there was something in her manner, her way of speaking that suddenly made me think she would be an absolute standout for the role of Irina Arcadina Trepleff in *The Sea Gull*. The visiting artist program, which had started with my leave of absence to Williams College, would be continued, so why not Frances Farmer in *The Sea Gull*?

I talked to Ross—who was always supportive—and presented my plan at a meeting of the entire Theatre Faculty. They agreed, with an understanding that I would be the one to approach her, and the Equity contract would be limited to $600. I called WFBM, talked to the manager, explaining who I was and that I wanted to talk to Miss Farmer. Could I have her home phone number? Those were the halcyon days when such requests were possible.

She was most receptive when I called. First, I cleared availability for performance dates, and the times I had scheduled rehearsals for her, explaining that I would first work on those scenes in which she was not involved and then concentrate on her scenes. She liked that plan because, of course, she had her daily afternoon TV program and would be unable to commute back and forth and be on campus from 7 to 10 for rehearsals. I then addressed the pay issue, prefacing it by saying I was a little ashamed of the amount, but there it was and I would understand if she felt it was too little. After she said that my offer, including a visiting artist Equity contract for $600 would suffice, she added that it was the play that counted. I then announced the role and play.

Her response was a stifled cry—a variation of the same reaction from every actor I ever contacted. I was fearless in contacting actors—Viveca Lindfors, Lee J. Cobb, Eileen Heckart, Barbara Loden, whomever—and although none of them appeared at Purdue, the reason was always availability, *never* money. The reason they came was because of a role in a play they had coveted for years and longed to perform.

Frances said she loved Chekov, telling me she had played Sonya in *Uncle Vanya* in her college days at the University of Washington, and had once rehearsed Olga in Clifford Odets' adaptation of *Three Sisters* for a production that had never materialized for the Group Theatre. She would dearly love to play Arcadina. And then almost in the same breath, "Come to think of it, I might be able to talk the producer of my TV show into letting it originate from The Loeb Playhouse during the time I'm involved in rehearsals and performances." And that is exactly what she did, which gave the show more coverage than we could ever have hoped for.

There was no question that she had been a major film star from 1935-1943 and starred in all but the first and last couple of the following films: *Too Many Parents; Border Flight; Rhythm On the Range* with Bing Crosby; *Come and Get It* (her best film) with Edward Arnold and Joel McCrea; *Exclusive* with Ray Milland; *Ride A Crooked Mile* with Leif Erickson; *South of Pago* with Jon Hall; *Flowing Gold* with John Garfield; *World Premiere* with John Barrymore; *Badlands of Dakota* with Robert Stack; *Among The Living* with Albert Dekker; *Son of Fury: The Story of Benjamin Blake* with Tyrone Power; *I Escaped from the Gestapo* with Dean Jagger; and then in the early 1950s *The Party Crashers* with Bobby Driscoll and Connie Stevens. As for Broadway, she was in The Group Theatre's productions of *Golden Boy, Thunder Rock,* and *Quiet City.*

During Christmas break before we started rehearsals, I was in New York to see shows and shared my good fortune that I would be working with Frances with Salem Ludwig, an acquaintance at The Actors Studio. Lee Strasberg actually spoke to me at the end of the next session when I was about to leave. "I hear you are going to direct Frances Farmer in *The Sea Gull.*" I acknowledged as much. "This is just a warning in case you don't know. She may never make it on stage. She's an alcoholic."

Under AEA's guest artist contract, in addition to what Frances was paid I saw to it that she would get transportation by automobile between Indianapolis and West Lafayette. I volunteered to drive her at no cost since these round trips afforded me three hours, five days a week for two weeks to talk with her about the play and the character. She would be provided a room at the Purdue Memorial Union for the dress rehearsal and performance period. I also saw to it that she was contracted for star billing over title and author, a star curtain call, and a star dressing room.

Informally, I asked her for three four-hour discussion periods in Indianapolis on Saturday afternoons prior to her starting rehearsals in order to talk about her character, the structural components of the play, plus its topic and Chekhov's point of view on the topic. Frances was 49 years old, I was 37, and I think she relived some of her college days during these sessions.

We read and discussed various writings: Maxim Gorki's address at Chekhov's funeral in which he interprets the playwright as saying, "You live badly, my friends, it is shameful to live like that," implying that people should live better, more productive lives; Ernest J. Simmons, *Chekhov: a biography* quotes the playwright on genre: "You say that you have wept over my plays. Yes, and not only you alone. But I did not write them for this purpose; it is Alekseev [Stanislavski] who has made such crybabies of them. I desired something other. I only wish to tell people honestly, 'look at yourselves, see how badly and boringly you live...' people should understand this, and when they do they will certainly create for themselves another and better life."

We discussed Stanislavski's *My Life In Art,* with special attention to the Moscow Art Theatre's production of *The Sea Gull* and his promptbook for this play. Reading various translations of the play resulted in the actual working script put together with two translations, Constance Garnett's and a more modern one—printed face-to-face. We found that we most often favored Garnett's translation, but if we were uncertain we had Katcha Singleton at most rehearsals who could both read and speak Russian and could translate from the original.

During these discussions, I found Frances prepared and extremely intelligent, with an understanding of the peripheral, historical milieu of the play's action and a wonderful insight into her character's humor.

I had the cast study all the same books as Frances, plus Vladimir Ivanovich Nemirovich-Danchenko's *My Life in the Russian Theatre.* I look back on these discussions and rehearsals as some of the most exciting learning experiences in my life. And I remember a moment in rehearsals at the end of Act

I when Masha confesses to Dr. Dorn that she loves Kostya. He replies, "...everyone seems to be in love... It must be the magic of the lake! (tenderly) But what can I do, my child. What can I do?" And on the words "my child," Cindy Miller, Bud Dixon, and I knew at the same moment that Dorn was actually Masha's biological father. He had been the tall dog around the lake. And we later read—in the Danchenko, I believe—the relationship had once been made explicit in the text, but had been cut prior to the play's first performance.

The week before opening with Frances in residence and doing her TV shows from The Loeb Stage, there was a magazine spread in the local newspaper that included comments by cast members about working with Frances in the show. Janet McGinniss who played Nina, graduate student Tom Holloway who played Trigorin, Cindy Miller who played Masha, and Stephanie Stein who played Pauline all had good things to say about Frances. With a generosity of spirit that was typical of Frances, she was quoted as saying, "The thing that's important about Chekhov is the ensemble."

In the actress-director relationship, I found her flexible and easy to work with. She did not feel that the parameters of the movements limited her creativity. She clued me in on this by saying quietly one day after I asked her if she "felt comfortable" with the blocking of a beat, "Joe, I don't feel any need to discuss blocking. Just tell me where you want me onstage to get the stage picture and when to cross." She never played the "star," never upstaged or gratuitously took focus, and she was generous and trusting with her fellow actors. And she *always* gave full measure in a rehearsal, never withheld emotionally or on vocal projection. She was adamant in believing the audience had the right to hear as well as see, that what the actor was feeling internally meant little unless that feeling was projected to the back of the house. In short, she was a dream to work with.

At no time to my knowledge, either at conferences or rehearsals, had she been drinking. Early in the afternoon of the day we opened, I thought about that warning from Lee Strasburg and went to her room to wish her a good performance. She was resting but not asleep, and on the dresser beside the bed was a fifth of whisky.

I made a quick decision. If it happened, it happened. We were too far out of the theatrical mainstream for the cancellation of a show to make a big difference to theatrical history. Her $600 salary plus the play's production costs of perhaps $2,000 was small potatoes compared to the staggering amount being spent on scientific research at Purdue. Further, I knew that she was enormously fond of the students and me, and that she had great love and respect, even reverence, for Chekhov. For these reasons alone she would never break faith. Suspicion on my part demeaned her; she was an extraordinary actress and a fine human being and for these reasons alone she rated absolute trust.

My confidence was rewarded that evening.

Random remembrances: her entrance, on the arm of Sorin; the smoking of the black Russian cigarette; and the difficult and quick transition from defensive anger, after she had interrupted the onstage performance of her son's play, to her genuine concern that she had wounded his pride.

In Act II: lying in the hammock under the lime tree projecting utter boredom while making her ennui theatrically interesting. The stinginess: disclaiming: "I am an actress not a banker!" Her persuading her lover Trigorin to leave with her, using excessive flattery, and her skills as a provincial actress walked a fine line: comedy for the audience while at the same time making the action believable enough to persuade the vain but intelligent writer. This was risk- taking to the nth degree since Frances herself might be thought to be a bad provincial type. It was also risky because many of those who had seen Chekhov's works were preconditioned to believe that they were all tragic.

In Act III, a delicious moment: when having gotten her way with Trigorin and about to leave, in a rare moment of generosity, she tips the cook "A ruble." But seeing his two helpers edge forward she adds pleasantly, "It's... for the three of you." And in the last act, after she brings Trigorin from the station, her playing lotto, and telling of her theatrical triumph in Karkoff.

In the offstage dinner scene she participated fully with the ensemble, improvising and laughing at times to counterpoint the tragic scene being played onstage between Nina and Constantine. And when Nina leaves and Constantine tears up his writing and goes offstage—and then the shot is heard—Irina, alarmed, enters, followed by the others. Dr. Dorn returns to explain that it was just a bottle of ether in his medicine case, quickly relieving her anxiety. Then pulling Trigorin downstage and dropping his voice Dorn says, "Somehow get Irina Nikolayevna away from here. The fact is, Konstantin Gavrilovich has shot himself."

The critic from the Lafayette paper in a review headlined "EVEN WRITER WOULD LIKE MISS FARMER'S PORTRAYAL" wrote:

> Miss Frances Farmer puts the magic in Chekhov's involved play... Her talent and theatre knowhow provide the magnetism.... A professional and convincing portrayal.... She puts glittering vitality into the part... bringing life and empathy to the role. She did wonderful things with the comic elements. Her articulation was superb and even Chekhov would have been delighted with her enactment of the role... every moment was graceful and she acted with the tremendous verve of a skillful performer.... *The Sea Gull* with Miss Frances Farmer as its star is an excellent and memorable offering....

Walter Spencer, who wrote for an Indianapolis newspaper and eventually for *The Village Voice* and a local radio station in New York said: "The role of Madam Trepleff is perfect for her ....with all the regal posturing of a Czarina, she plays the overbearing and over dramatic actress who wheedles and begs and thunders and browbeats to get her own... selfish ways.... The play has, in fact, been given a thoroughly professional production."

During *The Sea Gull* production, Ross had requested sabbatical leave for the academic year 1963-64 in order to spend the year in France. This would be his first leave since getting his PhD. The hitch was that if he took a full year he would only get half his regular salary. I offered to take his duties as Chairman of Convocations and Lectures, Gene Kildahl said he would teach his History of Theatre class, and we agreed to act as co-chairs of Theatre. President Hovde then approved full pay. Ross also applied and received a travel grant from the Fulbright Awards people. In addition to my new salary—$10,500—I also got $300 as an entertainment stipend to spend on celebrities who came to Purdue on the Convocations and Lectures program. Big deal!

⌘ ⌘ ⌘

I went into my summer theatre duties with a renewed vigor because of the McNeil Lowry article, plus a new sense of what I wanted for the theatre. I still would be doing shows that hopefully attracted large audience, but I no longer felt limited to summer stock fare. Our schedule included *The Fantasticks, A Taste of Honey, Misalliance, The Caretaker*, and we also did a children's musical by Stuart Howard, *Snaggletooth, Queen of the Gypsies* directed by its author, with scenery by Stuart Wurtzel and costumes by Lyn Carroll.

It was thanks to Stuart Howard, who was my assistant for the season, that we got Stuart Wurtzel, a Carnegie Tech student, as our designer. He stayed on for a second season and was one of the best designers I ever worked with, eventually designing several Off-Broadway and nine Broadway shows plus 45 major films including one nomination for an Academy Award, two wins for the Art Directors Award, and two nominations and one win for the Emmy Award.

Our *Fantasticks* cast was headed by Stuart Howard as The Narrator. The Mute was played by Cindy Miller, who was the first woman to play the role. Staging included her swinging over the heads of the audience from the back of the Experimental Theatre to the pit area on her first entrance. The Experimental Theatre was the perfect venue in which to produce this show and it seldom went on without extra seats being set up in the back of the house. The House Manager was instructed to have those who were so accommodated to buy first-night tickets for future productions; I, in turn, used them as comps for cafeteria workers in the Memorial Union, people who loaned us props, or in some cases people who had never before seen a live show. *Fantasticks* played to well over one hundred percent capacity, and since tickets were scarce it helped create a sense of urgency in ticket buyers for the rest of the season

In a review (6/12/63) in *The Lafayette Journal and Courier*, Alfred Chiscon wrote: "Local Playgoers long have realized that a production by Joseph Stockdale assures them of a close-up view of professional artistry at work. *The Fantasticks* proves no exception." And Charles Staff of the *Indianapolis News* (6/18/63) wrote: "A visit to the Purdue Summer Theatre does much to clear the foggy notion that Purdue University is a boiler factory hard by a cow pasture... with another rich vein to Hoosier summer theatre fare."

Shelagh Delaney's *A Taste of Honey* also had a fine cast which was open to experimentation. The mother was an alcoholic, and although not a prostitute, lived off the funds given her by the men she slept with. Being the drama teacher at West Lafayette High School, it was understandable that Mary Helen Kahn was a bit worried about how the community would take her playing this role. I said we would rehearse one scene in total darkness and the cast could improvise any business that came to them.

Prior to this I told Peter Bock, who played Helen's boyfriend, to be a bit outrageous in his scenes with her, making some semi-unacceptable sexual advances. When this happened (I never knew exactly what he did) I heard Mary Helen shriek with laughter, and after that she seemed to sense the joy and humor in the role. Her final line, when Jo, her daughter, pregnant by a black South African sailor, experiences her first birth pangs and pleads for advice from her mother, Helen's response is to grab her purse and head for the local bar, calling back, "Put it on the stage and call it blackbird!" This brought down the house, but the laughter seemed to stick in the throats of the audience when the terrified Jo contracts in another labor pain and the lights fade to out. Cindy Miller and Bill Lampe were brilliant in this production, as was Stuart Howard.

Shaw's 1910 play, *Misalliance,* subtitled *A Debate in One Setting,* would take more than three hours of playing time. There is a lot of extraneous political "stuff" plus the use of the "N" word which, at the time of Shaw's writing, could be used in fashionable society, but was certain to clear the Experimental Theatre of our audience. I assigned the cutting of the play to Bill Prosser and Stuart Howard, asking them to eliminate everything except what illustrated the ironies of the relationship between parents and children, a subject I was beginning to know well with a 13-year-old daughter at home.

In short, our production, sans talk of socialism, the life force, and other issues which Shaw was fond of, lasted 1 hour and 30 minutes plus a 10-minute intermission, which seemed more civilized. This cutting was later used in half a dozen other productions throughout the country, including two of my own.

I know! I know! You have caught me being inconsistent because I almost inevitably disapprove of directors who cut and reshape a playwright's work. But I also know that Emerson was right when he said that "a foolish consistency is the hobgoblin of little minds" and advised one to "speak what you think today in hard words and tomorrow speak what tomorrow thinks in hard words again, though it contradict everything you said today."

The production was a sold-out smash hit playing to one hundred twelve percent capacity. Stuart Howard, while trying to identify the face of a woman in a miniature ("Gunner's" mother with whom he had an affair), points to the small photograph lodged in a brooch and says: "I remember that brooch, I brought it from a man in Cheapside who wore a yellow wig and had a cast in his left eye, but for the life of me, I can't remember your mother." This line never failed to bring down the house far more effectively than most lines in contemporary summer stock comedy.

Critic William Tillson of *The Lafayette Journal and Courier* wrote (7/18/63) "Purdue Summer Theatre's stylish revival of G.B.S's *Misalliance* is the seasonal peak of the group's most successful series... most capably produced, directed and acted by the Stockdale Company, it is the affirmative, active-verb answer to a question Shaw posed to a group asking to do a play: 'of course you may, but can you?"

The Caretaker, which had been on Broadway and won a Tony nomination for "Best Play," was the first of three Harold Pinter productions I directed. Of all contemporary playwrights I think he had the widest background in theatrical experience. He started out as an actor, later turned to directing, and then writing, all skills at which he was successful. He was winner of several awards including the Nobel Prize.

I had seen The *Caretaker* in New York and was much impressed, especially by its sub-textual moments during pauses, which were interesting to work with since they required actors to risk long silences in which thoughts or actions, rather than dialogue, held an audience. I also loved the suspense created in the "comedy of menace" genre for which Pinter was known. And above all, I loved the mixture of comedy and tragedy.

Rehearsals were the most intense I ever had. Bill Lampe, who played Aston, was incredibly moving when he describes the electric shock treatments he had undergone, and Stuart Howard, playing the scrofulous old beggar Davies, saw the comedy in the role and was splendid. Bill Prosser was also a joy to work with. Of this production, Lewis Freed of *The Lafayette Journal and Courier* wrote (8/1/63) that it "provides a fitting close to a distinguished season of the Purdue Summer Season."

Chapter 17

WITH ROSS SMITH ON SABBATICAL, my major thrust in the first semester was preparing and directing the production of Brecht's *Mother Courage and Her Children*. The faculty had already agreed that I could hire a visiting artist for the title role, but whom? I called Allan Fletcher who had recently worked with Anne Revere and he thought her perfect for the role. A descendant of Paul Revere, after graduating from Wellesley College in 1926 she studied acting with Richard Boleslavsky and Maria Ouspenskaya at the American Laboratory School in New York.

Her Broadway career included a 691-performance run of Lillian Hellman's *The Children's Hour*, about two Scottish teachers accused of being lesbians, and also Hellman's 456 performance run of *Toys In the Attic* for which she received a Tony for best supporting actress. But it was in her 37 films, working with 64 actors who routinely received star billing such as Montgomery Clift, Bette Davis, Marlene Dietrich, Cary Grant, Gregory Peck, Barbara Stanwyck, Elizabeth Taylor, and Spencer Tracy, that she received her fame. She was a four-time nominee as best supporting actress. and winner for *National Velvet* as the mother of the young Elizabeth Taylor. But after the blacklists, *Red Channels*, and *Counterattack*, kicked in and she was called to testify before the House Un-American Activities Committee in 1947, she did not work for years.

I called her and went through the routine of dates of rehearsals and performances, availability, salary (for which I apologized) of $200 per week, and then let her have it by naming the play. She was *very* interested. I said I would be in town in a few days and could we meet? She agreed and gave me the address of her Upper West Side brownstone.

Mother Courage was a hot title at the time. Its Broadway premiere six months earlier had been directed by Jerome Robbins, with Anne Bancroft in the title role. I saw it and didn't think it worked. Rumor had it that there was dissention between Bancroft and Robbins caused by Lee Strasberg, her acting coach. The show closed after four previews and 52 performances.

During this time there was endless talk about Brecht's "A" effect—the alienation effect—for epic Theatre. In the 9/12/1959 issue of *The New Yorker* there was an article by Kenneth Tynan who wrote, "For every American who has seen a Brecht production, there are possibly a thousand who are armchair experts on the 'alienation effect'..." He was spot on! Much of the writing was just hot air. I've always been moved and persuaded by survival and I found this in abundance in the play.

I rang the doorbell of Anne Revere's home on West 104th Street and introduced myself as the guy who called from Purdue University concerning the possibility of her playing Mother Courage. She was 5' 5" and I was 6' 3" and I blurted out, "I thought you were taller."

"On the stage I'm any height I want to be," she said and ushered me into the living room, which was sparsely furnished. She pulled up a couple of chairs and we sat down. "Now what about this alienation business in the acting of Brecht?" she asked. I was taken aback by the directness and urgency of the question. It had been uppermost in my mind and I had decided it would be my opening gambit to her. "Well," I said, "I don't completely understand it, but if it means that you're not to act, then I'm against it."

"Good," she said putting on her glasses and opening the script, "Then we can work together."

At that moment my mind was made up about whom to cast, and her hiring taken for granted. I came to believe that this straight-forward, simple beginning was probably triggered by a lot of talk between herself and her husband, Sam Rosen. In my mind's ear I can imagine it. "Yes," Sam would say, "it would be great to get to act that role. But who is this guy? Another one of those academics with a head full of talk about the 'A' effect? If so, going out there will be a headache and you need that like you need a hole in the head." And in most cases Sam would have been right. But I had no such intention. Even though this is all about the professional relationship between Anne and me, it is important to know something about Sam.

I distinctly remember what Anne said after the production was over and we were seated next to each other on the plane to New York, talking about the show and possible others for the future. She suddenly said, "You've got to love Sam." And I always did, even though loving Sam meant listening to Sam and his ideas about the "unconditional reflex" in acting, which I still do not understand.

Sam had a career, of sorts in the theatre, as a small-part actor, sometimes stage manager, director and writer. When he died in 1984, he and Anne had been married for 49 years, and as far as I know for 45 years of the marriage his only work-for-money was investing the money she made in the stock market, plus teaching acting with her at their home (that was why the living room was almost bare of furniture) on 104th Street after she left Hollywood.

I did not approach *Mother Courage and Her Children* differently than any other play I directed. I read the script over and over, and then over and over again. First and foremost, I read to see if the play held my interest, and second to analyze the parts that comprised its structure and created suspense. I didn't see then, nor have I seen since, that Brecht's purpose was to lobotomize my emotions and substitute "a critical state of mind" so that I could sit back on my butt and contemplate the events enacted, having eliminated suspense and empathy. My brain never exploded with, "Oh, wow! This is about business being an extension of war."

Nor was I hoodwinked by the supposed fact that Brecht's *Verfremdungseffekt,* which was called the "A" effect, was something newly devised for the "epic" theatre, since the time-honored episodic form had been around since Homer's *The Iliad* and *Odyssey*. And regardless of Aristotle's admonishment that the epic was not as effective *for the theatre* as the dramatic form with limits on time, place, and action used by Aeschylus, Sophocles, or Euripides, it was used effectively by Shakespeare and most of the Elizabethan writers.

Nor was the genre of tragicomedy intended to alienate the audience from their emotions and enhance thinking. In fact, genre by definition (as far as theatre is concerned) deals exclusively with the audience's emotional reactions from laughter to tears. Neither was the music or lyrics in *Mother Courage* created to turn off emotion and turn on the brain. Nor was the subject matter, war, used to alienate emotions while expanding the intellect. Many shows, from *Lysistrata* (411 BC) to *Bury the Dead,* used war as their subject.

Our physical production would be as realistic as could be facilitated, which simply meant, rather than using traditional settings for the 12 different scenes in the play, we would use the style of selected realism. In short, as with any other episodic play that takes place in different locations, we designed stage props (in this case Courage's wagon), as realistically as possible

We also used slide projections of the etchings and engravings of German artist Kathe Kollwitz, who always thought of herself as "a realist." Her pictures depicting "Black Anna" urging the peasants on during their revolt was perfect, and after scene five we projected Kollwitz's peasant girl holding up a baby. We projected these as giant 30 by 40-foot images on a cyclorama as the audience entered, at intermission, and after the play ended. In addition they were used at the end of scenes: as the scene lights faded the images would appear momentarily to enforce the emotional point of the scene, prior to a spot hitting the narrator, Peter Bock, who would *tell* (not act) the audience of the time, place, and give a brief synopsis of the action that takes place in the next scene. None of this scenery or lighting was thought of as something that promoted the "A" effect or that hadn't been used before (think *periaktoi*: the three-sided scenic piece employed by the Greeks more than two thousand years prior to Brecht).

As soon as I returned from New York I went to the Purdue library and checked out for the entire semester all the *Congressional Records* in which Anne Revere's testimony appeared. Indiana was very conservative politically and a conservative snoop might wish to dredge up this Senator Joe

McCarthy inspired trash. Our production of this play was just the sixth in the United States. In addition to its Broadway showing, it had been presented by the Extension Division of UCLA with Eileen Heckart, The San Francisco Workshop, Butler University at Clowes Hall, and the University of Denver.

I believe Anne Revere was one of our country's best actresses. She was wonderful to work with and grew into a Mother Courage who was a lusty, bawdy, shrewd, materialistic street brawler, but a mother with real affection for her children, and a human being with a life-force and vitality that always catapulted her back to her canteen business. There were many iconic moments that I shall never forget, such as when she is forced to identify the dead body of her son, Swiss Cheese. Any hesitation or equivocation of looking directly at his face would be taken as evidence of an emotional relationship. She is forced to cross to where the body is laid out, all eyes on her reaction. There is that split second when she braces herself to look down at the corpse of a son she bore and suckled at her breast, and raised to young manhood. She steels herself for the task. Her face is cement, nothing changes, and the judging onlookers conclude that there can be absolutely no connection between the piece of meat on a slab and the mother. She goes back to the bench to sit beside the distraught Kattrin, who is about to break. Surreptitiously she reaches over and takes the girl's hand, injecting her white-knuckled strength into the girl. And only when the focus is no longer on her does she allow for cracks in her face of cement.

The cost of mere survival is unendurable, but she will endure. The bitterness at the end of scene six, when Kattrin has been attacked and her face scarred, and Courage knows she will never attract a husband and that her two sons are gone, makes her "curse the war," a cry from the gut and heart. But at the same time there is business to attend to.

The only scene that was totally visual with no dialogue was scene ten when Courage and Kattrin stop pulling the wagon on a snowy night and simply listen to the song by a girl in an offstage farmhouse. Both Cindy Miller and Anne were extraordinarily beautiful in their listening and feeling and doing absolutely nothing else: a magic, never to be forgotten moment in the theatre—in my life.

Sam Marks' wagon was the most beautiful and realistic piece of scenery he ever designed for a show I directed. He loved designing the wagon because there was something in him that was very like Mother Courage. He off-loaded the actual building to graduate student Peter Bock, who had a background in engineering. Peter added metal bushings on the wheels to make the wagon easy to move. It was Anne's acting that made it look lumbering and heavy but in reality she claimed she could have pulled it with her little finger. The following summer when Anne was hired by Catholic University to play the role again, she insisted that she had to have this wagon. If I remember correctly it was first sold to a Chicago Theatre, and then the Catholic University bought it from them. Sam Marks enjoyed and respected Anne Revere more than any other professional actor who came to Purdue, and their mutual enjoyment and respect included that young graduate student who constructed her wagon.

Before we opened, we had a few days off for Thanksgiving vacation. I was walking down that long underground hallway to my office on November 22nd after a bite to eat at the Union building when a kid came running up the hall and yelled: "Jack Kennedy has been shot!" Like everyone else I was dumbstruck and enormously affected by this and all that followed. I went home immediately. He was not yet dead, but then the announcement came that he was, and I sat for hours watching events on TV.

Runs and reruns of the assassination, the motorcade, Jackie with blood on her dress, the new man, Lyndon Johnson, being sworn in on Air Force One. The funeral: banners tied up in black crepe, the drums muffled, Jackie, dressed all in black with the two kids as the caisson holding the casket moved by, and suddenly the little boy—John-John everyone called him—stepped out and saluted, and we all wept. And of course, this epic tragedy in our history and its aftermath was in the hearts and on the minds of everyone who saw our production of *Mother Courage and Her Children*.

⌘ ⌘ ⌘

After *Courage* was over and I had some time before the summer theatre season was upon me, the first thing I did was write an article from the heart called "For A University Theatre" which was eventually published along with an article by Anne entitled "Oasis in Indiana" in *Equity* magazine, which is included in this book as Appendix A. Both outlined what we thought should happen as far as a liaison between the professional and educational theatres was concerned and the advantages for both in the training of theater students, as well as an adjunct educational benefit for both students and faculty.

Anne's article gave great praise to Purdue University administrators. She had had a meeting with President Hovde and said one of the most honest things that was ever said about me: "Dr. Joseph Stockdale, *disguised as a college professor,* proved in fact to be a talented and experienced young director." Let's face it, publicity helps and these articles gave important information to 35,000 AEA members about our theatre in Indiana.

⌘ ⌘ ⌘

For the summer of 1964 I was granted permission by Purdue to form an AEA company and I spent a great deal of time during the second semester getting together the Summer Theatre season: *Romeo and Juliet* June 12-27; *The Threepenny Opera* July 1-11; *Look Homeward, Angel* July 19-25; and *Pygmalion* July 29-August 7. In addition, *The Fantasticks* had two performances every Sunday from June 14th through July 25th and I was already thinking of Anne Revere as the Nurse in *Romeo and Juliet* and Frances Farmer as Mrs. Gant in *Look Homeward, Angel.*

⌘ ⌘ ⌘

In early 1964 choreographer Wayne Lamb and Director Barry Menagh were responsible for Purdue University Theatre's production of *West Side Story.* By that time it was routine for Gene Kildahl to handle Ross's academic responsibilities and me his responsibilities as producer. Barry and Wayne came to me and said that an actor/singer who could hit and sustain the high notes could not be found to play Tony. Someone needed to be brought in.

My first thought, which both agreed with, was to call Kenny Nelson. He had originated the role of the Boy in *The Fantasticks* and had been standby for Tommy Steele on Broadway for *Half a Sixpence,* taking over the role for the national touring company that played Purdue. I felt acquainted enough to call him, getting his home number from the AEA membership office.

Pleased that I thought of him for the role, he was otherwise engaged but asked me why I didn't just call Larry Kert, who had created the role on Broadway and played it throughout the entire run. He gave me Larry's home phone number. I called. Larry said yes immediately. My offer was $800 plus transportation.

All work on the show that did not include Larry was blocked and rehearsed. When he arrived on campus we had a greeting party for him at 435 Robinson St., during which he was perfectly charming, unassuming, and seemed glad to be with us. He was the same way throughout his put-in, ready to do the dances that Wayne had choreographed, and the blocking that Barry had directed. Wayne wanted me to be involved not only as producer for the theatre but in the production. Since they could not find anyone for the minor role of Lt. Schrank, I agreed to do it, and was at most rehearsals so Barry, Wayne, and I could talk about any problems. The show was a major success, and the large cast was thrilled to be working with Larry. Since it filled the theatre, it inadvertently led me to make my final decision to open our summer season with *Romeo and Juliet*. I was finally set to ask Frances Farmer if she would be interested in the role of Eliza Gant in *Look Homeward,* a character for whom sympathy is not easy to inspire. Her answer? She would love to play the part.

After *The Sea Gull* Frances had received a request to appear on the *Today* show in New York. Her TV show in Indianapolis had the best rating for a local station of any similar show in the nation and there was some thought that it might transfer to New York. The *Today* people sent a camera crew to Indianapolis to film Frances in her daily routine. While filming from the hood of her car as she was driving, she had a minor accident that greatly upset her. She went to New York and did the show with John Daly, the substitute host.

On April 21st we sent out her Equity contract. She had stayed in New York after the *Today* show and I was anxious to get contracts signed and plans firmed-up for this first professional Equity Company. A couple of days after she returned from New York, an Indianapolis friend of hers called saying she had returned drunk on the plane, gone to WFBM drunk, been fired, and was now locked in her home and would not see anyone.

I immediately drove to Indianapolis. At first she would not open the door but eventually she did. She was extremely drunk. This was the only time I ever saw her drunk and it was a frightening experience. She was dressed in black sateen pajamas, the waistband of which was ripped in several places revealing the elastic band, and the jacket was without buttons. Her hair was disheveled and she was generally a mess. The letter with the Equity contract was on the table next to her chair. I kept telling her that she had to pull herself together, that we were depending on her playing in *Look Homeward*.

The thing I remember most was the anger. She had been upset by the car accident in Indianapolis prior to going to New York. Once there she had been asked "humiliating questions" about her past, questions that had been submitted by the network in advance but which had never been passed on to her. She kept saying that she was who she was *now*, that her past was past, should remain so, and be forgotten.

She said she went to a luncheon following the show, started drinking and just stayed drunk the entire week. She had gone to the Broadway production of *Blues For Mr. Charley* and was so disturbed by the racial injustice presented that she became disruptive and the management requested she leave. She eventually managed to get to the airport and back home where she was too drunk to appear on her own show.

I kept veering the conversation back to *Look Homeward, Angel*. She kept insisting that I did not really want her for the play. I talked about Thomas Wolfe and even quoted poetic passages, saying she should start reading the novel. At that point she looked up, the anger was gone, and tears sprang to her eyes. She waited until she could speak and then said, "I have, Joe," as if I should have known this about her, and which I should have. She added, "I got it just as soon as you asked me if I would be interested in playing the role." Although I had begun to waver in my own conviction, seeing her in the condition she was in, I knew at that moment she had to play that part. I told her to sign the contract and I would take it back to Purdue with me.

Back home, I called the young priest, Father Melvin, of St. Thomas Aquinas, a friend and theatre supporter, told him about Frances and asked him if he knew any Indianapolis priests. He had seen Frances in *The Sea Gull*, as well as when she attended five o'clock Saturday mass when in residence for rehearsals. He shared my concern and yes, he did know an Indianapolis priest, who called Frances for an appointment and looked in on her the following day. Within the week, Robin also phoned and chatted about the family. She told her how happy she was to know that she would be with us in July for *Angel*.

Within two weeks the Indianapolis papers announced that Frances was to return to WFBM-TV on June 1st to her $18,000 per year job, and went on to report that she "...resigned in a flurry of controversy, April 28... The week before her resignation she had been in New York where she was profiled in a segment of NBC's *Today* show... in addition to rejoining WFBM-TV Miss Farmer plans to appear in a theatre production of *Look Homeward, Angel*, at Purdue in July."

⌘ ⌘ ⌘

I kept up with the New York Theatre scene by reading the Sunday edition of *The New York Times*. The big news in 1963 was about a repertory company being formed by Robert Whitehead and Elia Kazan. The plan was that this company would eventually play in true European repertory style, that there would be a permanent company that would train together for about a year, and from those being trained casts would be chosen for the first three shows. The company was to occupy what would be named the Vivian Beaumont Theatre at Lincoln Center. When that project was delayed it was decided to build a temporary theatre called ANTA Washington Square Theatre on a section of the New York University campus where the company would operate for the first couple of years, and open with Arthur Miller's *After The Fall* in January 1964. This project would hopefully be the beginning of an American National Theatre Company mirroring The National Theatre of Great Britain.

I began to want to be close to the project as it was being developed, especially during its first season. I had accumulated enough time to take a one-semester sabbatical which would pay full-time. I applied to be an observer of the Whitehead/Kazan project from September 1964 through mid-January 1965, which would allow me to attend all rehearsals of the three new productions to be mounted that season. This required letters of recommendation, one of which I got from Mildred Dunnock, whose brother was the doctor of the Health Center at Williams College, and others, which led quickly to interviews first with Robert Whitehead and then Elia Kazan, both of which went extremely well. Since the administrators at Purdue—Deans and President Hovde—had already approved the sabbatical for this specific project, it was to be finalized sometime in April. I was waiting for notification of this when an event occurred that was extremely important at this stage in my life.

⌘ ⌘ ⌘

It was a fairly warm mid-week day when Stephen [not his real name] came running across the backyard of 435 Robinson and into our kitchen. He was hysterical, crying and using his hands to claw at the skin of his arms. We got him upstairs to our bedroom, laid him down and Robin held his hand and talked to him while I got a cold washcloth to wipe the sweat from his forehead. Neither of us had ever seen anyone in such abject agony. His hands were trying to rip the skin from his bones and he kept blurting out that this was what he wanted to do.

The story came out, slowly, but eventually all of it, evidencing the absolute self-hatred imposed on him by what had happened when he had gone to the men's room of the Memorial Union. There was a person in the next booth who moved his foot just inside the stall Stephen occupied, raising it up and down several times. Next, came a note passed under the partition asking for sex.

Stephen went to the next booth, the door of which was ajar and saw that the man inside was fondling himself. Then he reached out for Stephen and immediately told him he was under arrest. Stephen was taken to the campus police station where he was photographed, interrogated and finally confessed that he had gone into the booth. He was told that he would have 24 hours to get his things together and get off the campus and out of town. No, he would not be allowed to finish his class work and receive his degree. He must leave now. Just as soon as he was out of the police station he started running to our house. Up to this point neither Robin nor I had ever speculated about Stephen's sexual orientation. Gene, Ross, and I had all cast him in roles which called for "regular guy" types because there was nothing stereotypically effeminate about him.

Here was Stephen admitting to us not only his complicity in the act, but that indeed he had always been a homosexual (l don't believe that the word "gay" was much used by the general public at that time). How was he going to explain to his family that he would not receive his degree? How in fact could he go on living? We both felt overwhelming pity for this kid and the trauma he was going through.

The thing that I felt was unfair was that he would not be able to complete his degree with graduation six weeks away. I told him that I would fight his being expelled. I got on the phone and called President Hovde's office. His secretary said he was not in, but if it was an urgent matter to call Vice President Donald R. Mallett. I did, explained what happened, and said I did not think the police had the power of cutting off this student from graduating.

Don differed with me, so I took another tack saying, of course, that I wasn't a lawyer but questioned how the policeman had handled this situation and suggested that if the family decided to fight the case in court, they might win. It wasn't long before Don came around to my point of view, but since it was already late afternoon he could not see me until the next morning. I figured that he was biding time to get the story from the policeman before our meeting.

After this glimmer of hope, Stephen pulled himself together enough so that we felt he could go to his apartment, but I told him to call us if he needed anything. Robin and I talked and she was the one who suggested—her undergraduate major was pre-law political science—that there might be a legal way out of this mess because of the interpretation of "entrapment." I went to the law section of the library and acquired specifics on this issue, which seemed to me to rest on one point: IF entrapment was legal, the act that caused the arrest had to be instigated by the suspect, but if it was motivated by the actions of the arresting policeman, it could be challenged.

As Stephen had told the story it seemed to us that a case could be made that it was not Stephen's actions, but rather the policeman's come-on that led to the incident. Of course, we both knew that we had only heard Stephen's side and that he might not be telling it exactly as it had happened. Robin was quick to say that although this was true and that a jury would likely take the side of the policeman, there were two other considerations. First, the case would be a "he said, he said" with no witnesses. Second, if it provoked interest by a sympathetic trial lawyer and was picked up by some liberal eastern newspaper, especially by *The New York Times,* Don might agree that simply allowing Stephen to finish his school work and graduate could be the wiser solution.

The next morning both Robin and I went to Don Mallet's office. The meeting was civil and very low-keyed. We simply mentioned that another of our theatre students had a video tape of his apartment being broken into by the campus police while he was supposedly away. I if Stephen's case came to trial it might open a beehive of feelings against the campus police and could prove harmful to Purdue's image.

Don Mallett was a reasonable man and I think he saw this whole thing—as compared to budget approval by the state legislature—as making a mountain out of a mole hill. He very soon said that he would deal with the police and they would not press charges. The student would be allowed to receive his degree if the two of us signed a statement that we would be responsible for his conduct until the end of the term. I think, in truth, Don had come down on our side of having feelings for the student.

The student finished his classes and graduated.

⌘ ⌘ ⌘

In a letter dated June 1st, Frances Farmer wrote, "I'm back in the saddle again… things have simmered down to an even keel; and I am feeling greatly refreshed and relaxed as the result of my sudden and unexpected vacation. Give my love to Robin and the family. I am really looking forward to *Look Homeward, Angel* in July. I understand that the station will grant me the full four weeks from my program, which will certainly enhance the project as far as I, as an actress, am concerned. Until later, with love, Frances."

⌘ ⌘ ⌘

Prior to rehearsals for the summer theatre I was in New York, and one of the shows I saw was *Dylan* with Alec Guinness, which had opened in January. When I opened my program I saw that Susan Willis was a stage manager doing small roles and understudying a couple of others. I thought perhaps it would be nice to see her again, hoping that she was no longer angry. I wasn't thinking of sex; all I wanted was for her not to be pissed off at me as I've never liked being not liked. After the show, I went back to say hello.

It was not exactly a warm greeting, but Kate Reid who played Caitlin, Dylan's wife in the show, was headed out. Susan introduced her to me and suggested that I accompany Kate to the Algonquin bar where she would join us. Kate was very friendly in the kind of way that made me feel she took a fancy to me. When we crossed the street she held onto my arm. She was a short woman—at least it seemed so to me—and she said she liked tall men. I did not know her background, but was sure I must have seen her at Stratford but had no recollection of it. So although I was excited and talked about our new AEA company, I was genuinely interested in her background as well.

When we came in the bartender greeted her warmly as did our waiter—obviously she was known there. I sensed she liked my enthusiasm and energy. She was not what I would call a beautiful woman but there was something about her that struck me as needy. She had dark short hair and her face was full—no Hollywood type cheekbones; her figure matched her face—and she tossed down the drinks. I could not keep up and had to pass. She was, in fact, perfect for the casting of Dylan Thomas' real-life wife who was also a drinker.

When Susan showed up, it was evident that she and Kate were good friends. She ordered a drink and seemed friendly enough, but soon said that she had to leave. I was a little disappointed, but Kate and I closed the bar. She had a tab there and insisted that the drinks were on her. By that time I was feeling no pain.

She took my arm when we crossed the street, and I walked her to her hotel. She did not say come up for a nightcap or anything like that, because by that time I had gotten the picture and just went with her up to her room. She was needy for hugs and closeness, and I was needy, too.

In the morning I gave her a kiss and she said how about meeting for lunch at Sardi's. Although I had passed it many times I had never been there. We set a time and I split. I called Susan. When I asked if I could see her that night after the show, she said she did not think it was a good idea. That was the end of that.

⌘ ⌘ ⌘

Our six-page summer theatre program was a 6" x 8" attractive fold-over with a picture of the experimental theatre on the front cover with me standing on stage beneath a row of lights. The program was designed so that only the center page needed to be reprinted for each new show, and on the back cover was a message from me that covered the entire page. It laid out our plans for the future, which followed many of the goals of the Whitehead/Kazan National Theatre project for the Repertory Theatre Company of Lincoln Center:

> This season, Purdue Summer Theatre realizes two dreams: A professional company and a bill of plays that is not only entertaining, but encompasses the finest in dramatic literature. Professional Equity standing will assure professional standards of production, will provide a yardstick against which our apprentices can measure their talent and will attract the best theatre students throughout the country. It will augment the cultural life of the university community by providing the best possible viewing experience for students,

staff and community during the summer months when there is little university-sponsored entertainment....

Occasionally we have been asked why we do not operate in the Loeb Playhouse. The Experimental Theatre provides an intimacy and informality that cannot be gained in the Loeb and certainly not in the Hall of Music. It is good, once in a while, to be able to view a play in a theatre where every seat allows one to hear, see and observe the action at very close range; where people may come in informal attire; and where the audience is greeted at the top of the stairs by a friendly and personal "good evening." Purdue already has the biggest bass drum in the world, as well as the biggest many other things —let's keep one of the smallest theatres and that sense of the personal and intimate.

As to our future, we would someday like to play in true European Repertory, with a different play each night. We would like to see the professional repertory idea expanded to include more than the summer-school session, and a professional curriculum closely connected to the repertory company... We already have some of the finest facilities and equipment in the country. But we must remember that buildings and equipment do not make a theatre; only talent and dedication can do that.... Joe Stockdale, director.

I have not mentioned many names in the narrative part of this book in order to save space, but this first Equity Company has to be an exception. Six AEA members were required by the union to make this Equity Company. I chose Merle Louise, Dale Helward, Donald Jacobs, Peter Simon, Jim Stephens, and Richard Newdick, and as director, I was also an AEA member.

Our Non-AEA company, which were paid a small stipend, consisted of Jeff Carter, Marilynne Black, William Hillis, Bill Lampe, and Cindy Miller. Our production staff consisted of set designer Stuart Wurtzel, costume designer Lyn Carroll, musical director Jane Bowman, business and publicity manager Robert Tolan, and Randy Earle as technical director and assistant lighting designer.

In our production of *Romeo and Juliet,* Peter Simon, who had made his AEA membership at The Barn Theatre, once again played Romeo for me. Had he lived in London he would have been a major professional Shakespearian actor. His wife, Merle Louise, whom he had met at The Barn and whom I had first met backstage at the stripper's dressing room for Broadway's *Gypsy,* was wonderful as Juliet, and so was Anne Revere as The

Nurse. The supporting cast, Dale Helward as Mercutio, Jim Stephens as Benvolio, Robert Tolan as Friar Laurence, and Bill Lampe as Tybalt were all first-rate.

The production did not do capacity business as I had hoped it would. I think this was because Shakespeare was often considered a yawn at Purdue, and also because the playwright's verse and actions were better served in a larger venue, a problem that had not occurred to me. Not only was a venue of a certain size important for the language and acting, but also for accomplishing scenic elements. Clearly, the Experimental Theatre itself was not really capable of a double story on which a realistic balcony scene could be mounted. Stuart Wurtzel attempted to accommodate my wishes in this matter, which on reflection I'm not sure that anyone could have solved it. The space, by its very size, was better suited to the realism of modem theatre.

Earl Harlan, who had played *Lear* as an undergraduate and had a magnificent vocal instrument (he eventually did the Narrator in *Unto These Hills*), said he thought it was the best Shakespearian production he had ever seen. But summer stock has an advantage; you are always in rehearsals directing the next production and do not have time to brood about the one that is on the boards. Our next show was Brecht's and Kurt Weill's *The Threepenny Opera* based on John Gay's 18th century *The Beggars Opera*. It sold out and was a great joy for the actors as well as the designers and me. For this production I jobbed-in Stacy Winter (*aka* Nanci Hall) for the role of Mrs. Peachum, since she not only was a talented actress but also had a first-rate singing voice.

In its original production in Berlin in 1928, at the musical's ending, when instead of being hanged, Macheath is pardoned by the Queen and given the title of Baron, and as the Street Singer pulled the flimsy front curtain, bright limelight was suddenly turned onto the audience and he yelled in a scowling voice, "There's your picture!" Then, after holding for a moment, the lights on the audience were cut, and the Street Singer returned to the smiling sweetness and highly entertaining mode that the song is written in. This spotlighting, of course, says that although the show has been done as pure entertainment with great parody and wonderful music, the true villains are the audience members who require such "sop" when they attend the theatre.

When we did the scene that way on opening night it so startled the audience, and annoyed them, that even with the Street Singer's sweet melodic rendering of the song's final words in the fading lights, the audience did not immediately applaud. When they did it was skimpy and perfunctory. I thought long and hard about this and decided to cut the lights slapping the audience in the face and just keep the ending as melodious and sweet as it was in the original Off-Broadway production. For the rest of the run we got incredible applause and the audience left the theatre happy.

Charles Preston of the *Indianapolis Times* wrote (7/3/64): "Purdue Summer Theatre's full-bodied presentation of *The Three Penny Opera*... is far beyond what one would expect from a university group.... Which could make Indianapolis based taxpayers wonder why we suffer through tiny-cast mediocrities while Purdue has all this."

Look Homeward rehearsals started on July 6th so Frances got to view *Threepenny* which delighted her as well as the full houses it played to. She was staying at a local motel and worked extremely well with all members of the cast. Her pay was $150 per week for both rehearsals and performance. The amount of detailed preparation we had was not nearly as long or as in depth as *The Sea Gull* but she and Victor Kilian—whom I jobbed in and had played the role on Broadway—worked well together and she relished their fight scene; she also greatly admired Dale Helward's acting, especially in his death scene, and her scenes with Peter Simon.

On opening night she was very nervous and her concentration was somewhat off during the first act. This was because she had never played in such close proximity to an audience. The Experimental Theatre seated 187; the first row of seats in the pit had leg room only in front of the stage's apron. She adjusted to the close proximity quickly and was fine during the play's two-week run. When Eugene confronts her about giving all her attention to the boarders, "when it is you we wanted for us, you we needed for us, Why? Why?" and Frances answers, "They don't hurt me like the rest of you do," it was an incredibly moving moment torn from her guts, probably by remembrances of her own dysfunctional family.

Fremont Power of *The Indianapolis News* wrote: "Praise be for this bit of drama among the froth of summer theatre. Miss Farmer... the mother, bitterly torn between love of family and of property... commanded the stage."

Walter Spencer of *The Indianapolis Times,* who saw the show a couple of nights after it opened, wrote under headlines "'ANGEL' AT PURDUE HAS RARE QUALITY."

It's almost too bad that someone can't put the Purdue University Theatre under glass. It should be preserved as the definitive example of what educational theatre can—and should–do. The group in residence at Purdue this summer is about the closest thing to a professional repertory theatre in Indiana. It also may well be providing the best theatre in the state.... Miss Farmer is Gant's wife. Of the various stage roles she has played since settling in Indianapolis, this is by far Miss Farmer's finest performance. She and Kilian play with and against each other as an exceptional well-matched team.... In her role as the earthy but self-centered mother, Miss Farmer shows great power.... The theatre offerings here, in their consistently fine quality, are on a higher standard than even the good professional efforts of a Playhouse such as Avondale in Indianapolis.

The day Frances left after the run she sent the following message:

Dear Joe, the longer I stay in this business, the more diffident I become about saying 'thank you' and God knows it's not false modesty. I honestly feel what George Santayana must have meant when he said at the age of ninety, 'The older I grow the more I realize how little I know.' Well, I have acted again, under your direction— what shall I say? This: that for you, I have done the best I could, because I respect, admire, marvel at, and yes, love you. Tell Robin I mean it, and wish the best for the future for you, her and the children. I enclose something I hope you will pin on the bulletin board... Do keep in touch—I will follow your plans with interest.

Enclosed was the following note: "To the cast and crew of *Look Homeward, Angel.* Dear people: Words can't say how much my engagement in this play has meant to me. You sometimes get discouraged about this thing called 'show biz' but, [as Eliza Gant] Law Saks! like the fellow says, this was a good one. Thanks, Thanks, to one and all—and good luck in the future, Frances."

Look Homeward, Angel was followed by Shaw's *Pygmalion* in which there were 21 roles, with Merle Louise doing a perfect Eliza Doolittle—absolutely wonderful—as was Dale Helward as Henry Higgins. But then the summer theatre season was over and soon I would be spending the next few months in New York City in one of the most important learning experiences of my life. But in the meantime we all took a vacation in Michigan, visiting Dad and Robin's folks, going swimming in Lake Michigan, and seeing Karen Jensen in *Irma La Douce* at The Barn. We also met Jack and Betty's newly adopted son, Brendan.

Chapter 18

I GOT INTO NEW YORK LATE afternoon. I had contacted Stuart Howard and asked him to find an inexpensive hotel near the ANTA Washington Square Theatre on West 4th Street. He sent me a couple of names but said he actually knew very little about hotels in that area. I am unable to remember the name of the one I arrived at. It was close to the theatre, but I was put off by the place the moment I entered. I asked to see the room, which was $21 a week. It was postage-stamp size with a window that looked out on an ugly air shaft. I thought of going up to the Y on 63rd Street where I had stayed while at the Feagin School, but I wanted something within walking distance. I told myself that I'd get used to it and went back to the desk and paid.

It was a terrible night. I didn't feel safe. The room did not smell good. I wondered if there were bed bugs in the lumpy mattress. The walls seemed to be made of cardboard and I could hear people talking. I tried to sleep but couldn't. It was September and I needed a window to open and get fresh air. I got up at one point and found the name of the other hotel Stuart had named. Next morning I walked up to The Albert at 23 East 10th Street and many years later, found out that this was a hotel where Hart Crane and many other artists had sometimes lived.

Miss Feldman was at the desk, and I told her—I was obviously upset and a little panicked because I hated the thought of losing the week's rent on the other place—who I was, what I was doing in New York, that I expected to be there through early December, and that I had foolishly gotten into a hotel that I did not want to stay in. I asked her the weekly rate for a renter on a budget. She listened sympathetically, and when I was finished she patted my arm and told me she had a room that rented for $5 a night, but for a long-term renter it would be $26.25 including tax, per week. It was on the fourth floor. She gave me the key and told me to go up and see if it was satisfactory.

It was three times the size of the room I had already paid for. Three big windows looked out on the cross street. There was a desk with a lamp and a straight-backed chair, an overstuffed one with a reading lamp beside it, a private bath with shower, a small apartment sized refrigerator, and yes, there were a couple of places in the ceiling where lath could be viewed through damaged plaster, but everything about the hotel, including the reception room in the lobby, and especially Miss Feldman, made me know that this was where I could comfortably live.

She obviously knew this when I stepped off the elevator. As I paid for the first week, she said she was glad to have me there and if I needed anything to just let her know. And, oh yes, just talk to the desk clerk at the other place and explain that you need more room and ask for a refund.

The desk clerk was the same person as when I had arrived and I was a little emotional in telling him my circumstances. He said he understood, had been in the same situation in his life, and refunded me $16. I was so happy I could have cried. New York was absolutely wonderful!

Once settled in at the Albert, I walked down to the ANTA Theatre where an understudy rehearsal with Hal Holbrook and Jennifer West was taking place for *After the Fall*. I didn't quite know what to do—I certainly wasn't going to interrupt a rehearsal—so I sat in a row near the back of the house and watched. I must have been there for almost an hour before Robert Downing, the stage manager, came and asked me who I was. I told him. He said I was welcome to stay, but that Kazan would be rehearsing *The Changeling* in a building over on Second Avenue.

It was a large space on the second floor. I hovered just inside the room until the stage manager, Fritz de Wilde, came over and told me where to sit.

On the break Kazan shook my hand, welcomed me, told me to come and go as I pleased, and if I needed anything to let him know. Wow! This was a big moment: Elia Kazan, arguably the greatest theatre and film director of the twentieth century—a man I admired, whose work I loved, and had only met the one time on the interview when I had applied to be an observer—now treated me like an old friend.

That was about it. I was always a good listener. I did not leave until rehearsal was over, and was back ten minutes early the next morning, before rehearsals started. Of course, I had read *The Changeling* before I left home, and had checked out a copy from the Purdue Library on semester loan to take with me. I also had a rare tape recording of the play copied from a British Broadcasting Company recording given to WBAA, the Purdue Radio Station, by someone from a radio station in Canada.

The question was: how was I going to approach, understand, and gain something from viewing rehearsals of this tragedy written by Thomas Middleton and William Rowley, first performed on January 4, 1623 (?) I always started with the plot, and usually on the first reading connected with something—subject, plot, characters—that hit me emotionally and intellectually. This didn't happen when I read *The Changeling*, nor when I listened to the BBC recording, so out of desperation I did a cutting of the script based on the recording to try to get me thinking *something* about the play. After I saw the actors who were playing the various roles, I at least became a little more familiar with the plot and the character relationships.

Why, I wondered, did Kazan want to direct this play? English critic Kenneth Tynan, literary advisor for The Old Vic, and Laurence Olivier liked the play, but after years of directing mostly naturalistic contemporary plays I wondered if Kazan was now attempting to forage into the forest of Elizabethan drama and reveal himself to be as capable in that area as Olivier. If so, the only connection he had with this Jacobean play was the gore (cutting off of a finger) and sex (Des Flores "deflowering" Beatrice) along with the sexual involvements with most of the other characters.

I also went to some weekly sessions at The Actors Studio and it was there that I heard that Kazan was divorcing his wife, Molly, and living with Barbara Loden. However, I kept my main focus on rehearsals at the Repertory company, being present on time and giving full attention to what was going on with the same degree of involvement as Laura Shaw taught me as an undergraduate. But that was tough sledding with this play. During one of the rehearsals Kazan asked if I could do some research for him on Bethlem, the first hospital in London for management of the mentally ill since it was the prototype for some of the scenes in the play. He had heard that there were etchings of the madhouse's inhabitances and he wanted to emulate them in the blocking of some of the scenes.

A really nice woman in the picture collection at the Fifth Avenue 42nd Street Library helped me. They were mostly Hogarth prints. The one I liked best was of a madman surrounded by other inmates (a tailor, a musician, a Catholic Bishop and another high ranking church member who believes he is King), plus two society women from fashionable London who have come to the asylum to while away an afternoon by watching the lunatics.

Kazan liked all the pictures and asked me to use the one of the madmen-astrologists as the central focus. He assigned half a dozen actors who were in the ensemble, or understudies, to work on the scene. I quickly came to the conclusion that the actors should choose one of the characters from any of the pictures, but that the basic stage picture would reflect the one with the astrologer. Each actor would live in the reality of his character's imaginary world and would include talking, screaming, or shouting—"Bedlam," being synonymous with clamor and confusion—and the stage picture would subliminally be recognizable to anyone who had ever run across the original.

I enjoyed doing this rather than always sitting and watching, and was grateful for Kazan's praise and thanks. I had not the slightest clue how what I was doing fitted into the production as a whole because I never heard Kazan discuss any unifying subject or point of view.

He also asked me to stand in for actors who were not present due to some screw up in scheduling. All he really needed was a body so he could see the total picture of any scene he was blocking or re-blocking. Shortly after this started, Frederick—"Fritz" as everyone called him—de Wilde (father of actor Brandon), one of the production stage managers, told me that I was not allowed to either direct actors or stand in for any of them because as an Equity member I would have to be put under contract if I did. Kazan, of course, was trying to get me more actively involved—a kindness on his part—but of course we could not break AEA rules.

He then asked me to try writing the production's program note and if accepted by the publicity department it would be used in *Playbill* magazine which would be in every playbill for a Broadway play. But what was I going to write about? I didn't have a handle on the production that could even start an interesting first paragraph. So I asked myself, what focus would I take if I was directing this turkey, which I never would have directed?

Structurally, the character who most interested me was Beatrice, so she would be the protagonist who is thrown out of adjustment by the decision of her father to marry her off to a man she does not like. In church she meets and falls in love with a young man and he falls head over heels in love with her. Her overall through-line objective then would be freedom of choice, in a society that denies it. The urgency of this objective is fueled by her sexual drive, which is a force of nature and pretty overwhelming—in conflict with society's rules and norms.

I liked Barbara Loden, probably because more than any other member of the acting company she was extra nice to me. She approached me the second day I was at rehearsals and said that she'd noticed I smoked Kent cigarettes. It was her brand; she was trying to stop, but could she bum one from me? She sat down, I lit her cigarette and we spoke of inconsequential matters. When the cigarette was down to a nub she took one final drag, stubbed it out, smiled, said thanks, and was gone. I think she sensed the fact that I was pretty much alone in New York and enjoyed her company. Second time bumming was easier, and after that we were old friends; I whipped out my pack as soon as I saw her approaching.

Innocence and kindness was what projected from her onstage, especially in Arthur Miller's *After The Fall* which was playing in repertory and in which she played the Marilyn Monroe prototype opposite Jason Robards. She got into the skin of the character and played what she felt and imagined, which basically was Monroe's attraction as an actress. But she could not play what was not true to her natural instincts. As Beatrice she did not seem to understand the restraint the character was under, fighting against her father's absolute control, or the moral dictates of a dominating male society in 1623.

There was something about her of a waif—same as with Marilyn—something unsure that said, "help me," "like me,"—the fragility and venerability that appeals, knowing she is in need of a cigarette, and you whip out a Zippo to fire her up and know her need is not faked but absolutely real. She simply did not have the background, education, imagination, or acting chops to play Beatrice, so I approached my program note hoping to write something that might help her see what she did not see, and at the same time help the audience connect with the feminist movement which was beginning to be an issue in the country. I did a great deal of research in manners, morals and costumes and came up with:

> The social customs of the time, especially relating to women, form a ... background for the play. They trigger the action and direct the plot by which Beatrice can achieve her objective, which is marriage to Alsemero.
>
> When Beatrice first meets him, two great opposing forces are suddenly brought into conflict: her social conditioning and her nature. Although she is a young Spanish girl and the play was written by English authors, this conditioning was in fact, if not always in degree, *the same* for all women throughout Western Europe.
>
> From early childhood a gentlewoman was taught the suppression and negation of self; her whole life was to be lived in unquestioning submission and according to Christian virtues: modesty, obedience, humility, piety, patience and, above all, virginity and chastity. Virginity was held to be the supreme and essential gift a woman must bring to her husband. The husband was chosen, not by the girl, but by her father. She could protest if the chosen one had any discernible vice or flaw but she was bound to defer to her father's wisdom and authority.
>
> Her education was in home crafts: the only vocations open to her were the church or marriage. During her leisure hours she was permitted to meditate and read holy books or those upholding and illustrating virtue in women.
>
> A noblewoman might study Greek and Latin (only approved selections, of course) but moral philosophy, history, oratory, rhetoric and poetry were not considered proper subjects for her mind. A mirror was to reflect neatness and cleanliness and not vanity. She was never to speak to young men on the street nor to dress conspicuously, lest she be suspected of conceit or of trying to attract men. She was to stand and sit quietly, feet and

knees together, and not make meaningless gestures; to walk slowly (but not too slowly lest it be thought she was meeting someone), eyes downcast (because through the eyes enters knowledge of worldly things). She was to eat and drink temperately without moving her mouth too much; to be silent unless spoken to, and then to answer with modesty and brevity. Laughter was objectionable because it might incite or indicate sensuality, and it displayed her teeth. In short, a woman was to do nothing that attracted attention to herself.

Since these social customs were imposed on women by men, they reveal men's thinking concerning women. A father (such as Capulet in *Romeo and Juliet*) could be gentle but severity was a safeguard against temptation and the natural heat of youth. Men knew women were as inclined to sensuality as they were, but deemed them weaker, less intelligent and therefore more vulnerable. Above all, men feared cuckoldry; an unfaithful wife made a man an object of ridicule and scorn with symbolic horns sprouting from his head....

The day after I handed Kazan this final draft of my program note, he walked down the aisle where the company was gathered at the front of the theatre, held up the copy, called out that this was the best damn program note he had ever read, and pointed me out. You don't know how happy that made me. It was published in *Playbill* (vol. I, November 1964. No. 11), but I doubt that it was read by many theatergoers.

I doubt that Barbara ever read the program note. *The Changeling*, playing in repertory with *After The Fall*, and then *Incident At Vichy*, opened on the 29th of October and had a total run of 32 performances, ending on December 23rd. I got comps for Anne Revere and Sam who were not impressed. The day after Kazan came up to me and said, "I saw the Duchess and Sam were here last night. What was their reaction?" "Not favorable," I told him and he laughed.

On November 6th, *Time* magazine printed the following review:

The Lincoln Center Repertory Theatre is working its way from mediocrity to absurdity. This season's starter was an Elizabethan potboiler full of sex, gore and lunacy. As Beatrice, a noblewoman of Spain, Barbara Loden is not on speaking terms with her lines, and the rest of the cast is unspeakable, except for Barry Primus, who plays Beatrice's low-born hatchet man and seducer. The message of the evening seems to be that a girl may love the man she loathes. It does not hold for a playgoer.

Barbara invited me to dinner one night, saying she would make a home-cooked meal for me. I was pretty thrilled about being invited to her and

Kazan's apartment, in the low sixties on Central Park West facing the park. When I arrived she explained that she had had an appointment that afternoon with her psychiatrist and had just arrived home so could not hold to her promise of a homemade meal. I said that was okay and that if she wanted to get some rest, I could always come back another time. No, Elia would be a little late, but she had called him. When he got there he would order out from a Chinese place they both liked.

She had been given a small amount of LSD at the psychiatrist's office in an attempt to take her back in time to help her figure out the basis of a recurring harrowing dream of trying—and being unable—to open something which was terrifyingly real but she didn't know what it was. She found out that afternoon under the LSD. As a little girl she was awakened by a sound and called out for her mother. There was no response. Terrified of the dark, she got out of bed sobbing and went to her mother's bedroom. She called out but her mother did not answer. She went to the bed and pulled on her mother's arm but she did not awaken. Going to the foot of the bed she managed to pull herself up and then crawled up to her mother's face and called out. There was no response. Fearfully, she placed her left index finger on the skin below her mother's eye, and her right index finger above it and pulling open the lid saw the bloodshot eyeball.

It was unclear to me what insights she had gained from this knowledge that could soothe her troubled psyche, but she seemed happy that she now knew that it was her alcoholic mother's eyelids that she could not open. This was the first time she ever told another person about solving this terrible dream that had so troubled her. When she finished, she took a long pause, then laughed slightly and apologized—"I seem to be doing all the talking"—and quickly managed the transition to the traditional "girl" in conversation with a guy; her duty to listen understandingly to *him*.

I, on the other hand, was interested in *her* background in North Carolina, and so we ping-ponged the conversation between us until Kazan came. He would call and order dinner, and of course I had to get his advice because I didn't—and still don't—know what to order from a Chinese menu.

While we were waiting the phone rang and he took the call. It was Tennessee Williams commiserating with him about the critics' panning of

The Changeling. After the call he explained that Tennessee hadn't called in a long time. He had been in bad shape since he lost his longtime companion, Frank Merlo, to lung cancer, and his *The Milk Train Doesn't Stop Here Anymore* (about the need for summing up before death) in its first revival, starring Tallulah Bankhead, had lasted only three performances.

Kazan said that Tennessee had a new "shrink" who had a questionable reputation ("Dr. Feel-good") because of his drug prescribing, but at least Tennessee had started to write again. Kazan was very sympathetic to Tennessee, and as I think back, I believe his empathy was greatly spiked by the fact that he saw in Tennessee's desperation, caused by negative critical reception, a reflection of what could be his own future. Sure, Tennessee was making millions from movie sales, but money was not the issue. He was a writer, and he could not write a play that was accepted on The Great White Way.

Kazan had directed some 28 major productions on Broadway plus acting in, and producing, 22 others. That evening while chowing-down Chinese, using a fork rather than chopsticks, I caught an oblique view of the beginning of the end of our greatest playwright and our greatest director.

After *The Changeling* Kazan never directed another Broadway production.

⌘ ⌘ ⌘

Arthur Miller's *Incident at Vichy*, the second show scheduled to open that season, was directed by Harold Clurman. I really liked this play and watched every rehearsal, as did its author, and I listened carefully to their observations and comments. I was invited to go with the company to the Museum of Modern Art and see documentary footage about Germany, which was important back story for the play's events. This included parts of famed German director Leni Riefenstahl's *Tiefland, Triumph of the Will* and *Olympia*.

I had always considered Harold Clurman a great theatre writer and critic. Up to this point in his career he had acted in four Broadway productions and directed/staged some 40 more. So understand that I am not suggesting that *Vichy* was typical of all his directing. But the following incidents epitomized what I felt was his actual command of the *craft* of directing on this, his last directed production on Broadway.

The Vichy section was in the South of France and controlled by French police who were searching for escaping or in-hiding Jews and other undesirables, including Gypsies, arresting them, and transporting them to a Paris suburb for deportation to Auschwitz. In short, it was the history of Vichy France's compliance with the Nazis. In the play the Jews are brought in, one by one, and seated next to each other on a bench while waiting to be interrogated. During blocking rehearsals, when the fourth or fifth actor playing one of the captives sat next to the man who preceded him, Clurman called out, "No, do not sit so close, leave a space." The perplexed actor paused and asked, "Why would I do that?" "Because that's where I want ..." (Clurman named another actor whose entrance was later) to sit. "But *I* (meaning the character he was playing) wouldn't know that!" the actor shot back with a fair amount of disgust, and remained seated next to the actor who had preceded him.

Another directorial incident that sticks in my mind was when Harold Scott, an African American playing the Gypsy, was given a direction and Clurman called him Henry. Scott dropped character, turned front, and said to Clurman in a voice filled with contempt, "My name's Harold. I'm Harold Scott. Perhaps you were thinking of Henry Scott who was in your production of *The Member of the Wedding*. Presumably you can't tell one black actor from another."

Clurman's legendary status in the theatre was achieved by his writing *The Fervent Years,* as well as being a very influential critic for both *The New Republic* and *The Nation*. To me, he seemed to lack any instinctive knowledge of theatre craftsmanship. To me his brilliance was in his philosophic viewpoint.

Kazan, in his capacity as co-producer with Robert Whitehead, asked me to write the *Vichy* program note for *Playbill.* I loved the play and think I did a really good job of writing this article. Final approval, of course, had to be with Arthur Miller, who was staying at the famed Chelsea Hotel on 23rd Street. When I got there he was very pleasant and pleased that I loved the play. But he did not think that my program note was quite right for *Playbill*. Kazan praised the essay and said he was sorry that Miller had rejected it.

⌘ ⌘ ⌘

My experience with the production of *Tartuffe* was rewarding even if a bit difficult. Director Bill Ball was a Carnegie Tech graduate and artistic director of the American Conservatory Theatre in San Francisco, as well as a first-rate actor and director. Rehearsals were held in the midtown Edison Hotel ballroom (Norman Kean had turned it into a theatre) which was a nice change of location for me. The production had a splendid cast. Michael O'Sullivan would win a Tony Award for his work in the title role.

Bill Ball rightly—and in agreement with George Bernard Shaw's *The Art of Rehearsal* "... no direction should ever be given to an actor in the presence of a stranger"—did not want anyone at rehearsals who was not professionally involved in the production. But the poet May Swenson was also an official observer because of friendship with Poet Richard Wilbur who had translated this *Tartuffe*, and since producers Kazan and Whitehead approved both of us as official observers, there wasn't much Bill could do to disallow it. He spoke with me only twice: the first time prior to starting the blocking when he told me that he did not like the fact that I was an observer and, if he had his say, would not have allowed it. He assigned me to a specific seat which was about a mile from the action and far enough away so I could not hear his direction. Of course, this was heard by Michael, who had recognized me from the University of Denver and had come over to chat. Michael was nothing if not compliant, and this action on Bill's part put the kibosh on any further acknowledgment of our past relationship, including even a "good morning."

The second time Bill spoke to me was a day he was fraught with frustrating problems and happened to glance over to where I sat writing a letter to Robin. He raced across the ballroom floor and hissed in my face, "Don't you *ever* take notes on what happens in rehearsals of my show. If you ever attempt to publish anything that relates to my direction, I will have you in a court of law!" "Sorry, to have upset you, Mr. Ball," I said, "but I was just writing a note to my wife. I'll not do so again at rehearsals." He took a long moment to look me in the eye, then turned and walked back to rehearsal and never spoke to me again.

During an early dress parade—costumes were designed by Jane Greenwood—he took a great dislike to the sleeve of one of Sada Thompson's (cast as Dorine) costumes. Since he had been trained in historic style by Bess Kimberly, Carnegie's legendary costume designer, he may have been historically correct, but his actions, although theatrically stunning were over the top. He turned to Miss Greenwood and said tensely, as his claw-like fingers traveled up the arm of the costume Sada was wearing, "You're not going to use this for the sleeve, are you?" Before she could answer, he ripped the offending sleeve off her arm. Actually, I enjoyed—although I did not dare laugh—the chutzpah of this temper tantrum, but of course, felt sympathy for Miss Greenwood, who was an absolute first-rate designer.

William Ball's life ended in suicide at age 60, rumored to be caused by AIDS. He was a brilliant young director at the top of his game when I was privileged to observe his work.

All in all this experience in the New York Theatre was not only informative but made me less starry-eyed and idealistic. And I know it gave me an edge as a director and teacher for all the students I was to come into contact with in the future. I no longer revered even the greatest of actors, writers, directors, or designers. I knew damn well that when they sat on the crapper, they didn't do anything different than any other human being.

⌘ ⌘ ⌘

I was immensely glad to get back to 435 Robinson Street the second week in December to be with Robin and the kids and have a wonderful Christmas at home. Amazing how we melted into one another as if no time had passed. And so good to be with my bed partner again, to spoon up against her and go to sleep and not hear "the things that go bump in the night"; and to go to campus and see student friends and faculty. Then almost too soon I was off to London on the second part of my sabbatical to see theatre and visit the Royal Academy of Dramatic Arts. My hotel was the

Jesmond Hotel at 63 Gower Street, W. C. 1. (we would call it a bed and breakfast), the same one Ross and Dorothea had stayed in when they visited London during their sabbatical the year before.

On Friday evening, January 1, 1965, I was seated at the Aldwych Theatre, home of the Royal Shakespeare Company (RSC) to see the first of their productions, which were done in repertory. That evening it was Harold Pinter's *The Birthday Party*, one of the funniest shows I saw, although the London critics were not amused and it would close with only one more performance. I also saw Christopher Marlowe's *The Jew of Malta* with its Machiavellian central character, which is one of those productions you can mention to a history of theatre class for shock and awe reactions because it is the least known of Marlowe's four major plays.

I vaguely remember *The Merry Wives of Windsor* as well produced, dutifully done, but dull; *Eh?* by Henry Livings was immediately erased from my short-term memory because I did not find it interesting enough to listen to. It was, however, produced later that year in the U.S. by Circle in the Square and a young unknown, Dustin Hoffman, won the Theatre World and Drama Desk Awards for best actor. The play won best in the Obie Awards and ran for 232 performances.

The fifth production by the RSC was Peter Weiss' *The Persecution and Assassination of Jean-Paul Marat as Performed by the Inmates of the Asylum of Charenton Under the Direction of the Marquis de Sade*, with music by Richard Peaslee. Directed by Peter Brook and influenced by Antonin Artaud's Theatre of Cruelty, Clive Revill played Marat, Patrick Magee played de Sade, and Glenda Jackson, Charlotte Corday. This was certainly the most important offering by the RSC and one of the most interesting productions of the mid-twentieth century.

At The Old Vic I saw Peter Shaffer's *The Royal Hunt of the Sun* about the destruction of the Inca civilization by Conquistador Francisco Pizarro, staged brilliantly by John Dexter; and *The Master Builder* and *Othello* with Sir Laurence Olivier starring in both. Of the former, the role of Solness has always seemed to me to lack an effective redemptive scene that can negate the character's hubris. As such, this was not a good role for Olivier. In contrast, his *Othello* was absolutely stunning, and the electronic kinescope which I later saw never captured the live performance, one of my great evenings in the theatre.

After several visits to the Old Vic box office the gatekeepers finally took pity on me and let me buy a 60¢ gallery ticket to see Noel Coward's sold-out production of *Hay Fever*. It had an outstanding cast that included Derek Jacobi, Robert Stephens, Maggie Smith, Lynn Redgrave and the incomparable Edith Evans as Judith Bliss (a character based on actress Laurette Taylor). It was an unforgettable evening. Coward had been the darling of the English Theatre, but after World War II the critics labeled his work inconsequential and him only with "a talent to amuse." Olivier disagreed and asked him to direct this revival, and once again he became acknowledged as a master craftsman and regained fame, and more important, the love of the English public.

As for 77-year-old Dame Edith, some 25 years older than her character, I shall *never* forget her entrance: The set was one of those center door fancies and on hearing her approach from the garden, one of the pretty young actors sprang forward to swing open the French doors where she was revealed—in an attractive long dress, of course—with a large floppy hat, garden snips and an *armful* of roses. The house went up for grabs with the longest entrance applause I have ever heard, which she acknowledged with bows.

When it finally quieted down, the young man relieved her of the snips and roses and holding out his arm to steady her, glided her down the raked stage to the down-stage-left sofa, where she removed her hat and remained seated until her exit, occasionally being prompted by the stage manager from the wings. On the curtain call the house rose. Remember, this is 1966 and unlike present day American audiences who give standing ovations for almost *anything*, the English audiences *expect* to have first-rate actors do their job. Of course, much more existed between them and Dame Edith after decades of love for her performances. If you are a female American actress today and have reached the age of 40, you are seldom, if ever, even considered for hiring, let alone playing a leading role unless you are Angela Lansbury.

A Collier's Friday Night at the Royal Court, which had housed the English Stage Society, was in a class by itself. The play, written by D.H. Lawrence when he was 21, pictures a Welsh coal-mining family in the early 1900s and dramatizes the thorny relationship between the young man's mother and father. The Royal Court prided itself on being "a people's theatre," producing plays of quality that could not get a hearing in the commercial West End by the RSC or The Old Vic. After a generation of neglect, it rose again in flames like the phoenix in the mid-1950s with the emergence of John Osborne's *Look Back in Anger*.

In addition I saw West End productions of *Toad of Toad Hall* by A. A. Milne; Agatha Christie's *The Mousetrap* (in its 13th year); *Wait a Minim!* a forgettable revue that played 656 performances (Brits love revues); the fashionable *Hostile Witness* and *The Right Honorable Gentleman;* the thinly-disguised farce about Nureyev's defection *Case Me, Comrade!;* and *Maggie May,* the hit London musical about a goodhearted Liverpool prostitute and a labor union supporter that ran 501 performances. All of these productions were impeccably produced (scenery, costumes, lighting) and slickly acted.

Perhaps the most extraordinary theatre of the entire trip was seeing Kenneth MacMillan's production for the Royal Ballet at Covent Garden of *Romeo and Juliet* with music by Prokofiev and danced by Rudolf Nureyev and Margo Fonteyn. Nureyev's entrance and cross from stage right to left was made in four leaps. I've never seen anything like the technical skill he transformed into *beauty,* and when Fonteyn and he were together—she 46 and he, 20—they were absolutely electric. This was one of the highlights of my life's viewing, and the fact that I had directed the play twice added greatly to my appreciation. It actually opened on the 9th of February so I was obviously seeing a preview, but none the less... incredible!

I spent the weekend of the 9th and 10th with Tony Buckley's mother (I think I remember his father being in Australia) in the Cotswolds, some of England's most beautiful countryside. During that wonderful weekend in the country I was treated to a tour of Bath, as well as being wined and dined and meeting the Buckley's' neighbors.

Upon my return to London I went to beautiful St. Paul's for a pre-arranged interview with George Devine, a man of 52 who had terminated his position of artistic director of the Royal Court. I told him that Purdue might need someone to teach the directing class next semester and asked if he would be interested. He said yes and mentioned a salary of $3,000 plus transportation (which was $435 round trip to Chicago).

In a letter I received from Ross he said that the Purdue University Theatre had accepted an invitation to represent the United States at the World Festival of University Theatres at Nancy, France, April 24th to May 3rd with a production of *The Fantasticks*. I wondered about the choice since the French were never noted for their love of commercial New York musicals, but wrote back only that if he used the same cast members from my Summer Theatre production of *The Fantasticks,* some of our best actors would not be able to appear in my production of *My Fair Lady*. But Life Happens! And there was nothing to be done about it since Purdue was obviously honored to be selected.

I was a passionate tourist in London and walked miles, rode the double-decker red busses, and also quickly learned how to get around on "the tube." In fact I had a tremendous feeling that I had been in London before, a sense of direction that suggested reincarnation, and in addition to St. Paul's—the one built by Inigo Jones (Campton, I did learn to spell it correctly!), I also saw the one near the vegetable markets which is the background for the first scene in Shaw's *Pygmalion*.

I marveled at London Bridge and the Tower of London built in 1067 by William the Conqueror and the home of the Crown Jewels. I visited the British Museum three times and saw the Elgin Marbles; the historic costume collection in the Victoria and Albert museum; the National Portrait Gallery (twice, I loved it!); Trafalgar Square; Piccadilly Circus and the statue of Eros; Buckingham Palace and the changing of the guard; Madame Tussauds Wax Museum; Westminster Abbey and the Poet's Corner; Parliament and Big Ben; Windsor Castle (upstream); Kensington Palace; the Old Bailey (and actually sat for a while and listened to a hearing in which some of the bluest language I had heard since backstage at *Gypsy* was being quoted from a letter by a prim white-wigged lawyer); Hyde Park and the famed Speaker's Corner near Marble Arch where anyone could talk about any subject they wished; and The Royal Academy of Dramatic Arts (RADA) where I had a prearranged interview with some official in attendance—not the headmaster. We discussed their training program for actors which favored all aspects of voice, speech, movement rather than acting classes and performance, performance, performance.

In fact, RADA was only a short way from the Jesmond Hotel, where I ate breakfast at the very last moment before the kitchen closed in order to quell hunger throughout the day. Then all I needed was a steak and kidney pie, or biscuits and slices of Stilton cheese, to last me through evenings in the theatre, after which I would rush to the nearest pub and order a pint of stout just about the time the bartender called "Last call" at 11:00 P.M.

On Sunday the 17th I flew back to New York and stayed at the Albert Hotel through Tuesday so I could see *Tartuffe*, which had opened on January 14th after I'd left New York. It was, I thought, an absolute first rate production. I also saw the new Edward Albee play *Tiny Alice* which was unrelentingly baffling, and flew back to West Lafayette on Wednesday, the 20th of January.

⌘ ⌘ ⌘

Expenses for my Sabbatical leave from September 4, 1964 through January 21, 1965.

Hotel Albert $315 from September 4th thru December 2nd; a trip to Stratford, CT from NYC and seeing three shows staying with Allen and Ann Fletcher in The Little Red House on the Housatonic, $12; food for 84 days was $420; transportation round trip from West Lafayette to NY (two trips) plus the round trip to London totaled $748.14. The 21 more days in 1965, sixteen of which were spent in London, the cost for 18 plays/musicals/ballets (including 5 matinee performances) of $40.34; the Jesmond Hotel in London cost $52.50 and back in New York at the Albert Hotel for 3 nights was $15.75 plus two shows; *Tartuffe*, $5 and at the Billy Rose, Edward Albee's *Tiny Alice* $4.80. Food and cost of sightseeing for these two, 21 days in London & New York @ $5 per day cost of $105.

Grand total for the entire sabbatical: $1,718.63.

Eat your hearts out, today's theatre lovers!

Chapter 19

MY PRODUCTION OF CHEKHOV'S *Three Sisters* in Randall Jarrell's translation played in early March and was a major highlight of my directing career. New to the faculty that year was the very talented but erratic designer Joe McArdle, with an undergraduate degree from Notre Dame and a graduate degree from Carnegie Tech. There were three sets: two interiors and one exterior of the Prozorov's home backed by a stand of birch trees. The multitalented Larry Randolph designed the costumes and played the old hard-of-hearing servant, Ferapont.

Our three sisters, Irina, Olga, and Masha were played by Michelle Dezerseran, Sharon Ryterband, and Cindy Miller. For the role of Vershinin, I jobbed in Louis Edmonds, who was a graduate of Carnegie Tech, and whose speech teacher Edith Skinner was arguably the most influential and brilliant in the history of U.S. theatre education. Louis was probably best known for his appearances in two daytime TV soaps, *Dark Shadows* and *All My Children,* and also credited with roles in episodes of many TV shows and an occasional film along with Off-Broadway productions including the musical *Earnest in Love,* and on Broadway in some half dozen productions starting with *Candide*. I had also seen him in the adaptation of the Forster novel *A Passage to India*. He accepted this guest artist job-in for minimum AEA pay, mainly because Vershinin was a role he coveted and was desperate to play. Our stage manager was Tom Moore and our technical director, Randy Earle.

⌘ ⌘ ⌘

With Ross and company headed to France on the 24th, we opened *My Fair Lady* on the 22nd for a six performance run. Our AEA actors, John Newton as Higgins and Janet Hayes as Eliza, were perfectly cast, enormously talented with Broadway credits. They were actors who understood the importance of playing in a university production, as well as their relationships with both students and theatre-goers. In fact, Stuart Main (who played Doolittle in the production) and his wife Porter became life-long friends with John and Janet, taking them to the Russian Tea Room on their New York junkets. "In thanks" for enlivening their lives, Stuart left John (Janet had already passed) $1,000 in his will.

The production was chosen for the annual Gala Week alumni show, so with all this, who would not be thrilled to direct such a great musical as *My Fair Lady*, with choreography and musical numbers staged by Wayne Lamb, and the university orchestra, a pit-full of 28 musicians under the direction of Alan H. Drake.

⌘ ⌘ ⌘

When *The Fantasticks* company returned from France on May 5th, news of its reception was not good. The problem was that the French audience was incensed by the fact that their great playwright Edmond Rostand's play, *The Romancers*, had been transformed into a commercial American musical. Peter Saputo, who played one of the fathers, recently told me that there was booing from the audience during the curtain call, and that many of them had turned their heads from the stage to stare down those in the balcony—Festival participants—who were applauding.

Prior to and during the run of *My Fair Lady* I was finishing plans for our sixth season (and second as an AEA company) of the Purdue Summer Theatre with a schedule of five shows, focusing on how an AEA company worked in an educational environment, not only as a part of student training but as a means of eventually gaining AEA membership if the student so desired.

I wanted to work again with Pamela Printy, who had played the lead in *The Glass Menagerie*, my first full-length directed play. Her mother still lived in West Lafayette, and she and her husband Bill Bohnert, who designed the Ed Sullivan TV show for a dozen years, were coming for a visit and would be in residence for much of the summer.

I decided to play both *Stop the World, I Want to Get Off* and *The Amorous Flea* in repertory because of the simplicity of the settings for both shows. The exact dates of each production are listed in Appendix D, which gives all information on each production.

For our opener we did *Stop the World, I Want to Get Off,* a show that carried special meaning for me. Miriam Birch from Santa Barbara was Evie (who also played the Russian Anya, the German Ilse) and Stuart Howard played Littlechap. On opening night when Littlechap, who marries the boss's daughter Evie but searches for love with other women, realizes that the woman who sustained him throughout his life, the woman he really loves, is in reality his wife and sings "What Kind of Fool Am I," it was an incredibly moving moment. On his star curtain call Stuart received the greatest applause of any production I ever directed.

The next night we opened *The Amorous Flea*, a small musical based on Moliere's *School for Wives*. I thought to myself that if this had been done in France they would have brought out the guillotine and beheaded every one of us for disrespecting their beloved Moliere. But the show was a riotous romp, the cast headed by Peter Stanton (*aka* Saputo) as Arnolphe. The story is of an older man who locks up his young bride so she can be kept from temptation.

In one performance when Stuart Howard, executing a piece of business, slapped Peter on the back, dislodging his wig so that it momentarily flew in the air before settling back in an askew manner on his head, neither Stuart nor Mimsy could keep from laughing. Then Peter broke, and I have never seen such a frenzy of uncontrollable laughter, with the actors desperately trying to regain straight faces and restart the scene, and then breaking again into laughter. Unprofessional? Well, yes, but what a wonderful spontaneous participation it created in the audience who, swept into the spirit of the moment, were also unable to control their laughter so the play could restart.

⌘ ⌘ ⌘

For the first and only time in my life I experienced a situation during this season involving the death of a parent of one of the actors. The final day of performances—a late matinee and evening of *Stop The World*—was on Saturday July 3rd. Just after the matinee, Stuart Howard got word that his father had suffered a massive heart attack. He was extremely upset and I told him that we could cancel the evening performance if necessary. He thought about it, and knowing the financial problems a cancelation would cause, he decided to play the second performance.

That last performance was incredibly well played, but with knowledge of his father's condition it was a heartbreaker. Friends insisted on having him stay with them overnight. At 3:00 A.M., I got the call that his father was dead. According to Jewish law he would be buried within 24 hours. The stakes were very high, not only because of the opening of *Streetcar* three days later in which he played Mitch, but for the rest of the season in which he was scheduled to play leading roles. He was fully aware of this and told me he would go home for the funeral, stay with family on Tuesday, and return on Wednesday for the opening of *Streetcar*.

Astonishingly, in *Streetcar*, when it seemed problematic that he could do it, he pulled himself together and seemed to omit all traces of bereavement in his performance, but broke down later and wept.

Our cast for *A Streetcar Named Desire* was headed by Pamela Printy as Blanche, Charles Hayman as Stanley, Stuart as Mitch, and Royce Lenelle as Stella, and it was a labor of love. In real life as on the stage, Charles Hayman was unrelentingly male. As an English major he was smart enough to instinctively know he did not have to imitate Brando's performance, and therefore he served Williams' point of view better than young actors who go that imitative route.

Pamela was also true to Williams, and her own creation of Blanche included the character's sense of ironic humor as well as the tragedy. As for this approach, one of the Indianapolis critics noted that she had something in her features—profile vs. full front—that struck him as a Janus quality of two totally different people, which I think was absolutely right.

The day after the return of Stuart from his father's funeral and the opening night of *Streetcar*, he was on time for rehearsal for the demanding role of Jack Tanner in *Man and Superman* opposite Pamela Printy as Ann Whitfield.

In this George Bernard Shaw play as is customary, we eliminated the third act—The "Don Juan in Hell" scene—and concentrated on a comedy of manners contained in the story of Ann Whitfield's convincing her dying father to name confirmed bachelor Jack Tanner her guardian, after which she accosts him with her desire for marriage. He flees in his car but she catches up with him in the Spanish Pyrenees, where he finally gives in to her wish, realizing she represents the unbeatable Life Force.

The philosophic inspiration for this play is based on Shaw's reading of Nietzsche's idea of the Superman. In today's world we might call Shaw's Life Force a new kind of understanding of Darwin's Evolution in creationism. But in our production we kept the thru-line objective clear, simple and conventionally human with the female as pursuer in the mating game. And if you check the program you will find that Bill Bohnert (yes, the TV designer!) was Hector Malone, in a small non-AEA role.

Our fifth production was Brendan Behan's *The Hostage*, set in a whorehouse owned by a former IRA officer in Dublin. The story centers around the impending execution of a never seen young IRA member charged with killing an Ulster policeman and awaiting execution in a Belfast jail. The hostage of the title is an innocent young British soldier captured on Ireland's border and being held captive in the brothel. Among its habitués are: Republican-Irish, drunkards, whores, revolutionaries, and lapsed hierarchies of the Catholic Church, along with a young orphan girl who falls in love with the young Cockney hostage who is also an orphan.

It is this young couple's love story that serves as the slim thread of the play's plot, which is sidetracked time and again with songs, as well as dialogue revealing the characters, the time and place, but undergirded *always* by the impending execution of the IRA member in Belfast. The climax of the play comes with the news of his hanging, followed by a raid on the brothel in which the young British soldier is killed. It ends with his rising from death to sing "The bells of hell / Go ting-a-ling-a-ling / for you but not for me. / oh death, where is thy sting-a-ling-a-ling / or grave thy victory?"

Since the central situation that hovers over everything is the hostage in the Belfast jail and thus unseen by the audience, I had a terrible time figuring out the dramatic structure of this play, especially at the climactic moment. This was true even when I saw the production Off Broadway in New York. I finally decided, at the very last moment, to have the brothel's characters line up across the stage listening to a broadcast of the Belfast hanging, and in their imagination seeing the young IRA officer being escorted through the streets of Belfast to his execution.

I did not think of this until two days before we opened, and when I did I called a meeting of the entire company and explained what I wanted. Randy Earle had to figure out a new lighting plot that lit only the faces of the brothel inhabitants, which could not be facilitated until the final Tuesday afternoon dress rehearsal. As always, Randy made it happen and the company was wonderfully cooperative.

Remember, this was 1965 when there was beginning to be more knowledge of the war in Vietnam that would eventually take the lives of 58,000 young men like the young prisoner in Belfast. You could read the incredible sadness in the faces of each of the characters when, in their imaginations, he was escorted to his execution, the same sad looks the members of the audience might wear when they read of the news of the war in Vietnam.

Incidentally, note in Appendix D that Purdue track star, Nate Adams, played the role of Rio Rita. This production was a wonderful ending to that rewarding summer season in 1965 and I entered the next semester as a full professor, having made it in record breaking time.

⌘ ⌘ ⌘

I took a much needed vacation in Michigan, taking along with me the Samuel French acting edition of *The Visit*. I had Frances Farmer in mind, and knew that Gene Kildahl would be perfect to play opposite her. By this time she had been "summarily fired" from WFBM-TV. The copy I had sent her in the spring was the "authorized acting edition" used by Lunt and Fontanne in their Broadway production, which was adapted by Maurice Valencia. Asking if she would be interested in playing the role of Claire Zachanassian at the Loeb Playhouse in October, she wrote back immediately.

> Dear Joe.... The play is, of course, a marvelous show case for whomever plays Claire but in reading it I found myself fascinated by the curious abstract quality of the showmanship... as if I were viewing pictures at a museum, of a most meticulous ballet, with overtones of Pirandello. In the end I think one feels one has witnessed the swallowing of a too willing rabbit by a glittering snake. If you would like me to do the role, I think I would very much like to do it.

The young Gene Kildahl was a sports-loving handsome young alpha male with tallest dog-on-the-block assurance and likeability. When he started college his right leg and hip were injured in a train accident. The family did not provide the funds for an operation that could have straightened the leg, so he moved with a slight limp. Over time he found ways to hide this, or at least to limp as little as possible. He would sit, his back straight, bent slightly forward, left leg straight and thrust forward, the right injured one tucked just behind it. This gave him the physical appearance of concentrated attentiveness, with the grace of a panther ready to strike. He trained as an actor under Gilmore Brown at the Pasadena Playhouse and, never highly driven, settled easily into his position at Purdue where he stayed until he retired.

We had been in reading rehearsals for a week and Frances was scheduled to start on Monday when some bright graduate student mentioned that there were really two versions of *The Visit*. For some reason I had never read the Patrick Bowles' "translation," a copy of which I had bought in London and that was in my office. I started reading and never stopped until I had finished. I was absolutely blown away by the beauty of the Bowles translation and the enormous differences between it and the Valency adaptation, not only in clarity but more poetic, more imaginative, and more theatrical.

As soon as I finished reading, I decided to switch. This meant my typing the play on those blue mimeograph sheets, which took me much of the night. I caught some sleep and finished by noon the next day, after which the theatre secretary ran off copies, and I assembled and bound them. At 6:55 P.M. I walked into rehearsal with 35 copies.

I welcomed Frances, and then with no fanfare announced that I had changed the script. I saw the panic and fear in Frances' face, but much to her credit, she said nothing about having already memorized all the lines of the Valency. As we read the Bowles translation she became captivated, and when we finished both she and Gene (who also had learned many of his lines) said that I was absolutely right, and the entire company agreed that the Bowles was a much more powerful show.

My most vivid remembrance of Frances' performance was her entrance: aged, red-haired, wearing a pearl necklace; a survivor, her scenes in the sedan chair, the lovely scene in the woods and later in the barn with Gene. Especially effective was the ending of the first act when she addresses the people of the village: "I'll give a million to your village if someone kills Alfred III." And in the scene with Alfred when she says: "Now we're old, the pair of us. You decrepit, and me cut to bits by the surgeon's knife." And her cigar smoking, and the power when she said, "The world turned me into a whore. I shall turn the world into a brothel." And there was her shattering final silent entrance and exit on her way to Capri, like an old stone idol, in the sedan chair, followed by her retinue which includes the two castrated men who first lied about her, and a coffin bearing the body of Alfred III.

After the performance, President Hovde gave a public reception for Frances in one of the ballrooms of the Memorial Union, where she was introduced to audience members. This was quite a gala event, a first time happening at Purdue and could not have provided better publicity and more support of theatre at the university.

We were not reviewed by the Indianapolis papers, but critic Frank Argenbright in the *Journal and Courier* wrote:

"STERLING PERFORMANCES GIVEN IN POWER-PACKED 'VISIT'"

Frances Farmer... and Erling Kildahl... gave sterling performances... Miss Farmer undoubtedly gave one of the finest performances of her career in the difficult and unsympathetic role... unlike many actresses who seem always to be themselves on stage or screen, Miss Farmer expertly assumes the personality and characteristics of the woman she portrays, with the aid of a terrific make-up job, she looks the part of a woman who had 'been around,' delving into prostitution—and switching husbands—after she first marries wealth. She faithfully gives the illusion that she has an artificial left leg and an artificial left arm—both lost as the result of an airplane crash.

⌘ ⌘ ⌘

At two o'clock the Sunday afternoon after the first three performances, I passed through the trap room and saw Frances' dressing room door ajar and the lights on. She was inside cleaning up, putting used Kleenex into the wastebasket, checking to see that her costumes were hung up properly, and jewelry secured. We talked for a few minutes and she said she had slept late, was exhausted, and was going to drive back to her motel, pack and be underway. She would be back on Wednesday for the brush-up rehearsal and the other three performances.

Tuesday someone called Robin and told her that there was a story in the Indianapolis paper that Frances had been arrested. The October 26, 1965 *Indianapolis News* had a story headlined:

FRANCES FARMER FINED $68.50 ON DRIVING CHARGES (Special to the News, Lebanon, Ind.) Frances Farmer Mikesell, 52, former Indianapolis television personality, was fined a total of $68.50 here Sunday on charges of reckless driving while under the influence of alcohol. Mrs. Mikesell, who, under her stage name, Frances Farmer, was appearing in a play at Purdue University, was arrested south of Lebanon about 3 p.m. She gave her occupation as interior decorator and her home address as 5107 N. Park, Indianapolis. She appeared in the court of Justice of the Peace, T. A. Robinson and pleaded guilty to the two charges.

Francis had not been drinking when I saw her in her dressing room on Sunday at two o'clock. I would have known instantly. What happened after I left her, of course, I cannot say, but I do know she had to drive back to the motel where she was staying, check out and then head back to Indianapolis, which would have taken her at least twenty minutes. I could not believe that she was drunk by the time she reached Lebanon.

Robin and I drove to Indianapolis. Frances was very upset. She told us she was not drunk but was tired and had apparently fallen asleep at the wheel. Whatever the truth, she was profoundly depressed. I said I would respect her decision. Whether she played the last three performances was not a matter of loss of revenues at the box office. But for her sake I urged her to come back and finish the run. Robin felt the same and Frances eventually agreed.

The next day she was back for the brush-up rehearsal. The cast and crew members were especially supportive, going out of their way to make her feel welcome and no one, to my knowledge, mentioned the incident. The next night, however, I knew would be very difficult for her. By that time most of the faculty, students and community who followed the theatre would know of the arrest and she would not just be facing supportive fellow cast and crew members, but the general public. I tried to make as little of the situation as possible. We all knew the anxiety she was going through, and when the stage manager called "Places, please," she had to go up to the right side-stage alone where she would join her "retinue" for her first entrance.

Robin had come to the theatre that evening. I always sat alone, in the back of the orchestra or balcony, or sometimes in the light booth, any place well out of the public's eye. That night when Frances made her entrance, Robin (god bless her!) applauded—certainly not from any prompting on my part since it was not customary in a University theatre production to give an actor entrance applause. Although at the very beginning I feared she might be applauding alone, she was joined by others, and then others joined in until the sound generously and warmly welcomed Frances back and gave her the support she needed. Her confidence restored, she gave us a hell of a great performance those last three shows.

For the final performance she wrote the cast: "To everyone in 'The Visit': I can't tell you how much I appreciate your interest, dedication, and real talent that made it possible for me to be Claire in this production. God bless you and good luck for the future, with love, Frances Farmer."

To me she wrote:

> Dear Joe: It was in 1935, when I left the University of Washington, with my head full of Stanislavski, my suitcase in my hand and hopes of becoming a professional actress in my heart. Now, in 1965, after all this time, I feel I have finally graduated. In the last three years you have opened my eyes, given me the tools. *The Visit* will remain in my mind always as the first real performance I finally achieved. Thank you. Frances.

After the opening night I had sent a program and a news story with a picture of Frances which appeared in the local paper to Elia Kazan. He wrote back, "Dear Joe: Thank you for sending me the clipping about Frances Farmer. I always liked Frances enormously. And I am glad she's working. And she does look happy in the photograph. I remember her when she was one of the best looking girls I have ever seen in my life, and had the grace and character to go with it. Best Regards, Gadge."

I sent the letter to Frances. In the meantime, in Walter Winchell's syndicated "Broadway and Elsewhere" column, the following appeared: "One-time screen star Frances Farmer of Indianapolis appears with obscure theatre groups in the small towns where the new generation enjoy her talent although most of the time they do not know she was once a movie star... She just starred in *The Visit* at Lafayette, Ind."

On November 10, Frances, having appeared on a TV interview, wrote:

> Dear Joe: Enclosed is the Kazan letter that impressed Leibo very much on last night's show. That and a Winchell squib helped a great deal for my image—and the questions and comments which I had forebodings about, turned into a very friendly session. Perhaps you heard it. Of course I had my carefully controlled (and not expressed) comment about the obscure town of Lafayette, where an obscure former movie actress mingles with a young generation in an obscure play, *The Visit*. Really, something should be done about New Yorkers!

⌘ ⌘ ⌘

After *The Visit* Erling directed a first-rate production of Tennessee William's *The Night of the Iguana* and cast Robin as Hannah, with Sharon

Spelman as Maxine. Since he wanted to bring in an actor for Shannon, the defrocked minister, I suggested Mark Lenard, who grew up near South Haven, Michigan, and whom I had seen briefly in Lillian Hellman's *My Mother, My Father and Me,* and off-Broadway with Anne Meacham in an interesting *Hedda Gabler.* I believe this is the best acting Robin ever did. Mark was wonderful to work with and helped her a great deal in their shared scenes.

My next production was the musical *Gypsy,* playing for nine performances (longest run for a University Theatre production we ever had in The Loeb Playhouse) March 17-19 and March 22-25, with double performances at 6:30 and 9:30 on Saturdays, with a cast of 75 characters, some actors doubling in brass. Sets were by a frantic Joe McArdle who was still painting one used in the second act when the curtain went up on our first performance. Again, the pit was filled with musicians. The house lights lowered and that best of all overtures ever written for a musical started as Randy Earle's lighting clicked in with one-at-a-time lights framing the proscenium, then the runway that stretched out over the orchestra into the audience The word G Y P S Y was spelled over the stage, and ended by flashing on and off at the climax of the overture.

Years later, Peter Gilman, a graduate of our department, told me that on a tip from a friend he had reluctantly come to check out Purdue, even though he thought of it as an improbable school to attend as a theatre major. His visit just happened to coincide with the opening night of *Gypsy* and he was so blown away by the production that he immediately signed up for the fall semester.

Choreography and musical numbers were staged by Wayne Lamb, and an absolutely fabulous singing actress whom I had first seen in Ross and Wayne's production of *Annie Get Your Gun,* Mary Margaret O'Brian, played Rose.

Gypsy was too big to rehearse in the Loeb's trap room so we booked the rehearsal space in the Hall of Music where we could have the whole shebang, including real live stage mothers, at rehearsals. A memorable moment was the very first time John Eldridge as Tulsa, who had worked privately with Wayne, did his "All I Need Is The Girl" song-and-dance number for Cindy Miller as Louise. All of us broke into shouts and applause for his talent and energy. Sharon Spelman as Tessie Tura, Sharon Ryterband as Mazeppa, and Karin Woodward as Electra knocked the audience out with their stripper number, and Don Treat was a low-keyed understanding Herbie, who was such a good-looking guy as to make no doubt about what Rose saw in him even though she had to be top-dog in the relationship. And Mary Margaret O'Brian's final "Rose's Turn" was as thrilling as when I first saw it done in New York and later on the road, with the "Mama" stammer (harking back to the character's own controlling mother which made credible and sympathetic her character) as a pushy, tough-loving, show-biz mother. In short, that production of *Gypsy* was a *total* show-biz, knock-their-sox-off finale. Not to mention David Stockdale with "the Russian Yaks" played by Wayne Lamb's two poodles in that first scene where pushy mothers are overseeing their kids' auditions.

The opening night party at 435 Robinson Street was memorable, if only for the high everyone was on with the success of the show. The only one unhappy was Joe McArdle, who got roaring screaming drunk and started to leave about midnight. I stopped him and said I'd drive him home but he lurched away across the backyard and up to Littleton Street. The problem was, he was ticked off at himself because he knew he had screwed up by not getting his sets done on time.

It wasn't more than 15 minutes later that I got a call from a West Lafayette policeman asking whether I knew a Professor Joe McArdle? Seems he had entered a fraternity house and been thrown out, and was now claiming that he was on the faculty and that the police should call me.

Joe was in a raging fit when I arrived, with threats of retaliation at the policeman, his over-the-top indignation on a par with Gloria Swanson's performance in *Sunset Boulevard*. I apologized to the officer and said I'd get him home and off the street. After the officer drove away, Joe was belligerent, but I managed to get him into the car, and we drove to his apartment where he wanted me to drop him off. I was not about to leave him drunk and incoherent, so I got him inside and told him to go to bed and sleep it off.

He turned violent and started throwing things—even a lamp and an ash tray which broke through the cheap wallboard construction, and I just said to hell with it—whatever was going to happen was going to happen. He was totally out of control, so I drove back home. The incident was just too much and I knew that for all his talent, he was really a mess and that his contract must not be renewed. But he was already contracted to design the summer theatre productions, and this worried the hell out of me. If he had been a job-in designer, he could have been fired, but academic contracts were hard to break.

⌘ ⌘ ⌘

Son Joe, who would be 15 in August, had saved his paper delivery money for several years and decided he wanted to go abroad. I suggested England where Tony Buckley's mother lived in the Cotswolds. Arrangements were made for him to sail on the last trip of the *Queen Elizabeth* and then to fly home in August. This would be the first of son Joe's world travels. He wrote about his trip for his high school paper and was the envy of other students because he had been allowed to go alone on such a journey.

⌘ ⌘ ⌘

I, like the people at Lincoln Center, fancied that rotating repertory would be absolutely wonderful for the actors. The standard eight performances a week on Broadway, and playing a show as long as it sold tickets, could lead to incredible monotony, and to a technical rather than felt impression-of-the-first-time performance. Why not try it? In addition there would be no star calls, only the standard repertory lineups with all the women downstage and the men upstage for the first call. On the second one the men walked between the women (who took one step backward) to the downstage position, and then the women joined them in a lineup, across the stage, for the third call.

The professional actors I thought might join me in this adventure, and did, were: John Newton, Janet Hayes, Merle Louise, Peter Simon, Dale Helward, Dorothy Harlan, and Al Hinckley (replaced after two weeks of rehearsal with first-rate, versatile actor and fast study Stuart Howard). In addition to Joe McArdle as set and costume designer, the repertory staff was: Randy Earle lighting designer and technical director; Dick Newdick stage manager assisted by Peter Simon; Paul Voelker assistant technical director assisted by Gary Craven and Steve Hodge; Sharon Ryterband property mistress and actress in *Ardele* and *A Doll's House;* Mary Jane Hargitt (mother of the three children Eden, Charles and Russell in the cast of *A Doll's House*) wardrobe mistress and her assistants Mary Arnold and Marty Van Cleef. House manager was Patrice Murphy and that was it: a total company of 20, including myself as director about to face an almost unheard-of venture in the contemporary regional theatre movement in this country.

As for the four shows, I was determined to add an original play to the others and we would rehearse all of them during a standard eight-hour day, six days a week for four weeks. In the fifth week we would open the first show on a Tuesday and play it for two more days, and open the second one on a Friday, playing it four performances over the weekend. In the second week we would open the third and fourth productions on the same schedule; after that we would rotate the bill *every single day* and play in rotating repertory until the end of the summer season. This was an American actor's dream, like the RSC and The Old Vic in London, and as it was done in Russia and the famous European state-subsidized theatres.

One show I had been dying to direct since I had seen a theatre company in Santa Barbara do it, and had read Simone de Beauvoir's *The Second Sex*, was Ibsen's *A Doll's House.* Another was *The Birthday Party*, which had not gotten a good reception when it first played in London but which I loved. I'd found Pinter a striking new voice in the theatre and had laughed myself silly at it.

As for the original choice, grad student Richard Busch had taken my playwriting class and written a play called *Talk of Another Day,* a William Inge-type work. Although it had some problems that I could not figure out, I thought perhaps that we could solve them and improve the show during its run. I insisted, however, that Richard be present to give advice so I would not encounter a situation like the one I went through during the opening of the Experimental Theatre.

Finally, I knew enough about modern drama to realize that Jean Anouilh was France's major playwright. His *Antigone* was not only taught in literature classes but was popular in community theatre and university theatre productions. I was convinced that of all the modern French dramatic literature I had been exposed to, Anouilh's work was better suited to our audience than Samuel Beckett's or Eugene Ionesco's.

I had seen several of his New York productions—*The Lark, The Waltz of the Toreadors, Becket* with Laurence Olivier and Anthony Quinn, and only a year before *Traveler Without Luggage* with Ben Gazzara and Mildred Dunnock. I started reading Anouilh's plays with cast listings of characters that would fit the number of actors in our company. If memory serves it was Peter Simon (French major at Williams under Professor Jack Savacool) who came up with *The Cry of the Peacock*, produced originally under the title *Ardele*.

Except for the replacement of one actor—which cost us two weeks' salary and transportation—the only thing that did not go well was the completion of the four sets. My plan was that the building and painting of all four sets, plus costumes, *had to be completed* in the four-week rehearsal period so the two week break-in periods would go smoothly. As it turned out, sets were not ready in time, so building and painting had to take place at the same time we were breaking in the four plays. Tech Director Randy Earle was totally capable of this, but the brilliant designer Joe McArdle was constitutionally unable to meet deadlines.

This resulted in the most difficult two weeks of my theatre career. I found it necessary to stay up all night keeping McArdle company while he painted the sets. I brought along a six-pack to keep him at it. My job was to encourage him and keep him focused, but by that time I was so exhausted from the planning and rehearsing that those nights were total hell. They reminded me of our return from Denver after getting my PhD when I literally had to lean my head out the car's window and slap myself to stay awake. We did make it; the sets were first-rate and everything got painted, and of course Randy had a lighting plot that worked for all four shows, with only minor changes in refocusing required.

The real pity of this situation was that McArdle knew of his own failures. He hated himself for his drinking problem and not having the discipline to meet schedules. I went to Ross and said that Joe could not be re-hired, and Ross called him in and told him.

Joe respected me enormously and kept in contact with me by phone for the rest of his life. At first I always took the drunken calls and listened to him talk about his success in Hollywood and elsewhere, knowing that most of what he said was pure fiction. He always ended up saying that I was the best director he had ever worked with, and me trying to get him to hang up. I finally told Robin to take all incoming calls, and she always told him that I was not there. She would listen, until even she got to the point where she could not take it any longer and would tell him she needed to go to the bathroom. His last communication was about how he and Bette Midler had been arrested for drunken driving and thrown in jail overnight. Then there was nothing. Neither his phone nor his snail or e-mail worked. Jerry Williams finally found his obit in a Pittsburgh newspaper.

The opening review complimenting us for showing our intent of introducing new works was by Charles Staff, Drama Critic of *The Indianapolis News*. The headline: PURDUE OPENER HAS FRESH CRISIS: LOVE.

> If, as Aristotle wrote, imitation is the beginning of art, the young playwright Richard Busch has begun. The Purdue University Summer Repertory Theatre opened its season last night in the Experimental Theatre, with the 25 year-old Wisconsin native's first full-length play, "Talk of Another Day." Busch, who will get his Master's Degree this August from Purdue, had only two one-act works under his belt when he started this two act domestic study a year ago. Although this reaction may sound lame, the play is a good first try, one that shows promise not so much for itself as for its author. A better opener could have been found, but the choice is commendable. A troupe that encourages fresh, creative urges deserves the blessings of anyone interested in the theatre as a living and not as a museum for musty, but tested items.
>
> Discovered Love In Small Town
>
> Throughout the evening one was struck by Busch's affinity for playwright William Inge. The setting, a small town hotel lobby, which serves the family owners as a living room; the crisis is of a young man who discovers love's "sweet hell" and the "lack of communication" theme that are Inge elements.

Like Tennessee Williams' "Glass Menagerie" Busch's treatment of the quiet desperation of two brothers and a female lodger is obviously a "memory" play. The title may refer if taken literally to Busch's memory of "another day."

There are flashes of fine theatrical sense such as the end of the first act. The younger brother and the spinster teacher reach for each other tenderly as the older brother and a carnival harlot participate noisily in an act of darkness upstairs during a storm.

This same device, the juxtaposition of extremes, is used effectively again at the conclusion as the two brothers go through their frustrated defeated paces as a parade passes outside accompanied by the laughter of their mother and her male companion.

What is missing is the kind of dialogue that illuminates, talks that break through the crust to the bubbling juices beneath. Busch has an ear for conversation but lacks the cleverness; the feel for language, for sounds and rhythms that are so dazzling in Williams and at his best in Inge to say old things in new ways.

Directed by Joseph Stockdale, the production is one which any author might be pleased with and this includes lighting effects, set design and execution, pacing and, most particularly, performances. Merle Louise makes a delightful tart. Dorothy Harlan is the most convincing figure as the mother, partly because Busch wrote it that way without strain, partly for Ms. Harlan's obvious ability.

Dale Helward and Peter Simon are excellent as the brothers, though Helward pushes a bit too hard. Janet Hayes drew sympathy as the teacher, but her character was not always clear, and John Newton presented a thorough portrait of the mother's friend....

If this first production is an indication, a trip to Purdue for one or all of the plays is a must for the Hoosier summer theatergoer.

Both *Birthday Party* and *A Doll's House* were liked by the audiences and critics, *Ardele,* less so. The ensemble curtain calls did not work because, for example, the audience wanted to applaud Merle Louise and show their appreciation for her playing Nora so breathtakingly in *Doll's House.* In truth, so did I, so we changed to standard curtain calls after all the shows opened. The rotating schedule was totally confusing to our public. Having the schedule printed in the local paper did not help, and once they understood that they could see plays later in the season they kept putting it off with the obvious result that things got jammed up at the end.

I do believe that a repertory system of four or five plays playing in big cities for at least two years is much more conducive to stimulating work for the actors, as well as an impression-of-the-first-time performance for the audience. Audiences are the ones who will teach the actors about their responses since they are, by definition, a part of the equation of what theatre is. And the productions will have an opportunity to grow and improve in such a system.

However, I came to the conclusion that repertory was *not* good for our customers. I would not try it again. But as an experience, I shall never forget it, nor would the actors in our company. A repertory of the four major plays of Anton Chekhov, or four or five plays by August Wilson with absolute first-rate actors who would commit to long-term contracts—that's always the catch—could thrive in large cities. What this idea does not serve, perhaps, is the great god of commercialism and competition. But then those were never the goals of art in the first place.

The Birthday Party was the only time I ever went through a rehearsal period where we broke up at every rehearsal with falling on-the-floor laughter. As soon as the interrogation scene of Stanley by Goldberg and McCann started, we steeled ourselves to keep from laughing but always failed. Stuart, with his Yiddish accent, John Newton with an Irish brogue, and Dale Helward, the English chap being interrogated, was a situation so bizarre that when Goldberg turns to McCann and says "Give us a blow," and the not too bright McCann goes over and blows in his mouth, we all became hysterical. It was only on opening night that the cast finally made it through without breaking up.

After we got all the shows up and playing, I was no longer trying to redo (improve) *Talk of Another Day* since I had come to believe that its protagonist's reason for traveling around southern Minnesota from one small bed-and-breakfast establishment to another was to search for the love that dare not be named. The character is really a man and I did not wish to confront the author with this. Further, Janet Hayes could not have played a cross-dressing male because she was one of the most beautiful and feminine women I have ever known. The play was not very well received, but we did the best we could under the circumstances. The author attended all rehearsals and I urged him to talk freely to the cast.

⌘ ⌘ ⌘

In mid-summer I got a call from Darwin Payne of the University of Southern Illinois at Carbondale asking me if I would direct *Brigadoon*. I accepted since our summer theatre shows were playing in repertory and there was nothing to keep me at Purdue. That musical is, of course, charming, and I enjoyed working with choreographers Gil and Nancy Green and Darwin, and meeting the legendary scene designer, Mordecai Gorelik, who was on the design faculty. I think we put on a pretty good show.

⌘ ⌘ ⌘

In October I again directed G.B.S.'s *Misalliance,* this time for the main stage of The Loeb Playhouse. I knew of the famed City Center revival of it directed by Cyril Ritchard, which transferred to the Ethel Barrymore Theatre for an extended run. The setting had been designed by John Boyt. I called Ritchard. He was extremely cordial and had high praise for Boyt's talent and taste, and said that he was certain he could serve as a designer of sets, costumes, and lighting.

I researched John and found that he had designed both sets and costumes for a Broadway production of *The Playboy of the Western World* in addition to the set for *Misalliance.* He had also costumed nine other Broadway shows, including the men's costumes for the legendary Katharine Cornell/Guthrie McClintock *Anthony and Cleopatra*. I called Boyt and he accepted the job.

This 44-year-old-guy, physically rotund and with a white beard, was immensely intelligent, talented and brutally honest. With a biting cantankerous wit, he endlessly pointed out the folly and stupidity of mankind and institutions; in short a classic curmudgeon. Although I have never known anyone so prone not to suffer fools, let alone not to suffer them gladly, we got along from the get-go and I thank my lucky stars. I used him not only for the set and lighting design, but to help out on costumes. Why?

The new faculty costumer was William G. Bruch, who had been hired by Ross to replace McArdle on the strength of academic recommendations from two California colleges. Soon after I got home from Carbondale I met Bill and his wife. They had bought one of the expensive old mansions on South Ninth Street and had settled in. His father-in-Law, Frank Capra—yes, the famed Hollywood film director of the Academy Award winners *It Happened One Night, Mr. Deeds Goes to Town, Mr. Smith Goes to Washington,* and *It's a Wonderful* Life—was coming to town for a visit. They threw a terrific bash for him which we all enjoyed. Later, when I got down to cases and started going over the requirements for costumes for *Misalliance,* I could see that although he was a nice guy, Bill didn't really have what I would call professional talent in the area of costuming. But not to worry. I had John Boyt to advise in that area. He was the one who told me about renting costumes from the Costume Collection in New York.

I had also contracted actor Eric Berry for the major role of John Tarleton. His background was pristine: He was 53 years old and had come from London originally to be in the hit musical *The Boy Friend.* He had acted in 17 Broadway plays, including three Shakespearian productions, as well as other classics, and had been in some 30 TV serials such at the *Hallmark Hall of Fame,* plus made-for-TV movies. His was perfect typecasting, although Stuart Howard's performance (who was *not* perfectly typed when he played it) engendered more laughs.

From the start Eric was wonderful to work with. Only once, perhaps on the third blocking rehearsal did he—very professionally, of course—challenge my blocking, saying, "I think I'll just sit on this line, do you mind?" I replied, "No you shouldn't be seated because..." and he smilingly interrupted me, very pleasantly and said, "Well, let me try it just this once," and I said, "All right, if you wish." Two lines later a line was addressed to him that read... "You dare stand there..." at which point he looked up, giggled, said, "Quite right!" and moved back to where I had him standing in the first place. After that he never questioned my blocking.

Before the first curtain rose on this production President Hovde came on stage and presented me with the Samuel French Award, presented to Purdue University for excellence in instruction in Playwriting. It was in recognition of the winning achievement of Richard Busch, who received second place in the annual National Collegiate Playwriting Contest for his *Talk Of Another Day*.

We received a vitriolic review of *Misalliance* by the theatre critic for the *Lafayette Journal and Courier*. But not only did the audience love the show, poetess May Swenson, whom I met during the *Tartuffe* rehearsals at Lincoln Center and who was now visiting artist in Purdue's English Department, wrote an extraordinary letter to the editor contradicting all that the reviewer said.

The opening-night party may have been the wildest I ever attended. Held in an apartment complex near Happy Hollow Road, I was late because we had a baby-sitting problem and Robin decided to stay home. As soon as I came through the door, I saw that a lot of liquor had been consumed. A short time later Eric Berry was on his knees in front of one of the young male actors, at which point the front door was broken down and an officer of Purdue's ROTC—who I was later told knew the young actor—stormed in, grabbed him, threw him over his shoulder, and stormed out. "Disguised as a professor," as Anne Revere had described me, I left quietly only minutes later.

⌘ ⌘ ⌘

In the spring of 1967 I was to direct a show I had desperately wanted to do for some time: O'Casey's *Juno and the Paycock*. But because at that point we did not have a really professional designer, and knowing that I was adamant about the necessity of such, Ross suggested we bring in a visiting designer. I chose Robert T. Williams. Once that decision was made I changed the schedule and did *The Plough and the Stars*, which had four sets, figuring that I could do *Juno* with its one set sometime in the future in the Experimental Theatre.

Randy Earle and Don Treat designed and built The Loeb's first turntable, divided into three sections; the four settings for *Plough* were easily facilitated simply by re-dressing one of the sections. Robert gave me his colored rendering of the sets, as had John Boyt for his brilliant *Misalliance* set, and they hang on a wall just above where I am writing this. The cast for

Plough was first-rate. We did a great deal of research about the "troubles" in 1915-16 culminating in the Easter Uprising, and put on a damn good production that became another favorite in my directing history.

⌘ ⌘ ⌘

We opened the summer theatre early—at the end of May 1967 just prior to the beginning of the summer school session—with Murray Schisgal's *Luv* shortly after it had closed its 929 performance run on Broadway directed by Mike Nichols, and with Alan Arkin, Anne Jackson, and Eli Wallach. Our cast was composed of Dale Helward, Stuart Howard, and Janet Hayes. We ran for two weeks, Tuesday through Sunday, with two performances on Friday and Saturday at 6:30 and 9:30 when the theatre—under AEA ruling—took the responsibility of serving supper for the cast and crew between these double-day performances. The rest of the summer season consisted of *The Importance Of Being Earnest, Little Mary Sunshine, Tartuffe,* and *Oh What A Lovely War,* and ended on August 12th.

One thought on *Luv*. I never cared for the piece and did it simply because of the small cast and the staggering track record it had in New York. But, of course, I wasn't Mike Nichols. Not that we didn't get off a good production. But these are not real people any more than a Jewish mother type is a real person. They are caricatures, and the piece's opening with a man about to commit suicide by jumping off the Brooklyn (or any other) Bridge is followed by Second City repartee between him and the guy who saves him. Their talk is mostly about their relations with women with a lot of competitiveness: *à la* my existentialist angst is bigger than yours. This is not really a play, as I understand plays. This is simply a sketch that might be funny for 20 minutes done by a stand-up comic in a Catskill-summer-resort style for that audience. But that wasn't me, nor was it our audience in West Lafayette, Indiana.

I loved Oscar Wilde's *The Importance in Being Earnest.* The problem for the director is that the characters walk a fine line between real things happening to real people—I feel real people is essential—and *style* (manners, morals and customs of 1895 London) which tends to breed types rather than individuals. The focus must be on Wilde's language, which in turn means that in two weeks of rehearsal the lines must be spoken *as the author wrote them* and does not allow for added handles on sounds ["ah"] connecting sentences or improvisation on what is written. I had to insist on this from the very beginning of rehearsals, which drove the actors absolutely mad, and was the acid test for the stage manager, Richard Newdick, whose job it was to correct the actors when they did not get the line as written and face a possible exasperated blowup in early rehearsals.

That's when I entered the picture, telling them the story of legendary actress Dame Sybil Thorndike. When a young stage manager interrupts to correct her line, she blows up. After she has vented her wrath, he respectfully, but firmly replies: "Dame Thorndike, every time you've said that line you've gotten it wrong." Hearing his tone, she immediately calms down and after a moment of thought says, "Quite right." In doing so she revealed her respect for theatrical professionalism regardless of titles to a young stage manager named Tyrone Guthrie.

⌘ ⌘ ⌘

For the musical *Little Mary Sunshine*, Robert Joyner took over as costume designer after Bill Bruch left. Stuart Howard staged the musical numbers and played Captain Billy Jester. Janet Hayes starred in the title role, and the handsome and talented Michael Sevareid (yes, the famed newscaster's son) played one of the forest rangers.

I'd seen and loved this show with Eileen Brennan at Off-Broadway's Orpheum where it played 1,143 performances. It's a parody of all those operettas such as Rudolf Friml's *The Vagabond King*, Sigmund Romberg's *The Desert Song*, and *The New Moon* that used to serve as standard fare for Purdue's spring Gala Week crowd.

In spite of the fact that I had been through the rehearsals of the Lincoln Center's *Tartuffe*, which was translated by the poet Richard Wilbur, I returned to English actor Miles Malleson's translation and adaptation when I designed Allan Fletcher's production. This version played the play for farce, not the beauty of poetry; in fact the only concession it allows poetry is a jokey rhymed couplet at the end of each scene. It played to full houses and lots of laughter.

Oh, What A Lovely War! by Joan Littlewood's theatre workshop is credited as being "based on official records, memoirs, commentaries, newspaper articles, and other factual data from World War I." But the reason I was interested in the show was that I had been reading Barbara Tuchman's extremely well written *The Guns of August,* which was on the *New York Times* bestseller list for almost a year. It won the Pulitzer Prize for nonfiction in 1963 and was a major book at this stage of my life, as well as subsequently for many statesmen and military officers of that period.

I suspect that my interest in this subject had to do with my dad and our lack of a traditional father/son relationship caused by his participation in trench warfare and being gassed in WW I. For this reason, perhaps, I was trying to understand more about that war. What I found out was absolutely devastating and I still feel a great sadness when I think of it. There was a thermometer on stage that measured the causalities resulting from WW I: Eight million soldiers, including more than 50,000 Americans. An estimated 12 million civilians died. German's losses 1,700,000 killed and over 4,200,000 wounded. France had 1,300,000 deaths and over 4,200,000 wounded. The total number of people killed during WWI, including civilians, was 16.5 million. Although these statistics were incomprehensible per se, in terms of this war's effect as it seeped down into the next generation—such as mine—they were overwhelming.

Our production was all about the human aspects of that great conflict: in the recruitment song "I'll make a man of you" sung suggestively by Karin Woodward in a see-thru blouse and backed by Ladies of the Ensemble; "There's a Long, Long, Trail A-Winding" sung by Tom Jennings; "*Stille Nacht, Heilige Nacht*" ("Silent night, holy night" as the war stopped for Christmas Eve, and the Germans and Americans locked voices); "I Don't Want to be a Soldier," sung by Dick Jeager, Dale Helward, and John Newton; and "Keep the Home Fires Burning" sung by Janet Hayes so beautifully and with such absolute simplicity as to break your heart.

The programs for the season were a two-fold. On the cover was a black-and-white picture of the Experimental Theatre and on the first page inside the fold, bannered by: "The School of Humanities, Social Science and Education and The University Theatre presents: The Purdue Professional Theatre Company," was information about the play and creative credits. The opposite third page listed the production staff, and the back cover had the photograph reprinted from "The John F. Kennedys: A Family Album" by Mark Shaw, of JFK walking (toward the sea?), half of which pictured a cloudy sky and the other half foliaged land, the president's back to us, walking a bright path toward a distant horizon.

Below this picture was printed the speech he gave about the importance of the arts. The act of typing this brought back the emotional memory of my feelings when I first read it and moved me to tears because I recognized in JFK's words my own hopes and dreams.

> A need within contemporary civilization, a hunger for certain values and satisfaction appears to be urging us all to explore and appreciate areas of life which in the past we have sometimes neglected in the United States. Too often in the past, we have thought of the artist as an idler and dilettante and the lover of the arts as somehow sissy or effete. We have done both an injustice. The life of the artist is, in relationship to his work, stern and lonely. He has labored hard, often amid deprivation, to perfect his skill....
>
> Today we recognize increasingly the essentiality of artistic achievement. This is part, I think, of a nationwide movement toward excellence—a movement which had its start in the admiration of expertness and skill in our technical society, but which now demands quality in all realms in human achievement. It is part, too, of a feeling that art is the great quality in all realms of human achievement. It is part, too, of feeling that art is the great unifying and humanizing experience. *We know that science, for example, is indispensable—but we also know that science, if divorced from a knowledge of man and of man's ways, can stunt a civilization.* And so the educated man—and very often the man who has the best scientific education—reaches out for the experience which the arts alone can provide. He wants to explore the side of life which expresses the emotions and embodies values and ideals of beauty. Above all, we are coming to understand that the arts incarnate the creativity of free society. [Italics mine.]

I think this program note helped make clear the importance of the connection between science and technology at Purdue University—engineering, aerospace, business, science, and agriculture—and what we were trying to accomplish. It justified every ounce of our effort.

But before I leave this summer season, I must mention that on August 19th we got word that Brian McMaster, my playwriting student, had received honorable mention for his play *All on an April Evening* in the 15th National Collegiate Playwriting Contest.

Chapter 20

I MENTIONED EARLIER THAT I FELL in love with the novel *The Grapes of Wrath* (1939) when I was 14 years old. After reading it I went back to the library and got *Of Mice and Men* (1937) and fell in love with it, too. The play based on that novel was staged on Broadway in late November of that year, and the novel received the Pulitzer Prize. Steinbeck had written several novels up to this time including *Tortilla Flat*, but *Of Mice and Men* was his first real money-making success, due in part to the Broadway production.

At this time George S. Kaufman was just reaching a midway point in one of the most successful theatre careers of the twentieth century that would include 90 Broadway productions in which he was either director/stager, writer/collaborator, producer, theater owner, lyricist, "uncredited book doctor" ("book" refers to the story in dramatic form), and performer (*Once In a Lifetime*.) Steinbeck had no theatre credits, and yet he was credited with writing the play.

I decided on *Of Mice and Men*, a quintessential piece of great American writing, as the opening production for "Purdue University Theatre's Professional Theatre Company –Indiana's Only Resident Professional Theatre." We were now under a LORT (League of Resident Theatres) Actors Equity contract right along with the very best regional theatres in the

United States, and the only one that was organically a part of the Theatre Department on a university campus.

When I read the acting edition of *Mice*, published by Dramatists Play Service, Inc. which leased the property, I was sorely disappointed. It just didn't have the same appeal as the novella which I read again and loved. I came to believe that George Kaufman had adapted the play and given it his upper-middle-class "genius of Broadway" touch, which reflected his own heart and brain along with a talent that richly serviced the vast majority of the theatre projects in which he was involved. But not this one. As a kid, I had been a seasonal farm worker and I knew damn well what it was to be poor and hungry and live on small dreams for the future.

Since I loved the novel and writing, why not make my own adaptation? We would pay the royalties of $50 per performance and buy the required number of scripts from Dramatists Play Service. I saw no point in advertising the fact of my adaptation since it would cause all sorts of dumb-assed legal complications which would inevitably suck all the energy and love out of the project for me.

But there was one reason why I had to contact the Steinbeck estate, and that was because I cast James Earl Jones, who at that time was not a household name. In my letter I stressed that I had to know by return mail if it would be okay for me to write a "few lines" which would justify this casting; specifically why The Boss allows a black Lennie to sleep in the bunkhouse, while the other African-American character in the play, Crooks, is forced to live in the harness room of the barn. The request was granted by return mail, most probably without a hell of a lot of thought since the bottom line of the leasing business was take the money and run. In addition there was that pervasive New York attitude that Indiana was somewhere out there between the Hudson River and Los Angeles, and no one of importance would see the production anyway.

In my letter, I only mentioned the one change, but this casting raised the stakes in almost every scene. The very first one is after George and Lennie arrive at the ranch, and Candy brings them into the bunkhouse. Candy will not be able to assign them bunks until he gets The Boss's approval and he clearly doubts this will happen. That's why, in describing The Boss, he tells the story of him giving the workers a gallon of liquor at their Christmas party, and the "nigger" (Crooks) shows up and is almost killed by another farmhand. Is Candy's motive in telling the story to forewarn the two that it isn't likely that The Boss will allow a black to stay in the bunkhouse and drive them away so that they should not even attempt to get the job?

The casting of a black actor also ups the ante for The Boss. He believes the races should be separated, but on the other hand he is shorthanded and the barley harvest is behind schedule. He sees that Lennie is endowed with unusual strength and endurance and figures he can buck more barley bags than any of the other workers. Also, with a black actor as Lennie, George can no longer claim that Lennie is his relative and is the reason why he looks after him. And there is also a new relationship between Crooks and Lennie since Crooks would be resentful that Lennie is accepted in the bunkhouse and he has to bunk in the harness room. And yes, having James Earl Jones's father, who is also an actor, play Crooks could change things. To some degree almost everything changed by casting a black actor as Lennie, and that was what was so exciting.

I found out through AEA that Lucy Kroll was his agent. She told me that Jim was at the Edinburgh Festival in Scotland and gave me a contact number. He was flabbergasted and overjoyed when I told him I wanted him for Lennie. He had been on the continent playing *The Great God Brown*, and had met Steinbeck in Paris where they'd talked about his playing that role.

Rehearsal and performance dates worked out perfectly. He would be back in New York and have a few days before flying out to Purdue to begin rehearsals on Monday, August 28th, and the matter was settled in minutes. In addition he suggested I call Ed Setrakian, with whom he had done scenes from the play, to see if he would play George. As soon as I hung up I did just that, and once again the casting was settled in minutes.

This first fall season of the Professional Company would be for 13 weeks, including two weeks of rehearsal for *Mice*, playing from Tuesday, September 12th through Sunday the 1st of October. I asked Wayne Lamb to direct a musical for the second show. His choice was *Irma La Douce*. I'd seen it with Karen Jensen at The Barn Theatre but had not listened to the recording. Wayne consulted with his partner, Angelo Mango, who had served as one of two assistant stage managers, plus being understudy for three small roles in the 625 performance run on Broadway. *Irma* would play from Wednesday October 4th through Sunday the 29th, and *Long Day's Journey Into Night* would open on Tuesday October 31st and play six nights a week for six weeks through Sunday November 26th.

I counted on the fact that we could save money on transportation by cross casting. In our New York auditions, with Connie Heaver who was my assistant, I cast Mark Dempsey as Slim: Wayne would use him in a role to be decided in *Irma* and he would play Jamie in *Long Day's*. But as the show I would start with should have reminded me, *"The best-laid schemes o' mice and men gang aft agley."*

After the show was on, Mark got a call from his agent who wanted him to come in and audition for a Broadway show. On his day off he did just that, was cast, and gave notice he would leave after the run of *Mice*. I was, of course, disappointed, because Mark was a terrific actor, but I certainly understood. As it turned out, hindsight is always easier than foresight. The David Merrick production of *Mata Hari*, a legendary disaster in which he was cast, closed out of town, which meant Mark missed playing in our other two shows including the dream role of Jamie in *Long Day's Journey Into Night*.

Rehearsals for *Mice* went extremely well because having adapted it, I knew the show backward and forward. Early on I had to tell Ed Setrakian that because I had only two weeks of rehearsal time, once a scene was blocked and I asked if it felt comfortable and he agreed, that he could not, at his discretion, change the blocking. This seemed to be a new way of working for him, but he understood and did not object.

In the scene when Curley quarrels with Slim and Carlson because he is jealous of what he thinks is their attention to his wife, Lennie is still smiling at memory of George's telling him that they are going to get a ranch of their own with a hundred dollars borrowed from Candy. However, Curley thinks Lennie is laughing at him and "like a terrier" slugs him in the face and pins him against a wall while Lennie holds his hands over his face and cries out to George to make him stop. Lennie's face is bloody from the pummeling. George yells to him to fight back. Lennie doesn't. Slim is about to intercede on Lennie's behalf but George yells, "Get him, Lennie!"

and in a moment Curley is "flopping like a fish on a line" as his hand is being crushed by Lennie.

Angelo Mango played Curley and was very anxious about this scene, so I suggested he and Jim go into the locker room and work it out together. They did, marking it out in 1, 2, 3 fashion as in choreography and then going over the action again and again until they were comfortable with it. It worked beautifully.

At one point when we were doing the scene in the barn between Lennie and Curley's wife, in which Lennie, in order to stop her yelling, shakes her and breaks her neck, Pamela Gruen's body went totally limp. But when Jim put her down he was right not to hold his hand under her head. Consequently it hit against the cement floor. Pam stopped the rehearsal and complained, holding her head as if she had been severely injured. I have no doubt that the bump hurt, but it was not a serious injury. However, I catered to her with the result that this incident forever undergirded Jim's playing of the scene. Lennie has to be terrified by what he has done; his concentration is not on placing her body down carefully. There was nothing to do about this. The actors should not have been rehearsing in a room with a cement floor and that is where the blame should have been leveled.

Robertearl (his spelling of his name at the time) kept his script in hand so long that I finally give a note that he must not use it again. The next day in a run-through he had the script in hand. I got up and took it, whispering, "Just keep on with the scene." I saw his panic and anger and later apologized to him, but we were nearing the end of the second week of rehearsals and everyone else had been off book after the first week. I did what had to be done. All else went smoothly during the rehearsals.

During former summer seasons, I had always scheduled a full day—meaning from the end of their Sunday matinee through 7:00 P.M. on Monday, when we had our first dress rehearsal (which could last up to midnight), and then the final dress on Tuesday afternoon before opening. When we approached the weekend prior to opening, I was informed by the stage manager that Equity deputy Louis Girard had contacted the Equity office. Under their LORT contract I could not call a rehearsal for Monday evening. I was upset by this news. I called a meeting of the company and told them that I had not been aware of this AEA/LORT rule, but of course would abide by it.

James Earl saw how upset I was. He said that he needed that Monday evening rehearsal and that he and Ed planned to be there. Although under the rules I could not be present, and no actor could be required to be there, he asked the stage manager and the other actors if they would join him. They all agreed.

I observed and took notes during the full-scale rehearsal from the light booth.

Other than Tennessee Williams, I have never seen dramatic writing so well written for the lighting and sound designer. At play's end, even before Lennie has arrived at the river, in his novel Steinbeck writes: "Already the sun had left the valley to go climbing up the slopes of the Gabilan Mountains, and the hilltops are rosy in the sun.... A rush of wind sounds and a gust drives through the tops of the trees like a wave. The sycamore leaves turned up their silver side; the brown, dry leaves on the ground scudder a few feet. As quickly as it had come, the wind dies down and the clearing goes quiet again." *Then* suddenly Lennie appears and throughout his monologue Steinbeck carefully orchestrates lighting and sound. "The light climbs out of the valley, and as it does so, the tops of the mountains seem to blaze with increasing brightness." And later when George quietly enters, "Only the topmost ridges are in the sun. The shadow in the valley is blue and soft. From the distance comes the sound of men shouting to one another." Still later: "A little evening breeze blows over the clearing and the leaves rustle and there are shouts of men, this time much closer than before."

By this time George has arrived at the river bank of the first scene prior to their reaching the ranch where he tells Lennie that they will meet if any trouble develops. He has coaxed Lennie into looking "across the river" and tells him, "So you can almost see it." And then he starts on the story about the life they will live together on their farm. As "Lennie looks off across the pool and up the darkening slopes of the Gabilans," George begins, "We're gonna get a little place ..." and as he paints the picture of their future he brings the gun in his shaking hand to the back of Lennie's head. "A man's voice calls from up the river, and another man answers" and finally "crashing footsteps are heard in the brush"—and then the shot.

We did not play the scene that follows in the novel with the posse arriving. The dialogue between Slim and Carson makes it clear that they would believe George killed Lennie as an act of vengeance because of the death of Curley's wife, and therefore he will not be prosecuted. This can be established in the scene when the posse is formed and the hunt commences.

We opened with an astoundingly moving show that found me in the light booth living and breathing every moment with these characters and their hopes, and then the shot.... And the same reaction that I have only experienced two or three times in the theatre—the blackout followed by absolute silence for perhaps thirty seconds before the response from the audience, which was overwhelming.

I cannot say which show I loved the most in my directing career because I loved so many of them, but this one was very close to the top of the list. It was a great success. I was told that in a speech much later, when James Earl Jones returned to Purdue, he said that at that stage in his career he was about to give up trying to make a living as an actor. But this show had changed his mind and he had gone on to the Arena Theatre in Washington D.C. to create the major role under Edwin Sherin's direction of *The Great White Hope*, for which he received a Tony Award for Best Performance by a Leading Actor, and the play received the Best Play Award plus the Pulitzer Prize and Drama Desk Award.

When *Of Mice and Men* was revived on Broadway, Ed Sherin again directed Jim. Jim was thoughtful enough to have me mentioned in his bio in the *Playbill*. "It is of interest to note that Mr. Jones first experimented with the role of Lennie some eight years ago at Purdue University under the direction of Dr. Joe Stockdale. That experiment and its results met with the full approval of playwright Steinbeck." He also mentioned me in his autobiography, *Voices and Silences*, published in 1993. And our production was remembered 40 years later when in October, 2007, Purdue invited Jim to speak in The Loeb Playhouse and I was introduced from my seat in the audience.

⌘ ⌘ ⌘

I have very little to reflect on about the rehearsals and production for *Irma La Douce* because I was in rehearsals for *Long Day's Journey Into Night*. During this time the stage manager and some actors in *Irma* told me that rehearsals were not going well, and that as artistic director for the Professional Theatre Company I should come and see what was happening. I did not feel comfortable with this situation. But the complaints continued until I could avoid it no longer. I finally dropped in on a rehearsal, which upset Wayne. He told me he was not ready yet "to invite me in" and I capitulated and tried to smooth over relations between us.

When I saw the show opening night, it just was not my cup of tea, and probably would not have been even if I had seen it on Broadway. But I knew in my heart that my handling of the situation was a mistake; Jack Ragotzy would never have done what I did. In fact, I should have chosen a musical myself, directed it, and asked Wayne to do what he was so good at, choreography and staging the musical numbers.

⌘ ⌘ ⌘

Long Day's Journey Into Night takes four hours to play and it was wonderfully acted in that amount of time when I saw it in New York. But as I read and reread it I became aware that there were places in the script where possible cuts could be made. I asked Sam Rosen (Anne Revere was cast as Mary) what he would cut. Many film directors are not so much interested in dialogue as they are the cinematic aspect of a film, and I knew that Sam and Anne went over all the scripts of films she had been in, not only changing lines but adding and cutting some. I had already made tentative cuts myself and the show ended up playing just a little over three and a quarter hours.

We got Robert Donley to play James Tyrone. He had been in three Broadway shows, national tours, and TV shows, and had extensive experience in professional regional theatres such as the Alley and Meadowbrook (at the University of Michigan). He was a perfect physical type, and had the trace of an Irish accent; he was not your typical NY actor, since he lived in a small Pennsylvania town, was married, had three kids, and was the least driven actor I ever met. But he was good, and character actors who can play father/husband/actor are very difficult to find, at least those who are willing to work for $150 a week.

Robert Browning had received his undergrad degree at Carnegie and completed his MA at Purdue, appearing in three major student productions and four professional summer theatre productions which I directed. I felt comfortable in awarding him an AEA contract for the role of Edmund, the prototype of O'Neill. Incidentally, two years later he was cast in the Broadway production of Shaw's *Candida* as Marchbanks in which Celeste Holm played the title role; later he became a fixture at the Alabama Shakespearian Festival.

Susan Murray, whom I cast as Cathleen, had done three major student productions for me, plus all four shows in the professional summer theatre's season. She had also written her MA thesis, under my direction, on the critical reception of the shows of the Irish National Theatre. She was talented, intelligent, and right for the role.

When I lost Mark Dempsey as Jamie, the rest of the cast had been decided upon. We did not have the money to audition in New York, but Wayne and Angelo said that Michael Walsh, who had been an actor at The Barn Theatre in the summer of 1963 and had done *The Hostage*, would be first-rate for James Tyrone, Jr. I read the New York and regional credits on his resume and looked at his picture. He was certainly not Jason Robards, Jr. who originally played the role on Broadway, but there was something of a "Black Irish" resemblance: black hair, eyes, fair skin and something in the sharpness of his look that told me his physical appearance was right for this older son who has always taken a backseat in the family to Edmund. I called him, we talked— his voice was right—he was available, and I hired him.

Only later did I find that the New York credits on his resume were not Main Stem, not even Off-Off Broadway, more probably from acting classes at the Herbert Berghof Studio. In rehearsals he was not as forthcoming as I would have liked, which could have been caused by a shyness working with Academy/Tony Award winner Revere. At one point in physical action between him and his brother Edmund, Robert Browning struck him a blow which Mike felt was too hard and complained about possible hearing loss. This became a worry for me and didn't do much for the relationship between the brothers. But Mike's look was good and he did a serviceable job.

In short, I felt that this was an excellent production; Jerry Williams' set and costumes were absolutely first-rate as was Randy Earle's lighting and Anne Revere, whom I considered one of our country's great actresses, was brilliant in the role of Mary Tyrone.

Anne was living in an attached apartment at the home of Henry and Phyllis Koeffler. He was chair of the Biology Department and both he and his wife were great supporters of the professional theatre. In August the head of the English Department had contacted me after seeing our schedule and wondered if we could play a special evening performance of *Long Day's* in the Loeb Playhouse for the national convention of the Modem Language Association. This association of language and literature scholars in the United States had some 20,000 members, of which over 2000 would be participants at the convention and most of them would be aware of Anne Revere's distinguished stage and film career. The event would not only be prestigious for Purdue University, and the English Department, but also for the new LORT Theatre Company.

The afternoon of this event Anne was taking a walk and fell. She was rushed by ambulance to the hospital where the doctor discovered a fine line fracture of her wrist. She insisted that she would be able to make the performance that evening. The doctor put her wrist in a cast to immobilize it, gave her a shot of pain killer, and advised bed rest.

That evening it took her extra time to get to the theatre and once there, the costume had to be altered to cover the cast and she needed time with the other actors to run a couple of scenes in which she would remain seated rather than following the blocking. Every seat in the theatre was filled, and I tried to appear calm, but inwardly was very emotional. I explained to the audience why we would delay the show half an hour and urged them to feel free to roam the foyer and lobby. We would give a ten-minute call prior to curtain.

Anne assured me she would be all right. Throughout, she gave one of the best performances I've ever seen. The drug-addiction scenes were so real that it was frightening, and her final scene, in which Mary Tyrone is under the influence of the drugs, was absolutely breathtaking. The show broke a little after 11:30 and received incredible applause. I drove her home to get a good night's rest.

The next night we were back in the Experimental Theatre and she was fine, but as the week wore on something troubling was happening. She started talking to herself in the dressing room and hitting the other actors, playfully at first, then harder. Phyllis and Henry called and told me she was not eating and was talking to herself in her room. The pace of her line readings became slower and more deliberate. By Friday night I was desperate—what was I going to do? Dorothy Harlan was the understudy for the role, but we had never had an understudy rehearsal and it would take days to get her up in the role. I kept hoping that things would improve, but on Saturday night the show was like a fog and unbearably real. As I watched it from the light booth I knew I had to cancel and we would have to refund the two sold-out weeks still scheduled.

At intermission I called Sam Rosen. He knew exactly what it was and explained that Anne was a manic-depressive. At one time she had been committed to the psychiatric ward of New York City's Flowers and Fifth Avenue Hospital. The fall, and the fractured wrist and medication, must have triggered a siege and he would be here just as soon as he could.

I told Richard Lake, the stage manager, to tell everyone without Anne's being aware, that there would be a company meeting just as soon as I could get her out of her dressing room and on her way home. He was to tell the others that the show was cancelled and that we would, of course, pay everyone through two more weeks. They could keep the rooms at the Krannert until they made arrangements to head home.

I drove Anne to the Koeffler's. She was talkative, almost against her will. I went in the apartment with her and explained that I was cancelling the show and that I had called Sam and he was on his way. She was devastated by this news and I asked her if it was okay for me to stay there until she got to sleep. She said that would not be necessary so I went home and told Robin what was happening. We must have just gotten to sleep when the phone outside our bedroom rang. I jumped out of bed with great fear and answered it. Anne said, "I've done something stupid and I need your help." I said, "I'll be right there," and threw on my clothes and drove fast. She was dressed and ready to go when I drove up. She said that she had taken an overdose of sleeping pills and would have to have her stomach pumped.

I got her into the car and drove to the emergency entrance of St. Elizabeth Hospital, took her in and told them that she was a friend and had overdosed. She was taken immediately into the operating room and I got her registered under the name of Mrs. Samuel Rosen. I stayed in the waiting room until she was out of the OR and was sedated and sleeping. I went home to Robin about 5:00 A.M. on Sunday morning.

A couple of days later, I took Sam out to the psychiatric hospital on River Road where he had Anne admitted after she was released from St. Elizabeth's. She stayed there for three months because Sam decided on long-range treatment at this small facility for two reasons: First when Anne had been in the hospital in New York City one of the ward attendants had dragged her across the floor by her hair. He felt that some of the minimum wage workers living in New York City were not qualified, and some should not have been working on a psychiatric ward. On the other hand, almost all of workers at the facility on the River Road were Purdue students. Sam, as well as Anne, fell in love with them and they with her.

Second, Sam thought the doctors were first-rate, and especially one young one who suggested that Sam allow him to use an "experimental" drug as treatment. He claimed that it was not experimental but had not yet been approved by the Food and Drug Administration. Why? Because it was salt of Lithium which could not be patented, cost very little, and therefore was of no interest to the pharmaceutical industry.

A year or so later there was an exposé on this issue published in one of the news magazines. It caused a defensive reaction in drug companies who used the same arguments used today: profit has to be made in order to finance research which is why drugs purchased in this country are so much higher than in Canada. Of course they omitted the adjective "sizeable" before the word profit.

The bottom line is that for the rest of her life Anne used Lithium to control her mood swings. But full disclosure is mandatory here: I vividly remember that one day when I was visiting them at their home at 1 Fox Lane in Locust Valley, New York, we were talking about her use of this drug and she raised her hand high and chopped it sideways down through the air, saying, "It cuts like a knife!"

Anne's illness was terribly upsetting to me, but something else happened that upset me even more. Within a week I got a call from Dad saying I had to come to Allegan because my sister Rae—who was now living in the house Bill and she had built on the property—was talking back to the television and had been doing so for some time. Something had to be done. He had called Bill in Detroit and could not get an answer but would continue trying.

I got his call in early evening and arrived about 11 o'clock. Rae was watching TV, my cousin Bob Stockdale was there, and Bill had been reached but not yet arrived. She actually believed as she watched TV that these people were in the same room with her. Bob and Dad had decided that they would take her to a small psychiatric hospital in Plainwell half an hour's drive away.

Dad drove his car and Bob and I sat on either side of her in the backseat. She grew very agitated during the trip. At one point she tried to crawl over the seat to get in front with Dad and had to be restrained. I could not do this on my side so Bob put both arms around her and restrained her as she screamed and pleaded with me to help her. I have never been so terrified and sick at heart.

We got her registered at the private hospital where they were going to give her electroshock treatments. I had to get back to West Lafayette to teach the next day. I did not tell anyone but Robin about this situation, I suppose because I felt others might think that it reflected on me. More horribly, I could not get the play *Streetcar* out of my mind, or what had happened to the department secretary Dorothy at Santa Barbara.

I kept in touch with Dad. Bill had arrived shortly after I left and was taking care of the situation. Within three weeks, because of the health insurance issues but mainly because their facilities were much better, he committed her to the psychiatric hospital in Kalamazoo where she stayed for almost a year before being released.

During the month of December I sometimes had the feeling that I was hanging on by a thread and fought against showing any indication of what I felt inside. This is the reason I was not, I'm afraid, very helpful to Sam Rosen, although we did have him over for Christmas dinner.

I welcomed early January because before classes started I held auditions with Connie in New York for the three shows I'd selected for the Professional Theatre's spring season: *Incident At Vichy; A Funny Thing Happened on the Way to the Form;* and *Uncle Vanya*. All would play eight performances a week with two performances on Friday and Saturday evenings at 6:30 and 9:30 P.M. and a Sunday matinee at 2:30.

It was also during this time that I applied to the Purdue Research Foundation for a six week leave—to start after *Vanya* opened—to view and study various theatres in Russia, Poland, East Germany, England and Ireland. I was overjoyed when I received it.

On the first rehearsal for *Vichy*, I told the cast that I had watched all the rehearsals of the first production of this show in New York, loved it, and had written a program note which although not published in the *Playbill*, I thought was worth reading to them. A number of them, including Reid Shelton, told me it was the best introduction by a director to what he wanted in a production of a play that they had ever heard. Rehearsals went smoothly. There were 17 men in the cast, the two leading roles played by Reid Shelton as Prince von Berg and Will Gregory as Dr. LeDuc. By this time Reid already had been in five Broadway productions, all of which were musicals, and was very glad to be entrusted with this role, and another in which he did not have to sing.

Will Gregory was a leading-man type who had from early December 1965 been one of two assistant stage managers of the hit play *Cactus Flower* starring Lauren Bacall. He also had the small role of Customer, and understudied the leading role of Julian played by Barry Nelson. Obviously this was a good, but boring, job which he left in a few months for a larger role in another Broadway show which lasted one performance, and then on to another that lasted a week. So in the winter of 1968 he was glad to be playing two excellent major roles and one minor one in Indiana.

I jobbed-in Dale Helward to play the Major, and Stuart Howard to play the actor. Jerry Williams, who joined the cast as a police captain, recently told me that although he had designed the set, he never could remember if the door to the waiting room opened in or out. One night in a panic he almost ripped the hinges off the door before he remembered that it opened out, not in.

While we performed this intense, intermission-less show, I rehearsed one of the greatest musicals written: *A Funny Way Happened On the Way to the Forum,* based on the plays of the classical Roman playwright Plautus, adapted by Bert Shevelove and Larry Gelbart, with music and lyrics by the great Stephen Sondheim. I cast the astounding Philip Polito as our Pseudolus. I called Robert T. Williams, who had designed the set and costumes for the Williamstown Summer Theatre production in which Phil played the role, and who said he was great and that I should cast him. I did, and oh how right Robert was! Phil was absolutely terrific. James McDonald was our Hysterium (Jim would later collaborate with others on the book of *Something's Afoot,* the most produced musical-mystery by community theatres in this country), Stuart Howard was our Lycus (using his Goldberg accent from *The Birthday Party*), and Reid Shelton our Miles Gloriosus. The girls from Lycus' house of ill repute were Cynthia Strickland, Alice Vaughn (a beautiful African-American), Karin Woodward, Rebecca Taylor, Connie Heaver, and Vicki Earle. Our season's leading man, Will Gregory, played the bit part of "A Soldier."

I cannot leave the history of this production without relating a major event of its run, and as I write this I'm wondering if Ripley ever published this record? In no other production in the history of the theatre were there two, yes I said *two!* emergency appendectomies. The first was Cindy Strickland, but there was time for Wayne to teach Sharon Ryterband the dance number. Then on the day of the final performance, Alice Vaughn was rushed to the hospital for an appendectomy. I talked to Wayne, and we decided to just cut that number since it was one of five dances by the girls from Lycus' brothel. I called the stage manager and told him to be sure and tell Phil Polito that Alice's dance was being cut.

Okay. The show is on and it's time for the courtesans' numbers. But when Stuart announced Panacea, the role Alice played—I thought he hadn't gotten the word that it was cut—there appeared one of the most delectable brown bodies ever seen, attired in a Jerry Williams' costume that consisted of a trace of faux feathery fur barely attached to a body stocking thong, above a décolletage cut of the same faux fur at her breast, and a thinly tantalizing matching strip of it around her right bicep. She executed a dance so torrid as to lift the, ah, spirits of any red-blooded Roman watching. Phil Polito's jaw dropped almost to the floor since unbeknownst to him Cathryn (*aka* "Skipper") Damon, having been informed by Wayne of the problem, had offered her considerable talents—as he hoped she would—to go on for that last performance. Incidentally, Connie Heaver was the only one with forethought enough to record this event. She did so with her little Kodak Brownie Hawkeye, and even with a bad flashbulb reflection off a window, it's worth viewing.

While we were playing Forum, which drew SRO every performance, we rehearsed my third Chekhov production, *Uncle Vanya*. In the title role I cast Reid Shelton, luring him away from a job offer to play Freddy in *My Fair Lady* a third time in one of those large regional tent theatres for $1000 a week to join our winter season company for two months at $150 per week.

The role of Dr. Astrov, the Chekhov prototype, was played beautifully by Will Gregory, and our Yelena rates special attention since she was played by Cathryn Damon, the most experienced of anyone in the company. She had just finished a two year "workshop" which was offered by Jerome Robbins and sponsored by the Ford Foundation in which the company mainly "danced" plays, seeing if the character's thoughts and the story could be expressed through movement rather than dialogue.

"Skipper" was a trained ballet dancer. Her first Broadway show, *By the Beautiful Sea,* starred Shirley Booth. Incidentally, Reid Shelton was in it as a singer. That was followed by *The Vamp* with Carol Channing, *Shinbone Alley* with Eartha Kitt, *A Family Affair* directed by Harold Prince, *Foxy* with Bert Lahr, *Flora the Red Menace* with Liza Minnelli, followed by more musicals and two straight plays that she loved, *Sweet Bird of Youth* and *The Cherry Orchard*. She also had many TV credits.

I only occasionally asked a cast of professionals to dance a show, communicating only in bodily movements. But one day I told the *Vanya* cast that without a break, we would dance the show and they should indicate passing of time through movement. I clearly remember Reid Shelton blanching. I asked him why and he said he didn't know if he could do it; he had never tried such a thing. I asked him if he had ever played charades. He said that he had. I suggested that if he did not feel he could dance, perhaps he could communicate through gestures. Reid was always an accommodating actor. At first he attempted gestures but eventually—he was physically a big man—he got into bodily movement and became more and more unconscious of his inability to do this exercise. The point is, he tried and did it.

Since I had told the cast that we would not stop between acts we did the entire show without a break. That rehearsal was the greatest dance improvisation of a show I ever saw. I did not know at the time that Cathryn had been in the Jerry Robbins company for two years, but none of us who saw this rehearsal will ever forgot the dance performance that afternoon in the trap room of The Loeb. Cathryn inspired the entire cast. She was a truly great artist and a wonderful Yelena. Sadly this major talent, with whom we were so fortunate to work, died in Los Angeles in 1987 of cancer at the age of 56.

⌘ ⌘ ⌘

When I was about to leave for Moscow, Robin happily announced—with both of us 43 years old!—that she was pretty sure she was once again pregnant. All I could think of was that I would be 61 years old when the kid started college and once again had hoisted myself on my own petard—so to speak. But as the French say, *c'est la vie!*

Chapter 21

CARRYING LETTERS OF INTRODUCTION FROM Elia Kazan, Martha Wadsworth Coigney, head of the International Theatre Institute, and Frederick L. Hovde, I left West Lafayette airport on Friday, March 29th, and after layovers in Chicago, London, and Helsinki, arrived at Leningrad at 9:50 P.M.

LENINGRAD: *Lohengrin* at the Kirov Theatre was second-rate, and I left after the second act. The experience taught me some things about going to the theatre in Russia. Everyone was required to check his coat; there were no ushers; you found your seat by checking the seating charts in the lobby. There were no programs (at least that I could find), and I never did find a place to buy one. The audience did not quiet down when the conductor appeared and raised his baton. The 70 member orchestra, whom I could clearly see from my seat in the front, seemed bored and talked out loud while the performance was in progress. Boredom was about the only emotion the singing chorus (with excellent voices) showed. At times there were almost 100 people on stage and I got the feeling they were going through their paces without a hell of a lot of interest. The scenery was gigantic and old-fashioned. The stage was raked, and there was a circular turntable to facilitate scene changes. The blocking was basically pictorial—and even gestures seemed arbitrary and unrelated to the character or situation. Like so much opera, the major roles were taken by singers who were much older and much fatter than the characters they played, with makeup literally caulking their facial wrinkles.

There was very little applause at the intermissions, and members of the audience were yawning as I left the theatre. I went back to my hotel and ordered a scotch at the bar and pondered: is it possible that subsidized repertory theater may not produce *exciting* theatre? Is competition a good thing? Or, maybe I was jet lagged and cranky and needed to go back to my room and sleep.

The Physicist by Durrenmatt (which I had seen in New York) was talky, and of course I do not speak Russian. The theatre was hot, the seats uncomfortable, and I had trouble staying awake. Set construction, properties and costumes were poor by Broadway standards. There was musical accompaniment which intrigued me because music aids emotional understanding (as in films).

As for content, there is a madhouse setting in which three psychiatrists, Isaac Newton, Albert Einstein, and another who believes he is in contact with King Solomon, reside. It turns out that both Newton and Einstein are spies who are attempting to get information from the third psychiatrist, who finally convinces them that mankind is incapable of dealing with scientific developments and that they should all remain in the madhouse. At this point a female enters and informs them that she has overheard and taken notes of the third psychiatrist's findings and intends to reveal all. In this production three thuggish American police types are the ones to obtain the information.

The author's intent of showing the consequence of scientific inventions [the atomic bomb and the hydrogen bomb] to a doomed mankind is skewed by the director (all directors of subsidized theatres, which are the only kind they have in Russia, have to be members of the Communist Party), who turns the play into a blistering anti-American cold-war diatribe! This performance was certainly not entertaining.

Oedipus Rex, produced by the Mayakovsky Players of Moscow on tour in Leningrad, was an absolutely memorable experience and beautifully acted, especially by the leading performers. The play opened with the sound of a kettle drum, harps, and cymbals. There was no formal choreography—but a great deal of swirling of the actors' cloaks. The set consisted of a raked platform backed by an elevated platform with the palace's entrance represented by an arch in Grecian style. On stage was King Oedipus' chair which looked like granite. Back-lighting was used effectively and there was no attempt to justify lighting cues via realistic light sources; lights just changed to fit the scene's mood. Makeup for Oedipus' final entrance after he has blinded himself was dark red-brown and in the shape of an inverted triangle in keeping with the whole nonrealistic presentational style of the production.

After gouging out his eyes, he entered, face lowered, still with great pride of manner [tragic flaw: overweening pride]. He walked downstage and tripped against one of the small side platforms, but caught himself, avoiding the fall. Fighting to retain his regal manner, but with face still lowered, he continued downstage but again tripped, this time falling full length, his body sprawling out on the raked platform. After a moment, using both hands, he raised himself suddenly, head held high so that the effects of his gouging were seen, one of the most stunning moments in a great performance and all the more effective because of the eyes being represented abstractly. And now, shattered by a loss of pride and fear and terror of the unknown, blinded and totally dependent, he is led off, self-banished from his country.

A great evening in the theatre.

Swan Lake, the ballet at the Kirov Theatre, was beautifully done in all aspects: dancing, acting, music, scenery, lights, and costuming, especially in theatricality. It was good to be back in the dance-theatre world, where the only language is music and movement, both of which were sublime.

Woe from Wit is a verse play by Aleksander Griboyedov from the early 1820s, which satirizes the author's characters' attitudes about the government and society of the time. The period for this production was changed to just prior to the Russian Revolution that replaced the Czar and seemed to demonize, rather than make fun of, those who opposed it. In short, the political message was pro-communism. What the production did tell me indirectly, because my guide told me the story, was of the love Russians have for their writers, whom they commemorate by erecting statues in public places, fresh flowers strewn on their birthdates.

The story about Griboyedov was that he married a 16-year-old girl, half his age, and was soon sent to Persia as a minister and slaughtered by a mob of Persians. His young wife, upon hearing of his death, loses their unborn child. I sensed that the tragedy in this writer's life—even though it had nothing to do with the play's plot—enhanced the spectator's love of the performance.

Anthony and Cleopatra as a ballet rehearsal at the Maly Opera Theater was terrifically choreographed with a slew of absolutely great dancers, as good as any I have ever seen anywhere—simply unbelievable talent in such abundance! I loved every moment of it.

MOSCOW: *Ten Days That Shook The World,* which I watched from the middle of the third row, was fantastic! Set in the ten days of the 1917 Revolution, the various scenes were framed by four young Russians in military service who played guitars, sang folk songs, and were backed by visuals of patriotic images. The sheer energy of the production was staggering: acting, singing, dancing, and incredible lighting effects including a "light curtain," "black light" (used in puppetry) and other matters that were beyond my technical knowledge. Toward the end of the show there was the visual of an actor in an Uncle Sam costume dropping bombs on Vietnam, reflecting the iconic images of the My Lai massacre which had happened in mid-March, less than a month before. This image inflamed the audience. It called out and there was flowing red, white, and blue bunting ripped apart while the stalwart young Russians from various branches of the military stood alongside greedy-looking American capitalists in black-and-white. The music swelled and the images of the young Russians grew larger and larger and more distinct while the capitalists diminished and faded away.

The young girl I sat next to spoke English and knew I was from the United States. When I asked if it wasn't terribly anti-America, she answered in a kindly and pleasant manner, "Yes, and rightly so." I couldn't wrap my head around this response because it was so contradictory! The whole theatre seemed alive with some kind of righteous indignation.

Three Sisters was superbly acted and directed by Yuri Lubimov. This production became famous world over. When the play started, my Intourist interpreter immediately whispered her translation. I finally had to tell her—hoping I would not offend—that I had directed the play, knew what they were saying, and could follow what was going on even though I did not speak Russian, but would feel free to ask questions if I needed anything explained.

I loved the production. There was a pole stage center with strings on which were attached cut-out art nouveau leaves made from lighting gels that matched both the backdrop, as well as the wings made of burlap and on which, painted in the same style, were nonrealistic-leafed birch trees. Set props were simple (but correct for the period): chairs, sofas and a piano for the first two acts, the living room and ballroom—followed by an intermission during which the prop crew cleared the stage and brought on two big bureaus containing the clothing for the fire victims in full view of the audience.

For the last act these were removed quickly and a park bench was added for an outdoor scene. Somehow, the lighting effectively, but subtly, changed the color of the leaves to indicate the seasons. Music often backed or framed the action—a leitmotiv of a military band which was sometimes danced to. The production received an ovation with even the director taking two curtain calls.

My interpreter told me the actor who played the doctor was one of the country's "honored actors." The staging of the fire scene had him playing a gramophone record of "If you knew Susie," and he danced to the music in a frantic but non-joyous manner, revealing how much he hated himself because as a doctor, he was drunk and could not attend to the fire victims. Vershinin's philosophy about the future in the scene with Tusenbach gave a pessimistic rendering rather than a positive spin, making the point of the play (which also fit Communist ideology) that things will *not* be better in the future unless *we act*. We cannot be like the indolent three sisters and lead a sort of moment-by-moment existence hoping that things will turn out well. The whole cast acted with true feeling and were wonderful. I thought that with *Ten Days* and *Three Sisters*, I had seen the best productions Moscow had to offer.

The Visit was very bad. And oh, my god, how sick and tired and bored I was with anti-Americanism. At the performance I wished I could drive a pink Cadillac down Gorky Street in a zoot suit, munch a hamburger, smoke a fat cigar, and throw dollar bills out the window! Our production at Purdue was fifty times better. Yes, we showed the horror of materialism—they showed the horror of *American* capitalism. And oh, how corny for the actress playing Clare and the actor playing Alfred III to weep glycerin tears at parting. This is not what Durrenmatt had in mind. He didn't want Clare to grow old and sick at the play's end, but rather to have her leave Gillian triumphantly in her sedan chair.

Anti-Worlds was a collection of poems by Andrei Voznesensky, which played in repertory at the same theatre as *Ten Days* and was directed by the same director. I absolutely loved the staging of these poems—no, I did not understand the words—but the emotions were totally clear, the subject universal, and the love of this poet by the audience overpowering. Taganka Square was crowded by those who hoped there might be an extra seat. I was lucky enough to get one through Intourist as a visiting American. I can't really describe why—the emotional subjects, the powerful feelings of the readers, the special rhythms—I *don't know why*, but I was swept away and bought a translation in English of the poet's works back in America.

My Whimsical Look was about the life of Chekhov, a sort of Hal Holbrook as Mark Twain narrative. The setting consisted of only a few set properties: a desk, bench, and sofa, backed by a black velour curtain which occasionally opened to reveal a scene on a platform that dramatized various periods in Chekhov's life, perhaps a scene with Olga Knipper or Stanislavski. The first act lasted an hour and a half and with so little action it was simply not a show that could command the attention of anyone who did not know the language. I left. The only thing I had noticed was that the pauses seemed interminable, which surprised me since I was under the impression that Vaktangov's direction—this was the Vaktangov Theatre—was historically the antithesis of the Stanislavski method of acting.

WARSAW: Ruth and Ida Kaminska's Panstwowy Teatr, Zydowski, in Warsaw was in dreadful condition outside and in. Poverty-stricken is the only way to describe it. The director, Ida Kaminska, met me at the box office and insisted that I be guest of honor at the theatre. The play—unknown to me at the time and still unknown—started at 7:15. Scenery, costumes and especially lighting (there were only a dozen lekos) were shockingly insufficient and inartistic—I mean bad, even by high school standards—as was the directing and acting. Only Ruth herself was competent, perhaps only by comparison. There were about 50 audience members. The spoken language was Yiddish, translated into Polish via phones for those who did not understand it, which was no help to me because I did not understand Polish! The play was a comedy but there was no Molly Picon in the cast and few, if any, laughs. Fortunately, it wasn't too long.

I also saw a production there of *The Glass Menagerie* and I could tell where the script was cut and changes made. It was not good. I had a feeling that the theatre was financially subsidized by the government because of a small loyal faction, and perhaps for fear of being considered anti-Semitic, maybe because of guilt over the horrible way the Jews, especially in Warsaw, were treated during WWII.

WROCLAW: The Teatr Laboratorium: *The Constant Prince* by Spanish playwright Calderon was extraordinary and the major reason I visited Poland. It was scheduled the day after I arrived, but due to some whim of director Grotowski at the last moment it was performed the evening of my arrival. Translated/adapted by Polish writer J. Slowalki, it starred actor Ryszard Cieslek in the title role. I was third in line when I arrived and was admitted ten minutes to the hour. The seating area was on the second floor and I sat on the far end as Pascal Monod, whom I met in the box office earlier when I went for my ticket, told me to do since it was the best seat in the house. The theater was full, 34 spectators. That was it. All of us were looking *down* upon the actors.

The doors were locked at seven and the performance was over at 8:00. That single hour was worth the trip. There was nothing comparable to this work that I had ever seen at that time or since, an incredible fusion between the talents of director and actor. Cieslek had the charismatic appeal of a Nureyev. I spent two days talking to various acolytes at the theatre and still do not know why this hour of movement and sound was so incredibly effective.

There have been only three well known theorists on how to re-create at every performance (which is what acting is) in the history of modern theatre: Stanislavski, Brecht, and Grotowski. At the time I was in Poland the most important figure in the theatre world was Grotowski. I cannot analyze, verbalize, and communicate the performances of his actors or connect their performance with any clear method, nor can I describe what I *felt* when I first saw this production.

In rehearsal for three years, *The Constant Prince* was a transforming experience. Grotowski's theater had existed for eleven years and had five productions in its repertory. The director was "busy" getting ready to birth another in June, one that had been gestating for over two years. His work started out in the city of Opole in 1959, and in January 1965 transferred to Wroclaw, the "capital" of the southeastern section of the country. The place, he felt, was important because the acting must come from *Polish* roots, which was only possible in a province in a provincial town where the problems of state and international matters did not take focus away from actors working to find the artistic "truth" of their bodies.

EAST BERLIN: *Man is Man* by Bertold Brecht takes place in India in the mid 1920s. Gayly Gay is a kind of World War II Sad Sack who goes out to buy a fish for dinner and gets hijacked into the Army by three soldiers, robbers of collection boxes from temples which resulted in a colleague—Jeraiah Jip—getting killed. Their tough-as-nails sergeant is looking for Hindu temple looters, and the three soldiers need a replacement for Jip. The story deals with their morphing Gayly into Jip. The funniest episode is when the three convince Gayly that Jip had an elephant. He becomes so convinced of this that he sells it to the Widow Bigbick (who is a kind of canteen-owning Mother Courage). As soon as she pays him and finds out that the elephant is only a figment of his imagination he is arrested and executed.

I loved the story but didn't see why the actor playing Gayly Gay imitated the acting style of Charley Chaplin's "Little Tramp" character instead of creating his own character. For me, the imitation made for a distancing that took precedence over the entire production.

The Mother starred Helene Weigel, one of the great actors of our time. She was simply magnificent as the title character, Pelagea Vlassova: very simple, truthful, and with a sense of humor of the true survivalist; she reminded me of Anne Revere. The story's form is episodic as in *Mother Courage*, but the great difference is that while *Courage* is an antiwar play, *The Mother* is a pro-communist play. Everything else is similar: the central character, the number of episodic scenes, the direct narration to the audience including quotes from Marx, Engels and Lenin; and the songs. The *mise-en-scene* is also the same: a basic background with stage properties, costumes in muted colors, visuals via slides and realistic lighting. The story's arc of action is of an ignorant peasant woman (but dutiful mother) and her journey from her prime consideration as a mother, the taking care of her own brood, to an understanding that a good mother must also be a human being. This means she should know how to read and think, since it is these qualities that will benefit all people. Her greatest dramatic moments occur in such situations as the death of her son (same as in *Mother Courage*), her learning to read, and at the end when she becomes politically active, symbolized by the red flag, the night prior to the 1917 revolution against the Czar. Weigel also had fantastic moments of comedy, especially when she learns to read, when she talks to the butcher, and even when she is ill. The audience loved her, and Weigel played the character to inspire empathy from them, certainly not to alienate them.

Caesar and Cleopatra, Shaw's play produced by the Berlin Ensemble, was a splendid production in all respects—acting, scenery and music. I was especially taken by the settings, costumes, and lighting. After the prologue, which is spoken directly to the audience, the curtain opens on a moonlit night in Egypt's Sahara desert in front of the Sphinx of Giza, with Caesar talking to himself. He is flummoxed when there is an answer from the Sphinx. But of course it is not this icon of Egypt but Cleopatra, who is resting between the Sphinx's paws. Other scenes are the Palace at Alexandria on the quay that looks across the eastern harbor at the famed lighthouse, and Caesar's fortification from which he dives into the water to swim to a

Roman ship in the eastern part of the harbor with Cleopatra clinging to him.

So much attention is given to the geography of east and west, Rome and Egypt. The island of Pharos is reached from the Palace via a causeway that separates the harbor into eastern and western sections, and at the tip of the eastern side is anchored Caesar's ship of escape. I wondered if perhaps this play was produced because of the similarity in geography. East Berlin/West Berlin, an island inside East Germany caused by the partition of Germany by the leaders of the Allies after WWII. Second, but probably more important, the production saw George Bernard Shaw as a supportive socialist—the mostly black-and-white program depicted him with a very red beard.

The Resistible Rise of Arturo Ui by Brecht was a play I read at the Brecht Archives before I saw it. Brecht was in Finland when he wrote it and didn't know anything about Al Capone's gang in our country except for the headlines. But he used America for the setting of the play, and pastes parallel events from the rise of Hitler in his own country onto the Capone story about gangsters trying to control the cauliflower racket in Chicago. The great scene is the ham actor teaching Hitler how to give a speech.

At the end of the play the man who played Hitler comes forward and removes his mustache before addressing the audience. I believe the audience thought he was taking his curtain call for they applauded wildly, and he had to wait to say his famous last line: "Although the bastard's crushed, but beware—the bitch that bore him is in heat again." I found the production not very good. Hitler was played as a complete madman—temper tantrums, melancholy and inferiority complex so exaggerated that he becomes an over-the-top caricature, not giving him 3-D psychological underpinning. Years later I saw a great production with student actor Nick Cascone playing Hitler.

For me, the terror comes from the fact that the people follow a madman and submit to him. But the fear and terror of this can only be realized if the character is probable. Perhaps the character was played as a caricature because it is the only picture of Hitler that the German audiences can stomach, not being able to face their own complicity in his rise.

Schweik in the Second World War by Brecht is based on *The Good Soldier Svejk*, an unfinished work (1923) dealing with the *first* World War, written by Czechoslovakian novelist Jaroslav Hasek. I sat center of the first row for this production and thought it was wonderful! It's the old story of "the little guy." This one's name is Schweik, and the story tells of how he makes it through the *second* World War by outfoxing and outwitting the big guys. He does so with a sly sense of humor and a twinkle in the eye. I laughed even though I didn't understand the language. The audience loved it, and the production was approaching its 250th performance in repertory. The specific setting is the Russian Front when the "little guy" Schweik [think *Kilroy* and *SNAFU* (Situation Normal: All Fucked Up)] meets Hitler at the end of the play in a snowstorm outside Leningrad and screws him over.

LONDON: *Edward II* by Christopher Marlowe and produced by the Old Vic, which I saw on its opening performance, was first-rate even though it lasted three hours and fifteen minutes. King Edward is in love with a young Irishman named Gaveston and rejects his wife, Queen Ann, by whom he has had a child, Edward the third. Back in England after being exiled, Gaveston is despised by the noblemen and King Edward is forced to banish him once again. After fifteen years of longing for him it is the Queen of France who urges Mortimer (who will be her lover) to have Edward recall Gaveston so he can be killed by the noblemen of the court.

When Gaveston returns from Ireland, Edward embraces him and asks Gaveston to embrace him back, whereupon Gaveston kisses him passionately full on the lips. I'm not sure the audience liked this moment of pure lust but Edward wins our respect as a tragic hero, not only because of his loyalty and love for Gaveston, but because he refuses to give up his crown, and even more so, because he knows who he is, accepts himself, and endures.

On this preview night there was a terrible moment. When Gaveston is to be hanged the actor playing the hangman threw the rope, but missed getting it over the pole and only succeeded after the fifth attempt The audience applauded, which broke the desired mood.

The Importance of Being Earnest by Oscar Wilde at the Haymarket gave star billing to Flora Robson, who played the minor role of Miss Prism! I dearly respect the English audiences for their homage and faithfulness to actresses of a certain age, but this was total nonsense, especially since she did no more than an adequate job. Her comedy was comprised of tricks and stage business rather than character, language and situation. Daniel Massey, who looks a lot like his father, Raymond, played John and is really an amateur. Dale Helward was head and shoulders superior to him in that role in our production. In fact, the only person I really liked was the young girl who played Cecily. English actors who think they can rely on technique rather than moment-to-moment reality have it all wrong.

Hadrian VII was one of the best productions in London. Alec McCowen starred in the title role and gave a brilliant performance. Although the staging is simple, the costumes are very complex because they have to be absolutely right historically as representatives of the hierarchy of the Catholic Church. The setting was utterly simple: two wagons lashed together with two smaller ones on their sides, black velour drape backing and one ornate chair. The show is beautiful in its visual simplicity, which focuses attention on the rituals—the procession of the Cardinal hierarchy—and I was riveted by the absolutism and certainty of the Catholic myth. The comfort of certainty that *we* (the United States) are the *best* and most honest country in the world had vanished with the series of assassinations and the death of *myths*. That parallel is what was so painful about the assassination of Hadrian at the end of the play.

Margaret Courtenay was in the cast and I fondly remember meeting her at a party at Page Karling's when she was at Purdue on an Old Vic tour. I went backstage and she remembered me, was very nice, poured scotch, and we talked. Then Bill Freedman, who also produced *Staircase*, came in and I told him I loved the production and wanted to do it. He said he knew about our professional company at Purdue but thought it might be impossible to get the rights because of an expected New York production. But he added that if I did decide on it, to write him and gave me his card.

Oedipus, by the Roman playwright Seneca, directed by Peter Brook at The Old Vic, was so idiotic that I was compelled to boo at the curtain call. Brook called it "...an experimental production the importance of which transcends such trivial considerations as the immediate success of the first night; or the satisfaction of audiences." Such balls!

In truth it was just bloody awful. There could be all sorts of reasons why one would want to see a straight production of the Roman playwright's version based on the original by Sophocles. For example, it has a lot more blood and gore when Jocasta impales herself on a sword through her vagina, which makes it nearer to a take by our own Quentin Tarantino. But such a prurient reason was eschewed by the director in favor of theories advanced by Artaud's Theater of Cruelty, a pinch of Brecht's "A" Effect, and possibly some Grotowski. When that first-rate actress Irene Worth impales herself she did it in some kind of slow-motion nonrealistic "Body Truth" way, which rendered it ineffective in arousing the terror and pity that creates catharsis, which is the essence of tragedy. The only thing it created was a yawn.

But the production's ending proved sillier still, which wasn't exactly what Seneca had in mind for his tragedy: A huge Trojan horse-object was wheeled onstage by actors in skimpy Roman togas which, when it was unveiled, proved to be a Size-Queen's wet dream: a nine foot lifelike penis made of gold around which members of the company (except Gielgud and Worth) danced joyfully to modern rock music, all apropos of *nothing*—except possibly giving the audience the big shaft! Although from the critics' reception and the length of run it did produce some of the best—however apocryphal—stories about rehearsals in the history of theatre.

As the stories go, the *Oedipus* rehearsal took weeks, but it took only a few days for the cast to grasp the fact that textual matters such as learning the author's lines were insignificant. They then settled down to such necessities as mastering difficult yoga positions while moaning the Indian-sounding word "Yabunghole." This was sometimes followed by the French form of African voodoo; or nose-rubbing greetings. Then there was the ensemble assistance in pulling a breech-birth baby from its mother's womb while chanting Tibetan haiku until they had shattered the false reality of their perceptions.

It was on the third day of the week devoted to primal scream—a non-cerebral method of releasing trauma based on society's imposed repressions—when Brook told the cast members to scream at the top of their lungs words they had been told by society were wrong, and to scream in a violent physical manner. As the cast ran around yelling dirty words, Sir John, with his perfect diction, primal-screamed, "We open in seven days! When will we get our fucking blocking? When will we learn our fucking lines?"

Three Sisters, directed by Laurence Olivier, was wise and conventional. Since I know it so well there isn't much to add. There is one problem. In my steno pad notes taken on the trip I list *Three Sisters* as the third production at the Old Vic that I got tickets for. Since everything else is right I cannot understand why this production is not listed as playing in 1968, although it is listed for 1967. So after a lot of research, I am assuming that it was kept in the repertory.

Perhaps what happened was that when I saw it in May 1968, negotiations were underway to have the production filmed. In the 1967 production Robert Stephens played Vershinin and Anthony Hopkins, who was hired in his first contract at the Old Vic as Olivier's understudy, played Andrei. In the production Olivier was not only listed as director, but also played Dr. Chebutikin, and Alan Bates played Vershinin. Both of them also appeared in the not very good film, released in 1970, designed by Czech designer Josef Syoboda. Perhaps what I saw the second week in May 1968 was scheduled to refresh the cast and give Olivier and Bates a chance to play the roles in preparation for the making of the film in which Joan Plowright was most memorable in the role of Masha.

DUBLIN: *In the Shadow of the Glen* by Synge, and *The Shadow of a Gunman* by O'Casey, were two one-acts opening on Monday the 13th at The Abbey. I was invited for an early afternoon dress rehearsal. The plot of *Glen*—which served as the curtain raiser—is about Nora, a young woman married to an elderly man who just died and for whom she is dutifully mourning, when a young tramp appears. The two are attracted to one another. When she goes out, the husband rises up and tells the tramp he is only feigning death. When Nora returns she tells the young man what it was like sitting and waiting for the old man to consummate the marriage, which he never did. The young man proposes and the old man rises up and orders Nora out of his house. She gladly leaves this loveless marriage and she and the young man go off together. The dialogue is the same kind of folk poetry found in

Synge's *Riders To The Sea,* and since I knew that play well, I readily understood this one in spite of the thick Irish accents.

The O'Casey—the main feature of the bill—was about a poet who comes to live with a friend in a slum apartment. The suspicious neighbors start to believe he is a member of the IRA, an organization they much admire. The poet takes advantage of this hero worship, especially with a young woman who falls in love with him. This aspect of the plot is similar to O'Casey's *The Playboy of the Western World* with its satirical view of romantic notions of the Irish. Because I was technical director for Gene Kildahl's production of that play, I found the comparison helpful in understanding the author's point of view. Vincent Dowling directed, and both plays were well mounted—set, costumes and lighting—and wonderfully well-acted.

That evening I had a ticket to the opening of *Is e Duirt Polonius,* scheduled for a week's run at the smaller venue in the Abbey, the Peacock Theatre. Ernest Blyth was the Abbey's general manager. He had once served as treasurer for the Irish Republic and had been instrumental in the Abbey receiving a government subsidy. But with it came the proviso that they do a play in Gaelic to keep the Irish language alive, and this was the play that opened that Saturday night. I did not understand a word. My main impression was an odd one: Gaelic sounded very much like the Yiddish I had listened to at the Ida Kaminski theatre in Warsaw.

INTERVIEWS: On this trip, I interviewed various directors, but since my questions dealt with matters of finance, government subsidy, management and student training, and since all the theatres in Russia, Poland and East Germany were about the same, I will give only a few summaries.

Nikolay Akimov of the Comedy Theatre in Leningrad, a director for over 30 years and a People's Artist of the USSR, said his theatre employs about 200, which includes 60 in the acting company. There are nine such theaters in Leningrad and close to 500 in the USSR. All productions play in rotating repertory and roles are double or triple cast, with the programs printing all the names. But the name of the actor playing a specific performance is checked (X). There are 15 productions in the repertory, with four or five new ones each year. They do seven to nine performances a week.

Cost [at the time the rate of exchange was one U.S. Dollar for 28.25 rubles, and there are 100 kopecks in a ruble] of tickets is between 60 kopeks to two rubles and there are special rates for students. The actors' pay per month ranges from a low of 75 rubles to an average of 275 with a few receiving 400.

Mr. Gorbunov, president of the Theatre Institute, told me that there were 2000 - 3000 applicants, between the ages of 17 to 23 for men and 17 to 20 for women, who audition for the 57 openings in the freshman class of aspiring performers. Courses taken are acting, speech, movement, dance, makeup, physical culture and fencing. In addition, they take courses in Russian and English Literature, History of World Theatre, History of the Russian Theater, three years of foreign language (mostly English), art and decor, architecture and paintings throughout the ages, Philosophy, and Political Science.

Mr. Chemyshov of the Maly Opera Theatre in Leningrad, where ballet and opera are produced, said that his company was comprised of 107 dancers (67 women and 40 men). The symphony orchestra was just over 100. The repertory consists of 18 productions of modern and classical works, with three or four performances per week of ballet and five of opera. There was a ballet school connected with the theatre where students are taken at age 10 and graduate at age 18. There are three ballet companies in Leningrad, and perhaps two in about 20 other cities throughout the USSR.

At the Gorky Theater the director, Georgy Tovstonogov, said he had 75 actors and 60 other workers, and 14 productions in their repertory with four new productions each year. The theatre holds 1,400 and the top price for a ticket is two rubles. Doors are locked at curtain time and no one is admitted to the orchestra or mezzanine. Latecomers are allowed to view from the back of the top balcony, which he said helps train them to be on time.

Miss Lukovna (Tanya), my Intourist guide, told me that tuition for preschooling preceding professional theatre training was paid for by the government, and that there was universal medical health care. As for specifics in the theatre, as an actress—she said she was not a very good one—she received 110 rubles per month; her small three-room apartment cost eight rubles a month—in fact the cost of all apartments could be no more than five percent of citizen's income—and this included heat, gas, lights, and water. There were also co-op apartments which one could buy and pay for over a period of time. She said the average wage for an actor was about 175 rubles per month, the highest being 400 and the lowest 80. She said that in her company for the third time in eight years the director would replace five actresses and six actors. If the actors being replaced did not want to accept assignments in provincial theatres because they did not want to leave Leningrad, they would have to find other occupations. There were approximately 400 professional theaters in the country, with an average company of 50, which would mean 20,000 actors employed.

HIGHLIGHTS: Before I left on this trip and early in the rehearsals of *Uncle Vanya*, we came across the following scene. A workman comes from the factory to summon Dr. Astrov because a worker has been injured. Astrov then says, almost to himself, "How could I then, how should I then," and starts to look for his cap, telling the workman to get him a glass of vodka. As he continues looking he says: "There is a man in an Ostrovsky play with a big mustache and little wit—that's me." Then repeats to himself, "How could I then, how should I then."

Both Cathryn Damon who played Yelena, and Will Gregory who played Astrov, wondered what the speech meant. I researched it but never found the answer, so I told them I would find out when I was in Russia. Even though the play would have finished its run, I would get back to them.

Tanya arranged for me to meet a young woman, an historian at the Theatre Museum, who did the research. I was able to find the place in the Russian script of *Vanya* simply because I knew the approximate number of pages before the workman enters. The young woman eventually found a copy of an Ostrovsky play, *The Girl Without A Dowry* (her translation), and it is interesting to note that this is one of two Ostrovsky plays with similar titles—which has a hero who says, "How could I then, how should I then." She concluded that Astrov is quoting this line because his situation is similar to the one in the Ostrovsky play. Astrov does not want to leave Yelena, whom he has just met because he is attracted to her. Yet as a doctor he feels he must aid the injured man at the factory. I later found out that this

Ostrovsky play was not translated into English, and of course I got the word to Cathryn and Will on my return.

⌘ ⌘ ⌘

When the *Oedipus Rex* produced by the Mayakovsky Players on tour from Moscow was finished, I decided to walk back to my hotel. On the way over in a cab I had memorized the signposts for every turn: pass the Winter Palace, the Peter and Paul Fort, cross the bridge over the Neva, turn left past the Naval School, turn right past the moored cruiser *Aurora* (of October Revolution fame), and turn right across another bridge.

When I approached the small guardhouse in front of the cruiser *Aurora*, the guard came from the door of his shelter with a rifle, his finger on the trigger, and called out (it sounded as if in fear), for identification. I responded in English, "American! I am a citizen of the United States," with all the bravado I could muster, slicing my right-hand through the freezing night air. Facing forward I walked on with great conviction, not turning back at his repeated calls. I suppose from his point of view I was like an apparition disappearing into the night's snowstorm. I was scared that he might try to follow or shoot me, but I walked on at a measured pace across the bridge.

⌘ ⌘ ⌘

I was going through the art gallery on the top floor of the Winter Palace, looking at Picasso, Matisse, Gauguin, and Cezanne paintings. The amount brought on sight-gluttony until finally my eyes had gorged so much that they couldn't look any longer. I was the only person in the gallery and was surprised to see three galvanized water buckets strategically placed. I asked my guide, who spoke a trace of English, what they were for. He pointed up to the ceiling, "Rain water. Roof leaks." And he informed me proudly in memorized English, "There are more blue-period Picassos here than any place on earth including Paris' Louvre."

⌘ ⌘ ⌘

The night I was scheduled to see *Galileo* at 8:00 I got a call from Intourist saying the theatre had changed schedule and was playing *Ten Days that Shook the World,* with the curtain at 7:00. I rushed to the subway escalator, which took me deeply underground to the immaculately clean platform, and was suddenly confused about which train to take. I had already been in Leningrad and developed my method to get help. I would hold up my hand flat to an oncoming pedestrian and say, "Excuse me!" and tapping my chest, add, "American!" On my second try a woman, obviously in a hurry, stopped. I must have looked desperate. I just started by pointing to myself and enunciating clearly: "I am from the United States and I'm trying to get to Taganka Square where there is a theatre playing *Ten Days that Shook the World."*

I could see that she was sympathetic so I tried again in pidgin-English and gestures. She either got what I meant through my facial expressions or gestures, or perhaps she knew a little English, because I saw in her face that she finally understood. She motioned for me to follow her to the other side of the platform where we caught the train. Seeing my worried face she would smile reassuringly and say "Teatro. Taganka Square" We finally arrived at the station. I said thanks and good-bye, but she took my hand pulled me on to the escalator and out into a square where she pointed to the theatre. I thanked her in English, French, and German and shook her hand. She opened her purse and took out four pieces of wrapped hard candy—butterscotch as I remember—and pressed them into my palm. I put the candy in my pocket and remembering a movie I had seen, I held both hands together, bowed my head several times bending slightly from the waist, and turned and ran toward the theatre.

⌘ ⌘ ⌘

It was at a scheduled meeting with Mr. Vadim Galushko and a friend of his at the Institute of Soviet-American Relations, at Kaliuim Street, 14, Moscow, where I finally connected the dots and understood the reason for the antagonism I sensed on the streets, in the theatres, and so obviously in the posters plastered on kiosks showing an Uncle Sam figure dropping bombs on natives in Vietnam.

There was an air of something like sadness or misunderstanding that hung over this meeting. Galushko's friend started off by asking me if I would write an article for *The Russian Times* about "my feelings on the event,"—I though he meant our meeting—and thinking he might be trying to get me to write something that could be used for purposes of propaganda I told him I would be glad to do so when I returned home, and asked for his address.

Mr. Galushko, who headed the Friendship Institute and who I was supposed to be interviewing, asked me, "When President Johnson spoke about the first peace talks with Vietnam was this just a political ploy? And was he serious when he said he would not seek or accept another term of office as President of the United States?" I was befuddled and just didn't feel comfortable. I said I wasn't aware the President had done so. He explained that he was talking about the President's talk on the last day of March. At last I understood why I didn't understand! That would have been just as I was arriving in Leningrad and had no knowledge of the speech or what he had said.

I felt so out of what was happening that I said I was unsure of what their sources were. I asked if I could take notes. Mr. Galushko explained that the "Friendship Society" dealt with Soviet-American Relations and was represented by 50 chapters in all 15 Republics of the USSR. He then asked me if I knew how many such organizations there were in the United States. I did not. In fact, I had never heard of such an organization. He told me there was The National Council of American-Soviet Friendship in N. Y. headed by Rev. Richard Morford and Rockwell Kent (whose name I recognized because some of his paintings hung in the Hermitage), plus chapters in San Francisco, Los Angeles, and Chicago. But he commented that the United States was a big country so why were there only four when the relationship between our two countries was so vitally important?

I told him that I was unsure, but perhaps it was because such organizations feared being put on a Communist-front list, something of the sort that started with the blacklist during the McCarthy investigations. I then asked him if their Friendship Societies were government sponsored. Absolutely not was his answer. They were all financed by concerned individuals who wanted to promote friendship between our two countries. Both had the Atomic bomb, and the antagonism was being referred to as The Cold War. "Our Friendship Societies feel we *must* learn to understand each other and coexist." His friend then said that is why he asked me to write my reactions to what just happened. When I explained I had no idea what he had been talking about, both he and Mr. Galushko were astonished.

Prior to our meeting, he had said that they had both attended a two-hour memorial service for Martin Luther King. I was stunned at this news. The first thing I thought about was the assassination of JFK. Tears welled up in my eyes and I kept shaking my head in total disbelief. "When did he die?" I asked, and they told me he had been assassinated three days earlier. How was such a terrible act possible? I needed to be at 435 Robinson in front of the television set with Robin and the kids, not here in Moscow, alone; I needed someone to talk with and try to come to grips with the awfulness of this crime.

They obviously sensed my deeply felt reaction and were very kind. I tried to make sense to connect the dots but my talk was oblique because all I could think to say was that when I left the United States, I sat next to a young man on the airplane whose name was Michael Mishler. He told me his father had been in *The Three Penny Opera* in New York and his mother, Jaclyn Jones, who worked at The Actors Studio, had said it was going to be closed for lack of funds, which I had thought a tragedy. Michael seemed to me to be an example of the exodus of the young, thinking student from the USA who considered the Vietnam War unjust and was not going to be drafted into the Army. He said he doubted he would return to the United States. As I talked, I felt the sympathy of both men from the Friendship Institute and when I finished they asked me if there was anything they could do to help me?

When I left I thought of my first theatre experience in Russia, seeing *Lohengrin* and finding out that I had to check my coat. When I left the show early I saw that the very old woman who had checked it had re-sewn the broken loop that was used to hang the coat up. I was so grateful I tried to tip her but she would not take the money. She was a mother taking care of a child. There had been so many kindnesses during my visit, so why had I been pissed off about a little hostility and propaganda?

⌘ ⌘ ⌘

In Warsaw I visited the Pawaik prison—saw the actual lists—sometimes 200 people named to be killed at a certain place, date and time in reprisal for the killing of one Nazi solder *unless* the killer was named or revealed himself. These lists were framed along with pictures drawn by prisoners of starving colleagues, 37,000 human beings killed in this one prison alone. Warsaw was eighty-five percent leveled by the Nazis on Hitler's orders. 700,000 people were killed between 1939 and 1945. Now the city was rebuilt, harsh gray concrete buildings to replace a city that took 800 years to build and two months to destroy.

⌘ ⌘ ⌘

I had a program of my production of *Mother Courage and Her Children* and asked the curator at the Brecht Archive to give it to Helen Weigel, who lived overhead. The next time I was there the curator said he had given the program to her and she said to give thanks and say that Anne Revere was the *only* actress in America who could play the role.

⌘ ⌘ ⌘

When I saw Brecht's 1943 play *Schweik in the Second World War*, I had moved to West Berlin and had to go back through Checkpoint Charlie to The Berliner Ensemble. When the play was over, Werner Hecht and I talked for some time and it was near midnight when I thanked him and split. As I walked toward Checkpoint Charlie I was dumbfounded. There were Russian tanks and soldiers with machine guns on every corner, but what was most surreal were the Russian flags and gigantic five-story banners hanging from buildings picturing Lenin, Marx and Stalin that had been put up while I was at the theatre. It came to me that it was almost May 1st.

It had started to rain and I was without my raincoat or umbrella. I was about to run for it but I thought I must not do that or they might suspect me of something. So I walked in the rain and got soaked. I made it to Checkpoint Charlie where I went through the grilling by the ones who held the power in the East, kept my mouth shut, took their rudeness until I was let go and got to the other side where I kept my mouth shut, took *their* rudeness, and was finally allowed to enter the West. I walked calmly to the street, caught a cab, returned through some ruins to a skuzzy street and up to my room. The next day I would leave for the airport and take off at 3:00 P.M., happy to get the hell out of a place where I did not dare run to get out of the rain.

⌘ ⌘ ⌘

Gabriel Fallon, artistic director of The Abbey Theatre in Dublin, told me its history. His tour of the building took us to the most needed of all rooms in any theatre, the rehearsal hall, which was on the theatre's roof affording plenty of sunshine, air and space. I recognized it immediately and congratulated him on the theatre's design for beauty and function, especially this magnificent rehearsal space, and asked if he had ever read Samuel Montefiore Waxman's *Antoine and The Theatre Libre*. He about fell out of his chair, understanding immediately that I was referring to Antoine's design printed in Waxman's book. He said I was the first person who had ever made this connection. Antoine (1858-1943) of course never got this wished-for theatre. but many of its features, particularly of the rehearsal hall, had at least been realized in the Abbey where actors did not live their lives like moles rehearsing in dark underground rooms so small there was not space enough to tape down a ground plan.

The two of us were no longer strangers. Both had read a book we loved, and instantaneously, by the look in each other's eyes, the tight skin of ordinary conventionality vanished, followed by laughter and the shock of recognition. We were old friends asking each other why in hell any other theatre designer hadn't caught on to that as far as the activity of creation was concerned, the rehearsal hall was the most important space in a theatre building?

The 70-year-old Ernest Blythe, who had been managing director of The Abbey Theatre since 1941, now retired, told the story of how the new Abbey eventually became erected.

The land on which it was to be built held a pub, which would have to be demolished. The owner, who was his own bartender and often served The Abbey's actors until last call, was an older man with an Irish sense of taking-the-advantage when possible. He had refused the original offer, which amounted to more than he would have gotten under the right of eminent domain. Mr. Blyth sweetened the pot a little, but the greedy old skinflint refused to budge and wanted twice what the property was worth.

Through years of dealing in Irish politics and understanding human nature, Mr. Blyth had not only gained the ability, but dearly loved the journey of telling how he had managed. "It was one thing I was sure of after all my years in dealings with actors—they are all curious and fond of gossip and unable to keep a secret. So I had the architect of the building we planned on building draw up another set of blueprints for a totally different piece of land, and I spread these out on a table so that anyone sitting in the only chair in front of my desk would notice them. No sooner was this done than an actor came in to tell me he had heard rumors about a certain older actor being caught *in flagrante delicto* with a pretty new ingénue. He would never have mentioned it except that he was afraid if it were true and ever came to light, the story would reflect badly on the honor of Ireland. While he talked, he kept glancing at the table where he could barely make out the blueprints. When he could no longer stand it he asked what they were.

"After hedging for a bit of time to bait his curiosity, I asked if he could keep a secret and never tell a soul if I told him, to which he swore on the sacred honor of his mother accompanied by a catholic crossing of his protestant self. I showed him the blueprints, told him about the pub owner's refusal to sell, and for that reason we had decided to build elsewhere.

"Within the hour the pub's owner appeared, cap in hand, and gave a gentle knock on the open door. I greeted him and asked him to come in.

Was there something I could do for him? Giving a slight glance at the table he seated himself and began to tell me of the grievously troubled dreams he had been having since our last talk during which had he rejected my offer to sell his pub. Only last night, he said, he had dreamed a dream leaving him in an agony of torment in which the Ghost of Greed, Marley himself, appeared. The dream had made him see clearly. Instead of making a profit he decided that he would sacrifice his pub for the glory of Ireland and the National Theatre and would accept my last offer.

"Oh, had you only made your decision sooner, I told him, reminding him that I was the former minister of finance for Ireland. The Board of Governors have come to realize that our last offer was twice what he could have expected if the theatre had pursued a suit of the right of eminent domain. And now they have decided not to pay a penny more.

"And that," he said with some relish, "is how the new Abbey was up and running by the year of our Lord in 1966."

Chapter 22

I ARRIVED BACK HOME EXHAUSTED BUT glad to be with the kids and back in bed with Robin, who was now certain she was pregnant. I needed to firm up plans for the summer theatre season which would start within the month. Before that I had to give a talk about my trip, which was scheduled in a week and would be held in the hall where we rehearsed *Long Day's Journey Into Night* at St. Thomas Aquinas. In the speech, I announced that in December I would direct a student production that would use Jerzy Grotowski's ideas so that our students and I would understand what was going on in Eastern Europe. The speech was basically a thank-you report on the trip, which had been paid for by a grant from the Purdue Research Foundation

⌘ ⌘ ⌘

Son Joe was getting ready to go abroad again, ostensibly to meet up with friends he had met in the Balkans the previous summer. This would be his third trip, traveling alone as a very mature young man who would be 17 in August. He was well aware of the general strike in France in mid-May, and though it lasted only two weeks there were still pockets of resistance in the French Quarter. As soon as he landed in Paris he joined students at the barricades of the Sorbonne until they found out his age and advised him to get out of town. He went to the Balkans.

⌘ ⌘ ⌘

I had read plays at the Samuel French book store in London and finally settled on the schedule for the summer season June 19th to August 10th: Moliere's *The School For Wives,* William Inge's *Bus Stop,* Harold Pinter's *The Homecoming,* and Emlyn Williams' old warhorse, *Night Must Fall.* And although I could not be much involved, I found that a major event was starting to take shape. It was years later that I realized that by this time my salary exceeded Ross'. This happened when I finally went on a 12-month salary schedule, which Ross had always been on. The two extra months' income tipped my salary over what he was making. Associate Dean of the School of History, Social Science and Education (forerunner of the School of Liberal Arts) Leon E. Trachtman, known as "Lee," had come to Purdue in 1958, and from the get-go understood and valued the theatre and was our biggest administrative supporter. But the bottom line on salaries of all faculty was Bladen Ogle, Dean of HSSE.

As head of Convocations and Lectures, Ross was nationally known, not only among his colleagues but also by the big booking agents in New York, one reason for his substantial clout; another, because he watched football practices with Coach Mollenkopf and President Hovde. But although he never mentioned the fact that my salary was greater than his, it obviously rankled, as well it should have since his first appointment was in 1942 and mine was in 1950. True, he had taken time away during World War II and later to earn his PhD during the '40s but still.... When he found out that the University of Minnesota was looking for someone to head its Convocations and Lectures program and who could also qualify for tenure in their Theatre Department, he did what he had always advised me to do when I wanted a raise or promotion—he applied for the job.

All through the years that theatre was under the leaky umbrella of the Speech Department, Ross pretty much had access to President Hovde, not only for the reasons stated above but because he was the official announcer for the football games in Ross-Ade Stadium. When the University of Minnesota made an offer, Ross went immediately to Hovde and explained that he wanted a raise in salary. The President genuinely wanted Ross to stay at Purdue and felt that a demand for a salary increase was not only understandable, it was perfectly manageable. He did note the academic politics, however. Ogle, who had replaced Ayers as Dean of HSSE, had been the choice of the heads of all the departments, as well as most of the tenured full professors. The salary issue decision would be up to him and not challenged by the President.

State politics were also involved. The reason for the rather strange name of HSSE (we all called it "Hissy"), which was obviously a school of liberal arts, was because President Hovde, rightly so, did not want to ruffle the feathers of administrators at Indiana University. The State Legislature, which frowned upon mixing the focus and objectives of their institutions of higher learning, considered Indiana University as their school of liberal arts, Purdue as their school of engineering and agriculture, and Ball State University and Indiana State University as their teacher colleges. For financial reasons never the twain should meet.

Ross, thinking the salary increase would be a fait accompli after his 25 years connection, saw Dean Ogle and said he wanted a raise or he would accept Minnesota's offer. Ogle read the letter offering Ross the job, looked up, smiled, and said he accepted Ross's resignation, wished him well, and bon voyage!

Ross was furious. He went back to Hovde but the President's hands were tied. Ross loved Purdue and felt he deserved credit for getting the Loebs to build the Playhouse, for running a first-rate Convocations and Lecture program, and for being a producer of what was now known as the best professional theatre in the state, a member of the prestigious League of Professional Theatres. He was naturally bitter about Ogle's decision. But he was also practical and resilient and there was nothing to do but be hopeful. He had received his master's degree at the University of Minnesota, whose reputation as a major university greatly exceeded that of Purdue's. He wrote his official letter of resignation and he and Dorothea started making plans to shift ground after 25 years by starting to house hunt in St. Paul.

If I had known at the time that the reason he'd applied for the Minnesota job was because my salary was greater than his, I would have felt badly about it. But I did not know and looked at the situation objectively, figuring he was fortunate in getting a substantial raise. I couldn't spend much time on this anyway because I had my work to do for the summer theatre season.

We had done Moliere's *The School for Wives* four years earlier as a musical, *The Amorous Flea*, but this was the straight play. John Newton would play Arnolphe, the old guy who has married a very young wife, played by Merle Louise, and Peter Simon would be the young guy she takes a shine to, and he to her. Stuart Howard would direct *Bus Stop*, which had been a major hit both on the stage with Kim Stanley and in the film with Marilyn Monroe. This would be Stuart's first professional directing job and the major hit of the summer season. I would then direct Pinter's *The Homecoming* and *Night Must Fall*, all shows having good roles for our AEA company members.

I had dearly loved directing both Pinter's *The Caretaker* and *The Birthday Party* and hoped to get some, if not the same, kind of kick out of *Homecoming*. The plot centers around a visit to his father by Teddy, a professor of philosophy at an American university, his three adult sons and his new wife Ruth to whom he has been married six years. It had received the 1967 Tony Awards for best play, best direction and best performance for both leading and supporting actor. I found this play tough sledding and to be fair, probably not only because of the play but because I was kicking a bad habit of heavy smoking and doing it cold turkey.

I think occasionally that sometimes very good actors get Academy Awards simply because they have been bypassed previously, and those who judge give them the award for lesser work to compensate for the oversight. The same happens to awards given to writers. I wish, like John Lahr, theatre critic for *The New Yorker* whom I greatly respect, that *The Homecoming* had "changed my life," as it did his in the 2007 revival when he credited it for allowing him "…to understand the eloquence of the unspoken: The position of a chair, the length of a pause, the choice of a gesture" that he "realized could convey volumes."

That didn't happen to me. There is a strangeness in this play; it lacks the humor of the other two and I could not identify with any of the characters.

For example, I did not believe it was possible that Ruth should react so sexually to her father-in-law and brothers-in-law.

Although I thought Janet Hayes did it extremely well, the famous scene in which Ruth spends so much time and care in crossing her legs didn't strike me as sexy; rather it seemed choreographed and laid on, "style" for its own sake rather than a distinctive or characteristic mode of expression. It just wasn't real. And this crossing of her legs did not make probable to me that she had been a prostitute prior to her marriage, or clarify why she was taking so damn much time to cross them—not even as a metaphor. In fact, hardly anything was clear.

That may have been why I had an idea of recording the heartbeat of a real person and subliminally playing it, occasionally bringing up the volume so it was audible, which I hoped might make it more human. Ross Smith came to the opening, and the only thing he said to me afterwards was, "What was that irritating sound that occasionally underscored some of the show?" I explained what it was and my intention. His response? "I found it pretentious and annoying."

I worried that he was right and had Randy Earle cut the sound way down. But it wasn't just the sound. The play itself was problematic. I tried to find some way to penetrate its "mystery" but in fact it may be, to paraphrase what Tallulah Bankhead said to Alexander Wolcott of a play they once attended together, "There was less there than meets the eye *or the ear.*"

We ended the summer season with Emlyn Williams' *Night Must Fall,* a first-rate melodrama about a young man named Dan who has impregnated Dora, a housemaid of Mrs. Bramson who is an elderly despot pretending to be an invalid confined to a wheelchair. Her nasty disposition is quickly revealed when early in the play, her niece Olivia cheerfully comments, "It's a beautiful morning!" and she replies, "I expect it'll cloud over." Eventually getting Dora to bring Dan home so she can talk to him, the old lady finds him so charming that she hires him to become her in-house caretaker.

A murder has been committed in Forest Corner, Essex, where Mrs. Bramson lives, and the victim's amputated hands are found, followed by the body whose head has been severed. The only clue is that the murderer likes to hum, whistle or sing "Mighty like a rose." Olivia distrusts and suspects

Dan, and with Nurse Libby and Mrs. Terrence, conducts a search of his suitcase in which they find a picture of him and the murdered woman. In addition, there is also a hat box.... oh, what fun!

I believe the most effective scene designed to scare the pants off an audience is in this play. Everyone has left the house and Mrs. Bramson becomes frightened thinking of the recent murder. Suspense builds when Dan suddenly slashes open the curtains that separate the living room from the foyer. This sudden sound never failed to lift the audience right out of its seats and cause a stifled scream or two. Our cast, uniformly excellent, all had a wonderful time playing this melodrama. During its run, and probably forever after, if someone said it was a beautiful day, the reply was sure to be: "I expect it'll cloud over."

⌘ ⌘ ⌘

It was a sad day in August when I packed Ross and Dorothea Smith's books that took up every space in my VW, leaving only enough room for me to drive to Folwell Avenue in St. Paul where I stashed the books in the order in which they'd been shelved on Littleton Street in West Lafayette. I spent a couple of good-bye days with these lifelong friends before returning home.

Son Joe had arrived from abroad after a wonderful summer, having sent us wonderful letters about his experiences, which I shared with everyone in the company. In late August the Democratic National Convention was being held in Chicago and he wanted to go. I was not in favor of it, but he insisted so I called Bert Berdis, now married and living in Chicago, and asked if Joe might stay with them. Bert said yes. I don't think Joe took him up on his offer. I do know that he joined the antiwar demonstrations in Grant Park. The Mayor escalated the conflict between police and protestors by calling for excessive police protection and getting the National Guard to put protestors down. Joe got clubbed over the head but he avoided being arrested and got home safely to start his senior year in high school.

At this point I became Administrative Head of the Theatre. Even though I realized the Theatre was soon to be included in a new Department of Creative Arts with a new Head, I knew damn well that being an academic administrator of even a section of such a department was definitely *not* my forte. Indeed, I had to get the fall and winter professional seasons scheduled, and with a cut in production money each would consist of two, rather than three plays.

⌘ ⌘ ⌘

The casting of James Earl Jones as Lennie the previous season probably had something to do with my idea to cast an African-American woman to play Billy Dawn in *Born Yesterday*. I mean, let's face it, no man rich or poor, red, yellow, white, or blue would not be attracted to a Lena Horne-type. So I figured everyone in the audience would accept the fact that the rich junk dealer Harry Brock would be proud to have such a woman as his live-in.

In its original production dumb-blonde Billy played by Judy Holiday gets wised up by reporter Paul Verrall to Beltway D.C. politics and eventually takes down Harry Brock and his political cronies. Sure, the original production worked beautifully and ran for 1,642 performances. But isn't the bar raised and the stakes higher if instead of the stereotype dumb blonde bimbo, she's an uneducated African-American whose ancestors were slaves? And wouldn't it take even more courage on her part to allow herself to fall for a guy who's a newspaper reporter and just happens to be white? And know that *her choice, as a black woman,* will be to deal with the prejudice she is bound to encounter—even by her own race and sex. And wasn't that the same thing that happened to Lena Horne?

I was in New York hoping to cast the nearest thing I could find to a Lena Horne look-alike. Obviously, getting the right actress was not easy, not when the pay was $150 a week, she would be coming out to West Lafayette, Indiana, and the gig would last only a month—two weeks of rehearsal and two of performance. In my favor, however, was how few young black actresses ever got a chance to play this role On, Off, or Off-Off Broadway or even in the remotest regional theatre?

I finally found a young woman, Lee Kirk, and it didn't take a rocket scientist to see she had the kind of looks I was looking for. But what about the talent? I asked her to read sections of the play and to do improvisations so I could judge potential skills, plus sensitivity-intelligence- imagination factor to see if I thought she had the right stuff. The answer was yes. So I cast her and she would be the first, and as far as I knew, *only* black Billy Dawn.

Lee did one hell of a great job.

It wasn't easy to find a Harry Brock, the rich junk dealer, either. The guy had to be a good-looking roughneck capitalist who made it in the junk business, yet someone who is probable for Billy Dawn to hook up with. Sure, he thinks of himself as a man in a man's world but he's not a mean SOB. It just never occurred to him that a woman would even be interested in the things men are interested in. And she's not just a sex kitten for him; he really likes her, likes the challenge of her and hates to be beaten by her in gin rummy.

The guy Connie and I found was maybe a little young for the role, but I recognized him from Kazan's *The Changeling* rehearsals. John Garces made a hell of a good Harry Brock. He had been in only one Broadway production, *Diamond Orchid* (1965) directed by Jose Quintero which lasted five performances. I never heard of him again after our production. What happens to young talent like John? Do they just give up and do something else?

The role of Paul Verrall is also not easy to cast. It takes a guy who can wear glasses, but whose package matches his brain and to whom Billy Dawn is attracted. For this role I cast young Thomas Connolly, who had just finished a long Broadway run of Brian Friel's *Philadelphia, Here I Come.* He was excellent. And it also must be noted in passing that Peter Schneider played a one-line waiter; yes, the same Peter Schneider who headed Disney's animation during its *Lion King*'s glory days and also served as president of the whole shebang for some time.

The result of all this thought and planning? This production was very *interesting* (hateful word to use backstage after viewing a show) but it *was* interesting because the casting brought so many values to the work that were not in the original. In September 1968 it was interesting; but does that justify the change? On reflection over the years I'm not at all sure it did.

A director's duty is to serve what is written by subsuming, emotionally and intellectually, what the writer of the piece created. In *Of Mice and Men*, that is what I actually did by going back to the original creator's creation. However, in *Born Yesterday* the entertainment value was most important, and that included both emotion and intellect. With my casting, the audience's focus was on the issues of race and sexual relationships. Those issues nullified and limited a lot of the laughter. What I should have said to myself was, "If that's what you're interested in, Joe, go write your own damn play! Changes are easy. It's the doing that's the bitch in showbiz!

But I was on some kind of what I thought of as a creative kick after my recent trip, especially after the Grotowski production in Poland. Or maybe it was the effect of a few tokes with a couple of my grad student buddies—and yes, I did inhale. In a way, the same thing I now questioned about my *Born Yesterday* also happened on *All My Sons*.

I had seen the original production in New York and loved it. Again, ours was an "interesting" production. but my "concept" of an all-gold set that visually stuck it to greed and capitalism was already obvious in the Arthur Miller text. Clearly, a decision to sell defective airplane parts for the purpose of "getting ahead," "making a buck," for *his* sons boomerangs because Joe Keller would eventually be forced to face the fact that one of those planes was piloted by his eldest son and had gone down in flames. Now Joe Keller understands.

Louis Girard played Joe and had difficulty with this classic recognition scene because there is so little time given to it after he recognizes the truth. All he says of his older son's death is, "I guess to him they were all my sons. And I guess they were. I guess they were" and goes into the house and we hear the shot. Unlike in *Death of Salesman* where Willy is given a scene in which he recognizes the truth of himself, makes his final decision accompanied by supportive music, and as Linda fearfully calls from the bedroom, Willy runs offstage, the car is heard starting, Biff runs downstairs shouting "Pop," and the music swells to a climax when we hear the sound of the crash.

We plainly solved the problem of the short period after Joe knows the truth and kills himself by letting the very talented Mary Hara, who played Joe's wife, feel great pity and fear for him when their younger son starts to tell his father the truth about his brother's death. She is fearful of what might happen, and when he goes into the house and the shot is fired her extraordinary vocal release did what tragedy is supposed to do. It nullified the emotion of pity by terror and left the audience drained.

Why should I have felt the necessity of hitting the audience over the head with the concept of a gold setting when the tragedy of Joe Keller was already illustrated by Arthur Miller's plot and characters and obvious to everyone? Jerry William's design was brilliant; my concept was wrongheaded. I know it now just as I knew it soon after the production.

⌘ ⌘ ⌘

Life Happens! On November 3, 1968, a beautiful baby, Larkin Anne (for Anne Revere) Stockdale, was born at St. Elizabeth's in Lafayette, Indiana. I remember how happy I was to have the symmetry and closure of another girl—bookends, first Laurel and last Larkin—with three boys in between. Holding and caring for a baby always regenerates a very special kind of love in a man—which is probably instinctive for most women—caused by the exercise of his ability to provide for a *totally* dependent human being and then rewarded by looks—always looks—that accompany giggles, coos, smiles and burps. Larkin was a wonderful baby, just as was Lory.

⌘ ⌘ ⌘

As chair of the theatre, I now faced administrative problems which were unique. As an artistic director I had the authority of enforcement of the bottom line, which I was not only familiar with but damn good at. But in the academy, the administrator is subject to the absolute rule—the authority—of the tenured professors of each department as long as they do not violate the rules of the academy, the state, or nation. *Robert's Rules of Order* was standard use for the democratic operation of faculty affairs in each Department. The result is what we have in the three branches—administrative, legislative, and judicial—of government, which fosters "politics" and "politicians" who operate within the Beltway and are subject to money, lobbying, and manipulation.

On the other hand, power corrupts and absolute power corrupts absolutely. So dictatorship in the academy is out as a form of government—except in art. Those who create architecture, literature, visual art and sculpture, music, dance and theatre might or might not listen to all advice. But eventually whoever paints the picture or composes the music, or directs the play has the final say, and the work of art must stand on that final judgment. Chairing the Theatre section of the Creative Arts Department was not easy for me. In fact, Gene Kildahl and I were actually, if not so named, co-chairs, he in academics and me in artistic matters.

The first problem I had was when I hired Wayne Lamb, who was without a college degree, full time to not only choreograph musicals, but to teach classes in dance. He had a tenure track line and membership on the faculty. Obviously, he had to have a place to teach. The only suitable space was The Loeb Playhouse stage and the criterion was established by AEA: it had a wooden floor.

The Loeb Playhouse was given to the University specifically for use by Purdue Playshop, which meant that a campus building would be controlled by the Theatre faculty who would be responsible for opening doors, turning on the lights, and closing and turning off the lights. In the Hall of Music were IATSE union members who worked all the national tours imported by Convocations and Lectures. They were overseen by the Hall's manager, John Ditamore, to do everything necessary within overseer parameters.

Since most of my duties were concerned with the Experimental Theatre in the basement, I didn't pay much attention to the tension resulting between Ross Smith and John Ditamore. The first time I felt animosity toward the Music Hall Union members was when one came to check fireproofing on my production of *The Diary of Anna Frank* and waterproofed the straw of the pussycat's cage, causing havoc for the first act which has been previously described.

But why was the theatre being charged for this Hall of Music inspector? The result was that through years of low-level conflict the Theatre head and staff no longer had keys to enter the stage of The Loeb for rehearsals or load-ins Now with a legitimate university-authorized dance class, why should the theatre pay to have a union man open and close the stage door?

I went to President Hovde, who understood that we had to have access for the class, and occasional use by other classes for rehearsals, especially for my up-and-coming Grotowski experiment. We felt we were professional and trustworthy enough to have a key to open the goddamn door.

In the greater picture, the theatre—both the student and the Professional Theatre—had been acknowledged by local and Indianapolis theatre critics as the best in the state. It had won support of the scientists and mathematicians in HSSE, all the administrators and faculty of the new Krannert School of Business Management, Engineering, including the powerful Aeronautical section (think of Purdue's reputation for astronauts), and later in statements by John Hicks, President Hovde's assistant.

But other, lesser forces were at work. We did not have the full support of the English Department. They argued that for the money spent on the professional theatre they could hire two or three full professors. University Treasurer Freehafer, who sided with Ditamore and the Hall of Music staff, had greater knowledge and insight of the constant struggle between the four state educational institutions in convincing a very conservative Legislature of the need for their support. He clearly viewed the professional theatre, which he seldom, if ever, attended, as a non-essential.

As an administrator I hated this kind of political/power struggle. I did not have the temperament to fight these issues, nor did Gene Kildahl. While winning the battle for the Loeb stage key, I distinctly remember being told that I may have won the battle, but would lose the war. I now had to have a place to rehearse *Oedipus/Antigone:* a dance/movement production which needed the wooden floor and the space of the Loeb stage for rehearsals. But this was, perhaps understandably, in reflection, about as important to the University, in Freehafer's view, as if the Ag Campus wanted to graft tits on a tomcat.

⌘ ⌘ ⌘

Oedipus/Antigone, scheduled for December 11-20, was based on the texts of Sophocles' *Oedipus Rex, Oedipus at Colonus* and *Antigone*. I directed, Jerry Williams designed the setting, Lyn Carroll, the costumes, and Randy Earle the lighting. We limited the actors to one dozen. The purpose of it was so reported in the show's program.

On 18 April, 1968 at the *Teatr Laboratorium* in Wroclaw, Poland, I saw a performance of Calderon's *The Constant Prince* adapted by the Polish writer, J. Slowacki (Yes, the same nineteenth century writer whose play, produced in Warsaw last year, criticized the USSR. Its withdrawal by the government caused the student riots).... for three days I talked with Pascal Monod and Ludwik Flaszen of the theatre staff and with students Jean Irwin (US), Francois Mirante (France) and Ingegerd Hellner (Sweden) concerning the work of the *Teatr Laboratorium*. Although there have been a few articles published in English on the theories of Grotowski *(Tulane Drama Review*, Vols. 24, 27, 56 and *Realities*, October, 1968) and he was a guest lecturer at the Professional Theatre Department at NYU for four weeks in November 1967, comparatively little is known of his work in our country. Perhaps we have felt his influence most through English director Peter Brook....

The "work in progress" tonight is frankly experimental and in the Grotowski manner, although our own problems have taken precedence over strictly derivative theories. This is as it should be. As Pascal Monod said when asked if he were going back to France to establish a school in the Grotowski manner: "no, each theatre in each region has its own problems and must arrive at its own solutions." Although it would be impossible to attempt to explain the manner in which we worked, we can share with you some of the ideas and questions.

Relevance: The performance presents a study of power: the causes of power, the retention of power, the corruption of power, and finally power vs. chaos. The scenario is a collaboration of director and actors after intensive study of the three plays. Causality, rather than being brought up as exposition in dramatic form, is linearized [historically sequential] into epic form. The scenario is then improvised by the actors, exploring all possibilities of action, including additional material brought in from their own backgrounds and experiences.

Since art evolves only when improvisation meets form, there is then a selective process of what to keep and what to discard in both the scenario and the montage. But *who* is to select? Thus, the nature of power is not only the backbone of the work, but we are all involved in and confronting power, the very thing we are illustrating. This is our artistic ethic.

Questions: What is distinctively theatre? Has the theatre borrowed too much from other media so that it has composited itself out of its true identity? More and more we come to understand that theatre *per se* exists only in the confrontation between actor and spectator—all else is irrelevant. The spectator, then, plays in the uniqueness which is theatre. Have we allowed [the spectators] the proper place outside of the proscenium arch? (Before another penny is spent on new Fine Art Centers this question should be answered, for it affects all theatre architecture.) What is the best arrangement of space for actor and spectator? Does it differ with each individual play? Yes. The space allotment must depend on the role the audience is to play and the nature of that role in relation to the central idea of the work of art. Should the role of the audience be one of passive involvement or active involvement? Does active involvement turn an audience off!

How are ritual and myth related to the uniqueness of theatre? What is the historical relationship? Is the Church dead and is it now time for the theatre to once again be the purveyor of these seemingly indispensable needs of mankind: myth and ritual? The search is always for truth. But have certain psycho-physical conditions (chairs and backs; telling our children not to lie when they introduce us to their imaginary companions) inhibited what may be the actor's truth in voice, body and mind? If so, can the mind and body stretch beyond what they now feel are their limitations? What exercises are best to achieve this stretch? Yoga? Actors Studio "private moments"? Meierhold's bio-mechanics?

Discovery and self-knowledge are ends, what are means? How can one learn to recreate the stimuli which produced a certain response (effect)? Acting is recreating what has been created—that's the whole bag. But how? And not only HOW, but how at a certain time each evening and two matinees a week? (An actor must create whether he feels like it or not.)

One acts for Truth—not for the audience (exhibitionism) or for oneself (self-indulgence). But what is the Truth of the performance and how does one achieve it? Should the confrontation between the actor's intellect and the text be kept from the audience? "I don't buy this motivation where Sophocles has Oedipus…"

Above are a few of the questions we have been trying to answer. The results? We don't know yet—it takes years before we even begin to know the questions.

JGS

Once again I come to a conclusion about directing: once a person has a first-rate approach to acting—as I had, studying with Laura Shaw—all that is needed is George Bernard Shaw's the "Art of Rehearsal" and Epps' translation of Aristotle's *Poetics*. Our Oedipus character was a newcomer to Purdue, a charismatic Randy Ade who rode a motorcycle and was in only two other productions that I remember. I would have bet that this would be the beginning of a Hollywood career for him. But in fact, although I have kept up with former students more than anyone else I know, I haven't a clue what happened to Randy. At any rate, this production, which was very *interesting*, concluded our fall season and we had won the battle of independence from union control of the space. But as we were to find out, we hadn't won the coming war.

Chapter 23

OUR WINTER SEASON CONSISTED OF a premiere of a musical of George Bernard Shaw's *You Never Can Tell* to be presented from February 11–March 1, 1969, followed by *The Little Foxes* from March 5–23. I loved turning Shaw's play into a musical, which also included bits and pieces from his *Misalliance*. I started on the book soon after I got *All My Sons* on and prior to *Oedipus/Antigone* rehearsals and had, curiously enough, received a resume from Julie Hayden postmarked from a little town in Wisconsin. I had seen her only once and that was as Laura in the original production of *The Glass Menagerie* on Broadway. But I knew she had played in *Shadow and Substance* and *The Time of Your Life* and other Broadway shows, and had been married to George Jean Nathan for the final three years of his life. She wanted to audition for the role of Birdie in our production of *The Little Foxes*.

I was stunned by the humility of this application, as if anyone would not know who she was when I thought of her as legendary. I answered immediately and told her that in addition to Birdie in *Foxes*, whoever was cast had to play the role of Mrs. Clandon in *You Never Can Tell*, a musical version, and I doubted that this would be right for her. She answered immediately and said she had recorded a couple of albums for Folkways. I thought she would be close to 70 years old but what the hell? She was a major star, and I would not think of insulting her by asking for an audition. I wrote telling her I would consider working with her an honor, and the AEA contract for $150 a week plus transportation was sent.

I held New York auditions with Connie Heaver. As the character Valentine we cast actor/singer Jay Stuart, who up to this point had no Broadway, Off Broadway, film or TV experience but who had a terrific voice, was a good actor, and had leading man looks and actions. He would be playing opposite Connie as Gloria, who was born to play the role. Eventually Jay's "career" would be three roles on Broadway including a revival of *The Music Man* (1980), and understudy for the leading role of Harold Hill. I would have sworn he would have made it big time. By now, however, having been in the business of training young talent, I know that all of the attributes that Jay possessed, and that are necessary, do not necessarily mean success in show business where ninety percent of "success" is luck of the draw.

The same was true for the juvenile, young Michael Stoddard who played Phillip. An actor/singer, he had just finished a short run in Tennessee Williams' three-character play, *The Seven Descents of Myrtle,* understudying leading man Brian Bedford. But after Purdue I could find nothing about him.

Finding a character man, always the most difficult to cast, was not so difficult this time because Robert Donley, who was in my *Long Day's Journey,* said he would love to play Crampton in *You Never* and Ben in *Little Foxes.* Thank our lucky stars that we auditioned David C. Jones for the wonderful role as the Waiter in *You Never* and could play Oscar in *Foxes.*

⌘ ⌘ ⌘

A brief catch-up necessary for understanding of the gathering storm: I had directed 67 shows in nine years. As artistic director of the Experimental Theatre, I had been producer of all the graduate student productions, which must have numbered at least 35; been responsible—except for Saroyan, Mark Connelly and Howard Bay—for bringing *all* the visiting artists to the campus; artistic director for the Summer Theatre as a non-Equity company, then under an AEA summer stock contract; then in 1967 expanding into a fall and winter 12 week season as a national Regional Professional Theatre Company under AEA's LORT contract.

I helped expand the Theatre department's curriculum from courses in speech to a point where we had a full professional curriculum, both undergraduate and graduate. I am listed in the course catalogue as teaching: Theatre Appreciation; Acting; Directing; Studies in Dramatic Structure; Comedy; Tragedy; Playwriting; The Development of the "Independent Theatre Movement"; Rehearsal and Performances; Directed Study of Special Theatre Problems; The History of Dramatic Theory and Criticism; Chekhov's Dramatic Art; and an Audio-tutorial in Play Analysis. And I had also assumed the responsibility of being Head of the Theatre program.

I had gone through Anne Revere's attempted suicide and my sister Rae's commitment to a mental institution. The truth was I was physically, mentally, and emotionally close to the end of my rope by January 1969 when I returned from the New York auditions and found out that son David, then almost 13, had startled to urinate blood. Robin took him to our doctor, who was uncertain of the cause.

Rehearsals for *You Never Can Tell* and a company read-through for *The Little Foxes* had begun and I was alarmed from the get-go and fearful that Julie Hayden simply did not have the chops to sing and act Mrs. Clandon, or to play Birdie. This was my fault for not having auditioned her. I kept hoping that things would improve as the first week of rehearsals progressed, but by Friday I knew I had to act.

We had auditioned an actress/singer in New York, Mary Nettum, who had a great singing voice and had been in three Broadway shows. I called her. She said she would be thrilled to come for the musical and especially thrilled to play Birdie. She could be here by Monday. I had to call Julie into one of the dressing rooms and in the presence of the stage manager explain that I would have to replace her. I cannot tell you how I dreaded doing this, and I was not certain of what to expect from her. When I had finished, she was completely understanding. She said she was sorry and that I was the best director she had ever worked for. I was incredibly vulnerable at this point and this just tore apart what was left of me.

At home, David's condition worsened. I told Robin we had to take him to the Children's Hospital in Indianapolis. We got an appointment with Dr. Carl Trigstat for a day during the next week when I would schedule music rehearsals only. Seeing his blood in the toilet made me almost beside myself with fear, which I dared not show David, or Robin who was nursing Baby Larkin.

What we thought would be a diagnosis at the hospital turned out to be a decision that it was necessity for him to be admitted for tests. We hadn't even brought his pajamas. Leaving him there alone that first time was almost unbearable.

In the next few days I blocked Mary Nettum into the scenes we had already completed, and she was absolutely first-rate. I visited David each day after rehearsals while Robin took care of the home front. I just fell apart each time I left him. David was an immensely likeable kid and the doctor and nurses loved him. I functioned on automatic pilot as the show progressed, and at my request, the stage manager told everyone I was under pressure and please not to mention anything dealing with my home situation.

Then Dr. Trigstat called and said we both should come to the hospital. David was diagnosed with acute kidney failure. Even all these years later as I write these words, the terror and sadness still live in me. The doctor told us, as gently as he could, that acute nephritis could be fatal. You have to realize that the first ever kidney transplant was just nine years earlier and that even if I was a donor, such an operation was still in the experimental stage and might not be successful. But the doctor said that there was a new experimental treatment that involved drugs that were still being tested. If David survived the experience all his hair might fall out and his sex organs might stop developing, so we would have to sign a waiver saying whatever happened we would not hold the hospital responsible. But the doctor said, "There is a chance." After struggling with our feelings, we signed.

While driving out of town I broke down completely and had to pull off the road. It was raining hard and difficult to see. We were very close to Frances Farmer's home, so we decided to go there. She was understanding of our grief and let us both fall apart. When we recovered she stressed our need to have absolute faith in the possibility of David's recovery. About "faith" she was a rock. I knew she was a devout convert to Catholicism, and that much of what she told us was based on her own life. Her incredible strength and support helped us that day and throughout the long ordeal.

I can't remember all of this well because the uncertainty of David's prognosis and treatment was the worst thing that had ever happened to us. Since the specifics of what had happened next at the theatre were really not as important to me as what we were going through at home, I am simply going to give you the facts.

⌘ ⌘ ⌘

February 5, 1969, I announced my resignation as Artistic Director of the Purdue Professional Theatre. What followed is included in Appendix B in this book, which I hope you will take the time to read. The letters and editorials are historic fact and should be read by anyone interested in the support for the professional theatre company. As I read over these documents after all these years, it seems to me that the Editor of *The Exponent,* in the second editorial on March 3rd, got it right when suggesting a good and workable solutions to the theatre's problems: applying for a National Arts and Humanities Foundation or Ford Foundation grant to fund the professional AEA company. But was that what the university treasurer wanted?

I had spoken the truth when I said that what I had done with the Professional Theatre had been done for love, and now I was no longer in love. I deeply appreciated the support which came from all sections of the university and the state. But Gerald MacLane's letter to the editor suggesting "some understanding and support" was needed in the one area—Freehafer's business office—which unfortunately trumped anything even President Hovde could do.

Our temporary battle to control our activity in The Loeb had been gained for classes and productions without the need of union stagehands—when we presented *The Visit, My Fair Lady,* and *Gypsy*—that were best viewed in a 1,200 seat house. This was important and necessary for the theatre program and for the training of our students. Now that this control was beginning to be lost, I told myself I still had the Experimental Theatre in which to operate. The majority of shows we produced were actually best viewed in that 187-seat house which was the best theatre I ever worked in, but only for a certain kind of theatre.

The face is the mirror of the mind, and the eyes are the mirror of the soul, and both revealed the secrets of the heart. Thus, the closer the actor is to the audience, the more the viewers will understand the thoughts of the character. That is why films and TV use close-ups, which arguably could mean that the best venue, not only for an audience's enjoyment but as a place to train actors, was the Experimental Theatre, because more of them will be involved in TV, film, regional, and Off and Off-Off Broadway houses than on Broadway. But of course, this was rationalization. We needed a full theatre training program which had to include The Loeb. But still half a slice of the pie was better than none.

⌘ ⌘ ⌘

There was another fight. The control of all ticket prices—including both The Loeb and Experimental Theatre—was unilaterally taken away from the theatre faculty by the business office. What followed next was that Randy Earle, the business manager of the theatre, my right-hand man and the backbone of productions, was disenfranchised and could no longer control any expenses for the theatre, including petty cash for meals for the actors between our two performances on Fridays and Saturdays, an AEA ruling, or film for our choice of photographer who recorded our productions. As I said previously, the specifics of this are detailed in Appendix B, which I urge you to read in order to understand the magnitude of the problem.

A year previous I still had some fight left in me, but realized that it was not sufficient for the continuing struggle. In fact, not only the control of The Loeb was usurped but for all intent and purpose the Professional Theatre program, as I had built it, was being taken away. The theatre faculty would no longer be able to control any financial aspect necessary to run such an operation, and it was finally obvious to me that this was the clear intent of the business office.

I would make it through the spring season of the Professional Theatre, but since I would no longer be able to function, I had to resign as artistic director. The backlash from the university faculty was not expected, and when it came it proved to be far too great for either administrators or the business office to ignore. The professional theatre was valued since theatre attendance, and good theatre, helped living in West Lafayette and even proved to be an attraction in getting the best faculty.

Within a couple of years our best faculty was replaced, and Randy Earle took a job at San Jose State University, where he eventually became chair of the department and served as president of the prestigious International Theatre Alliance. But what would my future hold?

⌘ ⌘ ⌘

After my experience with *Oedipus/Antigone*, which was interesting to those who worked on it, but less so for the audiences, I began to think again of my first love, writing. What I felt was most needed was a book on dramatic structure, so I set about filling my time with writing, finishing the book in the spring of 1975. A variation of it co-authored by David Letwin and Robin would be published in 2005 as *The Architecture of Drama*. But I still had one final play to direct for the professional theatre.

Although my mind was still taken up with David's illness, Lillian Hellman's *The Little Foxes* gave me something to think about and hold onto. Why did I like it? Why was it exciting theatre when so much of what was being taught as gospel, variously called post-modernism, Jacques Derrida's deconstruction, and the "new criticism," claimed that plays such as *Foxes'* were hopelessly old-fashioned.

Although constant thoughts of David's condition were undergirding my life, I could focus on the play's meaning, characters and their relationships, as well as the physical blocking. What I could not bear do was get into discussions with the cast because if anyone looked at me with even an iota of pity, or especially if they touched me—a laying on of sympathetic/

understanding hands to communicate that they knew what I was going through—I would simply fall apart and break down crying uncontrollably, which I could not allow to happen in rehearsals. The thing that held me together was automatic pilot, my ability to concentrate my focus on this production, which revealed itself on the least interrelation with cast members than any other play I had ever directed.

Larry Schumpert's review of *Foxes* appeared in *The Journal and Courier* under the headline: "*Little Foxes* Is Appropriate Swan Song for Stockdale." He wrote: "Lillian Hellman's 30-year-old play is an evening of engrossing theatre... populated by a lot of fine actors... and is the last play at Purdue that will be directed by Joseph Stockdale. It is a wonderful swan song... Stockdale says he has quit directing because of a running dispute with the business office over theatre finances. It is altogether fitting that he should end his Purdue directing career with a play about money."

March 14th, *The Exponent* review by William Newport was headed: "'Little Foxes' Dramatically Depicts Family Struggle." This excellent review started with "Under Joseph Stockdale's sure direction, The Purdue Theatre Company's current production of Lillian Hellman's 'The Little Foxes' proves that the 30-year-old drama still has impact and audience appeal...."

On March 28th, in the *Journal and Courier's* Letters to the Editor, was one written by distinguished professor and official biographer of Summerset Maugham, Richard A. Cordell of the English Department. Under the heading, "Dramatic Achievement," he wrote: "If a stranger in Lafayette after hearing the current argument over the educational classification of Purdue—is it a real university or a training institution—were to attend a performance of 'The Little Foxes' he would be puzzled. It would seem most unlikely to him to see the near flawless production of one of the best American plays ever, to appear in the campus theatre of a teleological institute."

And now to backtrack, but still on the subject of the reception of the Purdue Professional Theatre's productions under my direction. On Friday March 1st, on the next to the last performance of *You Never Can Tell*, Henry Hewes, distinguished drama critic for *The Saturday Review*, came from New York to review our production that preceded *The Little Foxes*.

In his article, "'Pros' and Cons," published on March 15, 1969 (p. 22) he wrote:

"The company's artistic director, teacher Joseph Stockdale, has just finished staging a new musical comedy version of Shaw's *You Never Can Tell*, which captures the charm of an English seaside resort in the 1890s. Although it is not a very good play, it does contain one marvelous role, that of the elderly waiter whose skill and tact make all the other characters seem foolish by comparison.

The musical, as adapted by Stockdale, emphasizes the romantic undercurrents in the script, and even brings together at the end, as Shaw did not, the play's two most irreconcilable characters. The music by Roz Aronson, wife of a Purdue professor, is melodic and excellent, with "If You Walk With Me" the most memorable of several lovely ballads. Though serviceable and singable, Stuart Howard's lyrics are less impressive. And this is perhaps the first musical ever to use its title song only during the curtain call.

Although the performances by a company chosen primarily for its ability to act in a variety of speaking roles are quite understandably best during the non-singing parts of the action, the song deliveries turn out to be agreeable and competent. As the waiter David C. Jones is amusingly imperturbable, Connie Heaver, as the immovable maiden, and Jay Stuart, as the irresistible impecunious dentist who pursues her, are attractive and vital. And Robert Donley as the terrible tempered father, and Angelo Mango, as the clear thinking lawyer who saves the day, both give strong portrayals.

Is there a future for this musical? Certainly in its present form it, like the play, suffers from an unclear attitude and a scattered romantic focus. Yet it compensates for these lacks for its old-fashioned charm and its one very playable character. Perhaps with a bit more ruthlessness on the part of its adapter (after all, the play is in public domain), it could become a thoroughly delightful intimate musical.

⌘ ⌘ ⌘

I was pleased by all the attention and reviews both plays of our spring season received. As for me personally, I felt honored and humbled by the outpouring of support at the local level and throughout the state for what had been accomplished through my efforts over the last decade. But in *fact and truth*, I was glad to let someone else come in and take over. In the end Robin was still nursing Larkin, and Son David survived and thrived; it was the experimental medicine and a great children's kidney specialist, Dr. Trigstat, who made the miracle happen that saved David's life.

I was no longer in rehearsals. I taught my 12 hours per week as did everyone else. And once it was decided, or rather I should say forced by the opinion of the faculty, that the Purdue Professional Theatre Company was indeed an important adjunct for the campus, a department search committee used in the hiring of *academic* personal—of which I asked not to be included—was formed to find my successor. The choice of the majority of the tenured-track members in agreement with the Dean's office was the affable Michael Flanagan of the Loretto Hilton Repertory Company in St. Louis; a new head of the Creative Arts Department was also selected by yet another *academic* committee, Mr. Robert Forth.

Michael lasted one year; Robert, two.

Chapter 24

IN THE PREFACE OF THIS book I quoted Aristotle's *Poetics* as to the differences between a poet and an historian. In this chapter I'll deal with the history of what happened after my resignation in as objective a manner as possible. I've always been interested in history. What follows are the facts during the 1970/1971 academic year.

But before I start I wish to make clear that although Michael Flanagan brought in four AEA actors under Equity's visiting artist contract for his first production, a professional AEA company *never again existed on the Purdue campus*, however the powers that be—some from understandable ignorance and others by calculated design—attempted to pass on the lie that there was.

September 9, 1969, Fremont Power, critic for *The Indianapolis News* wrote:

> In a rather raunchy little set-to between what might be called business and art, it appeared last spring that Purdue University's resident professional theatre might be kaput. It would have been a shame. By bringing in resident pros and blending them into student casts, Professor Joseph Stockdale had achieved a training program in dramatics and a theatre unmatched in this state.
>
> He was playing James Earl Jones in "Of Mice and Men" when Jones was known primarily only to those in the business. It was later that he was cast in New York as that old Negro fighter, Jack Johnson, in "The Great White Hope" and became a Broadway

and national celebrity. But Lytle J. Freehafer, Purdue treasurer, didn't like the way James Randolph Earle was handling things as Purdue's Theatre business manager. And so Freehafer put out a memo that hence fourth, Earle's signature would not be honored anywhere in Freehafer's jurisdiction.

With this, Professor Stockdale quit as the theatre's artistic director, declaring his business manager had been de-jobbed, which he certainly had. John W. Hicks, executive assistant to the Purdue President, said at the time "we may have to find a new director... but the administration's going to try to save the theatre." Well, summer has come and nearly gone, September is here and football coach Jack Mollenkopf has spoken approvingly of "hearing 'em hit" out on the Purdue practice fields. And the Purdue theatre is intact, with a new director, Michael Flanagan, and a new business manager, Frank Schmitt. The season will open Oct. 9, with "A Midsummer Night's Dream," with four professionals in the cast

"We wanted to keep it," Hicks said of the theatre. "We're proud of it." And he confided there was another factor beside the obvious one of not disassembling what had become a considerable achievement: "It certainly helped with keeping faculty."

Flanagan comes to West Lafayette from St. Louis, where he founded the repertory theatre at the Loretto Hilton Center for the Performing Arts and was Chairman of the Theatre Arts Department at Webster College. In the '64-65 season, he was playing Broadway in "Absence of a Cello."

Schmitt is a stage and company manager whose credits include the road company of "Porgy and Bess" (Clowes Hall, 1957) and touring with Gordon and Sheila McRae before they went their separate professional and marital ways. His stage management regiment includes the Dunes and Flamingo Hotels in Las Vegas.

Flanagan had decreed a modern tone for the opening "Midsummer" production and has commissioned some original rock music by Donald Heckman, Stereo Magazine who has done several movie scores.

Professionals in the cast will be Jill Tanner, English actress; Rona Dingle, recently in a west coast version of "Plaza Suite" directed by Mike Nichols; Barry Bostwick, member of the APA Theatre in New York, and Patrick Fox, Columbia Records vocalists.

And so the Purdue is not only alive, but stirring. Even Professor Stockdale will direct three of its works during the season and ex-business manager Earle is still there as technical director. Let us hear it for the old Gold and Black.

⌘ ⌘ ⌘

Of the four professionals hired under AEA visiting artist contract by Mr. Flanagan only twenty-four-year-old Barry Bostwick had appeared on Broadway (he was in two shows) prior to the summer of 1969 when Flanagan cast him in *Dream*. Whether it was a sharp eye for talent or simply luck of the draw, bringing Bostwick to the Purdue Campus was a real coup. What followed relates his career *after* his Purdue stint, when this gifted and charismatic talent achieved one of the most distinguished careers in the history of Broadway, film and television. He was a Golden Globe Award winner and chalked up half a dozen Broadway shows, including *Grease* (in which he originated the role of Danny Zuko), gained three nominations for Tony Awards and one win. In 1975 he was fortunate, or unfortunate enough, to be cast as Susan Sarandon's nerdy boyfriend in *The Rocky Horror Show*. Although he played many different kinds of characters in his career he is remembered mostly for being this glasses-wearing nerd named "Brad."

It is also important to know that *Midsummer* played from October 9-19, 1969, and Flanagan announced his season for the year in this program as follows:

"November 8-16, *Eh?* in the Experimental Theatre/Conservatory, directed by Bernie Passeltiner; December 12-18, *Bury the Dead* on The Loeb Stage/Conservatory, directed by Joseph Stockdale; February 5-March 15 in The Loeb Playhouse & Experimental Theatre, the Resident Theatre in Repertory, *King Lear*, directed by Joseph Stockdale; *Heartbreak House*, directed by Michael Flanagan; *A Flea In Her Ear*, directed by Joseph Stockdale; March 20 -27 in The Loeb Playhouse/Conservatory, *Celebration*, directed by Wayne Lamb; May 1-10, Loeb Playhouse/ Resident Theatre *The May-Day Spring Thing*, directed by Michael Flanagan."

In the above, "Resident Theatre" productions featured professionals augmented with students-in-training; "Conservatory" productions featured all-student casts under professional direction. I will not include the critical reception of the *Midsummer* production since Michael Flanagan will be quoted later on with his own reaction to this "mod" production.

⌘ ⌘ ⌘

Prior to David's illness and my resignation I had been thinking of writing Irwin Shaw to ask permission to produce his antiwar play *Bury The Dead*. But during the upset with the business office, I had not done so. When Michael Flanagan asked me what show I wished to direct for a "Conservatory" production in December, I remembered *Bury The Dead*. When it had been withdrawn soon after I was in the last production at Western Michigan, the author had explained his reasons in an article to the drama editor of *The New York Times*.

That letter became the program cover for our production, which is set "in the second year of the war that is to commence tomorrow night."

Several weeks ago I had to perform an unpleasant duty: I had to inform my agent to refuse permission to any group or person here or abroad to present my play, Bury the Dead. Perhaps it would be of interest to your readers to learn why a playwright feels he had to withdraw from possible production a fifteen year old play.

Bury the Dead was written in 1935 and produced in 1936. Since that time it has been done by many amateur collegiate groups and by little theatres throughout the country. It was a play that expressed the passionate revulsion against the horrors of war and the fear of another war which was so much a part of the emotional climate of the Nineteen-thirties, a revulsion that was reflected in such other war plays of the time as Idiot's Delight, Ten Million Ghosts, and Johnnie Johnson.

It also reflected a belief, which now seems impossibly naive, that by appealing to reason and sentiment war might be forever halted. Since then we have been forced into one war by men in Germany and Japan who clearly demonstrated their immunity to reason and sentiment. As a soldier I saw enough of the agony of war to make my original revulsion stronger than ever. Putting on my civilian clothes once more, I put on my civilian beliefs in the possibility of peace to reason and sentiment.

Now, five years later, the rulers of Russia have demonstrated that the gentle hopes of 1950 are as naive as they were in 1935. In invading, killing, destroying, they proclaim with monstrous cynicism that they are the supporters of worldwide peace. In a spectacle of complete moral corruption their adherents in this country wave peace pledges and petitions while communist guns are killing American soldiers.

It is to balk these double tongued gentlemen, with whatever small means are at my disposal, that I have withdrawn my play. I do not wish the forlorn longings and illusions of 1935 to be used as ammunition for the killers of 1950. I still hope passionately for peace— but peace that is selective and divisible at will, not peace that is a political slogan and a military instrument, but peace that is real, general and complete.

Irwin Shaw, Quoque, L. I.

His answer?

"Dear Professor Stockdale: Thank you for your letter… in regard to Bury The Dead. I am willing to let you put it on at the Purdue University Theatre.

Yours truly, Irwin Shaw. Hotel Ritz, New York."

At Purdue there had been one sit-in at the hiring office against Dow Chemical of Midland Michigan, manufacturers of Agent Orange. I was a sympathetic participant until I had to meet a scheduled class. There was also a protest against the tuition raise that met resistance from the campus police, who arrested over 200 students. There were also small flair-ups about Marine recruitment on campus. In an article in *Newsweek* about "hotbeds of unrest" at various U. S. colleges, Purdue was cited for its distinction as a "hotbed of student rest."

The first moratorium to end the Vietnam war was on October 15, 1969, followed by the first national moratorium on November 15th in Washington D.C. On December 12th, when we opened *Bury The Dead,* there was the first moratorium on the Purdue campus. We opened to a packed Loeb Playhouse, which was unusual. We received an extraordinary response with interruptions of applause and shouts from the audience, and by the time the lights came down on this one-act, which lasted an hour and a half, there was a standing ovation. But there were also some members of the audience heading up the aisle in disgust. We got this dual response at each performance.

The production undoubtedly pissed off various administrators who were in a position to make Michael Flanagan's job difficult, but there can be no denying that it was one hell of a hit with most of the students, and better attended than the "mod" "professional" production of *Midsummer Night's Dream,* the one production directed by the new artistic director during his year in residence.

⌘ ⌘ ⌘

When school commenced in early January, I had three students come to my office and tell me they had been thinking of trying out for *Dracula*—now a substitute production for the original schedule announced by Flanagan and published in the *Midsummer* program. But these students had heard that nudity would be required in the auditions. This was the first I had heard about it and I walked a tightrope in my reply. Of course, I did not think it proper to require college students to strip naked at call-outs. On the other hand, I had been very careful since my resignation to stay aloof from faculty conflicts during the fall that had caused Flanagan to make the schedule change.

I never understood why he wished to leave his three year old position at Loretto Hilton, since he had to know that the AEA contracted professional theatre at Purdue was kaput, or why he was the choice of the Purdue search committee as the new head. I advised the concerned students to talk to Father Melvin, a young liberal Catholic priest who was a personal friend, and I'm pretty certain this matter was also called to Dean Ogle's attention.

On Thursday, January 29, 1970 the following article appeared in the *Journal and Courier*:

Behind-Theatre Scenes
Staff 'Differences of Opinion' Drop Curtain on Four Plays

Purdue University's Professional Theatre Program will substitute four student productions for four professional cast plays originally scheduled during the second semester.

M. B. Ogle Jr., Dean of Purdue's school of Humanities, Social Science and Education, said the canceling of the professional productions stemmed from unreconciled differences of opinion about operating procedures among the theatre's staff members.

Dean Ogle sent a letter of explanation along with the theatre's announcement to season ticket holders, promising them refunds for the unused part of their subscription. The theatre program operates as a section of the Humanities School.

In his letter, Dean Ogle said the cancellation in no way reflected any shortage of financial support by the public or the university.

Michael Flanagan, the theatre's executive director, said the revised production schedule called for a world premiere of "Dracula" adapted by Leon Katz from Bram Stoker's novel, and the Award Winning Musical "Guys and Dolls." Both will show in Loeb Playhouse.

From its run from Feb. 24 through March 8, "Dracula" will have as its guest director Word Baker, who directed the original production of "Fantasticks." Guest designers will be Lloyd Burlingame [this did not happen] and Caley Summers.

Wayne Lamb, the theatre staff choreographer, will direct "Guys and Dolls" in its run from April 23 through May 2. Two other productions, to be in the Experimental Theatre in March and April with all-students casts, will be directing projects of graduate students. The April 6-8 show will be Chekhov's "Uncle Vanya."

Under the original schedule for the season, professional casts were to have presented a mid-repertory series of three plays: "King Lear," "Heartbreak House," and "A Flea In Her Ear." The professional spring production in May had not been selected.

The "Guys and Dolls" production will be a replacement for the previously scheduled musical "Celebration."

The Journal and Courier, Lafayette, Ind. [Feb. 4, 1970]

Department Split on Philosophy

Flanagan To Resign As Head of Theatre at Purdue

By Larry Schumpert

After only six months at Purdue, Michael Flanagan has announced he is resigning this spring as executive director of the university theatre program.

Flanagan, who came here from Webster College in St. Louis, said he was leaving because of frustration over direction taken by Purdue's theatrical efforts. He will supervise a production of "Dracula" that opens February 24 in Loeb Playhouse and continue teaching his theatre courses for the rest of this semester.

Flanagan said he made known his decision to some people in the theatre department on Jan. 1, and that it had no direct connection to last week's announcement of a drastic overhaul in this semester of plays. As a result of the shake-up, four plays using professional actors were replaced by four all-student productions.

SOME CONNECTION

But there obviously is some kind of connection between the two announcements, and it involves Flanagan's concept of a university theatre program. The experienced director had hoped to "integrate" professional and amateur talent in Purdue's theatre curriculum, much as he did at Webster College.

"I thought Purdue wanted this also," he said Monday, "but now I don't know exactly what is wanted here."

"The theater is changing greatly today," he went on, "and I think it's necessary for a university to bring representatives *of the real theatre* [my italics] onto the campus. There has to be a balance of the two -- amateur and professional. That's the direction I see for theatre education in this country."

Flanagan thinks students want to salvage some of their ties to professional theatre, because it gives them, "a standard of excellence." But the integration he speaks of involves more than student's rubbing shoulders with professional actors on a college stage. Purdue has mixed the two for several years in its professional theatre seasons and its use of name actors as "guest stars" in student plays.

TOTAL INTEGRATION

Flanagan, however, thinks the integration should involve every aspect of the campus theatre program. This is the only way, he argues, that a college theatre can remain current with the "real theatre" off campus. "It's difficult to keep a theatre relevant," he said, "when you're removed from a large metropolitan area. There is always the danger of it becoming static." Flanagan directed one play at Purdue that used both students and professionals -- the mod production of "A Midsummer Night's Dream." He says now it encountered trouble "on many levels" and he was quite unhappy with it.

As a result he decided to change things this semester and bring in more professional talent. During December he worked on what he called his "new season" and went to New York to scout for professionals. One of the actors he had in mind was John Voight, the appealing young man who reached sudden prominence last year in the film "Midnight Cowboy."

NO CONFIDENCE

But when he returned from New York in January, Flanagan walked into what he described as "unrest" among members of the theatre faculty. He asked for a vote of confidence in what he was trying to do, and the faculty wouldn't give it to him, he said.

It was, according to one university official, "a deep and fundamental difference of opinion among the faculty of the theatre concerning operations, procedures and professional values."

So the faculty drew up a new season of its own, switching to four student productions including a musical this spring directed by choreographer Wayne Lamb. For Lamb it's getting to be an old story. This makes the second theatre director to be shot out from over him in the last year.

Earlier in 1969 Dr. Joseph Stockdale resigned as artistic director of the Purdue University Theatre [*sic*] because of a dispute over theatre finances. Lamb took up some of the slack with a spring production of "Leave It to Jane," a vintage musical comedy that goes back to the first World War. This spring he'll try to help salvage a season with "Guys and Dolls."

INDECISION CITED

As for Flanagan he calls the faculty changes "a major departure from the kind of program I was brought here to do. The first thing Purdue needs to do about its Theatre program," he added, "is decide what it wants to do. A college theatre should not content itself with just churning out plays," he said. "It shouldn't be simply a play factory which exists for the sake of doing plays. It should experiment." "There is great freedom in a campus theatre," Flanagan said, "because there isn't the financial pressure you have in professional theatre. You don't have to worry about having a hit. We should use that freedom.

Feb. 6 1970: The Purdue Exponent

By Marsh Roush

University Theatre will lose their executive director this June when Michael Flanagan's recently announced resignation becomes effective. With Flanagan will go Frank Schmitt, publicity manager, and Bernie Passeltiner, instructor and director.

Flanagan has said he is leaving Purdue for a number of reasons. He is not satisfied with merely "choosing a season of plays"; rather he would have liked, and indeed tried, to make "a selection of a series of experiences to involve people." He explains that "a dialogue needs to be created between professionals and students and this happens on many levels." With this dialogue Flanagan said, students not only learn acting but learn about people as well.

Flanagan was formerly artistic director at Webster College in St. Louis, where he said he could "have an idea and was given a chance to use it. I am not a traditionalist—I am an innovator," he said.

The ideal situation for a professional theatre is if the theatre "can move to a shelter where they are free from money problems, then they can do 'research' like in other fields. They can open avenues for new ideas and find new ways to solve old problems," Flanagan said.

Stating the facts the way they appear to him, Flanagan said, "This University does not move in any direction. I wanted to experiment with something that would creatively involve the students." Thinking into the future, Flanagan plans to go to New York to "recharge my battery and get back into the swing of things."

Schmitt, publicity manager for the theatre, also considered handing in his resignation in December and in Christmas break he made a final decision to leave Purdue. The reason for leaving, Schmitt said, was that, "I don't dislike Purdue, but I don't think it is possible to get what I want here because of the nature of Purdue. It takes a long time to accomplish something, and I am not willing to spend that kind of time."

He also made it clear that he did not wish to "indict any one person," but he just wanted to get back to the commercially professional world.

"I have had my fill of academia," Schmitt said.

Schmitt came to Purdue, he said, after receiving a request from Flanagan to join him. At the time he was working with Word Baker at the Playhouse in the Park in Cincinnati. Baker is currently working on the upcoming "Dracula" presentation.

Passeltiner, who teaches acting to both graduates and undergraduates and who also directed a play this fall, was the third man in the theatre to hand in his resignation. Passeltiner gave his reasons for leaving as the institution itself. "I thought that the theatre at Purdue is not an important picture here." To Passeltiner this meant the institution was not willing to give the theatre the kind of money it needed to work with. "There was no chance to try to do the things I wanted to do."

Passeltiner made a remark on a statement made by the board of Trustees on the enrollment policy which discouraged Passeltiner for building up the Art school. The statement (Exponent, Sept. 12th) said "enrollment of freshmen will have to be limited to the academic curriculum unique to Purdue." John W. Hicks, executive assistant to the President, also said in the article that the university would "do its best to accept all qualified Indiana students to the unique professional schools such as pharmacy, agriculture, and engineering."

Passeltiner is now planning to go back to New York along with Flanagan and Schmitt and concentrate on professional work. "I am not going back to a school for a while," he commented. The resignation came some 14 months after Joseph Stockdale quit as the theatre's artistic director. Stockdale too had become irate over university business practices.

⌘ ⌘ ⌘

What was Purdue like in February 1970? The editor of the student newspaper *The Exponent* wrote the following editorial on the 25th, the day after opening night of *Dracula*.

> Please be very quiet this year. Few can forget the tumultuous events of last year. We passed through issue after issue with argument and action. People were involving themselves as never before in The Exponent crisis, in the fee decision movement.
>
> This year we have had only a ticking alarm clock thrown at Marine recruiters. Nothing has excited interest; very little has incited action. The campus seems to have gone back to the 'hothead of student rest' Newsweek called it two years ago.
>
> The issues are still there—they're just as crucial as they were last year. Even more crucial, actually, because a year has passed without solutions.
>
> Why the silence?
>
> One major cause is the emotional backlash among students from last spring's movement. The fee increase was a valid issue bringing into question the misuse of power by so few in a matter affecting so many. Students were hit hard financially, and responded as never before by boycotting, sitting in, marching in the Capitol, and living in the Union.
>
> The result? A $300-400 tuition increase and 229 arrests. And a bad taste in the mouth of supporters at the defeat of a just cause. So the great majority of the students, with the memory of a disintegrated movement and fruitless involvement are back to football games and beer parties. It's easier... Serious protests will be crushed....
>
> The Trustee's resolution providing automatic suspension for those involved in "destructive activity" is the most blatant form this attitude has taken. The stripping of faculty discipline over students, the anti-disturbance ordinance proposal in West Lafayette, the forced incorporation of the Exponent, police harassment of campus radicals—all have created psychological controls over involved students.
>
> The result is that these individuals have retreated from the line office. They realize that in a confrontation situation only a few people would be left standing up to the authorities, and so they've turned inward. They are not raising timely issues to a campus audience....

⌘ ⌘ ⌘

Now, after all the expense and hoopla about *Dracula*, the reviews.... Larry Schumpert on February 25, 1970 in the *Journal and Courier*, wrote:

'DRACULA' AUDIENCE TENSE, BUT EXPECTATIONS UNFULFILLED

The audience held its breath through much of "Dracula" Tuesday night expecting either to be sized by hallucinatory images or shocked by some disrobing Purdue coed showing it like it is. The anticipation provided most of the suspense at the opening in Loeb Playhouse, attended by a group of free-spirit students and jaded critics who literally packed the theatre. When the lights went out at 8:05p.m., they were still trying to squeeze in another reviewer or two from Indianapolis.

The tension was easily felt; especially when the play started so slowly and quietly that spectators became aware of one another's breathing patterns. During the first 10 minutes, while a chorus of witches glided from the sides of the altar toward the stage, the only thing that broke the silence was a series of good natured coughs.

Things picked up after that, but the expectations for this brand-new version of "Dracula" died in the audience. Despite a number of scanting scenes and some marvelous theatrical effects this production lacked the excitement and terror that had been promised.

All the clever lighting and spooky choreography of "Dracula" were unable to suggest much in the way of hallucinations or nightmares or even a good old fashioned bad dream. That tension in the audience never quite made it up on stage. And when the fair Lucy's head was chopped off and held aloft by the blonde tresses the audience reacted by laughing.

A FLASH OF NUDITY

As for the hysterical rumors of nudity in the production they too were somewhat disappointing. Throughout the evening the cast remained safely concealed by ample loincloths or choir robes, although there was a plethora of bare feet. Occasionally there was the exciting flash of a naked leg slipping out from behind the folds of a black gown. Like they say, it gets more interesting when you keep it covered up for a while. The only nudity in all this horror was a ritual scene in which Penelope Windust, a visiting professional actress who once played Melvin Douglas' daughter on Broadway, went topless for a few intriguing minutes. She was lovely.

Nevertheless the real attributes of "Dracula" were some exciting staging and sets by Ron Hall and Tom Oldendick, backed by a pulsating series of light effects by Charles Fletcher. The latter ranged from a projection onto the background of throbbing blood to a flickering sequence of lights that distorted the movement on stage and seemed to chop time up into little pieces.

Hall's scenic work was appropriately eerie and bathed in a deathly white light that achieved some of the feeling director Word Baker wanted for this production. But it failed to do something that might have made "Dracula" a lot more successful as an hallucinatory trip. That something would have been a spatial distortion offstage and players that might better have suggested the images in the mind's subconscious.

Instead "Dracula" presented a series of rituals and orgies more reminiscent of a gymnastics class than acts of exorcism or purgation. The dancing was frantic and enthusiastic, but like the rest of the play it didn't quite make it across the footlights to the audience. Everything was too slow, too self-conscious, too deliberate. The whole thing lacked atmosphere and it seemed devoid of spontaneity.

"Dracula" was something interesting to watch and puzzle over, but it needs to bridge a wide gap between sight and feeling. Its visual achievements have yet to be converted into emotional experience. Billed as a simulated trip on some exotic drug like LSD, "Dracula" has until March 8 to get off the ground.

Charles Staff, Drama Critic for *the Indianapolis News* **wrote:**

It's not uncommon for a production to get in the way of a play, but when a play gets in the way of a production, that's news. Last night in Loeb Playhouse, conservative Purdue University got a shock—"Dracula" in a version by Leon Katz based on the 1887 novel by Bram Stoker.

No stranger to the theatre, Stoker was the business manager for Sir Henry Irving, and the theatrical material inherent in the book is of its theme, overdrawn, overblown. The passing years have not helped with the parade of melodramatic films and purposely silly stage satires.

Katz and the director of the Purdue presentation, New York's Word Baker, were swimming upstream against a strong current awash with corn. As long as the play lay dormant, asleep, as it were, in its own coffin, Baker took Katz' script by the throat and, with an eye on Julian Beck and Judith Melina's Living Theatre, created electrifying moments.

Baker's credentials include the successful "The Fantasticks," and, most recently, the rock musical, "The Last Sweet Days of Isaac," which just opened in New York to raves.

Loeb was packed for the performance, which might be the first and last for reasons that will become evident. There had been rumors of nudity and, while these rumors proved only half true, at least two sequences were shocking enough to satisfy the curious.

The program listed Ron Hall as scenic designer, costumes by Caley Summers, lighting by Charles Fletcher and music by Worth Gardner and Gary Nelson, but the center force was Baker. The elements, excellently thought out and executed were all of a piece surely born, primarily, in his mind of one man.

BARE, BUT FOR A BIER

The play began with the curtain already up to reveal a steeply raked stage bare except for the bier. From the sides the cast, a coven of the "living dead" wrapped in black cloaks, slipped in one by one.

Then, in one of those electrifying moments, the figures formed a circle and started humming, at first almost inaudibly, then swelling to a frightening pitch, and the story began with the first bit of dialogue. All of this took at least 15 minutes or so, it seemed.

One, of the most fascinating devices was the use of a few of the hooded performers formed to make a coach and horses to drive Renfield, Dracula's first victim, to the count's castle. Done in about 90 minutes without intermission, the performance swept through the high points of Stoker's tale to the destruction of Dracula. Sections, or, as the playwright evidently called them, "events," were variously entitled, "Preparation," "Introit," "Witches Round," "Madman," "Rite" and "Betrayal," among others.

A black mass was celebrated; Dracula, in the form of the horned Satan, and another of his victims, Miss Lucy, consummated their unholy alliance and, later, the company, now with painted bodies, joined an explicit but stylized sexual orgy. At this last point, one could not help wondering whatever became of animal husbandry, electrical engineering and home economics at Purdue.

Only Penelope Windust, who enacted Miss Lucy with considerable conviction, appeared half naked but mass nudity would have been gilding the lily, even if it is improbable that witches and warlocks wear breechcloths and bras.

Every modern lighting trick was utilized. Strobe, black light, psychedelic lighting, rear projection and kaleidoscope effects. At the conclusion, the cast threw off the robes stood quietly dressed in jeans and t-shirts and departed up the aisle.

The acting core was provided by four professionals: Miss Windust; Bernie Passeltiner, an acting professor at Purdue who might consider dropping his German accent as Van Helsing; Charles Haid, as Seward and Donald Gantry, an excellent Renfield. The rest were students including Daniel Von Bargen who wisely underplayed Dracula.

Despite the honest evil created by Baker and his cast, Stoker's story brought giggles but everyone coped with the production and the play with skill, considering that conventional acting has little place in something of this sort.

Whether the production runs through March 8, remains to be seen, but Baker's method, like it or not, represents to a large degree, what advanced theatre is these days in sophisticated centers like Manhattan and Berlin, and wonder of wonders; it was Purdue that gave Hoosiers a glimpse.

⌘ ⌘ ⌘

Again, just the facts: When he came to Purdue, Flanagan's background in professional New York Theatre was a single credit: he acted on Broadway as a replacement in the role of Parry Littlewood in *Absence of a Cello*. In 1966 he became head of the Repertory Theatre of St. Louis at the behest of the Nuns who headed the theatre at this Catholic Girls School, Loretto Hilton. He came to Purdue three years later. After he left Purdue his New York career consisted of directing Off Broadway's *Rain* (1972) at the Astor Place Theatre, which lasted seven performances; *Ocean Walk* (1976) for Playwrights Horizons which ran for 11 performances, and *Boo Hoo* (1979) which may not have opened at all since the number of performances, as opposed to previews, is not listed. Michael (God bless him and I mean that sincerely) died at age 58 on March 31, 1993 of stomach cancer at his home in West Hollywood, California.

⌘ ⌘ ⌘

I believe I have been fairly objective in stating the above. Now I would like to make an observation about professionalism and Purdue. Professionalism was what Purdue was all about. Why then should the theatre have been different? Would I be allowed to go over to Aeronautical Engineering department and say, "Hey, guys, I'm in the language department and I need extra-curricular activities to wrap my head around when I'm not studying Chinese. I've decided I'd like to try designing and constructing a space rocket, Is that okay?"

"Whaddya mean okay?"

"Is it okay if I use your whatchamajiggies—supercollider, whatever—when I get tired of memorizing Chinese? Can I come over here and horse around in the lab?"

"Hell no!" they'd say.

"Well, why not?" I'd ask.

"Because we are not an extra-activities activity. You have neither the background, the experience, the expertise, the knowledge, the chutzpah or the *talent* and obviously not the brains for *aerospace engineering*, which is serious business."

In truth, the professional departments at Purdue are all serious business, and competitive as hell in seeking out the very best and most dedicated they could get. And not only in science and technology but also the best beef. I don't mean on the Ag campus but on the football field! So why in hell shouldn't theatre—or any of the arts—be given a little respect?

What was now left of the Purdue Theatre? There was a faction who loved and respected the professional theatre, but as new faculty was added who knew nothing about it, there developed an amateurish enthusiasm which did absolutely nothing for the students or the spectator except foster a kind of misguided dilettantism, which seemed perfectly accepted by those in charge.

Chapter 25

IN THE SUMMER OF 1970 I did not have a summer job, so when an African-American friend, Linda LaRue, administrative head of Upward Bound, a federally funded program that focused on kids from low income families from Gary, Indiana, offered me a job that paid a small stipend, I agreed to direct them in a workshop of *Day of Absence*.

My first day was absolute hell. They talked when I was talking about the play and I could not get them to stop interrupting. When we took a break, one of the guys got into a hassle with one of the girls and punched her in the stomach. She hauled off and slapped him, and that morphed into a fight in which they tried to throw one another on the cement floor of the trap room. I placed myself between them, and holding up both arms to keep them apart I yelled, "I can hardly believe this. Stop it! No fighting in my class! You're supposed to love one another!"

There was a moment of silence before all twenty-five of them went into the loudest laughing and slapping of thighs I've ever heard. Just as the laughter was about to die down so that I could scold them, one went into pelvic thrusts and said, "We gotta love one another," which brought down the house. I eventually got them quieted down enough to hand out the scripts of black playwright Douglas Turner Ward's play, with parts for all of them.

The play is a very funny minstrel show, except its cast of blacks is in whiteface and blond wigs rather than the other way around. It was well structured, starting early morning in a southern town with Clem and Luke, two lazy whites, sitting under signs reading "store" who would "lethargically" wave at imaginary passersby and occasionally talk between drowsy silences. After a page or so of dialogue they begin to realize that "somp'ums outta kilter" about the morning. What finally penetrates is that they haven't seen any "nigras" heading to work: "Not a darky in sight. We ain't laid eyes on nary a coon this whole mornin'!!!"

Throughout the play, which I had seen Off Broadway in the mid-sixties, scene after scene shows the results of a day of absence of the town's black workers. The whites are the laziest, most lame-brained and ineffectual human beings who ever existed. Ward sharply satirizes their habits with humor instead of hate, wisely knowing that hate is nullified by satire. One could not help but laugh at the over-the-top view of the manners and morals of these lazy Southerners.

When that first day was finished, so was I. I saw Linda and told her I couldn't do it. I quit. It was too much for me. I did this in a manner hoping she would understand, but she showed not an ounce of sympathy, even when I described the in-class fight and how I'd handled it. "Is that what you'd do in any other rehearsal?" she asked.

"Hell, no!"

"Well, why did you stand for it in this case? " Answering her own question, she said. "You did it because these kids are black!"

She had pinned me flat to the mat.

The next day I knew that I had to be honest with them. "We are going to do a show which is really fun and we are going to do it the best we possibly can," I said, before I started blocking. "If any of you not in the scene starts talking, I will tell you in no uncertain terms to keep quiet and to watch because you will be doing the same thing when I work on a scene you are in."

One line, and a piece of business that accompanied it, was particularly difficult for one of the kids. We were trying different ways to get him to understand when the boy who'd hit the girl in the stomach the day before yelled out, "Ah, Give up! He ain't no mother-fuckin' actor."

I grabbed the front of his shirt, slammed him against the wall of the trap room, and only inches from his face said, "If you ever make a comment like that again about someone who is trying to get something right in this play, you are out of this class, out of this program, and back in Gary, Indiana, for the rest of this hot summer! Do you understand?"

His 'yes' was barely audible, and he gave me no more trouble.

Everything didn't always go well. "C. T.", their acronym for "colored time," was pervasive. I hated waiting and kept demanding that they be professional and on time, and a lot of them started to improve. But one thing I was absolutely certain of. I got the majority on my side and if any of them got out of line—as happened—the majority got on the offender's back because I believe they had begun to enjoy the work and the play.

There was a particularly tricky timing for one scene that they couldn't seem to get right. I finally threw up my hands and said, "You kids just don't seem have any sense of rhythm!" Stunned silence followed for no more than a couple of seconds. Then one of them could not contain himself and started laughing and the others followed. When they would try to control themselves and someone couldn't, there would be another snigger which sent them back into gales of laughter.

It took a while but it finally dawned on me that this was probably the one thing they had *never* been accused of, and I couldn't help but start laughing.

The day of performance, I wrote individual notes to all of them, saying thanks and 'break a leg,' and let the stage manager get them ready. The theatre was filled with mothers and grandmothers and kids who were taking other classes in the program. We started on C.T. because the audience was late, which drove me up the wall as I hovered in the light booth. Finally the house lights dimmed, the curtain opened, and just as soon as they saw the actors in white face and blond wigs the audience got the point and whooped, yelled, and laughed. The two boys didn't break but stayed in character.

When they quieted down the guys started. I was a little annoyed when people in the audience began making their comments aloud. But the kids handled it correctly by waiting for the laugh to die down and then got in character. After about fifteen minutes I got used to these interruptions and, in a way, found that it somehow added as if the audience was a part of the show.

I was proud of the kids. After curtain calls, the house lights came up and the cast swarmed out into the audience. I was introduced and hugged by their mothers and grandmothers, who told me it was the best show they'd ever seen. I told them it couldn't have happened without the kids. Of course, I was pleased because they had done the best they had ever done—could do—and were as pleased with themselves as I was with them.

As produced by Robert Hooks, directed by Phillip Meister in the mid-sixties on a double bill with "Happy Ending" at the St. Marks Playhouse in New York, it had a splendid cast: Frances Foster, Moses Gunn, Douglas Turner, and Billy Dee Williams (a replacement). It ran for just over 500 performances, and was truly wonderful.

A week later Linda asked me if I was ever going to read the teacher evaluations. I told her I didn't dare since I had been so demanding. But I did read them and couldn't have been more pleased. "Joe's rough on us, but he's okay," was the one that expressed all the others. And that made me feel good, but not by any stretch of the imagination was it a well-done show. I got to thinking about how theatre art is misused by amateurs. Engineering and science have a sense of what getting it *right* means as a necessary and absolute requirement.

I never did another Upward Bound project and I'm not sure I would have done one if I'd been offered a chance. But I did love those kids.

⌘ ⌘ ⌘

Even though I was not officially on the summer school faculty getting paid, I volunteered to teach an independent study project, a lab project in acting that would give enough academic credit to the three graduate students Michael Flanagan had brought with him from Loretto Hilton so they could complete their master's degree requirements. This obviously saved them from staying for the fall semester. The project with no budget or scenery or lighting would culminate in a rehearsal performance of

The Glass Menagerie on July 17th, 18th, and 19th in the trap room for very small audiences. The three involved were Les Gruner in the role of Tom, Pam Mathews as Laura and Page Massman as Amanda. Michael Yelton supported them by playing the Gentleman Caller and helping me with props and costumes. Obviously, this was a jerry-rigged situation, but it would allow them to graduate and get on with their lives. But the project wasn't just a WPA lean-on-your-shovel-and-collect-your-30-bucks-a-month gig. I demanded decent work and they all gave it.

⌘ ⌘ ⌘

Fully recovered from the kidney problem, it was 14-year-old David's turn to travel. He decided on England and he went with a buddy, Bill Buroff.

Son Joe graduated from West Lafayette High School in June, flew to Paris, trained to Moscow, travelled from there down through Chekhov country, and took deck class passage across the Black Sea. On August 18th (his 17th birthday) he decided to jaunt through Turkey rather than come back to West Lafayette.

⌘ ⌘ ⌘

Thursday evening, July 28, 1970, Jean Ratcliff called at 10:00 P.M. to tell me that Frances Farmer was being given last rites and that if I was up to it I should come at once. We called Dick Newdick, a Catholic who had played her son in *The Sea Gull*, and asked him if he wanted to come with us.

The nurse in charge said that it might be best if only one of us went in. Frances lay on the bed and it looked as if she had already passed.

"Frances, Joe's here," Jean said.

There was a physical metamorphosis. She raised her head up off the pillow, smiled and held out her hand. I took it and said I had to pick up someone at the airport at midnight and just stopped by for a moment to say hello. It could not have been more than a couple of minutes before she fell back on the pillow and closed her eyes.

We drove back home and sat waiting. Jean did not call and we finally went to bed. Thursday, just after noon, the phone rang. It was Frances. The same voice, the same vitality! I could not believe it. "Jean has to go to the farm and take care of the cats," she said. "I have something to show you. Why don't you come down and baby-sit?"

Even though it was difficult for her to sustain conversation, and she occasionally dozed off, we did talk during those three hours until Jean returned. What she wanted to show me was a letter from Elia Kazan. I had called and told his secretary to tell him that Frances was dying of cancer and had given her the hospital address in case he wanted to send a card. He wrote her a lovely letter, which pleased her very much. I do not have it, but he also wrote one to me: "It is impossible to write a person about what she was, but I tried. I just sent her the news, along with good wishes and I hope that helps."

And I think it did.

There had been a thunder and lightning storm during the night. Just before I left she told me of waking and watching through the slats of the venetian blinds and thinking how good it was to be alive.

Saturday, Robin had taken the kids to Dad's place in Michigan for a visit. About 4:30, friends came over for a drink. At five o'clock the phone rang. It was Jean saying that Frances was dead. The funeral would be on Thursday. Would Robin be a pallbearer and would I speak? When I hung up I went back into the living room and told the friends what had happened. A husband asked, "Was Frances a lesbian?"

I could not answer at once. When I did, I said, "I don't know. I only know that when Frances vomited blood at the top of the stairs, Jean was there to hold her. I only know that it was Jean who sopped up the blood with towels... I only know... that... there are probably a lot of things people don't know or understand about one another."

Thursday, August 4, 1970, at 9:00 A.M., on a warm sunny day, a few friends had gathered at a run-down farmhouse in the northwest outskirts of Indianapolis where Jean and Frances lived. Inside the living room was an open coffin containing the body. An attempt at cocktail-party cheerfulness pervaded the talk, the way most thought she would want it. There was tension between Jean and Edith, Frances' sister, who had come out from Seattle. Edith suspected Jean of a cover-up concerning the will and finances. But there was no cover-up. During her illness, Frances had been accepted as a charity case at Community Hospital through the influence of her friends, Mozel and Dr. Ed Shafer, who had donated their services.

After coffee and breakfast rolls, the friends looked one last time at this legendary beauty, the lid of the casket was closed, and the group followed the hearse to St. Joan of Arc Catholic Church where a full Mass was read. The theme of the service was from a prayer of Saint Francis of Assisi: "Lord, make me an instrument of your peace..." and ended with, "It is in dying that we are born to eternal life." After the service the six women pall bearers—including Robin—bore the coffin to the hearse and rode with it to Oaklawn Memorial Gardens.

In a spacious marble mausoleum belonging to an Indianapolis family, a drawer had been donated where her body would lie in rest. It had been Jean's idea that although the service should be "high Catholic," the ceremony at the cemetery would be informal, with friends remembering Frances as she wanted to be remembered. At a small upright piano placed near the open door of the crypt, Indianapolis night club singer Flo Gavin played and sang Jimmy Dean's...

> Jean, Jean, roses are red and all the leaves have turned green
> And the clouds are so low you can touch 'em and so
> come out to the meadow, Jean.
> Jean, Jean, you're young and alive...

I said, "Frances' favorite playwright was Anton Chekhov. She had an innate understanding of his tragic humor and the absurd edge of his characters." Richard, Robin and I then read sections from his plays. I ended with Nina's line from *The Sea Gull:* "Now I know, I understand... that the essential thing in our profession... what matters is not fame or glory but how to endure."

The service ended and the mourners disappeared over the flat midlands of Indiana in the heat of early afternoon. It wasn't spring, but fall, and the leaves were turning red, not green.

⌘ ⌘ ⌘

I put in for a half-time (at full pay) sabbatical for the second semester in order to view Greek Theatres: Dionysus, Epidaurus and Delphi. I had read *The Greek Way* by Edith Hamilton and loved every word of it.

In September and October I directed *King Lear,* which played in The Loeb Playhouse. I had greatly enjoyed working with Erling Kildahl on *The Visit* and asked him if he would play Lear. He was thrilled as it was a role he had always wanted to play. I also had a first rate supporting cast. I loved the play and I think we all did. There wasn't a lot of money for the production so I asked Dusty (*aka* Donamarie) Reeds, who designed both costumes and setting, to just put a very big round platform stage center that was raked at about 15 degrees so it seemed that the action spilled out into the auditorium, and paint it like a cross-section of a skull that has been split open with an ax but do it so that only she and I would ever know what it was.

The rake meant that Lear's throne and any other stage props accommodated the angle of the rake so the back legs would be shorter than the front ones, making Lear's throne perpendicular to the Loeb's stage floor; seemingly steady in a wracked world, which I thought of as my own.

Everyone in the cast and on the crew gave it their all, and we had a good show. There was nothing visually theatrical—no "concept" that would require the cast to wear Mexican huaraches, thongs, and hula-hoops, no influence by Jan Kott, no allegory, and no Stonehenge objects hovering in the background.

My greatest influence was William Poel and the Elizabethan revivalists, who eliminated scenery, which facilitated pace, the heels of actors departing as the toes of the actors entered for the next scene. I had gone over the play more than any other I ever directed, color-coding every character in my script and making written notes of what they said about themselves, what others said about them, and analyzing their actions to decide what kinds of people they were.

Notes on physical descriptions were especially important for casting. Whoever played Cordelia had to be a lightweight if Kildahl, who was 52 at the time and had problems with his leg, was going to carry her on stage in that final scene. When I cast I had all of the physical requirements in mind, and I believe that with the talent pool available, I had the best cast that could be assembled. Such scenes as: Lear on the heath with the thunder and lightning; Cromwell's gouging out of Gloucester's eyes; characters such as Peter Schneider's Fool; Patty Murphy's Goneril, John Eldridge's Edmund, Dan von Bargen's Kent were all well done.

Gene's Lear was a first-rate accomplishment in the presentational style of acting in which he was trained at the Pasadena Playhouse. It depended first and foremost on a keen mind plus an ability to reason and choose what the actor felt was best vocally. Erling was blessed with a powerful vocal instrument and all aspects of good speech that intelligently spoke Shakespeare's poetry. If it lacked, it was in the subjective connection. We saw only the steady controlled self rather than the scrambled brains of a Lear thrust into a wracked world backed by a truth found only in his (mine really) unique experiences as a human being.

There were several issues that interested me. First and foremost was the idea of diminished status and the giving up of power. There had to be reasons for this action that were logical and true to the character. King Lear cannot be just a doddering old fool who divides his kingdom in three parts, one for each daughter, based on his judgment of how much they love him.

Is there a forecasting of his descent into madness in his acceptance of Goneril and Regan's false flattery and his inability to understand Cordelia's refusal to play the who-loves-me-most game to the point of disinheritance? Yes, of course. The need to be loved (liked) is a powerful primitive motive that I was beginning to think about. Was this a cautionary tale on giving up power, which I had done, and that ended the Professional Theatre Company?

I was 44 years old. Why my lifelong drive for perfection? For success? My endless energy? Now I was exhausted, both mentally and physically, worn out and stunned by David's brush with death, by my sister's commitment to a mental institution for almost a year, and being a new father to an absolutely adorable baby, smarting from my failure with my oldest daughter and her leaving the family for a relationship that I violently opposed, and Robin's (most probably correct) pragmatic acceptance of her actions. I was saddened by the death of Frances. And I was worried about the Vietnam War and my oldest son, my namesake, who would be eligible for the draft in a year. In short, I shared with many what was felt in the incredible 1960s.

Now in real time, when I Google Purdue University, then click on College/School, then the School of Visual and Performing Arts, then Theatre, and then History, I am astounded to see how the decade is recorded in mostly one liners that do not record its history factually.

"1957: Performances move to Elliott Hall of Music." In fact the theatre operated in the Hall of Music starting in September 1954 and all major productions were done there until we opened The Loeb in May 1958. In brief, The Loeb, which replaced Eliza Fowler Hall, took four years to build.

"1960: Beginning of Purdue Summer Theatre." But there should be added, "In the Experimental Theatre with a combination of local and student talent. The 1962/3/4 seasons used apprentices selected from all over the United States. In the summer of 1964 the Summer Theatre Company became The Purdue Summer Theatre, now under the School of Humanities, Social Science and Education of the greater University *as a full-fledged Actors Equity Association* Company in the Experimental Theatre."

Instead of listing degrees at the Master's level, why only list the MFA originating in 1976? Note should have been made that our first Master's degree [MS] students (Ditton, Hawley, Goodwin, and Staley) received their degrees twenty years earlier, in 1956.

And the one line note, "1967 Summer Theatre became The Purdue Professional Theatre Company," ignores the fact that this was under the prestigious League of Resident Theatres (LORT) contract. And in addition to a 12-week summer season, 12 week fall and winter seasons were added giving eight performances a week in The Experimental Theatre.

And finally, that 1969 was the end of the Professional LORT AEA company. The entry on the theatre's history says, "Purdue Professional Theatre Company becomes inactive in 1994!"

In a letter to the editor of THINK magazine (spring 2008) in reference to an article in the liberal arts magazine (Fall issue, 2007) entitled "Centennial Curtain Call" by David M. Williams on the history of the Purdue Theatre, a theatre faculty member wrote that "unfortunately the article left out an extremely important individual, " his colleague, Jim O'Connor. "Jim was passionate about theatre, not just as entertainment, but as a vehicle that could change people's lives. He felt strongly that an audience could be cultivated for intelligent, sophisticated theatre and proved his point by slowly building a reliable audience that regularly filled Purdue's Experimental Theatre to capacity."

Doesn't this imply that the only theatre up to this point was "just entertainment," that there was not an audience for "intelligent and sophisticated theatre" and that one had to be built up and was? Certainly the writer has a right to regret that Professor O'Connor's name was left out of the centennial article, but why would he defensively denigrate what had gone before?

And then there was the removal of all the pictures of programs I collected that were framed and lined the hallway and walls of the trap room of The Loeb. Whatever happened to them? Tear down every wall in Warsaw and no one will ever know what the city was like.

⌘ ⌘ ⌘

After the production of *Lear*, I received notice that my requested sabbatical for the second semester was approved. As soon as I found out I went to Raffael Nedomansky, who was new to the faculty and who had told me about a place he and his wife rented on the Italian Riviera that overlooked the Mediterranean, and behind which the Alps could be seen on a clear day. I asked him how much rent he paid. He said $50 a month. On the spot I asked him if I could rent it for half a year for $100 a month. He gladly agreed. Before I went to make arrangements for travel, I happened to see grad students Donn Ping and John Eldridge who were looking for a place to live. I told them 435 Robinson would be available; they said they would love to rent it and would pay all expenses (heat, lights, and water), the small mortgage payment to the Bank and to Page Karling, plus half a year's taxes. As I remember this came to a little over $300 per month.

I went home absolutely elated and told Robin to sit down because I had some good news: we were leaving prior to Christmas for Italy and returning at the end of May. When she said she wasn't sure she wanted to go, I replied that I had the tickets, had rented the house, and that she, David, John and Larkin were going.

This would be her first trip abroad and she got used to the idea fairly fast. In addition, I had another stroke of good fortune. Ed Loessin called from Greenville, North Carolina, where he headed the Theatre Department. One of his faculty members was taking a leave for the fourth quarter starting in late March. Could I come and teach two courses in Speech, and direct the spring play? The pay was $5,000, which would not only help pay all expenses for the sabbatical but leave enough money to make final mortgage payments on the house. I said YES! I was thrilled at the thought of being totally out of debt, and that Joe, who was now on an Israeli kibbutz, working in the banana fields, and hearing gunfire from the war, would come to visit us in Sori on his way home.

With baby Larkin in a new red coat trimmed in white faux fur and bonnet, we left soon after the first semester ended because we wanted to be in our house by Christmas. Flying to Brussels, we transferred to a train with a two-day stop in Basel, Switzerland. We had a great compartment, and the kids loved the ride.

Basel is where the Swiss, German, and French borders intersect in northwest Switzerland, on the Rhine River. Our hotel had adjoining rooms with beds one sunk deeply into, and bedcovers five inches thick. We stopped there because Robin had once heard her father say that this was where he was from and she wanted to find out. Her total effort to this end was a glance in the phone book. Finding no listing for Fastenrath, the search was ended. I decided we should explore the town but since a walking tour with baby Larkin was out of the question, I suggested taking a bus to the zoo, which pleased John and David.

Basel was mostly German speaking, and since I'd been there and done that, I thought I could still say "*Sprechen Sie Deutsch?*" with a perfect accent, tap my chest, shake my head, and say, *"Nein."* Nonetheless, this almost inevitably resulted in the addressee saying, "May I help you find something?" in English.

This trip to the zoo resulted in an event that has lived in infamy in Stockdale family history and has been repeated so often at family gatherings that it is layered with barnacles. But I will attempt to give the facts as closely as possible without enhancement. The boys loved the monkeys and apes, and must have spent an hour making faces, scratching their armpits and pounding their chests. I think the lion cage was probably their next most liked area, although the lions scared Larkin, and the boys tried to comfort her by saying they were only big "pussy cats." I hated the reptile cages but the boys loved them. We were near the end of our sightseeing when we arrived at huge watering tanks for the rhinoceros.

Rhinos hold the fewest qualities in the animal kingdom that afford humans empathy. Ask yourself, have you ever wanted to pet a rhino? The group that we saw 25 or more feet away were not just homely, they were grotesque, with muscular humps on their backs and faces that would stop a clock: square mouthed and two-horned; no knees, weighed a ton or more with hairy ears and backsides with patches of sparse hair. They are said to have the smallest brains for their size of any animal and have incredibly thick skins, which is probably a blessing since it protects them from hurt feelings when insults are hurled at them.

John was laughing and pointing at the rhinos' knobby toes, and David was having fun skylarking and remarking on what eyesores they were when one of the them laboriously turned her back on him, slowly lifted her ugly tail, and shot out a stream of urine the volume of which would make the latest fire-fighting hoses look like water pistols. David was soaked in rhino piss. It took only a moment before John, baby Larkin and I were laughing hysterically, although Robin was not amused.

We whisked David back to the hotel in a cab, with Robin telling the children in no uncertain terms that they should *never* make fun of the way people looked! "Do you think they heard us?" I questioned, which brought on more laughter and improvised scenes of what they said to one another as they planned their revenge.

Crossing the Alps and entering Italy was thrilling. The Nedomanskys had said that the easiest and least expensive way for us and our luggage to get to their place was to take a taxi. When we arrived in Genoa I cashed a traveler's check. English-speaking personnel led us to the cab, instructed the driver where we were going, and told us approximately how much the trip would cost. There are no friendlier people than in Italy, not only friendly but also joyful and emotional. That our darling bambino was dressed in her little red coat and bonnet, *and* it was only a couple of days before Christmas, gave us a hand full of trump cards.

When the taxi stopped, the sea was just on our right. Our driver pointed up the hill where we saw a small house that looked like it was made of marble. It was a climb and took a bit of doing to get up there but the driver helped with luggage. There were two bedrooms and a bathroom, a kitchen, dining room and small front room that looked out over a thin strip of beach, with underwater sand that faded as the water turned light green-blue and then deeper blue. There was also an unbelievably beautiful view of distant ships.

It was late afternoon when we were finally settled in. David wanted to explore and John wanted to tag along. There were paths that led up the hill behind us so we told David it would be all right, but that he must not lose sight of the house and was to always keep an eye on John, who was eight. They were off. Larkin needed a nap, and Robin said it was her period and didn't have any Kotex.

There was a path across the hill and then steps leading down to the village where I quickly found what we would call a convenience store. However, stores at home were self-serve; this one used the clerk-method of acquiring goods. There was a woman clerk. I scanned the shelves to see if I could see the familiar box. Failing to do so, I prefaced my talk with the usual. *"Parlez vous français,* (shaking my head) *no; Sprechen sie Deutsch? Nein. Italiano?"* Eyes downcast in shame, right-hand cupped, thumping my chest, shaking my head. *"Stupido, Americano!"*

This caused a totally unexpected reaction. The woman cried, "No, no, no, no!" She came from behind the counter and wrapped her strong arms around me. Then, holding me away, she shook her head, again saying "No, no, no, no!" to assure me I was not stupid.

This time I spoke cognates: "*Mon,* my, (another thump to my chest) *femme, protégé, épouse,* protection" (If I wore a wedding ring, all this would have been so easy.) Lines formed in her forehead. W*hat could he possibly buy in a grocery store to protect his wife?* I read her mind. Then something occurred to her. She went behind the counter, reached under and brought out a box of condoms, which I suspected were out of sight in case His Holiness was snooping around Sori. "No, no, no." I waved my hand, but at least she was on the right track I said, "Wife. Protection. Kotex!" and cupped my right-hand over my crotch.

Her face lit up. The box she brought fourth did not look anything like what they sold in West Lafayette, Indiana. But I knew she had gotten it right. I swiped my forehead as if to eliminate sweat, reached for my wallet, put some bills in my hand and held it out. She made change. When the transaction was finished I said, *"Gratzia, Madam!" "Bonna sera."* She answered in that wonderful flowing language and I hurried back up the steps that led to Robin and our house in the hills above Sori, Italy.

We had a chicken dinner for Christmas with all the trimmings I could find. Joe III came from Israel and spent a few days telling us of his travels and said he was thinking of joining the army. I urged him to enroll at Indiana University instead. He, David and John went out to explore. Joe and David got ahead of John, who became lost. We later found him in the loving care of an Italian family who probably felt we were terrible parents for not looking after our baby boy. Christmas passed and Joe left.

I loved the views, loved walking by the sea, and loved exploring the hills. David made friends with the Zilioli brothers at the pool hall, and Robin forced herself to drop an octopus that David caught into boiling water as its eye looked up at her.

David and I traveled to Greece to do those things I said I would do on my sabbatical to presumably make myself a better teacher. We took the train from Genoa to La Spezia and went to Pisa to see the Leaning Tower where Galileo dropped a couple of cannon balls to show that the speed of the fall was not related to the mass of the object—the story was said to be apocryphal—and to enjoy the sound of its bell-tower chimes. Then on to Rome where we stayed three days. We spent a day and a half at St. Peter's Basilica, going up to the dome and laughing ourselves silly when a New Yorker enquired of one of the guards, "So we've seen fifteen of these chapels, where's the sixteenth? We also visited the Coliseum, Trevi Fountain, Victor Emmanuel's Monument, and the Piazza della Republica.

We caught the train to Brindisi and boarded the Poseidon. Although we were not hit by a tsunami, we did get caught in a storm that brought big waves. We had thought it might be fun to join the deck-class clientele, but after the storm struck and everyone started throwing up, I booked a cabin, because I, too, was getting sick.

Arriving in Athens the next day we gladly went to the hotel that a student from Purdue, Andrew Antoniadis, had recommended. From our bathroom window we could see the Parthenon if we strained our necks. We walked up and around it and I knew firsthand that Edith Hamilton got the architecture right. We explored other great sights of Athens, and went to Delphi to see the shrine of the Oracle and the theatre, and to Epidaurus and tested the theatre's amazing acoustical properties. We dined at a place where a belly dancer, in the middle of her gyrations, broke her space to come toward us. I thought she had her eye on me but it turned out that she was more interested in 14½ year old David, who was incredibly handsome and had a head of black curly hair as big as a sagebrush.

We spent less than a week doing these things before boarding a very slow train that took us through Albania (the border of which was closed), Yugoslavia, Trieste, just slightly south through Bologna, and on to Genoa. We shared a compartment with four other men, and the ride took damn near three days. At night the seats were pulled together to form a bed where we slept head to foot. You have never smelled socks as sour as those of our compartment companions.

After a week or more of rest, I tried to get Robin and the family to train with me through the south of France and the Riviera to Barcelona, but she said it was too much of a hassle and she was more than happy overlooking the Mediterranean and getting acquainted with our village and its shopkeepers. I went alone. I remember the colors of the early morning sky as I went from France into Spain and thought of Picasso's works I had seen in the Hermitage in Leningrad.

At the Barcelona train station I enquired of an English speaking woman who sold tickets, cashed traveler's checks, and made hotel reservations, about a hotel room. How much did I wish to pay? she asked. I said I could afford $5 in American money but I would prefer something less expensive if possible. She booked me into a hotel on the main street, The Rambla, which sprouts many side streets to form an entire district. She gave me directions. Observing that I carried my bag with the strap over my head rather than my shoulder, she said that this was a wise choice. There were pickpockets and thieves even in early March, which was definitely not the tourist season.

The air was wonderful. In my walks along the un-crowded streets I saw newspaper kiosks and bought myself a copy of the *International Herald Tribune.* There were dozens of flower sellers and the same for exotic birds. One man sold monkeys. I found the hotel easily and was pleased that my rate would be the equivalent of $3.50 a night. My room, on the first floor, was very large and had a comfortable bed and a private shower.

The streets of The Rambla that go east and west lead to the sea and the mountains, and I walked in both directions. I took the guided tour up to Montserrat and the monastery that seemed to be pasted to the side of the mountain.

The architecture in Barcelona reveals influences of the Moorish, eschewing squares, horizontal and perpendicular lines in favor of rippling curves made of iron fretwork as delicate as lace.

Near the harbor were palm trees mixed with strange fir trees without pine needles. Parks and public gardens with fountains were plentiful, and along the streets, always and forever, were various shops. There was a famous opera theatre but I was not in the mood after feasting my eyes on the beauty of the city. In fact, the only thing I did other than walk and sightsee, and sit and people-watch, was to attend a bull fight in honor of Ernest Hemingway, although I knew that Barcelona was not Pamplona, but the music, the matadors, the bulls, the costumes, and the crowds are the same. It is a brutal spectacle. I watched but did not enjoy it any more than I enjoyed the pounding football players or boxers gave one another (unless I wanted Joe Louis to win.)

I wished I had insisted that Robin and the family come, but then what of Larkin, who was too young to do much walking and sightseeing? Perhaps if all of them went to Barcelona on a ship from Genoa and had a hotel to go to, as the one I was in, they could at least see something of this gorgeous city and enjoy the air, and strange food, and trees and fountains, and certainly the monkey seller on the avenue. With David's help I talked Robin into taking exactly that trip with the family after I departed for my job in March.

When I left, I trained to Hamburg where I had a gig as a visiting lecturer at the university. The person who arranged this was a Purdue student whose name I'm ashamed to say I have forgotten; it may have been Bob. I arrived early evening and after checking into my hotel, Bob and I went to dinner. Afterwards he wanted to show me the nightlife. Where he took me was the section called the Reeperbahn, where the whole area was devoted to sex.

There was a six-or seven-story building called Eros Center, which had recently opened. It was said to be the biggest whorehouse in the world. There was a sex museum and a street where prostitutes posed in glass showrooms. Bob, of course, wanted us both to pick a girl but I was embarrassed, although I would not have done so even if I had been alone.

The narrow street was crowded and everyone was there for only one thing. I watched as a young, very attractive prostitute, flashed a customer and then left her glass display case to go off with him to the Eros Center. I never considered myself a puritan but sex as commerce did not work for me. It was like the time when I was in the Navy when we went to the whorehouse.

But the streets were crowded, mostly men. There were live sex shows. We walked through the entire area but not for a moment was I aroused. I went back to my hotel room. The train ride to Hamburg had been an overnight. I was exhausted and just a little sick to my stomach.

The next day Bob came to tell me that Communist students had taken over the university, all classes were suspended, and that the students were gathering in the lecture halls to talk about Communism. He said one of the professors had offered to have me come and talk to the students at his home. I went, but only a couple of students showed up. The entire trip was a fiasco.

With no lecture, Bob wanted me to come back to the Reeperbahn with him. He was a Beatles fan and claimed they had played in the sex clubs there. He wanted me to go to one of the sex shows on stage, which offered various forms of fornication. I gave him the excuse that I was leaving for London the next day. But, I was perplexed. *The streets were crowded.* Why was I not part of the crowd?

Hamburg has access to the North Sea via the Elbe River. I loved this 12 hour trip up the river and out into the sea and on to London. This time, I stayed at the Jesmond on Gower Street and saw shows on the weekend before flying to West Lafayette where I stayed overnight at our house. I then drove our car down to Greenville, North Carolina, stopping at Fort Knox to visit Joe who had enlisted in the Army.

When I got there it was very clear that he was one unhappy kid; his joining the army was an impulsive mistake and he realized it. I talked to his commanding officer, Captain Don Wilburn, who was a very nice guy. During our talk I told him about our family and that I felt Joe's enlistment was a mistake. I also told him that I was opposed to the Vietnam War and wanted him to know that. He was very understanding.

⌘ ⌘ ⌘

My landlady in Greenville was Mavis Ray, the dance instructor and the real thing, not your typical academic. She choreographed the musicals as the real pro that she was. Her career started in 1949 in the Broadway production of *Carousel*. She had been with *Paint Your Wagon, Goldilocks, Finian's Rainbow, Brigadoon,* and *110 in the Shade* as either performer or assistant to the choreographer up through 1964 when she was hired by Ed Loessin. Her last appearance on Broadway was in the legendary *Ballroom* in 1979. She was a terrific person.

I had bought a book that was very popular and just recently published: *Everything You Always Wanted to Know About Sex (But Were Afraid to Ask)*, and another oversized picture book with photos and drawings about sexual anatomy and practices that made for popular reading/viewing/doing.

I have to admit that Mavis interested me sexually, but I never received a receptive signal, which I needed before making a pass. That was my history. In almost all instances it was the women who first made the pass and I was, in most cases, more than willing to participate. But I lacked the confidence of the aggressor. Why? Could it have been fear of rejection combined by my need to be loved/liked?

Son Joe got a general discharge from the Army and came to visit. We had a good time together. When at Sunday lunch I asked the waitress for two breasts and a couple of thighs, the way one actually ordered in that restaurant, he took the order the other way and got a big kick out of it.

It was Easter vacation when I drove up to Washington D.C. and visited Robin's brother, Jimmy, who had just divorced his first wife and was dating Anne, the woman he eventually married after 18 years of living together. Jim was planning a trip to Europe and stopping at Sori to see Robin and the kids. We had a terrific week together. We smoked more marijuana and drank more booze than I had ever done in my life.

Jimmy was a constant drinker. After his time in the Marines and their breakout from the Chosin Reservoir in Korea, he took a degree at Western Michigan and wound up at the Pentagon with a desk job in the bomb-shelter section. When atomic bomb drills ended in the public schools and people stopped buying air-raid shelters for their backyards, there wasn't a hell of a lot for Jimmy to do. He once told me he spent most of his time reading *The Wall Street Journal* in the men's john. With no children he was a hail-fellow, well-met provocateur, known and well-liked by all the bartenders he introduced me to when we did the town each evening. At the end of the week, I drove back to Greenville totally wiped out.

The main reason I was in Greenville was to direct the play. Ed, being head of the drama department, was the producer, but the choice of plays was influenced by his wife, Amanda. I was getting a nice sum for my work, but I didn't much care for *Little Murders*. It had a really strange history. A comedy by Jules Feiffer, its main character meets an emotionally stoned man whom she falls for and brings home to meet her dysfunctional family. The characters are caricatures and the humor is topical, with a sixties black-comedy ending when a stray bullet kills her.

The play received a production in London and played Off Broadway at the old downtown Circle in the Square where it ran for 400 performances, winning an Obie and an Outer Circle Award, primarily, I suspect, because of a masterful comic performance by Linda Lavin. No one ever mentions that in its original run on Broadway, Patsy was played by a petite blonde beauty with one of the great singing voices of our time, Barbara Cook. It opened on Broadway after 16 previews, followed by a run of seven performances.

The leading lady in the production I directed was Amanda Meiggs Loessin (program credit under Amanda Muir), who was Ed's wife and who looked a bit like a young Barbara Cook. But beauty alone cannot make this play work. The brilliant Robert T. Williams, whom I recommended to Ed, was the designer. The costumer was something else again. When I asked for a change in one of the costumes, she went to Ed and complained that I was too demanding. What could he do? She was highly satisfactory to the leading lady's taste, and I was just a short-term job-in.

In brief, this was a play I did not care for, and worse, even though as director I worked well with the designer, I did not have the final say about how it was to be approached and acted. I sure as hell wasn't going to wreck my long-standing friendship with Ed, who had been a rock when I first played at Cherokee. So I went to rehearsals, followed the basic Samuel French stage manager's blocking from the failed Broadway production which was what Amanda was used too, and let her do whatever she wished.

At the end of the quarter, I drove home to West Lafayette and had a party for eight friends, including Jim Cost, our neighbor, whose wife, Dona, had gone to Italy so she and Robin could take a trip to Paris. One of my friends whom I invited was an attractive woman. We all drank quite a bit and when everyone left, she gave me more than a receptive signal; in fact, she came onto me, and I was ready, willing and able! She was a remarkable woman, and reminded me of Susan Willis in a lot of ways. It was wild for a couple of weeks before Robin and Dona came home with John and Larkin. David was staying the summer in Italy with the Ziliolis and would return at the end of August.

It was great to have Robin and the two kids back and I figured the affair would end, but it did not because I could not let go, not for a year-and-a-half. She and her family left town for a year or so. When she moved back to West Lafayette I helped find her a nice rental and stopped by, but as it turned out only as a friend.

Chapter 26

IN OCTOBER 1971, I GOT to finish my Chekhov cycle by directing *The Cherry Orchard* in the Experimental Theatre. This time, of course, it was with an all-student cast. Lopahin was played by Dan von Bargen, a laid-back mensch and one hell of a fine actor who had an acting career that included regional, Broadway, films and TV. Within the past month as I write this there was sad news from Cincinnati that he had tried to commit suicide. The 911 call he made when the attempt failed was recorded and played on YouTube and was very difficult to listen to and watch. Apparently because of diabetes he had already lost a leg, and an appointment the next day to see the doctor about his other foot was the reason he wanted to end his life. I had attempted to contact him for the past seven years in order to nominate him for Purdue's School of Liberal Arts Distinguished Alumni Award but was unable to do so, as were others who attempted to contact him. After his failed suicide attempt we all tried again to send love and support but without success. Frustrating.

As I look at *The Cherry Orchard* program I can't help but note that although it is listed as the 206th major production of the Purdue University Theatre, the program is printed on a folded single sheet of 8½ x 12" paper, which may account for the fact that no record of it could be found in the Theatre's files even though it was given eight performances.

Although I had a fine cast with Kathy Yeager, Van Ibsen, Dan von Bargen, Paul Mazzaglia, David Noll, Cassie Wolfe, and Bob Walker, plus such technical experts as Peter Schneider and David Potts as co-lighting designers, in all honesty I do not have the same exciting and joyous memories of this production as I do of the other three Chekhov productions. It isn't just the acting that makes a production memorable. It's *everything*, including such seemingly minor details as the program. Not that it was a bad production; it was the best that could be done with the money available. I realized more and more that I was in this vise between what I knew was first-rate and what was the mediocre, which most of the theatre faculty had settled for. The majority of them had never attended a Broadway production, so our view of what qualified as excellent was different.

⌘ ⌘ ⌘

The next two chapters could be called "the Doldrums," and I meant exactly that. *I* was out of sync, *I* did not fit, *and I* did not see things as others saw them. But I had a family to support, so the only thing I could do was to find another job, which would not be easy since I was a full professor with tenure. In addition, I suspected that educational theatre throughout the country was probably much the same as it now was at Purdue.

I, along with everyone else, was glad when Vera Mowry Roberts, who headed the Theatre Department at Hunter College in New York City, published her book, *The Nature of Theatre*, (Harper and Rowe, N.Y.) with pictures of Purdue's productions. But no one mentioned (or realized) that all the pictures were of Purdue's Professional Theatre productions which I had directed: *Uncle Vanya, Romeo and Juliet, Of Mice and Men, Tartuffe, Misalliance, Born Yesterday, Oh What a Lovely War, Stop the World I want to Get Off,* and *Mother Courage and Her Children.*

The only area of work I now had access to, that I really loved—and that I could do by myself—was writing, the thing that at one time had been what I most wanted.

⌘ ⌘ ⌘

David, now 16, and his buddy Larry Anderson who played drums, performed under union musician contracts at various venues in and around Lafayette, with David singing and strumming his guitar and sometimes accompanying himself with a harmonica, which was strapped around his neck and fixed so he could mouth it and strum the guitar at the same time. Their repertoire included favorites such as James Taylor's "Sweet Baby James" and "Fire and Rain," Cat Steven's "Moonshadow," and John Lennon's "Working Class Hero" with lyrics that offended. But my favorite, which for some reason always made me cry when David sang it, was Elton John's "Your Song."

By June 1972 both Richard Newdick and Bill Prosser were teaching at Richmond's Virginia Commonwealth University where Tom Holloway, who had played opposite Frances Farmer in *The Sea Gull*, was now a long time tenured faculty member with a PhD from Purdue. Bill had started a summer theatre, very much like the one he and Richard had worked in at Purdue, and wanted me to direct *Hadrian VII*. Charles M. Dorn, the new head of the Creative Arts Department, had given me a summer course in Introduction to Theatre to teach and I told Bill I could not afford to give up the two months' half-time salary, which is what I would have had to do because my first day of teaching coincided with *Hadrian's* first dress rehearsal.

He immediately countered by saying he would take over for me at that point. What I believe he expected, knowing me, was that I could never leave a show I had directed until after opening night, and was put out when I flew back to West Lafayette the morning of the first dress rehearsal. He was right to feel put out because leaving before opening nights is like *coitus interruptus;* if you know you're going to pull out before the climax, all you're going to get is a dry hump, and in a way, that's all I gave and got.

What I loved most about the gig was the fact that my room was in one of the mansions just off famed Monument Avenue. I loved the atmosphere, and although June in Richmond is hot, I enjoyed walking along "one of the ten Great Streets in the country." I loved the statues of Robert E. Lee, J.E.B. Stuart, Jefferson Davis and Stonewall Jackson. But mostly I loved the fact that each of them rode a horse. I was told by an old-timer that in the lithograph of Lee, which was used by the Parisian sculptor as a model for the horse, it was not Lee's favorite, "Traveller," who for one reason or another had missed out on the lithographic op session. But, not being a connoisseur of Lee's stable, I still loved the stand-in and all the other horses. The look in their eyes carries total understanding, each knowing exactly the prancing pose needed to show off their glorious power.

⌘ ⌘ ⌘

In my spring playwriting class I had a young woman, Sheila Hofstetter, who showed talent, and who I thought needed practical theatre work writing in a rehearsal situation where the show she had written would be produced. We settled on a lab production of her adaptation of Arnold Wesker's *Roots* with an all-black cast.

What happened was that this project seemed so good as it went along that it morphed into a full production in the Experimental Theatre, which we decided to show for public performance. Obviously we had to apply for rights and get Wesker's approval for adapting it. Since he was a well-known socialist, the project would not only give a young female playwright experience, but would address racial and feminist issues that were important to socialism. I wrote that it would be produced on a tight budget in a theatre seating less than 100 and that I hoped for his approval without charging royalties.

He was furious, and let me know that he could pull the project entirely and raise hell with all our future producing negotiations through the Dramatists Guild. After his fury was spent he casually added that since we were so far along, and there were only five performances scheduled, he would let us do the adaptation for "only" $50 a performance.

Thanks for nothing! At that time we could have gotten the latest release of a hit Broadway musical for $50 a performance! Somehow Ron Reed, new Head of Theatre, managed to get the money. But under the circumstances as you might well guess, this was not a production that I remember fondly. It was a job. I did my best within the perimeters of talent and money and, incidentally chalked up some FTE (Faculty/Teacher/Equivalency) credit for the Theatre Department by giving academic credit for which I was getting only half-time pay for the speech course I was teaching.

Ron asked me to direct *Death Of A Salesman* as the first production of the fall season in The Loeb and bring in an AEA actor to play Willy, *and* to work with the students. I knew at the time that this was a kind of Band-Aid approach to justify professionalism and I talked to John Newton, who was a very good actor, known and liked in the community, and someone the kids could learn from. He was reluctant because he did not think he was right for Willy Loman. I agreed, but I persuaded him, saying he would be a first-rate example of a professional working actor.

I asked Dusty Reeds to re-create the original design by Jo Mielziner and the production was pretty good. John as always was generous with his time and talent and participated in training by going over scenes with the students when they wanted to try different approaches. But I believe that someone must have suggested to Paul Mazzaglia that one "educational" value of having a professional would be that he could listen to John's line delivery and learn a good deal about timing. Paul was an outstanding new student talent whom I cast as Biff, and who would study at Julliard for a couple of years. John came to me after an early rehearsal and asked me to talk to Paul because he was mouthing Willy's lines as John was saying them. One thing Paul learned was to *never* do this again!

After *Salesman* closed I had no more directing responsibilities until late spring. I went back to work on my book, dealing with the relationship of a play's dramatic structure and its acting, directing and design. It seemed a good idea since it would probably be more marketable than fiction, and I would do this in an authentic *op. cit., loc. sit.,* and *ibid.* academic style.

It took me three years to finish but it saved my life. I set the book's perimeters; I wasn't dependent on anyone else except Robin who was my editor. And although there was a lot of research, I could still use my imagination and creativity in the writing. It was all just between me, and a clean white sheet of paper, rolled into the Underwood. I still have the original copyrighted version which had 17 pages of "end notes," a detailed analysis of a one-act play to illustrate the points I had discussed in the narrative, and an addendum which included a list of plays that had been recorded. When this 474 page book was finished, my dedication read: "For my students, past, present and future after twenty-five years of teaching."

In April I directed the largest production—bigger than *Gypsy*—I ever did: *Cyrano de Bergerac* by Edmond Rostand in the original translation by Brian Hooker. It was to have been designed by Robert T. Williams, but other commitments intervened so I called Jerry Williams and he agreed to come from the Alley Theatre in Texas. What a blessing. It needed a professional designer. Ron Reed was so impressed with Jerry's work that he offered him a faculty position, but Jerry was aware of the bitter disagreements about the direction in which Purdue theatre was headed and declined the offer.

Jerry's work was brilliant, and once again I knew there was someone aboard who would work his ass off, as I would, because this was his life, the thing he loved. The design requirements were massive. The first four acts of *Cyrano* take place in 1610 and the fifth in 1655. Act one is in the Hotel de Bourgogne, Paris; Act two, Ragueneau's Pastry Shop; Act three, the Courtyard outside Roxane's home; Act four, the Battlefield at the siege of Arras which not only includes a battle scene but a horse and carriage, and Act five, the Garden of a Convent.

Every one of those sets was absolutely outstanding and scene shifts were no longer than two minutes. The costumes were beautiful. We rented them from the Costume Collection in New York. They had originally been created for the Lincoln Center production. When they arrived a week before opening night, were unpacked and hung on racks in the trap room, they were the most costumes I have ever seen for a show.

Sidney Pellisier, professor in the French Department, not only acted a leading role (the Comte de Guiche) but served as French pronunciation director. Leading roles were played by David Noll as Cyrano, Tami Ramaker as Roxane, Michael Maddux as Christian de Neuvillette and Paul Mazzaglia as Le Bret, and, let me add proudly, in the small role of the boy drummer, John Stockdale, who listened and learned all the lines in the play.

I became fascinated with the history of this show. I read and considered the Anthony Burgess translation/adaptation which was to be made into a musical that opened in New York only a few weeks after our production. But in my opinion, no one has done a better job of translating this play than Brian Hooker.

The show was a vehicle for actor Richard Mansfield in 1898 and again in 1900. It was also done in the Garden Theatre in New York in repertory with four other shows with Sarah Bernhardt and Benoit Constant Coquelin in 1900. After that it was not revived until 1924 when Walter Hampden played the title role. The reason? A pending lawsuit by an Illinois farmer who claimed that he had written the story first! That was the odd kind of research I fell in love with. I still rate this production as one of the most fulfilling, worthwhile, creative projects during my five years in the doldrums and the most spectacular of a lifetime.

In June, I directed *The Moon Is Down*. This production used a mimeographed folded 8½" x 11" sheet of paper for the program's front and back page, and the two inside pages for the creative and technical listing along with a program note:

Friends of the Theatre: After an absence of four summers the Purdue University Theatre once again has a summer company; but it differs somewhat from the one you may remember. We will still attempt to provide the best theatre possible; however, the emphasis will be upon students rather than professionals. This year's company is composed of graduate, undergraduate, and high school apprentices. Our ultimate aim is to have a small group of professionals acting with our advanced graduate and undergraduates and working with them to make the summer company the culminating experience of the students' training program. With the kind of support we received this past year and in past summer seasons and with your continued support, this goal can be achieved in the near future. I hope you enjoy the unique selection of plays to be presented this summer.

Sincerely, Ronald M. Reed, Director of theatre.

I had seen Steinbeck's *The Moon Is Down* at the Kalamazoo Civic Theatre when I was in high school and loved it. I'd also read the novel. Now, 30 years later, many experiences had coalesced, including my success with *Of Mice and Men,* and my misery in this five-year period which drew me to Steinbeck's point of view that in the long run the will of a person cannot be snuffed out by anything, including brute force. This novel had been turned into a play and then a film in the early 1940s. Incidentally, the exact situation was made into a mini-series in England a couple of years ago called *Island at War,* which I thought quite good. I had two first-rate actors: Dale Helward came in under a visiting artist AEA contract to play the very difficult role of Lanser, a Nazi colonel. The talented Stephen McKinley Henderson, whom I had auditioned at a URTA (University Resident Theatre Association) meeting and recommended as a graduate student, played the role of the Mayor. I consider this the worst physical production I ever saw. But let's face it, the patrons of the theatre should have been clued in when they arrived at the theatre and were handed that mimeographed sheet of paper with a note lauding "an attempt to provide the best theatre possible with students."

Sheila Hofstetter's *Busy Dyin'* had been written and read in my playwriting class and I thought it held a lot of promise. I made it clear that everything would be my way and I told the designer what I wanted. The set would consist of three slightly raked rectangular platforms, the living quarters of two old men on stage left, a mother and daughter on stage right, and in the middle platform the young couple. The rehearsals went extraordinarily well because we all loved the characters as revealed through their stories and the way Sheila had connected them. The visual and auditory elements concentrated only on lighting effects and music, and the production, on characters and honest acting.

Sheila chose her title from a Bob Dylan lyric, "If you ain't busy being born, you're busy dying" and it was originally scheduled for 12 performances as the last show of the summer season. It went so well that Ron Reed decided to open the fall season with it, playing ten performances with Marjorie Cody replacing Cassandra Wolfe, who had graduated. In early January it became Purdue's entry in the American Theatre College Festival in Ft. Wayne where it played a single performance.

I shall never forget the reaction at the ending. Members of the three family units, hearing the siren, look straight out as the rotating light from the police car hits their faces and the lights dim slowly to blackout. The audience remained in absolute silence and then someone said, "Jesus Christ," and suddenly the crowd was on its feet cheering and applauding.

Two of the judges for the Festival were unable to attend the performance at Ft. Wayne so Ron got them to come to West Lafayette later in January when we gave the show two more performances, one for a Purdue audience and the next night for another full house including the two judges.

Busy Dyin' won the regional competition but was not selected for the national competition that played Washington D.C. One of the judges told me it should have won, but said there was always politics in the selection of the shows. In March, however, it was selected for a public reading by Zelda Fichandler, Artistic Director of the famed Arena Theatre in Washington, D.C. for a reading performance, and in July it was produced by the prestigious Circle Rep Theatre in New York under the direction of Peter Schneider. This was the only other show during this five years in the doldrums that I felt had qualities that were first-rate. In my dealings both on production and in routine matters at faculty meetings, I was outspoken and said what I thought. I did not see eye to eye with anyone on the faculty except Wayne Lamb, nor did I have much in common with any of them. I was, in short, odd man out.

⌘ ⌘ ⌘

On January 10, 1974, I received my copy of the following interoffice memorandum:

To: Mennen, Stockdale, Reed, O'Connor, Lamb (tenured Theatre Division Faculty)

From: Charles M. Dorn, Head, Department of Creative Arts.

Subject: Structure of the Arts Division Faculty Procedures.

Following what has been for all of us a trying series of meetings regarding interpersonal tensions felt by the Theatre faculty, I believe we have arrived at the following general agreement which will be operative at least for the remainder of this semester and for the 1974/5 academic year:

Professor Stockdale has voluntarily agreed to withdraw himself from directing and from participation in all meetings which involve deliberations of the theatre faculty. It is understood that this action is voluntary and in general meets with the approval of all tenured Theatre faculty with the exception of Wayne Lamb who is not on campus this semester. It is further agreed that Professor Stockdale will be provided the opportunity to vote on all issues of substance affecting the Theatre Division and ... substantive actions recommended by the Theatre faculty.

The selection committee for new Theatre faculty is to consist of Professors Reed, O'Connor, Mennen and one full professor from outside the Division to recommend personnel. Weekly or bimonthly regular faculty meetings to include all Theatre faculty. The meetings are to encourage open discussions regarding curriculum, procedures, and Theatre productions. All probationary and tenured faculty will be eligible to vote on Theatre Division issues. Minutes are to be kept and votes recorded. Theatre Graduate faculty to include all on Creative Arts Department list. All Grad faculty have the right to vote on issues affecting Theatre Division.

All graduate forms to be signed by Department Head after being initialed by Director of Theatre.

At least 1 hr. conference to be scheduled by all Theatre personnel with the Head of Creative Arts each semester.

If feasible, the Theatre faculty will elect one representative to the Primary Committee. Vote to be taken by the beginning of fall semester to serve for 1 year.

That this Head of Creative Arts or his representative be included, as originally specified on this production committee. At least one open [meeting] each semester with Grad and Undergraduate students and Theatre faculty for open discussion of program development.

All discussions referred to in this memo were related to the direction in which the Theatre program would be moving between reestablishing professionalism for the benefit of the total university, town, and state that blended in extremely talented graduate and undergraduate students in acting and design and technical work, OR a student company for a summer theatre with high school apprentices and a yearly season of five or six shows that occasionally had an AEA member.

As for "inter-personal tensions" it was my view that in discussions where there is disagreement one should follow the standard forms of support to persuade and inform, rather than using caprice and skewed logic. With Wayne Lamb on sabbatical but having voted against my being excluded from faculty meetings, the only other tenured members who voted on it were Dorothy Mennen and Jim O'Connor. I decided not to vote on my own behalf so that Ron Reed would not have to tip his hand to break a tie vote.

At this point Ron directed a major production in The Loeb of *Long Day's Journey Into Night* with two guest stars, Irene Daily and Joseph Warren.

Miss Daily had been given a room at Page Karling's home and she got the cast to come there and talk over how the scenes should be played. For example, she decided that the play was too dark and the way to lighten it up was by having the family very happy and compatible during the first scene at breakfast.

This makes absolutely no sense. The inciting incident for this long day into night is that the night before, Mary Tyrone went back into the bedroom where she always went to shoot up. This is unmistakable. When she finally comes to breakfast, her husband and two sons are totally stressed-out, although attempting desperately not to show it. How this scene can be played as a truly happy family situation absolutely goes against O'Neill's obvious intent. When such a thing happens it is up to the director to set it right rather than letting an actor dictate. But "happy" was how the scene was played.

Chapter 27

ON SUNDAY, MARCH 17, 1974 at six o'clock in the morning, the phone at 435 Robinson rang. It was on a nightstand just outside our bedroom and Robin mumbled something to the effect that it was probably a wrong number. But after a couple more rings I got up and answered it. It was Bruce Caldwell, one of Joe III's buddies from Indiana University. He said he had some bad news. The way he said it brought on sudden fear. I knew that he and Joe were thinking of going to Mexico on spring break, but what I did not know was that they had decided to travel by hitching train rides like guys did during the Great Depression.

Bruce went on: that morning in Liberal, Kansas while running to catch the moving train Joe slipped—at the word "slipped" I was more fearful than I have ever been in my life.

"But," Bruce added, "we got him into the hospital. I think they are going to operate this afternoon. They might have to amputate."

I doubled up and tried to breathe.

"It's his foot... and I don't know..."

"I'm coming out. I'll be there just as soon as I can," I said.

Robin was out of bed and with me in that little space at the head of the stairs. "It's Joey," I said, and told her what had happened. They may have to amputate. I've got to get there. Right now!"

I called Wayne and asked him to drive me to the Indianapolis airport.

I dressed as fast as possible while Robin got some money together. I told her to call the Indianapolis airport and tell them I was on my way and that I needed to fly to Liberal, Kansas, or the town nearest to Liberal.

Wayne drove as fast as possible. It was hard to talk. It was worse to think about Joe's leg being amputated. It was unbearable. We reached the airport and they were waiting for me. They had me booked on a flight to Wichita where I could get a private plane to Liberal, another 200 miles.

Wayne stayed with me but I could not talk. An hour later I was onboard, the plane was in the air, and that's when I totally fell apart and started bawling, trying not to make any sound which only made more noise. An attendant came. It was hard to explain because every time I tried I broke down. She took my hand, and as soon as she did I could not contain even what was left of my shattered control. I couldn't pull myself back and I put my head down on the tray and let go.

We arrived in Wichita before noon. The people there knew what was happening because the attendant had told the pilot, who had called ahead. I could not take kindness because it just undid me. They wanted to know if I was going to need a private plane to take me to Liberal and I said yes. But when Robin answered my phone call she said no to having to charter a private plane. Joe had been operated on and was still in the recovery room. It would be hours before he was back in his room.

I had missed getting there in time. The woman at the desk helped me get a taxi. I thanked her but could not talk again, and she explained to the driver what had happened and where I was going.

At the bus station I was alone, waiting, and no one knew me. Now all I could do was try to wrap my brain around the fact that Joey might not have a leg—I did not know which one—and would be dealing with that for the rest of his life.

It took almost six hours to get to Liberal, a very small town about the size of Allegan. I got directions to the hospital. It was after seven o'clock. I identified myself at the desk and found out that Joe was out of recovery and in his room. I had to do everything in my power to pull myself together before I could walk into that room.

Joe was awake. His bandaged right leg—the whole leg—was in a sling and elevated. At the end, the gauze was very thick but I could see that the foot was missing. It was all I could do to hold myself in check. He knew that and was the first to speak. In a normal conversational tone, he said, "Dad, I won't mind, if you don't."

It was a bargain and the measure of the man my son had become. I knew right then and there I had to somehow equal his courage and maturity. I also knew I was unable to do this as well as I wished. There were times when my voice faltered and I could not go on. But I accepted the bargain. I did not break. He explained to me what the operation was. It was called a Syme's. The toughest skin of the body was the callused heel. The doctor had removed the part of the foot that had been run over but saved the skin that was under the heel and from it, made a flap that went over the bottom of the stump that was now the end of his right leg. The Doctor had explained this to him as the choice he made rather than amputate just below the knee.

It was, I realized, something he wanted me to know and understand, as well as something to keep my mind on things other than my feelings. Joey had Robin's mind. He was very smart. He wanted me to accept what had happened and go on; take one breath after another, think forward. He was assuring me he was going to be all right. He was 22 years old. I was 49. He had traveled more in his young life than I ever had. His life was ahead of him, mine was mostly behind.

That night, after calling Robin from the hotel room, I thought things I should not have thought but I could not help myself: Why could it not have happened to me instead? I wished I was home with Robin and John and little Larkin. I could not sleep. I just kept thinking "what ifs" and asking myself what Joey was going to do for the rest of his life?

The next day I talked to the doctor. Yes, this was a small town but its jobs all centered around what was raised on the nearby farms: wheat, corn, alfalfa, cotton. Had I not noticed the grain elevators from the window of the bus coming in? The machines used in harvesting often cut off arms or legs resulting in an operation. And that is why he knew about the Syme's.

I stayed at the hospital, much of the time in Joe's room, sometimes just watching him sleep and going over our life together and his travels, doubting he would ever be able to travel abroad again. On Wednesday the doctor said he would be able to leave the next day. I went to the airport and chartered a small single engine plane for $500. The young pilot's job was to do such things as needed to be done, taking the sick and injured to their homes. The next morning an ambulance took us to the airport and Joe was carefully strapped to a kind of bed. I sat beside him as we flew to Lafayette. Robin had an ambulance waiting to take him to Home Hospital, where I left him and came home.

The next day I wanted to talk to the orthopedic doctor who was in charge but he would not give me the time. I hated the bastard. Joe was measured for the necessary prosthesis. While it was being made there was some small adjustment that had to be done in the operating room. The doctor would not talk to either Robin or me. We were given two explanations: orthopedic surgeons were the prima donnas of the medical professions (but not the one in Liberal, Kansas), and what they had to worry most about were lawsuits for medical malpractice (but that fear had not reached the doctor in Liberal, Kansas).

My first thought when Bruce called was that I had to get Joe to a place where they had the best doctors. And now I realized that the best doctor had been in Liberal, Kansas.

A week or so later, I had a previously scheduled class where I was supposed to talk. It was over in University Hall. I went there but as soon as I stood behind the podium and faced them, I knew I could not do it. I tried to hold in my emotions. I tried to start but I could not. My breakdown was too difficult to explain. I fled back across Oval Drive and came home.

Sometime after that Joe was fitted with his prosthesis and was anxious to get back to Bloomington and make up what he had missed. I came home and told Robin. We were talking and I was questioning what he would be able to do back in Bloomington. "I don't know, "she said, "but he's just going to have to learn to stand on his own two feet."

I gasped for breath, and then started laughing and crying at the same time. It took her a minute to understand what I was laughing at, but when she did, she laughed too, but she did so without crying. I thought I would never stop my crying-laughter until all the tightly strung wires holding me together let loose, and there wasn't anything more left in me. After that, I did not cry again about Joey's foot being amputated.

After he became ensconced at I. U. and made up his class work, he came home for an overnight, and some of his friends had a party out at Happy Hollow. Robin and the kids and I went. There was a basketball game being played, and Joe was right in the middle of it, running and shooting baskets and acting as if he was the same as he had always been.

That picture has stayed with me forever.

The summer after, he was once again off to Europe, landing in England, and took a boat to Spain While there, he ran the bulls at Pamplona. And he never stopped traveling and living a fascinating life. Only recently he finally settled down in Asheville, North Carolina, and called to tell me that he had been kayaking and camping out for the last three days.

⌘ ⌘ ⌘

Spring and summer passed, and I was still "voluntarily" not attending faculty meetings with the theatre faculty. Bob Walker, who had been the young guy on the center platform of *Busy Dyin'*, was directing a project and asked me, I think out of kindness, to do the role of Crocker Harris in *The Browning Version*. It was a one-act, one of the first plays I had directed at Purdue. I thought I might try acting again, something I had not done for a long time. But acting did not come back easily and the thing that drove me crazy was that the day before we opened (October 13, 1974) I saw the set and it looked more like some tacky student digs than the apartment of an Oxford professor facing the end of his career. There was absolutely nothing to be done unless I refused to go on. I wasn't going to do that, so I did the best I was capable of, which was not much.

⌘ ⌘ ⌘

One of the self-help psychological books I read during this time was Thomas A. Harris's *I'm OK-You're OK*, which was on the *New York Times* best-seller list for a couple of years. It dealt with transactional analysis based on four possible positions in relationships. 1) I'm not OK, You're OK, 2) I'm not OK, You're not OK, 3) I'm OK, You're not OK, 4) I'm OK, You're OK. It seemed to me that I encompassed that third category on almost every issue that dealt with the theatre, and that made me feel as though something was wrong with me. That's why, as in the case of *The Browning Version*, I felt compelled in my interpersonal relations to just go along. But, of course, this was just coping. That kind of insincerity could not help. It only increased my frustration.

Harris said the first stage in life—"I'm not OK, You're OK"—takes place from infancy through learning to walk and encountering the world. Later, Eric Berne, one of the noted psychiatrists who inspired Harris's theory, and who was the originator of transactional analysis, disagreed with Harris, saying that the *first* stage for children is "I'm OK, You're OK" which seemed to me closer to the facts. Perhaps that was because I was raised by Aunt Floss, rather than a biological mother, and my father. I never remember being awed by her or any other grown-ups for any reason.

The reason I was attracted to Harris' work was that it was *self*-help, rather than Freudian analysis that could go on for years. It saved money and was more private. It was also much more uncomplicated than Freud's relationship between the id, ego, and superego. When dealing with interpersonal relationships Harris categorized simply, "parent, adult, child." His method involved reliving memories and experiences from childhood as in "private moments" in acting. And he made it clear that this kind of self-analysis should not include cases such as manic depressives who needed medical attention, drugs, or shock or hydrotherapy treatments.

The danger with self-help, of course, was in becoming a psychological dilettante. I now think that what the information in this book did for me was to help me try to find ways to accept, or at least cope with things that no matter how I tried I did not agree with. The downside to this was that in doing so, it seemed to categorize me as a child: "I'm *not* OK, You're OK," or in my interpersonal relations as *acting* like a child rather than an adult. Of course, I may have gotten this all wrong, but that is what I thought at the time, and I'm not going to restudy the book to find out.

All I knew emotionally was that I had to get away from the current environ, and I kept looking for job openings and writing queries for anything I thought I might be qualified for. But finding a job as a full professor with tenure was as tough as finding an acting job on Broadway. What was my future life going to be like? The thing that saved me from going bonkers was work, finishing my book on dramatic structure and teaching.

Christmas came and a New Year, 1975, and how I missed going to Ross and Dorothea's place and seeing him fire off his gun at the stroke of midnight. Just after the New Year, Robin and I were invited to a party at Ron Reed's home on the East side. I had a beard by that time and was unsure what we should wear since this was the first time we had visited them. I finally dressed in a jacket and tie, and Robin as always was beautiful in whatever she wore. We knocked on the front door. Ron opened it and immediately there were people swarming into the room singing Happy Twenty-Fifth Anniversary.

Yes, I had just finished 25 years—February 1950 to January 1975—at Purdue.

Ron and his wife had done everything possible to make this a joyous occasion. Desperate not to act like a child—"I'm wrong and You're right" rather than an adult—I tried my damnedest to be "happy." There were wonderful mementos including a telegram from Elia Kazan congratulating me. There was a photographer to record this "historic" event and who would paste pictures into a scrapbook. There were a lot of Townies such as Dotty Murphy and Patty, Page and Jack Karling, Alice and Tom Dowling, Stuart and Porter Main, Richard Cordell, the Al Chiscons and the Sidney Pellisiers, and so many more whom I liked and who had been so loyal and supportive of what I had been doing. But there were others on the theatre faculty with whom there were still "interpersonal tensions," even though I had not much to do with them since I was excluded from faculty meetings. I kept up the lie of happiness with a phony smile throughout, but the truth was I was miserable.

⌘ ⌘ ⌘

On January 28, 1975, Dad died. He had been ill, and his death was expected. Rae took care of all the arrangements, and our whole family went to the funeral, which was of a military nature at Gordon's Funeral Home on Ely Street in Allegan. The flag that covered his coffin was folded by the military attendants and given to me. His ashes were buried in the lower part of the Trowbridge Cemetery and the marker was provided by the military. I believe this was the first funeral our kids attended.

I did not cry. I did not have any feeling except general sadness. I tried to think about our relationship but there had been so little of it. I decided the reason for my lack of feeling was simply that I did not really know this man. And that was the truth. This was not thought in anger, only a fact of life and I wished I had loved him and that he had loved me. But maybe he had and I never knew it.

⌘ ⌘ ⌘

It was a couple of months after Dad died that I woke one night with my body absolutely rigid. I went downstairs and called Father Melvin, who by this time had been transferred to a state prison near Marysville as a spiritual councilor.

He said to come along. I did not wake Robin; I just got in the car and drove north.

He listened carefully. I told him about the frustrations in my job and my sister spending time in a mental institution, and that I thought perhaps I was going crazy. Of course, he could only listen, but I needed someone who wasn't family to talk to. When I left I had not resolved much, but I had vented and shared. I drove to Logansport where a state mental asylum was located. I identified myself and asked to see the head of the hospital. I told him I wanted to be committed because I needed help. He ended up recommending a psychiatrist in Lafayette. I drove home and told Robin where I had been and that I was going to see a shrink. I made an appointment and had three or four more sessions before I felt that this was not helping me.

I just felt like I was at the end of my life and I was doomed to stay exactly where I was.

One bright note in all this was a course during the second semester on the four major plays of Chekhov as if we (the group of kids I was teaching and I) were actually planning to do these plays in repertory in the Experimental Theatre. In addition to reading and analyzing the plays together we took notes on properties, costumes, lighting and casting (one set of professional actors only from Hollywood or Broadway and the other limited to actors at Purdue and the Lafayette area). They immediately saw that most of the actors used in one play could be cast in another, as well as a lot of properties and costumes that would serve all four plays. What the hell? Only two samovars needed and Masha's black dress could be used for her character in all the plays. And we always kept in mind the author's intent which was, of course, the same for all his plays.

For our final, we met one Sunday afternoon at 435 Robinson, each student as one of the characters from his plays, *in character*, and wearing an assimilated costume. The occasion was a dinner party. There were conversations all started from something talked about in one of his plays, and there were walks on the lawn. We talked in character and drank vodka and ate Russian foods. Steve Henderson was in that class and always reminds me of the joy of that day.

The semesters closed in and I had, without the slightest hope of receiving it, filled out the forms and written a letter to Farley Richmond of Michigan State applying for a State Department grant to go to India to observe art, architecture, theatre, music and dance for the following summer. I had found no openings for another job except one that would replace retiring Norris Houghton as Dean of Theatre and Film at the three-year-old newly invented School of the Arts at the State University, New York at Purchase. I didn't have any confidence that I'd get this top job in the country because I had so little administrative experience. In addition, I had no book-length publications, as did Norris.

Then a letter came.

April 23, 1975: Dear Joe: I am pleased to announce that you have been selected as the recipient of your Department's Outstanding Teacher Award for 1974-75. The fact that you have been selected for this honor by your students and colleagues is a testimony to your excellence and devotion as a teacher. As the Department recipient for this honor, you will receive a framed certificate at the fall convocation of the faculty of the School of Humanities, Social Science, and Education. I hope that you will be present then to receive the recognition you have earned. Best wishes for the continued success in your work as scholar and teacher.

Cordially. /s/ signed Robert L. Ringel, Dean, with CC: to Dr. Dorn

I had no job that summer for either teaching or directing and it was not until mid-June that I got a call from John Straus, Vice President of the School of the Arts at SUNY, Purchase, asking me to come for an interview. I went with high hopes, but in the back of my mind— probably the same protective device as actors carry with them into an audition—the knowledge that I actually had little hope of getting the job.

Since it was summer, John Straus and his wife Anne were living in their summer home at Pound Ridge. I had been instructed to take the train from Grand Central to White Plains where he would pick me up late-morning and give me a look-see at the campus, as well as a meeting with others. I would stay overnight at his place and meet the next day with Abbott Kaplan, the president, and then return home.

The campus was not particularly appealing. In the center of 500 prime acres of Westchester County, across the road from Pepsi Cola's National Headquarters, it was all brand new and laid out with the Performing Arts Center (still under construction) on the east end, the gym at the far west end. What separated about a third of this was the quad made of thousands of bricks, in the center of which was the first floor of the library (with other floors in the basement, and subbasement) along with a bookstore. Further west were the green playing fields and the gym. On the right of the bricked mall was an empty space where the Theatre Arts building was yet to be built, followed by Visual Arts, The Newburger Museum, Humanities, and Campus Center South, which were already constructed. On the north side of the mall, across from the hole in the ground, was the Music building, Dance building, Natural Science, Social Science, and Campus Center North (under construction). Facing the playing fields on the northwest side was an apartment complex, and on the southwest side dormitories and a dining hall.

Adrift from this formally laid out campus were the old farm buildings, which functioned as the Administrative/Admissions/Business/and Personnel offices. The old Gate House was on the south side with access from Lincoln Avenue, and just a bit toward the quad was what they called the Metal Building, which was made of corrugated steel and used by the Design/Technology students of the Theatre Arts and Film Division.

John Straus was obviously very pleased with what was there, including what he had made possible with private gifts of his own and money he had raised. The Music building was equipped with special soundproof rooms (were there 75 of them?), all containing Steinway grand pianos. In the Dance building the wooden floors were "sprung" in all sixteen studios. In one of the four theatres in the Performing Arts Center was the largest organ in the world (this may be an exaggeration) which John had imported piece by piece from Europe. To me, the campus was impressive, although strangely uninviting. Even the Henry Moore statue at the end of the mall and bordering the green playing field, comprised of entwining nudes, did not look comfortable.

After lunch John took me to be interviewed by Norris, a small man who was pleasant, positive, likeable, and to the point. I met Joe Anthony, who was strictly nonacademic. When I mentioned that I had not cast Karen Black in *No Exit* years previously, he wanted to know if I had made out with her.

I stayed with John and Anne at their gorgeous place at Pound Ridge and we had dinner prepared by their cook and served by a housemaid. A wonderful long evening talk followed in their living room. I had one drink too many and when John and Anne got into a minor altercation concerning their son, I sided with Anne and when I thought about it after getting into bed I worried that I may have pissed John off. But as I think back on it, I believe it helped him to make up his mind about me. He was a man who didn't want yes-men surrounding him. He valued other opinions; whether he accepted them or not was another matter.

It was early in July when he called and offered me the job of Dean of Theatre Arts and Film. I cannot tell you how glad and relieved I was. The offer included a tenured full professorship and $25,000 a year. I asked him if I could have a day to think it over because I wanted to talk to Robin, but that I might call him back earlier. Robin knew more than anyone else in the world how unhappy I had been and was all for me taking the job, although if I could have been happy staying at Purdue, she would rather have stayed at 435 Robinson, which had been our home where we had raised, and were still raising, our last two kids.

I called John back in a couple of hours and asked him if he could possibly sweeten the offer a bit, and he said, of course, and that he was glad I asked since it showed I was savvy about money He offered $2,000 more and I agreed. He said he would overnight the papers, which I should sign and send back as soon as possible.

To celebrate, Robin and I went to the Chinese Restaurant in West Lafayette for lunch. Dean Hass was there. When I told him I was leaving Purdue and about my new job he was stunned. He had always been a major supporter of my work, and didn't want me to leave. In fact, he went to President Hanson and talked to him about it. I was making $19,000 per year after more than 25 years. The new President called and said that I had been underpaid and offered to raise my salary by $6,000 if I would consider staying.

I think at that point I was rude in my answer. I said something to the effect that if they could suddenly raise my salary by that much, why in hell hadn't that been done during the years I had been working my butt off? He apologized (he was a very nice man), and then I said no, that nothing on earth could make me stay. They had treated me badly, not only me but the arts in general, and I was leaving. The truth is I had been out of love with my job for five years and was hurting badly.

Three days later John Straus called and told me that because of some bureaucratic hitch in Albany the tenured position that I had signed for in my contract could not be offered until sometime in November, but that Abbott Kaplan had promised that it would be honored and to please trust him. I knew that this was dangerous, but I accepted it because this was my lifeline. I was not going to stay at Purdue and drown. I also suggested that rather than starting September 1st, I should be on the payroll the 1st of August because I needed a month to get organized before school started. He thought this was an excellent idea and agreed.

We sold our house for $30,000 to Jim O'Connor and Kay Deaux. It was worth more but we took the offer. We gave away hundreds of books and sold as much as we could. Then late in the month we rented a U-Haul truck that I drove. Robin followed in the Volkswagen with John and Larkin and our little caravan headed to Rye, New York. I'll never forget the early morning at the end of July when we left West Lafayette. I never looked back. Son John, who was approaching the age of 13, had problems. He had made many friends in West Lafayette and the adjustment would be difficult. Larkin, who would be seven in November, was unaffected. Robin was apprehensive about driving such a long distance. We stayed overnight at a motel that first night and then headed out early the next morning.

On the road that would take us to into the city of Rye, I was driving in the far left lane when I saw a sign on the other side of the road that indicated that the turnoff was to the right and coming up in one mile. There were three lanes of traffic. I *had* to get to the right lane, and Robin had to follow. I flashed my turn signal several times to warn what was going to happen. I moved to the middle lane, screwing up traffic behind, but we both made it. Then, with less than a quarter of a mile to go, we ventured into what was dangerous traffic. Robin was panicked but followed behind, with John learning out the window and waving to the fast moving traffic to please not cut them off. We made it to the right lane just in time to turn off at the exit. We reached our rental and Robin followed me right into the driveway, totally exhausted. We were both half a year from being 50 years old. We had driven all that way with the two kids and all our possessions in a U-Haul and were about to start another new life.

Chapter 28

WE TOOK A WEEK DOING the millions of things it takes to get settled. Toward the end of that week I received a letter from Charles M. Dorn, Head of the Department of Creative Arts at Purdue.

Dear Joe: Following my return from Europe, Ralph informed me of your decision to resign and to accept a deanship at Purchase. It goes without saying that I was surprised at your decision, but also delighted at the opportunity that is presented to you in this fine position. Over the past three years I have known you, I have truly come to respect the many competencies you have as a teacher and scholar in the field of Theatre. I also am aware of your frustrations with Purdue and perhaps with me, but I sincerely hope you can look to a very bright future at Purchase and not back to the agony and frustration of these past few years in Creative Arts.

You have a lot to offer to that institution and I know you'll do a good job and I think the change will do a lot for you and perhaps help to improve your feelings toward this institution. You will be missed by many of your friends here and that should tell you that all your efforts here have not been in vain.

Good luck and if the spirit moves you, keep in touch. My best to Robin.

P.S. As an administrator, please also remember that the first three years are the hardest.

This saved him from having to decide whether to let me attend theatre faculty meetings after a year and a half, or to insist on my separation from them. Frankly, I was overjoyed not to have to do so.

⌘ ⌘ ⌘

I have written of the incredible effect of the W. McNeil Lowry article on my thinking about the connections between the University and theatre training. As Lowry wrote: "The University has largely taken over the function of professional training, but in the main has sacrificed professional standards in doing so." Lowry's views gave focus to my life for over a decade, even when I could not pursue what I knew to be true.

Now, by a stroke of luck, I had an opportunity to be in an environment where my belief in conservatory training—a School of The Arts—was up and running. I differed in a couple of ideas: I believe that the objective of a Liberal Arts institution—at SUNY Purchase called the College of Letters and Science (hereafter referred to as L&S)—was to create a thinking individual who uses the traditional tools of reasoning to arrive at logical conclusions. Such tools, however, were not antithetical to creativity; in fact in the analysis of plays, they were absolutely essential for the highly motivated and focused creative talents found in theatre and film students.

Another belief I had up to this point was that the working core of any production should consist of professionals with students, which was true for Purdue since the theatre was a necessary cultural adjunct for the campus and town. At SUNY's School of the Arts, less than an hour away from the heart of New York City, neither the campus nor the town of Purchase (which was so small it actually could not be located) had any such need to make life more interesting and livable. In addition, every student enrolled in the Arts School had been interviewed, auditioned and in the case of design/technology had to present portfolios, and in the case of film, actual films. Unlike Purdue, the competition for entry into the theatre was fierce. In acting, for example, we auditioned about 1,200 for a class of 30 students. And, of course, all faculty members were professionals who had gained membership in their unions through participation in productions that often included Broadway.

In this instance it made sense to use only student talent in theatre productions since their talent was at such a high level. I was to learn, however, that since the emphasis was basically on training its students' talent, strangely enough, the mounting of first-rate productions that audiences wanted to see was rare.

Another problem was that the year, 1975, was one of the worst years in the state and the city's history. There was talk of New York City going bankrupt. When asked if I wanted to go into the New York State retirement plan or keep my TIAA/CREF retirement plan from Purdue, the choice was a no-brainer. I also knew that if the worst happened, Abbott Kaplan and John Straus could renege on their promise of my tenure. But I had to take that risk for my own survival. The fact that the theatre arts and film building was still a hole in the ground was uppermost in my mind.

⌘ ⌘ ⌘

I found out some, but not all, of the school's history with the help of the Dean of Music Michael Hammond, a fellow enthusiast of McNeil Lowry. This campus, obviously built as an Arts School, would be a first in American education. Instigating the plan were such influential leaders as Governor Nelson Rockefeller, SUNY's Chancellor Sam Gould, and philanthropist Roy Neuberger who contributed his art collection as well as money. The State of New York would offer professional training, at low-cost tuition, for the young potential professional artist, not only from New York but from the nation and the world, but only if they were talented enough to be chosen through auditions and interviews. Thus the institution's uniqueness lay in the fact that it was a School of the Arts for the whole country. In the 1978 graduation class, I handed out diplomas to Ghasem Ebrahimian and Mohamed Reza Salavi, Iranian student film makers who, incidentally, desperate for older character types, cast me in one of their films, the first of about 25 student films in which I acted.

The school would offer hands-on skills courses taught by professionals leading to the Bachelor of Fine Arts. But since artists are judged not by degrees but by their art, provision was made for the granting of a certificate to outstanding students who did not finish the professional course of study or meet their minimal L&S requirements.

Everyone, from the governor to the chancellor, was fully aware that some of this training would have to be done on a one-to-one basis, such as film editing where one highly skilled professional editor, such as Miriam ("Mimi") Arsham, from the real world of film/television, would sit on one side of a "flatbed," and one highly selected and talented student would sit on the other while training in how to edit a film. But how were such occasional one-on-one, or even one-on-six film or design courses, to be financed?

The original nuts-and-bolts plan was drawn up by James A. Frost in arts-minded Chancellor Gould's office. There would be 800 students in the School of the Arts with a faculty/student ratio of one to six. In order to finance this necessary special training, Purchase would have a *separate* College of Letters and Science—Mr. Frost said that this was the only way the plan could work—so graduates from Westchester, Rockland and NYC's community colleges, or any other junior college, having completed a two-year associate degree, could *easily matriculate* to Purchase to complete their BA degree without losing credits. The College of L&S would be outstanding in this specific role: to serve students from public, low-tuition junior colleges in the state and city.

L&S was to enroll 4,500. Training was also to be offered in nursing, social work, communications (media), and teacher-training, for another 700. The college would be funded on a one-to-23 teacher/student ratio. The imbalance between the number of arts students and those in L&S would allow the expensive arts curricula its necessary level of support, without distorting the relative overall cost per student in comparison with SUNY's other four-year campuses.

What was so exciting about getting this job was that it trained highly selected pre-professional students by professionals. No teachers were required to have a university degree; they only had to have impressive credits in professional theatre/films/TV.

During my years as dean, I twice held the preliminary auditions for approximately 1,200 potential acting students. This took place during all of February, March and early April. By that time the new acting teacher who would be teaching those selected, 30 from approximately 150 call backs, would then be able to join the board-of-study for input on the final selections. As with most European and Russian actor training schools, more men than women were selected, 20 to 10, plus three or four of each sex on the waiting list. The reason for this gender imbalance was because it approximated the same gender imbalance of the vast majority of the roles in classical dramatic literature, which professional regional repertory companies would be, and were, producing.

The basic training requirement for actors was: acting, voice, speech, stage movement, stage makeup, beginning gymnastics, design/tech practicum (crew members for upper-class production), and my course in dramatic structure, plus a colloquium which met once a week with outside speakers such as Harold Clurman, Agnes de Mille, Uta Hagen, Elia Kazan, Arthur Miller, Otto Preminger, and Roberto Rossellini, all of whom had spoken there in the three years of the school's existence. The second semester added an L&S course of their choice; and circus arts took the place of gymnastics.

Keeping the basics of acting, speech, voice and movement, the sophomore year added History of the Theatre, Director's Scene Workshop, beginning fencing and/or combat choreography, plus an L&S elective both semesters. In both their junior and senior years, students took variations of the five basic courses they had taken in their first two years plus an L&S elective, and Rehearsal and Performance. This last course met in the evenings to rehearse for fully mounted shows that were presented to the public.

Lest you feel my positive spin is not quite real, I assure you euphoria soon came to a screeching halt as I went over the department's books to find that the actual money available was $500,000 *less*—yes, I said LESS—than our budget for 1975/1976 (my first year!) This had to somehow be acknowledged and hopefully squared by the vice president of the arts and the business office, with more money added or cuts made. It didn't take a Camas the Magnificent with a crystal ball to guess on which side Albany would come down on in this matter. But that wasn't all.

Of the 12 tenured lines I was told our division had been authorized, Norris had signed letters that would legally award tenure-track to two positions for which tenure-track had never been approved by Albany. Abbott Kaplan had to be informed that in his budget the first two tenure-track positions, now referred to as "phantom lines," had to go to Theatre Arts and Film or risk a possible breach of contract. And, of course, he also had to get another tenured line for me. These "little administrative glitches" had to be settled to avoid financial scandal, and had "to be kept in confidence—just between us boys."

And there were minor issues. Whoever provided copy for the annual course catalogue hadn't a clue about numbering courses in sequence so that the figure one (1) meant it was a freshman course, two (2) meant sophomore, etc., etc., as had been tradition throughout the history of higher education since the University of Parma was founded in the 11th century.

I was also taken aback to find out that Dean Houghton's original plan had been skewed somewhat by Joe Anthony, whom Norris hired as the first "mentor," and who headed the acting board of study. This skewing awarded the "mentors" absolute and total control of *their* companies. The dean had to deal with their various wishes. (The second mentor hired was George Morrison, the third was Kay Carney, and the fourth, who came to the school at the same time I did, was Joan Potter.)

What was left of Norris' original idea was that when the first class graduated in late May of the following year, they were to go as a group to some city in the hinterlands—Moose Jaw, Minnesota?—where they were eagerly expected to bring cultural, with a capital K, enhancement to the culturally starved masses. This expectation, based on Norris' observations in Moscow in 1934, had to be dealt with immediately. If it were to happen, a city for them to descend upon had to be found.

And the biggest blow of all? When I was interviewed by Abbott my first question was, "When is the Theatre and Film's building to be built?" He and John assured that it was to start immediately. But someone had gotten to Abbott and convinced him that since this was an Arts Campus—"jewel of the SUNY system"—and since there was no question that such a building as Theatre Arts and Film would not be funded, why not put the money he already had into the most problematic piece of infrastructure to receive funding: the Social Science building, which would complete the L&S part of the campus. This would delay the Theatre and Film building "for only another year." In a decision that placated the demanding L&S deans, he went back on his word to me.

This again alerted me to the fact that his promise of my tenured position might also be in jeopardy. Further, being in competition for funds with L&S might not be such a good idea. If I learned anything from my first 25½ years in the Academy, it was that the arts were the runt of the litter and always sucked on the hind tit.

But who's complaining? I told myself. From where we lived I was 40 minutes from Broadway! And that helped make life very pleasant. And there were seafood restaurants around Rye that were unbelievably good. This was the best of all possible worlds. Further, it was good for me to be responsible for a whole new aspect of theatre, and I absolutely believed in the talent of the students selected for our division.

In my first talk with the theatre/film faculty I told them that if any of them had problems I would do my best to solve them. If in the future anyone felt I no longer served them or the division as well as they wished, I would step down. I would eventually learn how unwise it is to make such a promise.

After this first talk, Edith Skinner—arguably the best speech teacher in this country— needed a lift into the city. I offered her a ride in my newly acquired faded blue 1959 Plymouth with ruptured upholstery. I confessed that I had been slightly nervous when I delivered my speech since I knew she would hear my Midwestern nasality. She laughed, patted my arm, and said, "Oh, darling Joe, don't worry. I never listen to anyone unless I'm being paid for it."

In November my tenure was approved by Albany, as well as the two "phantom lines" for the division, which I was told by John was a major coup. But when I retired after 16½ years, the space where the Theatre Arts and

Film building was to have been built remained just a hole in the ground. We were renters in four of the studios in the dance building for the actors plus space for the film section in the music building. Administration of design/tech was in the social science building, with classes meeting in the Metal building.

Once tenure had been granted I felt free to tell both John and Abbott what I thought of the division's mentor system for acting companies, which in effect made the acting teacher an artistic director of a "company" as in a regional theatre. Administratively, it was unworkable and did not best serve actor training. I took it upon myself to deal with the original plan by interviewing the senior class about their forming a company out in Crotchbound, Arkansas. Not a single one of them said they had any intention of being in such a company. I remember the answer of Jay O. Sanders, one of the most talented, saying, "Absolutely not. After four years of looking into the same sets of eyes, however pleasant, I'm eager to move on." I also asked for their opinion of the mentor/company system. They said it would be okay for a couple of years, but after that there should be different acting teachers so they could get used to different approaches and ideas, the way it would be in the real world.

Wisdom from the mouths of babes!

Breaking the mentor system and "their company" was received well by the design/tech board of study since it was impossible to be accountable to both a dean and four mentor/artistic directors, who had total control of the training of his/her company, including productions. In addition there was another problem: an irate parent discovered that Joe Anthony required occasional nudity from students in his classes, which, of course, was utterly stupid in a tax-supported public institution.

Edith Skinner, who also taught at Julliard, came to my office and said she would not take the rudeness of students in Joe's company who made fun of her speech. She broke down and cried when she told me this. I called Ron Jacobson and Jay Sanders, two of the leading actors in Joe's company, into my office and informed them that I would not tolerate rudeness to Edith. They said that Joe himself made fun of her mid-Atlantic "snobbish" accent.

I told them I was going to meet with their whole company and asked for help in making the others understand that their conduct was unacceptable.

I later met with Joe Anthony and told him he could not require nudity in his classes, and that he had to be more collegial with fellow faculty members. I had absolutely no problem in speaking my mind to this 64-year-old-icon of the entertainment world who I much respected for his career in Hollywood and on Broadway. The result of this talk with Joe, the first mentor and head of the acting board of study, was that he requested a leave of absence, which I granted, pretty much knowing he would not return. I do believe that he eventually resigned because he knew, as dean, I was out to break the mentor/company system.

As for getting this job originally, I eventually found out that it had been Anne Revere who called Abbott and urged him to hire me as the new dean. To thank her for this, Robin and I give a dinner party for Anne and Sam and invited Abbott and Bea Kaplan. I can't forget Anne, sitting there on the sofa with Abbott, reminding him that as members of the same communist cell, he had cautioned her that her voice was too loud for a woman. She told him that the first speech she gave took place in the Hollywood Bowl, the largest natural amphitheater in the United States, with a seating capacity of 18,000.

Robin and I decided to take John Straus (the grandson of Isador Straus, an owner of Macy's Department Store, who went down on the Titanic) and his wife Anne to *A Chorus Line* for which I had four tickets in the seventh row, ordered by mail before we left Purdue. It was one of those gala evenings in the theatre, and after the show John had made late supper reservations for us at the Algonquin.

As we came through the lobby, there was Olive Deering in a rather shabby coat. I gave her a hug, introduced her to the others, saying I would join them in a minute. Olive told me she was desperate to play one last role: Mary Tyrone in O'Neill's *Long Day's Journey Into Night*, and she wanted me to direct it. Was there any chance it could be done at Purchase? I told her I would love to direct her in that show but that I'd have to query my colleagues and get back to her. What was her address? She said she and her brother Alfred lived next door at the Iroquois Hotel. I later found out it was a welfare hotel with a major clientele of indigent actors. In my letter I explained that what she proposed was impossible at the time but if anything changed I'd let her know.

Two or three years later the acting board of study and I had finished the second day of final auditions at Minskoff's studios, viewing 150 callbacks. I took the board of study to dinner at one of those nice restaurants in the theatre district. We were already seated when I saw Olive with her brother, Alfred Ryder, seated at another table. Joan Potter knew him as director of *A Far Country*. We went over to their table. Olive was obviously down in the heels but glad to be recognized and renew the acquaintanceship.

Our visit was brief, but while Joan and Alfred were talking, Olive again mentioned the possibility of me directing her in *Long Day's Journey*. I said that if and when I got any offers to direct she could rest assured I would find out if it was a possibility and let her know. "Is your address the same?" "Yes," she answered.

Who was Olive Deering? Does it matter? Yes, I think it does because it told me something about our theatre which allowed an actress (and her brother who had married Kim Stanley) to spend her declining years living in a welfare hotel. Olive had attended the professional Children's School in New York, debuting at age 15, and appeared in her first three Broadway shows. At the height of her career she was in *The Eternal Road,* a musical spectacular at the Metropolitan Opera House, directed by legendary German director Max Reinhardt, and the same year she played the Queen to Maurice Evans' *King Richard III*. Her film credits included the role of Miriam in Cecil B. DeMille's *Samson and Delilah* and later in his *The Ten Commandments* in the same role. She also had many credits in TV.

When I met her in Bar Harbor she had been out of work since June of the previous year. After that she would be in the Actor's Studio production of *Marathon '33* starring Julie Harris, and due to the kindness of Tennessee Williams, she ended her career in 1977 in his *Vieux Carre,* starring Sylvia Sidney.

Olive died in March 1986 at age 68.

⌘ ⌘ ⌘

It was in the spring of my first year at an all-dean's meeting that Michael Hammond was slightly late and apologized to Abbott, saying that he was delayed getting there by some terrific news. He had been selected as one of 17 who would spend the summer in India on a State Department travel grant from the U.S. Office of Education to participate in a seminar on Indian art, music, dance and drama. Everyone of course gave him a round of applause. After the enthusiasm died, I said that I had also applied for this grant and had obviously not been chosen, but I was sincerely happy for him.

One week later I received a forwarded letter from Purdue that enclosed a letter from Farley Richmond, who headed the seminar, informing me that I had received the same grant. I called him immediately. He said he thought it was strange that I hadn't answered sooner. He had not intended to choose two applicants from the same institution, but since I was at Purdue when I applied he was glad to have me aboard. Things were shaping up beautifully. I went to see Abbott Kaplan, who was totally supportive. I would continue to be on my twelve month contract as a representative of the school, and he said that he considered this recognition for two of his arts deans a real honor.

⌘ ⌘ ⌘

The participant's first meeting was on June 15th at Columbia University where we spent a couple of days in briefings. After the instruction sessions were over, I called Richard Busch, whose play *Talk Of Anther Day* I had directed, and he asked me to come down to his apartment. When I got there he was obviously not the Richard I had known as a student at Purdue. He had left his teaching position at Sweetbriar College and gotten an apartment in New York City. Someone had slipped him some LSD at a New Year's Eve party. He had ended up in the hospital for two weeks and was still in recovery.

I told him I was due for briefings early the next morning and split. This was the sad last time I ever saw Richard. At least I thought so. But just a few months ago as I write this, he resurfaced with an email to tell me he had news that I had written a novel that was published and to congratulate me.

It was great hearing from him. Since that time we have been corresponding. I have found that he lives in upstate New York and is doing well.

For the trip, Farley Richmond assigned roommates. I can't remember the name of mine, but he was from Binghamton, I believe. He was an Asian with a wonderful sense of humor. Once early on, when we were joking around and I could not think of his name, I called him "Yellow Peril," and he instantly answered calling me "Yankee Pig," and that's what we called one another, to our mutual delight, for the rest of the trip.

⌘ ⌘ ⌘

Our travel agenda to India seemed odd to me, because it did not follow a path that would take us from our first city to the next closest city, visiting each place in geographical order. We were in New Delhi only to fill out papers. We then went to Bombay (now Mumbai), which is in the middle of the West coast bordering the Arabian Sea. Jet lagged, we saw the Rajabat Clock Tower, the great circular Roman arch which is "the Gateway to India" along with the harbor, which appeared haphazardly full of boats and ships. The temperature was in the eighties and the humidity high since this was the monsoon season.

On a bus tour we saw the Taj Mahal Hotel, a giant square building topped by minarets; Bollywood, home of the Hindi film industry which we would visit on our return to Bombay; temples galore; statues of the Buddha; and ancient Catholic Churches, which pleased our two Nuns who were on the trip. But mostly we saw incredible poverty, the likes of which I could not imagine: great flocks of beggars, mostly very young emaciated children or sometimes babies, having had their arms or legs pulled from their sockets by their parents in order to create greater sympathy and take in more money, and naked male children with their genitals mutilated. A little girl walked down a street in the rain. She lifted her dress and let loose a stream of diarrhea to be washed away by the rain and run off into the various water supplies. We were told *never* to drink tap water or even use it to rinse our toothbrushes. All of us at one time or another came down with dysentery with incredibly high fevers and stomach cramps. I threw all the coins I had to the children—which our guide said not to do—and when I had no more I just stayed on the bus to avoid looking into the faces of human misery.

Our next city was back up north, Baroda (now Vadodara), in Gujarat with amazing banyan trees near the Vishwamitri River. It is an industrial city vibrating with the sound of motor scooters, taxis and man-pulled rickshaws, which is how most of us traveled. There, we attended classes at Maharaja Sayajirao University. The city is known for its culture: music, classical and modern, much sitar playing (you should try staying awake in 100 degree heat listening to a three hour sitar concert). While there, I fell in love with two paintings by a student at the university and told him that I had $175 to spend but that I had to have both of them. He was torn, but ended by saying that he wished for more money. I told him that was okay and if I had it I would give it to him. In truth I didn't have it.

He called me a couple of hours later at the hotel and said if the offer was still open he would like to accept it. I said, "Are you absolutely sure?" He said, "Yes, because I know I cannot get more money for them and I need the money to complete my schooling. They are modern paintings and Gujarat is a very conservative section of the country." Both paintings are with us to this day. Several years ago I contacted Christie's and Sotheby's and gave them the name of the artist, Vinod Dave, and the titles "Game of Flesh. Both auction houses said his paintings were selling for about $6,000.

Back to Bombay, the largest city in India with the greatest population. In fact it is one of the two or three most populated cities in the world. It is a conglomerate in almost everything. In religions there are the Hindus, Buddhists, Muslims, Christians, Jains and a few Sikhs (the ones who never cut their hair), all with churches, shrines, festival days and foods.

This time we visited Bollywood studio, where we were treated like royalty. They even brought out a sexy young bleached blonde, introducing her as "Our Marilyn Monroe." I said I would like to see one of their films, and arrangements were made. Most audience members waited hours to buy a ticket for a future showing and the movie theatres were jammed to capacity. Ours were reserved seats and we went ahead of the lines. But what I saw, a random pasted-together mish-mash of a musical melodrama in Technicolor, was not my idea of a good film.

Bombay was also a traditional manufacturer of fine clothing because of the textile mills. I bought Robin a sari made of a special silk, as beautiful a garment as one could ever see and which she wore for years on special occasions.

Kerala is not a city. It is a state, a sliver of coastal land on the Arabian Sea, in the most southwest section of India. The weather was equatorial and in the monsoon season, the humidity fierce. There were coconut trees, exotic birds and butterflies, lagoons, harbors, and a river connecting the backwaters on which were year-round houseboats. The region encompasses three cities which are the top tourist attractions of the country.

Cochin (now Cochi) is the first of these cities we visited. It is noted for its international and domestic tourism, radiant sea coast, trading center and shipyard. Trichur is an inland city known for its temple dedicated to Lord Shiva. Inside are wooden carved highlights of the epic poem *Mahabharata* (nine hours of which (as a play) I later saw every boring minute of, as staged by Peter Brook at The Brooklyn Academy's Second Theatre). Cheruthuruthi is a small village and it was here we visited the professional school of Kathakali, Indian drama featuring dance and gestures. Speaking of very long theatre presentations, this one started at sundown and lasted until sunup. I was the only person in our group who lasted the entire night.

The next day we interviewed the administrators of the School. To perform in this kind of drama, students study for ten years for which they receive state subsidy. Applicants are selected through auditions at ages seven or eight. The training is disciplined and rigorously physical, like ballet in the Western world. They gave us a demonstration of the intricate makeup, which includes putting a small seed in the corner of the eye to turn the eyeball red, long enough to last through the overnight performance. They also held a dress parade showing us the elaborate costumes necessary for the various characters. The nearest I can analogize this form of drama is Kabuki.

Mahabalipuram is a port city on the Bay of Bengal about halfway up on the east coast of India. This is where "Shore Temple" architecture, including bas reliefs, is best viewed. Carved out of granite, this kind of temple construction is where young sculptors learn their art and craft.

We had a wonderful time that night, out of our beach huts on the shore in a moonlit night, listening to the sounds of the waves and waiting till the dawn came up like thunder out of China 'cross the Bay. I remembered Kipling's poem read by Miss Teusink at the Baseline County School.

> By the old Moulmain Pagoda, lookin' lazy at the sea,
> There's a Burma girl a sittin', and I know she thinks o' me
> For the wind is in the palm-tree, and the temple-bells they say:
> 'Come you back, you British soldier; come you back to Mandalay!
> "Come ye back to Mandalay,
> where the old Flotilla lay:
> Can't you 'ear their paddles chunkin' from Rangoon to Mandalay?
> On the road to Mandalay,
> Where the flyin'-fishes play,
> An' the dawn comes up like thunder outer China 'crost the Bay!

Inland Aurangabad is the site of the famed Ellora Caves, actually architectural structures cut into the side of a mountain. The most famous is said to be double the size of Athens' Parthenon and holds a statue of Buddha. An American tourist seeking a Kodak moment asked me to move since I was obstructing her view. "Why" I asked, "don't you just *look*, and *see* and store the sight in your memory?"

Jaipur, with walled fortified gates, is known as the "pink city," the capital and largest city in the state of Rajasthan. It is said to be India's most well planned city, perhaps due to British influence. The "pink" was to welcome Prince Albert in 1876. We saw the Maharaja Palace and famed Albert Hall, and it was here that I rode an elephant. All of us got to do so, but before I mounted, I went to the front and caught her eyes. I had smuggled out a cube of sugar from our breakfast and held it out in my open palm. She understood at once and the end of her trunk touched my palm as she delicately slipped the cube into her mouth. It took only a moment before I saw the expression in her eyes when it hit her taste buds. She smiled.

What a beautiful beast! I *knew* we were friends for life, and if I had laid my body out on the sun baked road, I *knew* she would not have stepped on me. Her next move was to bend down and hold out her left knee, which I mounted. She straightened up and lifted it high enough so I could grasp her back and crawl up just behind her ears where I bent down, patted her, and whispered sweet intimacies. It was just incredible. Such a huge animal and so gentle, an absolutely irresistible combination.

It was also in Jaipur where I bought Robin a special "dinner ring" which cost about 35 American dollars. I thought perhaps this might compensate for not buying an engagement ring when we decided to get married. Not the same, of course, as the diamond ring her mother had provided, but perhaps more *us,* of what we had become together.

The stone was from India (not Pakistan), a huge lapis lazuli reflecting the colors of violet and blue. I had it set in a delicate silver band that tightly held the stone. Robin said she was thrilled and wore it for the first time one evening when we went to dinner at our favorite seafood restaurant near Rye. I found out only some time later that when she went to the Ladies' room and washed her hands, she removed the ring and without thinking left it on the side of the sink.

Agra is in Upper Pradesh on the banks of the Yamuna River. It is the city of the Taj Mahal. That's distinction enough! Seeing the Taj was, for me, the highlight of the entire trip. It seemed that it and Jaipur were the only two exceptions to sprawl and chaos. The Taj was absolutely symmetrical, with the classic arch-shaped main doorway and matching minarets on all four sides topped by the onion-shaped dome, originally gilded in gold.

Ustad Ahmad Lahauri is credited as being its chief architect, but it was built (1632-1648) under the watchful eye of the Mughal Emperor Shah Jahan, who had enormous influence and input during construction of this mausoleum for his third wife Mumtaz Mahal, who died giving birth to their 14th baby. His inscribed verse was:

>Should guilty seek asylum here,
>Like one pardoned, he becomes free from sin.
>Should a similar make his way to this mansion,
>All his past sins are to be washed away.
>The sight of this mansion creates sorrowing sighs,
>And the sun and the moon shed tears from their eyes.
>In this world this edifice has been made,
>To display thereby the creator's glory.

New Delhi, the capital of India, is where Prime Minister Indira Gandhi addressed the Nation on August 15th, the 29th anniversary of India's independence from Britain in 1947. Our visit there was only long enough for a sightseeing bus tour plus hearing the Prime Minister's address the following day. We did get to see the India Gate (1914), which resembles Paris' *Arc de Triumph,* and we rode by Jantor Mantar, which has thirteen architectural instruments of astronomy (1724) whose purpose was to compile tables, and predict the times and movements of the sun, moon and planets. If you really want to see wealthy excess in a nation that for the most part reflects only abject poverty, there is the Presidential House built in 1911 for the appointed viceroy. It has 340 rooms, and is still the largest domain of any head of state in the world .

Indira Gandhi's address to the nation took place at Red Fort, a walled city covering 255 acres strewn with hoards of expensive buildings. It had been built as the residence of England's royal family, and the building itself made the prime minister's message of this socialistic and secular country seem more than slightly incongruous. I would have chosen another venue, such as a shack in the Dharavi slums in Bombay, rather than the epitome of the conspicuous consumption of the "2-percenters." In addition, at that time Red Fort was used almost exclusively by the Indian Army, whose quest for nuclear armament seemed to mock the ideal of one of India's most revered spiritual fathers, Mahatma Gandhi, whose mantra was nonviolence and civil disobedience.

⌘ ⌘ ⌘

It was not an easy trip. It wasn't really pleasurable, nor was my sense of the beauty of Indian art, architecture, music, dance and theatre heightened. The land itself seemed worn out and drained of all value from overuse without rotation. It looked like the deep wrinkles of an old person. I could see no reason for the divineness of cows when people were starving, or for not adopting modern methods of dairy farming so cows would yield five rather than one quart of milk a day.

I came to think of India as chaotic: a statue of Buddha sprouting many arms and adorned with monkeys placed here and there; effigies of the Hindu God Shiva with two right forearms and one left, or two heads, one a destroyer the other the creator or with three eyes, and holding back the Ganges River; the beautiful symmetry of the body of man in total disarray.

A couple of years after my visit I read E. M. Forster's novel *A Passage to India*, and I shall never forget the shock of recognition I felt when the author writes of Fielding's return from India to Europe via the Suez Canal, his slow entrance back to Western civilization.

>Egypt was charming—a green thick of carpet and walking up and down it four sorts of animals and one sort of man. Fielding's business took him there for a few days. He re-embarked at Alexandra—bright blue sky, constant wind, clean low coastline, as against the intricacies of Bombay. Crete welcomed him next with the long snowy ridge of its mountains, and then came Venice. As he landed on the Piazzetta a cup of beauty was lifted to his lips, and he drank with a sense of disloyalty. The buildings of Venice, like the mountains of Crete and the fields of Egypt stood in the right place, whereas in poor India everything was placed wrong. He had forgotten the beauty of form among idol temples and lumpy hills; indeed, without form, how can there be beauty? Form stammered here and there in a mosque, became rigid through nervousness even, but oh, these Italian churches! San Giorgio standing on the island which could scarcely have risen from the waves without it, the Salute holding the entrance of a canal which, but for it, would not be the Grand Canal! In the old undergraduate days he had wrapped himself up in the many-colored blanket of St. Mark's, but something more precious than mosaics and marbles was offered to him now: the harmony between the works of man and the earth that upholds them, the civilization that has escaped muddle, the spirit in a reasonable form, with flesh and blood subsisting. Writing picture postcards to his Indian friends, he felt that all of them would miss the joy he experienced now, the joys of form, and that this constituted a serious barrier. They would see the sumptuousness of Venice, not its shape, and though Venice was not Europe it was part of the Mediterranean harmony. The Mediterranean is the human norm. When men leave that exquisite lake, whether through the Bosporus or the Pillars of Hercules, they approach the monstrous and extraordinary; and the southern exit leads to the strangest experience of all. Turning his back on it yet again, he took the train northward and tender romantic fancies that he thought were dead forever flowered when he saw the buttercups and daisies of June.

Everyone we met in India was either an academic or someone who supported the arts. Those interested in the theatre spoke of once-a-year trips to London's West End for a couple of weeks of theater-going. If they didn't make this yearly trip—this lifeline—to culture, they were devastated. Every one of these people was an Anglophile, and none seemed happy about gaining independence from Britain. All revered British culture. And yet, from what I understood, they were not accepted socially in England or by the great majority of their fellow Indians. They seemed to huddle together as people without a country.

⌘ ⌘ ⌘

Our trip home took something like 36 hours since we were delayed in the Tehran airport. One of our trippers from South Carolina and I were bridge partners against the nuns, and we whiled away the time playing bridge. Some hours before we landed at JFK we were given papers to fill out about what we had bought abroad and what we might have to pay import tax on. Some asked the nuns if they would mind wearing the bracelets and other jewelry through customs, to which the nuns readily agreed. The Irish Catholic checkers greeted them warmly with "Welcome home, Sisters. Hope you had a nice journey. No need to wait, just go right on through with your luggage."

Chapter 29

AS ALWAYS, IT WAS GREAT to be home, and in a day or two I had recovered enough to go back to the office. In addition to everything else during my first year at SUNY Purchase, I found out that one of the most pressing problems was that the entire theatre, nay, almost the entire School of the Arts faculty, seemed to know nothing about the procedures and standard regulations of traditional university life.

I had never thought of how many hours I worked in a week. Now I was confronted with union ideas that I truly believed were as necessary for the university as for people who did what I thought was actual work. Now I had to think—to justify—how many hours a week I could reasonably expect of teachers who taught such skills as speech, voice, movement, and acting.

At most institutions of higher learning there is a standard that has been worked out of what is considered fair amount of work for full time employment. None of this had been thought out and established under Dean Houghton, whose only academic experience had been as a professor for three years at Vassar College. My 25½ years at Purdue had trained me exceptionally well in these aspects of the world of academe.

How I did this was to compare the work of a science lab technician at Purdue, who was expected to be in the lab 40 hours per week, with a professor who lectured four classes per week. I figured that in addition to the actual four hours in class lecturing, he spent an average of two hours in preparation for each class, plus another three hours for each class grading and recording of papers, quizzes, mid-term, final exams, and routine office hours which amounted to 32 hours plus eight more for meetings of sectional, divisional, and school faculty meetings. That met the 40 hours week of the Fair Labor Standards Act of 1938.

Each skills course teacher (we will take Chuck Jones, the voice teacher, as an example to illustrate) would have to teach two sections for our freshmen actors, two sessions for the sophomores, one session each for the juniors and seniors, which means six hours per day for five days a week, a total of 30 hours a week. The other ten hours per week would be devoted to attending one or two rehearsals for coming productions, viewing one public performance of the production, plus faculty meetings which gives him 40-hour work-weeks.

One also has to realize that this is 40 hours per week for two twelve-week semesters, plus the four-week winter session, which means that he works only 28 weeks a year for full-time employment with all peripheral benefits. This leaves 24 weeks of paid vacation a year; others in the world work force world would probably feel this was a pretty damn good deal.

I know this analysis is simplistic. All sorts of variations exist, and a comparable work-week for those in the Academy will *never* be achieved. I also know that some feel that getting advanced degrees should give them special salary consideration. I had some teachers who wondered if their daily drive into and out of the city should be considered as part of their work day, and I would point out that I knew of no job that paid a worker for their choice of where to live, or their commute time.

In short, I tried my damnedest to be reasonable. I believe that for the most part Chuck Jones saw that I was attempting to get the best education possible for our students, and that there was only so much money to go around. I put him on a tenure tract contract rather than keeping him as an adjunct employee, which paid peripheral benefits (health insurance, retirement benefits, etc.) and also made him a voting member of the faculty and therefore a part of the division's governing body. He groused occasionally about me being a slave driver, but the grousing was good natured, and I tried to make it clear how much I appreciated the work he was doing. He, in turn, began to feel needed and proud of his work and proud of those kids he trained who were making it in the real world.

I also listened carefully to arguments from all sides about acting and began to understand those who suggested that what young, carefully selected, pre-professional acting students needed most were the skills courses. Acting could not be taught; either the student had it or did not have it. And if the actors had it, what they most needed was training in skills such as voice projection, dialects, fencing, movement, and these skills could be taught by using scenes from plays like the dances and fights in *Romeo and Juliet*. Select a sensitive, imaginative, and intelligent student with X-factor chemistry ("spirit and fire"), energy, focus and drive, and teach him the *skills* he will need in a lifetime career working in all kinds of plays. That was what was important. The only other thing he or she really needed to know to survive and succeed was how the structure of a play works hand in glove with acting. Guru acting coaches and followers of L. Ron Hubbard can be counterproductive, especially if they are also anti-directors.

As dean, I started out with ten approved tenure track lines and after five years had 18¼, more than any other dean of either the School of the Arts, or the College of L&S had acquired. All 18¼ lines were fought for in a lion's den of stiff competition, especially against the L&S deans who knew the ins-and-outs of the academic world, including parliamentary procedure from *Robert's Rules of Order*.

My full-time "confidential management" contract as dean did not require any teaching. But when Linda LaRue, my Upward Bound buddy from Purdue now teaching in the Social Science Department at Purchase, asked me to join her and a young woman from Boston University to co-teach a "cluster" in Political Theatre, I was glad to do so. This class was a grossly inflated L&S 8-credit course taught by three professors from different disciplines. It was to be taken in the student's freshman year, and constituted the L&S teachers full-time load during the new twelve-week semesters (which left time for a four week January short course.)

No one from L&S foresaw that my teaching this course, which was approved by John Howard, dean of Social Science, acting for the entire L&S administration, would certify and qualify me to offer L&S credit. And why not? I had a PhD and had been on Purdue's graduate faculty for twenty years.

Once this appointment became a fait accompli, I started offering my Dramatic Structure and History of Theatre as L&S electives. This caused a big fight led by an irate L&S faculty member who manipulated some of her students to write thinly veiled hate letters published in the student newspaper, *The Load*. They referred to me only as "you all know who I'm talking about."

All L&S courses awarded four hours credit instead of the standard three. That now meant that our Theatre Arts and Film students, who were required to take only 24 hours of L&S credits of their choice (half in lower division and half in upper-division courses) only had 16 more credits to earn from the L&S faculty.

As a quid pro quo, I allowed L&S students into both my courses. A core of them from the Political Theatre cluster—Phil Miller, Ed Altman, Amy Wolfson, Michael Bailey, and Sarah Wolins—asked me to direct them in Michael Weller's *Moonchildren*, which I did in what was called the "short term" [four weeks in January in which the students could do special projects which mostly turned out to be just a four week vacation for both students and teachers]. This production gave participants four L&S credits in January 1978. David Potts [Google him on the Internet] from Purdue, who was then designing in New York, did the sets and costumes and was later hired part-time on the design/technology staff. Our technical director, Alan Kibee, designed the lighting, and an organized smart young L&S kid named Michael Lesser was stage manager. I loved working with these kids and frankly, after four years of not directing, it felt good to be back in harness.

⌘ ⌘ ⌘

In the spring of 1978 I got a letter from Harris Gordon, the very successful CEO of a transportation business, who lived in Woodstock, New York, and enjoyed its famed Playhouse. When news reached him that it was about to be destroyed and a shopping mall installed in its place, he bought the

Playhouse and was determined to restore some of its former glory. Both Janet Hayes and John Newton had been leading actors there the season before and had recommended me as artistic director for the upcoming summer season.

I said yes immediately, as recorded in a lengthy article in the *Ulster County Gazette* written by Sylvia Day [6/22/78 p. 14] which gave my background in detail and asked why I wanted to join the Playhouse in such a prestigious and demanding position. I explained that the summer before I had seen a production of *Candide* in which my friends John and Janet had starred, and recalled that when I was a high-school student I subscribed to *Theatre Arts* magazine. I remembered that the Playhouse was cited as one of the great summer theatres, so in a way my interest was really not new; I knew its history and wanted to do everything I could to bring back its former prestige. "God knows, it wasn't for the money!" she quotes me as saying.

After a hiatus of four years and being talked into directing the L&S production of *Moonchildren,* I guess I was like a retired fire horse who suddenly smelled smoke; my nostrils flared, I heard the fire bells clanging, and I was ready to be hitched up and run like hell. I was well aware one-a-week summer stock was the acid test. But I met and liked Harris. I could choose what I felt would make a good season, hire whom I wished, and do shows I felt would make an exciting play-going experience for the audience.

I had an idea that I thought would work, and asked Harris if the company could meet two weeks before the first show opened rather than one. During that extra week we would rehearse on the following schedule, which I maintained throughout the rest of the season: During mornings we would rehearse the second play on the schedule. In the longer afternoon period we would rehearse the opening show. Granted, after we opened the first show the time for rehearsals was cut to two hours in the morning and three in the afternoon. But this still gave us two weeks of rehearsal on every production, which allowed the actors more time to think about their characters and the play's plot, which I believed improved their performances.

The best way to let you know what happened that summer is for you to get it straight from the critic's mouth, rather than me telling you. Therefore, brief excerpts dealing only with the directing aspect of the offerings and how the show was received by the critics are attached in Appendix C. I'd appreciate your reading them.

⌘ ⌘ ⌘

In my years as dean, Mentor Joan Potter was my greatest antagonist. People are motivated by very complicated reasons and situations and I don't want to speculate why she was so difficult during my deanship. When later we became best friends, she often said that I was the only dean who understood what was needed for the creation of a School of the Arts.

I was also a one-person integrationist between the School of the Arts and the College of L&S. In the short term of 1978, I directed a production of *Equus,* a play I loved, and which was a great success. Phil Miller, who played Alan Strang, did something wonderfully outrageous and probably necessary.

We were all waiting in my office for the first read-through and everyone knew I took no hostages when it came to lateness. About five minutes before we were scheduled to start everyone was there except Phil. I was about to say something when the back door opened and Phil stepped in wrapped in a towel, closed the door, shed the towel and walked naked around the table saying something to the effect that he thought everyone might as well see it at the start of rehearsals as well as later. He then wrapped the towel back around him, stepped outside, and fully clothed reappeared and took his seat just prior to the time set for rehearsal.

Michael Hammond, who by that time was president of the entire institution of SUNY Purchase—and in my view was the best president we ever had—said the faculty of L&S came to his office and told him that *Equus* was the best show they had seen at Purchase, much better than the productions by the Theatre Arts and Film Division.

The only problem I had during the production was that lighting designer Jeff Nash and technical director Brian MacDevitt pointed out that the walls of Theatre B —the construction of which had just been completed—were a reflective off-white color, making it impossible to light until the walls and ceiling were painted black. They were right, of course, and this had to be done immediately. I went through the proper channels but could see that all I was going to get was dragging heels. I finally called Michael Hammond. I explained the situation and said that if the physical plant people didn't get their asses over there the next day I was going to Sears Roebuck, buy black paint and brushes, and Brian, Jeff and I were going to paint the walls and ceiling ourselves.

Jeff and Brian were the ones who knew the exact color of the paint needed. They got it, and the workers from the physical plant were there the next morning and starting painting.

⌘ ⌘ ⌘

Janet Hayes asked me to direct a production of *Rain* for her Off-Off Broadway group, The York Players, located at 90th and Fifth Avenue. The play would open in late February. I was glad to oblige. The money wasn't much but it gave me a New York credit. Reid Shelton was out of the city and offered me his apartment on West 43rd Street. The York operated in the Church of the Heavenly Rest where Janet's husband was choir director. I had to work around time restrictions and conflicting events, such as AA meetings, and we would have to rehearse in a totally unsuitable space or cancel rehearsals. Actors sometimes could not make rehearsals because they would get a commercial or voiceover. Worst of all, Jim Pritchett, who was cast as Rev. Davidson, could not join the company until halfway through rehearsals; the stage manager had to read his role. I was now finding out what the Off-Off Broadway scene was really like.

I knew the show well since I had directed it the summer before, and Janet had gotten great reviews as Sadie Thompson. She had her own group of production people, principally designer Jim Morgan and production stage and production manager Molly Grose. Basically my work was just understanding the space, blocking the scenes, and getting the rhythm of the beats and scenes. It was very difficult to do this with a stand-in for Jim, but I knew from my experience with him in The Barn's production of *Desire Is A Season*, that for him learning lines was a piece of cake. We got the show on and I think it was as good as it could be under the more than trying circumstances.

⌘ ⌘ ⌘

The summer of 1979 I opted out of directing all the plays at Woodstock myself and only did *The Subject Was Roses, Arms and the Man,* and *Tartuffe.* They all received excellent reviews. *Roses* was very special with John, Janet, and Tom Flagg, who was absolutely first-rate as Timmy Curry, the son. The play had won the Pulitzer Prize and the Tony Award. It dealt with a boy returning from World War II and portrayed his relationship with his mother and father, and their relationships with one another. I believe it to be autobiographically honest in characters and emotions.

The Playhouse had done so well in the previous season that a theatrical organization in Syracuse wanted to book one of our productions. Harris and I both knew that *The Subject Was Roses* would be the easiest to send, so the week after it played in mid-July, Chris Parietti, a School of the Arts design/tech student who was one hell of a great technical director, took a couple of the crew and transported and loaded in the set at Syracuse. None of the cast was in my next show so they drove up by themselves and were provided excellent accommodations in a local hotel. Brian MacDevitt and I went up together and we naturally talked about a lot of things other than the show, and as guys rather than teacher/student stereotypes.

His setting up of lights, and focusing, and running the cues for that dress rehearsal was incredibly professional, and he and Chris worked well together. Syracuse's auditorium was larger than Woodstock's, but John, Janet and Tom were real pros on projection. We finished the dress rehearsal, had something to eat, and the show went on at eight with a big, very appreciative audience.

Our company got an excellent review from the Syracuse critic. In fact, the show had done so well, and we all liked it so much, that Janet scheduled it for a run at the York Theatre where it played in early January 1980, with Brian still doing the lights and working with Janet's regular York Theatre crew. *The New York Times* hardly ever reviewed Off-Off Broadway productions, but somehow a critic who obviously favored Ionesco/Beckett, or who had a thorn up his ass that night, was sent and wrote a very mean-spirited review, not mentioning the actors or me, but trashed the play and its author Frank Gilroy. He felt so hurt, I was later told, that he stopped the release of the play for a while.

⌘ ⌘ ⌘

At Purdue Robin and I were used to, and enjoyed, social situations. 435 Robinson was where people gathered after opening nights. When we were in Rye and Port Chester, we had dinner parties for Joe and Perry Anthony, and they had us to their house, and the same was true for other members of the faculty with whom we were trying to keep some semblance of friendship. Within a year-and-a-half, our $30,000 for sale of the house was reduced to $10,000, and we had to buy a house, which we did in Pawling, NY, (where James Earl Jones lived). That made parties impossible since it was 40 miles upstate, and most of the faculty lived in the city. I asked Norris if we could use his apartment at 11 East 9th Street for parties for the theatre faculty. He said yes. But parties there never felt as warm and fuzzy as parties at Purdue.

⌘ ⌘ ⌘

The most difficult situation was when, after reading negative student evaluations about a teacher, or listening to them in person and observing the same behavior in faculty meetings, I felt that a teacher did not best serve our students and it was necessary to give him/her six months' notice. One mentor had a field day in retaliatory talks against me to his students, who felt they could not take sides. I did not dislike him personally, but he was not right for the job. The recommendation of the primary committee (full tenured professors) agreed, but their written and signed recommendation was confidential, so giving him notice fell to the dean along with the flak. In brief there was a lot of politics and not much getting together.

⌘ ⌘ ⌘

One of the most pleasant remembrances is of the striking redhead Melissa Leo, who was accepted into the acting program in the fall of 1979. It was clear she was a major talent. Bill Prosser was a professor at the community college in Key West but was ostensibly there to head the Tennessee Williams Fine Arts Center where, in January, he was directing the world premiere of Williams' *Will Mr. Merriweather Return From Memphis?*

He called me just after the New Year saying Tennessee had promised the ingénue role—the daughter—to an acquaintance in Texas. But after the first rehearsal he could tell that the girl was totally wrong for the part. Having met Bill's wife, Roxanna, a beautiful redhead, and knowing that she was playing the mother, I mentioned to Bill in a phone call that the situation was unfortunate because one of our students, Melissa Leo, a first rate talent, so resembled Roxanna she would be perfect as the daughter. Incidentally, in real time, I ran across the program yesterday and the resemblance—they are pictured next to one another—is staggering. Bill said it couldn't happen because Tennessee would not allow him to recast.

I knew in my gut that Melissa would be perfect and I could not rid myself of the possibility of her playing the role. This was during the short term month. I called and asked her to come to my office. I explained the situation: Bill was a former student and a very good friend. I asked if she had any money. She did. I advised her to take a bus to Key West and just show up at Bill and Roxanna's apartment, saying that I had sent her there. Ask Bill if she could possibly attend rehearsals and understudy the role of the daughter, which would give her a terrific learning experience, even though she would never play it.

Bill and Roxanna fell in love with her as soon as she arrived. Bill said he would be delighted to have her understudy and observe rehearsals. She did just that, learning the lines and blocking. Then, just shortly before final dress rehearsals, the girl playing the daughter told Bill she would not be at rehearsal the next day because she had gotten a commercial gig and it was being shot in Houston.

He feigned exasperation but told her to go ahead; they would "struggle on" without her. He called Tennessee and told him he had to be at rehearsal the next afternoon. Tennessee was there and Bill announced that it was a straight run-through with only a five-minute break between the acts, and that an understudy for the daughter would be reading from the script.

Later that day he called me and excitedly reported the following: On her first entrance without script, word-perfect and knowing the blocking, Melissa acted with a moment-by-moment spontaneity that was not only absolutely thrilling but energized the entire cast. The play suddenly took off. When the run-thru was over, Tennessee rose from his seat and said, "That girl is going to be a star." The stage manager was told to call the girl who had been in the part and tell her she was being replaced and would receive her two weeks' salary.

Melissa eventually had problems with Joan and quit her company during the second year. But Key West was Melissa's first professional break, which included reviews in national publications. Many years later she and Joan made up at the Actor's Studio and both said they valued one another.

⌘ ⌘ ⌘

George Morrison came to me in the late winter of 1980 and said he was taking me up on my offer to step down as dean if any single member of the department so wished. This so stunned me that I don't believe I asked why or argued my case. I just said all right, and informed President Michael Hammond. In the next scheduled colloquium I announced that I was stepping down as dean of the department, and told them the reason why without revealing the name of the faculty member who had requested it.

I was very hurt by this request and attempted to put a bravado spin on the situation in my talk to the students but was not successful. I had to stop several times to keep from breaking down. In truth, I believe it was probably a blessing. Being an administrator was not easy. In fact, I was in every aspect, except publicly, the dean who got the division up and running and in shape. But you wouldn't know this from reading Celestine Bohlen's obit for Norrie in the *New York Times* on October 10, 2001: "His last full-time position, from 1967 to 1980, was at the State University in Purchase, N.Y. where he was the first dean of the division of theatre and film." No clarification of exactly what that meant was offered, such as that from 1967 until 1972 there were no students on the campus since it was still being built. Norris was dean for three years, after which he retired at the age of 65, becoming dean *emeritus* when I replaced him prior to the graduation of the first full class. He taught a History of the Theatre class and directed one show, *Billy Budd,* during the next four-and-a-half years as a faculty member and not as dean, and had a full-time sabbatical leave for his final semester.

Once I resigned, my big problem was money. I had received $27,000 in 1975 when I came to The School of the Arts—a sum that I later found out made me the cheapest hire of any other dean at SUNY Purchase. In the winter of 1979 I was making $34,000, but my resignation from Confidential Management automatically reduced my salary by ten percent, which meant I would now have a salary of $30,600 a year, far below that of the average, full-tenured professor, especially one who been teaching for 30½ years. President Michael Hammond was outraged to hear this. He contacted the Chancellor in Albany and requested that because of my work, and because I was hired at a lower rate than any other dean, there should be no reduction in my salary. The Chancellor agreed.

⌘ ⌘ ⌘

In May 1980 I directed *Buried Child* for the L&S students in which Phil Miller gave an unforgettable performance as Tilden. His playing of the "carrying in the carrots" scene was the funniest scene, without much obvious basis in humor, I have ever seen an actor perform.

That summer of 1980 I again declined being artistic director at Woodstock, but directed *Chapter Two, Mrs. Warren's Profession, Relatively Speaking,* and ended up directing Agatha Christie's *The Hollow* as a fill-in for a director who was let go. I loved working on *Mrs. Warren* because Janet Hayes was playing the role and wanted to give a really outstanding performance, as did her daughter played by Nancy Nichols, a fine young actress.

Howard Stein arrived as the new dean of Theatre Arts and Film. As the retiring dean, I was not on the hiring committee. But I knew, of course, that Howard had been assistant dean to Brustein at Yale, and had only recently taken the headship at Austin, Texas. He had negotiated well and was hired for a salary exceeding $50,000. He knew I was interested in playwriting and asked me to write a play the department would produce as the opener for the following season. A stand-up guy, he had the wit to see what was happening at SUNY Purchase's School of the Arts. Only three and a half years later he found a better and less stressful job at Columbia in New York City.

During the fall semester I got a call from Bill Prosser, who was doing a four-show Equity season at the Tennessee Williams Fine Arts Center. He wanted me to direct *The Little Foxes,* which would play February 4 through 8, 1981. Howard made arrangements so that I could miss the first week of classes for the second semester, and as I remember he taught them himself.

It was, of course, a great pleasure not only to do this play again, but to spend almost a month in Key West. Some of the company stayed at the Banyan, a stately old house with the largest banyan tree I had seen anywhere including India. The weather, which I expected/hoped to be in the seventies, got down to the thirties at night but the sun was glorious during the days.

One evening I came home to the Banyan, and the manager said, "Hey, Joe. You wanna do a line?" I knew what he was talking about, because I saw the white powder on the coffee table. I thought what the hell? He handed me a rolled twenty-dollar bill, and I leaned over and breathed in, but nothing happened. "You gotta really sniff it up," he instructed. I did, and it was absolutely amazing as it took me back immediately to the *U.S.S. Wyoming* where the doctor had given me a seven percent solution of cocaine so I could breathe more easily. That evening in Key West, I enjoyed a great high, but that was the last opportunity I ever had to use it.

I remember arriving back home with the snow a couple of feet high in our driveway, which I could have done without. Howard Stein reminded me that I would be writing and directing the first production in September. I suggested a play about Frances Farmer, which I had already started, and he agreed. In the meantime, I went to Woodstock that summer and did two shows, *Talley's Folly* and *Same Time Next Year*, both two-handers.

The actress in *Talley's Folly* was Mary Hamill, who had been a standby for Trish Hawkins in the New York production which ran just short of 300 performances. Incidentally, the show's company manager was Purdue's own Mark Andrews. The man playing opposite Mary was David Rosenbaum, who had been an understudy in *Oh! Calcutta*. Both were good to work with. Mary especially wanted to explore the play anew. We also had an extraordinary set created by one of our Purchase students, a first-rate designer, Jim Bush, along with terrific lighting by Brian MacDevitt. As stage manager, Harris had hired Diana Banks, who had played in the 1966 revival of *Annie Get Your Gun* with Ethel Merman, and was now a dance instructor at New Paltz. She was absolutely great and knew exactly what to do. The show got terrific reviews.

Same Time Next Year had Natalie Ross, whom I knew from The Barn Theatre. She had taken over the leading role in *Come Blow Your Horn* on Broadway shortly after the show opened and was a great gal to work with. The guy was Peter De Maio, whom Harris hired saying he had been the understudy for this show on Broadway. At the first rehearsal, when I gave him my first direction he, pleasantly to be sure, declined. I asked him if he was going to take direction and he said he would just do his role as he had already done it, if I didn't mind. I spent the morning blocking Natalie and talking about character and we had a wonderful time. When lunch break came, stage manager Diana said she was going to the deli and could she get me anything. "Yes," I answered. "How about a ham and cheese on rye and tell them to hold De Maio," which brought down the house.

We got the show on, and since I did the blocking for Natalie there was no doubt that Peter had to be where she was. Natalie got rave reviews and Peter was hardly mentioned.

Chapter 30

WITH ONLY TWO SHOWS AT Woodstock, I had time to do research on my Frances Farmer play and I went to the two towns in upstate New York in which she had done summer stock before joining the Group Theatre. I soon set the through-line objective. The character Josh, played by Steven Weber, says to the audience:

> Did you ever try to fix a life? "Fix." To get a fix on, to fasten securely, to put into some kind of stable or unalterable form so that the life means something, can be explained. That's what I've been trying to do. Isn't it reasonable that if we have the facts—from birth to death—know the relationships, motives; have it all spread out before us, that on reflection, the life can be summed up? Because if it can't—this doesn't apply to just her, it's everyone—I mean... is it possible to ever know anyone?

The story was about a group of students doing research on Frances Farmer and trying to find out who she was. I wrote and directed the play, called it *God's Peculiar Care*, which was the title of her autobiography that was lost, and it premiered in October 11th 1982. The actors and I went to the Billy Rose Collection of Lincoln Center's Performing Arts Library, and wearing rubber gloves because the paper these dime movie magazines were printed on was so old and fragile, we went through all of them, starting from 1935, when Frances went to Hollywood. Our production designer, Glenn DeVino, set up a stationary camera with lights so he could photograph all her pictures. I believe we had the greatest collection of Frances

Farmer pictures ever assembled. Glen would use them as giant projections on the various flat surfaces of the proscenium arch theatre to back the scenes, which were staged in open space.

Since we also photo-copied the accompanying articles, when we started rehearsals we had a 500-plus page manuscript for our first read-through, which lasted several days. We even rehearsed various scenes from the stories we found in the film magazines, even though we knew we would have to cut them. I eventually turned over the manuscript, which was down to half the size, to L&S student Judy Hellman, my assistant, who did a really professional job of trimming it down to two hours traffic on the stage.

When I started, Joan Potter, mentor of that group of students, had urged me to have at least four different actresses play Frances at different points in her life, and had told the cast that this is the way it would happen. But Tracy Kolis was so breathtakingly beautiful and so absolutely right that I knew if I was going to have a terrific show, I needed her to play Frances throughout. Yes, that decision may not have served the acting training of three other women, but I wanted a good production, one that the audience would enjoy, because that is the way it is in the real world.

The scene when Frances is picked up by medics and incarcerated in the Steilacoom state mental asylum was very moving. Backed by female inmates moving endlessly back and forth with two guards walking among them, it was cross-lit at a low-level by lighting designer Brian Nason (he later did a dozen Broadway productions including Sting's *Three Penny Opera*) as the horrors of the institution were being narrated. It was a big chunk of the play and very theatrical and moving. Tracy's courage in the scene when Frances fellates Clifford Odets was simple and brilliantly done without shame. This show was a labor of love. I was madly in love with Tracy as an actor. The production was a great joy and the talk of the campus.

⌘ ⌘ ⌘

During the late winter that followed I was contacted by Jack Eric Williams, who had played The Beadle in Sondheim's *Sweeney Todd*. He'd found out that I had worked with Frances in three shows and wanted to speak with me. Our talk took place at his apartment in New York and resulted in my hope of getting a Broadway production of a musical dealing with the life of Frances. I loaned him my script and all those pictures and articles we had accumulated. I had every reason to believe that there was a real possibility that this musical called *Mrs. Farmer's Daughter*, with the book by this young musical genius Jack Eric Williams, Joseph Stockdale and Tom O'Horgan, (who had directed the Broadway productions of *Hair, Lenny* and *Jesus Christ Superstar*) might be successful. I also got a special line in the credits, "Research and Documentation by Joseph Stockdale." Jack used my script *God's Peculiar Care* as a basis for his work, and the fact that I had been Dean of Theatre and Film at SUNY Purchase, where the musical would have its world premiere under the banner of SUMMERFARE '83, gave me a bit of leverage, or so I thought.

I did not have an agent at this time but was a member of the Dramatists Guild. I was promised five percent for being one of the three writers of the book and for "research and documentation." [If anyone reading this is ever in the same situation, remember that verbal agreements are not binding in a court of law.] Along the way this promise dwindled away to three percent then two and finally, because someone with the title "creative consultant" needed more, one percent. Even that "one percent" failed to materialize.

I also acted in the show, playing the role of Frances' father, and did several bits including the abortionist. This was done because the employment of another card-carrying Actors' Equity Association member was deemed necessary by the union. But I was told that the production could not afford to pay for another union member so I donated (*aka* "kick-backed") my salary to the producer, PepsiCo SUMMERFARE '83, although at the time I did wonder if PepsiCo International really needed my financial aid, which was minimum AEA salary.

By that time, however, I had come to a conclusion about the commercial theatre and me. Spending my time laboring over contracts and fighting all the financial crap involved in legal negotiations sucked away my creative energy. What I loved was the work so I did not make any demands. I considered Jack Eric Williams a genius, and so I did not object when he insisted that the production incorporate William Arnold's *idée fixe*—that

Frances was lobotomized. Having known and worked with her, I do not believe she was, but this was the major premise of Arnold's book *Shadowland*. However often I requested the return of the pictures and other materials I had loaned Jack, they were never returned. After the original production, which was reviewed by all the major New York newspapers plus *Variety* and *Backstage,* Jack eventually got another try-out date.

Mrs. Farmer's Daughter, without Tom O'Horgan as director or with book-writing credit, played The American Music Festival at the Trocadero Theatre in Philadelphia the following summer, July 5-15, 1984. I was not given book credit, only credit for "research and documentation" which—let's be honest—I probably would not have received except for the fact that if the producers were sued for libel, I—not the producers or Jack—would take the rap. But what the hell? By that time, I thought a stretch in the pen would be pretty damn restful after this experience in big-time show biz. I showed up at the opening with Cindy Miller, who was now living and teaching in Philadelphia. It was show-off fun for me to be greeted with this beauty at my side by a bunch of the guys in the orchestra.

⌘ ⌘ ⌘

I did do one show toward the end of August at Woodstock, Paul Osborn's *The Vinegar Tree,* my designer was Salvatore Tagliarino who at that time was an adjunct instructor, School of the Arts at NYU, and already had an extensive resume for his design work in opera. I revised the floor plan of this two-set show into one set, which he gave a first-rate design. I had a terrific cast with John Newton, Janet Hayes, and Ruby Holbrook (Hal's ex). I also cast two supporting roles with SUNY Purchase actors, Andrea Morse (Bobby Morse's daughter) and Preston Maybank, who were both fine. At the time Paul Osborne's *Morning's At Seven* had a much acclaimed revival on Broadway that played 564 performances with Nancy Marchand, Maureen O'Sullivan, Teresa Wright and Gary Merrill. I had gone back and read other plays by Osborne and thought this one might have a good chance in revival.

While in rehearsals, someone from a film company called the box office and said they needed a couple of character men for a film being shot in the area. I passed this information on to John Newton and we decided to go for the tryout. This was a Larry Cohen film titled *The Stuff* starring Michael Moriarty and Andrea Marcovicci. John and I both read a scene and were hired, John under a Screen Actors Guild contract. But since I did not belong to SAG, I was not credited.

I asked one of the people in makeup where the scene was set and they hadn't a clue. Since the gal who had auditioned before us used a Southern accent, we figured it took place in a Southern state, and I thought maybe my character, named Grimsby, was grim. I guess none of this made any difference. On the day of the shoot we met with the two stars in a Winnebago dressing room and did some improvisations for Larry Cohen. Then we got in a car—John and the two stars seated on the backseat and me in the jump seat—with the photographer in a space in front where the pedestrian seat had been removed, and Larry on the floor behind the driver. We drove along the highway and did several takes of a short scene. When John had to be taken back to the theatre to meet curtain time, Larry asked me to stay and we drove the same route while he recorded me laughing. That was an interesting late-afternoon experience, and although I didn't get SAG pay, I got a hunk of money for what little I did.

⌘ ⌘ ⌘

Skipping ahead, Larry Kornfel replaced Howard Stein as Dean. Larry could not deal with Joan Potter's attitude and called a secret meeting in New York of everyone else on the acting board of study and proposed that she be excluded from all further board of study meetings. I abstained. Everyone else voted yes. But I was not against their purposed actions. She was difficult and some correction had to be made. Yes, it was humiliating. I certainly knew that from my similar experience at Purdue, but I figured the situation needed breathing space. And I remember my teacher Grace Mills' advice at Feagin: "Remember that all experience can be beneficial *if you make it so."*

⌘ ⌘ ⌘

In December of 1984 I directed *The Night of The Iguana* plus two one-acts called *Garden District* that were comprised of *Something Unspoken* and *Suddenly Last Summer*. Doing all three caused major problems with the design/technology faculty, but I said I would not do just one. I felt there had to be good roles for everyone in that acting company, and that was impossible if I only did *Iguana*. I finally convinced the powers-that-be that the major production would be *Iguana* in Theatre B (the proscenium arch theatre in the Performing Arts Center) and the two one-acts in the Dance Lab theatre with minimum technical support.

I loved doing these shows, especially *Iguana*. I did some cutting because the show is too long. I'm not going to say anything about individual actors except this: for one reason or another I think they were the most loving and fun group of young actors I worked with at the School of the Arts. I was very vulnerable at the time and remember one night at a rehearsal when I read them something I was writing and just broke down and fell apart. To an actor, they all made an attempt to comfort me.

The young actor who played Shannon had problems on his last long speech and I got him to analogize Mexico City, the subject of his speech, with New York where he lived. This helped him understand Shannon's attitude toward the specific place. Once that happened, we went back to the lines in the script.

On the final dress rehearsal he got to that point, froze up, and everything stopped. Silence hung in the air. After what seemed like an endless amount of time, I went on-stage and hugged him and assured him I had absolute confidence that he was going to be great in the role. We started again and he went through the speech fine. He had found his confidence and gave a hell of a fine performance throughout the run.

As for Mike Viola, our technical director, he was that kind of guy who not only knew his business but loved actors. I remember one night seeing him pick up—was it Michael Lenuskey?—and hold him high over his head in a playful gesture. I've worked with only a few techies who had so much enjoyment with cast members, and Mike gained the respect and love of all of them. He was basically responsible for the rain curtain for *Iguana*, which was a first at Purchase and a major undertaking.

Our set designer was James Youmans, one of the best I ever worked with. Later in life, Jim had four Broadway credits, including *West Side Story* and a revival of *Gypsy*, plus major achievements with perhaps 50 design credits for Off Broadway including *Hedwig and the Angry Inch*.

Randomly, scenes I shall never forget: the very "butch" Miss Fellows in her pursuit to save the vacuous Charlotte Goodall who had fallen for Shannon. This was one of the funniest scenes, and the entire company always watched it during rehearsals. Then there was the rain scene with Shannon, and the thunder and lightning and the scene between him and Hanna; Nonno's voice coming from offstage when he has finished his final poem and is dying; and the entrance of the German tourists in as little clothing as possible.

In *Something Unspoken*, when the two women, one dominant and the other submissive, come to the point when the something unspoken would like to be spoken but is not, was wonderfully acted. In *Suddenly*, there are two great arias: first, Mrs. Venable's monologue about her trip with her son to the Galapagos Islands and Herman Melville's description of the Encantadas, with Giant Sea Turtle eggs hatching, and as they raced toward the sea being devoured by the birds. And second, Catharine's speech about her cousin Sebastian on Cabezo de Lobo being literally devoured by the native boys. Both were brilliantly done. As for the scene in which the greedy Mrs. Holly and her son George appear, we never made it through rehearsals without breaking up.

The kids gave me an opening night birthday party with one of the posters that advertised the shows, the back of which they all signed with a note of remembrance. When I look up right now, it hangs in front of me above the computer. Prior to their going into final rehearsals I asked Joan to come to rehearsals of all three productions—for which I would not be present—and for her to feel free to give the students her valued opinion of their work. When we met, I talked to quite a different person than the one I had known up to this point. She gave her honest opinion but did so with humility. When she had finished, she took the time to say, with the emotion she felt, thanks for the opportunity. I thanked her. In another couple of weeks I suggested to Larry and the acting board of study that they invite her back to all meetings as a valued tenured faculty member. That happened and it changed Joan.

⌘ ⌘ ⌘

In April of 1985 I directed another doubleheader for George Morrison's company, *Misalliance* and *Buried Child,* to assure all members of his company good roles. I had already directed both shows so there is nothing much to say about the plays themselves. But there is something to say about the productions. The total budget for both was $1,500. I insisted that the costumes in *Misalliance* be of the time and place that Shaw wrote. In the first production meeting with the Design/Technical faculty and student designers and crew heads, I was told that building all those historic costumes would not be possible, even with the entire budget for the two shows. As if I would not know that!

I was so tired of this kind of negativism that I was not tactful, explaining that one costume might be designed and built and the others could be rented at the Costume Collection for $300, leaving $900. My estimate was challenged, indeed scoffed at, until I explained that I had just finished a production at Woodstock and personally had gone with the costumer and pulled all costumes from the Collection and rented them for $300. Since John Boyt was on the Design/Technical staff at this point, and in the room, I also said that I had done *Misalliance* at Purdue with him, and we had used costumes from the Collection. He confirmed that the cost was even less.

Shortly after that meeting I received a letter from Dean Kornfel castigating my behavior in front of students and accusing me of humiliating members of the Design/Technical faculty. Because of this I would not be asked to direct any more productions. This was my directing swan song at SUNY Purchase.

The head of costumes was Michael Cesario, a good costumer and faculty member, whom I sometimes unjustly, but fondly, referred to as "The Sicilian Twit." When Michael retired long after I did, he gave a farewell speech in which he said that I was the best Dean our department ever had. Long after his retirement—in fact within the last few years—we have had a good email relationship with lots of remembrances and laughs.

⌘ ⌘ ⌘

That summer at Woodstock I directed a play I loved, *Educating Rita,* a two-hander with exactly the right cast: Donald Gantry and Maddie Seide, a wonderful young actress who was in our first company to graduate at the School of the Arts. As designer I had Jim Youmans, and Robin Andrews was master carpenter. What I loved about this show was the relationship between these two incredibly different people, a bohemian hairdresser from Liverpool and a middle aged professor. In it I saw very clearly how much I had been affected by who my students were and what they had taught me.

My final show was *Shelter,* an original that Harris had co-authored with Nathan Scheib. Harris said that Howard Koch, who lived in Woodstock—and with the Epstein brothers is credited as one of the screenwriters of the film *Casablanca*—had read and liked the play. It had to do with a couple who were facing an atomic bomb blast and was close to the worst play I'd ever read. I told Harris that I did not want to direct it, but he kept after me. I had a soft spot in my heart for the little guy after all he had done for the Playhouse, so I finally said okay, but only if he honestly and freely agreed to allow me to make any and all changes in the script, including rewriting some of it. He said that was exactly what he wanted me to do. I hired Scott Rhyne, who had married Roxanna Stuart after she divorced Bill Prosser. I did rewrite a lot of the script while directing it. The production was not good, but the play was sure as hell better than what we started with. This is a rehearsal period that I do not remember with great fondness. But the show opened, and played, and garnered some good notices. Harris was pleased, and my directing career ended in late August 1985.

⌘ ⌘ ⌘

What follows was gained from Michael Hammond, Norris Houghton and Jim A. Frost, President Emeritus, of the Connecticut State University. After retiring I put this information into an essay which was informed by input by all of these men, although Michael's handwritten notes on the essay were the most significant.

Michael was one of the original four arts deans. He was appointed Dean of Music in 1967, five years before the first entering class at Purchase. You already know that in 1976 he and I were both on the trip to India, but even prior to that we shared our mutual admiration for W. McNeil Lowry's view on arts education. I was one of the faculty to nominate him for the office of president of SUNY Purchase when Abbott Kaplan retired. He was appointed, and I believe that he was the best president the institution ever had. However, he was literally drummed out of office by members of the L&S faculty and eventually accepted the position of dean and professor of music at the Shepherd School of Music, Rice University. Years later, he was confirmed by the U. S. Senate as head of the Art and Humanities but sadly died after seven days in office of the pancreatic cancer he had been fighting for years. The following information was included on my essay to which Michael, along with Norris Houghton and Jim Frost, contributed and affirmed.

A major reason for the failure of the School of the Arts was that in the original design there was absolutely no thought of L&S competing with other small private colleges. The plan—detailed in chapter 28—proposing a total of 6,000 students, was to justify The School of the Arts politically and economically. But these plans were systematically disapproved of and thwarted by the L&S Academic Vice-President, Deans, and their faculties. What they promoted was a small, selective, Amherst-Swarthmore-Oberlin type college that would mirror the small selective School of the Arts and have equal claims to quality, distinctiveness, and resources; they were especially interested in a more equitable faculty/student teaching ratio.

Albany saw this development—by this time Ernest Boyer had replaced Sam Gould as Chancellor—and protested. Boyer made it quite clear to all the SUNY Purchase Deans that Albany could not support the kind of cost that was implied in this new development. But no one in central administration ever came down with a clear decree saying, "Cut it out! That's not what was intended."

Even though the primary mission of the campus, as anyone can see by simply looking at the buildings, was clearly arts training, President Kaplan assigned the *academic* vice-president to draw up the campus's first mission statement, in which the plan called for a "matriculate year" including "clusters." Years two and three were to be viewed as a unit culminating in a "junior field exam" and a "publishable" senior thesis. There were to be "narrative evaluations" with an honors, pass-or-fail grading system, plus 12 week semesters to provide time for a January "short term." This mission statement expressly prevented students, even the best, from transferring in from the New York community colleges without losing at least a year, even though the original Frost plan had mandated that fully sixty percent of those in the L&S College be upper division students.

In short, the governance of the institution was controlled by L&S administrators and faculty, knowledgeable and used to the academy's often Byzantine mode of operation. After the skewing of the original objectives, there was no getting back on track. Decisions were made via the "democratic process," *Robert's Rules of Order*, lobbying and the promotion of self-interests. In short, it was academic politics as usual, in which the School of the Arts faculty were rank amateurs.

So what had been this extraordinarily pure idea from the 1960s, the creation of a school for conservatory training in New York State's university system, was wrecked by self-interest, obtuseness, naivety, lack of foresight, follow-through and control by both the central administration in Albany and the administration at Purchase. And the deciding factor, of course, was the drying up of funds when the state was hit by severe recessions. With the original purpose skewed by the first mission statement, all that could be done was to devise strategies to keep the place afloat, including a decade of "out-reach" for part-time adult students through Continuing Education.

According to Joan Potter, by the end of the century what existed had nothing in common with what Jim Frost had planned for Nelson Rockefeller and Chancellor Gould as SUNY's School of the Arts. The "School" was no longer even mentioned: no stationery, signs on the highway, nothing in print that tells that such a School ever existed. The Visual Arts Department no longer trained artists in the conservatory mode. Music became a part of what was called the School of Performing Arts (Dance, Music and Theatre) headed by a single Dean, a position that rotated among the three departments. Theatre, with an extraordinary record of accomplishment as seen by its distinguished alumni, clung to the idea of professional training, especially Joan Potter who kept me in touch after my retirement. But the division was soon given a general education spin mandating requirements consisting of courses in various branches of learning, including physical education.

The acting faculty still auditioned and interviewed prospective students, But instead of choosing the entering freshman class so acting, movement, speech and voice teachers could exchange opinions at a final call-back of those who had been judged talented in preliminary auditions, the final decision was made by the "Director" who headed the division, with the advice and consent of the admissions office controlled by L&S whose focus was academics.

⌘ ⌘ ⌘

By 1985 Larry Kornfel had left the deanship to assume his full tenured professorship. I did enjoy him as a person—I remember a drive with him to Yale to see a production—but the only thing I can remember of Larry as Dean was when he announced he was leaving Judaism and struggling to become a Quaker, which had no relevance at all to the desperate situation that existed after he and others allowed tenure track positions to be exchanged for money for adjunct professors and special studies. Of course, the Department of Theatre and Film never recovered.

When Larry—who actually never had any experience as a *faculty* member, but was at Yale for a few months as a visiting artist—resigned the deanship after three and a half years, the search committee chose Israel Hicks, a very likeable guy whom I loved to meet in New York for dinner at The All State Cafe on West End and 72nd St., and to whom I gave my old P.E. Lull academic robe that I used at Purdue to wear for graduation exercises.

Israel, probably wisely, went with the flow of what was happening at SUNY Purchase and seldom could be reached by phone. He spent a lot of his time directing a professional theatre in Denver where he apparently did excellent work, and later became head of the Theatre Department, Mason Gross School of Arts, at Rutgers University.

During my final five years I did major work on my play *Taking Tennessee to Hart*, which was first read at the Follow Spot. We finished the reading just past the stroke of midnight, got a lot of applause, and since it was then March 26, 1987, we all sang Happy Birthday to Tennessee on what would have been his 76th birthday.

I taught History of Theatre and Dramatic Structure classes, upping the credit (as well as the investment in time by the students) to four to conform with the rest of what was now known as The College. During those years there were always about 65 freshmen from Acting, Design/Technology, and Film who took Dramatic Structure, plus students from Drama Studies and others from of L&S. One semester the total was close to 100. In History I usually taught 50. So the FTE (Faculty/Teacher/Equivalence) I created for our Division more than tripled that for a full-time teacher in the college of L&S and allowed small enrollments in classes in both film and design/technology.

Instead of driving, I learned to take the train and bus from Pawling and to correct quizzes and record the marks on my white cards in transit. I worked at home correcting essay papers and mid, final and *Poetics* tests and papers. All students were also required to write a short play. I never once walked into the lecture hall without having reread the assigned play even if I had taught it for 25 years. And I still required what I considered professional conduct for a theatre student.

Of course, being closed out of directing, the names of such talented student friends as Rachel Hauben Combs, Michael DiGioia, John St Angelo, and Reese Madigan, and hundreds more unfortunately do not appear in this book. When I taught my last class, many other students showed up. After I gave my scheduled lecture, I took about ten minutes to sum up my career. As I remember, I said I did not have any great message. The only thing I could say was that I had been very fortunate in my work; what I got paid for doing was what I loved. The most I ever made was $64,000 per year and that was only for my last two years of teaching; money wasn't the important thing, work was, and work assured good health and one's ability to love.

Those few minutes of my life were sad because I knew it was the end of an opportunity for friendships, yet it was also exhilarating because now I would be able go back to a first love, writing. Very shortly after this last class Bill Prosser and Stuart Howard threw a splendid party for me at Sardi's in New York which was also a kind of "roast" with funny stories told from the kids' points of view about dealing with me. This was the true end of one kind of the *stages* in my life.

⌘ ⌘ ⌘

I now need to give, as closure, my view of The School of the Arts at SUNY Purchase. A notice in a Wikipedia posting states that in recent years SUNY Purchase has shifted away from the highly successful and well respected conservatory, to a more liberal arts/athletic program as found in other SUNY affiliated schools. I ask myself why? In fact, how is it possible considering the preponderance of buildings designed specifically for the arts?

The campus includes the performing arts center with four fully equipped theatres seating 1,400, 800, 700 and a "black box" with flexible seating; a 160,000 square foot visual arts building housing studios for painters and sculptors; a dance building with 16 studios with sprung floors along with a dance theatre; a music building with two theatres, 75 individual rehearsal studios, and 80 Steinways; and an art museum housing 7,000 works. And then there is the hole in the ground where there was to have been a theatre arts and film building with classrooms, two theatres with fully equipped scene shops, two film studios and editing rooms.

These buildings obviously indicate the institution's focus. SUNY Purchase was to be known as a School of the Arts, with a solid college where graduates from the state's two year community colleges could matriculate without losing any credits and graduate with a good liberal arts education in two years.

The Wikipedia article indicates that historically, the institution had more of an artistic focused *academic* program. Not true! That was never the main focus of SUNY Purchase. Academics are the focus of a college that grants the bachelor's degree in Liberal Arts. If Purchase's artistic focus was on academics, why would it build such unique and expensive buildings for conservatory training in the arts? A college can do with rooms accommodating 25-35 with good acoustics and a professor.

I am also perplexed by the statement that now the college has shifted even more toward a 'standard' education format with a greater emphasis on athletics, to the end that they are now offering recruitment incentives for athletes. I am aware that this new Purchase College claims to offer "a unique education that combines programs in the liberal arts, with conservatory programs in the arts in ways that emphasize enquiry, mastery of skills, and creativity" and that it has been included in the Princeton Review's Best 371 *Colleges* and Top 100 Best Value *Colleges*. I would advise whoever thinks this is possible to read W. McNeil Lowry's 1960's article "The University and the Creative Arts" which gave inspiration and guidance to the original idea.

The primary focus of SUNY Purchase, as its planned buildings clearly indicate, was to provide the best physical plant for conservatory arts training in this country for pre-professionals, whose admittance was to be controlled through auditions and interviews by the boards of study in each of the arts areas, rather than using traditional admission standards used by colleges .

To me the great success of this no-longer-existing School of the Arts lives on in spite of the fact that the original plan was not brought to fruition. The only way for me to bring closure, which I have done, is to tell myself that many idealistic plans go through an evolutionary process, thesis and antithesis, resulting in an inevitable synthesis which lasts for some time due to various influences, usually financial. But then the inevitable evolutionary process starts all over again as I hope it will with someone who understands the potential of The School of the Arts.

All that would be required to complete the original plans would be: fill the hole in the ground with a Theatre Arts and Film building, and reinstate what resulted from that something-in-the-air during the Sixties idea that

W. McNeil Lowry expressed so well in his essay on the Arts in American Education. It was this idea that struck a corresponding chord taken up by idealists Governor Nelson Rockefeller, Chancellor Sam Gould and Ernest Boyer, with James Frost as architect of the proposed plan.

As the second dean of the Theatre Arts and Film division (1975-80) and full professor until my retirement at the end of 1990, I believed that the potential for a resurrection of the original School lives on in the example of those who, in spite of the difficulties, graduated and found some success. The following incomplete list (apologies to those whose names I have not remembered) includes names from my time at the School of the Arts when it was wild and wonderful, glorious, and often funny as hell, and always filled with hard work. I do not regret a moment of the time spent with an extraordinary group unequaled in talent that included:

Todd Baker, Gina Belafonte, A. Dean Bell, Nancy Bell, Vebe Borge, Robert Burke, Nicholas Cascone, Orlagh Cassidy, Ed Check, Maria Chibas, Robert Clohessy, Matthew Colon, Jeff Croiter, John Danza, Daniel DaSilva, Lynne J. DeBerry, Matthew DeGanon, Traci-Ann DiGesy, Michael DiGioia, Brian Drillinger, Darryl Edwards, Ron Eldard, James Elmore, Dwight Ewell, Edie Falco, Peter Fanelli, George Feldenstein, Bert Fink, David Gallo, Brian Gaskill, Christopher Germon, Seth Gilliam, Nick Gomez, Susan\Gomez, Bob Gosse, Todd Graff, David Grill, Hal Hartley, Deidre Imershine, Peter Kaczorowski, Robert M. Jimenez, Ed Kershen, Stephanie Klapper, Tracy Kolis, Juliette Kurth, Liz Larsen, Melissa Leo, Jody Long, Reese Madigan, Matthew McClanahan, Brian MacDevitt, Matt Malloy, Jeffrey Markowitz, Preston Maybank, Tim McCann, Eric Mendelsohn, Ivan Menchell, Marcia Mitzman, Andrea Morse, Jeff Nash, Brian Nason, David Neumann, Adina Porter, Parker Posey, Kenneth Posner, Alan Pottinger, Louis Ramos, Ving Rhames, Scott Rhyne, Bill Sage, Tracy Sallows, Jay O. Sanders, Tim Saternow, Dan Schlachet, Paul Schulze, Karen Sillas, Wesley Snipes, Jim Spione, Pamela Stewart, Sherry Stringfield, Adam Trese, Stanley Tucci, Mark Viola, Steven Weber, Shea Whigham, Thom Widmann, Nancy Allyson Wolfe, Jim Youmans, and John C. Young.

Chapter 31

TO SUM IT UP:

The Kids? Laurel had three sons, and is now a very active grandmother, married to Tony Striedinger and living in Woodstock, Georgia. Joe III, who got his MA degree in English as a Second Language and taught for years in Saudi Arabia, was semi-retired in an area he loves: Asheville, North Carolina. However, weary of retirement, he went back to teach for Vinnell Arabia Company. David has one son and lives in Italy where he teaches English during the day and spends evenings composing songs, recording them, and appearing in various gigs. He lives with Sabrina in Gossolengo (near Piacenza), Italy. John, a drummer, lives in Saugerties, New York and shares a Bulgarian pooch named Ben with his long-time friend, Michelle Aizenstat. Larkin has two boys, Ben and Jake Hays, and has remarried a great guy, Art Walsh, several years after her first husband, Charles 'Chuck' Hays, Jr., died after a valiant seven-year battle with cancer. Art, Larkin, and the boys live in Roswell, Georgia. Living close together the girls—born twenty years apart—have now gotten to know one another. Our kids have all lived interesting and varied lives and are totally individualistic. During the past few years we have had reunions on Lake Michigan and great times together.

Health? At age 87 I've been through an operation to remove a cancerous left kidney at the Mayo Clinic, followed by cancerous polyps in the bladder, which were successfully treated with a couple rounds of chemo. I've passed kidney stones, had my gall bladder removed, had pneumonia, hemorrhoids, hives, and shingles, which qualifies me for roles as both Job and Sisyphus. But from age 65 when I retired to now—6,205 days later—I have actually been in a hospital *sick in bed* for only 14 days, so I have no right to play the curmudgeon.

Deaths? Blanche calls them "the long parade to the graveyard." There was the death of Ross Smith whose side I was at when he passed; Joan Potter who on my last call, unable to come to the phone, sent a message via her caretaker wanting me to know that she loved me; Erling Kildahl who called to say he was dying, and wanted me to know that I was his "best friend." I wrote a long obituary to send to his former students, and was about to do so when he called to say he was fine. I sent out the faux obit anyway explaining that he was still alive. Ten years later when death arrived, I informed his friends with Kent's last line in *King Lear*: "The wonder is, he hath endured so long," and added that he did tarry a trifle on the final exit.

In September 1986 my sister Rachel called and said that she was not going to make it and wanted to say good-bye. Jimmy, Robin's brother passed. And the saddest of all, Larkin's first husband, and so many more: Pamela Printy Bohnert, Chuck Jones, Dick Rogers, Aram Avakian, Eulalie Noble, Billy Mintzer, Bill Prosser, Anne Revere, Frances Farmer, David's wife Donatella Peroncini, Israel Hicks, Margaret Woodhouse, John Eldridge, Jim Pritchett, John Newton, Janet Hayes, Jack Watson, Page Karling, Angelo Mango, Linden Chiles, Bob Tolan, and many more.

As for retirement? It was Robin who sold our house in Pawling, for which we paid $50,000 and lived in for 12 years. She put it on the market for $237,000 and sold for $187,000! Who knew she was a real estate hawk? It was former student and longtime friend Joan Pape who got us settled into an apartment in the city: #3P, 20 River Road, Roosevelt Island, NY 10044-1128 in October 1990.

I joined The Shooting Gallery, consisting of many SUNY Purchase kids, who met every week in a building on lower Broadway where we read original plays, screenplays and sometimes short stories. I got to the theatre as often as possible. It was great to see former student Parker Posey on Broadway in

Taller Than A Dwarf; to have Peter Schneider of Disney give me comps for not only the film of *The Lion King* but also the stage play; and I shall never forget the opening night of *The Hunchback of Notre Dame* and the incredible party after held at St. John the Divine Cathedral.

During our seven years on Roosevelt Island I saw every Broadway, Off Broadway and Off-Off Broadway play worth seeing. Robin and I had season tickets to The Signature Theatre and The WPA. In addition, I had season tickets to The Manhattan Theatre Club, The Roundabout, The Pearl, Playwrights Horizons, BAM, The National Actors Theatre, and Circle in the Square. During these years I paid an average of $25 to $30 per show, often standing in line at the half-price ticket line in Times Square. The most I ever paid was $70 for *Sunset Boulevard*, and $50 to $60 for such shows as *Phantom of the Opera, The Secret Garden, Carousel* (Lincoln Center revival), *Miss Saigon, Perestroika* and *Salome*. I saw all the first-run movies at senior-rates prices in mid-town theatres on Third Avenue.

I read *Theater Week*—the best theatre magazine in the country—and when we saw Merle Louise in *Kiss of the Spider Woman* I asked her how many performances she had played on Broadway. Doing the math, we figured she would reach her 4,000th performance in mid-July. I thought that was worth an article in *TheaterWeek*, wrote it, took it to editor John Harris. He liked it, told me to cut 300 words, which I did. It was published and I made $150. And that was the first of a dozen or so pieces I wrote for the magazine where I eventually served as a contributing editor, which I absolutely loved.

My play *Taking Tennessee To Hart* got a great reader's report by Phil Bosco's wife, Nancy, who was the play-reader for the uptown Circle in the Square. She strongly recommended production. But that didn't happen. I had three New York readings, first by Janet Hayes' York Theatre Company with Jacqueline Brooks, Henderson Forsythe, Maureen Garrett, John Newton, Joe Godfrey, and Thomas G. Waites; then at the Nat Horn Theatre on West 42nd Street with the same cast except for Carol Morley replacing Jacqueline Brooks. The third reading was at the Shooting Gallery.

I had three productions of this play, first at Tallahassee's Florida State University School of Theatre in early November 1993. The only memorable thing to come out of it was scouting actor Saxton Palmer, who refused to be in his department's major production—a musical—to play bits and pieces in *Taking Tennessee To Hart.* This guy was so talented that I expanded the bits and pieces. The *Tallahassee Press* was encouraging and kind, but this was not a good production.

Theatre Artists of Marin, San Rafael, CA, produced it from March 17-April 15, 1995 which had just lost its AEA standing. This was the worst experience I have ever had in the theatre. The production was so bad I went home and had writer's block that lasted nine months.

Finally, at Actors and Playwrights Initiative in Kalamazoo, in a second-floor space entered by going through a back alley, it played from October 13th to 28th, 1995. It was far from even a semiprofessional production, but Bob Walker and cast gave it a good try, and I acknowledged that by a positive article for *TheaterWeek* to help him gain backing for the theatre.

It was after this production that I started to turn the play into a novel, which thanks to Donald Bain was eventually published two years ago. In addition, my play *Special Effects* was given a showing at the development reading series at the York Theatre in New York in March 1999. I wrote about a dozen short stories and settled into the habit of writing just because I loved the work. My last agent, Betsy Nolan, quit the business.

I also explored the city. I walked every avenue and all the side streets from the fifties down through the Village to the harbor, finding all the lesser known historic spots such as Edna St. Vincent Millay's apartment owned by the Cherry Lane Theatre and said to be the smallest apartment in New York City. I wrote in the mornings but walked in the afternoons. I explored the subway system, finding how to get to LaGuardia for senior citizen rates on the subway when I visited Ross and Dorothea at Gulf Pines, Florida, and when I went to Europe how to get to JFK without taking a taxi, and better still to pass JFK and get to Far Rockaway Beach.

I traveled to England and up to Terrington St. Clement in Norfolk County to do some family history research. I found my great grandmother Mary Gagen Stockdale buried in the churchyard, but could not find her husband Charles (whose grave I later found buried in Otsego, 15 miles away.) Of course I also saw shows in London, and when I got back someone asked me why I had made the trip to do family research, when all I had to do was go to the Mormon Building at Columbus and 66th Street that had the definitive family archives.

By that time son John was living in New York after a disastrous run-in with the leader of the band he was drumming for someplace in Maryland. I was reading Norman MacLean's *A River Runs Through It* when I got the call from John. I had already so identified him with the youngest son in MacLean's novel that after telling him to get up to New York so we would get him back into school, I closed the door of my room and cried for hours.

We found him an apartment, registered him in one of the city colleges so he could finish his associates degree on his G.I. Bill of Rights (his enlistment had been for three years and he spent a couple of years in Germany), and then move on to Hunter College where he graduated with a BA in English with honors. While I was doing the family research at the Mormon family research center he helped, and we had a great time doing this together.

In August 1991—talk about a bad idea—Robin and I went to Italy for a couple of weeks to visit David and his wife Donatella and their young son Michael. We all traveled to Sicily, living in Santa Teresa, a little fishing village, for a tough two weeks with no air-conditioning. We were on the seacoast just beneath that beautiful hotel in Taormina which Tennessee Williams and Frankie used to visit. Probably the best times we had in these two weeks were when David drove us through nearby mountain towns, and we had lunch and enjoyed the sights. Robin had had enough and wanted to get back home just as soon as we got back to Piacenza. I wanted to go to Paris for a week, so she flew home, and David and I traveled to Paris, where I was introduced to all the sights and fell in love with the "City of Light" and knew I had to return.

The years on Roosevelt Island were wonderful, except for a party we had one evening for John Newton, Janet Hayes, Merle Louise, and Peter Simon when Robin wore her sexy-spike red heels and decided to go smoke a cigarette down by the river. On her way to her favorite bench the heel of one of the sexy shoes settled into a crack between two bricks and sent her flying.

Instead of taking her to Manhattan, the ambulance took her to Queens General, charitably known as "The Butcher Block," where we waited until 3:00 A.M. to get any attention. When she was taken down the hall for an x-ray, I followed and heard the technician tell her to move over on the table. She said she could not, and he yelled "Move it" to her. I opened the door, read him the riot act, and told him to move the machine to her. He did without any effort, the X ray was taken, and about 8:00 A.M. she was moved upstairs to a room where she told the nurse she was in pain and the nurse said, "Get used to it, honey."

Her doctor was really terrific. When I said I wanted her moved out of that hospital, he said he didn't blame me. That very day we got her moved to a Jewish hospital further out in Queens, where her hip was set, she went through rehab, and was then released. Her diagnosis was arthritis with severe osteoporosis, and she had to be very careful because she could break bones very easily. That and the fact that our next rent was raised to $2,000 a month settled it: we knew it was time to move.

When I was in Kalamazoo for the production of *Taking Tennessee To Hart*, I visited the editor of the *Gazette*, Jim Mosby, whose son Josh had been an acting student at Purchase. Jim took me to lunch. Walking back to the *Gazette* office, I saw a tall building and asked him what it was. He said it was an apartment house called The Skyrise. I walked over to it —the tallest building in Kalamazoo—and enquired about apartments. Sharon, the woman who answered my rings from the foyer, showed me an apartment on the 21st floor which I found spectacular. It was three times the size of our NY apartment and included a laundry room and balcony and the rent was half of what our New York apartment cost.

I took a trip to the west coast, and Linden Chiles drove me from Malibu down to San Diego. We visited a goodly number of apartments in towns along the way. I did love some near the military cemetery on the hill in San Diego where one could see both the bay and the Pacific Ocean, and also those on the bay's island, but they were as expensive as those on Roosevelt Island. So I figured since Kalamazoo had an airport and a train station, why not go back there?

I did not use the train station much, but I did use the Kalamazoo/Battle Creek "International Airport" a good deal after we were settled in. Although Robin did not care to travel, she did not mind if I did. During our past 14 years I have gotten her to fly with me to Atlanta twice for Thanksgiving, and one of those times was also for Larkin's second marriage.

In April 2000 I went on a tour organized by Page Karling that included Spain's Costa del Sol: Malaga, Torremolinos, Majas, Marbella, Ronda, Seville, Cordoba, plus Granada, Gibraltar and Morocco. All the participants were old friends from Purdue, and I enjoyed the trip and found an exciting writing project after I had visited the Alhambra in Granada. I read a story called *The Pilgrim of Love* in Washington Irving's 1832 work *The Alhambra*, and had a wonderful time adapting it for the stage.

In 2001, many of the same group from Purdue went on a trip to Alaska. The trip lasted from August 3rd to the 17th. During a couple of days in Fairbanks, we took a sternwheeler cruise on the Chena and Tanana Rivers, and our tour guide boasted enthusiastically about the homes that withstood 60 degree below zero weather in the winter, and the glory of having daylight at 11:00 P.M. in August and darkness at 11:00 A.M. in December. I didn't share her enthusiasm.

We were then treated to a view of the Alaskan oil pipeline, spent a couple of days in Denali National Park, and for a moment saw Mt. McKinley in the far distance through the clouds. The tour guide assured us over and over that we were extremely lucky because no other group she had toured with that summer had had the thrill. But then I've not only seen but crossed the Alps four times on clear days.

The Alaska Railway train ride from Denali Park to Anchorage was fun for an hour or so, but how many fir trees can one look at before the thrill is gone? I saw a couple of moose in the distance, and at the Anchorage airport two caribou were stranded on the runway. But I'd seen moose and caribou up close at the Bronx Zoo.

Our "celebrity" cruise ship, The Mercury, carried 1,800 tourists—in every sense of the word including Kodak moments—and took us from Anchorage to Vancouver, detouring on such side trips (which I eschewed) as a 15-minute helicopter ride to stand on a glacier for ten minutes for

$200. We saw the Portage Glacier and small iceberg floats and some whales' backs. But I've seen whales and sharks close-up at Disney World in Orlando. Prince William Sound is beautiful, but how much water and how many islands and mountains can you see before you're brain dead?

At Sitka I got a "glimpse into the rich Russian heritage" of Alaska, sold to the US in 1867. But as you know, I'd been to Russia, so who needs a bad reproduction of it in Alaska via a couple of fake icons made in Korea? At Ketchikan, totem poles were featured, but actually I've never been crazy for totem poles; nothing personal, I just don't care for them. Anyway, if you see one you've seen 'em all.

So much for Alaska.

In 2002 I rented Cheryl Pearlman's apartment at 15 Rue Cler in Paris for six weeks in April and May, which was absolutely wonderful and from which I could see the Eiffel Tower lights turned off at 1:00 A.M. each night. I went again in 2003 and stayed for the same amount of time in the wonderful Hotel de Turenne, 28, Avenue de Tourville, which I had found the year before in the same area. David and I had had that whirlwind weekend in Paris after Sicily, but I really became acquainted with the city by living in it. On both trips David would come up from Piacenza on weekends, and we had wonderful days exploring the city .

I really experienced (saw, heard, touched, tasted, smelled) it without hurrying, sitting on benches and looking for as long as I wished; six days in the Louvre Museum; going up in the Eiffel Tower twice, once at night when there was a blue moon, the other time during the day to view Paris, as well as hanging out around its base many times. I loved the Pont d'Iéna, a bridge across the Seine leading to the steps up to Trocadero; the Arc de Triomphe (three times going to the top to see the layout of the Paris boulevards); the Champs Élysées; la Place de la Concorde; Notre Dame; Montmartre; Sacré-Coeur; Pont Neuf; The Museum National d'Historie; the Paris Opera, where I sat in a cramped seat (were people smaller when it was built?) for a student performance, and loved the grand staircase and the lobby's opulence; The Panthéon; the Comédie Française (twice seeing plays); the Jardin des Tuileries; the Statue de la Liberté, standing in the center of the River Seine on the southeast side of the Pont de Grenelle at the end of a long island walkway called the Allée des Cygnes; the Bastille; the Musée National d'Art Moderne at the Pompidou Center (the only building I disliked); the Conciergerie; the Père-Lachaise Cemetery (where Sarah Bernhardt, Oscar Wilde, Edith Piaf, and Jim Morrison are buried); the seldom visited museum of precious stones; and on and on among the endless treasures of the "City of Light."

I went to Versailles where I spent a day in the clipped and trimmed-to-a-tee gardens and the interior of the palace, but my feelings were the same about it as they were about the Presidential Palace in New Deli, India. My other out-of-city visit was with John and Karlene von Szeliski to Monet's gardens at Giverny with walks around the ponds of water lilies, and I took John, (who replaced me at Williams College, and after tenure and a sabbatical in California became an architect), to my special favorite in Paris, La Grande Arche de la Defense, a showcase for modern architecture on the Esplanade Du Général De Gaulle, from which one can look back at the Arc de Triomphe, the Champs-Élysées, the Tuileries, the Place De La Concorde, the Louvre, all on the exact same axis and see the Cathédral Notre Dame in the distance.

In 2004, after the national election, I decided to leave the country for some needed perspective. Linden Chiles said he would take the trip with me, so we landed in Milan, visited David and my grandson Michael in Piacenza, trained to Florence for three days, then Rome for a week (both of which I had visited twice before but always found wonderful), and from there flew to Valletta, the capital of Malta, where we stayed for more than two weeks. I explored this island daily via rickety and rattling buses, not only the main island, but also another island that is inhabited. Most of its other islands are home only to wild goats. All this was interesting and very inexpensive (I got a watch there for less than $5, which I still use), including a trip to the famed Blue Grotto.

Finally, in 2006 I went on a cruise down the Danube River organized by Charles Hays, Sr. On the first night out I suffered the attempted passing of a kidney stone. I waited in agony until morning when I alerted Charles, who had an ambulance waiting on an unscheduled stop on the Danube and who insisted in going with me some thirty miles to a hospital with siren blaring all the way, and traffic moving to the sides of the road. The diagnosis was confirmed but the doctor advised me to go to another hospital yet another thirty miles away. By that time, the pain was gone but we were unsure about whether the stone had passed or was taking a rest, so the doctor told me he thought it best to rejoin the tour. If the stone flared up again I was to seek a local hospital.

Fortunately, it didn't.

We met up with the tour in Budapest and saw the sights all the way back up the river, including stops in Vienna and Bratislava, after which I was glad to get back to the Kalamazoo/ Battle Creek International Airport, The Skyrise (with the hospital just across the street), and Robin.

National travel included trips to California for several visits with good friends Pam and Bill Bohnert in Beverly Hills; parties with former SUNY Purchase students at Ivan Mitchell and Karen Silas' home; a visit with Tom Moore to see him do his thing on the flying trapeze; walks with Peter Schneider on Venice Beach; a nearby visit with David Potts; and time with Karlene and John von Szeliski, who own a wonderful house in Baja, Mexico.

I also kept theater-going in New York, usually a couple of times a year until two and a half years ago when I tripped in especially so I could see Merle Louise go on in her understudy role as the grandmother in *Billy Elliott*. She was radiant in the role and I waited backstage until she was out of make-up. When we stepped outside the stage door there were 200 people waiting for autographs from cast members. They gave her a round of applause. I loved the show; my house seat cost $135, but it was worth every penny just to see Merle on and off stage once again.

⌘ ⌘ ⌘

The thing I missed most when moved from New York was that I no longer had an outlet for my writing. Even if we had stayed I would no longer have *TheaterWeek* because the magazine went bankrupt. In the final issue, which came out on December 30, 1996, my article, "New Kid On The Block," dealt with producer Julian Schlossberg. It was the longest article they ever published. Julian later informed Stuart Howard, who told me that

Julian's friends Mike Nichols and Elaine May commented on it by saying, "He got you. Exactly!"

Another of my articles was on the 50th anniversary of The Barn Theatre. Jack Ragotzy was at a point in his life where he wanted some historical record of The Barn, and he asked me to write its history. At first I thought no, but what other outlet for writing did I have? I had access to all Barn records, plus taped interviews with Jack and no demands on his part. After the manuscript was completed Jack read it, "almost in one sitting," as he told me, and loved it.

Entitled *Man in the Spangled Pants,* it very much emphasized Jack and caused some stir among those who felt I had slighted Betty. I believed the creative force behind The Barn Theatre was almost solely Jack's, although I certainly give due credit to Betty's contributions, especially in the area of publicity and attention to detail, essential for The Barn's success.

My next project was to redo my book on dramatic structure. My first thought was that if I had a bias it was against the *avant garde*, but one of my former students, David Letwin, was not only brilliant, but had belonged for many years to arguably the best *avant garde* theatre in New York, its artistic director Richard Schechner. I called David and asked him if he would collaborate on a revision of the original text and he agreed. We finally settled on the title *The Architecture of Drama: Plot, Character, Theme, Genre, and Style,* and the book, with Robin's editing, was published in August of 2008.

I then concentrated on *Taking Tennessee to Hart,* which I enjoyed enormously opening up and making into a screen play, and then a novel. It was finally published in 2011 by Hyphenates, Ltd. Publishers which is owned by Donald Bain and Renée Paley-Bain, and it garnered 25 excellent reader's reviews and keeps selling. Don is convinced it will eventually be sold and produced as an independent film. From his lips to God's ears! I love the novel and almost everything about it, and I, too, keep hoping it will be turned into a film.

In the past four years I have been working on this memoir and enjoying it enormously. I started just about the time The Skyrise turned over one of its spaces into an exercise room. I enjoyed exercising on the elliptical and tread-mill along with the rowing machine, and often burned 500 to 600 calories a morning before getting back up to our apartment, showering, having breakfast, and settling down to an uninterrupted morning of writing from 9 to 12:30. Now, just finishing the last chapter of this memoir, I am no longer John Wayne-ing it at the gym. I seldom burn more than 300 calories a morning before I write.

Every so often I go—Robin has not gone to the theatre since we left New York—with friends Michael Dombos and Ann Soukup to a Sunday matinee at the Farmers Alley Theatre. This is a small AEA house that reminds me of Purdue's Experimental Theatre (now used as a storage dump for electrical equipment) which mounts excellent productions. Michael and Ann then come up to our apartment on the 19th floor for a drink and some good talk, and the four of us go to one of our three favorite restaurants for a leisurely dinner.

⌘ ⌘ ⌘

Since I love writing, what will I do now when the memoir is published? Prior to *Taking Tennessee To Hart*, I had written a play called *April East*, the title of which came from my lifelong immersion into the works of Tennessee Williams. In a 1985 collection of 50 short stories by the playwright, I read "Ten Minute Stop," written by Tennessee in 1936 and prefaced with:

> He gulped and looked again at the movie poster. Jane Barlow had gorgeous breasts. In her picture she always wore gowns cut down low at the neck. You could often see the little groove between the two delectable promontories of her bust. Her hips were ample, too. They swayed when she walked even better than those of April East who was corseted a little too tightly, and she had a way of looking at a man with her lips parted and her eyes opened wide.

Had Tennessee come up with that fictitious name as a play on the name Mae West? All I know is that I wrote the name on the index page where it remained undisturbed until a few years ago when I decided to weave the play I had written, inspired by this figment of Mr. Williams vivid imagination, into a short novel. My publisher Donald Bain, who shares the same sense of humor, enjoyed this short novel, and maybe it will be next on the list.

You may well say that now that I'm 87, and when am I going to slow down? I have slowed down, believe me, *way down*, but I'm still here, and as Yogi Berra so wisely said, "It ain't over till it's over."

Fin

APPENDIX A

Oasis in Indiana

By Anne Revere
Published in *Equity Magazine* December, 1964 (Volume XLIX, no. 9)
(Article reprinted with the permission of *Equity News*.)

WHEN, IN MID-OCTOBER OF 1963, I received an invitation to play Bertold Brecht's "Mother Courage" at Purdue University, I recoiled at the multiple hazards. Under the best professional conditions the play is difficult. Witness five productions of which I have firsthand knowledge where it had failed despite the contribution of some very talented people.

Poor Brecht had tough enough sledding in New York. What would be his chances in the arid climate of Indianapolis, capital of the cultural desert of the Middle West, booby trap for any theatrical undertaking and a bare sixty miles from Purdue? And with an all-student cast, donating their spare time and residue of midnight energy painfully squeezed from a demanding university curriculum? And (most panicking of all) with an unknown director who was a college professor?

That, despite these hazards, I should have entertained the invitation measures the desperation to which the theatre sometime drives the professional actor. Two productions, about which I had with my usual folly been enthusiastic, vanished like Alice's rabbit. What, I asked myself, makes the hazards of Purdue more desperate than the hazards of Broadway?

A question to which, obviously, I had no rationale.

My decision (as such it can be called) was therefore subject, for better or worse, to that confluence of unpredictable forces known as luck.

Luck thereupon heralded my arrival at Purdue with a discovery doubly exciting in its total unexpectedness. Dr. Joseph Stockdale, disguised as a professor, proved in fact to be a talented and experienced young director.

The "amorphous, squeezed-out" student cast was discovery number two. Welded by a discipline of dedication, this student company devoting limitless time and energy emerged at last as integrated characters, several of whom attained a stature rivaling the professional.

Thus luck created Purdue University a "realm of gold," an oasis in which prior experience had evaluated as a "cultural desert," well meriting an expensive plant composed of three theatres: An Experimental Theatre of latest design seating 172, with an honorable record of testing the recent and the untried and recently initiated a series of Equity productions; second, the Loeb Theatre, in which we produced "Mother Courage," with excellent acoustics and equipment superior to that in our New York theatres; and most impressive of all, the Hall of Music, seating more than Radio City Music Hall and which, in my five weeks residence, I saw packed for two performances each of three productions. The enthusiastic response to the opera "Don Giovanni," the Bolshoi Ballet and the ovation accorded "Stop The World . . ." shattered the provincial complacency of this native New Yorker.

And what of the production itself?

Carefully shunning years-long theories spun endlessly by academicians to confuse performers and obscure Brecht, Dr. Stockdale directed a swiftly paced, imaginative performance, conveying effectively, excitingly, movingly, the spirit and intent of Mother Courage.

Toward the turbulent close of the rehearsal period, with the curtain revealing the crucial results of our sustained labors, luck seemed at last to have deserted us. Indianapolis papers blasted the area with grim reports of two Brecht flops, one a production of "Mother Courage." Brecht was now synonym for boredom. The outlook was bleak. And to compound the fracture, our opening night competition on campus was nothing less than the Bolshoi Ballet!

Would the impressive Hall of Music where I had so admired "Don Giovanni" and "Stop the World . . ." now overturn Mother Courage and her wagon?

Astonishingly, we opened to half a house—five hundred hardy souls who not only stayed to cheer but sallied forth as emissaries bruiting to future audiences the message, "Must see!"

Gratifyingly, they came.

An experience so richly rewarding prompts me not merely to share it but to explore in behalf of other professional actors possible benefits which might accrue from a liaison with the University Theatre.

Is there here an opportunity to exercise and improve techniques, expand audiences, heighten amateur standards with the creativity of the professional?

The most respected minds, John Reich of the Goodman Theatre and Professor Hoffman late of Carnegie Tech, for example, believe that amateurs cannot learn from amateurs and that the professional must take leadership.

My association with Joe Stockdale at Purdue and a prior association with Norris Houghton at Vassar College have convinced me that Equity members, through the love and quality of their creative labors, may here find a means for protecting and raising the standards and goals of our profession.

May we not say that helping to raise the level of the university production does more than develop a new audience with understanding and appreciation of fine theatre? More sensitive discrimination enriches the personal life.

Perhaps the end result will be reciprocal. As Brooks Atkinson has pointed out, it is possible the professional may learn from a head-on encounter with the academic world. There may be more things in the world of books than are dreamt of in our hurly burly.

The world of Academia appears ready to reciprocate interest. In Frederick L. Hovde, the distinguished scientist and educator and President of Purdue, I found a warm response. He was joined by Professor Paul Chenea, vice president in charge of academic affairs, and Dean M. B. Ogle in encouraging me to work toward a plan which further expands Purdue's association with Professional Actors. There are strong and level-headed forces reaching out from the university. I hope they will find a welcome response from our side.

APPENDIX B

LETTERS ON JOE'S RESIGNATION AS ARTISTIC DIRECTOR OF THE PURDUE PROFESSIONAL THEATRE COMPANY— February and March 1969

Feb. 5: Joe Stockdale's letter to the Editor of *The Purdue Exponent:*

Dear Editor: Before the new Theatre season starts, I think the ticket price policy of the Purdue University Theatre needs explaining. In December, several graduate students asked me why they had to pay regular rates rather than student rates for admittance. The answer is that on November 1968, T. B. Bittles of the Business Office sent a memorandum to L.J. Freehafer, Treasurer, which said that "any Purdue University student presenting a current validated passport" would be considered a student. This excluded graduate students, who for the most part do not have validated passports ... Not a single Theatre staff member was sent a copy of the memorandum, nor was a theatre staff member invited to the meeting that established the policy.

The Theatre staff, indeed, had disagreed with the business office not only on ticket prices but on the question of who constitutes a student. Last August I argued that high school students and students from other colleges should continue to be admitted under student rates as they were in the past. This is standard practice in theatres ... However, the business office, contrary to my arguments, decided that high school students and students from other institutions would be charged full rates. Only after three and a half months of arguing, and after the major portion of the first semester's theatre season was over, was the policy reversed by the business office ...

This is the first time in my nineteen years at Purdue that ticket prices and student rates have not been decided by the Theatre Faculty ... The theatre cannot be looked upon as just another section of another department because it affects the total university. The theatre should draw up a budget. Obviously, this must be approved by the Business Office. Once approved, however, autonomy should then rest with the Theatre staff without constant harassment and interference from people who are not experts in theatre. It is because this has not been the case that I have refused to be acting head of the Theatre.

Feb. 5: Letter was sent to Mr. C.B. Wise of the Business Office with copies to J.G. Stockdale and *The Exponent,* signed by three graduate teaching assistants in Mathematics: Judith M. Hutchens, Jane Stroupe, and Dorothy R. Hockema.

Dear Sir: We have just read the article by Joseph G. Stockdale, Professor of Theatre, in the Purdue Exponent. As graduate students we have always felt that it was unfair to be required to pay full prices for campus entertainment, while living on sub-poverty level incomes. Compared with our respective undergraduates schools, we find it difficult to understand why a large university like Purdue, with the aid of state and federal funds, charges higher prices to [graduate] students ... [and] object to the discriminatory policy of being charged as much for tickets as people who are making five or six times as much money as we are.

We are outraged to learn that the business office is forcing the Theatre to charge full prices for graduate students, when the theatre staff itself favors lower prices ... [and] that you did not respond to Dr. Stockdale's request to write a letter explaining your actions ....

Feb. 21: under headlines "Stockdale Resigns Theatre Position," Bert Oault of *The Exponent* wrote:

"In the third act of 'A Doll's House' Nora says, "Sit down here, Torvald," Prof. Joseph Stockdale told a special meeting of the Faculty Action Committee yesterday. She has had it, he continued, She's through. And I have had it, and I am through.

Thus, Stockdale announced his resignation as artistic director of the University Theatre effective after the completion of "You Never Can Tell" and "The Little Foxes." He cited "continual harassment' from the university business office as the sole factor behind his decision.

Stockdale will continue in his capacity as a professor in theatre in the creative arts department, but he stressed that "nothing would make (him) do shows on this campus this summer."

The event which climaxed a continual struggle between theatre and Vice President and Treasurer Lyle J. Freehafer was a memorandum issued by Freehafer on January 7 which said: "Effective 10 January 1969, the signature of M. James Randolph Earle will not be accepted on any official documents filed with any office under the jurisdiction of the Vice President and Treasurer of the university. This matter will be reviewed at the end of one year."

Earle is the business manager/technical director of the theatre, and according to Stockdale his signature was good for any supplies from boards and nails to food stuffs. However, in August of 1968, Earle authorized a requisition for photographic supplies from Foster's Film Services These supplies were picked up by David Umbarger, a photographer for Purdue News service who was performing in an additional capacity, on his own time, as theatre photographer, Stockdale said. According to Earle, the supplies were simply reimbursement for material which Umbarger had used at his own expense. However Freehafer maintains that they were barter and constituted a violation of university policy which prohibits double salaries, Earle said.

Earle added that he was simply following procedure carried out by his predecessor, Alan Light, who he replaced August 1. Light had arranged an identical system with another photographer, Steve Rose. This, accounting to Earle and Stockdale, was fully approved by Howard Lyon, business representative of the School of Humanities.

However, when Freehafer heard of the system, he notified Humanities School Dean Marbury B. Ogle and ordered it stopped. The message was transmitted to Earle and Umbarger, evidentially somewhat indirectly, and they complied.

Feb. 21: Editorial in *The Exponent* bears the headline: "Revoke Policy Decision!"

Prof. Joseph Stockdale's announcement that he will no longer head the University Theatre was hardly a shock to yesterday morning's session of the Faculty Action Committee. For an hour and a half, he and James R. Earle had voiced their grievances about the financial and legal interference they received from Vice President and Treasurer Lytle J. Freehafer. The meeting was called for this purpose, and Stockdale and Earle took full advantage of the opportunity...

[It ends with the following:]

The University Theatre cannot afford to lose Joseph Stockdale; his theatre productions are brilliant and his contributions to the cultural environment of the university are enormous. The financial office of the university can afford to amend its decision, however; the issue involved is minor, especially as compared to the disciplinary action taken.

Thus we join Dean Ogle, the Faculty Action Committee, and Stockdale in condemning the action taken by Freehafer, and we implore him to revoke his policy decision.

Accompanying this editorial is a cartoon picturing two men, Freehafer (labeled) with money flying out of his pockets as he dances with his left hand around a bloated longhaired figure with a sash on which is printed ENGINEERING. Freehafer's right foot has just kicked an infant who is flying askew wearing a sash HSSE. The caption is: "Get lost punk, There just ain't enough Bread to go around."

Feb.21: to Joseph Stockdale with CC to Deans Ogle and Felix Haas (Dean of Science) from Joseph F. Foster, Professor and Head of the Department of Chemistry:

Dear Professor Stockdale: I want to express my keen regret on learning of your resignation as Artistic Director of the University Theatre. I hasten to add, however, that I understand your position and realize that you probably had no alternative. Your resignation is a serious loss for the University. As administrative Officer of one of the largest technical departments at Purdue and as a member of the academic community I have looked on what you were doing as a tremendous asset! In recruiting staff members we have always made a point of stressing our outstanding theatre as a factor which makes life in Lafayette stimulating and exiting. I do want you to know that your efforts have been appreciated by countless faculty members in the technical areas, certainly by me, and your resignation is a serious blow, not just to the arts but to the entire University.

Feb. 21: *The Exponent* under a headline "Impossible To Continue," printed the following news story:

Dean Ogle heard of Freehafer's proposal concerning Earle in November and drafted a strongly worded letter of disapproval to President Hovde, Ogle said. On January 7, Freehafer issued his memorandum. Freehafer would not comment on his reasons for the action or his intentions in the future because the case is under review by a faculty committee. Stockdale contends that the utilization of Umbarger's services was less expensive and produced a better quality of pictures than if the Theatre had operated through university photographic services.

That is, for four summer productions and the initial three fall performances, the theatre allocated $39.20 to Umbarger for supplies. Early estimates that at the customary $6 per hour ($9 for overtime), the same services would have cost approximately $1,600.

As for the quality, Stockdale said, Umbarger was willing to devote hours of his time to watching the rehearsals for the high points of the performance then taking the pictures during the dress rehearsals. Stockdale said that any other arrangement would have involved posed shots instead of actual action pictures.

Stockdale also asserted that this is not an isolated case. In the summer of 1967, he said, two firemen were appointed by the university to attend every rehearsal and performance, costing the theatre approximately $600 in unbudgeted expenses.

Last year, due to a large turnout of students at reduced admissions prices and the illness of Anne Revere [cancellation of two weeks of the six week run of "Long Day's Journey Into Night"] the theatre produced a deficit of around $9,000.

Therefore, Freehafer's office has taken over the box office and raised the ticket prices ... [Stockdale] added that this will stifle the theatre's attempts to build up an audience ... [He] sent a letter to Prof. J.W. Wiley of University Senate which presents his opinions. These were that the theatre was probably wrong in its photographic arrangements, that Earle was unaware of the violation and ceased the process when he was informed and Freehafer's action had "the theatre operation 95% paralyzed."

In his letter of resignation to Dr. Ralph Beelike, head of the creative arts department, Stockdale said the future of a theatre program on this campus depends on the full cooperation with a "duly appointed head of theatre."

However, he said that he had not and would not accept such a position because "the academic and cultural policy of Purdue University concerning theatre as a performing art was not set by the theatre staff of experts, but by minor clerks of the business office."

Feb. 21: Larry Schumpert, under headlines that read "Theatre Director Quits In Business Dispute" in *The Journal and Courier,* Lafayette, Indiana, wrote:

... Dr. Joseph Stockdale has angrily resigned as artistic director of the Purdue University Theatre. Blaming his action on a "usurpation of authority," by the Purdue business office, of the Theatre's prerogatives, Stockdale said, "I've had it."

He said he would continue to teach theatre courses, but that the March production of "The Little Foxes" would be his final directing assignment. If he sticks to his decision, it will end an era at Purdue that has been praised both for its artistry and innovation.

"In the last 11 years I've directed 70 plays," Stockdale said, noting that the number exceeded any obligation to the university. "I didn't have to do it," he went on. "I already had tenure. I did it—and this may sound corny—I did it because I loved it. Well, I don't love it anymore."

Stockdale has been at Purdue for 19 years.

The other man who found himself at the center of the theatre's business office storm, James Randolph Earle, the theatre's business manager, said Stockdale would be difficult to replace.

The article then goes on to record the history of the problems with the business office in great detail. And

ends with...

In a letter to President Frederick L. Hovde last month Stockdale said the action of Freehafer would "paralyze the operation of the theatre, which must, by its very nature, function outside standard business hours and procedures. We feel very strongly that our business manager must be a person of the theatre, and continually in touch with its needs."

Feb. 24: An *Exponent* editorial under the headline "Theatre Needs Autonomy:"

· .. Autonomy and freedom are not characteristic of the Purdue atmosphere. And if this institution is going to be a university, they must be. We hold this to be true of the University Theatre, but in their case financial difficulties prevent complete autonomy. As in the case of many other university theatres, the operation of the Purdue University Theatre is dependent upon subsidy funds from the university.

However, we do believe that the theatre should operate under relative autonomy while remaining within the economic binds of the university. A project as demanding in time and talent as the theatre cannot undergo the constant political bickering and bureaucratic red tape employed by the computerized system.

Professor Joseph Stockdale's resignation as bead of the theatre pushes the issue to a climax which may ultimately result in a confrontation between the university business office and the theatre staff in which the theater would be backed by a large portion of faculty and students.

... Money, of course, will remain the major drawback to the completely efficient operation of the theatre. The university grants them approximately $30,000 while other universities go as high as $150,000. The university then should provide more funds and grant them as a block to the theatre.

The theatre's administrator would be bound to hold expenses within this block, but he would be able to channel them for the most effective use.

Unlike other, more controversial issues, this one should inevitably receive campus-wide support. People in all fields have voiced desires to see strong performing and creative arts programs to enhance technical, mass instruction. An excellent theatre program's also a tremendous factor in drawing outstanding faculty.

Feb. 25: Gerald R. MacLane who headed the Mathematics Department at one time writes

President F.L Hovde with a copy to Prof. Stockdale:

Dear President Hovde:

I feel compelled to comment on the recent developments related to the Purdue Professional Theatre. I am not sufficiently presumptuous to think that I know all that may be behind this fiasco ... rather I wish to make three statements which, to my mind are concerned with much more important issues than nit-picking-fault-finding.

The Purdue Professional is the sole ["Purdue created"] quality operation which Purdue runs on its own in the non-curricular area of art and culture.... and it is also very good indeed. I lived in Houston for 16 years and enjoyed many productions at the rather well-known Alley Theatre, which has been well-treated by the Ford Foundation. The Purdue Professional theatre, at its best (and that's a high percentage of the time) is just as good as the Alley. Professor Stockdale deserves a medal-or better; some understanding support.

I suspect that the real problem is dollars. How does the dollar loss of the Theatre compare with the dollar pumped into W-Bah or PMO, for instance? By no stretch of the imagination, can either of those two be rated as a quality production.

Surely every effort should be made to preserve and nurture the Purdue Professional Theatre.

Feb. 25: WASK RADIO voiced the following "Analysis and Comment;"

We note with considerable regret the resignation of Dr. Joe Stockdale as head of the Purdue University Theatre. At the very least the resignation removes a talented and experienced hand that has guided the Purdue Theatre to heights totally unexpected at an engineering school. Unfortunately, coupled with the resignation last summer of Ross Smith as head of both the theatre and convocations, it puts the future of the university's professional company in serious doubt. This summer's productions seem almost certainly doomed and there seems a good possibility that the entire project will go down the drain. Hence Purdue will lose something unique in Indiana and with it will go the distinction of being a pace-setter in what is fast becoming the important national trend of resident professional companies. The reasons behind Stockdale's resignation are significant in that they illustrate the constant battle the arts have faced with the technically oriented administration at Purdue. In the final analysis both Stockdale and Smith stepped aside for the same reason. They simply were tired of fighting. In Stockdale's words, "Enough is enough. There comes a point at which one person has had it. I've reached that point." The chief administration opponent has consistently been Purdue Vice-President Lytle Freehafer. Reliable sources say that he has been trying to cut down on the theatre operations and eliminate the professional company because of its need for subsidy. Among the members of the administration, The Theatre Department has found its most consistent friend in President Frederick Hovde. Unfortunately, it is not Hovde with whom the department must carry on its day-to-day dealings. The immediate loss of the summer theater will eliminate the Lafayette area's one oasis in what during the hot months is a cultural desert. The long term effects of the department's curtaining if that indeed develops will be more far reaching. It will rob both the Purdue community and the Greater Lafayette area of an important cultural activity and will see the devoted work of talented men fall by the wayside.

Feb. 25: *The Exponent,* headlined, "Students Voice Concern Over Theatre's Future."

Dear President Hovde:

We, the undersigned are deeply concerned about the future of the theatre at Purdue University. We believe that the theatre is an essential educational experience for all students, and as such should be considered as a service to the students. It is unfortunate that budget considerations are allowed to interfere with this service. Raising the price of student tickets this semester because too many students, at too low price, had developed the theatre-going habit, shows a lack of recognition of the educational function of the theatre. The role of the business office of the University should also be construed as one of service in that it should support rather than hinder the educational function of the various departments and should keep in mind that the function of the University is, after all, one of education.

Therefore, we urge you to use all of the powers you can command (1) to smooth out the differences between the theatre and the business office, (2) to provide the theatre such real autonomy as is necessary for its growth, and (3) as a first step in this direction to see that an Executive Director of the theatre is appointed soon who will have the authority to unite the resources of the University to continue to provide the University with theatre of quality. (Signed) James R. Cost, Professor of Metallurgy; H. J. Ewbank, Jr., Professor of Speech; Madeline Goulard, Professor of Aeronautical Engineering; Allen Hayman, Professor of English; John S. Karling, Professor and Dean Emeritus of Biology; Barnet Kottler, Professor of English; Paul Lykoudis, Professor of Nuclear Engineering; Dale W. Margerum, Professor of Chemistry; Alan McDonald, Professor and Head of Mathematics; S.P. Rosen, Professor of Physics; and Robert Toal.

Feb. 26: Letter to *The Exponent* from R. Goulard, Professor of Aeronautical Engineering.

The recent crisis at the Purdue Theatre brings out again the lack of a workable administrative structure where this group could flourish. The situation is not totally without parallel. Many Purdue departments have known the demoralization and losses which result from lengthy delays in replacing chairmen who have moved on to other things. A department chairman translates and promotes at all times the academic aspirations of students and faculty into dollars, square feet, and administrative decisions. His absence causes long lasting damage.

Amazingly enough not only is the theatre group currently deprived of such a coordinator but it never had one. It has had to rely for the academic welfare of the chairman of a much larger department and for all practical operations on the roles and judgment of a distant business office. No buffer exists which would relieve the theatre staff from the need to justify their every step in terms of a system each can understand.

If such daily frustrations can damage the morale of engineers and scientists, one can imagine what they do to the creative artist. Let us hope that our many Torvalds will at long last give our Theatre the structure and support it needs to maintain a leading educational role on campus.

Feb. 26, *The Exponent* printed the following letter written by The Association of Graduate Students in English.

Dear Editor: We, the Association of Graduate Students in English, view the recent resignation of Professor Joseph Stockdale, artistic director of the University Theatre, as another step in the enhancement of Purdue's reputation for cultural sterility.

The harassment Professor Stockdale and his staff were forced to undergo was deplorable, bordering on the ludicrous. When will the Administration recognize that there are some things which cannot or should not be justified by the profit motive? Must every semblance of culture at Purdue be subject to Mammon's throne?

James Joyce saw his native Ireland as a land which denied artistic creation and destroyed the artist. He spoke of it as "the old sow that eaters her farrow." It strikes us that this description is not wholly inappropriate to Purdue.

Feb. 26: *The Exponent* printed the following letter under the headline, "Administration
   Policy Causes Displeasure," from Glenn W. Howard, Jr.

Dear Editor:

It was with shock and regret that I read of Joe Stockdale's resignation as artistic director of the University Theatre. He has my support. I strongly suspect that the resignation of the theatre's director, Ross Smith, was also due in a large part to the attitude of the Business Office and the administration of the University Theatre.

Take a case in point: photography. The University Theatre uses photography as a means of recording their productions. Thus, for any given show they have a pictorial record of the acting, makeup, blocking, sets, lighting, and costumes. These pictures can then be used both for publicity and as aids in the classroom.

'… It is most strange that the University gripes about budget cuts by the Legislature, bitches about the Theatre budget deficit, and then complains because someone tried to save a little money. When the Theatre was a student organization they could spend their money as they pleased, and get the best-for-less if they could. Now they are not permitted to, even if they can.

Now for a couple of related gripes. The University maintains several "services" which may be used by the University Community, among these are the Photographic and Printing services and the Machine Shop. The University has a rule that if a "service" says that they can handle a job, then you cannot get it done off campus. This holds even if you can get it done better, faster, and for less if the job is given to a local business. And even if the quality and speed obtained from the university are good the job can usually be done for slightly less elsewhere.

It is time a few people raised their voices and asked, "What the — goes on here?

27 Feb.: Letter to the Editor of *The Exponent* from Victor H. Dennenberg, Professor of Psychology, headlined, "Prof. Praises Stockdale Productions."

I am writing concerning the recent situation involving Professor Joseph Stockdale. When I first arrived on this campus many years ago, my wife and I went to the various student theatrical productions given here. They were pathetic. These productions were at about the same level as one would expect from a third-rate Indiana junior high school.

Into this cultural desert came Professor Stockdale, bringing with him a rich imagination, an enthusiasm for his work, and the necessary energy to transform a desert into an oasis. He has succeeded magnificently. The student productions have now become near-professional in quality. The academic community has grown used to the idea of having professional Broadway actors appearing with students in plays. In fact, we are now so sophisticated that we no longer gawk when we see them casually wandering around the campus. Some of the productions I have seen are equal to or of better quality than plays I have seen on Broadway. And now a set of silly and arbitrary restrictions of a misguided Business Office has threatened to destroy one of the very few cultural activities of which this university can be proud.

I find this totally unbelievable. If Purdue were a profit-making industrial corporation, then I could understand-though I would not condone-the action of the Business Office. But this is a university with the responsibility of education in the broadest sense of that term. Within such a framework, how can one justify the restrictive pricing of theatre tickets, the failure to have special prices for students (including non-university students), and the persistent harassment of the Business Office?

If one does not wish to use a broad educational framework as a context for judging this problem, let me offer a more pragmatic one. Purdue is a good university with hopes and aspirations of becoming great. A university becomes great when and only when, it has a great faculty. I have never heard of a university which was great because of the business Office. There are few amenities at Purdue to attract, or to hold, those faculty members who can help this University become great. One of these few amenities is the theatre under the direction of Professor Stockdale.

Can this university afford to lose Professor Stockdale?

Feb. 27: *The Exponent* printed actions of the Student Senate as reported by Kaki Hinze:

In other business, the senate voted a resolution to recommend the selling of Purdue University theatre tickets at student prices to graduate students with invalidated passports. This resolution also applies to residence hall counselors.

Feb. 28: In a letter to *The Exponent* Professor Sidney Pellisier wrote:

Dear Editor: I am writing this letter to congratulate the Business Office for its recent victory. You, sirs, have finally crushed one of the last holdouts in this haven of Hoosier homogeneity: Joseph "Horse-before-the-cart" Stockdale. Now that you have won this battle you can forge forward to greater conquests. You may eventually win the coveted Anus Mundi Award for Neat Bookkeeping. Keep marching ever onward in your Crusade for Conformity.

Joseph Stockdale should be fired on the grounds of mental illness. He must be crazy to have stayed here for so long.

Mar. 3: Editorial in *the Purdue Exponent,* "University Theatre?"

... The first and major difficulty is, of course, money. The theatre now operates on a low budget compared to similar groups. Last year, the university allocated approximately $28,000 for theatre use and had to supply $9,000 more to cover a deficit. Other universities allow as much as $150,000 for theatre operations.

Because the state legislature doesn't seem to like the idea of supporting its universities, more funds from state allocations are impossible. However, the Purdue Research Foundation is set up to handle such special finances.

To implement this source, the theater must apply to the Board of Trustees for a national foundation grant. If the trustees approved, they would forward the request to the PRF directors, three of whom are members of the board and another is President Hovde. The directors would analyze the request in terms of the theatre's capability and desire to contribute to the total university concept. Under these terms, acceptance of the request seems inevitable. Then, PRF would apply for the grant as a sponsor of the university and the theatre to a national foundation.

By granting these additional funds, the theatre would be able to offer tickets at the rates which proved popular last year....

Mar. 5: Charles Staff, critic for the *Indianapolis News* under a headline "Purdue Theatre Group to End?" wrote:

Dr. Joseph Stockdale's resignation as artistic director of the Purdue Professional Theatre Company probably spells death for the troupe on the West Lafayette campus. Before the resignation is final and the fate of the company is sealed, Dr. Stockdale will direct one last production, Lillian Hellman "The Little Foxes," opening night to run-through March 23. According to a university spokesman, Dr. Stockdale resigned because of strained relations between the professional company, which he founded and headed, and the Purdue business office. This season, the business office required a price increase for tickets to offset a growing deficit. Attendance dropped and the financial situation did not improve. Dr. Stockdale, who has been at Purdue since 1950, will continue as a professor in the theatre department at the university....

Mar. 6: in Letter to the Editor from Mrs. Fred R. Gems, of West Lafayette, to the *Journal and Courier* of Lafayette, under headline, "Theatre's Loss:"

The news of Dr. Stockdale's resignation as director of the Purdue University Theatre is most distressing. In the final analysis it is both the university and the community that would suffer an inestimable loss with the withdrawal of Dr. Stockdale and the professional theater group he was so instrumental in bringing here.

Mar. 10: Editorial page of *The Exponent* devoted to a letter from Connie Heaver, with the headline: "Reader Praises Stockdale."

Dear Editor: When Joseph Stockdale resigned as Artistic Director of the Purdue University Theatre, those in authority in the Humanities School began to consider hiring a new director to replace him. For the record, I would like to summarize the amount of work Dr. Stockdale had fulfilled in the past eleven years here, and suggest that at least two directors be sought to assume his former output.

Since the Loeb Playhouse opened in May 1958, there have been 103 productions directed in the Loeb and Experimental Theatre by *eight staff and three guest directors* which played for 1110 performances. Of those 103 productions, Dr. Stockdale directed 63 which gave 916 performances...

... Dr. Stockdale has always carried a full teaching load, although the added director's duties have sometimes made his work load the equivalent of teaching six three-hour courses per semester .... 63 productions in eleven years (not counting the nine shows directed elsewhere) gives Dr. Stockdale a director's record unprecedented in either Broadway or Educational Theatre. One does not simply go out and hire a man to replace Joe Stockdale. If the Humanities administrators are merely looking for a director to continue play production on this campus, they had obviously better think of two or three men to assume Dr. Stockdale's level of output both academically and artistically.

... His great work output has not been mere performance of the job he was hired to do. It has been one special man's own drive to build a new theatre to offer to the people of Indiana. Men with the keen intelligence and dynamic energy necessary to forge something new and fight to develop it are rare. Joe Stockdale is such a man.

He will not be easy to replace.

Mar. 18: from "The News In Indiana" section of *The Indianapolis News,* an article by Fremont Power under the headline: "Theatre is Facing Crisis At Purdue."

Never mind how a resident professional theatre happened to develop at Purdue University, the state's engineering and agriculture school. It did. And under the aegis of Prof. Joseph Stockdale, became unquestionably the finest theatre in the state and a significant outpost for drama.

They have been doing things in drama at Purdue which were not being done elsewhere in the state.

Stockdale was playing James Earl Jones in "Of Mice and Men" when Jones' reputation was confined largely to theatrical casting offices. He since has become a Broadway celebrity in "The Great White Hope." And there was Anne Revere, the Academy award winner in the movie, "National

Velvet," appearing on the Purdue stage in "Long Day's Journey Into Night." Frances Farmer and Victor Kilian played "Look Homeward, Angel" and there was Bertold Brecht's "Three Penny Opera."

These Actors' Equity members were brought in a resident company for the purpose of pollinating Purdue's theatre students with professional approaches and concepts. There probably is no real way to assay the results, but as a cultural achievement the Purdue theatre has been a remarkable project.

Now it had fallen upon stormy times. Call it art versus the business office, or Stockdale and his theatre business manager, James Randolph Earle, versus Lytle J. Freehafer, Purdue vice-president and treasurer. Freehafer has been less than satisfied with some of Earle's fiscal operations: Payment of $39 to a photographer already on the university payroll, charging small stage property items at Lafayette stores, etc., etc. Earle said the $39 was only for supplies, that he was getting the photographer's service free in off-duty time and that if he hired a photographer "through channels" it would have cost $200-259 a production.

And so it goes.

"Somebody has to see that public funds are properly expended," Freehafer said. He notified fiscal officers of the university Jan. 7th that "the signature form. James Randolph Earle will not be accepted on any official documents filed with any office under the jurisdiction of the vice-president and treasurer of the university. This matter will be reviewed at the end of one year."

With this, Stockdale resigned as artistic director of the theatre, claiming his business manager had been virtually disenfranchised and his (Earle's) academic freedom as a theatre instructor violated. What remains to be seen now is whether this rhubarb, which, at least from an outside view, seems to have descended to some picayunish depths, is going to swamp the whole project.

The theatre's a deficit operation which was subsidized for about $35,000 last year from what Freehafer describes as general funds of the university, which would be a mix of tax and nontax monies. And, as they have gone to some pains to make known, universities have fallen upon "hard times" in the year of the Legislature. "We may have to find a new director and money is going to be short," John W. Hicks, said, executive assistant to the president. "But the administration is going to try to save the theatre.

Mar.1: on the next to the last performance of *You Never Can Tell*, Henry Hewes, drama critic for *The Saturday Review* had come from New York to review this production in an article called "Pros and Cons," which was published on March 15, 1969 (p. 22).

The concept of university theatre departments operating professional resident theatres as part of an educational program is being severely tested ... and there are recent indications that the burden of running a professional company within a university can become intolerable. For no matter how good the artistic results, there is too often a shortsighted inability on the part of university administrators to adapt their regulations to meet the special needs of theatrical production. The Purdue Professional Theatre Company is a case in point. This project which began its professional operation in 1967 had proved most popular with audiences and well worth the relatively small annual $28,000 deficit it required.

The company's artistic director, teacher Joseph Stockdale, has just finished staging a new musical comedy version of Shaw's *You Never Can Tell*, which captures the charm of an English seaside resort in the 1890s. . . .The musical, as adapted by Stockdale, emphasizes the romantic undercurrents in the script, and even brings together at the end, as Shaw did not, the play's two most irreconcilable characters. The music by Roz Aronson, wife of a Purdue professor, is melodic and excellent, with "If You Walk With Me" the most memorable of several lovely ballads. . . .

Unfortunately, this and the other achievements of the Purdue Professional Theatre Company have been accompanied by what has seemed to Stockdale to be a continual harassment by the regulation bound Purdue business office. As a result, Stockdale has just resigned as artistic director and will henceforth content himself with the less arduous chores of teaching and of directing student productions. This resignation presumably dooms an excellent company, for to hire a new artistic director would increase a deficit already considered onerous by the fiscal authorities....

APPENDIX C

Woodstock reviews

Man With A Load of Mischief

The Daily Freeman by John T. Sloper: "What gives it life, are the performances at Woodstock ... Director Joseph Stockdale is well aware of the style required and paced the piece well."

Poughkeepsie Journal by Jeffrey Borak: "The musical is at its most witty, most interesting, most subtly articulate in its non-musical moments .... The script is laced with subtle grace and urbanity, qualities which this expert company explores with great style and wit under Joseph Stockdale's smooth direction.... This is a handsomely mounted production and it moves fluidly through its nearly two-hours running time."

Charley's Aunt

Times-Union by Martin P. Kelly: "The dated farce Charley's Aunt, which had a revival 20 years ago as the musical Where's Charley, still has some life in it as shown in the production at the Woodstock Playhouse. The Brandon Thomas Comedy ... is staged by Joseph Stockdale at full tilt... it starts slowly, but once the deception starts, Stockdale's staging is brisk and sure. He exacts from his cast a 19th century style of acting whose artificiality is deceiving at first, but then fits into the pattern of the comedy....Charley's Aunt wheezes but the Woodstock cast brings enough fresh air to the production to make it work."

The Daily Freeman by John T. Sloper: "Farce required overdoing, with just the right attention to such details as facial and vocal expression and, of course, a very rapid pace ... All of these elements, and more, are present in the current production of this classic farce. It is a finely tuned bit of comic fun that is as entertaining now as it was in 1892 .... Director Joseph Stockdale has a talented cast to work with and he uses their talents to advantage. .. . The emphasis is on style and taste and both are just right for the piece .... The trick is to involve the audience and make it believe. This is accomplished with high style by the Company."

Ulster County Gazette by Marianne D. Darrow: "Charley's Aunt is certainly older (set in the 1890s) but in the hands of the Woodstock Playhouse cast, she is better than ever.... One word to describe the production? Hilarious.... Director Joseph Stockdale has tricks up his sleeve to focus the audience's attention – the way he moves people up and down stage and the other stage movements were just right, with the pace balanced between the madness and the moments of calm! Hope you don't miss this one!"

Ulster County Townsman by Sharon Cherven: "...Remarkably well done. Charley's Aunt is not an easy play to do. The cast was especially good resisting the temptation to overact. Director Joseph Stockdale is to be congratulated."

Rain

The Poughkeepsie Journal by Jeffrey Borak: "The play's forceful appeal, I suspect, has as much to do with the lucid, intelligent and dramatic production director Joseph Stockdale and his company have created as with the material itself. The production carries with an extraordinary sense of rhythm and timing.... This production of Rain begins slowly, almost languidly; building its force carefully like faint flecks of gray storm clouds building a thunderhead of enormous force and consequence on a far horizon.... Stockdale has managed to forge an extraordinary sense of ensemble in the playing of this piece."

The Times Herald Record by James F. Cotter: "The Playhouse is presenting a steamy, stormy revival. ... For summer repertory acting at its best you must see this production.... In directing Rain Joseph Stockdale has found a group of talented actors for the supporting roles.... The variety of roles, the harmony of acting styles, and the clean cut of conflict – this is the core of drama and the company has captured it whole.... The cast and its director have staged a lively revival of a timeless struggle."

The Knickerbocker News by Joan A. Jamison: "Rain as staged by Joseph Stockdale is a powerful drama that flexes the muscle in the third act. ... It is a well-balanced production of a thought provoking classic."

The Daily Freeman by John T. Sloper: "What emerges today from this revival of Rain is a deep and compelling character study. Given the honesty of approach that is on view, one cannot help but watch in total fascination as the tragic protagonist moves relentlessly towards his own undoing.... All of this is handled with exquisite taste, and considering the period in which the play was written, a quietly moving form of understatement that is combined with dramatic intensity... The main attribute of this production is the way the entire cast under the direction of Joseph Stockdale plays the rather archaic drama "straight" – and with complete honesty.... The performances themselves, with the effortless timing employed emphasize the poetic symbolism of the piece. This is definitely a performance that should not be missed."

Times Union by Martin P. Kelly, "A seldom produced drama is receiving a taut and intriguing production ... Director Joseph Stockdale gains good, solid performance[s] .... and keeps a firm hand on the staging, refraining from excessive melodramatics."

Misalliance

The Daily Freeman by John T. Sloper: "If there is a common dominator this season it is variety here coupled with persistent quality in production.... The quality of the acting and the polish of the production as a whole has been such that it has nearly overcome the inevitable talkers in the audience.... Misalliance is marked by consistently inspired performances and sparkles with polish.... But above all the stage is peopled with real humans, about whom one can develop interest and concern. The acting is so close to the ideal of ensemble playing that no one actor stands out. ... In any stylized period piece it is easy to stray from reality, but that temptation is resisted here. In the play, and in the production of it, everyone is a winner."

Times Herald Record by James F. Cotter: "The talented company of actors under the sensitive direction of Joseph Stockdale fills the bill to near perfection obviously enjoying every bit of foolishness and philosophy that Shaw has poured into his play."

The U. C. Gazette by Marianne Darrow: "This is a deliriously happy marriage between the genius of George Bernard Shaw and the Woodstock Playhouse Acting Company.... This comedy was such a triumph that Woodstock may be gaining a reputation for Shaw productions as the many Stratfords are for Shakespeare! ... Dr. Joseph Stockdale must have enjoyed directing this one, as he surely had a unified company performance, with every nuance of the Shavian comments on God, the generation gap, marriage partners and working classes as timely as today.... Misalliance at the Playhouse is Shaw and Woodstock at their very best."

The Poughkeepsie Journal by Jeffrey Borak: "One sparkling and radiant production of Shaw's Misalliance in an otherwise pedestrian summer season is an event. Two is a coincidence of remarkable proportions.... This production, directed by Joseph Stockdale hasn't the sunny, airy disposition of the production done earlier at Sharon Playhouse. It is a much more mannered and refined approach. And while its first act tended to move at a rather slow clip its second act moves at a brisk ebullient pace. Its cast is likeable and talented and, quite on its own merits it is a pleasant and engaging affair... It has its problems, not the least of which is Stockdale's staging; a series of static poses and line-ups with whatever movement there is, existing merely as a transition from one formal grouping to the next. I suspect there is a method to this design, but coupled with a solid, somewhat enclosed setting, it gives both the production and the play a somewhat stuffy and restrained feeling....[however] It all adds up to quite a delightful entertainment for a summer evening."

Suddenly Last Summer

Times Harold Record by James F. Cotter: "The production is polished to perfection, as flawless as the lines of Williams' own poetry when he spins his imaginary web and catches us in its diaphanous threads. When this playwright is good, he is very, very good, and this company is equal to the challenge.... Joseph Stockdale has directed "Summer" with inspiration and theatrical craft. Every gesture suits the word, and the result is an eloquent, honest version that remains close to the purity of the original play.... It is a tale you should not miss."

Old Dutch Post Star by Carole Costello: "The Woodstock Players skillfully handled this play whose intensity forbade even an intermission. Director Joseph Stockdale must be credited with displaying this difficult piece so successfully.... The entire cast has proven its ability to handle a diversity of plays from light musicals to something as chilling as "Suddenly Last Summer."

Kite by Eleanor Koblenz: "In choosing Suddenly Last Summer, one of Williams' most difficult plays, The Woodstock management placed itself more on the side of art than of commercialism. For those who availed themselves of the opportunity, the gamble was a good one.... The audience was rapt as an extremely competent company did full justice to Williams' strange work. ... The company which has been in residence all summer does an excellent job of filling the roles.... 'Suddenly' was directed by Joseph Stockdale.... With the exception of some weird movie-type music inserted to point up various parts of the plot, his staging was excellent."

Times-Union by Martin P. Kelley: "The Woodstock Playhouse closed out its week's run of Tennessee Williams' rarely performed work, Suddenly Last Summer, with a production that caught much of the poetic flights of the playwright but with not a great deal of success in penetrating the deep psychological structure of the play .... Director Joseph Stockdale wove the action of the play carefully through the maze of psychological meanderings by Williams. A good cast dealt earnestly with the script but was unable to overcome the obtuse nature of the plot."

The Poughkeepsie Journal by Jeffrey Borak: "Under Joseph Stockdale's direction, the production shifts awkwardly between poetry, intense drama, a calculated larger-than-life aspect and melodrama. He intrudes on the play with a choice and use of music which is annoying, obtrusive, and distracting and helps carry the production to almost ludicrous lengths."

Murder In the Vicarage

Times Herald Record by Marcus Kalipolites: "Director of this most engrossing play was Joseph Stockdale ... Even if you're not a mystery buff, the edge-sitting production offers a lot of excitement.

The Daily Freeman by John Sloper: "It is entertaining and that is what summer stock is all about."

A Little Night Music

Times Herald Record James F. Cotter: "The Playhouse has saved its best champagne for the last. The production of A Little Night Music bubbles with celebration and theatrical joy.... This is one party you must not miss.... This musical is a 10 course dinner that caters to everyone's taste....With a cast of 18, ably directed by Joseph Stockdale, the company savors the language and for the most part allows us to relish the musical dialogue."

The Daily Freeman by John T. Sloper: "There is a beautiful production of a thoroughly charming musical play currently occupying the boards at the Woodstock Playhouse ... For anyone who appreciates the wit, style, and saucy naughtiness of turn of the century Scandinavia, Night Music is a strong candidate for the must-see list. ... The season's company at Woodstock under the artful direction of Joseph Stockdale has consistently demonstrated their ability to handle the style, and rescue the wit. This time they again manage to make the richly-woven speech patterns from another era sound as believable as the people next door.... More than just trained professionals the resident company has, through the summer, molded an ensemble that makes a specialty of restoring the English language to its former glory.... Seeing it will light up your life."

From the local Woodstock paper: "The Woodstock Playhouse is celebrating the finish of their summer season with a ball. This is the spirit which comes through with their production of A Little Night Music.... Unquestionably, the upmost effort has been extended to do justice to this adult musicale.... With respect to all and every member concerned in the production praise must be given. Joseph Stockdale directed.... Applause for the playhouse!"

Kite by Bob Goepfert: "Lacking scenery, director Joseph Stockdale showed a lack of innovativeness and staged the production in the more traditional fashion... while the production was lackluster, it was not unpleasant."

Time-Union by Martin P. Kelly: "The Woodstock Playhouse has gathered together an excellent company for its final production of the season, a wry presentation of the musical A Little Night Music.... the sardonic humor of the piece is accentuated in the staging by Joseph Stockdale .... There is an air of the operetta about the musical that can delude a director but at Woodstock there is an understanding of the human foibles dissected in the work... The production is a fitting climax to a successful season at Woodstock which had a 12 percent increase in attendance over last season."

The Poughkeepsie Journal by Jeffrey Borak: "Woodstock Playhouse has mounted this complex musical handsomely and inventively and the whole affair is performed with a heady full sense of the play's wit, style and spirit. It is also a tribute to the cast and the director, Joseph Stockdale that its musical shortcomings do very little, if anything, to prevent this from being a lovely, radiant and intelligent production of a lovely, radiant and intelligent musical."

APPENDIX D

Productions Directed by Joseph G. Stockdale 1952-1985

Information on Venue, Production Dates, Cast and Crews Compiled from Programs by Patrice Murphy*

*Note regarding Appendix D and the *Stages* Index:

Joe Stockdale and his family have been a major influence in my life since I was 10 years old. Joe was, and remains, the best teacher and director I have ever had, and working closely on the book with him has allowed me a joyous trip back to my high school and college days, along with the 40 some years since.

My contributions to this book have been the research for and generation of Appendix D, which provides the detail from the programs of 118 productions that Joe Stockdale directed during his career, as well as compiling the alphabetized list that will form the Index to this book .

Appendix D contains approximately 3000 names; the production staff, crew heads and cast of each show. Given the extent of that appendix, Joe and I agreed that the Index content should cover those subjects and people that are mentioned in the memoir and that reflect specific situations, key relationships in, and major influences on his life so far. I'm sure you will agree, given the fact that it covers almost 87 years, that the Index is as eclectic as it is extensive .

Patrice Murphy

#1
Fowler Hall, Purdue
February 22, 23, 29 and March 1, 1952
The Glass Menagerie
By Tennessee Williams

Directed by Joe Stockdale

Set/Technical Direction	Burt Drexler
Music	Paul Bowles
Stage Manager	Robert Brunner
Rehearsal Assistants	Carolyn White, Joyce Buckner
Master Carpenter	Mike Swanson
Painting	Lowell Jackson
Props	Robert Wright
Make-up	Ann Townsend
Publicity	Pat Martin
Costume Mistress	Marilyn Monarch
House Manager	Lowell Jackson

CAST

The Mother	Pamela Printy
Her Son	Adrian Robinson
Her Daughter	Katie Neff
The Gentleman Caller	Lynn Chiles

#2
Fowler Hall, Purdue
February 20, 21, 27 & 28, 1953
Come Back, Little Sheba
By William Inge

Directed by Joe Stockdale

Set Design	Paul M. Talley
Technical Direction	Paul M. Talley
Stage Manager	William Seaton
Rehearsal Assistants	Mary Ellen Freel, Carolyn White
Sound	Mike Swanson & James Maloon
Master Carpenter	Chris Phelps
Scenic Artist	Philip Glessner
Master Electrician	Robert Hughes
Wardrobe Mistress	Alice Hadley
Make-up	Karlene Counsmen
Props	Paula Petty
Publicity	Betty Thompson
House Manager	Barbara Leroy

CAST

Doc	Lin Chiles
Marie	Shirley Boden
Lola	Katie Neff
Turk	Tom Tsatsos
Postman	Richard Ver Wiebe
Mrs. Coffman	Fleury LeSage
Milkman	Gene Vosicky
Messenger	Robert Wright
Bruce	Robert Ross
Ed Anderson	James Maloon
Elmo Hutton	Shelly Katz

#3
Hall of Music, Purdue
February 24, 25, 26, 1955
A Streetcar Named Desire
By Tennessee Williams

Directed by Joe Stockdale

Set Design	Sam Marks
Technical Assistance	Gerald Godwin, Bill Ditton, Jim Hawley & Geraldine Staley
Choreographer	Nancy Brock
Stage Manager	John Cox
Rehearsal Assistant	Marie Hooper
Master Carpenter	Tom Moran
Scenic Artist	Ann McCormick
Master Electrician	Jim Rhodes
Sound Effects	Roger Buel
Props	Alice Hadley
Make-up	Mary Ellen Freel
Costume Mistress	Helena Cowan
House Manager	Carole Sundling

CAST

Negro Woman	Bernice Davis
Eunice Hubbell	Mary Panages
Stanley Kowalski	Andy Rasbury
Stella Kowalski	Carolyn White
Steve Hubbell	J. Robert Ross
Harold Mitchell (Mitch)	Donald Bain
Mexican Woman	Judy Meyer
Blanche DuBois	Karlene Counsman
Pablo Gonzales	Humberto Valencia
A Young Collector	Keith Green
Nurse	Dorothy Allison
Doctor	Bob Lindsey
Dancers	Karen Nethery, Raymond Kressman, Sat Dev Sarna

#4
Lobero Theatre, Santa Barbara College
March 2 & 3, 1956
The Rainmaker
By N. Richard Nash

Directed by Joe Stockdale

Technical Director	David Hand
Rehearsal Assistants	Cynthia St. Clair, Esther Marshall
Stage Manager	Donna Crouch
Carpentry	Lew Kummerow
Costumes	Cynthia St. Clair
Properties	David Jones
Make-up	Jack Ford
Publicity	Jack Nakano
Lights	Judy Mills
Sound	Steve Roland

CAST

H. C. Curry	Holly Echols
Noah Curry	Ted Scott
Jim Curry	Bob Higbee
Lizzie Curry	Miriam Birch
File	Dale Pennington

Sheriff Thomas ....Michael Lally
Bill Starbuck .... Brian Hansen

#5
Music Hall, Purdue
December 6, 7 & 8, 1956
The Desperate Hours
By Joseph Hayes

Directed by Joe Stockdale

Set Design.......................................Sam Marks
Technical Director .... Carl White
Technical Assistant ....Douglas S. Denbow
Costumes .... William Ditton
Rehearsal Assistant ....Mary D. Rogge
Stage Manager ....Donald Heady
Master Carpenter ....Ozzie Hebert
Paint Lead ....Joanne Potlitzer
Master Electrician ....Roger Davidson
Wardrobe ....Evelyn Ivany & Liz Hoxsie
Property Master ....Al Brown
Make-up Artist ....Linda Budd
Ticket Manager ....John Upfield
House Manager ....Mary Jo Coling
Publicity ....Patricia O'Connell

CAST

Tom Winston ....Allan R. Burke
Jesse Bard ....Gene Selawski
Harry Carson ....Donald Porter
Eleanor Hilliard ....Patricia Porter
Ralphie Hilliard ....John J. Artopoeus
Dan Hilliard ....Alfred Culver
Cindy Hilliard ....Sharon Kelley
Glenn Griffin ....Douglas E. Streff
Hank Griffin ....Donald Rosenberg
Robish ....Randall Walti
Chuck Wright ....William M. Morehouse
Mr. Patterson ....Stanley D. Bogue
Lt. Carl Fredericks ....William D. Kalberer
Miss Swift ....Jeri Sorenson

#6
Music Hall, Purdue University
October 31, November 1 & 2, 1957
The Teahouse of the August Moon
By John Patrick

Directed by Joe Stockdale

Set Design .... Sam Marks
Choreographer .... Nancy Brock
Technical Director ....D. S. Denbow
Costume Design ....Donald Rosenberg
Stage Manager .... Dick Merz
Asst. Stage Manager ....Barbara Allen
Language Advisor ....Tom Miyazaki
Wrestling Advisor ....Jack Crider
Master Carpenter .... Erlene Ketcham
Scenic Artist.. Gail Linderman
Master Electrician ....Bob Henderson
Effects Master ....Dick Leinbach
Props .... Roger Davidson
Wardrobe ....Genvieve Robertson
Make-up ....Mary Margaret O'Brien
Publicity ....Jo Potlitzer
House Manager .... William Fowble

CAST

Sakini ....Jack Booch
Sargeant Gregovich .... Bert Berdis
Col. Wainwright Purdy, III.....................Ken Thomas
Captain Fisby ....Raymond Williams
Old Woman .... Patricia Albright
Old Woman's Daughter ....Jo Hulley
The Daughter's Children ....Steve Burdick, Nancy Burdick, Buddy Halsema
Lady Astor .... Saki
Ancient Man ....Sam C. Lin
Mr. Hokaida ....James Dean Musselman
Mr. Omura ....James H. Croy
Mr. Sumata .... Don Heady
Mr. Sumata's Father ....James R. Carter
Mr. Seiko...George Bogan
Miss Higa Jiga ....Julia Mathews
Mr. Keora .... Bill Donahue
Mr. Oshira .... Isaac L. Peltynovich
Villagers .... Marcia Allen, Judy Anuta, Jo Ann Baugh, George Bush, Bob Collins, Carolyn Eickhoff, Linda Halsema, John Hawkins, Mary Hebrank, Cynthia Horton, Judy Irvine, Jack Lambuth, Nancy Laufer, Tamara Holly Melcher, Bill Mellencamp, Joe Mizerak, Norma Pogrund, Brenda Rabinovitz, Loren Russakov, Syd Steele, Neal Stephenson, Bob Williams, Diana Williams, Bob Wingeard, Dennis Winstead, Shari Van Matre
Ladies' League for Democratic Action: Katie Burr, Ann Linder, Sonya Porter, Marilyn Aldrich, Patricia Albright
Lotus Blossom .... Nancy MacIvor
Captain McLean.............................. Robert L. Runda

#7
Inaugural production in the Experimental Theatre
at Purdue University
May 10, 14, 15, 16 & 17, 1958
Northern Lights
By Douglas S. Denbow

Directed by Joe Stockdale

Choreographer .... Robert Schiffmann
Technical Director ....James Newburger
Stage Manager .... John Hawkins
Rehearsal Assistant ....Mary Margaret O'Brien
Lighting .... David Bourchardt
Sound ....Robert Henderson
Props .... David Eggleston
Costumes ....Judy Irvine
Make-up ....Constance Krabbe

CAST

Scottie
Jimbo .... Bert Berdis
Bert .... Murray A. Sperber
Pete .... Dennis Winstead
Cooper .... Charles Lecht

Bill Downey .... James Maloon
Dorothy Downey .... Patricia Porter
                                              Joan Du Priest
Calypso .... Mary Yarnell
Waiter .... David Blakeslee
Dice Players .... Robert Schiffmann,
                         Bert Berdis, Murray A. Sperber,
                        Dennis Winstead, Thomas Leech,
                          David Blakeslee, John Hawkins
Groom .... Thomas Leech
Bride .... Judy Irvine
Preacher .... Murray A. Sperber
Hotel Clerk .... Thomas Leech
Bell Boy .... John Hawkins

8
Loeb Playhouse, Purdue
October 10, 11, 16, 17 & 18, 1958
Mister Roberts
By Thomas Heggen & Joshua Logan

Directed by Joe Stockdale

Production Designer .... James Newburger
Technical Assistant .... Bob Ackley
Stage Manager .... George E. Bush
Asst. Stage Manager .... Rita Bottomley
Asst. to the Director .... Constance Krabbe
Master Carpenter .... Ed Kenestrick
Scenic Artist .... Maralyn Emrich
Master Electrician .... David Hale
Sound Master .... Michael B. Stella
Property Mistress .... Earlene Ketchum
Wardrobe Mistress .... Donna Hoover
Make-up Artist .... Rita Bottomley
House Manager .... C.L. Schrader

CAST
Chief Johnson .... John W. Sadler
Lieutenant (jg) Roberts .... James Stephens
Doc .... Robert Runda
Dowdy .... Mickey Schrader
The Captain .... David Blakeslee
Insignia .... Bert Berdis
Mannion .... Dana F. Pellman
Lindstrom .... Dick Guhse
Stefanowski .... Jon Wirth
Wiley .... Thomas Fisher
Schlemmer .... Warren J. Davis
Reber .... W. Paul Grable
Ensign Pulver .... Ray Williams
Dolan .... Murray A. Sperber
Gerhart .... Charles Lanman
Payne .... Kirk Newell
Lieutenant Ann Girard .... Nancy Hall
Shore Patrolman .... Michael Mullen
Military Policeman .... Neal Stephenson
Shore Patrol Officer .... John R. Wright
Seamen, Firemen & Others....................... E. Bigelow,
                        W. Paul Grable, Bob Harrington,
                                     Dennis Winstead

9
Loeb Playhouse, Purdue
December 5, 6, 11, 12, 13, 1958
Death of a Salesman
By Arthur Miller

Directed by Joe Stockdale

Set Design .... James Newburger
Technical Assistant .... William K. Young
Stage Manager .... Aaron Monroe
Assistant to the Director .... Donna Hoover
Master Carpenter .... Warren Davies
Scenic Artist .... Maralyn Emerick
Master Electrician .... Dave Borchard
Sound Master .... Dana Pellman
Property Mistress .... Rita Bottomley
Wardrobe Mistress .... Sarah Campbell
Make-up Artist .... Lyn Quackenbush
Publicity ....Kirk Newell

CAST
Willy Loman .... Jon Wirth
Linda .... Nanci Hall
Biff .... David Blakeslee
Happy ....Dick Guhse
Bernard .... Robert Runda
The Woman ....Betty Smith
Charley ....Al Culver
Uncle Ben .... David A. Schobert
Howard ....Thomas King
Jenny .... Donna Hoover
Stanley ....William Grable
Miss Forsythe ....Ann Lloyd
Letta .... Lil Martin
Second Waiter .... Chuck Schelsky

10
Loeb Playhouse, Purdue
December 4, 5 10, 11 & 12, 1959
The Diary of Anne Frank
By
Frances Goodrich & Albert Hackett

Directed by Joe Stockdale

Set Design .... James Newburger
Technical Assistant .... Ned Bobkoff
Stage Managers .... Aaron Monroe, Elaine Goldman
Asst. Stage Manager .... Loren Russakov
Master Carpenter .... David Watkins
Scenic Artist .... Elaine Goldman
Master Electrician .... Anne Rhodes Hottell
Sound Master .... David Watkins
Property Master .... Hubert Frank
Wardrobe Mistress .... Pat McBride
Make-up Artist .... Martha Bottomley
Publicity ....Carolyn Wurm
House Manager .... Tom O'Connell

CAST
Mr. Frank .... Robert Cowan
Miep .... Marlis Gaildene Duncan
Mrs. Van Daan .... Nanci Hall
Mr. Van Daan .... William Shigley
Peter Van Daan .... Schorling Schneider

Mrs. Frank	Nancy Osborne
Margot Frank	Susan Buzney
Anne Frank	Susan Chodash
Mr. Kraler	Steve Van Matre
Mr. Dussel	Larry Tanzi

#11
Experimental Theatre, Purdue
June 15-19, 22-26, 1960
Tunnel of Love
By Joseph Fields & Peter DeVries

Directed by Joe Stockdale

Set Design	James Newburger
Technical Assistant	David Weiss
Stage Manager	Elaine Goldman
Properties	Lynne W. Bryant

CAST

Augie Poole	William M. Hardy
Isolde Poole	Helen McMahon
Dick Pepper	Robert Cowan
Alice Pepper	Jean Mahara
Estelle Novick	Millicent Loeb
Miss McCracken	Mary Lukens

#12
Experimental Theatre, Purdue
June 29 –July 3; July 6-10, 1960
Private Lives
By Noel Coward

Directed by Joe Stockdale & Elaine Goldman

Set Design	James Newburger
Technical Assistant	David Weiss
Stage Managers	Elaine Goldman, Jeff Hecht
Properties	Anne Hottell
Sound Master	Robert Sprafka
House Manager	Clifford L. Schrader

CAST

Sibyl Chase	Robin Stockdale
Elyot Chase	Joseph G. Stockdale, Jr.
Victor Prynne	Anthony Buckley
Amanda Prynne	Martha Nell Hardy
Louise	Mary Foley

#13
Experimental Theatre, Purdue
July 13-17 & 20-24, 1960
The Moon Is Blue
By F. Hugh Herbert
Directed by Joe Stockdale

Set Design	James Newburger
Technical Assistant	David Weiss
Assistant Director	Elaine Goldman
Stage Manager	Anne R. Hottell
Asst. Stage Manager	Susan Allen
Lights	R. J. Sprafka
Stage Crew	Jeff Hecht
Publicity	Robin Stockdale
House Manager	Thomas M. Elliott

CAST

Patty O'Neill	Sherry Risk
Don Greshem	Chuck Schelsky
David Slater	Erling Kildahl
Michael O'Neill	David Deacon

#14
Barn Theatre, Augusta MI
August 23 – 28, 1960
Look Homeward, Angel
By Ketti Frings
(from the novel by Thomas Wolfe)

Directed by Joe Stockdale

Set Design	Robert Cadman, Dusty Reeds
Lighting	Emmett Jacobs, Bill Leonard
Costumes	Lynn Eden, Ora Crofoot

CAST

Ben Gant	Emmett Jacobs
Marie "Fatty" Pert	Bobbie Byers
Helen Gant Barton	Sue Hopwood
Hugh Barton	Monty Aubrey
Eliza Gant	Susan Willis
Will Pentland	Robert Cadman
Eugene Gant	Dale Helward
Jake Clatt	Bill Leonard
Mrs. Clatt	Mary Ann Cottrell
Florry Mangle	Elaine Claire
Mrs. Snowden	Johanna De Salvo
Mr. Farrel	Dan Wilcox
Miss Brown	Barbara Reser
Laura James	Florence Di Re
W.O. Gant	Alfred Hinckley
Dr. Maguire	Francis Sattler
Tarkington	Christopher Jones
Madame Elizabeth	Betty Ebert
Luke Gant	Dean James
Newsboy	Norman Ornellas

#15
Loeb Playhouse, Purdue
December 2, 3, 8-10, 1960
Cat on a Hot Tin Roof
By Tennessee Williams

Directed By Joe Stockdale

Set Design	Bob G. Ackley
Technical Assistant	Carlo Spataro
Stage Manager	Warren Schwomeyer

CAST

Margaret	Virginia Carnes
Brick	George Dandrow, Jr.
Mae	Sharon Hubbell
Gooper	David Lakamp
Big Mama	Anne Rhodes Hottell
Sookey	Lonnell E. Johnson
Dixie	Janet McFadden
Big Daddy	Floyd Herzog
Reverend Tooker	Dan Blackburn
Doctor Baugh	Charles Lehman
Buster	Ken Machol
Sonny	David Stockdale

Trixie ....Margot Machol
Polly ....Laurel Stockdale

16
Experimental Theatre, Purdue
June 16-18, 20-25, 27 –July 2, 1961
The Marriage-Go-Round
By Leslie Stevens

Directed By Joe Stockdale

Set Design	James Newburger
Technical Assistant	Charles P. Lehman
Stage Manager	Elaine Goldman
Choreographer	Maida Rusk Withers
Sound	Don Paarlberg
Properties	Sayre Karling
Lights	Jeanine Low
Scenery	Sam M. Spelvin
Rehearsal Assistant	Ruby Davis
Stage Crew	Sayre Karling
Publicity	Erling Kildahl
House Manager	Erling Kildahl

CAST

Paul Delville	Erling Kildahl
Content Lowell	Martha Nell Hardy
Katrin Sveg	Maida Rusk Withers
Ross Barnett	Joe McClurg

17
Experimental Theatre, Purdue
July 5-9, 11-16, 1961
The Dark at the Top of the Stairs
By William Inge

Directed by Joe Stockdale

Set Design	James Newburger
Technical Assistant	Charles P. Lehman
Stage Manager	Elaine Goldman
Set Construction	Dave Eggleston
Lights	Sheldon Jennings
Properties	Jerry Lintner
Sound	Pete Altman
Rehearsal Assistants	Tom Moore, Anne Hottell, Ruby Davis
Costumes	Sondra Herriman
Publicity/House Manager	Erling Kildahl

CAST

Rubin Flood	Arlen Withers
Cora Flood	Robin Stockdale
Sonny Flood	Mark Goldman
Reenie Flood	Pam Ridder
Flirt Conroy	Merrily Hogg
Morris Lacey	Roger Hill
Lottie Lacey	Mary Helen Kahn
Sammy Goldenbaum	Jerry Lintner
Punky Givens	John A. Covely

18
Experimental Theatre, Purdue
July 18-23, 25-30, 1961
Two for the Seesaw
By William Gibson

Directed by Joe Stockdale

Set Design	Charles P. Lehman
Technical Assistant	James Newburger
Stage Manager	Elaine Goldman
Rehearsal Assistant	Jan McGinniss
Set Construction	Dave Eggleston
Stage Crew Head	Sayre Karling
Lights	Joe McClurg
Sound	Dave Eggleston
Properties	Jan McGinniss
Publicity/House Manager	Erling Kildahl

CAST

Jerry Ryan	William M. Hardy
Gittel Mosca	Millicent Loeb

19
Experimental Theatre, Purdue
August 2-6, 8-13, 1961
Charley's Aunt
By Brandon Thomas

Directed by Joe Stockdale

Set Design	Charles P. Lehman
Technical Assistant	Carlo Spataro
Stage Manager	Charles P. Lehman
Set Construction	Sayre Karling
Sound	Jeff Hecht
Lights	Joe McClurg
Costumes	Sondra Herriman
Properties	Bob Jones
Publicity/House Manager	Erling Kildahl

CAST

Brassett	Anthony J. Buckley
Jack Chesney	Jon Farris
Charley Wykeham	Phil Johnson
Lord Fancourt Babberley	Roger Hill
Kitty Verdun	Stina Cox
Amy Spettigue	Sherry Risk
Col. Sir Francis Chesney	Brian D, Deacon
Stephen Spettigue	Robert T. Corbin
Farmer	Don Paarlberg
Dona Lucia d'Alvadorez	Mary Ellen Cain
Ela Delahay	Janet McGinniss
Maud	Jeanine Low

20
AMT, Williams College
November 2, 3, 4, 1961
Death of a Salesman
By Arthur Miller

Directed by Joe Stockdale

Set Design	Robert T. Williams
Lighting Design	Jack Watson
Music Composer	Alex North
Technical Director	Jack Watson

Stage Manager ....William J. Anderson
Asst. Stage Manager ....John Bouldan
Master Electrician ....Jim Evans
Master Carpenter ....Clarke Hobbie
Sound Master ....Alex M, Schwartz
Properties Master ....John Bouldan
Electrician .... Jon Rose
Wardrobe Mistress .... Linda Chase
Asst. to Director ....Alex J. Pollock
Flyman .... Gordon Stonington
Publicity ....Jim Wick

CAST

Willy Loman .... Wood Lockhart
Linda ....Deborah Hayes
Happy .... Peter Noel Simon
Happy ....Philip Rhinelander McKnight
Bernard ....William L. Prosser
The Woman ....Robin Stockdale
Charley ....Jon Spelman
Uncle Ben ....Jan Berlage
Howard Wagner .... Roger Grimes
Jenny .... Linda Chase
Stanley .... Peter Van Campen Quaintance
Miss Forsythe ....Betsie Brodie
Letta ....Nina Pelikan
Waiter .... Alex Pollock

21
AMT, Williams College
January 10, 12, 1962
Oedipus Rex
By Sophocles
Translated by William Butler Yeats

Directed by Joe Stockdale

Choreographer ....Wayne Lamb
Set Design ....Clarke Hobbie
Technical Director ....Jack Watson
Asst. Director ....Wood A. Lockhart
Lighting Design ....James Evans
Costume Design ....Tom Sietz,
Rita Bottomley
Stage Manager .... T. Lincoln Morrison
Electrician ....Henry Citron

CAST

Oedipus .... Claude M. Duvall
Priest ....Benjamin Zelermyer
Creon ....Jon Spelman
Tiresias ....Ash Crosby
Jocasta ....Robin Stockdale
1st Messenger ....William J. Anderson
Herdsman .... Benjamin Zelermyer
2nd Messenger .... Ted Cornell
Antigone .... Kathy O'Brien
Ismene ....Martha McFarland
Chorus Leader ....John Wilson
Chorus .... Ted Cornell,
George Fourier, Philip R. McKnight,
Tim O'Leary, Peter Simon,
King Sorenson, Christopher C. Welch
Children ....Wendy DuBois,
David Stockdale, Joe Stockdale

22
AMT, Williams College
March 9, 10, 15-17, 1962
Guys and Dolls
Based on a story & characters by Damon Runyan
Music & Lyrics by Frank Loesser
Book by Jo Swerling & Abe Burrows

Directed by Joe Stockdale

Set & Costumes .... Robert T. Williams
Choreographer ....Wayne Lamb
Lighting/Tech Director ....Jack Watson
Musical Direction .... Monte Aubrey
Asst. Musical Director ....Bob Ciulla
Asst. Director .... Philip Meeder
Stage Manager .... Laurent A. Daloz, Jr.
Assistant Stage Managers......Ted Cornell, Bill Mensel
Assoc. Light/Tech Director.........................Jim Evans
Master Carpenter ....Clarke Hobbie
Electricians ....Jim Evans, Tom Gregory
Spotmen .... Dave Mellenkamp, Ralph Temple
Flymen ....Larry Favrot, Steve Thomas
Crew Chiefs .... Price Comly, Eric Crabb
Properties ....Jim Wick
Wardrobe .... Rita Bottomley
House Manager .... Alec Schwartz

CAST

Nicely-Nicely Johnson .... Bill Prosser
Benny Southstreet .... Stuart Brown
Rusty Charlie ....Peter Simon
Sarah Brown ....Miriam Piper
Arvide Abernathy ....Ash Crosby
Calvin ....Claude Duvall
Agatha ....Carolyn Rider
Martha .... Lyn Serdahely
Harry the Horse ....Jon Finklestein
Lt. Brannigan ....William Anderson
Nathan Detroit .... Wood Lockhart
Angie the Ox .... Steve Lavino
Miss Adelaide ....Barbara Barden
Sky Masterson ....David Macpherson
Joey Biltmore .... Rick Arms
Mimi ....Barbara Widen
Gen'l Matilda B. Cartwright .... Belle Boch
Big Jule .... T. Lincoln Morrison
Society Max .... Ralph Mastroianni
Brandy Bottle Bates ....Tim O'Leary
Liver Lips Louie .... Rick Arms
Drunk ....Chris Simonds
Cops ....Richard Berger, Ken Hatcher
Waiters ....Alex Pollock, Jim DeJongh
Bobbie Soxers .... Ann Scott, Chris Talarico
Master of Ceremonies ....Steve Rose
Spectators/Others ....Tom Boschen, Elinore Herne,
Josetta Knopf, Stefany Kocsis, Ellen Widen
Hot Box Girls .... Vesla Boyd,
Joan Bushnell, Brenda Johnson,
Pamela Littlefield, Sophie Schneer,
Barbara Widen
Scarecrow ....Christopher Welch
Crap Game Dancers ....John Calhoun,
Jin DeJongh, Clark Hobbie,
David Kieffer, Philip R. McKnight,

Peter Moock, Tim O'Leary,
Alex Pollock, Steve Rose, Peter Simon,
King Sorenson, John-Maurice Sundstrom
Cubana Dancers .... Vesla Boyd,
Joan Bushnell, John Calhoun,
Clarke Hobbie, Brenda Johnson,
David Kieffer, Pamela Littlefield,
Philip R. McKnight, Peter Moock,
Sophie Schneer, Peter Simon,
John-Maurice Sundstrom, Barbara Widen
Singers .... Rick Arms,
Richard Berger, Tom Boschen,
John Calhoun, Ken Hatcher,
Elinor Herne, Dave Kieffer,
Stefany Kocsis, Steve Lavino,
Rick Mastroianni, Philip R. McKnight,
Peter Moock, Tim O'Leary,
Alex Pollock, Steve Rose,
Lynn Serdahely, Peter Simon,
King Sorenson, John-Maurice Sundstrom

Orchestra
Piano .... Monte Aubrey
Bass .... Mike Scott
Drums .... Terry Collison

23
AMT, Williams College
May 11, 12, 17-19, 1962
Romeo and Juliet
By William Shakespeare

Directed by Joe Stockdale
Set & Costumes .... Robert T. Williams
Lighting & Tech Direction .... Jack Watson
Assoc. Costume Designer .... Rita Bottomley
Fencing .... Gilbert Leigh
Choreographer .... Wayne Lamb
Stage Manager .... Peter Hayes
Asst. Stage Manager .... George Spelvin
Asst. Lighting Director.................................. Jim Evans
Master Electricians .... Larry Daloz, Ted Cornell
Flymen .... Jim DeJongh
George Fourier, Clarke Hobbie
Set Crew Head... Larry Daloz
Costume Execution .... Rita Bottomley,
Wardrobe .... Angela Boyden,
Nina Fersen, Mary Foehl,
Alice Hall, Suzanne Kemper,
Peggy Pierson, Ina Root,
Julia Smith, Ann Waite
Music & Sound ...Maryanne Conheim, Bill Anderson
Stage Crew .... Tom Boschen, Tim O'Leary,
H. B. Stauffer and cast
Properties .... Robert McKittrick
Publicity .... Ted Cornell
House Manager .... Price Comly

CAST
An Elder of Verona .... Philip Meeder
Escalus .... Claude Duvall
Paris .... Philip R. McKnight
Montague .... Robert Anderson
Capulet .... John-Maurice Sundstrom
Romeo .... Peter Simon
Mercutio .... Wood Lockhart
Benvoleo ....Bill Mensel
Tybalt ....Richard Berger
Old Man of Capulet Family .... Nick Rawlings
Friar Laurence .... Jon Spelman
Friar John .... C. H. Simonds
Balthasar ....Ash Crosby
Gregory ....Christopher Welch
Sampson .... Rick Arms
Abraham .... Peter Moock
An Apothecary .... Steve Lavino
Three Musicians .... Peter Hayes,
Maryanne Conheim, Ken Hatcher
Page to Paris .... Alex Pollock
Watchman .... John Calhoun
Lady Montague .... Sue Macksoud
Lady Capulet .... Anne Andersen
Juliet ....Deborah Hayes
Nurse to Juliet ....Belle Boch
Capulet Guests .... Barbara Barden,
Vesla Boyd, Tonia Noell,
Sophie Schneer, Barbara Widen

24
Experimental Theatre, Purdue
June 19-24, 26 – July 1, 1962
The Fourposter
By Jan deHartog

Directed by Joe Stockdale
Sets & Lighting .... Jack Watson
Stage Manager .... Dick Newdick
Asst. Technical Director .... George Wood
House Manager/Publicity .... Paul Lane
Properties .... Jeffrey Carter
Stage Crew .... Joseph Johnson,
Cynthia Miller, Bill Prosser, Annalee Rossi,
Deborah Sprague, Phil Thorpe
Lights .... Benjamin Milligan
Sound ....William F. Hillis
Costumes .... Lois Myers, Dick Newdick
Dresser .... Marilynne Black
Construction .... Ed Kenestrick,
Don Paarlberg, Don Regan, Bob Sprafka

CAST
Agnes ....Helen McMahon
Michael ....William M. Hardy

25
Experimental Theatre, Purdue
June 23-24, June 30-July 1, July 7-8, 1962
Tom Sawyer
By Austin O'Toole

Directed by Joe Stockdale
Stage Manager ....Deborah Sprague
Set Design .... Jack Watson
Costumes .... Cynthia Miller
Properties ....Annalee Rossi
Lights ....Jeffrey Carter
Sound ....Ben Milligan
Technical Guidance .... Jack Watson,
Dick Newdick, George Wood

Publicity .... Paul Lane
Accompanist .... Marilynne Black

CAST

Tom Sawyer .... Phillip Thorpe
Huckleberry Finn .... Bill Prosser
Ben ....William F. Hillis
Injun Joe ....Joseph Johnson
Judge ....George Spelvin
Aunt Polly .... Cynthia Miller
Becky Thatcher ....Annalee Rossi

26
Experimental Theatre, Purdue
July 4-8 and 10-15
Angel Street
By Patrick Hamilton

Directed by Joe Stockdale & Ross D. Smith
Sets/Lighting ....Jack Watson
Stage Manager .... Dick Newdick
Asst. Technical Director .... George Wood
House Manager/Publicity .... Paul Lane
Properties .... Bill Prosser, Annalee Rossi
Stained Glass Windows ....Deborah Sprague
Lights ....Jeffrey Carter, Cynthia Miller
Sound ....Benjamin Milligan
Set Crew/Painting ....Don Regan, Dick Thayer
Miss Hardy's Costumes ..... Lois Myers, Dick Newdick

CAST

Mrs. Manningham ....Martha Nell Hardy
Mr. Manningham ....Joe Stockdale
Elizabeth ....Deborah Sprague
Nancy ....Annalee Rossi
Rough .... Paul Lane
Policemen ....Joseph Johnson, Bill Prosser

27
Experimental Theatre, Purdue
July 14-15, 22, 28, 29 & August 4
A Circus is a Happy Thing
By Joe Gage
Music & Lyrics by Jack Foley Horkheimer

Directed by Joe Stockdale
Musical Direction/Organ............................ Jack Foley Horkheimer
Sets/Lighting ....Jack Watson
Stage Manager .... Dick Newdick
Costumes .... Phillip Thorpe
Lights .... Dick Newdick
Sound .... George Wood
Set Crew .... The Company

CAST

Danny ....Jeffrey Carter
Mother ....Marilynne Black
Little Egypt .... Cynthia Miller
The Great Sardo ....William F. Hillis
Simba ....Deborah Sprague
Samba .... Bill Prosser
Bozo the Clown ....Joseph Johnson
Hercules ....Phil Thorpe

Miss Lillie White ....Annalee Rossi
Jeeves .... Benjamin Milligan

28
Experimental Theatre, Purdue
July 18-22, 24-29, 1962
Suddenly Last Summer
By Tennessee Williams

Directed by Joe Stockdale
Sets/Lighting ....Jack Watson
Stage Manager .... Dick Newdick
Asst. Technical Director .... George Wood
House Manager/Publicity .... Paul Lane
Properties ....Marilynne Black, Joseph Johnson
Lights .... William F. Hillis, Annalee Rossi
Sound ....Cynthia Miller, Ben Milligan, Jack Foley Horkheimer
Set Crew ....Don Paarlberg, Chris Westphal, Dick Thayer, Ed Hubbard

CAST

Mrs. Venable ....Dorothy Harlan
Dr. Cukrowicz .... William McPherson
Miss Foxhill ....Deborah Sprague
Mrs. Holly .... Nell Braswell
George Holly .... Bill Prosser
Catherine Holly ....Millicent Loeb
Sister Felicity ....Marilynne Black

29
Experimental Theatre, Purdue
August 1-5, 7-12, 1962
The Teahouse of the August Moon
By John Patrick

Directed by Joe Stockdale
Sets/Lighting ....Jack Watson
Stage Manager .... Dick Newdick
Asst.Technical Director .... George Wood
Properties .... The Company
Lights ....Jeffrey Carter
Sound .... Benjamin Milligan
House Manager/Publicity .... Paul Lane

CAST

Sakini .... Bill Prosser
Sargeant Gregovich ....Phil Thorpe
Col. Wainwright Purdy, III....................George Wood
Captain Fisby .... William McPherson
Old Woman (week 1 .... Marilynne Black
(week 2.....................................Deborah Sprague
Old Woman's Daughter ....Annalee Rossi
The Daughter's Children .... Lisa Hardy, Lindy Lu Burdick
Lady Astor .... Esther
Ancient Man ....George Spelvin
Mr. Hokaida ....Joseph Johnson
Mr. Omura ....Charles Helmetag
Mr. Sumata .... Bill Daugherty
Sumata's Father ....Al Chiscon
Mr. Seiko ....Joe Williams
Miss Higa Jiga (week 1) .... Deborah Sprague
(week 2).. Marilynne Black

Mr. Keora .... Biz Harlan
Mr. Oshira ....William F. Hillis
   Ladies' League for Democratic Action:
      Marilynne Black, Annalee Rossi,
          Deborah Sprague
Lotus Blossom .... Cynthia Miller
Captain McLean .... Paul Lane

#30
Bar Harbor Summer Theatre, ME
August 7-11, 1962
Private Lives
By Noel Coward

Directed by Joe Stockdale
Set Design ....Allan Stevens
Lighting ....Christopher Welch

CAST
Sibyl Chase .... Gretchen Walther
Elyot Chase ....Phillip J. Smith
Victor Prynne ....Richard A. Dysart
Amanda Prynne ....Olive Deering
Louise .... Nancy Kittredge

#31
Bar Harbor Summer Theatre, ME
August 14-18, 1962
The Moon Is Blue
By F. Hugh Herbert

Directed by Joe Stockdale
Set Design ....Allan Stevens
Lighting ....Christopher Welch

CAST
Patty O'Neill .... Gretchen Walther
Don Gresham ....Paul Day
David Slater ....Richard A. Dysart
Michael O'Neill ....Edgar B. Hess

#32
Loeb Playhouse, Purdue
October 12, 13, 18-20, 1962
Our Town
By Thornton Wilder

Directed By Joe Stockdale
Set Design ....Sam Marks
Technical Assistant .... Paul Lane
Costume Design ....Lyn Carroll
Stage Manager .... Patricia McBride
Assistant Stage Mgrs. ....Judy Skomp,
      Barb Eggeman, Sally Murphy
Master Electrician ....Randy Earle
Sound Master .... Doug Reid
Make-up .... Ed Kenestrick
Wardrobe Mistress ....Alison Kirk
Construction/Paint .... Carol Arden
House Manager ....Susan Aycock
Choir Master/Organist ....Jack Foley Horkheimer
Director's Assistants .... Vivian Van Camp,
     Ame Eggers, Tamara Andrews,
         Marianne Locke

CAST
Stage Manager ....E. Allyn Thompson
Dr. Gibbs ....George Wood
Joe Crowell ....Joe Stockdale III
Howie Newsome .... Allen Herdle
Mrs. Gibbs ....Joan Pape
Mrs. Webb ....Cynthia Miller
George Gibbs ....Stuart Howard
Rebecca Gibbs ....Janet McGinniss
Wally Webb ....Schorling Schneider
Emily Webb .... Lana Shaw
Professor Willard .... Paul Lane
Mr. Webb ....Bud Dixon
Man in Auditorium .... Dick Ewing
Woman in Auditorium ....Martha Van Cleef
Lady in Balcony .... Margery Hughes
Simon Stimson .... Dick Newdick
Mrs. Soames ....Bonnie Pottlitzer
Constable Warren .... Bob Stern
Si Crowell ....Bruce Shannon
Baseball Players .... Dick Ewing,
       Don Born, Henry Janes
Sam Craig ....Fred Lash
Asst. Stage Manager .... Don Born
Asst. Stage Manager .... Dick Ewing
1st Dead Man ....Ted Hazeldine
2nd Dead Man ....Don Perlis
1st Dead Woman .... Mary Jo Siewert
2nd DeadWoman ....Martha Van Cleef
Organist ....Jack Foley Horkheimer
Townspeople...................................Baana Lee Barker,
    Marilynn Brom, Judith English,
     Marge Hasse, Natalie Ellis,
    Thomas Anderson, Steve Barnard,
     Clarence Hansell, Bill Clark,
   John Robert Ditamore, James Eminhizer,
    Mike Fryer, Gary Lee, Paul Voelker,
     Linda Brewer, Gail Gramling,
   Sue Lineback, Sharon Luther, Louise Senf,
       Sandra Dwornicki

#33
Loeb Playhouse, Purdue
March 8, 9, 14-16, 1963
The Sea Gull
By Anton Chekhov
Translated by Stark Young

Directed by Joe Stockdale
Sets/Lighting .... Don Treat
Costume Design ....Lyn Carroll
Technical Assistant ....Stuart Howard
Master Carpenter ....Randy Earle
Set Crew .... Chuck Birchenough
Properties ....Joan Benedix
Master Electrician ....David Little
Sound Masters ....Joyce Pahl, John Beihl
Costumes ....Sandra Lawson
Make-up .... Ed Kenestrick
Publicity ....Carolyn Roberts
House Manager ....Susan Aycock

CAST

Irina Arcadina Trepleff	Frances Farmer
Constantine Trepleff	Dick Newdick
Peter Sorin	E. Allyn Thompson
Nina Zaryechny	Janet McGinniss
Ilya Shamrayeff	Peter Bock
Pauline Andreyevna	Stephanie Stein
Masha	Cynthia Miller
Boris Trigorin	Thomas Holloway
Eugene Dorn	Bud Dixon
Semyon Medvedenko	William Lampe
Yakov	Donald Perlis
Maid	Margery Hughes
Workman	George Wood

34
Experimental Theatre, Purdue
June 11-31, 1963
The Fantasticks
Book and Lyrics by Tom Jones
Music by Harvey Schmidt

Directed by Joe Stockdale

Assistant to Director	Stuart Howard
Technical Director	Peter Bock
Master Electrician	David Little
Stage Manager	Dick Newdick
Production Stage Manager	Jeffrey Carter
Wardrobe	Dick Newdick
Properties	Peter Bock
House Managers	Karen Fish, William Hillis

CAST

The Narrator	Stuart Howard
The Girl	Marilynne Black
The Boy	William Lampe
The Boy's Father	George Wood
The Girl's Father	Dick Newdick
The Actor	Bill Prosser
The Man Who Dies	Peter Bock
The Mute	Cindy Miller

35
Experimental Theatre, Purdue
July 3 -13, 1963
A Taste of Honey
By Shelagh Delaney

Directed by Joe Stockdale

Sets & Lighting	Stuart Wurtzel
Stage Manager	Dick Newdick
Technical Director	Stuart Wurtzel
Technical Assistant	Peter Bock
Assistant to Director	Stuart Howard
Master Electrician	William Hillis
Sound	Jeff Carter
Wardrobe	Dick Newdick
Properties	Marilynne Black, Bill Prosser
House Manager	Bill Prosser
Publicity	Robin Stockdale

CAST

Helen	Mary Helen Kahn
Josephine	Cindy Miller
Peter	Peter Bock
The Boy	William Lampe
Geoffrey	Stuart Howard

36
Experimental Theatre, Purdue
July 17 - 27, 1963
Misalliance
By George Bernard Shaw

Directed by Joe Stockdale

Sets & Lighting	Stuart Wurtzel
Costume Designer	Sandra Lawson
Stage Manager	Dick Newdick
Asst. Stage Manager	Jeff Carter
Technical Director	Stuart Wurtzel
Asst. Technical Director	Peter Bock
Assistant to Director	Stuart Howard
Master Electrician	Karen Fish
Sound	Jeff Carter
Properties	Cindy Miller
Publicity	Robin Stockdale
House Manager	Leslie Johnson

CAST

Johnny Tarleton	Bill Prosser
Bentley Summerhays	William Hillis
Hypatia Tarleton	Marilynne Black
Mrs. Tarleton	Robin Stockdale
Lord Summerhays	Dick Newdick
Mr. Tarleton	Stuart Howard
Joey Percival	William Lampe
Lina Szczepanowska	Cindy Miller

37
Experimental Theatre, Purdue
July 31 – August 10, 1963
The Caretaker
By Harold Pinter

Directed by Joe Stockdale

Sets & Lighting	Stuart Wurtzel
Stage Manager	Dick Newdick
Technical Director	Stuart Wurtzel
Assistant to Director	Stuart Howard
Master Electrician	Marilynne Black
Sound	Cindy Miller
Properties	William Hillis
Publicity	Robin Stockdale
House Manager	Jeff Carter
Head Usher	Leslie Johnson

CAST

Mick	Bill Prosser
Aston	William Lampe
Davies	Stuart Howard

38
Loeb Playhouse, Purdue
December 6, 7, 12-14, 1963
Mother Courage and Her Children
By Bertolt Brecht

Directed by Joe Stockdale
Adapted by Eric Porter
Music by Paul Dessau

Set Design	Sam Marks
Costume Designer	Margo Chandley
Musical Director	Dorothy Runk Mennen
Technical Director	Peter Bock
Stage Manager	Paul Voelker
Assistant Stage Managers	Joan Pape, Laurieanne Shufflebotham
Assistant to Director	Jac Cole
Master Carpenter	James Hayes
Master Electrician	Randy Earle
Sound Masters	Doug Reid, Brian Wesley
Stage Crew Chief	Bill Brooke
Properties	Marilyn Peterink
Wardrobe	Karen Arthurhultz, Jeff Nathan
Make-up	Joan Benedix, Stuart Howard
Poster Design	Kaki Work
House Manager	Karen Arthurhultz

MUSICIANS

Piano	Jane F. Bowman
Flute	Peter Wollan
Trumpet	Stephen Phillips
Accordionist	Lynda Bell
Percussion	Phil Phillips

CAST

Narrator	Peter Bock
Recruiting Officer	Bob Stern
Protestant Sergeant	Sam King
Mother Courage	Anne Revere
Kattrin	Cindy Miller
Eilif	William Lampe
Swiss Cheese	James Stephens
Cook	Stuart Howard
Swedish Commander	Robert Tolan
Chaplain	Dick Newdick
Ordnance Officer	Charles Hayman
Yvette Pottier	Linda Zimmer
Protestant Soldier	Rob Elias
One Eye	Don Perlis
Catholic Sergeant	R. Gene Carsten
Old Colonel	Bud Dixon
Stretcher Bearer	Charles Mayer
2nd Stretcher Bearer	Philip Menagh
Regimental Clerk	Jeff Nathan
Young Soldier	Peter Saputo
Older Soldier	Daniel Dunn
1st Soldier	Rob Elias
2nd Soldier	Steve Jaffe
Peasant Woman	Martha Van Cleef
Peasant	Charles Mayer
The Clerk	Neal Stephenson
Soldier 1	Ed Hubbard
Soldier 2	Charles Hayman
Young Man	Don Perlis
Old Woman	Joan Benedix
Sergeant	Bob Stern
Soldiers	Rob Elias, Charles Hayman, Sam King, Charles Mayer
Lieutenant	R. Gene Carsten
Peasant Woman	Dorothy Harlan
Young Peasant Boy	Richard Ewing
Peasant Man	R.C. Newton

39
Experimental Theatre, Purdue
June 12- 13, 16-20, 23-27, 1964
Romeo and Juliet
By William Shakespeare

Directed By Joe Stockdale

Sets & Lighting	Stuart Wurtzel
Costumes	Lyn Carroll
Stage Manager	Dick Newdick
Technical Director	Stuart Wurtzel
Choreographer	Dick Ewing
Master Electrician	Randy Earle
Sound Technician	Jeff Carter
Properties	Sheila Daly
Wardrobe	Marilynne Black
Publicity	Robert Tolan
House Manager	Leslie Johnson

CAST

Romeo	Peter Simon
Juliet	Merle Louise
Nurse to Juliet	Anne Revere
Friar Laurence	Robert Tolan
Mercutio	Dale Helward
Benvolio	James Stephens
Prince Escalus	Anthony Buckley
Paris	Peter Bock
Tybalt	William Lampe
Capulet	Donald Jacob
Montague	Dick Newdick
Lady Capulet	Cindy Miller
Lady Montague	Marilynne Black
Sampson	Peter Saputo
Gregory	Craig Halliwell
Abraham	John Fabricius
Balthazar	Dick Ewing
Peter	Bill Hillis
Friar John	Joseph Walsh
Page	Dick Barton
Apothecary	Bill Hillis
Citizens	Janice Baty, Pete Lazarus, Connie Heaver, Carole Lockwood

#40
Experimental Theatre, Purdue
June 14, 21, 28 July 5, 12, 19, 26
1964
The Fantasticks
Music by Harvey Schmidt
Lyrics by Tom Jones

Directed by Joe Stockdale

Musical Director	Jane Bowman
Lighting	Stuart Wurtzel
Stage Manager	Dick Newdick
Technical Director	Stuart Wurtzel
Master Electrician	Randy Earle
Costume Coordination	Dick Ewing
Publicity	Robert Tolan
House Manager	Leslie Johnson

CAST

The Narrator	Donald Jacob
The Girl	Merle Louise
The Boy	William Lampe
The Boy's Father	Dale Helward
The Girl's Father	Dick Newdick
The Old Actor	Peter Simon
The Man Who Dies	James Stephens
The Mute	Cindy Miller

#41
Experimental Theatre, Purdue
July 1 - 4 & 7 - 11, 1964
The Threepenny Opera
Music by Kurt Weill
Book by Bertolt Brecht
English Adaptation by Marc Blitzstein
Directed by Joe Stockdale

Musical Director	Jane Bowman
Sets & Lighting	Stuart Wurtzel
Costumes	Lyn Carroll
Stage Manager	Dick Newdick
Technical Director	Stuart Wurtzel
Master Electrician	Randy Earle
Properties	Peter Saputo
Publicity	Robert Tolan
House Manager	Leslie Johnson
Company Photographer	Ellis Ralston

CAST

A Street Singer	Peter Simon
Mr. Peachum	Donald Jacob
Mrs. Peachum	Stacey Winter
Polly Peachum	Merle Louise
Macheath	Dale Helward
Filch	Bill Hillis
Jenny	Connie Heaver
Lucy Brown	Janice Baty
Reverend Kimball	Dick Newdick
Messenger	Robert Tolan

The Gang

Matt	William Lampe
Jake	Peter Saputo
Walt	John Fabricius
Bob	Craig Halliwell

The "Girls"

Betty	Cindy Miller
Dolly	Carole Lockwood
Molly	Lyn Carroll
Coaxer	Marilynne Black
Holly	Louise Whitney
Suky	Sheila Daly

The Law

Tiger Brown	James Stephens
Smith	Joe Walsh
Darlington	Vaughn von Merwald
Merriweather	Dick Ewing
The Beggars	Dick Barton, Dick Ewing, Jeff Carter, Tom Moore, Joe Walsh
The Orchestra	Jane Bowman, Jan Baty, Dick Ewing, Bill Hillis, Carole Lockwood, Vaughn von Merwald

#42
Experimental Theatre, Purdue
July 15-18 & 21-25, 1964
Look Homeward, Angel
By Ketti Frings
Based on the novel by Thomas Wolfe

Sets	Stuart Wurtzel
Lighting	Sheila Daly
Costumes	Lyn Carroll
Stage Manager	Dick Newdick
Technical Director	Stuart Wurtzel
Master Electrician	Jeff Carter
Sound Technician	Richard Barton
Properties	Randy Earle
Wardrobe	Dick Ewing, Louise Whitney
Publicity	Robert Tolan
House Manager	Leslie Johnson
Company Photographer	Ellis Ralston

CAST

Ben Gant	Dale Helward
Mrs. Marie "Fatty" Pert	Connie Heaver
Helen Gant Barton	Cindy Miller
Hugh Barton	James Stephens
Eliza Gant	Frances Farmer
Will Pentland	Donald Jacob
Eugene Gant	Peter Simon
Jake Clatt	Vaughn von Merwald
Mrs. Clatt	Sheila Daly
Florry Mangle	Carole Lockwood
Mrs. Snowden	Louise Whitney
Mr. Farrell	Bill Hillis
Miss Brown	Marilynne Black
Laura James	Merle Louise
W.O. Gant	Victor Killian
Dr. Maguire	Peter Saputo
Tarkington	Joseph Walsh
Madame Elizabeth	Dorothy Harlan

Luke Gant ....William Lampe
Newsboy ....Dick Ewing

43
Experimental Theatre, Purdue
July 29 -31 & August 1 -7, 1964
Pygmalion
By George Bernard Shaw

Directed by Joe Stockdale

Set Design	Stuart Wurtzel
Lighting Design	Randy Earle
Costume Design	Lyn Carroll
Stage Manager	Dick Newdick
Technical Director	Stuart Wurtzel
Stage Coordinator	William Lampe
Master Electrician	Richard Barton
Sound Technician	John Fabricius
Wardrobe	Marilynne Black, Dick Ewing
Properties	William Lampe, Louise Whitney
Publicity	Robert Tolan
House Manager	Leslie Johnson
Company Photographer	Ellis Ralston

CAST

Miss Eynsford Hill	Carole Lockwood
Mrs. Eynsford Hill	Cindy Miller
A Bystander	Bill Hillis
Freddy Eynsford Hill	Peter Simon
Eliza Doolittle	Merle Louise
Colonel Pickering	Dick Newdick
Henry Higgins	Dale Helward
A Sarcastic Bystander	William Lampe
The Taximan	Peter Saputo
Mrs. Pearce	Marilynne Black
Alfred Doolittle	Donald Jacob
Mrs. Higgins	Dorothy Harlan
The Parlor Maid	Connie Heaver
Other Bystanders	Janice Baty, Jeffrey Carter, Dick Ewing, Craig Halliwell, Tom Moore, Vaughn von Merwald, Joseph Walsh, Louise Whitney

44
March 12-13 & 18-20, 1965
Loeb Playhouse, Purdue
Three Sisters
By Anton Chekhov
Translation by Randall Jarrell
Directed by Joe Stockdale

Set Design	Joe McArdle
Costume Design	Larry Randolph
Design Assistant	Sue Revzan
Movement Consultant	Wayne Lamb
Musical Director	Dorothy Runk Mennen
Production Stage Manager	H. Thomas Moore
Stage Manager	Mary Alice Wigmore
Technical Assistant	Randy Earle
Set Crew Head	Paul Voelker
Paint Crew Head	Marilyn Paradiso
Carpentry	Jim Larimer
Lighting Assistant	Jim Nichols
Sound	Jim Coomes
Wardrobe	Maxine Gootzeit
Properties	Sue Revzan
Make-up	Joan Benedix, Ann Poiry
Publicity	William Haddad
House Manager	Karen Rieffel

CAST

Prozorov	Richard Busch
Natalya	Joan Pape
Olga	Sharon Ryterband
Masha	Cindy Miller
Irina	Michelle Dezseran
Kulygin	Dick Newdick
Vershinin	Louis Edmonds
Tuzenbach	Bill Shigley
Solyony	William Lampe
Chebutykin	E. Allyn Thompson
Fedotik	Charles Potts
Rode	Richard Davis
Ferapont	Larry Randolph
Anfisa	Sharon Spelman
Maid	Ruby Matthies
Orderly	H. Thomas Moore
Nurse	Martha Van Cleef
Gypsy Street Musicians	Brian Smith, Martha Van Cleef
Soldiers	Gary Evans, Michael Maish, Richard Rusz, Peter Saputo, Peter Wollan, Carl Zurcher
Accordion (off stage)	Gerald Lambuth
Violin (off stage)	Hung Fan

45
Loeb Playhouse, Purdue
April 22-24 28, 29 & May 1, 1965
My Fair Lady
Book & Lyrics by Alan Jay Lerner
Music by Frederick Loewe
Adapted from George Bernard Shaw's Play and
Gabriel Pascal's motion picture "Pygmalion"
Directed by Joe Stockdale

Set Design	Donald Treat
Choreography & Musical Numbers	Wayne Lamb
Musical Direction	Alan H. Drake
Costumes	Larry Randolph
Vocal Direction	Dorothy Runk Mennen
Lighting	James Nichols
Technical Assistants	Jerry Bledsoe, Richard Busch
Stage Manager	Sue Revzan
Assistant Stage Managers	Don Bush, Joan Benedix, Marilyn Paradiso
Rehearsal Pianists	Bob Farris, Jackie Jo Anderson
Master Carpenter	Norman Birnbaum
Master Electrician	Brian Wesley
Follow Spots	Donna Clark, Doug Reid
Sound Master	Jim Coomes
Pinrail	John Andrews
Properties	Sue Reynolds
Wardrobe	Maxine Gootzeit, Darrelyn Milne
Ladies Opera Coats	Curt McDowell
Ascot Hats	Dick Ewing
Make-up	Joan Benedix
Publicity	Charles Potts
House Manager	Karen Rieffel

CAST

Mrs. Eynsford Hill	Joan Pape
Eliza Doolittle	Janet Hayes
Freddy Eynsford Hill	Dick Rusz
A Bystander	Bill Shigley
Col. Pickering	John Tully
Henry Higgins	John Newton
Selsey Man	Michael Shapiro
Hoxton Man	Richard Davis
Another Bystander	David Polinsky
1st Cockney	Richard Davis
2nd Cockney	David Polinsky
3rd Cockney	Bill Shigley
4th Cockney	Allan Keller
Bartender	Wayne Galman
Harry	Wayne Lamb
Jamie	Richard Busch
Alfred P. Doolittle	Stuart Main
Mrs. Pierce	Dorothy Runk Mennen
Mrs. Hopkins	Sharon Pankey
Butler	Allan Keller
Servants	Bill Shigley, David Polinsky, Richard Davis, M. Christina Rickards, Phyllis Denny, Sheryl Smith, Sharon Pankey, Mary Ann McGraw, Marilyn Holt, Pat Belden, Kathy O'Neil
Mrs. Higgins	Dorothy Harlan
Chauffeur	Don Bush
Lord Boxington	Michael Shapiro
Lady Boxington	Sharon Watkins
Constable	George Kessen
Flower Girl	Leslie Barth
Zolton Karpathy	Jon Spelman
Queen of Transylvania	Darrelyn Milne
Consort	Wayne Lamb

The Dancers & Singers
Gary Craven, Richard Davis, Charles R. Deible, George Kessen, Bill Mueller, H. Joe Scott, John Van Epps, Leslie Barth, Diane Beckwith, Ann Foster, Martha Kendrick, Ruby Matthies, Darrelyn Milne, Sharon Pankey, Ann Poiry, Susan Weiss

The Orchestra

Flute	William Bauer
Oboe	James Green
Clarinets	Anthony Marra, Steve Pater, Carla Jean Murphy
Bassoon	Jack Reynolds
Trumpets	Larry Walters, Bill Kerchival, Al Jarvis
Trombones	Mike Heath, David Wampler
Horns	Richard Fry, Steve Van Dellen
Tuba	Winfred Blevins
Percussion	Gregg Murphy, Rena Smith
Violin	Hung Fan, Martha Bradley, Peggy Shay, Debbie Golomb, Mike Phillips, Leslie Klein, Everett Klontz
Viola	Darwin Sarnoff
Cello	Richard Findley
Basses	Ben Timms, Tom Fitch
Piano	Bob Farris

46
Experimental Theatre, Purdue
June 9-11, 16, 18, 20, 22, 24, 26, 29 &
July 1& 3, 1965
Stop the World - I Want To Get Off
Book, Music & Lyrics by
Leslie Bricusse & Anthony Newley

Directed by Joe Stockdale

Sets & Costumes	Joseph McArdle
Lighting	Randy Earle
Musical Director	Jane Bowman
Stage Manager	Dick Newdick
Technical Director	Randy Earle
Master Electrician	Randy Earle
Follow Spots	Marilyn Paradiso, Paul Voelker
Wardrobe Mistress	Mary Moltz

CAST

Evie	Miriam Birch
Jane	Royce Lenelle
Susan	Carole Lockwood
The Boy	Richard Newburger
Littlechap	Stuart Howard
Chorus	Richard Davis, Susan Hummel, William Lampe, Leslie Johnson, Thomas Moore, Patricia Merrill, Richard Rusz, Laurel Stockdale, Peter Stanton

47
Experimental Theatre, Purdue
June 12, 13, 15, 17, 19, 23. 25. 27, 30 & July 2, 1965
The Amorous Flea
Based on Moliere's "School For Wives"
Book by Jerry Devine
Music & Lyrics by Bruce Montgomery

Directed by Joe Stockdale

Sets & Costumes	Joe McArdle
Lighting	Randy Earle
Musical Direction	Jane Bowman
Stage Manager	Dick Newdick
Technical Director	Randy Earle
Asst. Technical Director	Paul Voelker
Technical Assistants	Patrice Murphy, Marilyn Paradiso
Master Electrician	Randy Earle
Pinrail	Richard Davis
Follow Spots	Marilyn Paradiso, Paul Voelker
Wardrobe Mistress	Mary Moltz
Costume Assistants	Maxine Gootzeit, Darrelyn Milne

CAST

Arnolphe	Peter Stanton
Chrysalde	Dick Newdick
Alain	Stuart Howard
Georgette	Miriam Birch
Agnes	Royce Lenelle
Horace	William Lampe
Oronte	Richard Rusz
Enrique	H. Thomas Moore

Jane Bowman, pianist

#48
Experimental Theatre, Purdue
July 7-11, 13-17, 1965
A Streetcar Named Desire
By Tennessee Williams

Directed by Joe Stockdale

Sets & Costumes	Joe McArdle
Lighting	Randy Earle
Stage Manager	Dick Newdick
Master Electrician	Randy Earle
Sound	Paul Voelker, Brian Smith
Properties	Carole Lockwood, Richard Davis
Wardrobe	Mary Moltz, Pat Merrill, Pat Murphy

CAST

Negro Woman	Sharon Ryterband
Eunice Hubbell	Susan Hummel
Stanley Kowalski	Charles Hayman
Stella Kowalski	Royce Lenelle
Steve Hubbell	William Lampe
Harold Mitchell (Mitch)	Stuart Howard
Mexican Woman	Carole Lockwood
Blanche DuBois	Pamela Printy
Pablo Gonzales	Peter Stanton
A Young Collector	Richard Davis
Doctor	Dick Newdick
Matron	Mary Moltz

#49
Experimental Theatre, Purdue
July 21-25, 27-31, 1965
Man and Superman
By George Bernard Shaw

Directed by Joe Stockdale

Sets & Costumes	Joe McArdle
Lighting	Randy Earle
Stage Manager	Dick Newdick
Technical Director/Sound	Randy Earle
Master Electrician	Paul Voelker
Properties	Pat Merrill
Wardrobe	Mary Moltz

CAST

Roebuck Ramsden	Dick Newdick
The Maid	Susan Hummel
Octavius Robinson	Richard Busch
John Tanner	Stuart Howard
Ann Whitefield	Pamela Printy
Mrs. Whitefield	Dorothy Harlan
Miss Susan Ramsden	Mary Moltz
Violet Robinson	Royce Lenelle
Henry Straker	Peter Stanton
Hector Malone	William Lampe
Hector Malone, Sr.	Bill Bohnert
Mr. Mendoza	Richard Davis

#50
Experimental Theatre, Purdue
August 4 – 13, 1965
The Hostage
By Brendan Behan

Directed by Joe Stockdale

Sets & Costumes	Joe McArdle
Lighting	Randy Earle
Stage Manager	Dick Newdick
Technical Director	Randy Earle
Master Electrician	Randy Earle
Follow Spots	Paul Voelker, Marilyn Paradiso
Properties	Pat Murphy
Wardrobe	Mary Moltz

CAST

Pat	Stuart Howard
Meg	Sharon Ryterband
Monsewer	Dick Newdick
Mr. Mulleady	Peter Stanton
Miss Gilchrist	Carole Lockwood
Princess Grace	Joseph McArdle
Rio Rita	Nate Adams
Leslie	William Lampe
Teresa	Royce Lenelle
IRA Officer	Charles Hayman
Volunteer	Brian Smith
Polish Sailor	Paul Voelker

The "Girls"

Colette	Susan Hummel
Bobo	Mary Moltz
Ropeen	Pat Merrill
Mary	Lory Stockdale
Lucy	Mary Ellen Curtin
Lady Gregory, at the piano	Jane Bowman

#51
Loeb Playhouse, Purdue
October 22, 23, 28-30, 1965
The Visit
By Friedrich Duerrenmatt

Directed by Joe Stockdale

Sets	Joe McArdle
Costumes	Larry Randolph
Vocal Direction	Earl Harlan
Music Director	Dorothy Runk Mennen
Lighting	Paul Voelker
Asst. to Director	Jon Spelman
Technical Director	Randy Earle
Production Stage Manager	Donna Clark
Stage Manager	Gary Craven
Asst. Stage Managers	Mary Moltz, Joan Benedix, Irene Matlon
Design Assistant	Jerry Bledsoe
Technical Assistant	Christopher Welch
Master Carpenter	Steve Hodge
Master Electrician	Steve Hodge
Asst. Electrician	Steve Craig
Stage Crew Head	James Nichols
Paint Crew	Dick Eterno
Properties	Susan Ayres

Sound Master ....Michael Shapiro
Miss Farmer's Wardrobe Mistress.....Maxine Gootzeit
Costume Crew .... Georgia McKinley,
Kristine Grebezs
House Manager .... Mary Ann Shean

CAST
VISITORS:
Claire Zachanassian .... Frances Farmer
Her Husbands VII –IX ....Larry Randolph
Butler (Boby) .... Bill Prosser
Roby ....Lloyd Smith
Toby ....William Cripe
Koby ....Alan Mong
Loby .... Dan Mullet

VISITED:
Alfred III ....Erling Kildahl
His Wife .... Sharon Lea Spelman
His Son .... Gary Craven
His Daughter .... Rose Marie Bennett
Mayor ....Jerry Bledsoe
Priest .... Timothy Dewey
Schoolmaster .... Robert Browning
Doctor ....David Lucterhand
Policeman .... Charles Hayman
Man One ....John Sanders
Man Two ....Phil Thorpe
Man Three ....James Kenyon
Man Four ....Samuel Platt
Painter ....David Suits
First Woman ....Karlalea Cody
Second Woman .... Leslie Barth
Miss Louisa ....Sharon Ryterband

EXTRAS:
Station Master .... Tom Marlowe
Ticket Inspector .... Peter Iverson
Guard ....John Orr
Bailiff .... Roy R. Van Dusen

DISTRACTORS:
First Reporter ....William Robison
Second Reporter ....Patricia Merrill
Radio Commentator ....Richard Busch
Cameraman ....Joan Benedix
Reporter .... Kitty Boots

TOWNSPEOPLE:
Ramona Adamski, Suzy Ayers, Dan Bobek,
Mike Boyer, Jan Schmidt, Ruth Brown,
R. Alan Brubaker, Tom Builta,
Lynne Burnham, Bonnie Butler,
Suzanne Wiscaver, Sandra Cannon,
Joanne Chrystal, Susan Coers, Dean Crawn,
Linda Cussen, Clark L. Engebreth,
Richard Evans, J. Fleck, Mike Gannon,
David L. Geary, David German, Vivian Stair,
Bob Harvey, Jr., Lucy Hazeldine,
John R. Holmes, Brian Thevenin,
Jane Kinn, Catherine Kibby,
Richard Kroviak, Larry Lorenz, John Lux,
Mary Martin, Susan Mason, Nancee Mates,
Carol Wallace, Thomas McClure,
Juliet McConnell, Sara McCullough,
Sharon McEmber, Rita McMullin,
Roy Walz, Pamela Miller,
Nancy Monagle, Michael Shapiro,
Annette Tortorella, Pamela Offen,
Ruth Pahle, Susan Peterson, Pamela Phend,
Roberta Preston, Maxine Reifer,
Marsha Richman, Christina Rickards,
Kathy Rinehart, James Ritchey, Patrick Scully,
Orville, Sauter, Marjorie Schalliol

52
Loeb Playhouse, Purdue
March 17-19, 22-25, 1966
Gypsy
(Suggested by the Memoirs of
Gypsy Rose Lee)
Book by Arthur Laurents
Music by Jule Styne
Lyrics by Stephen Sondheim
Directed by Joe Stockdale
Choreographed by Wayne Lamb

Sets .... Joe McArdle
Costumes ....Larry Randolph
Music Director .... Alan H. Drake
Vocal Direction .... Dorothy Runk Mennen
Lighting Design ....Randy Earle
Technical Director ....Jack Shink
Asst. to Director ....Sandra Wood
Production Stage Manager.....................Dan C. Bobik
Stage Manager ....Susan Ayres
Asst. Stage Manager .... Ruth Christy
Draftsmen ....Charles R. Hayman,
Tom Builta, Richard Kroviak
Scenic Artist ....Jerry Bledsoe
Properties .... Maxine Reifer
Master Carpenter .... Steve Hodge
Master Electrician .... Gary Craven
Stage Crew Head .... Steve Hodge
Sound Effects ....Strother Brann
Wardrobe Mistress .... Maxine Gootzeit
Costume Crew Head .... Caroline Merrill
House Manager ....Janice Brewton

CAST
Uncle Jocko ....Robert Ankrom
George ....Peter Wellman
Casper & his Cornet ....Greg Sciarrotta
Balloon Girl .... Kathy L. Gregor
Baby Louise ....Beth Ullman
Baby June ....Lorna Prentiss
Twinkle Toes .... Robin Pyle
Angel Wings .... Debbie Treat
The Fairy Queen ....Kimberly Armstrong
Clown ....Chris Ullman
Casey at the Bat .... Don Wagner
With the Slide Trombone ....Jean Gailar
Boy With Russian Yaks .... David Stockdale
Russian Yak # 1 ....Dobrolyubov Stockdalewitz
Russian Yak # 2 ....Lermentov Lambwitz
Stage Mothers ....Pat Ekola, Marjorie M. Klein,
Carol S. Sarnoff, Sandra Wood
Rose ....Mary Margaret O'Brien
Pop .... E. Allyn Thompson
Rich Man ....Richard Busch
Rich Man's Son ....Greg Sciarrotta
Urchent Tap Dancer ....Steve Schuh
Cub Scout Pack # 34 .... Eric Christiansen,

Jim Shurig, Larry Stanford, David Stockdale, Gary Thoe, Alex Tons
Boy Scout Master ....Peter Wellman
Boy Scout ....Mike Sharp
Mr. Weber ....Joe Ullman
Herbie ....Donald Treat
Louise ....Cindy Larimer
June ....Sharon McEmber
Tulsa ....John R. Eldridge
Yonkers ....Richard Busch
Angie ....Bill O'Brien
L.A. .... Bill Prosser
Mr. Kringelein ....James Knox
Mr. Goldstone .... Bob Gregoire
Hotel Guests .... Pat Ekola, Marjorie Klein, Carol S. Sarnoff, Michael Shapiro, Peter Wellman
Gladys ....Sandra Wood
Waitress ....Marjorie Klein
Miss Cratchitt .... Patti Lee
Farmboys ....Richard Busch, John R. Eldridge, Bill O'Brien, Bill Prosser
Hollywood Blondes & Toreadorables
Agnes .... Susan Murray
Marjorie May .... Sharon Pankey
Dolores .... Diane Beckwith
Thelma .... Ruby Matthies
Edna ....Elizabeth Ann Butler
Olga .... Marjorie M. Klein
Cow, front end...................................... Peter Wellman
Cow, back end .... H. Joe Scott
Pastey .... Dick Newdick
Tessie Tura .... Sharon Spelman
Mazeppa ....Sharon Ryterband
Electra .... Karin Woodward
Cigar ....Michael Shapiro
Renee .... Maxine Gootzeit
Phil .... Bill Prosser
Bougeron- Cochon ....Will Gersch
Chorus Boys ....Richard Busch, Wayne Lamb
Showgirls & Strippers ....Leslie L. Barth, Diane Beckwith, Elizabeth Ann Butler, Kristine Grebezs, Marjorie M. Klein, Susan V. Mason, Ruby Matthies, Susan Murray, Sharon Pankey, Rebecca Taylor

53
Experimental Theatre, Purdue
June 14, 15, July 1, 12, 16, 21, 28 & August 7 & 9, 1966
Talk of Another Day
By Richard Busch

Directed by Joe Stockdale
Sets & Costumes...................................... Joe McArdle
Lighting ....Randy Earle
Stage Manager .... Dick Newdick
Asst. Stage Manager ....Peter N. Simon
Technical Director .... Randy Earle
Asst. Technical Director .... Paul Voelker
Properties ....Sharon Ryterband
Technical Assistants .... Gary Craven, Steve Hodge
Wardrobe .... Marea Jane Hargitt
Seamstress ....Martha Van Cleef
Asst. Seamstress ....Mary Arnold
House Manager .... Patrice Murphy

CAST
Larry Martz .... Dale Helward
Mitzy .... Merle Louise
Elizabeth Martz ....Dorothy Harlan
David Martz ....Peter N. Simon
Henry Langsworth ....John Newton
Lois Handley ....Janet Hayes

54
Experimental Theatre, Purdue
June 16-19, 28
July 6. 9, 14, 17, 22, 26, 30
August 3, 8 & 12, 1966
Ardele
By Jean Anouilh

Directed by Joe Stockdale
Sets & Costumes...................................... Joe McArdle
Lighting ....Randy Earle
Stage Manager .... Dick Newdick
Asst. Stage Manager ....Peter N. Simon
Technical Director .... Randy Earle
Asst. Technical Director .... Paul Voelker
Properties ....Sharon Ryterband
Technical Assistants .... Gary Craven, Steve Hodge
Gowns .... Marea Jane Hargitt
Wardrobe .... Marea Jane Hargitt
Seamstress ....Martha Van Cleef
Asst. Seamstress ....Mary Arnold
House Manager .... Patrice Murphy

CAST
The General ....John Newton
His Wife ....Dorothy Harlan
The Count ....Stuart Howard
The Countess ....Janet Hayes
Villardieu .... Dale Helward
Nicholas ....Peter N. Simon
Toto ....Greg Sciarrotta
Marie-Christine ....Beth Ullman
Ada ....Sharon Ryterband
Nathalie .... Merle Louise

55
Experimental Theatre, Purdue
June 21, 22, 30 July 2, 3, 8, 13, 19, 29, 31
August 4, 6, 10, 1966
A Doll's House
By Henrik Ibsen
Directed by Joe Stockdale
Sets & Costumes...................................... Joe McArdle
Lighting ....Randy Earle
Stage Manager .... Dick Newdick
Asst. Stage Manager ....Peter N. Simon
Technical Director .... Randy Earle
Asst. Technical Director .... Paul Voelker
Properties ....Sharon Ryterband
Technical Assistants .... Gary Craven, Steve Hodge
Gowns .... Lyn Carroll

Wardrobe .... Marea Jane Hargitt
Seamstress .... Martha Van Cleef
Asst. Seamstress .... Mary Arnold
House Manager .... Patrice Murphy

CAST
Torvald Helmer .... Dale Helward
Nora .... Merle Louise
Dr. Rank .... John Newton
Mrs. Linde .... Janet Hayes
Nils Krogstad .... Stuart Howard
The Helmers' Children .... Eden Hargitt,
     Charles Hargitt, Russell Hargitt
Anne-Marie .... Dorothy Harlan
Helene .... Sharon Ryterband
A Delivery Boy .... Peter N. Simon

#56
Experimental Theatre, Purdue
June 23-26, 29 July 5, 7, 15, 23, 24, 27
August 2, 5 & 11, 1966
The Birthday Party
By Harold Pinter

Directed by Joe Stockdale

Sets & Costumes .... Joe McArdle
Lighting .... Randy Earle
Stage Manager .... Dick Newdick
Asst. Stage Manager .... Peter N. Simon
Technical Director .... Randy Earle
Asst. Technical Director .... Paul Voelker
Properties .... Sharon Ryterband
Technical Assistants .... Gary Craven, Steve Hodge
Gowns .... Marea Jane Hargitt
Wardrobe .... Marea Jane Hargitt
Seamstress .... Martha Van Cleef
Asst. Seamstress .... Mary Arnold
House Manager .... Patrice Murphy

CAST
Petey .... Dick Newdick
Meg .... Dorothy Harlan
Stanley .... Dale Helward
Lulu .... Merle Louise
Goldberg .... Stuart Howard
McCann .... John Newton

#57
Southern Illinois University
August 19-20, 26-27, 1966
Brigadoon
Book & Lyrics by Alan Jay Lerner
Music by Frederick Loewe

Directed by Joe Stockdale

Musical Director .... William Taylor
Choreographer .... Gilbert Reed
Sets .... Darwin Payne
Costumes .... Richard Boss
Lighting .... Larry Wild
Chorus Master .... Janet Cox
Asst. Musical Director .... Jeordano Martinez
Asst. to Director .... Richard Hylland
Stage Manager .... Roy Harnetiaux
Technical Asst .... Richard Mizdal
Wardrobe .... Elizabeth Weiss, Jan Heston
Set Crew Head .... Robert Pevitts
Lighting .... Steve Gross
Make-up .... Alfred Erickson
Properties .... Alfred Erickson
Hair Dresser .... Charles A. Stone
Box Office .... Linda Sublett
Rehearsal Pianists .... Pete Martinez,
   Jack Ridley, Andrea Shields, Susan McClary
House Manager .... Rudy Barello
Publicity .... Richard Hylland

CAST
Tommy Albright .... Robert Guy
Jeff Douglas .... William McHughes
Archie Beaton .... Alfred Erickson
Harry Beaton .... Michael Telvin
Fishmonger .... Denyce Ross
Angus MacGuffie .... Jere Dawe
Sandy Dean .... Cliff Baker
Andrew MacLaren .... Mike Craig
Fiona MacLaren .... Susie Webb
Jean MacLaren .... Linda Sublett
Meg Brockie .... Elizabeth Weiss
Charlie Dalrymple .... Bill Wallis
Maggie Anderson .... Sondra Sugai
Mr. Lundie .... James Fox
Sword Dancers .... Gary Paben, Tom Overholser
Frank .... Albert Hapke
Jane Ashton .... Susan Frenkel
Bagpipers .... James Sullivan, Mary Ann Cambridge
Stuart Dalrymple .... Guy Klopp
MacGregor .... Norbert Krausz

Townsfolk of Brigadoon
Singers: .... Susan Carruthers, Elaine Ellison,
    Susan Frenkel, Ruth Gordon,
    Brenda Hall, Ruth Hastings,
    Becky McLaughlin, Marilyn Nix,
    Roberta Rodin, Judy Sink, Linda Sparks,
    Pam Worley, Cliff Baker, Earl Belk,
    Mike Craig, Al Erickson, Fred Fallen,
    Naggy Faltas, Al Hapke, Guy Klopp,
    Norbert Krausz, Bruce Miller, Jeordano
    Martinez, Bruce Potts, Ron Rendleman
Dancers: .... Nanett Cox, Sue McConnell,
    Denyce Ross, Jane Somogy, Priscilla Ryan,
    Cynthia Vogler, Tom Overholser,
    Gary Paben

#58
Loeb Playhouse, Purdue
October 21, 22, 27-29, 1966
Misalliance
By George Bernard Shaw

Directed By Joe Stockdale

Sets & Lighting .... John Boyt
Costumes .... William G. Bruch
Technical Director .... Randy Earle
Stage Manager .... Jim Waller
Asst. to Director .... Joyce White
Technical Assistant .... Charles Hayman

Master Carpenter	Gary Craven
Master Electrician	Dave Sigafoose
Properties	Alexa Smith
Wardrobe	Leila Hawkin
Sound	Dane Bernard
Paint Crew Head	Suzanne Ayers Stockdale

CAST

John Tarleton, Jr.	Bill Prosser
Bentley Summerhays	Roy Kirkpatrick
Hypatia Tarleton	Nova Young
Mrs. Tarleton	Susan Murray
Lord Summerhays	E. Allyn Thompson
John Tarleton	Eric Berry
Joseph Percival	Robert Browning
Lina Szczepanowska	Cindy Larimer
Julius Baker	Brian McMaster

59
Loeb Playhouse, Purdue
February 10, 11, 16-18, 1966
The Plough and the Stars
By Sean O'Casey
"To the Gay Laugh of my mother at the gate of the grave"

Directed by Joe Stockdale

Sets & Lighting	Robert T. Williams
Costumes	William G. Bruch
Technical Director	Randy Earle
Music Director	Dorothy Runk Mennen
Technical Advisor	Donald Treat
Speech Consultant	Dorothy Runk Mennen
Production Stage Manager	Donna Hodge
Asst. to Director	Donna Pflug
Asst. Stage Manager	Cindy Kite
Master Carpenter	Gary Craven
Master Electrician	Steve Hodge
Asst. Electrician	Dan Bobek
Sound Master	Strother Brann
Sound Asst.	Jim Waller
Properties	Jim Knox, Maxine Reifer
Scene Painter	Jon-Roger Miranda
Wardrobe Mistress	Patrice Murphy
House Manager	Janice Brewton

CAST
Tenement Residents

Jack Clitheroe	Charles Hayman
Nora Clitheroe	Cindy Larimer
Peter Flynn	Brian McMaster
The Young Covey	Roy Kirkpatrick
Bessie Burgess	Karin Woodward
Mrs. Gogan	Susan Murray
Mollser	Nova Young
Fluther Good	Robert Browning

Others in the Cast

Lieut. Langon	Warren Knorr, Jr.
Capt. Brennan	Sterling Johnson
Corp. Stoddart	Paul Mayberry
Sgt. Tinley	Jay Gluck
Rosie Redmond	Rebecca Taylor
A Bar-Tender	Ronald Newton
A Woman	Carole Lockwood
Irish Band	Robert J. Schlatter & Members of the West Lafayette H.S. Band

60
Experimental Theatre, Purdue
May 23-28, 30, 31 June 1-4, 1967
Luv
By Murray Schisgal

Directed by Joe Stockdale

Set Design	Robert T. Williams
Technical Director	Randy Earle
Costumes	William G. Bruch
Stage Manager	Dick Newdick
Wardrobe	Rosalie Clements Diane Bachert, Vickie Kuhl
Master Carpenter	Paul Voelker
Sound Master	Michael Yelton
Master Electrician	Jim Waller
Production Crew	Brian McMaster, Jim Fox, Nova Young, Carole Lockwood, Karin Woodward, Rebecca Taylor

CAST

Harry Berlin	Dale Helward
Milt Manville	Stuart Howard
Ellen Manville	Janet Hayes

61
Experimental Theatre, Purdue
June 6-11, 13-18, 1967
The Importance of Being Earnest
By Oscar Wilde

Directed by Joe Stockdale

Set Design	Robert T. Williams
Costumes	William G. Bruch
Technical Director	Randy Earle
Stage Manager	Dick Newdick
Wardrobe	Rosalie Clements Diane Bachert, Vickie Kuhl
Master Carpenter	Paul Voelker
Sound Master	Michael Yelton
Master Electrician	Jim Waller
Production Crew	Brian McMaster, Jim Fox, Nova Young, Carole Lockwood, Karin Woodward, Rebecca Taylor

CAST

John Worthing	Dale Helward
Algernon Moncrieff	Stuart Howard
Rev. Canon Chasuble	John Newton
Merriman	Robert Browning
Lane	Brian McMaster
Lady Bracknell	Dorothy Harlan
Hon. Gwendolyn Fairfax	Janet Hayes

Cecily Cardew	Nova Young
Miss Prism	Susan Murray
Footman	James Fox

62
Experimental Theatre, Purdue
June 20-30, July 1-9, 1967
Little Mary Sunshine
Book, Music & Lyrics by
Rick Besoyan

Directed by Joe Stockdale

Set Design	Robert T. Williams
Musical Direction	Dick Jaeger
Choreography	Stuart Howard
Costumes	Robert Joyner
Technical Director	Randy Earle
Stage Manager	Dick Newdick
Sound Master	Michael Yelton
Wardrobe	Diane Bachert, Patrice Murphy
Production Crew	Brian McMaster, Jim Fox, Nova Young, Carole Lockwood, Karin Woodward, Rebecca Taylor

CAST

Chief Brown Bear	William L. Engaas
Cpl. Billy Jester	Stuart Howard
Capt. Big Jim Warington	Dale Helward

The Forest Rangers

Pete	Robert Browning
Tex	William Prosser
Slim	Dick Newdick
Buster	Brian McMaster
Hank	Michael Sevareid
Tom	James Fox
Little Mary Sunshine	Janet Hayes
Mme. Ernestine von Liebedich	Dorothy Harlan

Young Ladies from Eastchester Finishing School

Cora	Elizabeth Porter
Henrietta	Rebecca Taylor
Mabel	Susan Murray
Maud	Susan Mason
Gwendolyn	Nova Young
Blanche	Diane Bachert
Nancy Twinkle	Karin Woodward
Fleet Foot	David Michael Thomas
Yellow Feather	Joel Levinson
Gen. Oscar Fairfax, Ret.	John Newton

63
Experimental Theatre, Purdue
July 11-23, 1967
Tartuffe
By Moliere
Adapted by Miles Malleson
Rhyming Couplets by Sagittarius

Directed by Joe Stockdale

Set Design	Robert T. Williams
Costumes	Robert Joyner
Technical Director	Randy Earle
Stage Manager	Dick Newdick
Wardrobe	Diane Bachert
Master Carpenter	Paul Voelker
Sound Master	James Waller
Master Electrician	Michael Yelton

CAST

Monsieur Orgon	John Newton
Damis	Brian McMaster
Mariane	Elizabeth Porter
Madame Pernelle	Dorothy Harlan
Elmire	Janet Hayes
Cleante	Dale Helward
Valere	Robert Browning
Dorine	Nova Young
Filipote	Susan Murray
Tartuffe	Stuart Howard
Tartuffe's Man	Jim Knox
Loyale	James Fox
The Officer	Michael Sevareid
Sergeants	David Michael Thomas, William L. Engaas

64
Experimental Theatre, Purdue
July 25-30, August 1-12, 1967
Oh What A Lovely War
By
Joan Littlewood's Theatre Workshop, Charles Chilton, and the members of the cast

Directed by Joe Stockdale

Set Design	Robert T. Williams
Costumes	Robert Joyner
Musical Director	Richard Jaeger
Technical Director	Randy Earle
Stage Manager	Dick Newdick
Wardrobe	Diane Bachert
Master Carpenter	Paul Voelker
Sound Master	James Waller
Master Electrician	Michael Yelton

CAST
The Pierrots

Robert Browning	Stuart Howard
John Newton	William Engaas
Dick Jaeger	Elizabeth Porter
James Fox	Tom Jennings
Michael Sevareid	Janet Hayes
Susan Mason	Ted Simmons
Dale Helward	Brian McMaster
Rebecca Taylor	Dick Newdick
Susan Murray	Karin Woodward

| Piano | Tom Berg |

65
Experimental Theatre, Purdue
September 12-October 1, 1967
Of Mice and Men
By John Steinbeck

Directed by Joe Stockdale

| Sets & Costumes | Jerry Williams |

Lighting ....Randy Earle
Stage Manager ....Wayne Lamb
Asst. Stage Managers ....Jim Fox,
          K.L. Coughenour, Richard Lake
Technical Director ....Randy Earle
Pianist ....Tom Berg
Master Electrician .... Michael Yelton
Master Carpenter ..........................K.L. Coughenour
Properties ....James Knox
Wardrobe Mistress ....Vickie Earle
Sound Master ....Michael Shapiro

CAST
George ....Ed Setrakian
Lennie ....James Earl Jones
Candy ....Joseph Boley
The Boss ....Louis Girard
Curley ....Angelo Mango
Curley's Wife .... Pamela Gruen
Slim .... Mark Dempsey
Carlson .... George Stauch
Whit ....Brian McMaster
Crooks .... Robertearl Jones

66
Experimental Theatre, Purdue
October 31 – November 26, 1967
Long Day's Journey Into Night
By Eugene O'Neill

Directed by Joe Stockdale
Sets & Costumes ....Jerry Williams
Lighting ....Randy Earle
Stage Manager ....Wayne Lamb
Asst. Stage Managers ....Jim Fox,
          K.L. Coughenour, Richard Lake
Technical Director ....Randy Earle
Pianist ....Tom Berg
Master Electrician .... Michael Yelton
Master Carpenter ..........................K.L. Coughenour
Properties ....James Knox
Wardrobe Mistress ....Vickie Earle
Sound Master ....Michael Shapiro

CAST
James Tyrone ....Robert Donley
Mary Craven Tyrone ....Anne Revere
James Tyrone, Jr. ....Michael Walsh
Edmund Tyrone .... Robert Browning
Cathleen .... Susan Murray

67
Experimental Theatre, Purdue
February 2-18, 1968
Incident at Vichy
By Arthur Miller

Directed by Joe Stockdale
Sets & Costumes ....Jerry Williams
Lighting ....Randy Earle
Stage Manager ....Wayne Lamb
Asst. Stage Managers .... Michael Yelton,
          Brian McMaster, Richard Lake
Technical Director ....Randy Earle
Pianist ....Tom Berg
Master Electrician .... Michael Yelton
Properties ....James Knox
Wardrobe Mistress ....Vickie Earle
Sound Master ....Michael Shapiro

Follow Spots ....Andy Andrews, Suzy Ayres

CAST
Lebeau ....Brian McMaster
Bayard ....John Morrow, Jr.
Marchand ....Leon Benedict
Police Guard .... Michael Yelton
Monceau ....Stuart Howard
Gypsy .... Peter Shawn
Waiter .... Roy Kirkpatrick
Boy .... Ted Simmons
Major .... Dale Helward
First Detective ....Gene Kramer
Old Jew ....Joseph Boley
Second Detective ....Richard Lake
Leduc ....Will Gregory
Police Captain ....Jerry Williams
Von Berg .... Reid Shelton
Professor Hoffman .... Tom Jennings
Ferrand ....Don Laffoon

68
Experimental Theatre, Purdue
February 21-March 17, 1968
A Funny Thing Happened on the Way to the Forum
Book by Bert Shevelove & Larry Gelbert
Music & Lyrics by Stephen Sondheim

Directed by Joe Stockdale
Choreography & Musical Staging
by Wayne Lamb
Musical Direction .... Dorothy Runk Mennen
Sets & Costumes ....Jerry Williams
Lighting ....Randy Earle
Stage Manager ....Wayne Lamb
Asst. Stage Managers .... Michael Yelton,
          Brian McMaster, Richard Lake
Technical Director ....Randy Earle
Pianist ....Tom Berg
Master Electrician .... Michael Yelton
Properties ....James Knox
Wardrobe Mistress ....Vickie Earle
Sound Master ....Michael Shapiro

CAST
Prologus .... Philip Polito
The Proteans ....Tom Jennings,
          Beecher Ketchum, Roy Kirkpatrick
Senex ....Leon Benedict
Domina ....Jean Repp
Hero .... Peter Shawn
Hysterium ....James McDonald
Lycus ....Stuart Howard
Pseudolous .... Philip Polito
Tintinabula ....Cynthia Strickland
Panacea ....Alice Vaughn
The Geminae .... Rebecca Taylor, Karin Woodward
Vibrata ....Connie Heaver
Gymnasia .... Vicki Earle

Philia	Susan Lehman
Erronious	Joseph Boley
Miles Gloriosus	Reid Shelton
A Soldier	Will Gregory

69
Experimental Theatre, Purdue
March 21-31, 1968
Uncle Vanya
By Anton Chekhov
Translated by Constance Garrnett

Directed by Joe Stockdale

Sets & Costumes	Jerry Williams
Lighting	Randy Earle
Asst. Director	Wayne Lamb
Asst. Stage Managers	Michael Yelton, Brian McMaster, Richard Lake
Technical Director	Randy Earle
Pianist	Tom Berg
Master Electrician	Michael Yelton
Properties	James Knox
Wardrobe Mistress	Vickie Earle
Sound Master	Michael Shapiro

CAST

Marina Timofeyevna	Dorothy Harlan
Mihail Lvovitch Astrov	Will Gregory
Ivan Petreovitch Voynitsky	Reid Shelton
Alexander Vladimirovitch Serebryakov	Joseph Boley
Ilya Ilyitch Telyegin	Brian McMaster
Sofya Alexandrovna	Susan Lehman
Yelena Andreyevna	Catherine Damon
Marya Vassilyevna Voynitsky	Jeanne Repp
Yefim	Michael Yelton

70
Experimental Theatre, Purdue
June 19-29, 1968
The School For Wives
By Moliere

Directed by Joe Stockdale

Sets & Costumes	Jerry Williams
Stage Manager	Richard Lake
Technical Director	Randy Earle
Master Carpenter	Dick Barton
Master Electrician	Michael Yelton
Sound Master	Perry White
Set Technicians	Jack Bourland, Andrew Biro
Properties	Cathy Taylor
Wardrobe Mistress	Vicki Earle
Seamstress	Bernadette Gorgosz
Assistants to Director	Connie Heaver, Brian McMaster
Hair Stylist	Mary Lou Riley

CAST

Arnolphe	John Newton
Chrysalde	Brian McMaster
Oronte	Andrew Jarkowsky
Enrique	John LeGrand
Horace	Peter Simon
Alain	Stuart Howard
Georgette	Janet Hayes
Agnes	Merle Louise

71
Experimental Theatre, Purdue
July 17-27, 1968
The Homecoming
By Harold Pinter

Directed by Joe Stockdale

Sets & Costumes	Jerry Williams
Stage Manager	Richard Lake
Technical Director	Randy Earle
Master Carpenter	Dick Barton
Master Electrician	Michael Yelton
Sound Master	Perry White
Set Technicians	Jack Bourland, Andrew Biro
Properties	Cathy Taylor
Wardrobe Mistress	Vicki Earle
Seamstress	Bernadette Gorgosz
Assistants to Director	Connie Heaver, Brian McMaster
Hair Stylist	Mary Lou Riley

CAST

Max	Reid Shelton
Lenny	Stuart Howard
Sam	John LeGrand
Joey	Peter Simon
Teddy	John Newton
Ruth	Janet Hayes

72
Experimental Theatre, Purdue
July 31-August 10, 1968
Night Must Fall
By Emlyn Williams

Directed by Joe Stockdale

Sets & Costumes	Jerry Williams
Stage Manager	Richard Lake
Technical Director	Randy Earle
Master Carpenter	Dick Barton
Master Electrician	Michael Yelton
Sound Master	Perry White
Set Technicians	Jack Bourland, Andrew Biro
Properties	Cathy Taylor
Wardrobe Mistress	Vicki Earle
Seamstress	Bernadette Gorgosz
Assistants to Director	Connie Heaver, Brian McMaster
Hair Stylist	Mary Lou Riley

CAST

The Lord Chief Justice	
Mrs. Bramson	Dorothy Harlan
Olivia Grayne	Janet Hayes
Hubert Laurie	John Newton
Nurse Libby	Connie Heaver
Mrs. Terrence	Karin Woodward
Dora Parkoe	Merle Louise
Inspector Belsize	Reid Shelton
Dan	Peter Simon

#73
Experimental Theatre, Purdue
September 16-October 6, 1968
Born Yesterday
By Garson Kanin

Directed by Joe Stockdale

Set Design ....Jerry Williams
Costume Design ....Lyn Carroll
Lighting/Technical Director ....Randy Earle
Stage Manager ....Wayne Lamb
Assoc. Technical Director ....Michael Yelton
Scenic Artist/Sound ....Jack Bourland
Master Carpenter ....Perry White
Master Electrician ....Paul Abe
House Electrician ....Andrew Biro
Sound Technician ....Michael Shapiro
Scene Technician ....Gary Hofmeister
Wardrobe Mistress ....Vicki Earle
Properties ....Janet Koplos
Hair Stylist ....Mary Lou Riley

CAST

Billie Dawn ....Lee Kirk
Harry Brock ....John Garces
Paul Verrall ....Thomas Connolly
Ed Devery .... Alexander Reed
Sen. Norval Hedges ....Louis Girard
Mrs. Hedges ....Dorothy Harlan
Eddie Brock ....Brian McMaster
The Assistant Manager ....Richard Lake
Helen, a maid ....Alice Vaughn
A Bellhop ....K.M. Rhodes
Another Bellhop ....David Gottschalk
A Barber ....Gary Anthony
A Manicurist ....Connie Heaver
A Bootblack ....Jesse Gore
A Waiter .... Peter Schneider

#74
Experimental Theatre, Purdue
October 9-27, 1968
All My Sons
By Arthur Miller

Directed by Joe Stockdale

Sets ....Jerry Williams
Costumes ....Lyn Carroll
Lighting/Technical Director ....Randy Earle
Stage Manager ....Wayne Lamb
Assoc. Technical Manager .... Michael Yelton
Scenic Artist ....Dusty Reeds
Master Carpenter .... Jack Bourland
Master Electrician .... Paul Abe
Set Technician .... Gary Hofmeister
Sound Master ....Michael Shapiro
Sound Technician ....Gary Nelson
Wardrobe Mistress ....Vicki Earle
Properties .... Kathy Waisner
Hair Stylist ....Mary Lou Riley

CAST

Dr. Jim Bayliss .... Alexander Reed
Joe Keller ....Louis Girard
Frank Lubey ....Richard Lake
Sue Bayliss .... Karin Woodward
Lydia Lubey ....Donna Wilshire
Chris Keller .... Thomas Connolly
Bert .... Kevin Gartenhaus
Kate Keller .... Mary Hara
Ann Deever ....Connie Heaver
George Deever .... Richard Sterne

#75
Experimental Theatre, Purdue
December 5-20, 1968
Oedipus/Antigone
Based on the text of *Oedipus Rex, Oedipus at Colonus, and Antigone*
By Sophocles

Directed by Joe Stockdale

Set ....Jerry Williams
Costumes ....Lyn Carroll
Lighting ....Randy Earle
Stage Manager .... Kathy Waisner
Electricians .... Steve Hodge,
Dave Sigafoose, Steve Perkins
Properties ....Lynn Brown
Wardrobe Mistress ....Curryanne Chalkley
House Manager ....Linda Mussman

CAST

Randy Ade ....Jerry Bledsoe
Jesse Gore, Jr...................................Davis Gottschalk
Donna Hodge...................................Andy O'Donnell
K.M. Rhodes .... Peter Schneider
Gayle Stahlhuth................................. Dan Von Bargen
Marsha Waterbury............................. Ellen Zitterbart

#76
Experimental Theatre, Purdue
February 11- March 2, 1969
You Never Can Tell
Based on the play by George Bernard Shaw
Book by Joe Stockdale
Music by Roz Aronson
Lyrics by Stuart Howard

Directed by Joe Stockdale

Choreographer ....Wayne Lamb
Musical Arrangements .... Roz Aronson, Tom Berg
Vocal Direction .... Dorothy Runk Mennen
Sets ....Jerry Williams
Costumes ....Lyn Carroll
Lighting/Technical Director ....Randy Earle
Production Stage Manager ....Richard Lake
Assoc. Technical Manager .... Michael Yelton
Scenic Artist ....Dusty Reeds
Master Carpenter .... Harris Bershatsky
Shop Foreman .... Paul Abe
Set Technicians ....Gary Hofmeister,
Robert Woolf, Jack Bourland
Master Electrician .... Steve Hodge
Sound Master ....Gary Nelson
Wardrobe Mistress ....Curryanne Chalkley
Properties .... K.M. Rhodes,
Alexa Smith

Hair Stylist	Mary Lou Riley
Follow Spots	Robert Woolf, Tricia Remich
Dolly	Candy Coles
Valentine	Jay Stuart
Philip	Michael Stoddard
Mrs. Clandon	Mary Nettum
Gloria	Connie Heaver
Parlor Maid	Marsha Waterbury
Crampton	Robert Donley
McComas	Louis Girard
Walter	David C. Jones
Bohun	Angelo Mango
Ensemble	Randy Ade, David Gottschalk, Donna Hodge, Cynthia S. Mc Kay, Diane McMaster, K.M. Rhodes, Peter Schneider, Gayle Stahlhuth, Dan Von Bargen, Marsha Waterbury, Cassandra Wolfe, Ellen Zitterbart
Chorus	Gary Anthony, Wayne Lamb, Brian McMaster, Dusty Reeds, Richard Williams
Piano	Tom Berg

77
Experimental Theatre, Purdue
March 5-23, 1969
The Little Foxes
By Lillian Hellman

Directed by Joe Stockdale

Sets & Costumes	Jerry Williams
Costume Execution	Lyn Carroll
Lighting/Technical Director	Randy Earle
Production Stage Manager	Richard Lake
Assoc. Technical Manager	Michael Yelton
Scenic Artist	Dusty Reeds
Master Carpenter	Harris Bershatsky
Shop Foreman	Paul Abe
Set Technicians	Gary Hofmeister, Robert Woolf
Master Electrician & Sound	Paul Abe
Wardrobe Mistress	Curryanne Chalkley
Properties	Linda Magnuson
Hair Stylist	Mary Lou Riley

CAST

Addie	Carolyn Y. Cardwell
Cal	Tom Bradley
Birdie Hubbard	Mary Nettum
Oscar Hubbard	David C. Jones
Leo Hubbard	Michael Stoddard
Regina Giddens	Connie Heaver
William Marshall	Angelo Mango
Benjamin Hubbard	Robert Donley
Alexandra Giddens	Candy Coles
Horace Giddens	Louis Girard

78
Loeb Playhouse, Purdue
December 12-18, 1969
Bury The Dead
By Irwin Shaw

Directed by Joe Stockdale

Sets & Costumes	Dusty Reeds
Choreography	Wayne Lamb
Lighting/Technical Director	Randy Earle
Projections	Brian McMaster
Vocal Coach	Dorothy Runk Mennen
Stage Manager	Jesse Gore, Jr.
Assistant Stage Manager	Amy Kirby
Rehearsal Assistant	Melanie Ray
Assistant to Designer	Donn Ping
Master Carpenter	Steve Placke
Make-up	Michael Yelton
Wardrobe Mistress	Kathy Yeager
Master Electrician	David Sigafoose
Sound Master	Gary Nelson
Property Mistress	Holly Hunt

CAST
LADIES OF THE CHORUS
Patrice L. Murphy, Moe Gaynor,
Sandra Mitchell, Susan Clark,
Candy Yelton, Trisha Hagen,
Karen Weedman, Jeanine King,
Nan Yarnelle, Vicki Earle
THE BURIAL DETAIL
David A. Gottschalk, John R. Eldridge,
Guy Gardner, George Jillich, Ken Werbinski
THE CORPSES

Private Driscoll	Randy John Williams
Private Schelling	Tom Belleville
Private Morgan	Robert H. Dein
Private Webster	Daniel Von Bargen
Private Levy	Larry A. McVey
Private Dean	Peter Schneider

THE CHURCH

| Priest | Gary Stanek |
| Rabbi | Randall Lemon |

THE OFFICER

| Captain | Les Gruner |

THE HIGH COMMAND

First General	Michael Yelton
Second General	John Obert
Third General	Rick Olafson

THE MEDICINE MEN

| The Doctor | David T. Moore |

OTHER SOLDIERS

| Bevins | Carl Morehouse |
| Charley | Edward Vendley |

THE 4TH ESTATE

Reporter	Sandy Langner
Editor	Fred Haskins
NEWSBOY	Jesse Gore

THE WHORES

First Whore	Moe Gaynor
Second Whore	Nan Yarnelle
Soldier	James David Smith

THE BUSINESSMEN
First ....Steve Heller
Second .... Randall Lemon
Third .... David T. Moore

THE MINISTER & THE CONGREGATION
Minister .... Gary Stanek
Members ....John Gareffa, Diane Henderson, Dennis Lavelle, Karyn Stresser

RADIO ANNOUNCER
Patrice L. Murphy

THE WIVES
Bess Schelling ....Kathy Yeager
Joan Burke .... Candy Yelton
Julia Blake .... Pamela Mathews
Katherine Driscoll .... Cassandra Wolfe
Elizabeth Dean .... Jo Sabel
Martha Webster .... Paige Massman

THE EXORCISM
Bishop .... Les Gruner

OTHERS
Carl Morehouse, David T. Moore, Thomas Reiser, Edward Vendley, Les Schoof, Steve Woods, John Gareff
PIANIST .... Tom Berg

In order to produce the large cast BURY THE DEAD as a Conservatory production, it was necessary to recruit additional student actors to augment the students-in-training in the Purdue Professional Theatre Program. We wish to acknowledge our appreciation to these students of diverse disciplines on the campus whose generous contribution of time and skills have made it possible.

79
Trap Room, Purdue
July 17-19, 1970
The Glass Menagerie
By Tennessee Williams

Directed by Joe Stockdale

Set ....Richard Teubert
Lighting/Technical Direction ....Randy Earle
Stage Manager .... Lesa Doades
Scenic Artists ....Jerry & Sherry Bledsoe
Master Electrician .... Naomi Saper
Sound Master ....Marsha Verbik
Properties ....Pam Biggs

CAST
Tom .... Les Gruner
Amanda ....Paige Massman
Laura .... Pamela Matthews
Jim .... Michael Yelton

80
Loeb Playhouse, Purdue
October 23, 24, 27-31, 1970
King Lear
By William Shakespeare

Directed by Joe Stockdale

Sets & Lighting ....Dusty Reeds
Costumes .... Stormie Lineberger
Vocal Coach .... Dorothy Runk Mennen
Technical Director .... Michael Yelton
Make-up .... Sarah Gumerson
Scenic Artist ....Donn Ping
Properties ....John Kessler
Assistant to Director .... Katherine Wiens

CAST
Earl of Gloucester ....E. Allyn Thompson
Edmund ....John R. Eldridge
Earl of Kent .... Daniel Von Bargen
King Lear ....Erling Kildahl
Goneril ....Patrice L. Murphy
Regan .... Ellen Zitterbart
Cordelia ....Kathy Dutton Yeager
Duke of Cornwall .... Charles A. Smith
Duke of Albany ....David Gottschalk
King of France ....Jerry Bledsoe
Duke of Burgundy ....James D. Smith
Edgar .... Lester Gruner
Knight .... Randy Howe
Oswald .... David Potts
Fool .... Peter Schneider
Gentleman .... Garry Montanari
Curan .... Randall W. Lemon
Gloucester's Servant ....Kim Muston
Old Man ....Arthur Scharbrough
Cornwall's Messenger ....Michael Immel
Doctor ....Donn Ping
Captain ....Bob Heiber
Herald ....Michael Immel

81
East Carolina Playhouse, UNC
May 12-15, 1971
Little Murders
By Jules Feiffer

Directed by Joe Stockdale

Sets & Costumes .... Robert T. Williams
Lighting ....Andrew Gilfillan
Production Stage Manager .... Juanda LaJoyce
Asst. Stage Manager .... George Merrell
Technical Director ....Conwell Worthington
Master Carpenter ....Mark McMillan
Master Electrician ....Lin Shehdan
Properties ....Don Squires
Paint Crew Lead .... Harry W. Bushwitz
Costume Mistress ....Mary Ann Perry
Special Effects ....Deby Childers, Donna Butrick
Sound .... William F. Doeg, Kit Hunter

CAST
Kenny Newquist .... Chris Jones
Marjorie Newquist ....Anita Brehm
Carol Newquist ....James Slaughter
Patsy Newquist ....Amanda Muir
Alfred Chamberlain ....Mark Ramsey
Judge Stern ....Gregory Smith
Henry Dupas .... Kirk Thayer
Miles Practice ....Frank Wieczeerzak
Wedding Guests, Photographer & Caterer:
Jane Bushway, Beth Cayton,
Jim Fleming, Donna Goodnight,
Tom Llewellyn, Bruce McKeown,

George Merrell, Linda Darnell Simpson, Viv Speight, Don Squires, Kleist Wideman

82
Experimental Theatre, Purdue
October 21, 23, 24, 28-30, 1971
The Cherry Orchard
By Anton Chekhov

Directed by Joe Stockdale

Set Design	Dusty Reeds
Costumes Design	Stormie Lineberger
Lighting	Peter Schneider & David Potts
Technical Director	James MacRostie
Choreographer	Wayne Lamb
Asst. Technical Director	Steve Placke
Stage Manager	Les Schoof
Properties	Mary Uttermohlen
Sound	Peter Schneider
Wardrobe Mistress	Jean Routt
Make-up	Lisa Osborne
Paint Crew	Sally Gumerson, Tim Emswiller, Phil Cross

CAST

Lyubov Andreyevna	Susan Clark
Anya	Debbie Dennis
Varya	Kathy Dutton Yeager
Leonid Gaev	Van Ibsen
Yermolay Lopahin	Dan Von Bargen
Pyotr Trofimov	Paul Mazzaglia
Boris Semyonov-Pishchik	Kimit Muston
Charlotta Ivanova	Karen Saperstein
Semyon Epihodov	Dave Noll
Dunyasha	Cassandra Wolfe
Feers	Tim Funcheon
Yasha	Bob Walker
A Tramp	Brian Ward Winne
Post Office Clerk	Patrick Flanagan
Station Master	Tim Funcheon

Orchestra

Cello	Sara Wollan
Violin	Carlis Favrot
Flute	Barbara Kornblum

83
Richmond Professional Institute
School of The Arts
June 21-24, 27- July 1, 1972
Hadrian the Seventh
By Peter Luke

Directed by Joe Stockdale

Sets & Lights	Bradford Boynton
Costumes	Lynn Sams
Stage Manager	Larry Verbit
Asst. Stage Manager	Gil Shaw
Master Electrician	Gridley McAdams
Properties	Victoria Jones
Vocal Coach	Wayne Hamilton
Asst. Technical Director	Tom Barrett
Assistant to Set Designer	Tom Magee
Costume Design Assistant	Betty Martin
Publicity	Sam Maupin
Costume Crew Head	Deeter Allmond
Box Office	Ralph MacPhail

CAST

Fr. William Rolfe	Richard Newdick
Mrs. Crowe	Donna Van Winkle
1st Bailiff	Jim Buss
2nd Bailiff	Richard Rivera
Agnes	Bonnie Roe
Dr. Talacryn	Jim Buss
Dr. Courtleigh	Richard Rivera
Jeremiah Sant	C. Thomas Holloway
The Cardinal-Archdeacon	Kirk Condyles
Fr. St. Albans	Lee Chew
Cardinal Berstein	Maury Erickson
Cardinal Ragna	Gene Johnson
Rector of St. Andrews College	David Williams
George Arthur Rose	Sam Maupin
Cardinals	Rex M. Ellis, Wayne Hamilton, Bill Jones, Gil Shaw
Seminarists, Swiss Guards, Acolytes	Chip Holloway, Bob Pemberton, David Williams, Michael Woolard

84
Experimental Theatre, Purdue
July 26-29, 1972
Roots
Sheila Hofstetter's Adaptation of Arnold Wesker's play

Directed by Joe Stockdale

Sets & Costumes	Dusty Reeds
Lighting/Technical Direction	D.G. Klovstad
Stage Manager	Sally Eldridge
Properties	Jane Wilbur, Tami Ramaker
Shift Crew	Dave Noll, Larry Yeager
Sound Master	Eric Helmer
Master Electrician	Joel Schell
Costume Mistress	Bennie Loro

CAST

Jenny Beales	Marcella Ann Hammer
Jimmy Beales	John T. Wolfe, Jr.
Stella Bryant	Mary L. Rowley
Bill Archer	Isaac Johnson
Mrs. Bryant	Agatha D. Sampson
Mr. Bryant	Joseph G. Wayne, Jr.
Mr. Hadley	James L. Russell
Frank Bryant	Reginald F. Davis
Pearl Bryant	Jo-Alice Hicks

85
Loeb Playhouse, Purdue
September 22, 23, 28-30, 1972
Death of a Salesman
By Arthur Miller

Directed by Joe Stockdale

Set Design	Donnamarie Reeds
Costumes	Stormie Lineberger
Lighting	D.G. Klovstad
Stage Manager	Les Schoof
Master Electrician	Jay Thompson

Sound Master	Peggy Wiese
Properties	David Veazey
Wardrobe Master	Tim Emswiller
Dressers	Jean Routt, Keith Hyatte
Pinrail	Mark Rogers
Make-up	Patti Elliott

CAST

Willy Loman	John Newton
Linda	Georgia Lowrey
Biff	Paul Mazzaglia
Happy	Richard Pigg
Bernard	David Noll
The Woman	Pat Frank
Charley	Donald Dickherber
Uncle Ben	Thom Culbertson
Howard Wagner	Robert Walker
Jenny	Georgene Martella
Stanley	Robert Heiber
Miss Forsythe	Joann Naylor
Letta	Tamara Ramaker
A Waiter	Patrick Flanagan

86
Loeb Playhouse, Purdue
April 20, 21, 26-28, 1973
Cyrano de Bergerac
By Edmond Rostand
Translated by Brian Hooker

Directed by Joe Stockdale

Set Design	Jerry Williams
Lighting Design	J.E. MacRostie
Technical Director	D.G. Klovstad
Costumes	Tim Emswiller
Properties	David Potts
Choreography	Wayne Lamb
Stage Manager	Sally Eldridge
Asst. Stage Manager	Jill Crary
Shop Foreman	Mike Lowther
Master Carpenter	Dan Warrick
Master Electrician	Steve Easley
Sound Master	Doug Hughes
Properties	Kathy Humbert
Pinrail	Gary Adams
Make-up	Stormie Lineberger

CAST

Cyrano de Bergerac	David Noll
Christian de Neuvillette	Michael Maddox
Roxane	Tami Ramaker
Comte de Guiche	Sidney Pellisier
Le Bret	Paul Mazzaglia
Ragueneau	Norm Lichtenfeld
Carbon de Castel-Jaloux	Jack Cahill
The Duenna	Donna Cost
Cadets	Patrick M. Flanagan, Grafton Houston, Randy Johns, John Gallagher, Kevin Sullivan, Marque Fullerton, Dan Irvin, Paul Cloyd
Mthr. Marguerite De Jesus	Dusty Reeds
Sister Marthe	Cassandra Wolfe
Ligniere	James Van Winkle
Vicomte De Valvert	Larry Fisher
Guigy	Enos Caudill
Brissaille	Ian Cassell
Lise	Karlalea Coyle
The Orange Girl	Diane Troxel
The Capuchin	Bob Zink
Montifleury	James MacRostie
A Marquis	Tim Emswiller
2nd Marquis	David Potts
3rd Marquis	C. Phillip Toombs
Bellerose	Dennis Monesmith
Jodelet	Robert Whitesel
The Citizen	Richard Demkovich
Citizen's Son	J. Crary
The Meddler	Robert Walker
The Old Citizen	Wayne Lamb
A Musketeer	Truel West
The Porter	Jeff Rossen
A Cut-Purse	John Constant
Cut-Purse Apprentice	Ron Kaden
A Lackey	William Blades
A Guardsman	John Hofstetter
Flower Girl	Sarah Bowers
Pastry Cooks	Ed Estridge, Todd Cannon, David Chudzynski
Pastry Cook Apprentice	Thea Vorbeck
Corneille	Barry Klemm
Bertrandou the Fifer	Manuel Teijelo
Musicians	George Novotney, Susan Goldsmith
An Actress	Sarah Bowers
Madam Aubray	Linda Maxwell
M. de Guemene	Myra Alexander
M. de Chavigny	Patricia Parsley
Barthenoide	Patti Elliott
Urimedonte	Pat Frank
Felixerie	Dawn Jakes
Obsequious Gentleman	Jeff Smith
Men Eating	Dennis Kaster, Carl Kloepfer, Jack Hennies
Boy Drummer	John Stockdale
Pages playing the Theorbo	Tom & Steve Pounders

87
Experimental Theatre, Purdue
June 20-24, 26-30, 1973
The Moon Is Down
By John Steinbeck

Directed by Joe Stockdale

Set Design	Joel Stoehr
Costumes	Tim Emswiller
Lights & Sound/Technical Direction	James Smythe
Stage Manager	Patti Elliott
Asst. Stage Manager	Bob Walker
Properties	Linda Maxwell
Lighting	Mariann Blaine
Sound	Rob Brindley

CAST

Doctor Winter	David Noll
Joseph	Sidney Pellisier
Captain Bentick	Richard Pigg
Sentry	Geoffrey Pfaff
Mayor Orden	George Novotney

Madame Orden	Susan Berg
Annie	Cassandra Wolfe
Orderly	Greg Hjort
Col. Lanser	Dale Helward
George Corell	Steve Henderson
Major Hunter	Don Dickherber
Lt. Prackle	Ken Renner
Lt. Tonder	David Lyles
Captain Loft	Bob Walker
Molly	Ann Lingel
Alex Morden	John Goff
Tom Anders	John Gallagher
Will Anders	Dave Franks

88
Experimental Theatre, Purdue
July 4-8, 10-14, 1973
Busy Dyin'
By Sheila Hofstetter

Directed by Joe Stockdale

Set Design	Joel Stoehr
Costumes	Tim Emswiller
Lighting	James Christopher Rice
Technical Director	James Smythe
Sound	Rob Brindley
Stage Manager	Don Dickherber
Asst. Stage Manager	David Lyles
Properties	Linda Maxwell
Production Assistant	Sally Eldridge
Lighting Execution	Mariann Blaine
Sound Execution	Geoffrey Pfaff

CAST
Rima	Ann Lingel
Junior	Robert Walker
Ray	Steve Henderson
Benny	George Novotney
Hazel	Cassandra Wolfe
Susie	Tami Ramaker
Mr. Pratt	David Lyles
Policeman	Don Dickherber

89
SUNY, Purchase
January 25 - 28, 1978
Moonchildren
By Michael Weller

Directed by Joe Stockdale

Set Design	David Potts
Lighting Design	Alan Kibbe
Sound	John Vail
Stage Manager	Michael Lesser
Asst. Stage Manager	Dorothy Sherman
Master Carpenter	Chris Parietti
Master Electrician	Marty Goldenberg
Properties	Craig Martin
Pianist	Antoine Zemor

CAST
The Students
Mike	Edward S. Altman
Ruth	Amy Wolfson
Cootie	Daniel Onzo
Norman	David Rodgers
Dick	Michael Bailey
Kathy	Penny Alger
Bob	Phil Miller
Shelly	Sarah Wolins

The Others
Ralph	Rod A. Lansberry
Mr. Willis	David S. Kapp
Lucky	Jody P. O'Neil
Bream	John Averill
Effing	Mark Wierman
Uncle Murray	Bill Marcus
Milkman	Kevin McCabe
Plumber	John Ray
Cootie's Mother	Dorothy Sherman

90
Woodstock Playhouse, NY
July 5 - 9, 1978
The Man With a Load of Mischief
By John Clifton & Ben Tarver
Based on the play by Ashley Dukes

Directed by Joe Stockdale

Set Design	Jonathon Arkin
Costume Design	Dean Reiter
Lighting Design	Michael Mazzola
Asst. Set Designer	Fran Pitchon
Music Director	Howard Houghtaling
Percussionist	Don Watrous
Stage Manager	Phillip R. Karnoff
Technical Director	Brian MacDevitt
Master Carpenter	Chris Parietti
Properties	Colin Keith Gregory
Costume Assistant	Ellen Shlasko

CAST
Innkeeper	John Newton
Innkeeper's Wife	June Helmers
Lady	Janet Hayes
Maid	Nancy Nichols
Lord	Louis Edmonds
Man	Robert Stoeckle

91
Woodstock Playhouse, NY
July 12-16, 1978
Charley's Aunt
By Brandon Thomas

Directed by Joe Stockdale

Set Design	Jonathon Arkin
Costume Design	Dean Reiter
Lighting Design	Michael Mazzola
Asst. Set Designer	Fran Pitchon
Music Director	Howard Houghtaling
Percussionist	Don Watrous
Stage Manager	Phillip R. Karnoff
Technical Director	Brian MacDevitt
Master Carpenter	Chris Parietti
Properties	Colin Keith Gregory
Costume Assistant	Ellen Shlasko

CAST

Jack Chesney	Robert Stoeckle
Brassett	James Morgan
Charley Wykeham	Christopher Gorman
Lord Fancourt Babberly	Robin Haynes
Amy Spettigue	Madeline Seide
Col. Sir Francis Chesney	John Newton
Stephen Spettigue	Andy Backer
Donna Lucia D'Alvadorez	Janet Hayes
Ela Delahay	Jennifer Campbell

#92
Woodstock Playhouse, NY
July 19 – 23, 1978
Rain
By John Colton & Clemence Randolph
Founded on the story "Miss Thompson" by Somerset Maugham

Directed by Joe Stockdale

Set Design	Jonathon Arkin
Costume Design	Dean Reiter
Lighting Design	Michael Mazzola
Asst. Set Designer	Fran Pitchon
Music Director	Howard Houghtaling
Percussionist	Don Watrous
Stage Manager	Phillip R. Karnoff
Technical Director	Brian MacDevitt
Master Carpenter	Chris Parietti
Properties	Colin Keith Gregory
Costume Assistant	Ellen Shlasko

CAST

Mrs. Horn, Ameena	Susan Zelouf
Corporal Hodgson	Christopher Van Doren
Private Griggs	Mark Brotherton
Sergeant O'Hara	Robert Stoeckle
Joe Horn	Andy Backer
Mrs. Davidson	Virginia Downing
Dr. McPhail	Robin Haynes
Mrs. McPhail	Nancy Nichols
Sadie Thompson	Janet Hayes
Quartermaster Bates	Christopher Gorman
Rev. Alfred Davidson	John Newton
Natives	Madeline Seide, Jennifer Campbell, Andrew La Piana

#93
Woodstock Playhouse, NY
August 2 – 6, 1978
Misalliance
By George Bernard Shaw

Directed by Joe Stockdale

Set Design	Jonathon Arkin
Costume Design	Dean Reiter
Lighting Design	Michael Mazzola
Asst. Set Designer	Fran Pitchon
Music Director	Howard Houghtaling
Percussionist	Don Watrous
Stage Manager	Phillip R. Karnoff
Technical Director	Brian MacDevitt
Master Carpenter	Chris Parietti
Properties	Colin Keith Gregory
Costume Assistant	Ellen Shlasko

CAST

John Tarleton, Jr.	Christopher Van Doren
Bentley Summerhays	Christopher Gorman
Hypatia Tarleton	Nancy Nichols
Mrs. Tarleton	Virginia Downing
Lord Summerhays	Andy Backer
John Tarleton	John Newton
Joseph Percival	Robert Stoeckle
Lina Szczepanowska	Janet Hayes
Julius Baker	Robin Haynes

#94
Woodstock Playhouse, NY
August 9 – 13, 1978
Suddenly Last Summer
By Tennessee Williams
Directed by Joe Stockdale

Set Design	Jonathon Arkin
Costume Design	Dean Reiter
Lighting Design	Michael Mazzola
Asst. Set Designer	Fran Pitchon
Music Director	Howard Houghtaling
Percussionist	Don Watrous
Stage Manager	Phillip R. Karnoff
Technical Director	Brian MacDevitt
Master Carpenter	Chris Parietti
Properties	Colin Keith Gregory
Costume Assistant	Ellen Shlasko

CAST

Mrs. Venable	Janet Hayes
Dr. Cukrowicz	Robert Stoeckle
Miss Foxhill	Jennifer Campbell
Mrs. Holly	Virginia Downing
George Holly	Robin Haynes
Catherine Holly	Nancy Nichols
Sister Felicity	Susan Zelouf

#95
Woodstock Playhouse, NY
August 16 – 20, 1978
Murder at the Vicarage
By Agatha Christie

Directed by Joe Stockdale

Set Design	Jonathon Arkin
Costume Design	Dean Reiter
Lighting Design	Michael Mazzola
Asst. Set Designer	Fran Pitchon
Music Director	Howard Houghtaling
Percussionist	Don Watrous
Stage Manager	Phillip R. Karnoff
Technical Director	Brian MacDevitt
Master Carpenter	Chris Parietti
Properties	Colin Keith Gregory
Costume Assistant	Ellen Shlasko

CAST

The Vicar	John Newton
Griselda	Nancy Nichols
Dennis	Christopher Gorman
Mary	Susan Zelouf

Ronald Hawes	Robin Haynes
Lettice Protheroe	Madeline Seide
Miss Marple	Eleanor Schlomann
Mrs. Price Ridley	Sara Mulligan
Anne Protheroe	Janet Hayes
Lawrence Redding	Robert Stoeckle
Dr. John Haydock	Christopher Van Doren
Inspector Slack	Andy Backer

96
Woodstock Playhouse, NY
August 23 – September 3, 1978
A Little Night Music
Music & Lyrics by Stephen Sondheim
Book by Hugh Wheeler
Suggested by a film by Ingmar Bergman
Originally Produced & Directed on Broadway by
Harold Prince

Directed by Joe Stockdale

Choreography	Janet Hayes
Music Director	George Malloy
Cello Performance	Nancy Koch
Set Design	Jonathon Arkin
Costume Design	Dean Reiter
Lighting Design	Michael Mazzola
Asst. Set Designer	Fran Pitchon
Music Director	Howard Houghtaling
Percussionist	Don Watrous
Stage Manager	Phillip R. Karnoff
Technical Director	Brian MacDevitt
Master Carpenter	Chris Parietti
Properties	Colin Keith Gregory
Costume Assistant	Ellen Shlasko

CAST
Mr. Lindquist	Robert Paul
Mrs. Nordstrom	Carol Toscano
Mrs. Andersen	Constance Craig
Mr. Erlanson	Robert Alpaugh
Mrs. Segstrom	Judy Leopold
Frederika Armfeldt	Ann Casapini
Madame Armfeldt	Eleanor Schlomann
Frid, *her butler*	Christopher Van Doren
Henrik Egerman	Robin Haynes
Anne Egerman	Nancy Nichols
Fredrik Egerman	John Newton
Petra	Merle Louise
Desiree Armfeldt	Janet Hayes
Malla, *her maid*	Susan Zelouf
Bertrand, *a page*	Andrew La Piana
Count Carl-Magnus Malcolm	Robert Stoeckle
Countess Charlotte Malcolm	Sharlie Stuart
Osa	Madeline Seide

97
Theatre D, SUNY Purchase
January 24 – 27, 1979
Equus
By Peter Shaffer

Directed by Joe Stockdale
Sets & Costumes	Dean Reiter
Choreography	Paul Thompson
Lighting	Jeff Nash
Technical Director	Brian MacDevitt
Stage Manager	Antonia Lasicki
Asst. Stage Manager	Bonnie Friedman
Production Manager	Bill Marcus
Master Electrician	Jonathon Vall
Properties & Wardrobe	B. Buchanan

CAST
Martin Dysart	Edward Altman
Alan Strang	Phil Miller
A Nurse	Jean Marie Freebody
Hesther Salomon	Judith Cole
Frank Strang	Jim Horan
Dora Strang	Amy Wolfson
A Young Horseman	Joseph Fanelli
Harry Dalton	A. M. Horn
Jill Mason	Stephanie Menuez
Horses	Robert C. Klein, Sarah Wolins, Alexander David Morrison, Elizabeth Poulos, John David Zeik

98
The York Players, NYC
February 24 & 25, March 3, 4, 9 - 11, 1979
Rain
By John Colton & Clemence Randolph
Based on the story *'Miss Thompson'* by Somerset Maugham

Directed by Joe Stockdale
Set Design	James Morgan
Costumes	Neil Cooper
Lighting	Jesse Ira Berger
Sound/Production Engineer	Joseph D. Sukaskas
Production Stage Manager	Molly Grose
Technical Director	Sally Smith
Stage Manager	Judy Zolan
Wardrobe Mistress	Sue Wurster

CAST
Mrs. Horn, Ameena	Gail Bearden
Corporal Hodgson	Archie Harrison
Private Griggs	Steven Orr
Sergeant O'Hara	Robert Stoeckle
Joe Horn	Andy Backer
Mrs. Davidson	Blanche Cholet
Dr. McPhail	Ralph David Westfall
Mrs. McPhail	Maria Hasen
Sadie Thompson	Janet Hayes
Quartermaster Bates	Lium O'Begley
Rev. Alfred Davidson	James Pritchett
Natives	Martitia De Witt, Gigi McHugh, Steven Metcalf
Policeman	Fred Schroeder

99
Woodstock Playhouse, NY
July 11 – 15, 1979
The Subject Was Roses
By Frank D. Gilroy

Directed by Joe Stockdale
| Set Design | Dean Reiter |

Costume Design .... Judianna Makovsky
Lighting Design .... Brian MacDevitt
Production Stage Manager .... Richard S. Viola
Stage Manager .... Lloyd Carbaugh
Technical Director .... Chris Parietti
Master Carpenter ....Bruce Farnworth
Master Electrician .... Andrea Jurgrau
Properties .... Mary Vivona
Costume Assistant ....Ellen Shlasko

CAST
John Cleary .... John Newton
Nettie Cleary ....Janet Hayes
Timmy Cleary ....Tom Flagg

#100
Woodstock Playhouse, NY
July 25 – 29, 1979
Arms and the Man
By George Bernard Shaw

Directed by Joe Stockdale

Set Design .... Dean Reiter
Costume Design .... Judianna Makovsky
Lighting Design .... Brian MacDevitt
Production Stage Manager .... Richard S. Viola
Stage Manager .... Lloyd Carbaugh
Technical Director .... Chris Parietti
Master Carpenter ....Bruce Farnworth
Master Electrician .... Andrea Jurgrau
Properties .... Mary Vivona
Costume Assistant ....Ellen Shlasko

CAST
Raina .... Nancy Nichols
Catherine Petkoff .... Mary Diveny
Louka ....Elizabeth Torgersen
Capt. Bluntschli .... Dale Helward
Russian Officer ....Conal O'Brien
Nicola ....Ron Boulden
Major Paul Pertkoff .... Vince O'Brien
Major Sergius Saranoff ....Robert Stoeckle

#101
Woodstock Playhouse, NY
August 8 – 12, 1979
Tartuffe
By Moliere

Directed by Joe Stockdale

Set Design .... Dean Reiter
Costume Design .... Judianna Makovsky
Lighting Design .... Brian MacDevitt
Production Stage Manager .... Richard S. Viola
Stage Manager .... Lloyd Carbaugh
Technical Director .... Chris Parietti
Master Carpenter ....Bruce Farnworth
Master Electrician .... Andrea Jurgrau
Properties .... Mary Vivona
Costume Assistant ....Ellen Shlasko

CAST
Madame Pernelle .... Eleanor Schlomann
Monsieur Orgon .... John Newton
Damis .... Tom Flagg
Mariane .... Gwendolyn Lewis
Elmire ....Janet Hayes
Valere ....Bram Lewis
Cleante .... Vince O'Brien
Dorine ....Elizabeth Torgersen
Filipote .... Madeline Seide
Tartuffe .... Dale Helward
Loyal ....Ron Boulden
Police Officer ....Conal O'Brien

#102
The York Players, NYC
January 11, 12, 18, 19, 25-27, 1980
The Subject Was Roses
By Frank D. Gilroy

Directed by Joe Stockdale

Set Design ....James Morgan
Costumes .... Robert W. Swasey
Lighting Design .... Brian MacDevitt
Technical Director ....Sally Smith
Production Stage Manager .... Molly Grose
Stage Manager ....Janet Stott
Properties .... Madeline Seide
Sound ....Andy Hoover
Master Carpenter ....Stephen Guntli
Chief Electrician .... Gayle Butler
Sound Design ....Charles Dodsley Walker

CAST
John Cleary .... John Newton
Nettie Cleary ....Janet Hayes
Timmy Cleary ....Tom Flagg

#103
Theatre B, SUNY Purchase
April 30, May 1-3, 1980
Buried Child
By Sam Shephard

Directed by Joe Stockdale

Set Design .... David Potts
Lighting Design ....Bubba Fanneli
Stage Manager ....Judy Hellman
Producer .... Kevin Wallin
Technical Director ....Robert Grahm Small
Master Carpenter ....Mark Freij
Master Electrician .... John Kreutz
Lighting Execution .... Nelson Otero
Properties ....Ann McGovern
Costumes ....Anne Holen
Seamstress .... Charlotte O'Donoghue

CAST
Dodge .... Edward Altman
Halie ....Amy Wolfson
Tilden .... Phil Miller
Bradley ....Robert Bernstein
Shelly .... Evie Owens
Vince .... Clay Hapaz
Father Lewis ....Jack Sawyer

#104
Woodstock Playhouse, NY
July 2 – 6, 1980
Chapter Two
By Neil Simon

Directed By Joe Stockdale

Set Design	James Morgan
Costume Design	Konnie Kittrell Berner
Lighting Design	David Gotwald
Production Stage Manager	Stephen Jarrett
Technical Director	David Moore
Master Carpenter	Al Miller
Master Electrician	John Conway
Assistant to Set Designer	Art Govin
Properties	Lynn Donoghue

CAST

George Schneider	Jerry Sroka
Leo Schneider	James Harper
Jennie Malone	Jan Pessano
Faye Medwick	Mary McTigue

#105
Woodstock Playhouse, NY
July 9 – 13, 1980
Mrs. Warren's Profession
By George Bernard Shaw

Directed by Joe Stockdale

Set Design	James Morgan
Costume Design	Konnie Kittrell Berner
Lighting Design	David Gotwald
Production Stage Manager	Stephen Jarrett
Technical Director	David Moore
Master Carpenter	Al Miller
Master Electrician	John Conway
Assistant to Set Designer	Art Govin
Properties	Lynn Donoghue

CAST

Vivie Warren	Nancy Nichols
Praed	William Cain
Mrs. Kitty Warren	Janet Hayes Walker
Sir George Crofts	James Harper
Frank Gardner	Kenneth Garner
Rev. Samuel Gardner	Ralph David Westfall

#106
Woodstock Playhouse, NY
July 16 – 20, 1980
Relatively Speaking
By Alan Ayckbourn

Directed by Joe Stockdale

Set Design	James Morgan
Costume Design	Konnie Kittrell Berner
Lighting Design	David Gotwald
Production Stage Manager	Stephen Jarrett
Technical Director	David Moore
Master Carpenter	Al Miller
Master Electrician	John Conway
Assistant to Set Designer	Art Govin
Properties	Lynn Donoghue

CAST

Greg	James Harper
Ginny	Nancy Nichols
Philip	William Cain
Sheila	Janet Hayes Walker

#107
Woodstock Playhouse, NY
July 23 – August 3, 1980
The Hollow
By Agatha Christie

Directed By Joe Stockdale

Set Design	James Morgan
Costume Design	Konnie Kittrell Berner
Lighting Design	David Gotwald
Production Stage Manager	Stephen Jarrett
Technical Director	David Moore
Master Carpenter	Al Miller
Master Electrician	John Conway
Assistant to Set Designer	Art Govin
Properties	Lynn Donoghue

CAST

Henrietta Angkatell	Jan Pessano
Sir Henry Angkatell, K.B.E.	Sam Stoneburner
Lady Angkatell	Eleanor Schlomann
Midge Harvey	Donna Pelc
Gudgeon	Dean Schambach
Edward Angkatell	Kenneth Garner
Doris	MaryAnn Urbano
Gerda Cristow	Nancy Nichols
John Cristow, M.D., FRCP	Robert Stoeckle
Veronica Craye	Janet Hayes
Inspector Colquhoun, CID	Ralph David Westfall
Detective Sgt. Penny	Jens Krummel

#108
Tennessee Williams
Fine Arts Center, Key West, FL
February 4 – 8, 1981
The Little Foxes
By Lillian Hellman

Directed by Joe Stockdale

Set Design	John Kavelin
Costume Design	Jeff Hendry
Lighting	John Toia, John Merriman
Stage Manager	John Toia
Technical Director	John Merriman
Master Carpenter	Gary McDonald
Master Electrician	Stewart Shaw
Properties	Lucile Kravitz
Costume Mistress	Nancy Weintraub
House Manager	Tom Sloan

CAST

Addie	Alyce Webb
Cal	Clarence Thomas
Birdie Hubbard	Marjorie Lovett
Oscar Hubbard	David Schramm
Leo Hubbard	Warren Keyes
Regina Giddens	Roxana Stuart
William Marshall	Philip Bratnober

Benjamin Hubbard ....William Simington
Alexandra Giddens ....Mary Ewald
Horace Giddens ....Scott Rhyne

#109
Woodstock Playhouse, NY
June 17-21, 23-28, 1981
Talley's Folly
By Lanford Wilson

Directed by Joe Stockdale
Set Design ....Jim Bush
Lighting .... Bryan MacDevitt
Stage Manager .... Diana Banks
Technical Director ....Al Miller
Costume Designer .... Nancy Galloway
Asst. Stage Manager ....Lynn Donoghue
Master Electrician .... Scott Gagnon
Properties .... Annie O'Keefe
House Manager .... Franklin Heller

CAST
Matt Friedman ....David Rosenbaum
Sally Talley .... Mary Hamill

#110
Woodstock Playhouse, NY
July 1-5, 7 – 12, 1981
Same Time, Next Year
By Bernard Slade

Directed by Joe Stockdale
Set Design ....Jim Bush
Lighting .... Bryan MacDevitt
Stage Manager .... Diana Banks
Technical Director ....Al Miller
Costume Designer .... Nancy Galloway
Asst. Stage Manager ....Lynn Donoghue
Master Electrician .... Scott Gagnon
Properties .... Annie O'Keefe, Joyce Gagnon
House Manager .... Franklin Heller

CAST
Doris ....Natalie Ross
George .... Peter De Maio

#111
Theatre B, SUNY Purchase
October 11, 12, 14, 15, 1982
God's Peculiar Care
By Joe Stockdale

Directed by Joe Stockdale
Asst. Director ....Judith Hellman
Set Designer .... Glenn R. DeVino
Costume Coordinator ....Alison B. Hubblard
Lighting Design ....Brian D. Nason
Sound Design .... Chuck Noble
Stage Manager .... Marla Falchi
Technical Director .... Dan Niccum
Master Carpenter ....Holbrook Hayes
Properties .... Michael Cioffi
Scenic Artist ....Brian Covington

Master Electrician .... Steve Challman
Costume Mistress ....Susan Gomez

CAST
Frances Farmer .... Tracy Kolis
Lillian Farmer .... Juliette Kurth
Josh .... Steven Weber
Mrs. John Fortner ....Gina Belafonte
Louella Parsons ....Katie Bull
Clifford Odets .... John Chardiet
Judge Hickson ....Jonathon Failla
Jean Ratcliffe ....Lynne D. Gugenheim
Belle McKenzie ....Leslie Kincaid
Ernest Melvin .... Preston Maybank
Sophie Rosenstein ....Andrea B. Morse
Stella Adler .... Kathryne Peterson
Arthur .... Christopher Shobe
Harold Clurman ....Saul Stein
Leif Erickson .... Richard Vecchiarello
Zucker .... Mark Zeisler

#112
Woodstock Playhouse, NY
August 8-19, 1984
The Vinegar Tree
By Paul Osborn

Directed By Joe Stockdale
Set Design .... Sal Tagliarino
Costume Design ....Robert Kracik
Lighting Design ....John Conway
Stage Manager .... Nancy Rifkind

CAST
Max Lawrence ....Chet London
Augustus Merrick .... John Newton
Winifred Mansfield .... Ruby Holbrook
Louis .... Dean Schambach
Laura Merrick ....Janet Hayes
Leone Merrick .... Andrea Morse
Geoffrey Cole .... Preston Maybank

#113
Abbott Kaplan Theatre, SUNY Purchase
December 6-9 & 14 – 16, 1984
The Night of the Iguana
By Tennessee Williams

Directed by Joe Stockdale
Set Design ....James Mark Youmans
Costume Design ....Michelle Zimmerman
Lighting Design ....James Parsons
Sound Design .... David Grill
Technical Direction ....Mark Viola
Stage Manager .... Steven Loehle
Asst. Stage Manager .... Lausanne Davis
Properties ....Michael Beetham
Master Carpenter .... Christopher Pierce
Scenic Artist ....Amy Parsons
Master Electrician .... Bave Brown
Wardrobe ....Pamela Ross
Sound Execution .... Mark O'Connor
Follow Spot Operators ....Kimberly M.
Collister, John R. Quinlivan

CAST

Pancho	Harlin Kearsley
Maxine Faulk	Kathleen Taber
Pedro	Thomas J. Edwards
Rev. T. Laurence Shannon	Michael Grieco
Herr Fahrenkoph	Michael Lenuskey
Frau Fahrenkoph	Elizabeth Geraghty
Hilda	Karen Silas
Wolfgang	Matthew M. McClanahan
Hank	Michael Costa
Miss Judith Fellowes	Tricia Sullivan
Hannah Jelkes	Pamela Stewart
Charlotte Goodall	Tracy Jane Sallows
Nonno (Jonathon Coffin)	David Troup
Jake Latta	Scot Robinson

#114
Dance Lab Theatre, SUNY Purchase
December 10 – 13, 1984
Garden District
*(Something Unspoken &
Suddenly Last Summer)*
By Tennessee Williams

Directed by Joe Stockdale

Set Design/Props	Serafina Risalvato
Lighting Design	Michael S. Egna
Sound Design	Wyatt De Freitas
Technical Director	W.A. Nelson, III
Master Electrician	Kade Mendelowitz
Sound Execution	Leila L. Torres
Electrician	Fred Geffken

Something Unspoken
CAST

Miss Cornelia Scott	Elizabeth Geraghty
Grace Lancaster	Daphne D. Fowler

Suddenly Last Summer
CAST

Mrs. Venable	Elizabeth Logun
Dr. Cukrowicz	Matthew M. McClanahan
Miss Foxhill	Tricia Sullivan
Mrs. Holly	Elizabeth Burnette
George Holly	Michael Lenusky
Catharine Holly	Tracy Jane Sallows
Sister Felicity	Karen Sillas

#115
Abbott Kaplan Theatre, SUNY Purchase
April 20, 24 – 27, 1985
Misalliance
By George Bernard Shaw

Directed By Joe Stockdale

Set Design	Tim Prinzing
Costumes	Michelle Zimmerman
Lighting Design	David Grill
Technical Director	Michael Beetham
Stage Manager	Jonathon D. Secor
Asst. Stage Manager	Margaret Flood
Master Carpenter	Jeff Mahler
Master Electrician	Benjamin Solotaire
Properties	Laurence C. Clark
Wardrobe	Ann Raleigh
Sound	Kenneth Griffin
Scenic Artist	Lausanne Davis
Sound Execution	Rob Ward
Hair Stylist	Kay Kurta

CAST

John Tarleton, Jr.	Joshua Cox
Bentley Summerhays	Gary C. Sauer
Hypatia Tarleton	Deirdre L. Imershein
Mrs. Tarleton	Edith Falco
Lord Summerhays	Bruce Bell
John Tarleton	Alan Pottinger
Joseph Percival	Edward Wasser
Lina Szczepanowska	Farryl Lovett
Gunner	Nick Cascone

#116
Theatre B, SUNY Purchase
May 2 – 5, 1985
Buried Child
By Sam Shephard

Directed by Joe Stockdale

Set Design	Tim Prinzing
Costumes	Erin Hennessy
Lighting Design	Russ Behrens
Technical Director	Michael Beetham
Stage Manager	Dara Hershman
Master Carpenter	Jeff Mahler
Master Electrician	Benjamin Solotaire
Properties	Laurence C. Clark
Wardrobe	Ann Raleigh
Sound	Kenneth Griffin
Scenic Artist	Lausanne Davis
Sound Execution	Boni Becker

CAST

Dodge	Matthew M. Malloy
Halie	Martha Holmes
Tilden	Jeffrey Howard
Bradley	Larry Wiedemann
Vince	Thomas Bruno
Shelly	Georgina M. Corbo
Father Lewis	Ron Potesky

#117
Woodstock Playhouse, NY
June 26 – July 7, 1985
Educating Rita
By Willy Russell
Directed by Joe Stockdale

Set Design	Jim Yeomans
Costumes	Cathy Lee Cawley
Lighting Design	James Parsons
Stage Manager	Jonathon Secor
Technical Director	Christopher Pierce
Master Carpenter	Robin Andrews
Master Electrician	Ben Solotaire
Wardrobe	Natalie Cyr, Katey Goodman
Properties	Daniel Kester
Scenic Artist	Matthew Moore

CAST
Frank .... Donald Gantry
Rita .... Madeline Seide

#118
Woodstock Playhouse, NY
August 21 – 24, 1985
Shelter
By Nathan Scheib & Harris A Gordon
Directed by Joe Stockdale

Set Design .... Jim Yeomans
Costumes .... Cathy Lee Cawley
Lighting Design .... James Parsons
Stage Manager .... Jonathon Secor
Technical Director .... Christopher Pierce
Master Carpenter .... Robin Andrews
Master Electrician .... Ben Solotaire
Wardrobe .... Natalie Cyr, Katey Goodman
Properties .... Daniel Kester
Scenic Artist .... Matthew Moore

CAST
Capt. Robert McDowell .... Scott Rhyne
Edith Quincy .... Roxana Stuart

Fin...

Acknowledgments

FIRST AND FOREMOST, THANKS TO Donald Bain and Renée Paley-Bain of Hyphenates Books for editing and publishing *Stages*. Peter Bock, Professor *Emeritus* of Engineering at The George Washington University, for photographs of pictures used in this book.

Dr. Sharon Carlson, Director of Archives and Regional History Collection at Western Michigan University; and also Central Reference at Western's Waldo Library, especially their student helpers who were absolutely terrific at finding almost anything regardless of how obscure. After my greatful thanks they always ended with, "Not a problem."

Connie Clark, actress, writer, and Purdue English major, for proofreading and advice.

Helaine Feldman, editor, *Equity News* for Anne Revere's "Oasis in Indiana," appendix A, which first appeared in *Equity* magazine December 1964, bringing the news of the Purdue Professional Theatre to 30,000 AEA members .

Willem Homan, who when after three years of work, the *Stages* file crashed and was pronounced "corrupt" and "irretrievable" by sympathetic professionals from AT&T and the Geek Squad from Best Buy, and I feared it was lost. It was Don Bain who first said "scan it" and then friend and neighbor Willem saw me through the long complicated process of resurrection that started with Beckett's "You must go on, I can't go on, I'll go on."

Mr. and Mrs. Ross Landers (Ross and Michiko), graphic editors.

Patrice Murphy for shepherding me through the final months of this project, plus researching and creating Appendix D, a listing of the 118 full-length productions directed by me. It credits crew heads as well as designers and casts. As editor of the index, she submitted photos from my file in The Virginia Karnes Archives and Special Collections at Purdue University Library, with the help of faculty and staff: Sammie Morris, Susan J. Calvert, Elizabeth Wilkinson, Mary Sego, Neil Harmeyer and Stephanie Schmitz.

Professor Rich Rand, who headed the Purdue University Theatre during much of the time the book was being written, and his colleague David Lageveen who aided in research and emailing verification of program information from the theatre files.

Anne Revere as the author of appendix A, which first appeared in *Equity* magazine, bringing the news of the Purdue Professional Theatre to 30,000 AEA members.

Robin Stockdale for unlimited patience during three years of proofing as the book was being written, although for full disclosure I should thank her for her collaboration on all my writing over our 65 years of marriage. Son Joseph G. Stockdale III read the first completed draft and offered advice and editing.

The majority of the photographs were taken by David Umbarger, who worked as a Purdue University photographer. His work for the theatre was especially first-rate since he was willing to go on stage and snap pictures, including close ups, when a production was in final dress rehearsals. Other photographs were contributed by Connie Heaver Clark, Randy Earle, Tracy Kolis, and Jerry Williams.

Accreditation goes to many others

Writers of letters to the Editor which constitute Appendix B published in the Purdue *Exponent* commenting on my resignation as artistic director of the Purdue Professional Theatre Company: James R. Cost,

Professor of Metallurgy; Richard Cordell, Distinguished Professor of the English Department; Victor H. Dennenberg, Professor of Psychology; H. J. Eubank, Jr. Professor of Speech; Joseph F. Foster, Professor and Head of the Department of Chemistry; Mrs. Fred R. Gems; Robert Goulard, Professor of Aeronautical Engineering; Madeline Goulard, Professor of Aeronautical Engineering; Allen Hayman, Professor of English; Connie Heaver, Student; Henry Hewes, critic for the *Saturday Review*, New York; Glenn W. Howard, Student; John S. Karling, Professor and Dean Emeritus of Biology; Barnet Kottler, Professor of English; Paul Lykoudis, Professor of Nuclear Engineering; Gerald R. MacLane, Professor and Head of the Department of Mathematics; Roush Maesh, editor of the student newspaper *The Exponent*; Dale W. Margerum, Professor of Chemistry; Alan McDonald, Professor and Head of the Mathematics Department; Bert Oault, Student; Sidney Pellisier, Professor of French; Robert Toal, Student; and S. P. Rosen, Professor of Physics.

Excerpts from the critical reviews in Appendix C for the plays I directed during my first year as artistic director of the Woodstock Playhouse (N.Y): Jeffrey Borak of *The Poughkeepsie Journal*; Martin P. Kelly of the *Times Union*; John T. Sloper of *The Daily Freeman*; James F. Cotter of *The Times Herald*; Marianne Darron of *The Ulster County Gazette*; Carole Costello of *The Old Dutch Post Star*; Joan A Jamison of *The Knickerbocker News*; and Bob Goefert and Eleanor Kobenz of *Kite*.

From articles, books, letters, poems, songs, lyrics and speeches: W. McNeil Lowry, Director of the Ford Foundation Program in Humanities and the Arts, in a speech delivered before the Association of Graduate Schools in New Orleans, October 24, 1961; John F. Kennedy's "The Arts in America" (December 18th, 1962) magazine article accompanied by a picture from Mark Shaw's "The John F. Kennedys: *A Family Album*"; FDR's first Inaugural Address (Mar. 4, 1933); E. M. Forster's 1924 novel, *A Passage to India*; John Steinbeck's *The Grapes of Wrath* (1939); the epigraph for Tennessee Williams' *A Streetcar Named Desire* from Hart Crane's final poem, "The Broken Tower"; Edna Vincent Millay's "Epitaph for the Race of Man"; Noel Coward's *Private Lives*; John Lahr's article from *The New Yorker* on Pinter's *The Homecoming*; Ernest J. Simmons' *Chekhov: a Biography*;

and Thornton Wilder's play *Our Town*; songs: "Isle of Capri" (1934) music by William Grosz, lyrics by Jimmy Kennedy; Jimmy Dean's song "Jean"; Alfred Noyes' poem, "The Highwayman" (1906); Leigh Hunt's (1784-1859) "About Ben Adhem"; and Benjamin Franklin's letter to a young friend dated June 25, 1745, "Advice on Choosing a Mistress."

Critics and Newspapers: Vestal Taylor of the University of North Carolina at Chapel Hill's *The Daily Tar Heel*; Fremont Power and Charles Staff of *The Indianapolis News*; Walter Spencer and Charles Preston of *The Indianapolis Times;* Larry Schumpert, Frank Arganbright, Alfred Chiscon, and Sidney Pellisier in *The Lafayette Journal and Courier;* George Dolliver and Hugh Humphrey of *The Battle Creek Enquirer;* Jack Bell of *Variety;* Jack Bell, Phillip Mayer and Louis Bockstanz of *The Kalamazoo Gazette; The Williamstown (MA) Record,* Michael Pilley of *The Albany Times Union;* Gordon Bullett of *The North Adams Transcript;* William Gibson in a letter to the Editor of *The Berkshire Eagle.*

On the Keubler affair, *The New York Times, The Chicago Daily Tribune, The Los Angeles Times, The Santa Barbara News Press* and *The Washington Post.* On the Norman Kean suicide, detective Jeremy Gerard in the *New York Times* on February 9, 1988.

Thanks also to literary agent Rogers Terrill for his ten years of work on my behalf with a never ending faith that I would be published, and to the editors of major publishing houses who kept encouraging me. Likewise to my first literary agent Bertha Klausner; play agents Janet Cohn and Harold Friedman of Brandt and Brandt; and John Bender, editor of *Argosy* Magazine. Letters from Page Karling and Alice Dowling; Irwin Shaw's letter to the drama editor of *The New York Times* along with his letter to me on the release of the one-act play *Bury The Dead.* Plus miscellaneous letters from Ruth Bronson, Paschal Sherman, John Ehle, Gov. Harold W. Hanley, and Alan Monroe. Al Stewart, director of the Purdue Glee Club.

And last but certainly not least to the on-line research engines: Wikipedia (and I urge everyone to give generously to this free encyclopedia during their fund drive each year), IMDb (data for films and television), IBDB (data for Broadway), and data for Off-Broadway the Lortel Off-Broadway data base.

A

Actors and Playwrights Initiative, 574
Actors Studio, The, 258, 263, 269, 312, 343, 425
Adams Memorial Theatre, 251-2, 266, 276
Ade, Randy, 445
After The Fall, 330, 342, 345-7
Akimov, Nikolay, 419
Allegro, 86, 270
Allen, Kelcey, (Women's Wear Daily), 126
Altman, Ed, 69, 544
American Conservatory Theatre, 351
American National Theatre and Academy, 114
American National Theatre Company, 331
Judith Anderson, 46, 86, 277, 306
Andrews, Mark, 554
Andrews, Robin, 563
Anthony, Joe and Perry, 517, 526, 528-9, 549
Anton, Thelma, 124
Archy and Mehitabel, 30
The Architecture of Drama, 453, 581
Ardrey, Robert, 155
Argosy, 133, 142, 146, 148, 151, 225, 231
Aristotle, 2-3, 92, 94, 323, 375, 445, 457
Arkin, Alan, 381
Arnold, William, 557
Arsham, Miriam, ("Mimi"), 524
The Art of Rehearsal, 134, 351, 444
Ashley, Elizabeth, 265
Aubrey, Monte, 260, 273
Avakian, Aram, 572
Ayers, Dean, 141-2, 170, 179, 192

B

Bailey, Blake, *(Cheever: A Life)*, 227-8
Bailey, Michael, 544
Bain, Donald ("Don"), 173, 574, 581-2
Baker, George Pierce, 98
Baker, Todd, 570
Baker, Word, 463, 466, 469-471
Ball, Bill, 351
Banks, Diana, 554
Bar Harbor, Maine Summer Theatre, 303-5, 308-9, 530
Barn Theatre, The, 69, 151-2, 160, 165, 230, 237, 241, 336, 389, 395, 554, 581
Barrett, Jan, 233
Barrow, Bernie and Jane, 120
Baseline School, The, 9, 11, 15
Battles, John, 86, 270

Baxter III, James Phinney, 251-2, 278
Bay, Howard, 448
Behan, Brendan, 265, 363
Beirge, Violet, Dr., 79
Belafonte, Gina, 570
Bell, A. Dean, 570
Bell, Campton, 141, 151, 172
Bell, Jack, 165, 654
Bell, Nancy, 570
Bender, John, 142-3, 146-8, 654
Berdis, Albert J., Jr,, 215, 220, 436
Berry, Eric, 379-380
Birch, Miriam ("Mimsy"), 193, 207, 281, 287, 361
Black Beauty, 13
Black, Karen, 205-6, 517
Black, Marilynne, 286, 336
Blakeslee, David, 220, 236
Blyth, Ernest, (Abbey Theatre, Dublin), 419, 428
The Bobbsey Twins, 13
Bock, Peter, 318, 324, 326
Bockstanz, Louis, (The Kalamazoo Gazette), 248
Bohlen, Celestine, 551
Bohnert, Bill, 361, 363, 580
Bond, Ray, 150, 239
Bond, Rudy, 85
Bond, Sudie, 270
Bonfils, Helen, 155
Booch, Jack, 212
Borge, Vebe, 570

Born Yesterday, 86, 114, 122, 296, 437-9, 496
Bostwick, Barry, 458-9
Bottomley, Rita, (Mrs. Jack Watson), 260
Bowman, Jane, 336
Boyt, John, 378-380, 562
Boyer, Ernest, 564, 570
Bramley, William, 165
Brenner, Carolyn, 126
Bronson, Mrs. Ruth M., 175-6, 178, 180, 184, 214
Brooks, Jacqueline, 270, 573
Brooklyn Naval Hospital, 56-7
Brown, Chamberlain, 48-9
Brown, Gilmore, 365
Brown, Joe E., 37, 126
Browning, Robert, 395,
Bruch, William G., 378, 382
Buckley, Tony, 240, 355, 372
Bullett, J. Gordon, 266
Burdick, Tex, 122
Burge, Lofton, (Dean), 79
Burke, Robert, 570
Bury the Dead, 75, 324, 459-61
Busch, Richard, 373, 375-6, 379, 531
Busy Dyin', 502-3, 511

C

Caesar and Cleopatra, 133, 214, 413
Caldwell, Bruce, 507
Camarillo State Hospital, 194

Candida, 395
Cap and Bells, 262-3, 266
Capra, Frank, 379
Carnes, Virginia, 251
Carney, Kay, 526
Carpenter, Juanita, 172
Carroll, Lyn, 317, 336, 443
Carter, Jeff, 336
Cascone, Nicholas, 414, 570
Cassidy, Orlagh, 570
Cat On A Hot Tin Roof, 250
The Cave Dwellers, 305-6
Cesario, Michael, 562
The Changeling, 342-3, 347, 349, 438
Charley's Aunt, 70, 257, 607-8
Chase, Mary, 144
Check, Ed, 570
Chemyshov, Maly Opera Theatre, 420
Chibas, Maria, 570
Chiles, Linden, 134-5, 144-6, 572, 576, 579
Chiscon, Alfred, 317, 513
Christman, Solomon, 8
Cieslek, Ryszard, 411
Claire, Helen, 45
Clohessy, Robert, 570
Clurman, Harold, 300, 349-350, 525
Cody, Marjorie, 502
Cohn, Janet, 151, 172-3, 175-8, 184
Cohen, Larry, 559

Coigney, Martha Wadsworth, 405
Coleridge, Samuel, 257
Combs, Rachel Hauben, 567
Come and Get It, 312
Come Back, Little Sheba, 149
Congressional Record, 324
Colon, Matthew, 570
Conn, Billy, 39
Connelly, Marc, 448
Connolly, Thomas, 438
The Constant Prince, 411-412, 443
Cordell, Richard, 236, 454, 513
Cornell, Katharine, 46, 65, 133, 252, 378
Cost, Donna and Jim, 224, 493
Counsman, Karlene, 173, 212
Country Mile, 164
Courtenay, Margaret, 416
Cowan, Bob, 235
Crane, Hart, 173, 341
Craven, Gary, 373
Croiter, Jeff, 570
Cronyn, Hume, 302
Crosby, Ash, 267
Culligan, Rosemary, 48
Culver, Al, 202
Cyrano de Bergerac, 500

D

DaSilva, Daniel, 570
Daily, Irene, 504
Daily Tar Heel, 103-4

Damon, Cathryn, 292, 402, 421
Dandrow, George, 251
Dane, Faith, 230
Danza, John, 570
The Dark at the Top Of the Stairs, 247, 250, 256
Darvas, Lili, 264
Darwell, Jane, 27
Day, Sylvia, (*Ulster County Gazette*), 545
Day of Absence, 473
Dave, Vinod, 533
Davis, Bette, 27, 97, 143, 265, 321
Davis, Harry, 90, 116, 118, 137, 177, 196
Davis, Susie, 117
Dawson Elementary School, 23
Day, Paul, 303-5
de Wilde, Fritz, 342, 344
DeBerry, Lynn J., 570
DeMaio, Peter, 554
DeVino, Glenn, 555
Death of a Salesman, 100, 220-1, 258, 499
Deaux, Kay, 519
Deep Are the Roots, 68, 74
Deering, Olive, 305, 529-530
DeGanon, Matthew, 570
Dempsey, Mark, 390, 395
Denbow, Douglas, 214-215
Denver Civic Theatre, 155
Denver, University of, 141, 144, 147, 152, 156, 166, 179, 325, 351

Desire Is A Season, 162-6, 172, 547
The Desperate Hours, 202-3, 234
Devine, George, 355
Dezerseran, Michelle, 359
The Diary of Anne Frank, 233, 235
Dietrich, Charley, 224, 309
DiGesy, Traci-Ann, 570
DiGioia, Michael, 567, 570
Dingle, Rona, 458
Ditamore, John, 441, 443
A Doll's House, 193, 373, 376, 590
Dolliver, George, (*Battle Creek Enquirer*), 163-4
The Doctors, 165
Dom, Charles M. 497, 503, 521,
DonHowe, Gwyda, 167-8
Donley, Robert, 297, 394, 448, 455
Douglas, Paul, 86
Dowling, Alice, 178, 189
Dracula, 462-3, 466-470
Drake, Alan H., 360
Drake, Alfred, 265
Drillinger, Brian, 570
Dunkley, Miss (Frances), 35
Durfee, Ross, 116, 119
Duvall, Claude M., 266
Dwan, John, 17
Dwan, Nell, 16-17
Dylan, 334

E

Earle, Randy, 336, 360, 364, 370, 373-4, 380, 396, 435, 443, 452, 458, 591, 605

Earle, Vicki, 401

Eaton, Walter Prichard, 98-9, 103

Ebert, Betty, 67, 69, 84, 160

Ebrahamian, Ghasem, 523

Edmonds, Louis, 359

Edward II, 415

Edwards, Darryl, 570

Ehile, John 102, 216

Eldard, Ron, 570

Eldridge, John, 370, 481, 483, 572

Eliot, T. S., 200-3

Elmore, James, 570

Engels, Rabbi Gerald and Marilyn, 224

Equus, 546

Epps, Preston H., 92, 94, 444

Evans, Dame Edith, 354

Ewell, Dwight, 570

Experimental Theatre, 188, 214, 216, 240, 262, 302, 317, 335-8, 373, 375, 389, 383, 397, 441, 448, 452, 459, 463, 482, 495, 498, 515, 582,

F

Falco, Edie, 570

Fallon, Gabriel, Abbey Theatre, Dublin, 427

Fanelli, Peter, 570

The Fantasticks, 317, 327, 329, 356, 360, 463, 469

A Far Country, 264, 530

Farmer, Frances, 288, 310-312, 316, 327-339, 365, 367, 450, 477, 497, 554-9, 572, 605

Farmers Alley Theatre, 582

Fastenrath, Jimmy, 85, 492, 572

Fastenrath, Robin, (Stockdale) (Throughout)

FDR: First Inaugural Address, (Federal Emergency Relief Act), 19, 40, 109

Feagin School of Dramatic Art, 43

Feltenstein, George, 570

Fisher, Lily, 236

Flagg, Tom, 548

Flanagan, Michael, 456-466, 471, 476

Fletcher, Allen, 109, 111-13, 134, 183, 265, 321, 382

Fletcher, Louise, 102, 198

Foley, Chotzi, 230

Foley, Martha, (*Best American Short Stories, 1954*), 225

Foley, Mary, 240

Fonteyn, Margo, 355

Forster, E.M., (*A Passage to India*), 359, 538

Forsythe, Henderson, 573

Forsythe, John, 102

Forth, Robert, 456

The Fourposter, 133, 159-60, 302
Frances Farmer Presents, 310
Franz Radio Shop (and soda fountain), 38
Freed, Lewis, 320
Freehafer, Lyle, 442, 451, 458, 589, 591-7, 605
Freistadt, Hans, 90
Friedman, Harold, (President, Brandt and Brandt Agency), 152
Frost, James A., 524, 564-5, 570
Fulton, Al, 236
A Funny Thing Happened on the Way to the Forum, 294, 400

G
Gallipoli, 2
Gallo, David, 570
Galushko, Vadim, (Institute of Soviet-American Relations), 423-5
Gam, Rita, 263
Gantry, Donald, 470, 563
Garces, John, 438
Garland, Judy, 27
Garrett, Maureen, 573
Gaskill, Brian, 570
Gavin, Flo, 479
Gault, Lynn, 90
Gazzara, Ben, 374
George, Grace, 37
Gerard, Jeremy, 168
Germon, Christopher, 570
Gibson, William, 274
Gielgud, John, 46, 417
Gilliam, Seth, 570
Gilroy, Frank, 549
Girard, Louis, 391, 439
The Glass Menagerie, 65, 134-6, 174, 177, 229, 236, 361, 376, 411, 447, 477
God's Peculiar Care, 297, 555, 557
Godfrey, Joe, 573
Goldman, Elaine, 235, 240
Gomez, Nick, 570
Gomez, Susan, 570
Gorbunov, 420
Gordon, Harris, 544
Gorki, Maxim, 313
Gosse, Bob, 570
Gould, Sam, 523-4, 564, 570
Graff, Todd, 570
The Grapes of Wrath, 26, 39, 196, 387
Grease, 256, 459
Great Lakes Boot Camp, 6, 54
Great Lakes Hospital Corps School, 55-6
The Great White Hope, 393, 457, 604
Green Candle Tea Room, (Mrs. Stilson's), 39
Green, Paul, 91, 98, 102
Greenberg, Richard, 227
Greenwood, Jane, 352
Gregory, Will, 292, 400-2, 421
Griboyedov, Aleksander, 407-8
Griffith, Andy, 102

Grill, David, 570
Grizzard, George, 102
Grose, Molly, 547
Groseclose, Frank, 102
Grotowski, Jerzy, 411-12, 417, 431, 439, 442-3
Gruen, Pamela, 391
Gruner, Les, 477
Guhse, Dick, 220
The Guns of August, 383
Guthrie, Tyrone, 382
Guys and Dolls, 258, 260, 262, 273-4, 282, 462-465
Gypsy, 225, 229-230, 252-4, 269, 306, 336, 356, 370-371, 451, 500, 561

H

Haas, Felix, Dean of Science, 592
Hackett, Hal, 128, 225-6, 230
Hadrian VII, 416, 497
Hagen, Uta, 58, 133, 525
Hall, Nancy, 220
Hamill, Mary, 554
Hamilton, Edith, 480, 488
Hammond, Michael, 523, 531, 546-7, 551-2, 564
Hand, David Hale, 182, 184, 193
Handley, Harold W., 233
Hanson, Arthur, 213
Hara, Mary, 439
Hardy, William ("Bill"), 96, 114, 236, 240, 257, 302,
Hardy, Martha Nell, 114, 236, 240-1, 255, 302, 306
Hargitt, Mary Jane, Eden, Charles and Russell, 373
Harlan, Dorothy, 122, 137, 189-190, 308, 372, 376-7
Harlan, Earl, 109-111, 137, 308, 337
Harris, Thomas A., (*I'm OK, You're OK*), 512
Harrison, William Henry, 137, 175
Hart, Richard, 65
Hartley, Hal, 570
Hasek, Jaroslav, 415
Hatlen, Edna, 181-2
Hatlen, Theodore ("Ted"), 174, 181-3, 187-8
Hayden, Julie, 447, 449
Hayes, Janet, 291, 360, 372, 376-7, 381, 383, 435, 545, 547, 552, 558, 572-3
Hayman, Charles, 362
Hays, Deborah ("Deb"), 261
Heaver, Connie, 297, 390, 401, 448, 455, 603
Heckart, Eileen, 311, 325
Hedda Gabler, 111, 123, 370
Heffner, Hubert, 99
Hellman, Judy, 556
Helms, Jessie, 101

Helward, Dale, 246-250, 285-291, 336-9, 372, 376-7, 381-3, 401, 416, 501

Henderson, Archibald, 98-9

Henderson, Stephen McKinley, 502, 515

Hewes, Henry, (*Saturday Review*,) 454, 606

Hicks, Israel, (Dean of Theatre), 566, 572

Hicks, John W., 442, 458, 466, 606

High Time Along The Wabash, 258

Hill, Roger, 257

Hill, Steven, 264

Hill, Tom, 124, 126

Hillis, William, 336

Hinckley, Alfred ("Al"), 372

Hodge, Steve, 373

Hofstetter, Sheila, 498, 502

Hoffman, Clair E., 40

Holbrook, Hal, 342, 410

Holbrook, Ruby, 558

Holliday, Judy, 86

Holloway, Tom, 314, 497

Horkheimer, Jack Foley, 302, 304

The Hostage 265, 363, 395

Houghton, Norris, 515, 526, 541, 564, 587

Householder, Frank, 70

Hovde, Frederick L., (Purdue President), 170, 233, 289, 316, 327, 331-2, 366, 379, 406, 432, 451, 587

Huban, Rachel,

Hull, Josephine, 71,

Hulley, Jo, 212

Humphrey, Hugh, (*The Battle Creek Enquirer*), 248

Hunt, Leigh, 12

Hunter, Kermit, 116, 198

Huntley, Mo and Doodle, 98, 138

I

Ibsen, Van, 496

Imershine, Deidre, 570

International Theatre Alliance, 453

Incident At Vichy, 295, 347, 349, 400

Inge, William, 144-5, 250, 373, 375, 432

Iowa, University of, 139, 141

Irma La Douce, 340, 389, 394

Is e Duirt Polonius, 419

J

Jackson, Anne, 381

Jacobs, Donald, 336

Jacobs, Jessie, 183

Jacobson, Ron, 528

Jeager, Dick, 383

Jennings, Tom, 383

Jensen, Karen, 340, 389

Jimenez, Robert M., 570
Johansson, Alma, 85
Jones, Charles, ("Chuck"), 47, 542, 572
Jones, Inigo, 156, 356
Jones, James Earl, 270, 293, 388, 393, 457, 604
Joyner, Mr. Henry, 117, 198
Joyner, Robert, 382
Jurgensen, Kai, 91-2, 98, 115, 120, 197
Justice, Charley "Choo-Choo", 102

K

Kaczorowski, Peter, 570
Kaechele, Lloyd, 21, 24, 33-4, 37
Kahn, Mary Helen, 256, 318
Kalamazoo Civic Players, 37, 51, 69, 501
Kaminsky, Ruth and Ida, 411
Kaplan, Abbott, 516, 518, 523, 526, 529, 531, 564
Kaplan, Bea, 529
Karling, Page, 122, 189, 204, 224, 416, 483, 505, 572, 577
Karnilova, Maria, 230
Kaufman, George S., 387-8
Kazan, Elia, 68, 229, 330-1, 342-351, 369, 405, 438, 478, 513, 525
Kean, 265
Kean, Norman, 155, 161, 163, 165-7, 351

Kelly, Eugene R., 185
Kelly, Peter, 143
Kennedy, John F., 326, 385
Kershen, Ed, 570
Kert, Larry, 229, 328
Kibee, Alan, 544
Kildahl, Erling ("Gene"), 109, 113, 121, 143, 241, 255, 288, 316, 327, 365, 367, 419, 441, 489, 572
Kilian, Victor, 338-9, 605
The Killing, 128
Kimberly, Bess, 270, 352
King, Martin Luther, 425
Kinsey, (film), 228
Kirk, Lee, 437
Kirkpatrick, John, 49
Kirsten, Lincoln, 128
Kismet, 225-6
Klapper, Stephanie, 570
Klausner, Bertha, 124, 126, 133, 142, 148
Koeffler, Henry and Phyllis, 396-7
Kolis, Tracy, 297, 556, 570
Kopit, Arthur, 274
Koch, Frederick, 91, 98
Koch, Howard., 563
Kornfel, Larry, 559, 562, 566
Kubrick, Stanley, 128
Kuebler, Clark G., 184-7
Kurth, Juliette, 570
Kyser, Kay, 102

L

LaRue, Linda, 473, 543
La Sage, Flurry, 146
Lafayette Little Theatre, 122, 132, 241
Lake, Richard, 397
Lamb, Wayne, 84, 260, 263, 273, 308, 327, 360, 370, 3 89, 441, 459, 463-4, 503-4
LaMonte, Louise, 102
Lampe, William ("Bill"), 318-9, 336
Lang, Harold, 144
Lansbury, Angela,45, 354
Larsen, Liz, 570
Laurel and Hardy, 27
Lawrence, D.H., 355
Lederer, Francis, 63
Lees, Dr. Lowell, 140
Leigh, Vivian, 27, 133, 276
Leighton, Margaret, 265
Lenuskey, Michael, 560
Leo, Melissa, 550, 570
Lesser, Michel, 544
Letwin, David, 453, 581
Letowt, Merle, 230
Louise, Merle, 230, 284, 286, 336, 372, 434, 573, 580
Lightcap, Edna and Judge, 121, 132
Linney, Romulus, 186, 269
Littlewood, Joan, 383
Lobero Theatre, 192-3
Lockhart, Wood, 261
Locklair, Wink, 115
Loden, Barbara, 311, 343, 345, 347
Loeb Playhouse, 188, 212, 214, 217, 312, 336, 365, 370, 378, 393, 396, 441, 459, 462, 480, 604
Loeb, Millie, 257
Loessin, Amanda Meiggs, 493
Loessin, Ed, 117, 186, 269, 484, 491
Logan, Joshua, 156
Lohengrin, 405, 425
Lohmann, Otto, 126
Long, Jody, 570
Long Day's Journey Into Night, 209, 221, 270, 390, 394, 432, 448, 504, 529, 530, 593, 605
Look Homeward, Angel, 63, 70, 177, 237, 242-250, 327-330, 334-9, 605
Louis, Joe, 39-40, 489
The Love Suicide at Schofield Barracks, 186-7
Lowry, W. McNeil, 299-301, 317, 522-3, 564, 569
Lubimov, Yuri, 409
Lukovna, Tanya, 420

M

Mabie, Edward Charles, 141
MacDevitt, Brian, 546,548, 554, 570
MacIlwinen, William ("Bill"), 115

MacLane, Gerald, 451, 596
Madigan, Reese, 567, 570
Maddux, Michael, 500
Mahon, Helen, 240
Main, Stuart, 122, 360
Make Your Voice Heard, 47
Mallett, Donald R., 332-3
Malloy, Matt, 570
The Man Downstairs, 242
The Man in The Spangled Pants, 69, 581
Mango, Angelo, 389, 391, 455, 572
Manual Training, 32
Marat/Sade, 353
Markowitz, Jeffrey, 570
Marks, Sam, 109, 111, 121, 131, 136, 173, 204, 212, 235, 326
Marquis, Don, 30
Marcovicci, Andrea, 559
Martin, Ann, 93, 96, 102, 116
Marx, Karl, 77
Masque and Sandal, 36-7
Massman, Page, 477
Mata Hari, 390
May, Elaine, 581
Mayakovsky Players of Moscow, 406, 422
Maybank, Preston, 297, 558, 570
Mazzaglia, Paul, 496, 499-500
McArdle, Joe, 359, 370-4, 378
McCann, Tim, 570
McClanahan, Matthew, 570

McDonald, James, 401, 598
McGinniss, Janet, 314
McKnight, Phil, 261
McMahon, Helen, 302
McMaster, Brian, 385
McNeil, Claudia, 229
Mead, Robert, ("Bob"), 150
Medea, 86, 193, 277
Meeder, Philip ("Phil"), 258-9
Menchell, Ivan, 570
Mendelsohn, Eric, 570
Mennen, Dorothy, 503-4
Merman, Ethel, 86, 133, 157, 225, 230, 252-5, 554
Michiana Summer Theatre, 162, 171, 179, 247
Millay, Edna St. Vincent, 200, 574
Miller, Arthur, 100, 220-1, 330, 345, 349-350, 439, 525
Miller, Cindy, 314, 317, 325, 336, 359, 370, 558
Miller, Phil, 544, 546, 552
Mills, Grace, 45, 58, 86, 559
Mintzer, Billy, 572
Misalliance, 317-9, 378-380, 447, 496, 562, 609,
Mister Roberts, 219-220
Mitchell, Burroughs, 152, 171, 187-9, 192
Mitchell, Thomas, 100
Mitzman, Marcia, 570
Miyazaki, Tom T., 212
Molnár, Ferenc, 86, 264

Monad, Pascal, 411, 443
Monroe, Alan H., 103, 109, 170, 174, 179, 192, 269, 299
Moonchildren, 544-5
The Moon Is Down, 501
Moore, H. Thomas ("Tom"), 256, 360, 580
Morgan, James ("Jim"), 547
Morgen, Ralph A., 205, 216
Moriarty, Michael, 559
Morrison, George, 526, 551, 562
Morse, Andrea, 558, 570
Mother Courage and Her Children, 284, 321-6, 413, 426, 496, 585
The Mother, 413
Mrs. Farmer's Daughter, 557-8
Murphy, Dorothy ("Dottie"), 513
Murphy, Patrice, 373, 481, 615
Murphy, Rosemary, 270
Murray, Susan, 395
My Fair Lady, 209, 356, 360, 402, 451
My Life In Art, 313
My Life in the Russian Theatre, 313
My Mother, My Father and Me, 370
My Whimsical Look, 410
Mystic River, 271

N

Nash, Jeff, 546, 570
Nason, Brian, 556, 570
Nazimova, Alla, 45, 63
Neal, Patricia, 144
Nedomansky, Raphael, 483
Neff, Katie, 135
Nelson, Barry, 133, 400
Nelson, Kenny, 328
Nemirovich-Danchenko, Vladimir Ivanovich, 313
Nettleton, Lois, 165
Nettum, Mary, 449-450
Neuberger, Roy, 523
Neumann, David, 570
New Yorker, The, 17, 172, 210, 322, 434
Newdick, Richard ("Dick"), 286, 304, 336, 373, 382, 477, 497,
Newton, John, 160-1, 165, 360, 372, 376, 383, 434, 499, 545, 558, 572, 575
Nichols, Mike, 381, 458, 581
Nichols, Nancy, 552
Niggli, Josefina, 102
The Night of the Iguana, 265, 290, 369, 560
'night, Mother, 256
Noble, Eulalie, 572
No Exit, 205, 207, 517
Nolan, Betsy, 574
Noll, David, 496, 500
No Time For Comedy, 211
Nobbs, Lucille, 71-2

Northern Lights, 214, 216
Noyes, Alfred, 13
Nureyev, Rudolf, 355

O

O'Brian, Mary Margaret, 370-1
O'Brian, Michael, 236
O'Connor, James, 483, 519
O'Horgan, Tom, 557-8
O'Sullivan, Michael, 155, 351
Obey, Andre (Noah), 76
October In The Spring, 101-4, 114, 124, 126, 133, 141, 149, 178
Oedipus Rex, 111, 113, 260-7, 406, 416-22, 442,
Of Mice and Men, 293, 387, 393, 438, 457, 496, 604
Ogle, Dean Bladen, 432-3, 462, 587, 591-3
Oh! Calcutta!, 167-8, 554
Oh What a Lovely War, 292, 381, 496
Olivier, Laurence, 13, 133, 276, 343, 353, 374, 418
O'Neal, Patrick, 264-5
O'Neill, Eugene, 74, 98, 163-4, 209, 221, 253, 270, 395, 505, 529
Orbach, Jerry, 274
Originals Only, 124
Othello, 58, 130, 353
O'Toole, Austin, 302
Our Dancing Daughters, 7
Our Town, 229, 231, 309-10

P

Page, Geraldine, 144, 229, 263
Pal Joey, 144
Panstwowy Teatr, Zydowski, (Warsaw, Poland), 411
Parietti, Chris, 548
Park, Win, 193
Parker, John, 114
Pasadena Playhouse, 365, 481
Pawaik Prison, (Warsaw, Poland), 426
Payne, Darwin, 378
Peachen, Rosemary, 130
Peckham, Bob, 38
Pellisier, Sidney, 513
Penn, Arthur, 274
Pepsico SUMMERFARE '83, 557
Picon, Molly, 265, 411
Pine Cobble School, 259, 267, 278
Ping, Donn, 483
Pinter, Harold, 265, 319, 353, 373, 432, 434
Playfair, Giles, 251, 261, 266, 268
The Plough and the Stars, 380
Poetics, 2, 92, 94, 444, 457, 567
Poel, William, 480
Polito, Philip, 401-2
Porter, Adina, 570
Posey, Parker, 570, 572
Posner, Kenneth, 570
Potts, David, 496, 544, 580

Potter, Joan, 264, 526, 530, 546, 556, 559, 565, 572
Pottinger, Alan, 570
Power, Fremont, *Indianapolis News*, 339, 457, 604
Preston, Charles, *Indianapolis Times*, 338
Priebe, Herman, 35
Principles and Types of Speech, 109
Printy, Pamela ("Pam"), 122, 135, 270, 361-3, 572,
Pritchett, James T., 102, 161-2, 165, 242, 547, 572
Private Lives, 240, 299, 305-8
Prosser, William ("Bill"), 262, 266, 276, 318, 497, 550, 553, 563, 568, 572
Psacharopoulos, Nikos, 252, 274
Purdue Research Foundation, 204, 213, 217, 400, 431, 602
Purdue Exponent, The, 232-3, 465, 589
Purdue University Theatre's Professional Theatre Company, 387

Q
Quinn, Anthony, 374
Quintero, Jose, 231, 438

R
Rabb, Ellis, 275
Ray, Mavis, 491

Ragotzy, Jack, 67, 69, 84, 151, 167, 230, 237, 248, 394, 581
Ramos, Louis, 570
The Rainmaker, 193
A Raisin In the Sun, 228
Ramaker, Tami, 500
Rand, Sally, 39
Randolph, Larry, 137, 359
Rasbury, Andy, 173, 241
Ratcliff, Jean, 477
Rattigan, Terrence, 121, 265
Rawls, Eugenia, 102
Razutto, Tommy, 102
Reed, Florence, 46, 86
Reed, Ronald ("Ron") 498, 500-4, 513
Reeds, DonaMarie (Dusty"), 480, 499
Regent Theatre, 25
Reid, Kate, 334
Revere, Anne, 284, 321-7, 336, 347, 380, 394, 413, 426, 440, 449, 529, 572, 585, 593, 604
Reynolds, Jo, 92, 129
Rhames, Ving, 570
Rhyne, Scott, 563, 570
Richmond, Farley, 515, 531-2
Ringel, Robert L, , Dean, 516
Ritchard, Cyril, 229, 378
Robards, Jason, Jr., 209, 274, 345, 395
Roberts, Vera Mowry, 496
Robeson, Paul, 58, 69
Robinson, Adrian, 135

Robinson Street, 224, 259, 287, 328, 331, 352, 371, 425, 483, 507, 515, 518, 549,

Rockefeller, Nelson, 305, 523, 565, 570

Rogers, Richard ("Dick"), 572

Romeo and Juliet, 258, 260, 275-7, 327, 336, 347, 355, 496, 543

Romeo, Vince, 270

Rose, George, 264

Rosen, Sam, 322, 394, 397, 400

Rosenbaum, David, 554

Rosenberg, Don, 202

Ross, Natalie, 554

Roush, Marsh, 465

Rowles, Polly, 209

Royal Academy of Dramatic Arts, 352, 356

Royal Ballet at Covent Garden, 355

Royal Shakespeare Company (RSC), 353

Ryder, Alfred, 530

Ryterband, Sharon, 359, 371, 401

S

Sage, Bill, 570

Sallows, Tracy, 570

Sailor From Nowhere, 137, 151, 225

Salaskie, Gene, 202

Salavi, Mohamed Reza, 523

Samuel French Award, 379

Sanders, Jay O., 528, 570

Sanford, Ruth, 251

Santa Barbara College, (University of California), 179, 181-195, 202, 204, 207

Santa Barbara Repertory, 193

Saroyan, William, 257, 305, 448

Sartre, Jean-Paul, 205

Saternow, Tim, 570

Saugutuck Summer Theatre, 86

Sawyer, John "Jack", 260, 268, 274

Schisgal, Murray, 381

Schlachet, Dan, 570

Schmit, Frank, 458, 465-6

Schneider, Peter, 438, 481, 496, 503, 573, 580

Schneider, Schorling, 202

Scheib, Nathan, 563

Schulze, Paul, 570

Schumpert, Larry, (*Lafayette Journal and Courier*), 454, 463, 468, 594

Scofield, Paul, 264

The Seagull, 275

Seibert, Russell, 77, 79, 82

Seide, Mattie, 563

Selden, Samuel ("Sam"), 87, 90, 93, 98, 102, 141, 173

Sellman, Hunton D., 99, 173

Setrakian, Ed, 293, 389, 390

Sevareid, Michael, 382

Shafer, Mozel and Dr. Ed, 479

Sharkey, Jofine, 102

Shaw, George Bernard, 134, 255, 351, 363, 414, 444, 448
Shaw, Irwin, 75, 460-1
Shaw, Laura V., 72
Shelton, Reid, 294, 400-3, 547
Sherin, Edwin, 393
Shooting Gallery, 572-3
Sillas, Karen, 570
Simon, Peter, 261, 276, 336, 372, 434, 575
Singleton, Katcha, 313
Skinner, Edith, 244, 253, 270, 359, 527
Slowalki, J., 411
Smalley, Webster, 265
Smith, Abbie, 28, 51, 63, 67
Smith, Betty, 102
Smith, Dorothea, 154, 162, 247, 436
Smith, Milton, 183
Smith, Pete, (aka Peter Kelly), 143
Smith, Ross, 103, 105, 109, 113, 130, 136, 139, 247, 321, 435, 441, 572, 597, 600
Snaggletooth, Queen of the Gypsies, 317
Snipes, Wesley, 570
Sobotka, Ruth, 128, 133
Somes, George, 155
The Sound of Music, 274
South Pacific, 123, 131, 133, 165
Spayde, Sidney, 51
Spencer, Walter, 316, 339
Spione, Jim, 570
St. Angelo, John, 567
Staff, Charles, 112, 317, 375, 469, 603
Stage Door Canteen, 58. 65
Stage Scenery and Lighting (1959), 99, 173
Stallard, Owen, 109, 112
Stanislavski, Constantin, 50, 73-4, 86, 137, 313, 369, 410, 412
Stanley, Kim, 264, 434, 530
Stanton, Netha A., 126
Stanton, Peter, 361
Saputo, Peter, 360
Stein, Howard, (Dean of Theatre), 553, 559
Stein, Stephanie, 314
Steinbeck, John, 26, 39, 196, 387-9, 392, 501
Stephens, James P. ("Jim"), 219, 336
Stewart, Albert P. ("Al"), 233
Stewart, Pam, 570
Straus, John, (Vice President of the Arts), 516-18, 523, 529
Stringfield, Sherry, 570
Stoddard, Michael, 448
Stop the World, I Want to Get Off, 287, 361-2, 496
Strader, Peter and Helen, 125, 137
Strasburg, Lee, 258, 314
Straus, John, 516-18, 523, 529
Street, James, 102

A Streetcar Named Desire, 85, 164-5, 172-4, 177, 170, 194, 212, 221, 241, 362-3, 399, 616, 630, 653
Streff, Doug, 202
Streisand, Barbra, 274
Strickland, Cynthia, 401
The Stuff, 559
Suddenly Last Summer, 303, 560, 610
Sweeney Agonistes, 200-201
Sweet Bird Of Youth, 229, 402

T

Tagliarino, Salvatore, 558
Take Me Out, 227
Taking Tennessee To Hart, 271, 567, 573-6, 581-2
Tandy, Jessica, 302
Tanner, Jill, 458
Tartuffe, 111, 123, 155, 258, 291, 351, 381-3, 496
A Taste of Honey, 317-18
Taylor, Laurette, 65, 229, 354
Taylor, Rebecca, 401
Taylor, Vestal, 103
Teatr Laboratorium (Wroclaw, Poland), 411, 443
Ten Days That Shook The World, 408, 423
Ten Nights In a Barroom, 206
Terrill, Rogers, 148
Teusink, Miss (Baseline School), 13, 535
Theater Week, 573

Thompson, Sada, 352
Thorndike, Dame Sybil, 382
Three Sisters, 312, 360, 409, 418
The Threepenny Opera, 285, 327, 337
Thunder Rock, 155, 312
Tillson, William, 319
Desire is a Season, 162-66
Tinsley, Ben and Evelyn, 224
Tobias and the Angel, 155
Tolan, Robert, 336, 572
Tom Sawyer, 302
Tovstonogov, Georgy, (Gorky Theatre), 420
Towne, Miss (Mildred), 43
Trachtman, Leon E., ("Lee"), Dean, 432
Treat, Donald ("Don"), 102
Trese, Adam, 570
Trigstat, Dr. Carl, 450
Trotman, William ("Bill"), 102
Tsatsos, Tom, 145
Tucci, Stanley, 570
Tuchman, Barbara, 383

U

Uncle Vanya, 400, 402, 421, 463, 496
Unto These Hills, 116, 129, 137, 180, 197-8, 236, 337
URTA –University Resident Theatre Association, 502
USS Wyoming, 60, 64

V

Vaktangov Theatre, 410
Valency, Maurice, 366
Van Cleef, Marty, 373
Van Riper, Charles, 72, 266
Variety, 654
Vaughan, David, 128, 133
Vaughn, Alice, 401
Village Players, 69, 71, 83, 86-7, 248
Viola, Mark, 570
The Visit, 289, 367-9, 410, 451, 480
Voelker, Paul, 630
von Bargen, Daniel, 470
von Cott, Vladimir, ("Wally") 113
von Szeliski, John, 212, 579
von Szeliski, Karen, 580
Voznesensky, Andrei, 410, 511

W

Walker, Bob, 496, 574
Walkup, Fairfax Proudfit, 131
Wallace, Henry, 108
Wallach, Eli, 210, 381
Walsh, Michael, 395
Warden, Bud (Mgr., Kroger Store), 41
Warren, Joseph, 504
Waites, Thomas G., 573
Watson, Douglas, 102
Watson, Jack, 252, 259, 261, 276, 278
Watson, Warner, 114
Wayne, David, 86
WBAA, (Purdue Radio Station), 343
Webb, Alan, 265
Weber, Steven, 555, 570
Weigel, Helene, 413
Weiss, Peter, 353
Weller, Michael, 544
Wesker, Arnold, 498
West Side Story, 165, 229, 286, 327, 561
West, Mae, 31, 172, 582
Whigham, Shea, 570
White, Carolyn, 173
White, Lou and Nat, 144
Whitehead, Robert, 331, 350
Widmann, Thom, 570
Williams, Annie Laurie, 265
Williams College, 251, 258, 274, 276, 278, 282, 311, 331, 579
Williams, David M., 432
Williams, Jack Eric, 556-7
Williams, Jerry, 375, 396, 402, 442, 500, 652
Williams, Robert T., 259, 273, 275, 380. 401, 493, 500
Williams, Tennessee, 85, 141, 144, 163-4, 167, 174, 209, 221, 303, 348, 376, 392, 448, 530, 550, 553, 575, 582, 611
Willis, Susan, 241, 248, 252, 334, 493

Will Mr. Merriweather Return From Memphis?, 550
Winch, Lee, 107-8
Windust, Penelope, 468, 470
Winter, Stacy, 337
Withers, Arlen, 256
Withers, Maida Rusk, 256
Woe from Wit, 407
Wolfe, Cassie, 496
Wolfe, Nancy Allyson, 570
Wolfe, Thomas, 63, 70, 91, 102, 149, 172, 177, 244-5, 329
Wolfson, Amy, 544
Wolins, Sarah, 544
Woodhouse, Edward and Margaret, 90
Woodward, Karin, 371, 383, 401
Wurtzel, Stuart, 317, 336-7
Wyeth, Buz, 208-210

Y

Yeager, Kathy, 496
Yelton, Michael, 477
You Can't Go Home Again, 177
York Players, 547
York, Zack, 102
Youmans, Jim, 563, 570
Young, John C., 570

www.ingramcontent.com/pod-product-compliance
Lightning Source LLC
Chambersburg PA
CBHW081206230426
43666CB00015B/2664